CLEARLY VISUAL BASIC®

PROGRAMMING WITH MICROSOFT® VISUAL BASIC® 2010

SECOND EDITION

CLEARLY VISUAL BASIC®

PROGRAMMING WITH MICROSOFT® VISUAL BASIC® 2010

DIANE ZAK

COURSE TECHNOLOGY
CENGAGE Learning™

Australia • Brazil • Japan • Korea • Mexico • Singapore • Spain • United Kingdom • United States

COURSE TECHNOLOGY
CENGAGE Learning™

Clearly Visual Basic:
Programming with Microsoft
Visual Basic 2010, Second Edition
Diane Zak

Executive Editor: Marie Lee

Acquisitions Editor: Brandi Shailer

Senior Product Manager: Alyssa Pratt

Freelance Product Manager: Tricia Coia

Associate Product Manager:
  Stephanie Lorenz

Marketing Manager: Shanna Shelton

Senior Content Project Manager: Jill Braiewa

Quality Assurance: Green Pen QA

Art Director: Faith Brosnan

Cover Designer: Cabbage Design Company

Text Designer: Shawn Girsberger

Print Buyer: Julio Esperas

Proofreader: Suzanne Huizenga

Indexer: Alexandra Nickerson

Compositor: Integra Software Services

Library of Congress Control Number: 2011921829

ISBN-13: 978-1-111-53015-0

ISBN-10: 1-111-53015-7

Course Technology
20 Channel Center Street
Boston, MA 02210
USA

Some of the product names and company names used in this book have been used for identification purposes only and may be trademarks or registered trademarks of their respective manufacturers and sellers.

Course Technology, a part of Cengage Learning, reserves the right to revise this publication and make changes from time to time in its content without notice.

Example: Microsoft® is a registered trademark of the Microsoft Corporation.

Cengage Learning is a leading provider of customized learning solutions with office locations around the globe, including Singapore, the United Kingdom, Australia, Mexico, Brazil, and Japan. Locate your local office at: **www.cengage.com/global**

Cengage Learning products are represented in Canada by Nelson Education, Ltd.

To learn more about Course Technology, visit
www.cengage.com/coursetechnology

To learn more about Cengage Learning, visit **www.cengage.com**

Purchase any of our products at your local college store or at our preferred online store **www.cengagebrain.com**

Printed in the United States of America
1 2 3 4 5 6 7 15 14 13 12 11

Brief Contents

CONTENTS

Contents

Preface

Clearly Visual Basic: Programming with Microsoft Visual Basic 2010, Second Edition is designed for a beginning programming course. The book assumes students have no previous programming knowledge or experience. However, students should be familiar with basic Windows skills and file management. The book's primary focus is on teaching programming concepts, with a secondary focus on teaching the Visual Basic programming language. In other words, the purpose of the book is to teach students how to solve a problem that requires a computer solution. The Visual Basic language is used as a means of verifying that the solution works correctly.

Organization and Coverage

Clearly Visual Basic: Programming with Microsoft Visual Basic 2010, Second Edition contains 27 chapters and two appendices. In the chapters, students with no previous programming experience learn how to analyze a problem specification and then plan and create an appropriate computer solution. Pseudocode and flowcharts are used to plan the solution, and desk-check tables are used to verify that the solution is correct before it is coded. Students code the solutions using the Visual Basic 2010 language, and then desk-check the code before it is executed. An entire chapter is devoted to teaching students how to select appropriate test data. By the end of the book, students will have learned how to write Visual Basic statements such as If...Then...Else, Select Case, Do...Loop, and For...Next. Students also will learn how to create and manipulate variables, constants, strings, sequential access files, structures, classes, and arrays. In addition, they will learn how to connect an application to a Microsoft Access database, and then use Language Integrated Query (LINQ) to query the database. They also will learn how to create simple Web applications. The text also introduces students to OOP concepts and terminology. Appendix A provides a listing of the data types available in Visual Basic. Appendix B contains the answers to the Mini-Quizzes and TRY THIS Exercises in each chapter.

Approach

Rather than focusing on a specific programming language, *Clearly Visual Basic: Programming with Microsoft Visual Basic 2010, Second Edition* focuses on programming concepts that are common to all programming languages—such as input, output, selection, and repetition. Concepts are introduced, illustrated, and reinforced using simple examples and applications, which are more appropriate for a first course in programming. The concepts are spread over many short chapters, allowing students to master the material one small piece at a time. Because its emphasis is on teaching the fundamentals of programming, the book covers only the basic controls, properties, and events available in Visual Basic.

Each chapter provides the steps for creating and/or coding an application that uses the concepts covered in the chapter. The videos and PDF files that accompany each chapter are designed to help students master the chapter's concepts.

Features

Clearly Visual Basic: Programming with Microsoft Visual Basic 2010, Second Edition is an exceptional textbook because it also includes the following features:

READ THIS BEFORE YOU BEGIN This section is consistent with Course Technology's unequaled commitment to helping instructors introduce technology into the classroom. Technical considerations and assumptions about hardware, software, and default settings are listed in one place to help instructors save time and eliminate unnecessary aggravation.

VIDEOS These notes direct students to videos that accompany each chapter in the book. The videos explain and/or demonstrate one or more of the chapter's concepts, provide additional information about the concepts, or cover topics related to the concepts. The videos are available online at *www.cengagebrain.com*. Search for the ISBN of your title (from the back cover of your book) using the search box at the top of the page. This will take you to the product page where free companion resources can be found.

WANT MORE INFO? FILES These notes direct students to files that accompany each chapter in the book. The files contain additional examples and further explanations of the concepts covered in the chapter. The files are in PDF format. The files are available online at *www. cengagebrain.com*.

FIGURES Figures that introduce new statements, functions, or methods contain both the syntax and examples of using the syntax. Including the syntax in the figures makes the examples more meaningful.

OBJECTIVES Each chapter begins with a list of objectives so you know the topics that will be presented in the chapter. In addition to providing a quick reference to topics covered, this feature provides a useful study aid.

MINI-QUIZZES Mini-Quizzes are strategically placed to test students' knowledge at various points in each chapter. Answers to the quiz questions are provided in Appendix B in the book.

SUMMARY Each chapter contains a Summary section that recaps the concepts covered in the chapter.

KEY TERMS Following the Summary section in each chapter is a listing of the key terms introduced throughout the chapter, along with their definitions.

REVIEW QUESTIONS Each chapter contains Review Questions designed to test a student's understanding of the chapter's concepts.

EXERCISES The Review Questions in each chapter are followed by Exercises, which provide students with additional practice of the skills and concepts they learned in the chapter. The Exercises are designated as TRY THIS, MODIFY THIS, INTRODUCTORY, INTERMEDIATE, ADVANCED, FIGURE THIS OUT, and SWAT THE BUGS.

TRY THIS EXERCISES The TRY THIS Exercises should be the first Exercises students complete after reading a chapter. These Exercises are similar to the application developed in the chapter, and they allow students to test their understanding of the chapter's concepts. The answers to TRY THIS Exercises are provided in Appendix B in the book.

MODIFY THIS EXERCISES In these Exercises, students modify an existing application.

FIGURE THIS OUT EXERCISES These Exercises require students to analyze a block of code and then answer questions about the code.

SWAT THE BUGS EXERCISES The SWAT THE BUGS Exercises provide an opportunity for students to detect and correct errors in an existing application.

New to This Edition!

DESIGNED FOR THE DIFFERENT LEARNING STYLES The book provides videos for visual and auditory learners, and tutorial sections and Want More Info? files for kinesthetic learners.

 VIDEOS The videos that accompany each chapter have been updated and now contain self-review quizzes.

WEB APPLICATIONS The Web Application chapter (Chapter 27) is now in the book rather than online. The chapter now shows students how to create a Web application that contains two Web pages. It also covers the LinkButton tool.

REVIEW QUESTIONS AND EXERCISES Additional Review Questions and Exercises have been added to each chapter.

APPENDIX B Appendix B contains the answers to each chapter's Mini-Quizzes and TRY THIS Exercises. The answers are provided to give students immediate feedback and more opportunity for learning.

POSTTEST LOOPS AND STRING CONCATENATION In the previous edition of the book, posttest loops and string concatenation were covered in the same chapter. In this edition, posttest loops are covered in a separate chapter (Chapter 13). String concatenation is now covered along with counter-controlled loops in Chapter 14.

ARITHMETIC ASSIGNMENT OPERATORS These operators are covered along with pretest loops in Chapter 12.

SELECTION STRUCTURES The selection structure chapters (Chapters 8, 9, and 10) now refer to the different forms of the selection structure as single-alternative, dual-alternative, and multiple-alternative.

REPETITION STRUCTURES The repetition structure chapters (Chapters 12, 13, and 14) were revised to include the following terms: looping condition and loop exit condition.

STRING MANIPULATION The Remove method was added to the string manipulation chapter (Chapter 23).

AUTO-IMPLEMENTED PROPERTIES Auto-implemented properties are covered in the video that accompanies the chapter on classes (Chapter 26).

Instructor Resources and Supplements

All of the resources available with this book are provided to the instructor on a single CD-ROM. Many also can be found at *www.cengagebrain.com.* At the CengageBrain.com home page, search for the ISBN of your title (from the back cover of your book) using the search box at the top of the page. This will take you to the product page where free companion resources can be found.

ELECTRONIC INSTRUCTOR'S MANUAL The Instructor's Manual that accompanies this textbook includes additional instructional material to assist in class preparation, including items such as Sample Syllabi, Chapter Outlines, Technical Notes, Lecture Notes, Quick Quizzes, Teaching Tips, Discussion Topics, and Additional Case Projects.

EXAMVIEW® This textbook is accompanied by ExamView, a powerful testing software package that allows instructors to create and administer printed, computer (LAN-based), and Internet exams. ExamView includes hundreds of questions that correspond to the topics covered in this text, enabling students to generate detailed study guides that include page references for further review. The computer-based and Internet testing components allow students to take exams at their computers, and also save the instructor time by grading each exam automatically.

POWERPOINT PRESENTATIONS This book offers Microsoft PowerPoint slides for each chapter. These are included as a teaching aid for classroom presentation, to make available to students on the network for chapter review, or to be printed for classroom distribution. Instructors can add their own slides for additional topics they introduce to the class.

DATA FILES Data Files are necessary for completing the computer activities in this book. The Data Files are provided on the Instructor Resources CD-ROM and also may be found at *www. cengagebrain.com.*

SOLUTION FILES Solutions to the chapter applications and the end-of-chapter Review Questions and Exercises are provided on the Instructor Resources CD-ROM and also may be found at *www.cengagebrain.com.* The solutions are password protected.

DISTANCE LEARNING Course Technology is proud to present online test banks in WebCT, Blackboard, and Angel to provide the most complete and dynamic learning experience possible. Instructors are encouraged to make the most of the course, both online and offline. For more information on how to access the online test bank, contact your local Course Technology sales representative.

Acknowledgments

Writing a book is a team effort rather than an individual one. I would like to take this opportunity to thank my team, especially Jill Braiewa (Senior Content Project Manager), Alyssa Pratt (Senior Product Manager), Tricia Coia (Freelance Product Manager), Nicole Ashton (Quality Assurance), Suzanne Huizenga (Proofreader), and the compositors at Integra. Thank you for your support, enthusiasm, patience, and hard work. Last, but certainly not least, I want to thank the following reviewers for their invaluable ideas and comments: Wayne Payton, Gadsden State Community College; Annette Kerwin, College of DuPage, Matthew Alimagham, Spartanburg Community College; Anthony Basilico, College of Rhode Island; Frank Malinowski, Darton College; Craig Brown, Boston College; and Laura Gipson, Beaufort Community College.

Diane Zak

Read This Before You Begin

Technical Information

Data Files

You will need data files to complete the computer activities in this book. Your instructor may provide the data files to you. You may obtain the files electronically at *www.cengagebrain.com*, and then navigating to the page for this book.

Each chapter in this book has its own set of data files, which are stored in a separate folder within the ClearlyVB2010 folder. The files for Chapter 3 are stored in the ClearlyVB2010\Chap03 folder. Similarly, the files for Chapter 4 are stored in the ClearlyVB2010\Chap04 folder. Throughout this book, you will be instructed to open files from or save files to these folders.

You can use a computer in your school lab or your own computer to complete the chapter applications and Exercises in this book.

Using Your Own Computer

To use your own computer to complete the computer activities in this book, you will need the following:

- A Pentium® 4 processor, 1.6 GHz or higher, personal computer running Microsoft Windows. This book was written and Quality Assurance tested using Microsoft Windows 7.

- Either Microsoft Visual Studio 2010 or the Express Editions of Microsoft Visual Basic 2010 and Microsoft Visual Web Developer 2010 installed on your computer. This book was written using Microsoft Visual Studio 2010 Professional Edition, and Quality Assurance tested using the Express Editions of Microsoft Visual Basic 2010 and Microsoft Visual Web Developer 2010. At the time of this writing, you can download a free copy of the Express Editions at *www.microsoft.com/express/downloads* (Visual Basic 2010 Express) and *http://www.microsoft.com/express/Downloads/#2010-Visual-Web-Developer* (Visual Web Developer 2010 Express). If necessary, use the following information when installing the Professional or Express Editions of the software:

To configure Visual Studio 2010 or Visual Basic 2010 Express:

1. Start either Visual Studio 2010 or Visual Basic 2010 Express. If the Choose Default Environment Settings dialog box appears when you start Visual Studio, select the Visual Basic Development Settings option.

2. If you are using Visual Basic 2010 Express, click Tools on the menu bar, point to Settings, and then click Expert Settings.

3. Click Tools on the menu bar and then click Options to open the Options dialog box. If necessary, deselect the Show all settings check box. Click the Projects and Solutions node. Use the information shown in Figure 3-3 in Chapter 3 to select and deselect the appropriate check boxes. (Your dialog box will look slightly different if you are using Visual Basic 2010 Express.).

4. Expand the Projects and Solutions node in the Options dialog box and then click VB Defaults. Verify that both Option Explicit and Option Infer are set to On. Also verify that Option Strict and Option Compare are set to Off and Binary, respectively. Click the OK button to close the Options dialog box.

To configure Visual Web Developer 2010 Express:

1. Start Visual Web Developer 2010 Express. Click Tools on the menu bar, point to Settings, and then click Expert Settings.

2. Click Tools on the menu bar and then click Options to open the Options dialog box. If necessary, select the Show all settings check box. Click the Projects and Solutions node. Use the information shown in Figure 27-5 in Chapter 27 to select and deselect the appropriate check boxes. When you are finished, click the OK button to close the Options dialog box.

Figures

The figures in this book reflect how your screen will look if you are using Microsoft Visual Studio 2010 Professional Edition and a Microsoft Windows 7 system. Your screen may appear slightly different in some instances if you are using another version of Microsoft Visual Studio, Microsoft Visual Basic, or Microsoft Windows.

Visit Our Web Site

Additional materials designed for this textbook might be available at *www.cengagebrain.com*. Search this site for more details.

To the Instructor

To complete the computer activities in this book, your students must use a set of data files. The files are included on the Instructor's Resource CD. They also may be obtained electronically at *www.cengagebrain.com*.

The material in this book was written using Microsoft Visual Studio 2010 Professional Edition on a Microsoft Windows 7 system. It was Quality Assurance tested using the Express Editions of Microsoft Visual Basic 2010 and Microsoft Visual Web Developer 2010 on a Microsoft Windows 7 system. The book assumes that both Option Explicit and Option Infer are set to On, Option Strict is set to Off, and Option Compare is set to Binary. To verify these settings, start either Visual Studio 2010 or Visual Basic 2010 Express. Click Tools on the menu bar and then click Options. Expand the Projects and Solutions node in the Options dialog box and then click VB Defaults. Verify the four Option settings and then click the OK button to close the Options dialog box.

Course Technology Data Files

You are granted a license to copy the data files to any computer or computer network used by individuals who have purchased this book.

I Am *Not* a Control Freak! (Control Structures)

After studying Chapter 1, you should be able to:

◎ Describe the three control structures

◎ Write simple algorithms using the sequence, selection, and repetition structures

Control Structures

All computer programs, no matter how simple or how complex, are written using one or more of three basic structures: sequence, selection, and repetition. These structures are called **control structures** or **logic structures**, because they control the flow of a program's logic. You will use the sequence structure in every program you write. In most programs, you also will use both the selection and repetition structures. This chapter gives you an introduction to the three control structures. It also introduces you to a computerized mechanical man named Rob, who will help illustrate the control structures. More detailed information about each structure, as well as how to implement these structures using the Visual Basic language, is provided in subsequent chapters.

The Sequence Structure

You already are familiar with the sequence structure, because you use it each time you follow a set of directions, in order, from beginning to end. A cookie recipe, for instance, provides a good example of the sequence structure. To get to the finished product (edible cookies), you need to follow each recipe instruction in order, beginning with the first instruction and ending with the last. Likewise, the **sequence structure** in a computer program directs the computer to process the program instructions, one after another, in the order listed in the program. You will find the sequence structure in every program.

You can observe how the sequence structure works by programming a mechanical man named Rob. Like a computer, Rob has a limited instruction set. This means that Rob can understand only a specific number of instructions, also called commands. For now, you will use only three of the commands from Rob's instruction set: *walk forward, turn right 90 degrees,* and *sit down.* When told to *walk forward,* Rob takes one complete step forward. In other words, he moves his right foot forward one step and then moves his left foot to meet his right foot. For this first example, Rob is facing a chair that is two steps away from him. Your task is to write the instructions, using only the commands that Rob understands, that direct Rob to sit in the chair. Figure 1-1 shows Rob, the chair, and the instructions that will get Rob seated properly. The five instructions shown in the figure are called an **algorithm**, which is a set of step-by-step instructions that accomplish a task. For Rob to be properly seated in the chair, he must follow the instructions in order—in other words, in sequence.

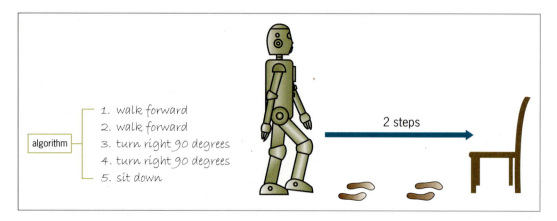

Figure 1-1   An example of the sequence structure

The Selection Structure

As with the sequence structure, you already are familiar with the **selection structure**, also called the **decision structure.** The selection structure indicates that a decision needs to be made, followed by an appropriate action derived from that decision. You use the selection structure every time you drive your car and approach a railroad crossing. Your decision, as well as the appropriate action, is based on whether the crossing signals (flashing lights and ringing bells) are on or off. If the crossing signals are on, you stop your car before crossing the railroad tracks; otherwise, you proceed with caution over the railroad tracks. When used in a computer program, the selection structure alerts the computer that a decision needs to be made, and it provides the appropriate action to take based on the result of that decision.

You can observe how the selection structure works by programming Rob, the mechanical man. In this example, Rob is holding either a red or yellow balloon, and he is facing two boxes. One of the boxes is colored yellow and the other is colored red. The two boxes are located three steps away from Rob. Your task is to have Rob drop the balloon into the appropriate box: the yellow balloon belongs in the yellow box, and the red balloon belongs in the red box. To write an algorithm to accomplish the current task, you need to use four additional instructions from Rob's instruction set: *if the balloon is red, do this:*, *otherwise, do this:*, *drop the balloon in the red box*, and *drop the balloon in the yellow box*. The additional instructions allow Rob to make a decision about the color of the balloon he is holding, and then take the appropriate action based on that decision. Figure 1-2 shows an illustration of the current example, along with the correct algorithm. Notice that the *drop the balloon in the red box* and *drop the balloon in the yellow box* instructions are indented within the selection structure. Indenting in this manner clearly indicates the instructions to be followed when the balloon is red, as well as the ones to be followed when the balloon is not red.

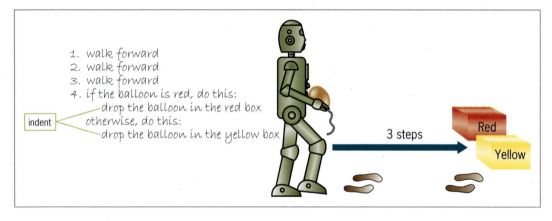

Figure 1-2   An example of the selection structure

The Repetition Structure

The last of the three control structures is the repetition structure. Like the sequence and selection structures, you already are familiar with the repetition structure. For example, shampoo bottles typically include the repetition structure in the directions for washing your hair. Those directions usually tell you to repeat the "apply shampoo to hair," "lather," and "rinse" steps until your hair is clean. When used in a program, the **repetition structure** directs the computer to repeat one or more instructions until some condition is met, at which time the computer should stop repeating the instructions. The repetition structure is also referred to as a **loop** or as **iteration**.

You can observe how the repetition structure works by programming Rob, the mechanical man. In this example, Rob is facing a chair that is 50 steps away from him. Your task is to write the algorithm that directs Rob to sit in the chair. If the repetition structure was not available to you, you would need to write the *walk forward* instruction 50 times, followed by the *turn right 90 degrees* instruction twice, followed by the *sit down* instruction. Although that algorithm would work, it is quite cumbersome to write. Imagine if Rob were 500 steps away from the chair! The best way to write the algorithm to get Rob seated in a chair that is 50 steps away from him

4

CHAPTER 1   I Am *Not* a Control Freak! (Control Structures)

is to use the repetition structure. To do so, however, you need to use another instruction from Rob's instruction set. In this case, you need to use the command *repeat x times:*, where *x* is the number of times you want Rob to repeat something. Figure 1-3 shows the illustration of Rob and the chair. It also shows the correct algorithm, which contains both the sequence and repetition structures. Notice that the instructions to be repeated (*walk forward* and *turn right 90 degrees*) are indented below their respective *repeat x times:* instruction. Indenting in this manner indicates that the instruction is part of the repetition structure and, therefore, needs to be repeated the specified number of times. Although both repetition structures shown in Figure 1-3 include only one instruction, a repetition structure can include many instructions.

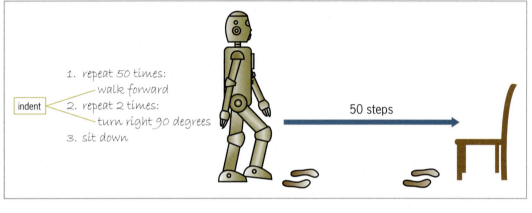

It's time to view the Ch1-Control Structures video.

Figure 1-3   An example of the repetition structure

Summary

- An algorithm is the set of step-by-step instructions that accomplish a task.

- The algorithms for all computer programs contain the sequence structure and either one or both of the following control structures: selection and repetition.

- The control structures, also called logic structures, control the flow of a program's logic.

- The sequence structure directs the computer to process the program instructions, one after another, in the order listed in the program.

- The selection structure, also called the decision structure, directs the computer to make a decision and then select an appropriate action based on that decision.

- The repetition structure directs the computer to repeat one or more program instructions until some condition is met.

Key Terms

Algorithm—the set of step-by-step instructions that accomplish a task

Control structures—the sequence, selection, and repetition structures, which control the flow of a program's logic; also called logic structures

Decision structure—another term for the selection structure

Iteration—another term for the repetition structure

Logic structures—another term for control structures

Loop—another term for the repetition structure

Repetition structure—the control structure that directs the computer to repeat one or more instructions until some condition is met, at which time the computer should stop repeating the instructions; also called a loop or iteration

Selection structure—the control structure that directs the computer to make a decision and then take the appropriate action based on that decision; also called the decision structure

Sequence structure—the control structure that directs the computer to process each instruction in the order listed in the program

Review Questions

1. The set of instructions for adding together two numbers is an example of the _____ structure.

   a. control c. selection
   b. repetition d. sequence

2. The recipe instruction "Beat until smooth" is an example of the _____ structure.

   a. control c. selection
   b. repetition d. sequence

3. The instruction "If it's raining outside, then take an umbrella to work" is an example of the _____ structure.

   a. control c. selection
   b. repetition d. sequence

4. Which control structure would an algorithm use to determine whether a credit card holder is over his credit limit?

   a. repetition
   b. selection
   c. both repetition and selection

5. A company pays a 10% commission to salespeople whose monthly sales are at least $5000; other salespeople receive a 7% commission. Which control structure would an algorithm use to calculate every salesperson's commission?

   a. repetition
   b. selection
   c. both repetition and selection

6. Which control structure would an algorithm use to determine whether a customer is entitled to a senior discount?

   a. repetition
   b. selection
   c. both repetition and selection

7. Which of the following control structures is used in every program?

   a. logic c. selection
   b. repetition d. sequence

6

CHAPTER 1 I Am *Not* a Control Freak! (Control Structures)

Exercises

You will use Rob (the mechanical man) and the instruction set shown in Figure 1-4 to complete Exercises 1, 3, 4, and 6.

walk forward

sit down

stand up

pick the flower with your right hand

pick the flower with your left hand

drop the toy in the toy chest

turn right 90 degrees

jump over the box

throw the box out of the way

if the box is red, do this:

if the flower is white, do this:

otherwise, do this:

repeat x times:

repeat until you are directly in front of the chair:

repeat until you are directly in front of the toy chest:

Figure 1-4 Rob's instruction set

TRY THIS

1. As illustrated in Figure 1-5, Rob is five steps away from a box that is an unknown distance away from a chair. Using only the instructions shown in Figure 1-4, create an algorithm that directs Rob to sit in the chair. Assume that Rob must jump over the box before he can continue toward the chair. (See Appendix B for the answer.)

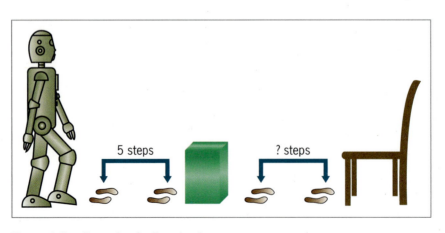

Figure 1-5 Illustration for Exercise 1

TRY THIS

2. Using only the instructions shown in Figure 1-6, create an algorithm that shows the steps an instructor takes when grading a test that contains 25 questions. (See Appendix B for the answer.)

```
if the student's answer is not the same as the correct answer, do this:
repeat 25 times:
read the student's answer and the correct answer
mark the student's answer incorrect
```

Figure 1-6   Instruction set for Exercise 2

3. Modify the answer to TRY THIS Exercise 1 as follows: Rob must jump over the box if the box is red. If the box is not red, Rob must throw the box out of the way. Use the instructions shown earlier in Figure 1-4.

    MODIFY THIS

4. Rob is facing a toy chest that is zero or more steps away from him. Rob is carrying a toy in his right hand. Using only the instructions shown earlier in Figure 1-4, create an algorithm that directs Rob to drop the toy in the toy chest.

    INTRODUCTORY

5. You have just purchased a new personal computer system. Before putting the system components together, you read the instruction booklet that came with the system. The booklet contains a list of the components that you should have received. The booklet advises you to verify that you received all of the components by matching those that you received with those on the list. If a component was received, you should cross its name off the list; otherwise, you should draw a circle around the component's name in the list. Using only the instructions shown in Figure 1-7, create an algorithm that shows the steps you should take to verify that the package contains the correct components.

    INTRODUCTORY

```
cross the component name off the list
read the component name from the list
circle the component name on the list
search the package for the component
if the component was received, do this:
otherwise, do this:
repeat for each component name on the list:
```

Figure 1-7   Instruction set for Exercise 5

6. As illustrated in Figure 1-8, Rob is standing in front of a flower bed that contains six flowers. Your task is to create an algorithm that directs Rob to pick the flowers as he walks to the other side of the flower bed. Rob should pick all white flowers with his right hand. Flowers that are not white should be picked with his left hand. Use the instructions shown earlier in Figure 1-4.

    INTERMEDIATE

Rob should end up on the other side of the flower bed

Figure 1-8   Illustration for Exercise 6

8

CHAPTER 1 I Am *Not* a Control Freak! (Control Structures)

INTERMEDIATE

7. A store gives a 10% discount to customers who are at least 65 years old. Using only the instructions shown in Figure 1-9, write two versions of an algorithm that prints the amount of money a customer owes. Be sure to indent the instructions appropriately.

assign 10% as the discount rate
assign 0 as the discount rate
calculate the amount due by subtracting the discount rate from the number 1,
and then multiplying the result by the item price

if the customer's age is greater than or equal to 65, do this:
if the customer's age is less than 65, do this:
otherwise, do this:
print the amount due
read the customer's age and item price

Figure 1-9 Instruction set for Exercise 7

ADVANCED

8. Create an algorithm for making a jelly sandwich.

ADVANCED

9. The algorithm shown in Figure 1-10 should instruct a payroll clerk on how to calculate and print the gross pay for five workers; however, some of the instructions are missing from the algorithm. Complete the algorithm. If an employee works more than 40 hours, he or she should receive time and one-half for the hours worked over 40.

_____
read the employee's name, hours worked, and pay rate
_____
    calculate gross pay = hours worked times pay rate
otherwise, do this:
    calculate regular pay = pay rate times 40
    calculate overtime hours = hours worked minus 40
    calculate overtime pay = _____
    calculate gross pay = _____
print the employee's name and gross pay

Figure 1-10 Algorithm for Exercise 9

FIGURE THIS OUT

10. Study the algorithm shown in Figure 1-11 and then answer the questions.

   a. Which control structures are used in the algorithm?

   b. What will the algorithm print when the user enters Mary Smith and 2000 as the salesperson's name and sales amount, respectively?

   c. How would you modify the algorithm so that it also prints the salesperson's sales amount?

   d. How would you modify the algorithm so that it can be used for any number of salespeople?

   e. How would you modify the algorithm so that it allows the user to enter the bonus rate, and then uses that rate to calculate the bonus amount?

repeat 5 times:
    get the salesperson's name and sales amount
    calculate the bonus amount by multiplying the sales amount by 3%
    print the salesperson's name and bonus amount

Figure 1-11 Algorithm for Exercise 10

11. The algorithm shown in Figure 1-12 does not get Rob through the maze illustrated in the figure. Correct the algorithm.

SWAT THE BUGS

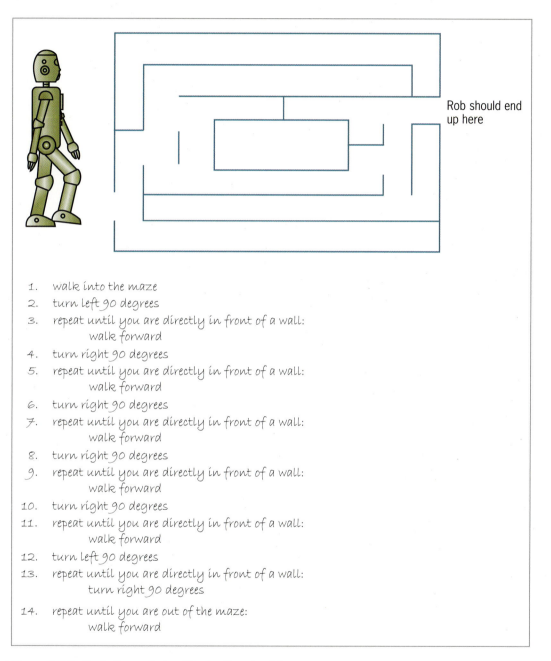

Rob should end up here

1. walk into the maze
2. turn left 90 degrees
3. repeat until you are directly in front of a wall:
        walk forward
4. turn right 90 degrees
5. repeat until you are directly in front of a wall:
        walk forward
6. turn right 90 degrees
7. repeat until you are directly in front of a wall:
        walk forward
8. turn right 90 degrees
9. repeat until you are directly in front of a wall:
        walk forward
10. turn right 90 degrees
11. repeat until you are directly in front of a wall:
        walk forward
12. turn left 90 degrees
13. repeat until you are directly in front of a wall:
        turn right 90 degrees
14. repeat until you are out of the maze:
        walk forward

Figure 1-12 Illustration and algorithm for Exercise 11

CHAPTER 2

First You Need to Plan the Party (Problem-Solving Process)

After studying Chapter 2, you should be able to:

◎ Identify the output and input in a problem specification

◎ Plan an algorithm using pseudocode and flowcharts

◎ Desk-check an algorithm

How Do Programmers Solve Problems?

Figure 2-1 lists the steps that computer programmers follow when solving problems that require a computer solution.

1. Analyze the problem
2. Plan the algorithm
3. Desk-check the algorithm
4. Create the user interface
5. Code the algorithm into a program
6. Desk-check the program
7. Rigorously test the program using the computer

Figure 2-1   Steps for solving a problem using a computer

This chapter covers the first three steps in the problem-solving process shown in Figure 2-1. The fourth step, which is to create the user interface, is covered in Chapters 3 and 4. The last three steps are explored in the remaining chapters.

Step 1—Analyze the Problem

You cannot solve a problem unless you understand it, and you cannot understand a problem unless you analyze it—in other words, unless you identify its important components. The two most important components of any problem are the problem's output and its input. The **output** is the goal of solving the problem, and the **input** is the item or items needed to achieve the goal. When analyzing a problem, you always search first for the output and then for the input. The first problem specification analyzed in this chapter is shown in Figure 2-2.

As a salesperson at J & J Sales, Addison Smith receives an annual commission, which is calculated by multiplying her annual sales by a commission rate. Addison wants a program that will both calculate and display the amount of her annual commission.

Figure 2-2   Problem specification for Addison Smith

A helpful way to identify the output is to search the problem specification for an answer to the following question: *What does the user want to see printed on paper, displayed on the screen, or stored in a file?* The answer to this question typically is stated as nouns and adjectives in the problem specification. For instance, the problem specification shown in Figure 2-2 indicates that Addison (the program's user) wants to see the amount of her annual commission displayed on the screen; therefore, the output is the annual commission. In this context, the word *annual* is an adjective, and the word *commission* is a noun.

After determining the output, you then determine the input. A helpful way to identify the input is to search the problem specification for an answer to the following question: *What information will the computer need to know to print, display, or store the output items?* Like the output, the input typically is stated as nouns and adjectives in the problem specification. When determining the input, it helps to think about the information that you would need to solve the problem manually, because the computer will need to know the same information. In this case, to determine Addison's annual commission, both you and the computer need to know her annual sales and the commission rate; both of these items, therefore, are the input. In this context, *annual* and *commission* are adjectives, and *sales* and *rate* are nouns. This completes the analysis step for the Addison Smith problem. Figure 2-3 summarizes the problem's output and input items.

Output: annual commission

Input: annual sales
          commission rate

Figure 2-3   Output and input items for the Addison Smith problem

Now you will analyze the problem specification shown in Figure 2-4.

Aiden Turner is paid every Friday. He is scheduled to receive a raise next week; however, he isn't sure of the exact raise percentage. Aiden wants a program that will both calculate and display the amount of his new weekly pay.

Figure 2-4   Problem specification for Aiden Turner

First, answer the following question: *What does the user want to see printed on paper, displayed on the screen, or stored in a file?* In this case, Aiden wants to see his new weekly pay displayed on the screen; therefore, the output is the new weekly pay. In this context, the words *new* and *weekly* are adjectives, and the word *pay* is a noun. Now answer the following question: *What information will the computer need to know to print, display, or store the output items?* To determine Aiden's new weekly pay, the computer needs to know Aiden's current weekly pay and his raise percentage; both of these items, therefore, are the input. In this context, *current*, *weekly*, and *raise* are adjectives, and *pay* and *percentage* are nouns. You have completed the analysis step for the Aiden Turner problem. The problem's output and input items are listed in Figure 2-5.

Output: new weekly pay

Input: current weekly pay
          raise percentage

Figure 2-5   Output and input items for the Aiden Turner problem

Unfortunately, analyzing real-world problems is not always as easy as analyzing the problems found in a textbook. The analysis step is the most difficult of the problem-solving steps, and it requires a lot of time, patience, and effort. If you are having trouble analyzing a problem, try reading the problem specification several times, as it is easy to miss information during the first reading. If the problem still is unclear to you, do not be shy about asking the user for more information. Remember, the more you understand a problem, the easier it will be for you to write a correct and efficient solution to the problem.

Mini-Quiz 2-1

See Appendix B for the answers.

For more examples of analyzing problems, see the Analyzing Problems section in the Ch2WantMore.pdf file.

1. Treyson Liverpool pays a state income tax on his yearly taxable wages. He wants a program that allows him to enter the amount of his yearly taxable wages. The program then should calculate and display the amount of his state income tax. Identify the output and the input.

2. Max Jones belongs to a CD (compact disc) club that allows him to buy CDs at a much lower price than charged at his local music store. He wants to know how much he saves by buying all of his CDs through the club rather than through the music store. Identify the output and the input.

3. Suman Patel saves the same amount of money each day. She wants to know the total amount she saves during a specific month. Identify the output and the input.

Step 2—Plan the Algorithm

The second step in the problem-solving process is to plan the algorithm, which is the set of instructions that, when followed, will transform the problem's input into its output. Most algorithms begin with an instruction that enters the input items into the computer. Next, you usually record instructions to process the input items to achieve the problem's output. The processing typically involves performing one or more calculations on the input items. Most algorithms end with an instruction to print, display, or store the output items. *Display*, *print*, and *store* refer to the computer screen, the printer, and a file on a disk, respectively. Figure 2-6 shows the output, input, and algorithm for the Addison Smith problem. The algorithm begins by entering the input items. It then uses the input items to calculate the output item. Notice that the algorithm states both what is to be calculated and how to calculate it. In this case, the annual commission is to be calculated by multiplying the annual sales by the commission rate. The last instruction in the algorithm displays the output item. To avoid confusion, it is important that the algorithm is consistent when referring to the input and output items. For example, if the input item is listed as *annual sales*, then the algorithm should refer to the item as *annual sales*, rather than using a different name, such as *sales* or *yearly sales*.

```
Output:   annual commission

Input:    annual sales
          commission rate


Algorithm:
1. enter the annual sales and commission rate
2. calculate the annual commission by multiplying the annual sales by the
   commission rate
3. display the annual commission
```

Figure 2-6 Output, input, and algorithm for the Addison Smith problem

The algorithm in Figure 2-6 is composed of short phrases, referred to as **pseudocode**. The word *pseudocode* means *false code*. It's called false code because, although it resembles programming language instructions, pseudocode cannot be understood by a computer. Programmers use pseudocode to help them while they are planning an algorithm. It allows them to jot down their ideas using a human-readable language without having to worry about the syntax of the programming language itself. Pseudocode is not standardized; every programmer has his or her own version, but you will find some similarities among the various versions. Programmers use the pseudocode as a guide when coding the algorithm, which is the fifth step in the problem-solving process.

Besides using pseudocode, programmers also use flowcharts when planning algorithms. Unlike pseudocode, a **flowchart** uses standardized symbols to visually depict an algorithm. You can draw the flowchart symbols by hand; or, you can use the drawing or shapes feature in a word processor. You also can use a flowcharting program, such as SmartDraw or Visio. Figure 2-7 shows the Addison Smith problem's algorithm in flowchart form. The flowchart contains three different symbols: an oval, a parallelogram, and a rectangle. The symbols are connected with lines, called **flowlines**. The oval symbol is called the **start/stop symbol**. The start oval indicates the beginning of the flowchart, and the stop oval indicates the end of the flowchart. Between the start and stop ovals are two parallelograms, called input/output symbols. You use the **input/output symbol** to represent input tasks (such as getting information from the user) and output tasks (such as displaying, printing, or storing information). The first parallelogram in Figure 2-7 represents an input task, while the last parallelogram represents an output task. The rectangle in a flowchart is called the **process symbol** and is used to represent tasks such as calculations.

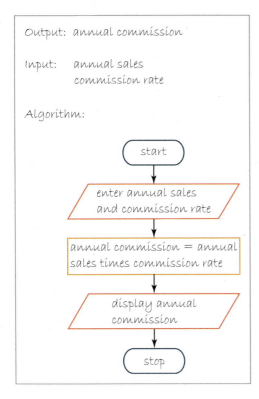

Output: annual commission

Input: annual sales
          commission rate

Algorithm:

Figure 2-7   Flowchart for the Addison Smith problem's algorithm

When planning an algorithm, you do not need to create both a flowchart and pseudocode; you need to use only one of these planning tools. The tool you use is really a matter of personal preference. For simple algorithms, pseudocode works just fine. When an algorithm becomes more complex, however, the program's logic may be easier to see in a flowchart. As the old adage goes, a picture is sometimes worth a thousand words.

Figure 2-8 shows the output, input, and algorithm for the Aiden Turner problem. Here too, the algorithm begins by entering the input items. It then uses both input items to calculate the output item. Again, notice that the calculation instructions state both what is to be calculated and how to calculate it. The last instruction in the algorithm displays the output item.

Output: new weekly pay

Input: current weekly pay
          raise percentage

Algorithm:
1. enter the current weekly pay and raise percentage
2. calculate the new weekly pay by multiplying the current weekly pay by the raise percentage, and then adding the result to the current weekly pay
3. display the new weekly pay

Figure 2-8   Output, input, and algorithm for the Aiden Turner problem

Even a very simple problem can have more than one solution. For example, Figure 2-9 shows a different solution to the Aiden Turner problem. In this solution, the weekly raise is calculated in a separate instruction rather than in the instruction that calculates the new weekly pay. The weekly raise is neither an input item (because it's not provided by the user) nor an output item (because it won't be displayed, printed, or stored in a file). Instead, the weekly raise is a special item, commonly referred to as a processing item. A **processing item** represents an intermediate value that the algorithm uses when processing the input into the output. In this case, the algorithm uses the two input items to calculate the weekly raise (an intermediate value), which the algorithm then uses to compute the new weekly pay. Keep in mind that not all algorithms require a processing item.

Output: new weekly pay

Processing: weekly raise

Input: current weekly pay
             raise percentage

Algorithm:
1. enter the current weekly pay and raise percentage
2. calculate the weekly raise by multiplying the current weekly pay by the raise percentage
3. calculate the new weekly pay by adding the weekly raise to the current weekly pay
4. display the new weekly pay

Figure 2-9   A different solution to the Aiden Turner problem

The solutions shown in Figures 2-8 and 2-9 produce the same result and simply represent two different ways of solving the same problem. Figure 2-10 shows Figure 2-9's algorithm in flowchart form.

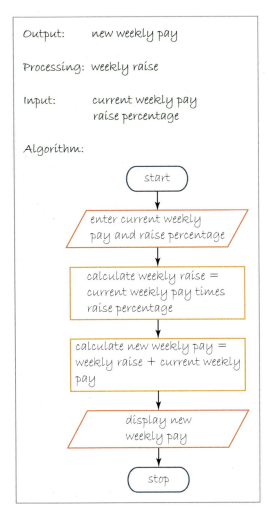

Output: new weekly pay

Processing: weekly raise

Input: current weekly pay
               raise percentage

Algorithm:

start

enter current weekly
pay and raise percentage

calculate weekly raise =
current weekly pay times
raise percentage

calculate new weekly pay =
weekly raise + current weekly
pay

display new
weekly pay

stop

Figure 2-10 Flowchart for the algorithm shown in Figure 2-9

Mini-Quiz 2-2

See Appendix B for the answers.

1. Treyson Liverpool pays a state income tax on his yearly taxable wages. He wants a program that both calculates and displays the amount of state income tax he must pay. The output is the annual state income tax. The input is the yearly taxable wages and the state income tax rate. Write the algorithm using pseudocode.

2. Rewrite Question 1's algorithm using a flowchart.

3. Max Jones belongs to a CD (compact disc) club that allows him to buy CDs at a much lower price than charged at his local music store. He wants to know how much he saves by buying all of his CDs through the club rather than through the music store. The output is the savings. The input is the number of CDs purchased, the club CD price, and the store CD price. The algorithm should use two processing items: one for the cost of buying the CDs through the club, and the other for the cost of buying the CDs through the store. Write the algorithm using pseudocode.

For more examples of planning algorithms, see the Planning Algorithms section in the Ch2WantMore.pdf file.

Step 3—Desk-Check the Algorithm

After analyzing a problem and planning its algorithm, you then desk-check the algorithm. The term **desk-checking** refers to the fact that the programmer reviews the algorithm while seated at his or her desk rather than in front of the computer. Desk-checking is also called **hand-tracing**, because the programmer uses a pencil and paper to follow each of the algorithm's instructions by hand. You desk-check an algorithm to verify that it is not missing any steps, and that the existing steps are correct and in the proper order.

Before you begin the desk-check, you first choose a set of sample data for the input values, which you then use to manually compute the expected output values. For the Addison Smith solution, you will use input values of $85000 and .08 (8%) as Addison's annual sales and commission rate, respectively. Addison's annual commission should be $6800 ($85000 times .08); therefore, $6800 is the expected output value. You now use the sample input values to desk-check the algorithm, which should result in the expected output value.

It is helpful to use a desk-check table when desk-checking an algorithm. The table should contain one column for each input item, as well as one column for each output item and one column for each processing item (if any). You can perform the desk-check using either the algorithm's pseudocode or its flowchart. Figure 2-11 shows the Addison Smith solution along with an appropriate desk-check table. (The flowchart for this solution is shown earlier in Figure 2-7.)

```
Output:   annual commission


Input:    annual sales
          commission rate


Algorithm:
1. enter the annual sales and commission rate
2. calculate the annual commission by multiplying the annual sales by the
   commission rate
3. display the annual commission



Desk-check table:
```

annual sales	commission rate	annual commission

Figure 2-11 Addison Smith solution and desk-check table

The first instruction in the algorithm is to enter the input values: $85000 for the annual sales and .08 for the commission rate. You record the results of this instruction by writing 85000 and .08 in the annual sales and commission rate columns, respectively, in the desk-check table, as shown in Figure 2-12.

annual sales	commission rate	annual commission
85000	.08	

Figure 2-12 Input values entered in the desk-check table

The second instruction in the algorithm is to calculate the annual commission by multiplying the annual sales by the commission rate. The desk-check table shows that the annual sales are 85000 and the commission rate is .08. Notice that you use the table to determine the annual sales and commission rate values; this helps to verify the accuracy of the algorithm. If, for example, the table did not show any amount in the commission rate column, you would know that your algorithm missed a step; in this case, it would have missed entering the commission rate. When you multiply the annual sales (85000) by the commission rate (.08), you get 6800. You record the number 6800 in the annual commission column, as shown in Figure 2-13.

annual sales	commission rate	annual commission
85000	.08	6800

Figure 2-13 Output value entered in the desk-check table

The last instruction in the algorithm is to display the annual commission. In this case, the number 6800 will be displayed because that is what appears in the annual commission column. Notice that this amount agrees with the manual calculation you performed prior to desk-checking the algorithm, so the algorithm appears to be correct. The only way to know for sure, however, is to test the algorithm a few more times with different input values. For the second desk-check, you will test the algorithm with annual sales of $3000 and a commission rate of .1 (10%). The annual commission should be $300. Recall that the first instruction in the algorithm is to enter the annual sales and commission rate. Therefore, you write 3000 in the annual sales column and .1 in the commission rate column, as shown in Figure 2-14. Notice that you cross out the previous values of these two items in the table before recording the new values; this is because each column should contain only one value at any time.

annual sales	commission rate	annual commission
~~85000~~	~~.08~~	6800
3000	.1	

Figure 2-14 Second set of input values included in the desk-check table

Next, you need to calculate the annual commission by multiplying the annual sales (3000) by the commission rate (.1); this results in an annual commission of 300. So you cross out the 6800 that appears in the annual commission column in the desk-check table and write 300 immediately below it, as shown in Figure 2-15. The last instruction in the algorithm is to display the annual commission. In this case, the number 300 will be displayed, which agrees with the manual calculation you performed earlier.

annual sales	commission rate	annual commission
~~85000~~	~~.08~~	~~6800~~
3000	.1	300

Figure 2-15 Results of the second desk-check included in the desk-check table

Next, you will desk-check the Aiden Turner algorithm twice, first using $400 and .03 (3%) as the current weekly pay and raise percentage, respectively, and then using $600 and .15 (15%). The new weekly pay for the first desk-check should be $412. The new weekly pay for the second desk-check should be $690. The Aiden Turner solution and completed desk-check table are shown in Figure 2-16. (The pseudocode is shown earlier in Figure 2-9.)

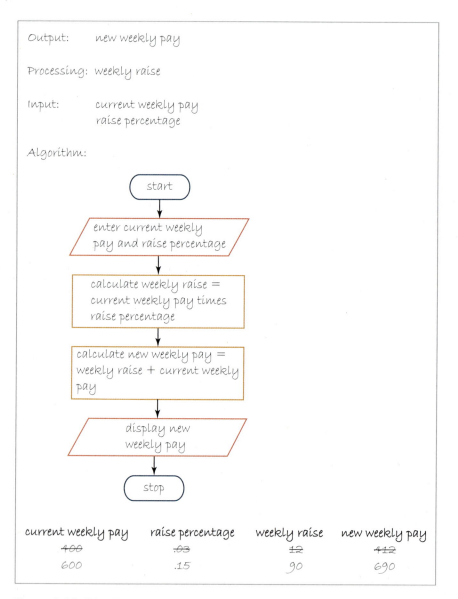

Figure 2-16 Aiden Turner solution and desk-check table

The amounts in the table agree with the manual calculations you performed earlier, so the algorithm appears to be correct. To be sure, however, you should desk-check it several more times, using both valid and invalid data. **Valid data** is data that the algorithm is expecting the user to enter. The Aiden Turner algorithm, for example, expects the user to provide positive numbers for the input values (current weekly pay and raise percentage). **Invalid data** is data that the algorithm is not expecting the user to enter. You should test an algorithm with invalid data because users sometimes make mistakes when entering data. The Aiden Turner algorithm, for instance, is not expecting the user to enter a negative value as the current weekly pay. A negative weekly pay is obviously an input error, because an employee cannot earn a negative amount for the week. In later chapters in this book, you will learn how to write algorithms that correctly handle input errors. You also will learn more about selecting good test data. For now, however, you can assume that the user of the program will always enter valid data.

Mini-Quiz 2-3

See Appendix B for the answers.

1. Desk-check the following algorithm twice. First, use a yearly taxable wage of $23000 and a 3% state income tax rate. Then use a yearly taxable wage of $14000 and a 2% state income tax.

   Algorithm:
   1. enter the yearly taxable wages and state income tax rate
   2. calculate the annual state income tax by multiplying the yearly taxable wages by the state income tax rate
   3. display the annual state income tax

2. Desk-check the following algorithm twice. First, use 20, $10.50, and $14.99 as the number of CDs purchased, the club CD price, and the store CD price, respectively. Then use 5, $9.99, and $11.

   Algorithm:
   1. enter the number of CDs purchased, the club CD price, and the store CD price
   2. calculate the club cost by multiplying the number of CDs purchased by the club CD price
   3. calculate the store cost by multiplying the number of CDs purchased by the store CD price
   4. calculate the savings by subtracting the club cost from the store cost
   5. display the savings

For more examples of desk-checking algorithms, see the Desk-Checking Algorithms section in the Ch2WantMore.pdf file.

It's time to view the Ch2-Planning Algorithms video.

Summary

- The first three steps in the problem-solving process are to analyze the problem, plan the algorithm, and desk-check the algorithm.

- When analyzing a problem description, the programmer first determines the output, which is the goal or purpose of solving the problem. The programmer then determines the input, which is the information needed to reach the goal. Some algorithms use intermediate values, called processing items.

- Programmers use tools, such as pseudocode and flowcharts, to organize their thoughts as they analyze problems and develop algorithms. These tools are used when coding the algorithm into a program, which is the fifth step in the problem-solving process.

- Most algorithms begin by entering data (the input items), followed by processing the data (usually by performing some calculations), followed by displaying, printing, or storing data (the output items).

- The calculation instructions in an algorithm should specify both what is to be calculated and how to perform the calculation.

- After completing the analysis and planning steps, a programmer then desk-checks the algorithm to determine whether it works as intended.

Key Terms

Desk-checking—the process of manually walking through each of the steps in an algorithm; also called hand-tracing

Flowchart—a tool that programmers use when planning an algorithm; consists of standardized symbols

Flowlines—the lines connecting the symbols in a flowchart

Hand-tracing—another term for desk-checking

Input—the items an algorithm needs to achieve the output

Input/output symbol—the parallelogram in a flowchart; used to represent input and output tasks

Invalid data—data that an algorithm is not expecting the user to enter

Output—the goal or purpose of solving a problem

Process symbol—the rectangle in a flowchart; used to represent tasks such as calculations

Processing item—an intermediate value that an algorithm uses when transforming the input into the output

Pseudocode—a tool that programmers use when planning an algorithm; consists of short phrases

Start/stop symbol—the oval in a flowchart; used to mark the beginning and end of the flowchart

Valid data—data that an algorithm is expecting the user to enter

Review Questions

1. Programmers refer to the items needed to reach a problem's goal as the _____ .

   a. input   c. processing
   b. output   d. purpose

2. The calculation instructions in an algorithm should state _____ .

   a. only what is to be calculated
   b. only how to calculate something
   c. both what is to be calculated and how to calculate it
   d. both what is to be calculated and why it is calculated

3. Most algorithms follow the format of _____ .

   a. entering the input items; then displaying, printing, or storing the output items; and then processing the output items
   b. entering the input items; then processing the output items; and then displaying, printing, or storing the output items
   c. entering the input items; then processing the input items; and then displaying, printing, or storing the output items
   d. entering the output items; then processing the input items; and then displaying, printing, or storing the output items

4. In a flowchart, the _____ symbol is used to represent an instruction that gets information from the user.

   a. enter

   b. input/output

   c. process

   d. start/stop

5. When desk-checking an algorithm, you should set up a table that contains _____ .

   a. one column for each input item and one column for each output item

   b. one column for each input item and one column for each processing item

   c. one column for each processing item and one column for each output item

   d. one column for each input item, one column for each processing item, and one column for each output item

6. The instruction sales tax = sales times tax rate would appear in a(n) _____ in a flowchart.

   a. oval

   b. parallelogram

   c. rectangle

   d. square

7. What is the purpose of a processing item in an algorithm?

Exercises

1. Jerry Feingold wants a program that will help him calculate the amount to tip a waiter at **TRY THIS** a restaurant. The program should subtract any liquor charge from the total bill and then calculate the tip (using a percentage) on the remainder. Finally, the program should display the tip on the screen. Desk-check your solution's algorithm using $85 as the total bill, $20 as the liquor charge, and 20% as the tip percentage. Then desk-check it using $35 as the total bill, $0 as the liquor charge, and 15% as the tip percentage. (See Appendix B for the answer.)

2. Party-On sells individual hot/cold cups and dessert plates for parties. Sue Chen wants a **TRY THIS** program that allows her to enter the price of a cup, the price of a plate, the number of cups purchased, and the number of plates purchased. The program should then calculate the total cost of the purchase, including the sales tax. Finally, the program should display the total cost on the screen. Desk-check your solution's algorithm using $.50 as the cup price, $1 as the plate price, 35 as the number of cups, 35 as the number of plates, and 2% as the tax rate. Then desk-check it using $.25, $.75, 20, 10, and 6%. (See Appendix B for the answer.)

3. Modify the answer to Exercise 1 as follows. Jerry will be charging the total bill, including **MODIFY THIS** the tip, to his credit card. Modify the solution so that, in addition to calculating and displaying the appropriate tip, it also calculates and displays the amount charged to Jerry's credit card. Desk-check the algorithm using $50 as the total bill, $5 as the liquor charge, and 20% as the tip percentage. Then desk-check it using $15 as the total bill, $0 as the liquor charge, and 15% as the tip percentage.

4. Wilma Peterson is paid by the hour. She would like a program that both calculates and **INTRODUCTORY** displays her weekly gross pay. For this exercise, you do not need to worry about overtime pay, as Wilma never works more than 40 hours in a week. Desk-check your solution's algorithm using $10 as the hourly pay and 35 as the number of hours worked. Then desk-check it using $15 as the hourly pay and 25 as the number of hours worked.

5. When Jacob Steinberg began his trip from California to Vermont, he filled his car's tank **INTRODUCTORY** with gas and reset its trip meter to zero. After traveling 324 miles, Jacob stopped at a gas station to refuel; the gas tank required 17 gallons. Jacob wants a program that calculates his car's gas mileage at any time during the trip. The gas mileage is the number of miles

his car can be driven per gallon of gas. The program should display the gas mileage on the screen. Desk-check your solution's algorithm using 324 as the number of miles driven and 17 as the number of gallons used. Then desk-check it using 280 and 15.

INTERMEDIATE   6.   Jenna Williams is paid based on an annual salary rather than an hourly wage. She wants a program that both calculates and displays the amount of money she should receive each pay period. Desk-check your solution's algorithm twice, using your own set of data.

INTERMEDIATE   7.   Rent A Van wants a program that calculates the total cost of renting a van. Customers pay a base fee plus a charge per mile. Currently, the base fee and charge per mile are $50 and $.20, respectively; however, the program should allow the user to enter both items. The program should display the total cost on the screen. Desk-check your solution's algorithm twice, using your own set of data.

INTERMEDIATE   8.   To celebrate her birthday, Sydney Pomeroy is taking a group of friends (adults and children) to a movie. If they attend the matinee showing, the price for adults and children is $7; otherwise, it is $12 for adults and $7 for children. Sydney wants a program that calculates how much less it would cost to take her friends to the matinee showing. Desk-check your solution's algorithm twice, using your own set of data.

INTERMEDIATE   9.   The manager of Mama Calari's Pizza Palace wants a program that both calculates and displays the number of pizza slices into which a circular pizza can be divided. The manager will enter the radius of the entire pizza. For this exercise, use 14.13 as the area of a pizza slice, and use 3.14 as the value of pi. Desk-check your solution's algorithm twice. For the first desk-check, use 10 as the pizza's radius; use 8 for the second desk-check. (Hint: For the first desk-check, the number of pizza slices should be a little over 22.)

ADVANCED   10.   The River Bend Hotel needs a program that both calculates and displays a customer's total bill. Each customer pays a room charge that is based on a per-night rate. For example, if the per-night rate is $55 and the customer stays two nights, the room charge is $110. Customers also may incur room service charges and telephone charges. In addition, each customer pays an entertainment tax, which is a percentage of the room charge only. Desk-check your solution's algorithm twice, using your own set of data.

ADVANCED   11.   The Paper Tree store wants a program that both calculates and displays the number of single rolls of wallpaper needed to cover a room. The salesclerk will provide the room's length, width, and ceiling height, in feet. He or she also will provide the number of square feet a single roll will cover. Desk-check your solution's algorithm twice, using your own set of data.

FIGURE THIS OUT   12.   The manager of a video store wants a program that calculates the amount a customer owes when he or she returns a video. A customer can return only one video at a time. The rental fee is $3.50 for four days. Customers are charged a late fee (currently, $2) per day when the video is returned after the due date. Study the algorithm and desk-check table shown in Figure 2-17, and then answer the questions.

a.   What will the algorithm display when the user enters 3 as the number of late days? What will it display when the user enters 0 as the number of late days?

b.   How would you modify the solution and desk-check table to include the total late charge as a processing item?

c.   How would you modify the solution from Question b to also display the total late charge?

```
Output:    amount due

Input:     number of late days
           daily late fee

Algorithm:
1.  enter the number of late days and daily late fee
2.  calculate the amount due by multiplying the number of late days by the daily late
    fee, and then adding 3.50 to the result
3.  display the amount due

Desk-check table:
number of late days        daily late fee        amount due
        3                        2                   9.50
        0                        2                   3.50
```

Figure 2-17 Algorithm and desk-check table for Exercise 12

13. Correct the algorithm shown in Figure 2-18. The algorithm should calculate the average of three numbers.

SWAT THE BUGS

```
Output:        average

Processing:    sum

Input:         first number
               second number
               third number

Algorithm:
1.  enter the first number, second number, and third number
2.  calculate the average by dividing the sum by 3
3.  display the average number
```

Figure 2-18 Algorithm for Exercise 13

CHAPTER 3

I Need a Tour Guide (Introduction to Visual Basic 2010)

After studying Chapter 3, you should be able to:

- ◎ Create a Windows application in Visual Basic 2010
- ◎ Use the Label and PictureBox tools to add controls to a form
- ◎ Set the properties of an object
- ◎ Save a solution
- ◎ Size and align objects using the Format menu
- ◎ Lock the controls on a form
- ◎ Start and end an application
- ◎ Close and open an existing solution

Ok, the Algorithm Is Correct. What's Next?

As you learned in Chapter 2, the first three steps in the problem-solving process are to analyze the problem, plan the algorithm, and then desk-check the algorithm. When you are sure that the algorithm produces the desired results, you can move on to the fourth step, which is to create the user interface. A **user interface** is what appears on the screen, and with which you interact, while using a program. In this book, you will create the user interfaces for your programs using the tools available in Visual Basic 2010. Visual Basic 2010 is available as a stand-alone product, called Visual Basic 2010 Express, or as part of Visual Studio 2010—Microsoft's newest integrated development environment. An **integrated development environment** (**IDE**) is an environment that contains all of the tools and features you need to create, run, and test your programs. In the following steps, you learn how to start either Visual Studio 2010 or Visual Basic 2010 Express.

To start Visual Studio 2010 or Visual Basic 2010 Express:

1. Click the **Start** button on the Windows 7 taskbar and then point to **All Programs**.

2. *If you are using Visual Studio 2010*, click **Microsoft Visual Studio 2010** on the All Programs menu and then click **Microsoft Visual Studio 2010**. If the Choose Default Environment Settings dialog box appears, click **Visual Basic Development Settings** and then click **Start Visual Studio**.
   If you are using Visual Basic 2010 Express, you will need to either click **Microsoft Visual Basic 2010 Express** on the All Programs menu or click **Microsoft Visual Studio 2010 Express** on the All Programs menu and then click **Microsoft Visual Basic 2010 Express**.

3. Click **Window** on the menu bar, click **Reset Window Layout**, and then click the **Yes** button. When you start Visual Studio 2010 Professional, your screen will appear similar to Figure 3-1. When you start Visual Basic 2010 Express, your screen will appear similar to Figure 3-2. As both figures indicate, the startup screen contains the Start Page window, Toolbox window, and Solution Explorer window. The startup screen in Visual Studio 2010 Professional also contains the Team Explorer window.

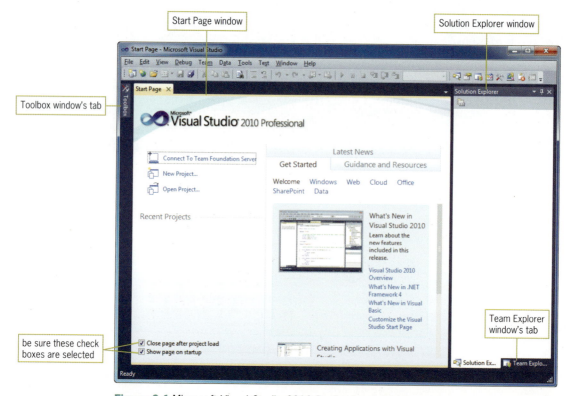

Figure 3-1 Microsoft Visual Studio 2010 Professional startup screen

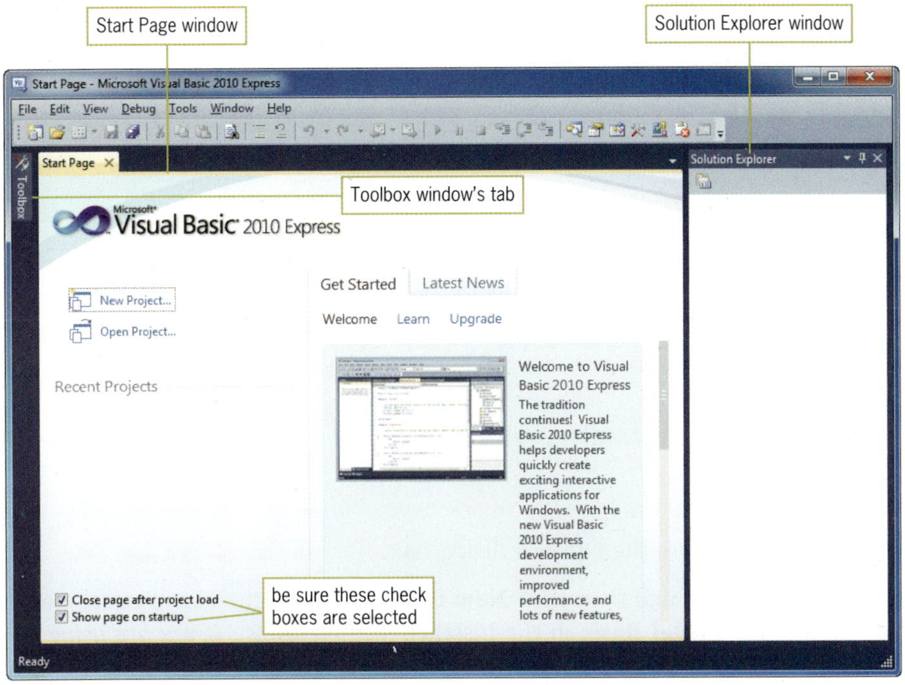

Figure 3-2 Microsoft Visual Basic 2010 Express startup screen

Included in Visual Studio 2010 are the Visual Basic, Visual C++, and Visual C# programming languages. You can use these languages to code your algorithms into programs, which is the fifth step in the problem-solving process. The combination of the user interface and the program's code is referred to as an application. You can create various types of applications in Visual Basic, such as Windows applications and Web applications. A Windows application has a Windows user interface and runs on a desktop computer. A Web application, on the other hand, has a Web user interface and runs on a server. You access a Web application using your computer's browser. This book focuses on Windows applications; however, Web applications are covered later in the book.

Creating a Visual Basic Windows Application

Windows applications in Visual Basic are composed of solutions, projects, and files. A solution is a container that stores the projects and files for an entire application. Although most solutions contain only one project, a solution can contain several projects. A project also is a container, but it stores only the files associated with that particular project. The following steps show you how to create a Windows application in Visual Basic 2010. The first two steps are necessary so that your screen agrees with the figures and subsequent steps in this book.

To create a Visual Basic 2010 Windows application:

1. *If you are using Visual Basic 2010 Express*, click **Tools** on the menu bar and then point to **Settings**. If necessary, click **Expert Settings** to select it.

2. Click **Tools** on the menu bar and then click **Options** to open the Options dialog box. If necessary, deselect the **Show all settings** check box. Click the **Projects and Solutions** node. Use the information shown in Figure 3-3 to select and deselect the appropriate check boxes. (Your dialog box will look slightly different if you are using Visual Basic 2010 Express.)

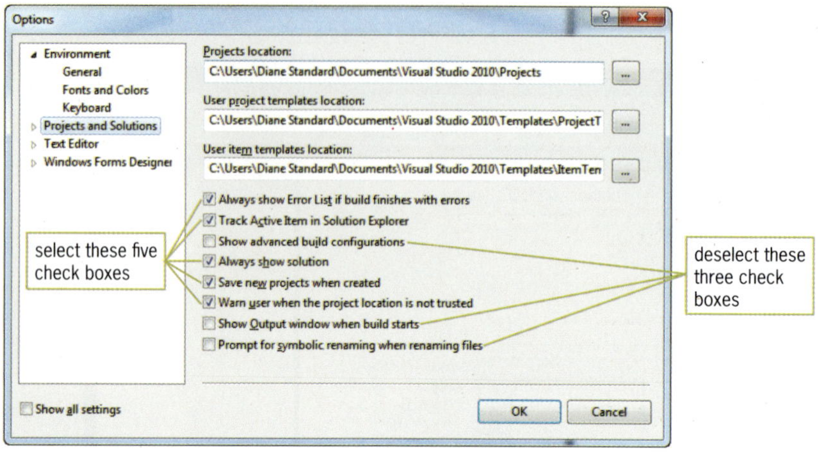

Figure 3-3 Options dialog box

3. Click the **OK** button to close the Options dialog box.

4. Click **File** on the menu bar and then click **New Project** to open the New Project dialog box. If necessary, click **Visual Basic** in the Installed Templates list. *If you are using Visual Studio*, expand the Visual Basic node, if necessary, and then click **Windows**.

5. If necessary, click **Windows Forms Application** in the middle column of the dialog box.

6. Change the name entered in the Name box to **My Pet Project**.

7. Click the **Browse** button to open the Project Location dialog box. Locate and then click the **ClearlyVB2010\Chap03** folder. Click the **Select Folder** button to close the Project Location dialog box.

8. If necessary, select the **Create directory for solution** check box in the New Project dialog box. Change the name entered in the Solution name box to **My Pet Solution**. Figures 3-4 and 3-5 show the completed New Project dialog box in Visual Studio 2010 Professional and Visual Basic 2010 Express, respectively. The drive letter will be different if you are saving to a device other than your computer's hard drive—for example, if you are saving to a flash drive.

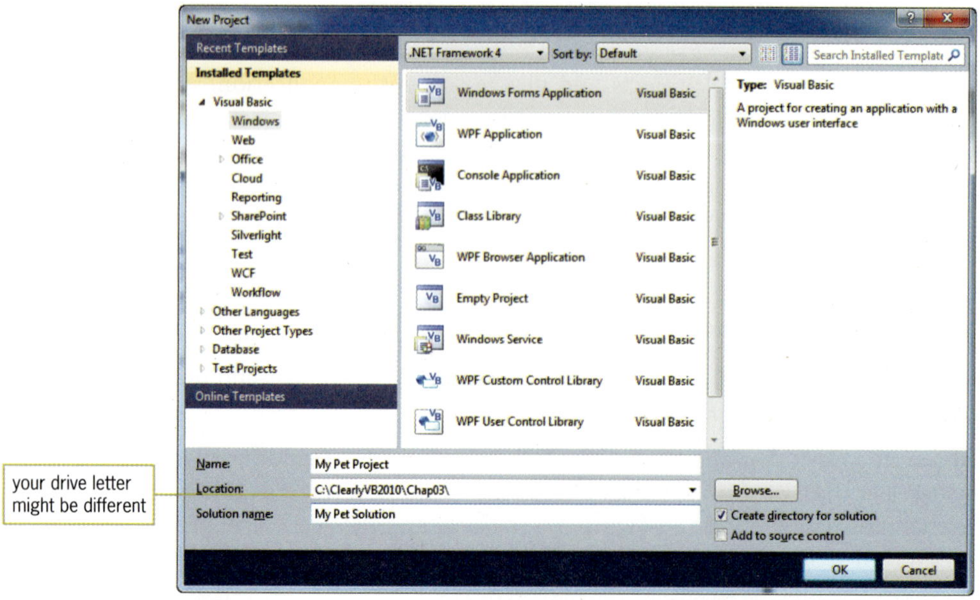

Figure 3-4 Completed New Project dialog box in Visual Studio 2010 Professional

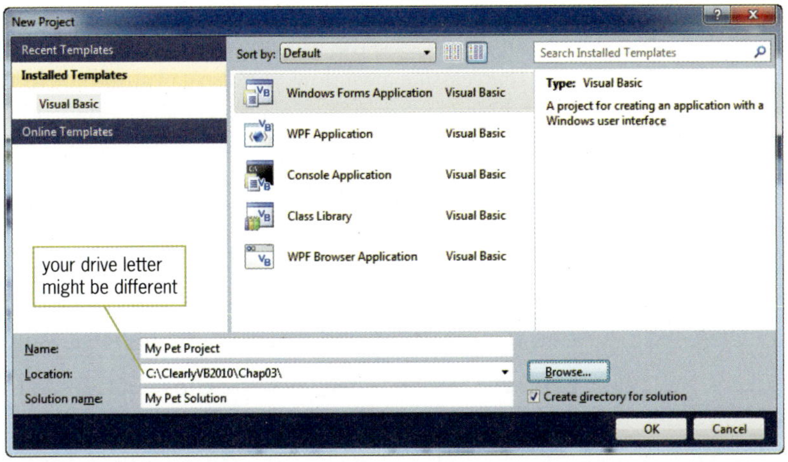

Figure 3-5   Completed New Project dialog box in Visual Basic 2010 Express

9. Click the **OK** button to close the New Project dialog box. The computer creates a
solution and adds a Visual Basic project to the solution, as shown in Figure 3-6. The
solution and project names appear in the Solution Explorer window. Notice that, in
addition to the windows mentioned earlier, three other windows appear in the IDE:
Windows Form Designer, Properties, and Data Sources. (If you are using Visual Basic
2010 Express, your title bar will say "My Pet Solution – Microsoft Visual Basic 2010
Express". In addition, your screen will not have the Team Explorer window.)

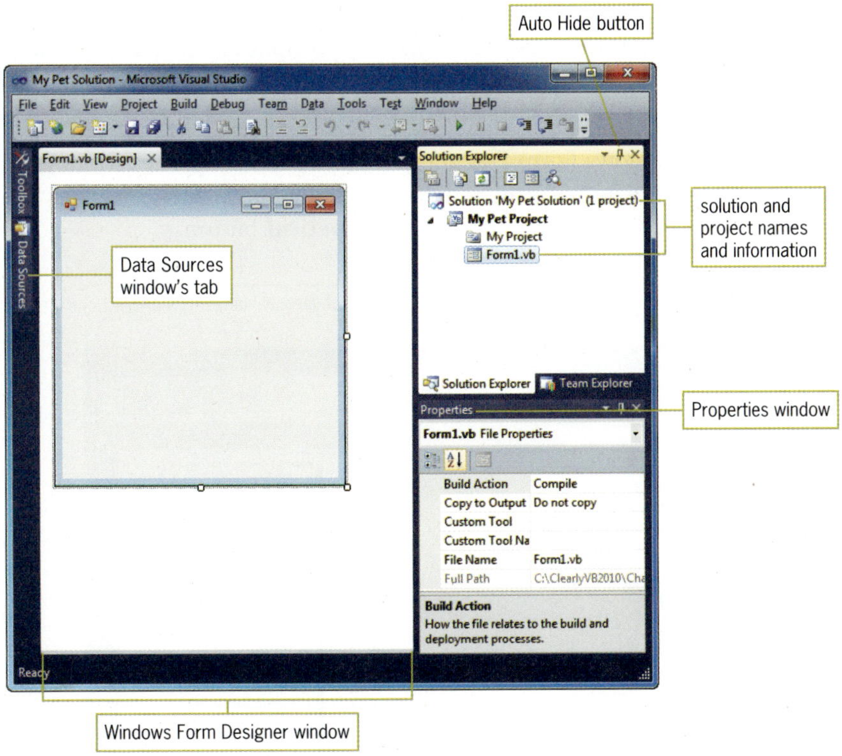

Figure 3-6   Solution and Visual Basic project

So Many Windows!

Having so many windows open in the IDE at the same time can be confusing, especially when you
are first learning the IDE. In most cases, you will find it easier to work in the IDE if you either close or

auto-hide the windows you are not currently using. The easiest way to close an open window is to click the Close button on the window's title bar. In most cases, the View menu provides an appropriate option for opening a closed window. Rather than closing a window, you also can auto-hide it. You auto-hide a window using the Auto Hide button (shown earlier in Figure 3-6) on the window's title bar. The Auto Hide button is a toggle button: clicking it once activates it, and clicking it again deactivates it. The Toolbox and Data Sources windows shown in Figure 3-6 are examples of auto-hidden windows.

To close, open, auto-hide, and display the windows in the IDE:

1. Click the **Close** button on the Properties window's title bar to close the window. To open the window, click **View** on the menu bar and then click **Properties Window**.

2. If necessary, click the **Team Explorer** tab, and then click the **Close** button on the Team Explorer window's title bar.

3. Click the **Auto Hide** button (the vertical pushpin) on the Solution Explorer window's title bar. The Solution Explorer window is minimized and appears as a tab on the right edge of the IDE.

4. To temporarily display the Solution Explorer window, place your mouse pointer on the Solution Explorer tab. The Solution Explorer window slides into view. Notice that the Auto Hide button is now a horizontal pushpin rather than a vertical pushpin.

5. Move your mouse pointer away from the Solution Explorer window. The window is minimized and appears as a tab again.

6. If necessary, close the Data Sources window.

7. To permanently display the Toolbox window, place your mouse pointer on the Toolbox tab and then click the **Auto Hide** button (the horizontal pushpin) on the window's title bar. The vertical pushpin replaces the horizontal pushpin on the button. If necessary, expand the **Common Controls** node in the Toolbox window.

8. Click the **Form1.vb [Design]** tab. Figure 3-7 shows the current status of the windows in the IDE. Only the Windows Form Designer, Toolbox, and Properties windows are open. The Solution Explorer window is auto-hidden. If the items in the Properties window do not appear in alphabetical order, click the **Alphabetical** button.

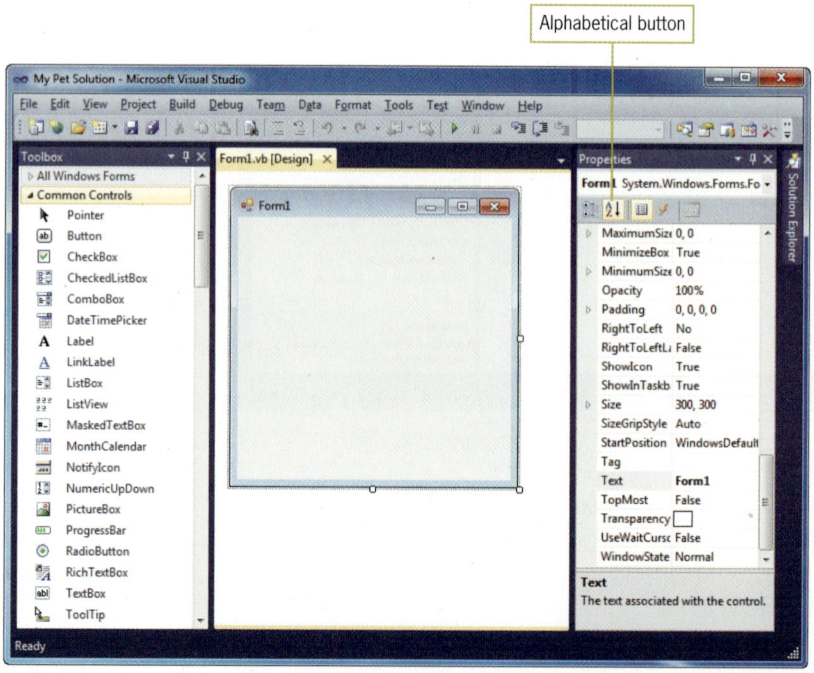

Figure 3-7   Current status of the windows in the IDE

Creating the User Interface

The **Windows Form Designer window** is where you create (or design) your application's user interface. The designer window shown in Figure 3-8 contains a **Windows Form object**, or form. A **form** is the foundation for the user interface in a Windows application. A form automatically includes a title bar that contains a default caption—in this case, Form1—as well as Minimize, Maximize, and Close buttons. At the top of the designer window is a tab labeled Form1.vb [Design]. [Design] identifies the window as the designer window. Form1.vb is the name of the file on your computer's hard disk (or on the device designated by your instructor or technical support person) that contains the Visual Basic instructions associated with the form.

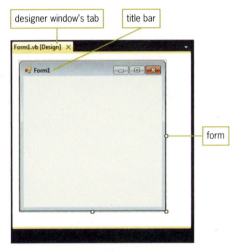

Figure 3-8 Windows Form Designer window

You create the user interface by adding objects (such as buttons, check boxes, and list boxes) to the form. The objects added to a form are called **controls**. Because the controls are graphical in nature, the user interface is often referred to as a graphical user interface, or **GUI**. You add the controls to the form using the tools contained in the **Toolbox window**. In the next set of steps, you begin creating the Pet Application interface shown in Figure 3-9. The interface contains four controls: two picture boxes and two labels. You use a **picture box** to display an image on the form. You use a **label control** to display text that the user is not allowed to edit while the application is running. Some label controls simply identify the contents of other controls. The label controls in Figure 3-9, for example, identify the contents of the picture boxes. Label controls also are used in an interface to display program output, such as the result of calculations. As you are creating the interface in the following steps, you also will learn how to move, delete, undelete, and size a control.

Figure 3-9 Pet Application user interface

To begin creating the Pet Application user interface:

1. Click the **Label** tool in the toolbox, but do not release the mouse button. Hold down the mouse button as you drag the mouse pointer to the lower-left corner of the form. As you drag the mouse pointer, you will see a solid box, as well as an outline of a rectangle and a plus box, following the mouse pointer. See Figure 3-10. Notice that a blue line appears between the form's left border and the control's left border, and between the control's bottom border and the form's bottom border. The blue lines are called margin lines, because their size is determined by the contents of the control's Margin property. The purpose of the margin lines is to assist you in spacing the controls properly on a form.

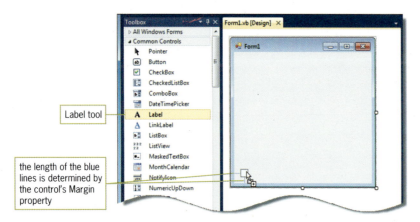

Label tool

the length of the blue lines is determined by the control's Margin property

Figure 3-10 Label tool being dragged to the form

2. Release the mouse button. A label control appears on the form, as shown in Figure 3-11. Notice that an asterisk (*) appears on the Form1.vb [Design] tab in the designer window. The asterisk indicates that the form has been changed since the last time it was saved.

the asterisk indicates that the form has been changed since the last time it was saved

Figure 3-11 Label control added to the form

3. Now you will practice repositioning a control on the form. Place your mouse pointer on the center of the label control, and then press the left mouse button and drag the control to another area of the form. (Don't worry about the exact location.) Release the mouse button.

4. Next, you will practice deleting and then restoring a control. Press the **Delete** key on your keyboard to delete the label control. Click **Edit** on the menu bar, and then click **Undo** to reinstate the label control.

5. Drag the label control back to its original location in the lower-left corner of the form.

6. Add another label control to the form. Place the label control in the center of the form.

7. Drag the Label2 control until its left border is aligned with the left border of the Label1 control, but don't release the mouse button. When the left borders of both controls are aligned, the designer displays a blue snap line, as shown in Figure 3-12.

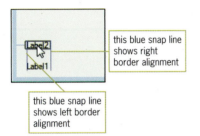

this blue snap line shows right border alignment

this blue snap line shows left border alignment

Figure 3-12 A blue snap line appears when the borders are aligned

8. Release the mouse button.

9. Now drag the Label2 control so that the Label2 text is aligned with the Label1 text. When the text in both controls is aligned, the designer displays a pink snap line, as shown in Figure 3-13.

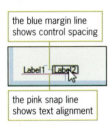

the blue margin line shows control spacing

the pink snap line shows text alignment

Figure 3-13 A pink snap line appears when the text is aligned

10. Release the mouse button.

11. Use the PictureBox tool to add two picture boxes to the form. See Figure 3-14. (You do not need to worry about the exact location of the controls in the interface.)

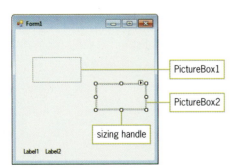

PictureBox1

PictureBox2

sizing handle

Figure 3-14 Picture boxes added to the form

To learn more about adding controls to a form, as well as sizing, moving, deleting, and undeleting the controls, view the Ch03-Controls video.

12. The sizing handles on the PictureBox2 control indicate that the control is selected. You can use the sizing handles to make the control bigger or smaller. First, use the sizing handles to make the picture box bigger. Then, use the Undo option on the Edit menu to return the control to its original size.

Save, Save, Save

It is a good practice to save the current solution every 10 or 15 minutes so that you will not lose a lot of your work if the computer loses power. You can save a solution by clicking File on the menu bar and then clicking Save All. You also can click the Save All button ![icon] on the Standard toolbar. When you save a solution, the computer saves any changes made to the files included in the solution. It also removes the asterisk that appears on the designer window's tab.

To save the current solution:

1. Click **File** on the menu bar and then click **Save All**.

Mini-Quiz 3-1

See Appendix B for the answers.

1. A _____ control displays text that the user is not allowed to edit while an application is running.

2. The _____ window contains the tools you use to add objects to a form.

3. GUI stands for _____.

Whose Property Is It?

Every object in a Visual Basic application has a set of attributes that determine the object's appearance and behavior; the attributes are called **properties**. When an object is created, a default value is assigned to each of its properties. The name and current value of each property appear in the **Properties window** when the object is selected.

To view the form's properties:

1. Click the **form** (but not a control on the form) to select it. Sizing handles appear on the form to indicate that the form is selected, and the form's properties appear in the Properties window.

2. Scroll up to the top of the Properties window. If necessary, click the **Alphabetical** button in the Properties window to display the property names in alphabetical order. Most times, it's easier to work with the Properties window when the property names are listed alphabetically.

3. Click **(Name)**, which is the third item in the Properties list, to select the form's Name property. Figure 3-15 shows a partial listing of the form's properties. Notice that items within parentheses appear at the top of the Properties list.

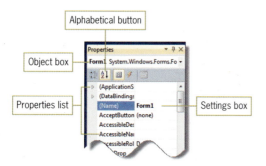

Figure 3-15 Partial listing of the form's properties

As indicated in Figure 3-15, the Properties window has an Object box and a Properties list. The **Object box** contains the name of the selected object—in this case, Form1. The **Properties list** has two columns. The left column displays the names of the selected object's properties. The right column contains the Settings box for each property. The **Settings box** displays the current value (or setting) of the property. For example, the current value of the form's Name property is Form1. Depending on the property, you can change the default value assigned to a property by selecting the property in the Properties list and then either typing the new value in the Settings box or selecting a predefined value from a list or dialog box. Although not shown in Figure 3-15, a brief description of the selected property appears in the Description pane located at the bottom of the Properties window.

In the next set of steps, you will change the values assigned to the form's Text, StartPosition, and Font properties. A form's Text property controls the text displayed in the form's title bar. The text also appears when you hover your mouse pointer over the application's button on the Windows 7 taskbar while the application is running. The StartPosition property specifies the position of the form when it first appears on the screen after the application is started. The Font property determines the type, style, and size of the font used to display the text on the form. A **font** is the general shape of the characters in the text. Segoe UI, Tahoma, and Microsoft Sans Serif are examples of font types. Font styles include regular, bold, and italic. The numbers 9, 12, and 18 are examples of font sizes, which typically are measured in points, with one **point** equaling 1/72 of an inch.

To change the values assigned to some of the form's properties:

1. Scroll down the Properties window and then click **Text** in the Properties list. Type **Pet Application** and press **Enter**. The Pet Application text appears in the Settings box and in the form's title bar.

2. Click **StartPosition** in the Properties list and then click the **list arrow** in the Settings box. Click **CenterScreen** to display the form in the center of the screen when the application is started.

3. Click **Font** in the Properties list and then click the **...** (ellipsis) button in the Settings box. Doing this opens the Font dialog box.
   Important note: The recommended font for applications created for systems running Windows 7 (or Windows Vista) is Segoe UI, because it offers improved readability. Segoe is pronounced SEE-go, and UI stands for user interface. For most of the elements in the interface, you will use the 9-point size of the font. However, to make the figures in the book more readable, some of the interfaces created in this book will use the 11-point Segoe UI font. You can change the Font property for each control individually; however, an easier way is to change the form's Font property. Any control whose Font property has not been set individually will be assigned the same font as the form.

4. Click **Segoe UI** in the Font list box and then click **9** in the Size list box. Click the **OK** button to close the Font dialog box. The form's Font property setting changes to the new value. The Font property setting for each label control also changes to the new value. To verify that fact, click the **Label1** control and then view its Font property setting. Click the **Label2** control and then view its Font property setting.

Next, you will change the Text and Location properties of the two label controls. A label control's Text property specifies the text displayed inside the control. Its Location property controls the location of the upper-left corner of the control on the form. (Although you can simply drag a control to the desired location, many times you will be provided with the setting for the Location property so that your screen agrees with the figures in this book.)

To change two properties of each label control:

1. Click the **Label1** control to select it, and then change its Text property to **Dog**.

2. Click the **Location** property in the Properties list. The first number in the Settings box specifies the control's horizontal location on the form; the second number specifies its vertical location. In other words, the first number is the location of the control's left border, and the second number is the location of its top border. Type **55, 212** and press **Enter**.

3. Click the **Label2** control. Set its Text property to **Cat** and its Location property to **240, 212**.

Finally, you will change the Image and SizeMode properties of the picture boxes. The Image property specifies the name of the file containing the image to display. The SizeMode property handles how the image is displayed and can be set to Normal, StretchImage, AutoSize, CenterImage, or Zoom. The images for the Pet Application's interface are stored in two image files contained in the ClearlyVB2010\Chap03 folder. Both image files were downloaded from the Microsoft Office site at *http://office.microsoft.com/en-us/images/*.

To change two properties of each picture box:

1. Click the **PictureBox1** control to select it. A box containing a triangle appears in the upper-right corner of the control. The box is referred to as the task box because, when you click it, it displays a list of the tasks associated with the control. Each task in the list is associated with one or more properties. You can set the properties using either the task list or the Properties window.

2. Click the **task box** on the PictureBox1 control. A list of tasks associated with a picture box appears. See Figure 3-16.

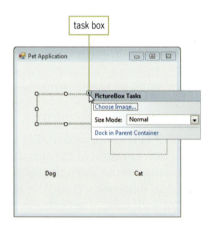

Figure 3-16 PictureBox1 control's task list

3. Click **Choose Image** to open the Select Resource dialog box. The Choose Image task is associated with the Image property in the Properties window.

4. Verify that the Project resource file radio button is selected, and then click the **Import** button to open the Open dialog box.

5. Open the ClearlyVB2010\Chap03 folder. Click **Dog (Dog.gif)** in the list of filenames and then click the **Open** button. A portion of the dog image appears in the Select Resource dialog box. See Figure 3-17.

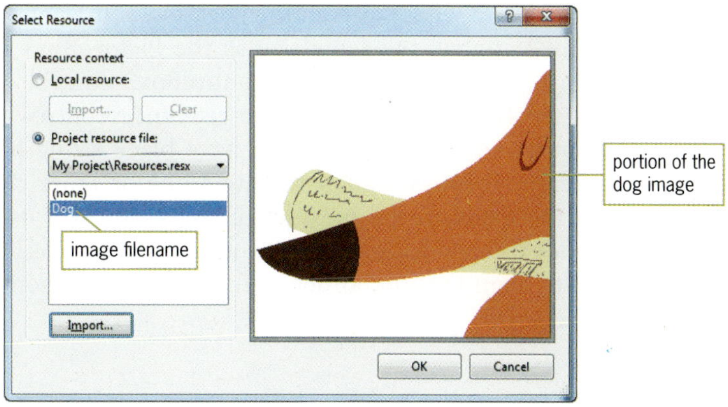

Figure 3-17 Select Resource dialog box

6. Click the **OK** button to close the Select Resource dialog box. Click the **Size Mode** list arrow in the task list and then click **StretchImage**. The dog image appears in the PictureBox1 control.

7. Click the **PictureBox1** control to close its task list, and then change its Size property to **115, 145**.

8. Drag the PictureBox1 control so that it is located above the Dog label. See Figure 3-18.

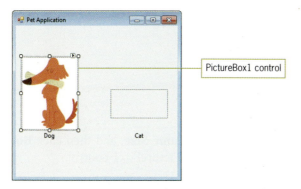

Figure 3-18 Location of the PictureBox1 control

9. Click the **PictureBox2** control and then click its **task box**. Use the task list to display the image contained in the **Cat** (**Cat.gif**) file. Also use the task list to set the SizeMode property to **StretchImage**.

10. Save the solution by clicking the **Save All** button on the Standard toolbar. (You also can click File on the menu bar and then click Save All.)

Using the Format Menu

The two picture boxes in the Pet Application interface are not the same size: PictureBox1 is larger than PictureBox2. You can make both picture boxes the same size by setting their Size properties to the same value in the Properties window. However, an easier way is to use the Format menu, which provides several options for manipulating the controls in the interface. The Align option, for example, allows you to align two or more controls by their left, right, top, or bottom borders. You can use the Make Same Size option to make two or more controls the same width and/or height. Before you can use the Format menu to change the alignment or size of two or more controls, you first must select the controls. You select the first control by clicking it. You select the second and subsequent controls by pressing and holding down the Control (Ctrl) key as you click the control. The first control you select should always be the one whose size and/or location you want to match. For example, to make the PictureBox2 control the same size as the PictureBox1 control, you first select the PictureBox1 control and then select the PictureBox2 control. The first control you select is referred to as the **reference control**. The reference control will have white sizing handles, whereas the other selected controls will have black sizing handles. The Format menu also has a Center in Form option that centers one or more controls either horizontally or vertically on the form. In the next set of steps, you will use the Format menu to make the PictureBox2 control the same size as the PictureBox1 control. You also will use the Format menu to align the top border of the PictureBox2 control with the top border of the PictureBox1 control.

To size and align the PictureBox2 control:

1. Click the **PictureBox1** control to select it. Now press and hold down the **Control** (**Ctrl**) key as you click the **PictureBox2** control, and then release the Control key. The two picture boxes are now selected. See Figure 3-19.

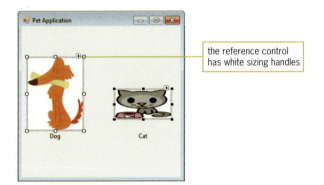

the reference control has white sizing handles

Figure 3-19 Both picture boxes selected on the form

2. Click **Format** on the menu bar, point to **Make Same Size**, and then click **Both**. The PictureBox2 control is now the same size as the PictureBox1 control.

3. Click **Format** on the menu bar, point to **Align**, and then click **Tops**. The top border of the PictureBox2 control is now aligned with the top border of the PictureBox1 control.

To learn more about the Format menu, view the Ch03-Format Menu video.

4. Click the **form** to deselect the picture boxes, and then set the form's Size property to **340, 305**. (You may need to reposition one or more of the controls after setting the form's Size property.)

5. Save the solution.

Lock Them Down

In the next set of steps, you will lock the controls in place on the form. Locking the controls prevents them from being moved inadvertently as you work in the IDE.

To lock the controls:

1. Right-click the **form** and then click **Lock Controls** on the context menu. Notice that a small lock appears in the upper-left corner of the form. (You also can lock the controls by clicking Format on the menu bar and then clicking Lock Controls.) See Figure 3-20.

Figure 3-20 Controls locked on the form

2. Click the **PictureBox1** control. The small lock in the upper-left corner of the control indicates that the control is locked.

3. Try dragging the PictureBox1 control to a different location on the form. You will not be able to do so.

If you need to move a control after you have locked the controls in place, you can change the control's Location property setting in the Properties window. You also can unlock the control by changing its Locked property to False. To unlock all of the controls, right-click the form and then click Lock Controls on the context menu; you also can use the Lock Controls option on the Format menu. The Lock Controls option on both the context menu and the Format menu is a toggle option: clicking it once activates it, and clicking it again deactivates it.

To unlock and then lock the controls:

1. Right-click the **form** and then click **Lock Controls** to unlock the controls. Notice that the small lock no longer appears in the upper-left corner of the form.

2. Right-click the **form** and then click **Lock Controls** to lock the controls.

Ok, Let's See the Interface in Action!

Now that the user interface is complete, you can start the application to see how it will look to the user. You can start an application by clicking the Start Debugging option on the Debug menu; or you can simply press the F5 key on your keyboard.

To start and then stop the current application:

1. Save the solution. Click **Debug** on the menu bar and then click **Start Debugging** to start the application. (You also can press the F5 key on your keyboard.) See Figure 3-21. (Do not be concerned about any windows that appear at the bottom of your screen.)

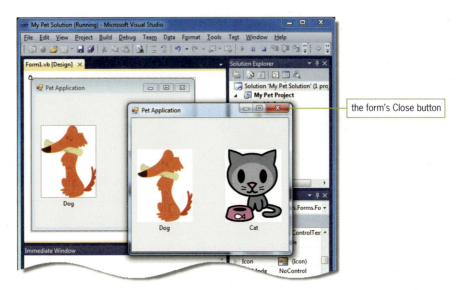

the form's Close button

Figure 3-21 Result of starting the Pet Application

2. Click the **Close** button on the form's title bar to stop the application. (You also can click the designer window to make it the active window, click Debug on the menu bar, and then click Stop Debugging.) When the application ends, you are returned to the IDE.

Closing the Current Solution

When you are finished working on a solution, you should close it. Closing a solution closes all projects and files contained in the solution. If unsaved changes were made to the solution, project, or form, a dialog box opens and prompts you to save the appropriate files. You close a solution using the Close Solution option on the File menu. Be careful to use the Close Solution option rather than the Close option. The Close option does not close the solution; instead, it closes the designer window.

To close the current solution:

1. Click **File** on the menu bar and then click **Close Solution**.

2. Temporarily display the Solution Explorer window to verify that no solutions are open in the IDE.

Opening an Existing Solution

You can use the File menu to open an existing solution. If a solution is already open in the IDE, it is closed before another solution is opened.

To open the My Pet Solution:

1. Permanently display the Solution Explorer window.

2. Click **File** on the menu bar, and then click **Open Project** to open the Open Project dialog box.

3. Locate and then open the ClearlyVB2010\Chap03\My Pet Solution folder. If necessary, click **My Pet Solution** (**My Pet Solution.sln**) in the list of filenames, and then click the **Open** button.

4. If you do not see the form in the designer window, right-click **Form1.vb** in the Solution Explorer window and then click **View Designer**.

Exiting Visual Studio 2010 or Visual Basic 2010 Express

You can exit Visual Studio 2010 or Visual Basic 2010 Express using either the Close button on its title bar or the Exit option on the File menu.

To exit Visual Studio 2010 or Visual Basic 2010 Express:

1. Click **File** on the menu bar and then click **Exit** on the menu.

Mini-Quiz 3-2

See Appendix B for the answers.

1. The name of the image file assigned to a picture box control is stored in the control's _____ property.

2. The value assigned to a label control's _____ property appears inside the control.

3. A control's Location property specifies the location of the control's _____ corner on the form.

4. To make the PictureBox1 control the same size as the PictureBox2 control, you first select the _____ control.

5. To start a Visual Basic application, click Debug on the menu bar and then click _____ .

Summary

- Creating the user interface is the fourth step in the problem-solving process.

- Windows applications in Visual Basic are composed of solutions, projects, and files.

- You create a user interface by adding controls to a form in the Windows Form Designer window. You add a control using a tool from the Toolbox window.

- Label controls display text that the user is not allowed to edit while an application is running.

- You use picture boxes to display images on a form.

- A blue snap line appears when the border of one control is aligned with the border of another control. A pink snap line appears when the text in two or more controls is aligned.

- It's a good practice to save a solution every 10 or 15 minutes.

- The Properties window lists the properties of the selected object.

- The value assigned to a form's Text property appears in the form's title bar. It also appears when you hover your mouse pointer over the application's button on the Windows 7 taskbar while an application is running. The value assigned to a label control's Text property, on the other hand, appears inside the control.

- A form's StartPosition property specifies the position of the form when it first appears on the screen after the application is started.

- The Font property determines the type, style, and size of the font used to display the text on the form or inside a control. Segoe UI is the recommended font for applications created for systems running either Windows 7 or Windows Vista. Any control whose Font property has not been set individually will be assigned the same Font property value as the form.

● The value assigned to a control's Location property specifies the location of the upper-left corner of the control on the form.

● A picture box control's Image property specifies the name of the file containing the image to display. Its SizeMode property handles how the image is displayed.

● The Format menu provides options for aligning, sizing, and centering the controls on a form. The first control you select is called the reference control and is the one whose size and/or location you want to match. The reference control will have white sizing handles, whereas the other selected controls will have black sizing handles.

● It's a good practice to lock the controls in place on the form.

● To start an application, click Debug on the menu bar and then click Start Debugging. You also can start an application by pressing the F5 key on your keyboard.

● You use the Close Solution option on the File menu to close a solution.

Key Terms

Controls—objects (such as labels and picture boxes) added to a form

Font—the general shape of the characters used to display text

Form—the foundation for the user interface in a Windows application; also called a Windows form object

GUI—an acronym for graphical user interface

IDE—an acronym for integrated development environment

Integrated development environment—an environment that contains all of the tools and features needed to create, run, and test programs; also called an IDE

Label control—the control used to display text that the user is not allowed to edit while an application is running

Object box—the section of the Properties window that contains the name of the selected object

Picture box—the control used to display an image on a form

Point—used to measure font size; 1/72 of an inch

Properties—the attributes that determine an object's appearance and behavior

Properties list—the section of the Properties window that lists the names of the properties associated with the selected object, as well as each property's value

Properties window—the window that lists the selected object's attributes (properties)

Reference control—the first control selected in a group of two or more controls; this is the control whose size and/or location you want the other selected controls to match

Settings box—the right column of the Properties list; displays the current value (setting) of a property

Toolbox window—the window that contains the tools used to add controls to a form; referred to more simply as the toolbox

User interface—what the user sees and interacts with while an application is running

Windows Form Designer window—the window in which you create your application's GUI

Windows Form object—the foundation for the user interface in a Windows application; referred to more simply as a form

Review Questions

1. A Windows form automatically contains which of the following?

    a. Close, Maximize, and Minimize buttons   c. a title bar

    b. a default caption   d. all of the above

2. When a form has been modified since the last time it was saved, what appears on its tab in the designer window?

    a. an ampersand (&)   c. a percent sign (%)

    b. an asterisk (*)   d. a plus sign (+)

3. You use the _____ window to set the characteristics that control an object's appearance and behavior.

    a. Characteristics   c. Object

    b. Designer   d. Properties

4. Which property determines the location of a form on the screen when the application is started?

    a. StartPosition   c. StartLocation

    b. Location   d. InitialPosition

5. When aligning two or more controls, the first control selected is called the _____ control.

    a. initializer   c. reference

    b. positioning   d. none of the above

6. You can run an application by pressing the _____ key on your keyboard.

    a. F4   c. F6

    b. F5   d. F7

7. The Close option on the File menu closes the current solution.

    a. True   b. False

Exercises

1. In this exercise, you create the Scottsville Library application. (See Appendix B for the answer.)   **TRY THIS**

    a. If necessary, start Visual Studio 2010 or Visual Basic 2010 Express and permanently display the Solution Explorer window. Create a Visual Basic Windows application. Use the following names for the solution and project, respectively: Library Solution and Library Project. Save the application in the ClearlyVB2010\Chap03 folder.

    b. Create the interface shown in Figure 3-22. Use the 9-point Segoe UI font for the form and the label. The form should appear centered on the screen when the application starts. The label should be centered horizontally on the form. The Book_opens.gif image file for the picture box is stored in the ClearlyVB2010\Chap03 folder. (The file was downloaded from the Animation Library site at *www.animationlibrary.com*.) The picture box should be centered both horizontally and vertically on the form.

    c. Lock the controls on the form. Save the solution and then start the application. Stop the application by clicking the form's Close button, and then use the File menu to close the solution.

Figure 3-22 Interface for Exercise 1

MODIFY THIS   2.   In this exercise, you modify the My Pet application created in the chapter.

   a.   Use Windows to make a copy of the My Pet Solution folder. Save the copy in the ClearlyVB2010\Chap03 folder. Rename the copy Modified My Pet Solution.

   b.   If necessary, start Visual Studio 2010 or Visual Basic 2010 Express and permanently display the Solution Explorer window. Open the My Pet Solution (My Pet Solution.sln) file contained in the Modified My Pet Solution folder. Open the designer window by right-clicking Form1.vb in the Solution Explorer window and then clicking View Designer.

   c.   Unlock the controls and then modify the interface as shown in Figure 3-23. The monkey image is stored in the ClearlyVB2010\Chap03\Monkey.gif file. (The file was downloaded from the Microsoft Office site at *http://office.microsoft.com/en-us/images/*.)

   d.   Lock the controls. Save the solution and then start the application. Stop the application by clicking the form's Close button, and then use the File menu to close the solution.

Figure 3-23 Interface for Exercise 2

INTRODUCTORY   3.   In this exercise, you create an application for Scenic Vacations.

   a.   If necessary, start Visual Studio 2010 or Visual Basic 2010 Express and permanently display the Solution Explorer window. Create a Visual Basic Windows application. Use the following names for the solution and project, respectively: Scenic Solution and Scenic Project. Save the application in the ClearlyVB2010\Chap03 folder.

   b.   Create the interface shown in Figure 3-24. Use the 9-point Segoe UI font for the form. Use the 18-point Segoe UI font for the label. The form should appear centered on the screen when the application starts. The scenic image for the picture box is stored in the ClearlyVB2010\Chap03\Lightsnow.gif file. The label and picture box should be centered horizontally on the form.

   c.   Lock the controls on the form. Save the solution and then start the application. Stop the application by clicking the form's Close button, and then use the File menu to close the solution.

Figure 3-24 Interface for Exercise 3

4. If necessary, start Visual Studio 2010 or Visual Basic 2010 Express and permanently display the Solution Explorer window. Create a Visual Basic Windows application. Use the following names for the solution and project, respectively: Arrows Solution and Arrows Project. Save the application in the ClearlyVB2010\Chap03 folder. Create the interface shown in Figure 3-25. The interface contains four picture boxes and four labels. Use the 11-point Segoe UI font. The form should appear centered on the screen when the application starts. The arrow images are stored in the following files, which are contained in the ClearlyVB2010\Chap03 folder: Up.gif, Down.gif, Right.gif, and Left.gif. (The files were downloaded from the Microsoft Office site at *http://office.microsoft.com/en-us/images/*.) Lock the controls on the form. Save the solution and then start the application. Stop the application and then use the File menu to close the solution.

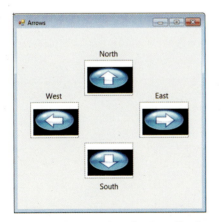

Figure 3-25 Interface for Exercise 4

5. If necessary, start Visual Studio 2010 or Visual Basic 2010 Express and permanently display the Solution Explorer window. Create a Visual Basic Windows application. Use the following names for the solution and project, respectively: Homestead Solution and Homestead Project. Save the application in the ClearlyVB2010\Chap03 folder. Create the interface shown in Figure 3-26. You can use any font style, size, and color for the label control's text. (The color of a label's text is determined by the label's ForeColor property.) The form should be centered on the screen when the application is started. The VACANCY image is stored in the ClearlyVB2010\Chap03\00223754.gif file. (The file was downloaded from the Microsoft

INTERMEDIATE

INTERMEDIATE

Office site at *http://office.microsoft.com/en-us/images/*.) Lock the controls on the form. Save the solution and then start the application. Stop the application and then close the solution.

Figure 3-26   Interface for Exercise 5

ADVANCED   6.   Create a Visual Basic Windows application. Use the following names for the solution and project, respectively: Show Hide Solution and Show Hide Project. Save the application in the ClearlyVB2010\Chap03 folder. Create the interface shown in Figure 3-27. The interface contains a picture box and three button controls. The wizard image is stored in the ClearlyVB2010\Chap03\Lightning_bolts.gif file. (The file was downloaded from the Animation Library site at *www.animationlibrary.com*.) The picture box should have a border around it; set the appropriate property. The form should appear centered on the screen when the application is started. Lock the controls on the form. Save the solution and then start the application. Stop the application and then close the solution.

Figure 3-27   Interface for Exercise 6

Do It Yourself Designing (Designing Interfaces)

After studying Chapter 4, you should be able to:

◎   Use a text box to get user input

◎   Perform an action with a button control

◎   Code a control's Click event procedure

◎   Stop an application using the `Me.Close()` instruction

Delegating the Work

In Chapter 2, you learned how to analyze a problem, plan an appropriate algorithm, and desk-check the algorithm. Then, in Chapter 3, you learned the mechanics of creating a user interface in Visual Basic. In this chapter, you will learn how to design the interface, using a problem's output and input items and its algorithm. More specifically, you'll learn how to design an interface for the Addison Smith problem from Chapter 2. Figure 4-1 shows the Addison Smith problem's output, input, and algorithm. As you may remember, the algorithm calculates and displays an annual commission based on the annual sales and commission rate entered by the user.

Output: annual commission

Input: annual sales
          commission rate

Algorithm:
1. enter the annual sales and commission rate
2. calculate the annual commission by multiplying the
   annual sales by the commission rate
3. display the annual commission

Figure 4-1   Output, input, and algorithm for the Addison Smith problem

When designing an interface for a problem, you need to examine each step in the problem's algorithm, along with its output and input items. The first step in the Addison Smith algorithm is to enter the annual sales and commission rate, which are the two input items. Visual Basic provides many controls that allow the user to enter data; in this case, you will use two text boxes. Step 2 in the algorithm is to calculate the annual commission. The user should have control over when (and if) the calculation task is performed. This is the perfect place to use a button control, because buttons perform their tasks only when the user clicks them. Examples of buttons with which you already are familiar include the Open, Save, and OK buttons. In this case, you will assign the calculation task to a button marked Calculate Commission. The Calculate Commission button also will be assigned the display the annual commission task from Step 3, because the user will want to view the annual commission immediately after it has been calculated. As Figure 4-1 indicates, the annual commission is an output item. In most interfaces, output items appear in label controls, because users should not be able to edit the value of an output item while an application is running. In this case, for instance, the user should not be able to edit the annual commission after it has been calculated. Based on the information shown in Figure 4-1, the interface will use two text boxes to get the annual sales and commission rate, a button to calculate and display the annual commission, and a label to show the annual commission to the user. In addition to the controls required by the algorithm, every interface also needs a control that allows the user to end the application. In this interface, you will use a button marked Exit for this purpose. Figure 4-2 lists the controls mentioned in this section.

Control	Purpose
Label	show the annual commission
Text box	get the annual sales
Text box	get the commission rate
Button (Calculate Commission)	calculate and display the annual commission
Button (Exit)	end the application

Figure 4-2   List of controls

You should assign a meaningful name to each of the controls listed in Figure 4-2, because doing so will help you keep track of the various objects included in the interface. In addition, as you will learn in Chapter 6, the programmer uses an object's name to refer to the object in code. The name must begin with a letter and can contain only letters, numbers, and the underscore character. You cannot include punctuation characters or spaces in the name. There are several conventions for naming objects in Visual Basic; in this book, you will use a naming convention called Hungarian notation. Names in Hungarian notation begin with a three (or more) character ID that represents the object's type. Label control names, for example, begin with lbl. Names of buttons begin with btn, and text box names begin with txt. The remaining characters in the name represent the object's purpose. For instance, using Hungarian notation, you might assign the name lblCommission to the label that displays the annual commission. The "lbl" identifies the object as a label, and "Commission" reminds you of the label's purpose. Hungarian notation names are entered using **camel case**, which means you lowercase the ID characters and then uppercase the first letter of each word in the name. Camel case refers to the fact that the uppercase letters appear as "humps" in the name because they are taller than the lowercase letters. Figure 4-3 lists the name and purpose of each of the controls listed in Figure 4-2.

Control name	Purpose
lblCommission	show the annual commission
txtSales	get the annual sales
txtRate	get the commission rate
btnCalculate (Calculate Commission)	calculate and display the annual commission
btnExit (Exit)	end the application

Figure 4-3 Name and purpose of each control

Mini-Quiz 4-1

See Appendix B for the answers.

1. It is customary to show the result of a calculation in a _____ control in the interface.
2. Using Hungarian notation, which of the following is a good name for a text box that accepts the name of a city?
   a. cityTextBox
   b. textBoxCity
   c. txtCity
   d. TxtCity
3. The three-character ID for a button control's name is _____.

Before you begin creating the Commission Calculator application, you may want to view the Ch04-Commission Calculator video. The video demonstrates all of the steps contained in this chapter. You may find it helpful to view the steps before you perform them.

To begin creating the Commission Calculator application:

1. Start Visual Studio 2010 or Visual Basic 2010 Express and permanently display the Solution Explorer and Toolbox windows. Create a Visual Basic Windows application. Use the following names for the solution and project, respectively: Commission Calculator Solution and Commission Calculator Project. Save the application in the ClearlyVB2010\Chap04 folder.

2. Permanently display the Properties window. Click the **form** to select it, and then change the following properties:

Font **Segoe UI, 9pt**

StartPosition **CenterScreen**

Text **Commission Calculator**

3. A project can contain many forms; therefore, it's a good programming practice to give each form a meaningful name. The name of each form in a project must be unique. In other words, the name of each form must be different from the name of any other form in the same project. The three-character ID for form names is frm. Change the form's Name property to **frmMain**. (The Name property is the third item in the Properties list.)

4. You also will change the name of the file (on your disk) that contains the form. Right-click **Form1.vb** in the Solution Explorer window and then click **Rename**. Type **frmMain.vb** and press **Enter**.

5. Next, you will begin adding the controls listed in Figure 4-3 to the form. For now, you do not have to worry about the exact location of the controls. Use the Label tool to add a label to the form, and then change the label's name to **lblCommission**.

6. Use the TextBox tool to add two text boxes to the form. Name the first text box **txtSales**, and name the second text box **txtRate**.

7. Use the Button tool to add two buttons to the form. Name the first button **btnCalculate**, and name the second button **btnExit**.

8. Position the controls as shown in Figure 4-4.

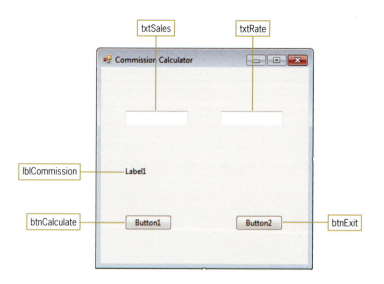

Figure 4-4 Controls added to the form

You will need to add descriptive identifying labels above the two text boxes; otherwise, the user won't know where to enter the input items. An identifying label should be from one to three words only, with the entire label appearing on one line. It is customary in Windows applications for identifying labels to end with a colon. The colon allows some assistive technologies, which are technologies that provide assistance to individuals with disabilities, to locate the identifying labels in the interface. It also is customary to enter identifying labels using **sentence capitalization**, which means capitalizing only the first letter in the first word and in any words that are customarily capitalized.

To continue creating the Commission Calculator application:

1. Add two more labels to the form. Position one of the labels above the txtSales control. Position the other label above the txtRate control. Use the blue snap lines to align the left border of each label with the left border of its respective text box.

2. Change the Text property of the txtSales control's identifying label to **Enter sales:**. Change the Text property of the txtRate control's identifying label to **Enter decimal rate:**.

3. The lblCommission control also needs a label to identify its contents for the user. Add another label to the form. Position the label above the lblCommission control, aligning both controls by their left borders. Change the label's Text property to **Commission:**.

4. Save the solution.

Next, you will change each button's Text property to a value that indicates the task performed when the button is clicked. The value in a button's Text property appears on the button's face and is often referred to as the button's **caption**. As with identifying labels, a button's caption should be from one to three words only, with the entire caption appearing on one line. However, unlike identifying labels, a button's caption does not end with a colon and is entered using book title capitalization. With **book title capitalization**, you capitalize the first letter in each word, except for articles, conjunctions, and prepositions that do not occur at either the beginning or the end of the caption.

To continue creating the Commission Calculator application:

1. Change the btnCalculate control's Text property to **Calculate Commission**. Drag the button's right border until the entire caption is visible. Also make the button slightly taller. (If necessary, reposition the button.)

2. Change the btnExit control's Text property to **Exit**, and then use the Format menu to make the Exit button the same height as the Calculate Commission button.

3. The lblCommission control should be empty when the user interface appears on the screen. In addition, it is customary to put a border around a label that displays the application's output, and to prevent the label from changing its size while the application is running. Click the **lblCommission** control on the form. Change its AutoSize property to **False**, and then change its BorderStyle property to **FixedSingle**. Click **Text** in the Properties list. Press the **Backspace** key on your keyboard and then press **Enter**.

4. Make the lblCommission control slightly taller. Then make it the same width as its identifying label.

5. Lock the controls on the form and then save the solution. Figure 4-5 shows the current status of the interface.

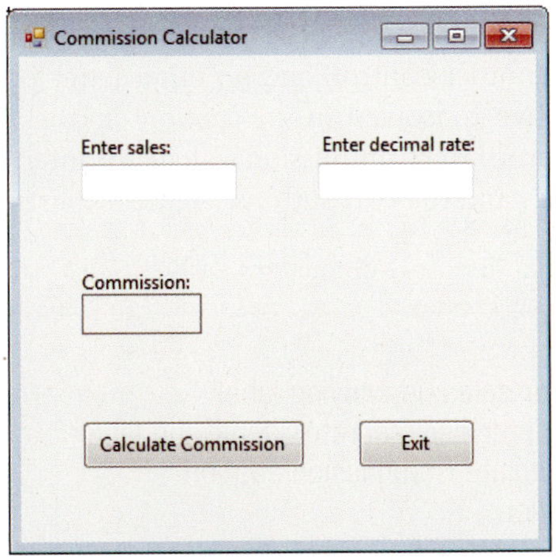

Figure 4-5   Current status of the interface

Making the Interface More User-Friendly

Looking closely at the Visual Studio menu bar in Figure 4-6, you will notice that the menu titles contain an underlined letter. The underlined letter is called an **access key**, and it allows the user to select a menu using the Alt key in combination with a letter or number. For example, you can select the File menu in Visual Studio by pressing Alt+F, because the letter F is the File menu's access key. Access keys are not case sensitive; therefore, you can select the File menu by pressing either Alt+F or Alt+f. Depending on your system's settings, the access keys may or may not appear underlined on your screen. If you do not see the underlined access keys, you can display them temporarily by pressing the Alt key. You can subsequently hide them by pressing the Alt key again. (To always display access keys, see the Summary section at the end of this chapter.)

access key ——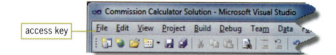

Figure 4-6 Visual Studio menu bar

You should assign an access key to each control (in the interface) that can accept user input. Examples of such controls include text boxes and buttons, because the user can enter information in a text box and click a button. The only exceptions to this rule are the OK and Cancel buttons, which typically do not have access keys in Windows applications. Access keys are important because they allow a user to work with the interface even when their mouse becomes inoperative. In addition, some fast typists prefer to use access keys, because the access keys allow them to keep their hands on the keyboard. Finally, access keys are important for people with disabilities that prevent them from working with a mouse.

You assign an access key by including an ampersand (&) in the control's caption or identifying label. If the control is a button, you include the ampersand in the button's Text property, which is where a button's caption is stored. If the control is a text box, you include the ampersand in the Text property of its identifying label. (As you will learn later in this lesson, you also must set the TabIndex properties of the text box and its identifying label appropriately.) You enter the ampersand to the immediate left of the character you want to designate as the access key. For example, to assign the letter C as the access key for the Calculate Commission button, you enter &Calculate Commission in the button's Text property. To assign the letter s as the access key for the txtSales control, you enter Enter &sales: in the Text property of its identifying label.

Each access key in an interface should be unique. The first choice for an access key is the first letter of the caption or identifying label, unless another letter provides a more meaningful association. For example, the letter x is the access key for an Exit button, because it provides a more meaningful association than does the letter E. If you can't use the first letter (perhaps because it already is used as the access key for another control) and no other letter provides a more meaningful association, then use a distinctive consonant in the caption or label. The last choices for an access key are a vowel or a number. In the Commission Calculator interface, four controls can accept user input: the two text boxes and the two buttons. Figure 4-7 lists the four controls along with their access keys.

Control name	Access key
txtSales	the first letter s in the Enter sales: identifying label
txtRate	the second letter r in the Enter decimal rate: identifying label
btnCalculate	the first letter C in the Calculate Commission caption
btnExit	the letter x in the Exit caption

Figure 4-7 List of controls and their access keys

To assign access keys to the controls that can accept user input:

1. Change the Text property of the Enter sales: label to **Enter &sales:**, and then change the Text property of the Enter decimal rate: label to **Enter decimal &rate:**.

2. Change the btnCalculate control's Text property to **&Calculate Commission**, and then change the btnExit control's Text property to **E&xit**. Figure 4-8 shows the access keys in the interface. (If you do not see the access keys, press the Alt key.)

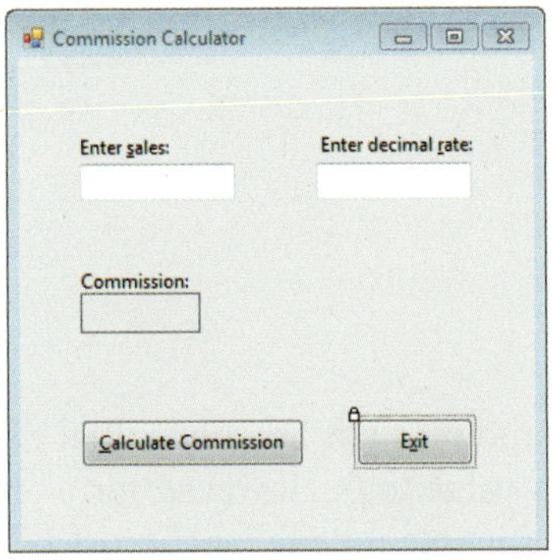

Figure 4-8   Access keys shown in the interface

Notice that the Commission: label in Figure 4-8 does not have an access key. This is because the label does not identify a control that accepts user input. Instead, it identifies the lblCommission control, whose purpose is simply to show the annual commission after it has been calculated. Users cannot access the lblCommission control while the application is running; therefore, it is inappropriate to assign an access key to the control.

In addition to assigning access keys for an interface, you also should set the interface's tab order, which is the order in which the controls receive the focus when the user presses either a Tab key or an access key. The tab order is determined by the number stored in each control's **TabIndex property**. When the interface is first created, the TabIndex values reflect the order in which each control was added to the form. The first control added to a form has a TabIndex of 0, the second control a TabIndex of 1, and so on. You can use the Properties window to reset the TabIndex property of each control so that it reflects the desired position of the control in the tab order. However, an easier way is to use the Tab Order option on the View menu. The Tab Order option is available only when the designer window is the active window. When using the Tab Order option, you need to set the TabIndex values in numerical order, beginning with the number 0. If you make a mistake while you are performing the next set of steps, press the Esc key to remove the TabIndex information from the form and then repeat all of the steps.

To set the tab order:

1. Click the **form** to select it. Click **View** on the menu bar and then click **Tab Order**. The numbers in the blue boxes indicate the value stored in each control's TabIndex property. The numbers reflect the order in which the controls were placed on the form. See Figure 4-9.

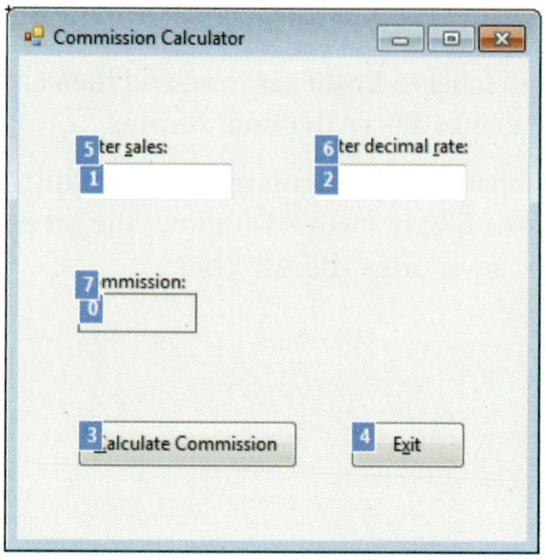

Figure 4-9 Current TabIndex values for the interface

2. Most times, the user will want to enter the sales amount first. So your initial thought might be to change the txtSales control's TabIndex value to 0. However, for a text box's access key to work properly, the TabIndex value of its identifying label must be one number less than the text box's TabIndex value. Therefore, you will need to set the Label1 control's TabIndex to 0, and the txtSales control's TabIndex to 1. Click the **blue box that appears on top of the Enter sales: label**. The number 0 replaces the current number in the box, and the color of the box changes from blue to white to indicate that you have set the TabIndex value for that control. Next, click the **blue box that appears on top of the txtSales control**. See Figure 4-10.

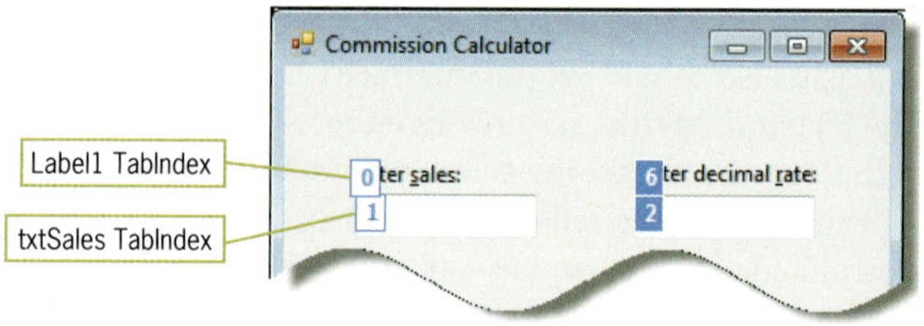

Figure 4-10 TabIndex values for the Label1 and txtSales controls

3. The user will want to enter the rate next. Here again, before setting the txtRate control's TabIndex, you will need to set the TabIndex of its identifying label. Click the **blue box that appears on top of the Enter decimal rate: label**, and then click the **blue box that appears on top of the txtRate control**. The white boxes now show TabIndex values of 2 and 3.

4. After entering the input items, the user will probably want to calculate the commission. Therefore, the next control in the tab order should be the Calculate Commission button. Click the **blue box that appears on top of the Calculate Commission button**. The white box indicates that the button's TabIndex is set to 4.

5. The only remaining control that can accept user input is the Exit button. Click the **blue box that appears on top of the Exit button** to set the button's TabIndex to 5.

6. Controls that cannot accept user input (such as the lblCommission control) and those that do not identify controls that accept user input (such as the Commission: label) should be placed at the end of the tab order. Click the **blue box that appears on top of the lblCommission control**, and then click the **blue box that appears on top of the Commission: label**. When you have finished setting all of the TabIndex values, the color of the boxes will automatically change from white to blue, as shown in Figure 4-11.

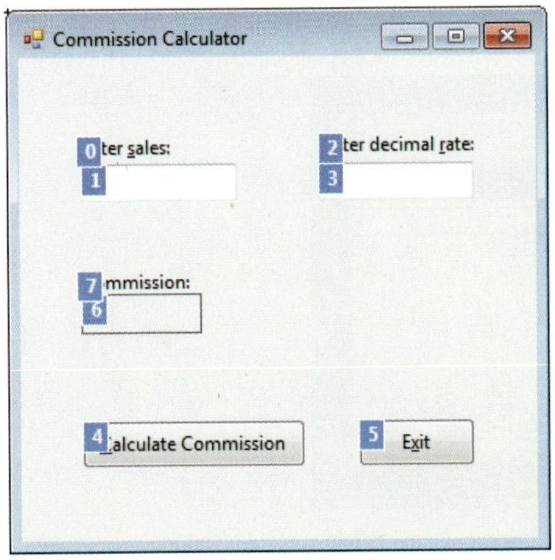

Figure 4-11 Correct TabIndex values for the interface

7. Press the **Esc** key to remove the TabIndex boxes from the form.

8. Now you will test the tab order. Save the solution and then start the application. The insertion point appears in the txtSales text box. The insertion point indicates that the text box has the focus. When a control has the focus, it can accept user input. Press the **Tab** key two times. The focus moves to the txtRate control and then to the Calculate Commission button. When a button has the focus, its border is darkened. Press **Tab** two more times. The focus moves to the Exit button and then to the txtSales control.

9. For now, you will test the access keys for the text boxes only. Press **Alt+r** (press and hold down the Alt key as you tap the letter r). The focus moves to the txtRate control. Press **Alt+s** to move the focus to the txtSales control.

10. Click the **Close** button on the form's title bar to close the application.

Do What I Tell You to Do

After creating the interface, you can begin entering the Visual Basic instructions, or **code**, that tell the controls how to respond to the user's actions. Those actions—such as clicking and double-clicking—are called **events**. You tell an object how to respond to an event by writing an **event procedure**, which is simply a set of Visual Basic instructions that are processed when a specific event occurs. In this chapter, you will write a Click event procedure for the Exit button, which should end the application when it is clicked. (You will code the Calculate Commission button in Chapter 5.) You enter an event procedure's code in the **Code Editor window**.

To open the Exit button's Click event procedure in the Code Editor window:

1. Auto-hide the Solution Explorer, Properties, and Toolbox windows.

2. Right-click the **form** and then click **View Code** on the context menu. The Code Editor window opens in the IDE. Click the **list arrow that appears in the lower-left corner of the window** and then click **150 %** in the list; doing this increases the size of the code font. See Figure 4-12. Notice that the Code Editor window already contains some Visual Basic instructions. It also contains a Class Name list box and a Method Name list box. The Class Name list box lists the names of the objects included in the user interface. The Method Name list box, on the other hand, lists the events to which the selected object is capable of responding. You use the Class Name and Method Name list boxes to select the object and event, respectively, that you want to code.

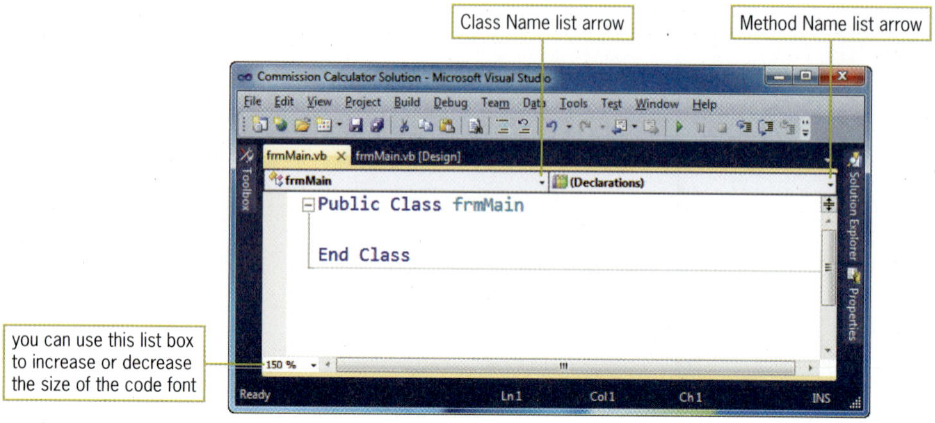

Figure 4-12 Code Editor window

3. Click the **Class Name** list arrow and then click **btnExit** in the list. Click the **Method Name** list arrow and then click **Click** in the list. A code template for the btnExit control's Click event procedure appears in the Code Editor window, as shown in Figure 4-13.

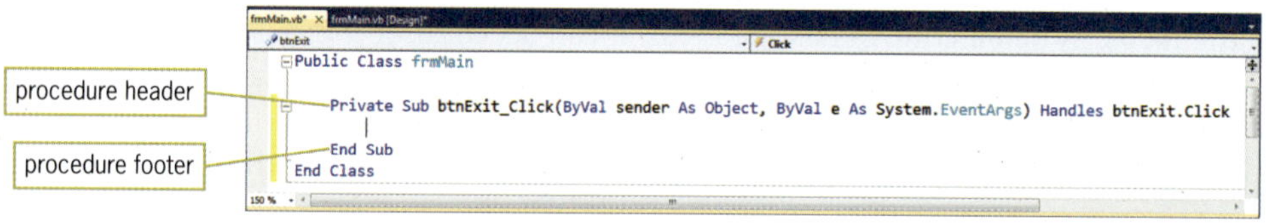

Figure 4-13 Code template for the btnExit control's Click event procedure

The Code Editor provides a code template for every event procedure. The code templates help you follow the rules of the Visual Basic language. The rules of a programming language are called its **syntax**. The first line in a code template is called the **procedure header**, and the last line is called the **procedure footer**. The procedure header begins with the two keywords Private Sub. A **keyword** is a word that has a special meaning in a programming language. Keywords appear in a different color from the rest of the code. The Private keyword in Figure 4-13 indicates that the button's Click event procedure can be used only within the current Code Editor window. The Sub keyword is an abbreviation of the term **Sub procedure**, which is a block of code that performs a specific task. Following the Sub keyword is the name of the object, an underscore, the name of the event, and parentheses containing some text. For now, you do not have to be concerned with the text that appears between the parentheses. After the closing parenthesis is Handles btnExit.Click. This part of the procedure header indicates that the procedure handles (or is associated with) the btnExit control's Click event. It tells the computer to process the procedure when the btnExit control is clicked.

The code template ends with the procedure footer, which contains the keywords End Sub. You enter your Visual Basic instructions at the location of the insertion point, which appears between the Private Sub and End Sub clauses in Figure 4-13. The Code Editor automatically indents the line between the procedure's header and footer. Indenting the lines within a procedure makes the instructions easier to read and is a common programming practice. In this case, the instruction you enter will tell the computer to end the application when the btnExit control is clicked.

The Me.Close() Instruction

The Me.Close() instruction tells the computer to close the current form. If the current form is the only form in the application, closing it terminates the entire application. In the instruction, Me is a keyword that refers to the current form, and Close is one of the methods available in

Visual Basic. A **method** is a predefined procedure that you can call (or invoke) when needed. For example, if you want the computer to close the current form when the user clicks the Exit button, you enter the `Me.Close()` instruction in the button's Click event procedure. Notice the empty set of parentheses after the method's name in the instruction. The parentheses are required when calling some Visual Basic methods. However, depending on the method, the parentheses may or may not be empty. If you forget to enter the empty set of parentheses, the Code Editor will enter them for you when you move the insertion point to another line in the Code Editor window.

To code the btnExit control's Click event procedure:

1. You can type the `Me.Close()` instruction on your own or use the Code Editor window's IntelliSense feature. In this set of steps, you will use the IntelliSense feature. Type **me.** (but don't press Enter). When you type the period, the IntelliSense feature displays a list of properties, methods, and so on from which you can select.

   Important note: If a list of choices does not appear, the IntelliSense feature may have been turned off on your computer system. To turn it on, click Tools on the menu bar and then click Options. If necessary, select the Show all settings check box. Expand the Text Editor node and then click Basic. Select the Auto list members check box and then click the OK button. Delete the **me.** that you typed in Step 1 and repeat Step 1.

2. If necessary, click the **Common** tab. The Common tab displays the most commonly used items, whereas the All tab displays all of the items. Type **cl** (but don't press Enter). The IntelliSense feature highlights the Close method in the list. See Figure 4-14.

```
         Private Sub btnExit_Click(ByVal sender As Obj
            Me.cl|
         End Sub  btnExit_Click
                   Close              Public Sub Close()
      End Class    MemberwiseClone    Closes the form.
                   Common  All
```

Figure 4-14   List displayed by the IntelliSense feature

3. Press **Tab** to include the Close method in the instruction and then press **Enter**. See Figure 4-15.

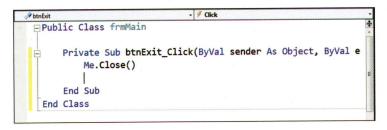

```
 btnExit                          ▾   Click
 Public Class frmMain

         Private Sub btnExit_Click(ByVal sender As Object, ByVal e
            Me.Close()
            |
         End Sub
 End Class
```

Figure 4-15   Completed btnExit Click event procedure

It's a good programming practice to test a procedure after you have coded it. By doing this, you'll know where to look if an error occurs. You can test the Exit button's Click event procedure by starting the application and then clicking the button. When the button is clicked, the computer will process the `Me.Close()` instruction contained in the procedure.

To test the Exit button's Click event procedure:

1. Save the solution and then start the application. Click the **Exit** button to end the application.

2. Now you will test the Exit button's access key. Start the application and then press **Alt+x**. When you employ a button's access key, the computer processes any instructions contained

in the button's Click event procedure. In this case, the instruction directs the computer to end the application.

3. Close the Code Editor window and then close the solution.

Mini-Quiz 4-2

See Appendix B for the answers.

1. If a text box's TabIndex is set to 7, its identifying label's TabIndex should be set to _____.

2. If a text box's access key is the letter t, you can move the focus to the text box by pressing _____.

   a. Alt+t   c. Esc+t

   b. Ctrl+t   d. Shift+t

3. The first line in a procedure is called the _____.

Summary

- You use a problem's input, output, and algorithm when designing the solution's interface.

- Text boxes provide an area for the user to enter data.

- Buttons are used to perform an action when clicked.

- Output items typically appear in label controls so that their values cannot be edited by the user.

- Object names in Hungarian notation begin with an ID that identifies the object's type. The rest of the name identifies the object's purpose. Object names are entered using camel case.

- Form names begin with frm. Button names begin with btn. Label names begin with lbl. Text box names begin with txt.

- Identifying labels and button captions should be from one to three words, with the entire label or caption appearing on one line. Identifying labels should end with a colon and be entered using sentence capitalization. Button captions should be entered using book title capitalization.

- To prevent a label from changing its size while the application is running, change its AutoSize property to False.

- A label's BorderStyle property determines whether the label has a border.

- You should assign an access key to each control that can accept user input.

- An interface's tab order is determined by the number stored in each control's TabIndex property.

- When a control has the focus, it can accept user input.

- When an event occurs on an object, the computer processes any instructions contained in the associated event procedure.

- Event procedures, which are procedures that tell an object how to respond to an event, are entered in the Code Editor window.

- The Handles part of a procedure header indicates the object and event associated with the procedure.

- You can use the `Me.Close()` instruction to end an application.

- To always display access keys in Windows 7, click the Start button on the Windows 7 taskbar. Click Control Panel and then click Appearance and Personalization. In the Ease of Access Center section, click Turn on easy access keys. Select the Underline keyboard shortcuts and access keys check box, and then click the OK button. Close the Control Panel window.

- To always display access keys in Windows Vista, click Start on the Windows Vista taskbar. Click Control Panel and then click Appearance and Personalization. In the Ease of Access Center section, click Underline keyboard shortcuts and access keys, and then select the Underline keyboard shortcuts and access keys check box. (You may need to scroll down to view the check box.) Click the Save button and then close the Ease of Access Center dialog box.

- To always display access keys when using the Classic View in Windows Vista, click the Start button on the Windows Vista taskbar. Click Control Panel, double-click Ease of Access Center, click Make the keyboard easier to use, and then select the Underline keyboard shortcuts and access keys check box. Click the Save button and then close the Ease of Access Center dialog box.

Key Terms

Access key—the underlined character in an object's identifying label or caption; allows the user to select the object using the Alt key in combination with the underlined character

Book title capitalization—the capitalization used for a button's caption; refers to capitalizing the first letter in each word, except for articles, conjunctions, and prepositions that do not occur at either the beginning or end of the caption

Camel case—used when entering object names in Hungarian notation; the practice of entering the object's ID characters in lowercase and then capitalizing the first letter of each word in the name

Caption—the text that appears on a button's face

Code—Visual Basic instructions

Code Editor window—the window in which you enter your Visual Basic instructions (code)

Event procedure—a set of Visual Basic instructions that tell an object how to respond to an event

Events—actions to which an object can respond; examples include clicking and double-clicking

Keyword—a word that has a special meaning in a programming language

Method—a predefined procedure that you can call (invoke) when needed

Procedure footer—the last line in a procedure

Procedure header—the first line in a procedure

Sentence capitalization—the capitalization used for identifying labels; refers to capitalizing only the first letter in the first word and in any words that are customarily capitalized

Sub procedure—a block of code that performs a specific task

Syntax—the rules of a programming language

TabIndex property—determines the position of a control in the tab order

Review Questions

1. You can allow the user to determine when (and if) a task is performed by assigning the task to a _____ control in the interface.

   a. button   c. picture box

   b. label   d. text box

2. Which of the following designates the letter Z as an access key?

   a. @ZIP code: c. ^ZIP code:

   b. &ZIP code: d. #ZIP code:

3. The computer processes a button's Click event procedure when the user _____.

   a. clicks the button

   b. employs the button's access key

   c. presses the Enter key when the button has the focus

   d. all of the above

4. Which of the following appears in a procedure header and associates the procedure with the btnSave control's Click event?

   a. `Handles btnSave.Click`   c. `Header btnSave.Click`

   b. `Handles Click.btnSave`   d. `Event Click.btnSave`

5. Which of the following tells the computer to stop an application?

   a. `Close.Me()`   c. `Me.End()`

   b. `Me.Close()`   d. `Me.Stop()`

6. A button's caption should be entered using _____ capitalization.

   a. book title

   b. sentence

7. Which of the following is a keyword in Visual Basic?

   a. `Me`   c. `Sub`

   b. `Private`   d. all of the above

Exercises

TRY THIS

1. In this exercise, you create an interface for the Aiden Turner problem from Chapter 2. (See Appendix B for the answer.)

   a. If necessary, start Visual Studio 2010 or Visual Basic 2010 Express and permanently display the Solution Explorer window. Create a Visual Basic Windows application. Use the following names for the solution and project, respectively: New Pay Solution and New Pay Project. Save the application in the ClearlyVB2010\Chap04 folder.

   b. Use the Properties window to change the form's name to frmMain. Change the name of the form file in the Solution Explorer window to frmMain.vb.

   c. Create a suitable interface using the information shown in Figure 4-16. Also include an Exit button. Be sure to assign names to the appropriate controls. Also be sure to assign access keys and set the tab order.

   d. Code the Exit button's Click event procedure so that it ends the application. You will code the algorithm in Chapter 5's Exercise 1.

e. Save the solution and then start the application. Test the interface's tab order and access keys.

f. Use the Exit button to stop the application. Close the Code Editor window and then use the File menu to close the solution.

Output: new weekly pay

Input: current weekly pay
               raise percentage

Algorithm:
1. enter the current weekly pay and raise percentage
2. calculate the new weekly pay by multiplying the current
   weekly pay by the raise percentage, and then adding the
   result to the current weekly pay
3. display the new weekly pay

Figure 4-16   Information for Exercise 1

2. In this exercise, you modify the interface created in Exercise 1.

   MODIFY THIS

   a. Use Windows to make a copy of the New Pay Solution folder. Save the copy in the ClearlyVB2010\Chap04 folder. Rename the copy Modified New Pay Solution.

   b. If necessary, start Visual Studio 2010 or Visual Basic 2010 Express and permanently display the Solution Explorer window. Open the New Pay Solution (New Pay Solution.sln) file contained in the Modified New Pay Solution folder. In addition to calculating and displaying the new weekly pay, Aiden Turner would now like to calculate and display his weekly raise. Modify the interface to include a label for showing the weekly raise. Be sure to also include an identifying label.

   c. Save the solution and then start the application. Stop the application and then close the solution.

3. In this exercise, you create an interface for an application that calculates and displays a 10%, 15%, and 20% tip on a restaurant bill.

   INTRODUCTORY

   a. If necessary, start Visual Studio 2010 or Visual Basic 2010 Express and permanently display the Solution Explorer window. Create a Visual Basic Windows application. Use the following names for the solution and project, respectively: Tip Solution and Tip Project. Save the application in the ClearlyVB2010\Chap04 folder.

   b. Use the Properties window to change the form's name to frmMain. Change the name of the form file in the Solution Explorer window to frmMain.vb.

   c. Create a suitable interface using the information shown in Figure 4-17. Also include an Exit button. Be sure to assign names to the appropriate controls. Also be sure to assign access keys and set the tab order.

   d. Code the Exit button's Click event procedure so that it ends the application. You will code the algorithm in Chapter 5's Exercise 4.

   e. Save the solution and then start the application. Test the interface's tab order and access keys.

   f. Use the Exit button to stop the application. Close the Code Editor window and then use the File menu to close the solution.

Output: 10% tip
         15% tip
         20% tip

Input: restaurant bill

Algorithm:
1. enter the restaurant bill
2. calculate a 10% tip by multiplying the restaurant bill by 10%
3. calculate a 15% tip by multiplying the restaurant bill by 15%
4. calculate a 20% tip by multiplying the restaurant bill by 20%
5. display the 10% tip, 15% tip, and 20% tip

Figure 4-17   Information for Exercise 3

INTERMEDIATE

4. In this exercise, you create an interface for an application that calculates and displays an annual property tax. Currently, the property tax rate is $1.02 for each $100 of a property's assessed value. However, the tax rate changes each year.

a. Complete the algorithm shown in Figure 4-18.

b. Create a Visual Basic Windows application. Use the following names for the solution and project, respectively: Property Tax Solution and Property Tax Project. Save the application in the ClearlyVB2010\Chap04 folder.

c. Change the name of the form file on your disk to frmMain.vb. If necessary, change the form's name to frmMain.

d. Create a suitable interface using the information shown in Figure 4-18. Also include an Exit button. Be sure to assign names to the appropriate controls. Also be sure to assign access keys and set the tab order.

e. Code the Exit button's Click event procedure so that it ends the application. You will code the algorithm in Chapter 5's Exercise 6.

f. Save the solution and then start the application. Test the interface's tab order and access keys.

g. Stop the application. Close the Code Editor window and then close the solution.

Output: annual property tax

Input: assessed value
            property tax rate

Algorithm:
1. enter_____
2. calculate _____
3. display _____

Figure 4-18   Information for Exercise 4

INTERMEDIATE

5. In this exercise, you create an interface for an application that calculates and displays the total amount a customer owes.

a. Complete the algorithm shown in Figure 4-19.

b. Create a Visual Basic Windows application. Use the following names for the solution and project, respectively: Total Solution and Total Project. Save the application in the ClearlyVB2010\Chap04 folder.

c. Change the name of the form file on your disk to frmMain.vb. If necessary, change the form's name to frmMain.

d. Create a suitable interface using the information shown in Figure 4-19. Also include an Exit button. Be sure to assign names to the appropriate controls. Also be sure to assign access keys and set the tab order.

e. Code the Exit button's Click event procedure so that it ends the application.

f. Save the solution and then start the application. Test the interface's tab order and access keys.

g. Stop the application. Close the Code Editor window and then close the solution.

```
Output:        total due

Processing:  subtotal
             sales tax

Input:        number of folders purchased
             folder price
             sales tax rate

Algorithm:
1. enter _____
2. calculate _____
3. calculate _____
4. calculate _____
5. display _____
```

Figure 4-19 Information for Exercise 5

6. In this exercise, you create an interface for an application that calculates and displays the total cost for running a party at a local restaurant. The restaurant charges a fee for renting its party room. It also charges a fee per guest.

   INTERMEDIATE

   a. Complete the algorithm shown in Figure 4-20.

   b. Create a Visual Basic Windows application. Use the following names for the solution and project, respectively: Party Solution and Party Project. Save the application in the ClearlyVB2010\Chap04 folder.

   c. Change the name of the form file on your disk to frmMain.vb. If necessary, change the form's name to frmMain.

   d. Create a suitable interface using the information shown in Figure 4-20. Also include an Exit button. Be sure to assign names to the appropriate controls. Also be sure to assign access keys and set the tab order.

   e. Code the Exit button's Click event procedure so that it ends the application. You will code the algorithm in Chapter 5's Exercise 8.

   f. Save the solution and then start the application. Test the interface's tab order and access keys.

   g. Stop the application. Close the Code Editor window and then close the solution.

```
Output:  total cost

Input:   room rental fee
         number of guests
         fee per guest


Algorithm:
1. enter_____
2. calculate_____
3. display _____
```

Figure 4-20 Information for Exercise 6

ADVANCED

7. In this exercise, you create an interface for RM Sales. The company divides its sales territory into four regions: North, South, East, and West. The sales manager wants an application that allows him to enter each region's sales amount. The application should calculate and display the total sales, as well as the percentage of sales attributed to each region. For example, if the sales manager enters the numbers 4000, 2000, 1000, and 3000 as the North, South, East, and West regions' sales amounts, respectively, then the total sales amount is $10,000. 40% of the sales come from the North region, 20% from the South region, and so on.

   a. List the output and input items, and then create an appropriate algorithm.

   b. Create a Visual Basic Windows application. Use the following names for the solution and project, respectively: Sales Solution and Sales Project. Save the application in the ClearlyVB2010\Chap04 folder.

   c. Change the name of the form file on your disk to frmMain.vb. If necessary, change the form's name to frmMain.

   d. Create a suitable interface. Include an Exit button. Be sure to assign names to the appropriate controls. Also be sure to assign access keys and set the tab order.

   e. Code the Exit button's Click event procedure so that it ends the application. You will code the algorithm in Chapter 5's Exercise 11.

   f. Save the solution and then start the application. Test the interface's tab order and access keys.

   g. Stop the application. Close the Code Editor window and then close the solution.

SWAT THE BUGS

8. Open the SwatTheBugs Solution (SwatTheBugs Solution.sln) file contained in the ClearlyVB2010\Chap04\SwatTheBugs Solution folder. Start the application and then click the Exit button. Notice that the Exit button does not end the application. Locate and then correct the error. (Hint: Look closely at the procedure header in the Exit button's Click event procedure.)

CHAPTER 5

The Secret Code (Assignment Statements)

After studying Chapter 5, you should be able to:

◎ Include a comment in the Code Editor window

◎ Use the Val function to convert text to a number

◎ Write expressions containing arithmetic operators

◎ Write an assignment statement

The Fun Starts Here

You completed the Addison Smith problem's interface in Chapter 4. You also coded the Exit button's Click event procedure. Now it's time to code the problem's algorithm. As you learned in Chapter 2, coding the algorithm is the fifth step in the problem-solving process. For most programmers, this is the most rewarding step, because this is where they give life to the interface. At the end of this step, the interface will change from one that the user can simply look at to one with which the user can interact. Figure 5-1 shows the Addison Smith problem's interface, and Figure 5-2 shows the problem's output, input, and algorithm.

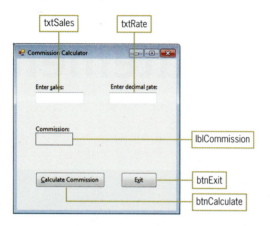

Figure 5-1   Interface for the Addison Smith problem

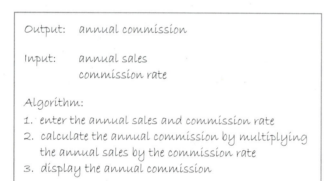

Figure 5-2   Output, input, and algorithm for the Addison Smith problem

 Before you begin coding the Calculate Commission button, you may want to view the Ch05-Commission Calculator video. The video demonstrates all of the steps contained in this chapter. You may find it helpful to view the steps before you perform them.

Step 1 in the algorithm is to enter the annual sales and commission rate. The user will enter the values in the two text boxes in the interface. A text box is designed to accept information from the user, and it automatically stores the information in its Text property. Therefore, no special coding is necessary for Step 1. Steps 2 and 3 are to calculate and display the annual commission. Recall that you assigned the tasks in these steps to the Calculate Commission button. The tasks should be performed when the user clicks the button. Obviously, the Calculate Commission button needs you to tell it *how* to calculate the annual commission when the Click event occurs. It also needs you to tell it *where* to display the calculated result. You do this by coding the button's Click event procedure.

To open the Calculate Commission button's Click event procedure:

1. Start Visual Studio 2010 or Visual Basic 2010 Express and permanently display the Solution Explorer window. Open the **Commission Calculator Solution (Commission Calculator Solution.sln)** file contained in the ClearlyVB2010\Chap05\Commission Calculator Solution folder. If the designer window is not open, double-click **frmMain.vb** in the Solution Explorer window.

2. Auto-hide the Solution Explorer window. Right-click the **form** and then click **View Code** on the context menu. The Code Editor window contains the btnExit control's Click event procedure, which you coded in Chapter 4.

3. Use the Class Name and Method Name list arrows to open the code template for the btnCalculate control's Click event procedure.

It's a common programming practice to include one or more comments in a procedure. A **comment** is a message to the person reading the code and is referred to as **internal documentation**. Many programmers use comments to document a procedure's purpose, as well as to explain various sections of the procedure's code. Comments make the code more readable and easier to understand by anyone viewing it. You create a comment in Visual Basic by placing an apostrophe (') before the text that represents the comment. The computer ignores everything that appears after the apostrophe on that line. Although it is not required, some programmers use a space to separate the apostrophe from the comment itself, and they follow the comment with a blank line.

To internally document the btnCalculate control's Click event procedure:

1. Type ' **calculates and displays the annual commission** (notice the space after the apostrophe).

2. Press **Enter** twice. See Figure 5-3. (For readability, the font size was changed to 150 %. It's not necessary for you to change the font size.)

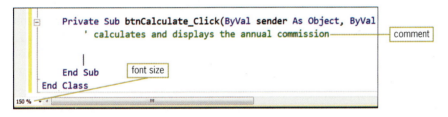

Figure 5-3   Comment entered in the procedure

First you need to tell the procedure *how* to calculate the annual commission. According to the algorithm, the annual commission is calculated by multiplying the annual sales by the commission rate. The annual sales and commission rate are stored in the Text property of the txtSales and txtRate controls, respectively. However, before you can use the Text property value in a calculation, you need to convert the value to a number. One way to do this is by using the Visual Basic Val function.

The Val Function

The characters entered in a text box can be numbers, letters, or special characters (such as the dollar sign, comma, or percent sign). Because of this, the value stored in a control's Text property is always treated as alphanumeric text, even when the value contains only numbers. For example, the computer treats a Text property value of 589 as three separate characters (a 5, an 8, and a 9) rather than as the number 589 (five hundred and eighty-nine). As a result, before you can use the Text property in a calculation, you must convert its alphanumeric value to a number. Visual Basic provides several ways of performing the conversion; the easiest way is to use the Val function. Therefore, in this chapter (and only in this chapter), you will use the Val function to convert text to numbers. A **function** is a predefined procedure that performs a specific task and then returns a value after completing the task. The **Val function**, for instance, temporarily converts one or more characters to a number; it then returns the number. The number is stored in the computer's internal memory only while the function is processing.

The syntax of the Val function is **Val**(*text*), where *text* is the characters you want treated as a number. The item within parentheses in the syntax is called an **argument**, and it represents information that is passed to the function while the function is processing. To temporarily convert the Text property of the txtSales control to a number, you use txtSales.Text as the *text* argument, like this: `Val(txtSales.Text)`. For the *text* argument to be converted to a number, it must contain only numbers and an optional period; it cannot contain a letter or a special character. When an invalid character is encountered in the *text* argument, the Val function stops the conversion process at that point. Figure 5-4 shows the numbers returned by the `Val(txtSales.Text)` function, using various Text property values. Notice that the function returns the number 0 when the txtSales control is empty. It also returns the number 0 when the first character in the *text* argument is invalid. However, when the invalid character occurs after the first character, the function returns the numbers previous to the invalid one.

txtSales.Text value	Number returned by the Val(txtSales.Text) function
456	456
24,500	24
$56.88	0
Abc	0
Empty text box	0

Figure 5-4   Examples of the Val function

As mentioned earlier, you can convert the txtSales control's Text property to a number using the `Val(txtSales.Text)` function. Likewise, you can convert the txtRate control's Text property to a number using `Val(txtRate.Text)`. To calculate the annual commission, you multiply the sales number by the rate number. You perform the calculation using an arithmetic expression, which is an expression that contains one or more arithmetic operators.

Who's in Charge of This Operation?

Most programs require the computer to perform one or more calculations. You instruct the computer to perform a calculation by writing an arithmetic expression that contains one or more arithmetic operators. Figure 5-5 lists the most commonly used arithmetic operators available in Visual Basic, along with their precedence numbers. The precedence numbers indicate the order in which the computer performs the operation in an expression. Operations with a precedence number of 1 are performed first, followed by operations with a precedence number of 2, and so on. However, you can use parentheses to override the order of precedence, because operations within parentheses always are performed before operations outside of parentheses.

Operator	Operation	Precedence number
^	exponentiation (raises a number to a power)	1
–	negation (reverses the sign of a number)	2
*, /	multiplication and division	3
\	integer division	4
Mod	modulus	5
+,–	addition and subtraction	6

Figure 5-5   Most commonly used arithmetic operators and their order of precedence

Some of the operators in Figure 5-5 have the same precedence number. For example, both the addition and subtraction operators have a precedence number of 6. When an expression contains more than one operator having the same priority, those operators are evaluated from left to right. In the expression 5 + 12 / 3 − 1, for instance, the division is performed first, followed by the addition and then the subtraction. The result of the expression is the number 8, as illustrated in Figure 5-6. You can use parentheses to change the order in which the operators in an expression are evaluated. For example, the expression 5 + 12 / (3 − 1) evaluates to 11 rather than to 8, as illustrated in Figure 5-6. This is because the parentheses tell the computer to perform the subtraction operation first.

Original expression	5 + 12 / 3 − 1
The division is performed first	5 + 4 − 1
The addition is performed next	9 − 1
The subtraction is performed last	8 ——————— result
Original expression	5 + 12 / (3 − 1)
The subtraction is performed first	5 + 12 / 2
The division is performed next	5 + 6
The addition is performed last	11 ——————— result

Figure 5-6   Examples showing how expressions are evaluated

Two of the arithmetic operators in Figure 5-5 might be less familiar to you: the integer division operator (\) and the modulus operator (Mod). The **integer division operator** divides two integers (whole numbers) and then returns the result as an integer. For example, the expression 211 \ 4 results in 52, which is the integer result of dividing 211 by 4. (If you use the standard division operator [/] to divide 211 by 4, the result is 52.75 rather than 52.) You might use the integer division operator in a program that determines the number of quarters, dimes, and nickels to return as change to a customer. For instance, if a customer should receive 53 cents in change, you could use the expression 53 \ 25 to determine the number of quarters to return; the expression evaluates to 2.

The modulus operator also is used to divide two numbers, but the numbers do not have to be integers. In other words, the numbers may contain a decimal place. After dividing the numbers, the **modulus operator** returns the remainder of the division. For instance, 211 Mod 4 equals 3, which is the remainder of 211 divided by 4. You can use the modulus operator to determine whether a number is even or odd. If you divide the number by 2 and the remainder is 0, the number is even; if the remainder is 1, however, the number is odd. Figure 5-7 shows examples of using arithmetic operators in expressions.

Expression	Result
2 ^ 3	8
4 * −3	−12
25 / 4	6.25
25 \ 4	6
25 Mod 4	1
7 + 6 * (5 − 2)	25

Figure 5-7   Expressions containing arithmetic operators

 For more examples of using arithmetic operators, see the Arithmetic Operators section in the Ch5WantMore.pdf file.

Recall that you need to tell the btnCalculate control's Click event procedure *how* to calculate the annual commission. You can do this using the expression `Val(txtSales.Text) * Val(txtRate.Text)`. You also need to tell the procedure *where* to display the result of the calculation. In this case, you want to display the result in the lblCommission control. To display the annual commission in the label control, you need to assign it to the control's Text property. You can accomplish this using an assignment statement, which you learn about next.

Mini-Quiz 5-1

See Appendix B for the answers.

1. Write an expression to add the number 100 to the contents of the lblTotal control.

2. If the user enters $67.45 in the txtTax control, the `Val(txtTax.Text)` function will return the number _____.

3. If the user enters 23 in the txtTotal control, the `Val(txtTotal.Text) Mod 2` expression evaluates to the number _____.

Your Assignment, if You Choose to Accept It

An **assignment statement** is used to assign a value to something (such as the property of a control) during **run time**, which occurs while an application is running. The syntax of an assignment statement is *destination = value*, where *destination* is where you want to assign (or store) the *value*. The *value* can be anything, such as numbers, letters, special characters, the property of a control, or an expression. To assign the result of the annual commission calculation to the Text property of the lblCommission control, you use `lblCommission.Text` as the *destination*, and the expression `Val(txtSales.Text) * Val(txtRate.Text)` as the value. The appropriate assignment statement looks like this: `lblCommission.Text = Val(txtSales.Text) * Val(txtRate.Text)`. The equal sign in an assignment statement is referred to as the **assignment operator**. When the computer processes the assignment statement, it first performs the calculation that appears on the right side of the assignment operator. It then assigns the result of the calculation to the location that appears on the left side of the assignment operator. You can either type the assignment statement into the procedure on your own or use the Code Editor window's IntelliSense feature. You learned about the IntelliSense feature in Chapter 4.

To code the btnCalculate control's Click event procedure:

1. *If you want to type the assignment statement on your own*, type **lblCommission.Text = Val(txtSales.Text) * Val(txtRate.Text)** and press **Enter**. See Figure 5-8.

   If you want to use the IntelliSense feature, type **lbl** to highlight lblCommission in the list and then press **Tab** to enter lblCommission in the statement. Type **.te** to highlight the Text property in the list. Now you can either press the Tab key or type the equal sign, which is the character that comes after the Text property in the assignment statement. Type **=** to include the Text property in the statement. Next, type **va** to highlight the Val function in the list. Type **(txts** to highlight txtSales in the list and then type **.te** to highlight the Text property. Type **)*va** to highlight the Val function in the list and then type **(txt** to highlight txtRate in the list. Type **.te** to highlight the Text property, press **Tab**, type **)** and then press **Enter**. See Figure 5-8.

```
Private Sub btnCalculate_Click(ByVal sender As Object, ByVal e As
    ' calculates and displays the annual commission

    lblCommission.Text = Val(txtSales.Text) * Val(txtRate.Text)      assignment statement

End Sub
```

Figure 5-8   Assignment statement entered in the procedure

2. Now you will test the procedure to verify that it is working correctly. Save the solution and then start the application. First, you will use a sales amount of 2000 and a commission rate of 10%. Type **2000** as the sales amount, press **Tab**, and then type **.1** as the commission rate. Click the **Calculate Commission** button. The button's Click event procedure calculates and displays the annual commission. See Figure 5-9.

Figure 5-9   Annual commission shown in the interface

3. On your own, test the application using different sales and rates. Also test the application when one or both text boxes are empty. When you are finished testing the application, click the **Exit** button.

Before closing the solution, you will add a few more comments in the Code Editor window. More specifically, you will enter the comments in the window's **General Declarations section**. The comments will document the project's name and purpose, your name, and the date the project was either created or modified. You also will center the annual commission in the lblCommission control. You center the contents of a control by setting the control's **TextAlign property**.

To enter additional comments and also center the annual commission:

1. Position the insertion point at the beginning of the Public Class clause and then press **Enter** to insert a blank line above the clause.

2. Press the **up** arrow on your keyboard to move the insertion point into the blank line. As the Class Name and Method Name list boxes indicate, the area above the Public Class clause is called the General Declarations section.

3. Type the comments indicated in Figure 5-10, replacing <your name> and <current date> with your name and the current date, respectively.

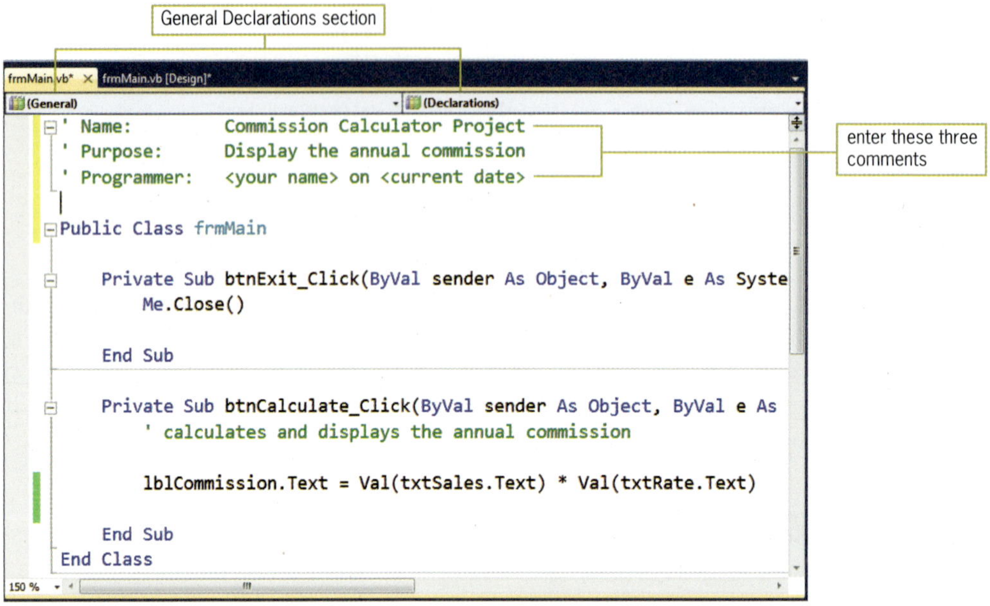

General Declarations section

```
frmMain.vb*  ×  frmMain.vb [Design]*
(General)                                              ▼  (Declarations)
     ' Name:          Commission Calculator Project
     ' Purpose:       Display the annual commission
     ' Programmer:    <your name> on <current date>

   Public Class frmMain

         Private Sub btnExit_Click(ByVal sender As Object, ByVal e As Syste
             Me.Close()

         End Sub

         Private Sub btnCalculate_Click(ByVal sender As Object, ByVal e As
             ' calculates and displays the annual commission

             lblCommission.Text = Val(txtSales.Text) * Val(txtRate.Text)

         End Sub
   End Class
150 %
```

enter these three comments

Figure 5-10 Comments entered in the General Declarations section

4. Close the Code Editor window.

5. Click the **lblCommission** control and then click **TextAlign** in the Properties list. Click the **list arrow** in the Settings box and then click the **rectangle that appears in the second row, second column**. Doing this changes the TextAlign property's value to MiddleCenter.

6. Save the solution and then run the application. Type **3000** as the sales amount, press **Tab**, and then type **.2** as the commission rate. Click the **Calculate Commission** button. The annual commission (600) appears centered in the lblCommission control.

7. Click the **Exit** button and then close the solution.

Mini-Quiz 5-2

See Appendix B for the answers.

1. Write an assignment statement that assigns the result of the Val(txtHours.Text) * Val(txtRate.Text) expression to the lblGross control.

2. Write an assignment statement that increases the contents of the txtOldPrice control by 5 and then assigns the result to the lblNewPrice control.

3. The equal sign in an assignment statement is called the _____.

4. The area above the Public Class clause in the Code Editor window is called the _____.

Summary

- The fifth step in the problem-solving process is to code the problem's algorithm.

- A procedure needs to know *how* to make a calculation and *where* to store the result.

- You use comments to internally document a project's code. A comment begins with an apostrophe.

- The Val function temporarily converts one or more characters to a number; it then returns the number.

- You instruct a computer to perform a calculation by writing an expression that contains one or more arithmetic operators.

- Arithmetic operators having the same precedence number are evaluated from left to right in an expression.

- You can use parentheses to override the order of precedence for arithmetic operators.

- You use an assignment statement to assign a value to something while an application is running.

- When an assignment statement contains a calculation, the calculation is performed before the resulting value is assigned to its destination.

- A control's TextAlign property determines the position of the text within the control.

Key Terms

Argument—appears within parentheses after a function's name; represents information that the function uses while it is processing

Assignment operator—the equal sign in an assignment statement

Assignment statement—a statement that assigns a value to a destination (such as the property of a control)

Comment—a message entered in the Code Editor window for the purpose of internally documenting the code; begins with an apostrophe; also referred to as internal documentation

Function—a predefined procedure that performs a specific task and then returns a value after completing the task

General Declarations section—the area above the Public Class clause in the Code Editor window

Integer division operator—one of the arithmetic operators; represented by a backslash (\); divides two integers and then returns the quotient as an integer

Internal documentation—the comments entered in the Code Editor window

Modulus operator—represented by the keyword Mod; divides two numbers and then returns the remainder of the division

Run time—the state of an application while it is running

TextAlign property—determines the position of the text within a control

Val function—temporarily converts one or more characters to a number, and then returns the number

Review Questions

1. Comments in Visual Basic begin with _____.

    a.   ' (apostrophe)   c.   ^ (caret)
    b.   * (asterisk)   d.   none of the above

2. If the user enters $5 in the txtPrice control and enters 3 in the txtQuantity control, the `Val(txtPrice.Text) * Val(txtQuantity.Text)` expression will evaluate to _____.

    a.   0   c.   15
    b.   3   d.   none of the above

3. If the user enters 75 in the txtNum control, which of the following changes the control's contents to −75 (a negative 75)?

    a.   `-txtNum.Text = Val(txtNum.Text)`
    b.   `txtNum.Text = -txtNum.Text`
    c.   `txtNum.Text = -Val(txtNum.Text)`
    d.   both b and c

4. If the txtNum control contains the value 82, which of the following expressions evaluates to the number 4?

    a.   `(Val(txtNum.Text) + 6) / 22`   c.   `Val(txtNum.Text) \ 20`
    b.   `Val(txtNum.Text) Mod 6`   d.   all of the above

5. The expression in which of the following assignment statements will not calculate correctly?

    a.   `lblTotal.Text = Val(txtSales1.Text) + Val(txtSales2.Text)`
    b.   `lblTotal.Text = Val(txtSales1.Text + txtSales2.Text)`
    c.   `lblTotal.Text = Val(txtRed.Text) * 2`
    d.   `lblTotal.Text = Val(txtBlue.Text) * 1.1`

6. The expression 2 ^ 3 * 43 Mod 3 * 6 evaluates to _____.

    a.   2   c.   10
    b.   3   d.   12

7. The expression 44 Mod 3 ^ 2 \ 4 evaluates to _____.

    a.   0   c.   2
    b.   1   d.   3

Exercises

TRY THIS ▶

1. In this exercise, you code the Aiden Turner problem's algorithm from Chapter 2. (See Appendix B for the answer.)

    a. Open the New Pay Solution (New Pay Solution.sln) file contained in the ClearlyVB2010\Chap05\New Pay Solution folder. If necessary, open the designer window. Figure 5-11 shows the problem's output, input, and algorithm. Complete the application by coding its algorithm. The calculation instruction associated with Step 2 in the algorithm will be fairly long. For readability, you can enter the instruction on more than one line in the Code Editor window. You do this by pressing the Enter key after typing either the equal sign or any of the arithmetic operators. For example, to enter the assignment statement shown earlier in Figure 5-10 on two lines, you could type `lblCommission.Text =` on the first line and then press the Enter key to move the insertion point to the next line, where you would type the remainder of the assignment statement.

b. Include comments in the Code Editor window. The contents of the lblNewPay control should be centered; set the appropriate property. Save the solution and then start the application. Test the application using various values for the current weekly pay and raise percentage. When you are finished testing the application, close the Code Editor window and then close the solution.

Output: new weekly pay

Input: current weekly pay
                raise percentage

Algorithm:
1. enter the current weekly pay and raise percentage
2. calculate the new weekly pay by multiplying the current weekly pay by the raise percentage, and then adding the result to the current weekly pay
3. display the new weekly pay

Figure 5-11 Information for Exercise 1

2. In this exercise, you modify the Commission Calculator application created in the chapter.

   a. Use Windows to make a copy of the Commission Calculator Solution folder. Save the copy in the ClearlyVB2010\Chap05 folder. Rename the copy Modified Commission Calculator Solution.

   b. If necessary, start Visual Studio 2010 or Visual Basic 2010 Express and permanently display the Solution Explorer window. Open the Commission Calculator Solution (Commission Calculator Solution.sln) file contained in the Modified Commission Calculator Solution folder. Currently, the application is designed to accept the decimal version of the commission rate. For example, if the rate is 6%, the application expects the user to enter .06. Modify the application so that it expects the user to enter the rate as a whole number. For example, if the rate is 6%, the user should enter 6. First, change the Enter decimal rate: label to Enter % rate:. Next, modify the Calculate Commission button's code appropriately.

   c. Save the solution and then start the application. Test the application using 2000 as the sales amount and 10 (for 10%) as the commission rate. The annual commission should be 200. Close the Code Editor window and then close the solution.

3. Open the Skate Away Solution (Skate Away Solution.sln) file contained in the ClearlyVB2010\Chap05\Skate Away Solution folder. The Calculate Order button should calculate and display the total number of skateboards ordered and the total price of the order. Each skateboard costs $100. Code the button's Click event procedure. Save the solution and then start and test the application. Close the Code Editor window and then close the solution.

4. Open the Tip Solution (Tip Solution.sln) file contained in the ClearlyVB2010\Chap05\Tip Solution folder. Figure 5-12 shows the problem's output, input, and algorithm. Complete the application by coding its algorithm. Include comments in the Code Editor window. Save the solution and then start and test the application. Close the Code Editor window and then close the solution.

MODIFY THIS

INTRODUCTORY

INTRODUCTORY

Output: 10% tip
             15% tip
             20% tip

Input: restaurant bill

Algorithm:
1. enter the restaurant bill
2. calculate a 10% tip by multiplying the restaurant bill by 10%
3. calculate a 15% tip by multiplying the restaurant bill by 15%
4. calculate a 20% tip by multiplying the restaurant bill by 20%
5. display the 10% tip, 15% tip, and 20% tip

Figure 5-12 Information for Exercise 4

INTERMEDIATE

5. In this exercise, you create an application for the Vans & More Depot, which rents vans for company outings. Each van can transport 10 people. The interface should allow the user to enter the number of people attending the outing. The application should calculate and display the number of vans that can be filled completely. It also should calculate and display the number of people who will need to find another way to get to the outing. For example, if 48 people are attending the outing, 40 of them will fit into four vans; the remaining eight people will need to arrange for their own transportation. The output for this problem is the number of vans that can be filled completely, and the number of people remaining. The input is the number of people attending the outing.

   a. Write the problem's algorithm.

   b. Create a Visual Basic Windows application. Use the following names for the solution and project, respectively: Vans Solution and Vans Project. Save the application in the ClearlyVB2010\Chap05 folder.

   c. Change the name of the form file on your disk to frmMain.vb. If necessary, change the form's name to frmMain.

   d. Create an appropriate interface. Also include an Exit button.

   e. Code the Exit button's Click event procedure and the algorithm. Include comments in the Code Editor window.

   f. Save the solution and then start and test the application. Close the Code Editor window and then close the solution.

INTERMEDIATE

6. In this exercise, you finish coding the Property Tax application from Chapter 4's Exercise 4.

   a. If necessary, complete the algorithm shown in Figure 4-18 in Chapter 4.

   b. Open the Property Tax Solution (Property Tax Solution.sln) file contained in the ClearlyVB2010\Chap05\Property Tax Solution folder. Code the problem's algorithm. Include comments in the Code Editor window.

   c. Save the solution and then start and test the application. (Using 104000 and 1.02 as the assessed value and property tax rate, respectively, the tax is 1060.8.) Close the Code Editor window and then close the solution.

7. In this exercise, you finish coding an application that calculates and displays the total amount a customer owes.

   a. Open the Total Solution (Total Solution.sln) file contained in the ClearlyVB2010\Chap05\Total Solution folder. Center the contents of the lblTotal control. Code the Calculate button's Click event procedure. Include comments in the Code Editor window.

   b. Save the solution and then start and test the application. Close the Code Editor window and then close the solution.

8. In this exercise, you finish coding the application from Chapter 4's Exercise 6.

   a. If necessary, complete the algorithm shown in Figure 4-20 in Chapter 4.

   b. Open the Party Solution (Party Solution.sln) file contained in the ClearlyVB2010\Chap05\Party Solution folder. Center the contents of the lblTotal control. Code the problem's algorithm. Include comments in the Code Editor window.

   c. Save the solution and then start and test the application. Close the Code Editor window and then close the solution.

9. In this exercise, you modify the application from Exercise 5. In addition to renting vans, Vans & More Depot also rents cars. Each van can transport 10 people, and each car can transport five people. The modified application should calculate three values: the number of vans that can be filled, the number of cars that can be filled, and the number of people who will need to arrange other means of transportation. As an example, if 48 people are attending the outing, the company will need to rent four vans (to transport 40 people) and one car (to transport five people). The remaining three people will need to arrange for their own transportation.

   a. Use Windows to make a copy of the Vans Solution folder. Save the copy in the ClearlyVB2010\Chap05 folder. Rename the copy Modified Vans Solution.

   b. Open the Vans Solution (Vans Solution.sln) file contained in the Modified Vans Solution folder. Make the appropriate modifications to the interface and code.

   c. Save the solution and then start and test the application. Close the Code Editor window and then close the solution.

10. The payroll clerk at Sun Projects wants an application that computes an employee's net pay. The clerk will enter the employee's name, hours worked, and rate of pay. For this application, you do not have to worry about overtime, because employees are not allowed to work more than 40 hours. The application should calculate and display the gross pay, federal withholding tax (FWT), Social Security tax (FICA), state income tax, and net pay. The FWT is calculated by multiplying the gross pay by 20%. The FICA tax is 8% of the gross pay, and the state income tax is 2% of the gross pay.

   a. List the output and input items, and then create an appropriate algorithm.

   b. Create a Visual Basic Windows application. Use the following names for the solution and project, respectively: Sun Solution and Sun Project. Save the application in the ClearlyVB2010\Chap05 folder.

   c. Change the name of the form file on your disk to frmMain.vb. If necessary, change the form's name to frmMain.

   d. Create a suitable interface. Include an Exit button.

e. Code the Exit button's Click event procedure and the problem's algorithm.

f. Save the solution and then start and test the application. Close the Code Editor window and then close the solution.

ADVANCED

11. In this exercise, you finish coding the RM Sales application from Chapter 4's Exercise 7. If you did not complete Chapter 4's Exercise 7, you will need to do so before you can complete this exercise. Use Windows to copy the Sales Solution folder from the ClearlyVB2010\Chap04 folder to the ClearlyVB2010\Chap05 folder. Open the Sales Solution (Sales Solution.sln) file contained in the ClearlyVB2010\Chap05\Sales Solution folder. Center the contents of the label controls in the Percentage column and also the contents of the lblTotalSales control. Code the problem's algorithm. Include appropriate comments in the Code Editor window. Save the solution and then start and test the application. Close the Code Editor window and then close the solution.

FIGURE THIS OUT

12. A Calculate button's Click event procedure contains the `lblDue.Text = Val (txtDaysLate.Text) * 2 + 3.5` statement.

a. If the user enters the number 3 in the txtDaysLate control, what will be assigned to the lblDue control when the user clicks the Calculate button?

b. If the user enters the letters AB in the txtDaysLate control, what will be assigned to the lblDue control when the user clicks the Calculate button?

c. If the txtDaysLate control is empty when the user clicks the Calculate button, what will the button's Click event procedure assign to the lblDue control?

SWAT THE BUGS

13. Open the SwatTheBugs Solution (SwatTheBugs Solution.sln) file contained in the ClearlyVB2010\Chap05\SwatTheBugs Solution folder. Start and test the application. Notice that the code is not working correctly. Locate and correct any errors.

Where Can I Store This? (Variables and Constants)

After studying Chapter 6, you should be able to:

◎ Declare variables and named constants

◎ Convert text to a numeric data type using the TryParse method

◎ Understand the scope and lifetime of variables

◎ Desk-check a program

◎ Format a program's numeric output

82

CHAPTER 6   Where Can I Store This? (Variables and Constants)

Using Storage Bins

Inside every computer is a component called internal memory. The internal memory of a computer is composed of memory locations. It may be helpful to picture memory locations as storage bins, similar to the ones illustrated in Figure 6-1. However, unlike the storage bins in the figure, each storage bin (memory location) inside a computer can hold only one item of data at a time. The item can be a number, such as 5 or 45.89. It also can be text, which is a group of characters treated as one unit and not used in a calculation. Examples of text include your name, the part number ABN123X, the phone number 111-2345, and the Visual Basic statement `Me.Close()`. Some of the storage bins (memory locations) inside the computer are automatically filled with data while you use your computer. For example, when you enter the number 5 at your keyboard, the computer saves the number 5 in a memory location for you. Likewise, when you start an application, each program instruction is placed in a memory location, where it awaits processing.

Figure 6-1   Illustration of storage bins

Some of the memory locations inside a computer are special in that they can be reserved by a programmer for use in a program. You reserve a memory location using a Visual Basic instruction that assigns both a name and data type to the memory location. The data type indicates the type of data—for example, numeric or textual—the memory location will store. But why would a programmer need to use one of these special memory locations? In Chapter 5, you calculated Addison Smith's commission using the expression `Val(txtSales.Text) * Val (txtRate.Text)`. Typically, programmers do not use the Text properties of controls in arithmetic expressions. One reason for this is that such expressions can get rather long and difficult to understand. Imagine writing an expression that calculates a value using the Text properties of 10 controls! And then imagine trying to understand the instruction a year after you wrote it! Instead, programmers store the Text property values in special memory locations called variables. The memory locations are called **variables** because their contents can change (vary) as the program is running. The programmer then uses the variable's name, rather than the Text property of its associated control, in the arithmetic expression. Because variable names typically are more concise than control names, using variable names in an expression makes the expression much shorter and easier to understand. Before learning how to reserve a variable in Visual Basic, you will learn how to select an appropriate data type and name for the variable.

So, What's Your Type?

Like storage bins, variables come in different types and sizes. The type and size you use depends on the item you want the variable to store. Some variables can store a number, while others can hold text, a date, or a **Boolean value** (True or False). The item that a variable will accept for storage is determined by the variable's data type, which the programmer assigns to the variable when it is reserved. In this chapter, you will learn about numeric data types, which are used to reserve variables that will store numbers. The three most commonly used numeric data types available in Visual Basic are listed in Figure 6-2, along with the range of values they can store and the amount of memory needed to store each value. (You will learn about other data types in later chapters in this book. Appendix A in this book contains a complete listing of the Visual Basic data types.)

Data type	Stores	Memory required
Integer	an integer	4 bytes
	Range: −2,147,483,648 to 2,147,483,647	
Decimal	a number with a decimal place	16 bytes
	Range with no decimal place: +/−79,228,162,514,264,337,593,543,950,335	
	Range with a decimal place: +/−7.9228162514264337593543950335	
Double	a number with a decimal place	8 bytes
	Range: +/− $4.94065645841247 \times 10^{-324}$ to +/−$1.79769313486231 \times 10^{308}$	

Figure 6-2   Most commonly used numeric data types

As Figure 6-2 indicates, variables assigned the Integer data type can store integers. An integer is a whole number, which is a number that does not contain a decimal place. Examples of integers include the numbers 0, 45, and −678. If the Text property of a control contains a whole number that you want to use in a calculation, you would assign the Text property value to an Integer variable and then use the Integer variable in the calculation. However, if the Text property contains a number with a decimal place, and you want to use that number in a calculation, you would assign the Text property value to either a Decimal variable or a Double variable. Both data types allow variables to store numbers that have a decimal place. The differences between the two data types are in the range of numbers each type can store and the amount of memory each type needs to store the numbers. As indicated in Figure 6-2, Decimal variables take twice as much room in memory as do Double variables. However, calculations involving Decimal variables are not subject to the small rounding errors that may occur when using Double variables. In most cases, the small rounding errors do not create any problems in an application. One exception, however, is when the application performs financial calculations that require accuracy to the penny. In those cases, the Decimal data type is the best type to use.

84

CHAPTER 6 Where Can I Store This? (Variables and Constants)

Let's Play the Name Game

Every variable that a programmer uses must be assigned a name. The name should be descriptive in that it should help you remember the variable's purpose. In other words, it should describe the contents of the variable. A good variable name is one that is meaningful right after you finish a program, and also years later when you (or perhaps a co-worker) need to modify the program. A variable name must begin with a letter or an underscore. The name can contain only letters, numbers, and the underscore character. No punctuation marks or spaces are allowed in the name. In addition, the name cannot be a reserved word, such as Val.

There are several conventions for naming variables in Visual Basic. In this book, you will use Hungarian notation, which is the same naming convention used for controls. Variable names in Hungarian notation begin with a three-character ID that represents the variable's data type. The names of Integer variables, for example, begin with int. The remaining characters in the name represent the variable's purpose. Using Hungarian notation, you might assign the name intAge to an Integer variable that stores a person's age. Like control names, variable names are entered using camel case, which means you lowercase the ID and then uppercase the first letter of each word in the name. Figure 6-3 lists the three-character ID associated with each data type listed in Figure 6-2. The figure also includes examples of variable names.

Data type	ID	Example
Integer	int	intAge
Decimal	dec	decPayRate
Double	dbl	dblPrice

Figure 6-3 Data type IDs and examples of variable names

You'll Need a Reservation

Now that you know how to select an appropriate name and data type for a variable, you can learn how to reserve a variable for your program to use. Reserving a variable is often referred to as declaring a variable. To declare a variable in an event procedure, where most variables are declared, you use the Visual Basic **Dim statement**. Figure 6-4 shows the Dim statement's syntax. Items in boldface in the syntax are required, while italicized items represent information that the programmer must provide. In the syntax, *variableName* and *dataType* are the name and data type, respectively, you want assigned to a memory location. The computer stores a default value in the variable when it is declared; the default value depends on the variable's data type. Integer, Decimal, and Double variables are automatically initialized to—in other words, given a beginning value of—the number 0. Also included in Figure 6-4 are examples of declaring variables.

Declaring a Variable
Syntax
Dim *variableName* **As** *dataType*

Examples
Dim intAge As Integer
Dim decPayRate As Decimal
Dim dblPrice As Double

Figure 6-4 Syntax and examples of the Dim statement

Mini-Quiz 6-1

See Appendix B for the answers.

1. Which of the three data types listed in Figure 6-2 is appropriate for storing the number of desks purchased by a customer?

2. Which of the following is not a valid name for a variable?
   a. `decRate`
   c. `decRate_Of_Pay`
   b. `dblRate`
   d. `dblPay.Rate`

3. Write a Dim statement to declare a Double variable named `dblHoursWorked`.

How Many Variables Should I Use?

You use a problem's solution—in other words, its output, processing, and input information and its algorithm—to determine the variables to use when coding the application. Most times, you will use a different variable for each unique output, processing, and input item listed in the solution. The Circle Area problem's solution shown in Figure 6-5 will utilize two different variables: one to store the output item and the other one to store the input item. Looking at the algorithm, you will notice that both items are involved in calculations. The items may contain a decimal place, so you should assign their values to variables of either the Decimal or Double data type. In this case, because the values don't involve money, you'll use the Double data type. Suitable names for the two variables are `dblArea` and `dblRadius`.

Output: circle's area

Input: circle's radius

Algorithm:
1. enter the circle's radius
2. calculate the circle's area by multiplying the circle's radius by itself and then multiplying the result by 3.141593 (which is pi rounded to six decimal places)
3. display the circle's area

Figure 6-5   Circle Area problem's solution

For more examples of using variables, see the Variables section in the Ch6WantMore.pdf file.

Before you begin coding the Circle Area application, you may want to view the Ch06-Circle Area video. The video demonstrates all of the steps contained in this chapter. You may find it helpful to view the steps before you perform them.

To open the Circle Area application:

1. Start Visual Studio 2010 or Visual Basic 2010 Express and permanently display the Solution Explorer window.

2. Open the **Circle Area Solution (Circle Area Solution.sln)** file contained in the ClearlyVB2010\Chap06\Circle Area Solution folder. If the designer window is not open, double-click **frmMain.vb** in the Solution Explorer window. The application's interface is shown in Figure 6-6.

86

CHAPTER 6   Where Can I Store This? (Variables and Constants)

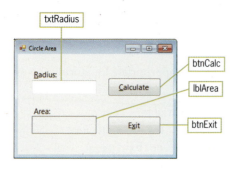

Figure 6-6   Circle Area application's interface

The user will enter the circle's radius (the input item) in the txtRadius control. When the user clicks the Calculate button, the button's Click event procedure will use the circle's radius to calculate the circle's area (the output item). The formula for calculating the area of a circle is πr^2, where π stands for pi. Before the procedure ends, it will display the circle's area in the lblArea control.

To begin coding the Calculate button's Click event procedure:

1.   Auto-hide the Solution Explorer window and then open the Code Editor window, which contains the code for the btnExit control's Click event procedure.

2.   Open the btnCalc control's Click event procedure. First, you will enter the instructions to declare the necessary variables. It is customary to enter the variable declaration statements at the beginning of the procedure. Type the comments and two Dim statements indicated in Figure 6-7, and then position the insertion point as shown in the figure. The green jagged line below each variable's name indicates that the variable has been declared, but it is not used by any other statement in the procedure.

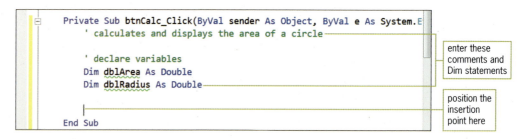

Figure 6-7   Comments and Dim statements entered in the procedure

Now you can begin coding the application's algorithm. The first step in the algorithm is to enter the circle's radius. Recall that the user enters the radius in the txtRadius control. The second step is to calculate the circle's area by multiplying the radius by itself, and then multiplying the result by 3.141593 (the value of pi rounded to six decimal places). Using what you learned in Chapter 5, you could calculate the circle's area using the expression `Val(txtRadius.Text) * Val(txtRadius.Text) * 3.141593`. The expression tells the computer to multiply the contents of the txtRadius control's Text property (converted temporarily to a number) by the contents of the txtRadius control's Text property (again converted temporarily to a number), and then multiply the result by the number 3.141593. However, although the Val function has been a part of the Visual Basic language since its inception, there is no guarantee that it will always be a part of the language. As a result, most programmers now use the TryParse method to convert text to numbers.

The TryParse Method

Every numeric data type in Visual Basic has a **TryParse method** that can be used to convert text to that numeric data type. The basic syntax of the TryParse method is *dataType*.**TryParse**(*text, variable*). In the syntax, *dataType* is one of the numeric data types available in Visual Basic, such as Double, Decimal, and Integer. The *text* argument is the text you want converted to a number of the *dataType* type and typically is the Text property of a control. The *variable* argument is the name of a numeric variable where the TryParse method can store the number. The numeric variable must have the same data type as specified in the *dataType* portion of the syntax. In other words, when using the TryParse method to convert text to a Double number, you need to provide the method with the name of a Double variable in which to store the number.

The TryParse method parses the text, which means it looks at each character in the text, to determine whether the text can be converted to a number of the specified data type. If the text can be converted, the TryParse method converts the text to a number and then stores the number in the variable specified in the *variable* argument. However, if the TryParse method determines that the text cannot be converted to the appropriate data type, the method assigns the number 0 to the variable. Figure 6-8 shows the basic syntax of the TryParse method and includes examples of using the method. (To learn more about the TryParse method, complete FIGURE THIS OUT Exercise 12 at the end of the chapter.)

Basic Syntax of the TryParse Method

<u>Syntax</u>
dataType.**TryParse**(*text, variable*)

<u>Example 1</u>
```
Double.TryParse(txtRadius.Text, dblRadius)
```

If the text entered in the txtRadius control can be converted to a Double number, the TryParse method converts the text and then stores the result in the dblRadius variable; otherwise, it stores the number 0 in the dblRadius variable.

<u>Example 2</u>
```
Decimal.TryParse(txtSales.Text, decSales)
```

If the text entered in the txtSales control can be converted to a Decimal number, the TryParse method converts the text and then stores the result in the decSales variable; otherwise, it stores the number 0 in the decSales variable.

<u>Example 3</u>
```
Integer.TryParse(txtNum.Text, intNum)
```

If the text entered in the txtNum control can be converted to an Integer number, the TryParse method converts the text and then stores the result in the intNum variable; otherwise, it stores the number 0 in the intNum variable.

Figure 6-8   Basic syntax and examples of the TryParse method

Before entering the instruction to calculate the circle's area, you first will use the TryParse method to convert the Text property of the txtRadius control to a number. You will have the method assign the resulting number to the dblRadius variable. You then will use the dblRadius variable in the circle area calculation.

88

CHAPTER 6   Where Can I Store This? (Variables and Constants)

To continue coding the Circle Area application:

1. The insertion point should be positioned as shown earlier in Figure 6-7. Enter the following comment and TryParse method. Press **Enter** twice after typing the method. (Notice that when you press Enter after typing the method, the Code Editor removes the jagged green line below the dblRadius variable.)

' store radius in a variable
Double.TryParse(txtRadius.Text, dblRadius)

2. Now you can use the dblRadius variable in the expression that calculates the circle's area. You will assign the result of the calculation to the dblArea variable. Enter the following comment and assignment statement. Press **Enter** twice after typing the statement. (You also can use the dblArea = dblRadius ^ 2 * 3.141593 assignment statement.)

' calculate area
dblArea = dblRadius * dblRadius * 3.141593

3. Step 3 in the algorithm (shown earlier in Figure 6-5) is to display the circle's area. Enter the comment and assignment statement indicated in Figure 6-9.

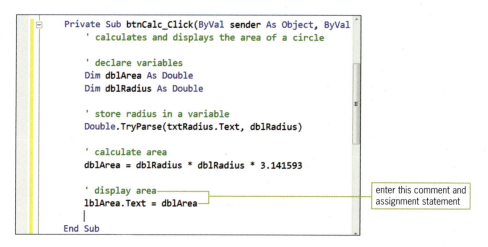

```
Private Sub btnCalc_Click(ByVal sender As Object, ByVal
    ' calculates and displays the area of a circle

    ' declare variables
    Dim dblArea As Double
    Dim dblRadius As Double

    ' store radius in a variable
    Double.TryParse(txtRadius.Text, dblRadius)

    ' calculate area
    dblArea = dblRadius * dblRadius * 3.141593

    ' display area
    lblArea.Text = dblArea

End Sub
```

enter this comment and assignment statement

Figure 6-9   Code entered in the btnCalc control's Click event procedure

Most variables are declared in procedures, such as event procedures. These variables are referred to as **procedure-level variables** and are said to have **procedure scope**, because they can be used only by the procedure in which they are declared. **Scope** refers to the area where a variable is recognized in an application's code. The dblRadius and dblArea variables in Figure 6-9 are procedure-level variables that can be used only by the btnCalc control's Click event procedure. When a procedure ends, its procedure-level variables are removed from the computer's internal memory. Programmers refer to the length of time a variable remains in memory as its **lifetime**. A procedure-level variable has the same lifetime as the procedure in which it is declared.

Check, Please...I'm Ready to Go

Before testing the Circle Area application using the computer, which is Step 7 in the problem-solving process from Chapter 2, you will perform Step 6, which is to desk-check the program. You can do this using a desk-check table, similar to one that you use when desk-checking an algorithm. The desk-check table for a program will contain one column for each variable. As an example, you will desk-check the Circle Area program using radius values of 6.5 and 10. Figure 6-10 shows the completed desk-check table. On your own, desk-check the program using other values.

dblRadius	dblArea
~~6.5~~	~~132.73230425~~
10	314.1593

Figure 6-10 Desk-check table for the Circle Area program

To test the Circle Area application using the computer:

1. Save the solution and then start the application. Type **6.5** in the Radius box and then click the **Calculate** button. See Figure 6-11. The button's Click event procedure tells the computer to reserve two Double variables named db1Radius and db1Area. The TryParse method in the procedure converts the 6.5 entered in the Radius box to a number, and then stores the number in the db1Radius variable. Next, the computer multiplies the contents of the db1Radius variable by itself, and then multiplies the result by 3.141593. It then stores the result in the db1Area variable. The last statement in the procedure displays the contents of the db1Area variable in the lblArea control. When the procedure ends, the db1Radius and db1Area variables are removed from the computer's internal memory.

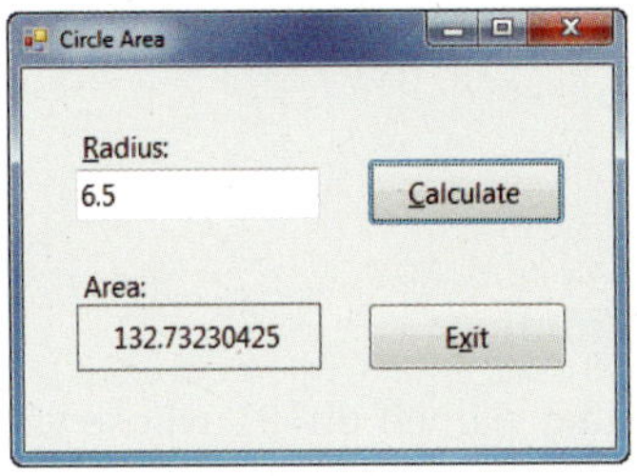

Figure 6-11 Circle's area shown in the interface

2. Change the radius from 6.5 to 10 and then click the **Calculate** button. The circle's area is 314.1593.

3. On your own, test the application using other values for the radius. When you are finished testing, click the **Exit** button.

Using Constants to Keep Things...Well, the Same

In addition to reserving (or declaring) variables in a program, you also can declare named constants. A **named constant** is a memory location whose value cannot change while the application is running. The programmer assigns a value to the named constant when it is declared. It might be helpful to picture a named constant as a locked storage bin that no one but the owner (in this case, the programmer) can open. When a named constant's value needs to be changed, the programmer must change its value in its declaration statement.

Programmers use named constants to give names to constant values. After a named constant is created, the programmer then can use the constant's name (rather than its value) in the application's code. For example, rather than using the number 3.141593 in the area calculation statement shown earlier in Figure 6-9, you could assign a name (such as db1PI) to the number and then use the name in the calculation statement. Named constants make code more self-documenting and easier to modify, because they allow a programmer to use meaningful words in place of values that are less clear. The name db1PI, for example, is much more meaningful than is the number 3.141593. Using a named constant to represent a value has another advantage: If the value changes in the future, the programmer will need to modify

90

CHAPTER 6 Where Can I Store This? (Variables and Constants)

only the named constant's declaration statement, rather than all of the program statements that use the value.

You create a named constant using the **Const statement**. The statement's syntax is shown in Figure 6-12. In the syntax, *constantName* is the name you want assigned to the named constant. To distinguish the named constants from the variables in a program, many programmers use a modified form of Hungarian notation for the named constant names. In the modified notation, the ID characters in the name are still entered in lowercase, but the remaining part of the name is entered in uppercase, like this: dblPI. *DataType* in the syntax is the named constant's data type, and *value* is the value you want stored in the named constant. Also included in Figure 6-12 are examples of declaring named constants.

Declaring a Named Constant
<u>Syntax</u>
Const *constantName* **As** *dataType* = *value*

<u>Examples</u>
Const dblPI As Double = 3.141593
Const intMAX_HOURS As Integer = 40
Const decTAXRATE As Decimal = .05

Figure 6-12 Syntax and examples of the Const statement

To declare a named constant in the Circle Area application:

1. In this step, you will declare a Double named constant named dblPI whose value is 3.141593. Like the variables declared in the procedure, the dblPI named constant will have procedure scope and will remain in memory until the procedure ends. Click the **blank line** above the ' declare variables comment and then press **Enter**. Enter the following comment and declaration statement:

   ' declare named constant
   Const dblPI As Double = 3.141593

2. In the statement that calculates the area, replace 3.141593 with **dblPI**.

3. Save the solution and then start the application. Type **2** in the Radius box and then click the **Calculate** button. The interface shows that the area is 12.566372.

4. Click the **Exit** button.

Dressing Up the Output

Many times you will want to control the number of decimal places and the special characters that appear in an application's numeric output. For example, numbers representing monetary amounts typically are displayed with either zero or two decimal places and usually include a dollar sign and a thousands separator. Similarly, numbers representing percentage amounts usually are displayed with zero or more decimal places and a percent sign. Specifying the number of decimal places and the special characters to display in a number is called **formatting**. You can format a number using the syntax *variable*.**ToString**(*formatString*). In the syntax, *variable* is the name of a numeric variable, and ToString is a method that can be used with any of the numeric data types. The **ToString method** converts the contents of the numeric variable to text. The *formatString* argument in the syntax is a string that specifies the format you want to use. A **string** is text that is enclosed in double quotation marks. The *formatString* argument must take the form "*Axx*", where *A* is an alphabetic character called the format specifier, and *xx* is a sequence of digits called the precision specifier. The format specifier must be one of the built-in format characters. The most commonly used format characters are listed in Figure 6-13. Notice that you can use either an uppercase letter or a lowercase letter as the format specifier. When used with one of the format characters listed in Figure 6-13, the precision specifier controls the number of digits that will appear after the decimal point in the formatted number. Also included in Figure 6-13 are examples of using the ToString method.

Formatting a Number

Syntax

variable.**ToString(***formatString***)**

Format specifier (Name)	Description
C or c (Currency)	displays the text with a dollar sign; includes a thousands separator (if appropriate); negative values are enclosed in parentheses
N or n (Number)	similar to the Currency format, but does not include a dollar sign and negative values are preceded by a minus sign
F or f (Fixed-point)	same as the Number format, but does not include a thousands separator
P or p (Percent)	multiplies the value by 100 and displays the result with a percent sign; negative values are preceded by a minus sign

Example 1
```
lblCommission.Text = intCommission.ToString("C2")
```

if the `intCommission` variable contains the number 1250, the statement assigns the text $1,250.00 to the Text property of the lblCommission control

Example 2
```
lblTotal.Text = decTotal.ToString("N2")
```

if the `decTotal` variable contains the number 123.675, the statement assigns the text 123.68 to the Text property of the lblTotal control

Example 3
```
lblRate.Text = dblRate.ToString("P0")
```

if the `dblRate` variable contains the number .06, the statement assigns the text 6 % to the Text property of the lblRate control

---

Figure 6-13 Syntax and examples of formatting numeric output

To format the area output to include only two decimal places:

1. Change the last assignment statement to **lblArea.Text = dblArea.ToString("N2")** and then click the **blank line** below the statement. See Figure 6-14.

92

CHAPTER 6 Where Can I Store This? (Variables and Constants)

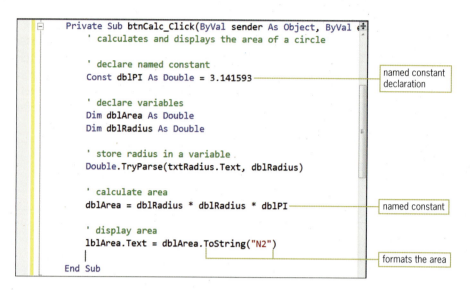

```
Private Sub btnCalc_Click(ByVal sender As Object, ByVal
    ' calculates and displays the area of a circle

    ' declare named constant
    Const dblPI As Double = 3.141593

    ' declare variables
    Dim dblArea As Double
    Dim dblRadius As Double

    ' store radius in a variable
    Double.TryParse(txtRadius.Text, dblRadius)

    ' calculate area
    dblArea = dblRadius * dblRadius * dblPI

    ' display area
    lblArea.Text = dblArea.ToString("N2")

End Sub
```

named constant declaration

named constant

formats the area

Figure 6-14 Completed btnCalc Click event procedure

2. Save the solution and then start the application. Type **2** in the Radius box and then click the **Calculate** button. The interface shows that the circle's area is 12.57.

3. Click the **Exit** button. Close the Code Editor window and then close the solution.

Mini-Quiz 6-2

See Appendix B for the answers.

1. Write a TryParse method that converts the value entered in the txtIncome control to the Decimal data type and then stores the result in the `decIncome` variable.

2. Write the statement to declare the `intMINIMUM` named constant whose value is 55.

3. The `dblSales` variable contains the number 56.78. Write the assignment statement to display the value with a dollar sign and no decimal places in the lblSales control.

Summary

-   The internal memory of a computer is composed of memory locations. Programmers can reserve some of the locations for variables and named constants.

-   A memory location can store only one value at any one time.

-   The value in a variable can change during run time. The value in a named constant, on the other hand, cannot change during run time.

-   The Integer data type stores integers. The Decimal and Double data types store numbers with a decimal place. The Decimal data type typically is used for numbers involved in monetary calculations, because it is not subject to the small rounding errors that may occur with the Double data type.

- You use the Dim statement to reserve a procedure-level variable. A procedure-level variable can be used only by the procedure in which it is declared, and it is removed from memory when the procedure ends.

- Most times, you will use a different variable for each unique output, processing, and input item listed in a problem's solution.

- Most programmers use the TryParse method, rather than the Val function, to convert text to numbers.

- You use the Const statement to declare named constants.

- You can use the ToString method to convert a number to text that contains a specific number of decimal places and optional formatting characters.

Key Terms

Boolean value—the values True and False

Const statement—the statement used to declare a named constant

Dim statement—the statement used to declare a procedure-level variable

Formatting—specifying the number of decimal places and the special characters to display in a number

Lifetime—indicates how long a variable or named constant remains in the computer's internal memory

Named constant—a computer memory location whose value cannot be changed during run time; created using the Const statement

Procedure scope—the scope of a procedure-level variable; refers to the fact that the variable can be used only by the procedure in which it is declared

Procedure-level variables—variables declared in a procedure; a procedure-level variable has procedure scope

Scope—indicates where a memory location (variable or named constant) can be used in an application's code

String—text enclosed in double quotation marks

ToString method—formats a number stored in a numeric variable and then returns the result as text

TryParse method—converts text to a numeric data type

Variables—computer memory locations where programmers can temporarily store data, as well as change the data, while an application is running

Review Questions

1. Which of the following statements declares a variable named `intNumSold`?

   a. `Dim intNumSold As Integer`

   b. `Dim As Integer intNumSold`

   c. `Const intNumSold As Integer`

   d. none of the above

94

CHAPTER 6 Where Can I Store This? (Variables and Constants)

2. If the user enters the text A34 in the txtPrice control, the TryParse(txtPrice.Text, decPrice) statement will assign _____ to the decPrice variable.

   a. A   c. 0

   b. A34   d. 34

3. Which of the following statements adds together the contents of the intScore1 and intScore2 variables and then multiplies the sum by 2, assigning the result to the intTotal variable?

   a. intScore1 + intScore2 * 2 = intTotal

   b. (intScore1 + intScore2) * 2 = intTotal

   c. intTotal = intScore1 + intScore2 * 2

   d. none of the above

4. Which of the following statements declares the dblRATE named constant and initializes it to .15?

   a. Con dblRATE As Double = .15

   b. Const dblRATE As Double = .15

   c. Constant dblRATE As Double = .15

   d. none of the above

5. Which of the following statements formats the contents of the dblDue variable with a dollar sign and two decimal places?

   a. lblDue.Text = dblDue.ToString("C2")

   b. lblDue.Text = dblDue.ToCurrency("C2")

   c. lblDue.Text = ToString(dblDue, "C2")

   d. lblDue.Text = dblDue.ToFormat("C2")

6. If the intNum variable contains the number 5, which of the following assigns the number 125 to the intCubed variable?

   a. intCubed = intNum ^ 3

   b. intCubed = intNum * intNum * intNum

   c. intCubed = intNum * intNum ^ 2

   d. all of the above

7. If intPRICE is a named constant, which of the following statements is incorrect?

   a. intTotal = intPRICE * intQuantity

   b. intPRICE = intPRICE * .9

   c. lblPrice.Text = intPRICE.ToString("C2")

   d. none of the above

Exercises

TRY THIS

1. In this exercise, you modify the Commission Calculator application from Chapter 5. Open the Commission Calculator Solution (Commission Calculator Solution.sln) file contained in the ClearlyVB2010\Chap06\Commission Calculator Solution folder. Modify the code so that it uses Decimal variables and the TryParse method. Format the commission with a dollar sign and two decimal places. Save the solution and then start and test the application. Close the Code Editor window and then close the solution. (See Appendix B for the answer.)

TRY THIS

2. In this exercise, you code an application that calculates and displays the amount of an employee's new weekly pay. (See Appendix B for the answer.)

   a. Open the New Pay Solution (New Pay Solution.sln) file contained in the ClearlyVB2010\Chap06\New Pay Solution folder. Code the algorithm shown in Figure 6-15. Be sure to use the TryParse method. Use the Double data type for the variables. Use a Double named constant for the raise rate of .03. Format the new weekly pay with a dollar sign and two decimal places.

   b. Save the solution. Desk-check the program twice, using 200 and 330 as the current weekly pay.

   c. Start and then test the application. Close the Code Editor window and then close the solution.

```
Output:        new weekly pay

Processing:    weekly raise

Input:         current weekly pay

Algorithm:
1. enter the current weekly pay
2. calculate the weekly raise by multiplying the current weekly pay by.03
3. calculate the new weekly pay by adding the weekly raise to the current weekly pay
4. display the new weekly pay
```

Figure 6-15 Information for Exercise 2

MODIFY THIS

3. In this exercise, you modify the Circle Area application created in the chapter.

   a. Use Windows to make a copy of the Circle Area Solution folder. Save the copy in the ClearlyVB2010\Chap06 folder. Rename the copy Modified Circle Area Solution.

   b. Open the Circle Area Solution (Circle Area Solution.sln) file contained in the Modified Circle Area Solution folder. Modify the code so that it uses a separate calculation for the radius squared. Assign the result of the radius squared calculation to a variable, and then modify the statement that calculates the circle's area.

   c. Save the solution and then start the application. Test the application using 4.6 as the radius. The area should be 66.48. Close the Code Editor window and then close the solution.

INTRODUCTORY

4. The cashier at Jackson College wants an application that displays the total amount a student owes for the semester, including tuition and room and board. The tuition is $100 per semester hour, and room and board combined is $1800 per semester. The cashier will need to enter the number of hours the student is enrolled. Use Integer named constants for the semester hour fee and the room and board fee. Use Integer variables for the input

96

CHAPTER 6   Where Can I Store This? (Variables and Constants)

and output items, as well as for any processing items you choose to use. Format the output with a dollar sign and no decimal places.

a. List the output and input items, as well as any processing items, and then create an appropriate algorithm.

b. Create a Visual Basic Windows application. Use the following names for the solution and project, respectively: Jackson Solution and Jackson Project. Save the application in the ClearlyVB2010\Chap06 folder. Change the name of the form file on your disk to frmMain.vb. If necessary, change the form's name to frmMain.

c. Create a suitable interface. Include an Exit button.

d. Code the Exit button's Click event procedure and the problem's algorithm. Be sure to use the TryParse method.

e. Save the solution. Desk-check the program using your own sample data.

f. Start and then test the application. Close the Code Editor window and then close the solution.

INTRODUCTORY   5.   A concert hall has three seating categories: Orchestra, Main floor, and Balcony. Orchestra seats are $25, Main floor seats are $30, and Balcony seats are $15. The manager wants an application that allows him to enter the number of tickets sold in each seating category. The application should calculate the amount of revenue generated by each seating category; format the revenue using the "N0" format. It also should calculate the total revenue; format the total revenue using the "C0" format.

a. List the output and input items, as well as any processing items, and then create an appropriate algorithm.

b. Create a Visual Basic Windows application. Use the following names for the solution and project, respectively: Concert Solution and Concert Project. Save the application in the ClearlyVB2010\Chap06 folder. Change the name of the form file on your disk to frmMain.vb. If necessary, change the form's name to frmMain.

c. Create a suitable interface. Include an Exit button.

d. Code the Exit button's Click event procedure and the problem's algorithm. Be sure to use the TryParse method.

e. Save the solution. Desk-check the program using your own sample data.

f. Start and then test the application. Close the Code Editor window and then close the solution.

INTERMEDIATE   6.   In this exercise, you modify the application from Exercise 5. In addition to calculating and displaying the revenue for each seating category, as well as the total revenue, the application should now display the percentage of the total revenue contributed by each seating category.

a. Use Windows to make a copy of the Concert Solution folder. Save the copy in the ClearlyVB2010\Chap06 folder. Rename the copy Modified Concert Solution.

b. Open the Concert Solution (Concert Solution.sln) file contained in the Modified Concert Solution folder. Make the appropriate modifications to the interface and code. Use Decimal variables to store the percentages. Display the percentages with a percent sign and one decimal place.

c. Save the solution and then start and test the application. Close the Code Editor window and then close the solution.

7. In this exercise, you modify the Circle Area application created in the chapter. For this exercise, the circle will represent a pizza. In addition to displaying the area of the pizza, the modified application also will display the number of slices into which you can divide the pizza. For this exercise, use the number 14.13 as the area of a pizza slice. INTERMEDIATE

   a. Use Windows to make a copy of the Circle Area Solution folder. Save the copy in the ClearlyVB2010\Chap06 folder. Rename the copy Pizza Circle Area Solution.

   b. Open the Circle Area Solution (Circle Area Solution.sln) file contained in the Pizza Circle Area Solution folder. Make the appropriate modifications to the interface and code. Display the number of slices with no decimal places.

   c. Save the solution and then start the application. Test the application using 10 as the circle's radius. The area is 314.16, and the number of slices is 22. Now test it using 6 as the radius. The area and number of slices should be 113.10 and 8, respectively. Close the Code Editor window and then close the solution.

8. In this exercise, you create an application that converts the number of fluid ounces entered by the user to the equivalent number of cups, quarts, and liters. Research the number of fluid ounces in a cup, a quart, and a liter. Use Double named constants for these values. INTERMEDIATE

   a. List the output and input items, as well as any processing items, and then create an appropriate algorithm.

   b. Create a Visual Basic Windows application. Use the following names for the solution and project, respectively: Ounces Solution and Ounces Project. Save the application in the ClearlyVB2010\Chap06 folder. Change the name of the form file on your disk to frmMain.vb. If necessary, change the form's name to frmMain.

   c. Create a suitable interface. Include an Exit button.

   d. Code the Exit button's Click event procedure and the problem's algorithm. Be sure to use the TryParse method. Display the output using the "N2" format.

   e. Save the solution. Desk-check the program using your own sample data.

   f. Start and then test the application. Close the Code Editor window and then close the solution.

9. In this exercise, you create an application for Starbeans. The application's interface should allow the user to enter two items: the number of pounds of regular coffee ordered and the number of pounds of decaffeinated coffee ordered. The application should display the total number of pounds of coffee ordered and the total price of the order. A pound of coffee at Starbeans costs $11.65. INTERMEDIATE

   a. List the output and input items, as well as any processing items, and then create an appropriate algorithm.

   b. Create a Visual Basic Windows application. Use the following names for the solution and project, respectively: Starbeans Solution and Starbeans Project. Save the application in the ClearlyVB2010\Chap06 folder. Change the name of the form file on your disk to frmMain.vb. If necessary, change the form's name to frmMain.

   c. Create a suitable interface. Include an Exit button.

   d. Code the Exit button's Click event procedure and the problem's algorithm. Be sure to use the TryParse method. Format the total price with a dollar sign and two decimal places.

   e. Save the solution. Desk-check the program using your own sample data.

   f. Start and then test the application. Close the Code Editor window and then close the solution.

98

CHAPTER 6 Where Can I Store This? (Variables and Constants)

ADVANCED ▶ 10. In this exercise, you modify the application from Exercise 10 in Chapter 5. If you did not complete Chapter 5's Exercise 10, you will need to do so before you can complete this exercise.

    a. Use Windows to copy the Sun Solution folder from the ClearlyVB2010\Chap05 folder to the ClearlyVB2010\Chap06 folder.

    b. Open the Sun Solution (Sun Solution.sln) file contained in the ClearlyVB2010\Chap06\Sun Solution folder. Modify the code so that it uses Decimal variables and Decimal named constants. Be sure to use the TryParse method. Format the gross pay and taxes with two decimal places. Format the net pay with a dollar sign and two decimal places.

    c. Save the solution and then start the application. Test the application using 35.5 as the hours worked and 9.56 as the pay rate. The gross pay will be 339.38. The taxes will be 67.88, 27.15, and 6.79. The net pay will be $237.57. Notice that the total of the taxes and net pay differs by a penny from the gross pay. The "penny off" problem occurs because the ToString method rounds the gross pay and taxes before they are displayed. However, the amounts are not rounded when they are used to calculate the net pay. Stop the application.

    d. You can fix the "penny off" problem using the Math.Round method. The method's syntax is **Math.Round(**_number_**,** _decimalPlaces_**)**. In the syntax, _number_ is the number to be rounded, and _decimalPlaces_ indicates the number of decimal places to include in the rounding. For example, `Math.Round(4.658, 2)` evaluates to 4.66. Use the Math.Round method to fix the "penny off" problem.

    e. Save the solution and then start the application. Test the application using 35.5 as the hours worked and 9.56 as the pay rate. This time, the net pay is $237.56. Close the Code Editor window and then close the solution.

ADVANCED ▶ 11. Allen County's Property Tax Administrator wants an application that calculates the amount of property tax owed based on a property's assessed value. Seven different tax rates are involved in the calculation. Each tax rate is per $100 of assessed value. The state rate is .124, the county rate is .096, and the school rate is .557. The remaining four rates are for special services as follows: ambulance is .1, health is .038, library is .093, and soil conservation is .02. The application should display each tax as well as the total tax.

    a. List the output and input items, as well as any processing items, and then create an appropriate algorithm.

    b. Create a Visual Basic Windows application. Use the following names for the solution and project, respectively: Allen Property Solution and Allen Property Project. Save the application in the ClearlyVB2010\Chap06 folder. Change the name of the form file on your disk to frmMain.vb. If necessary, change the form's name to frmMain.

    c. Create a suitable interface. Include an Exit button.

    d. Code the Exit button's Click event procedure and the problem's algorithm. Be sure to use the TryParse method. Use the Decimal data type for the variables and named constants. Display the state, county, school, ambulance, health, library, and soil conservation taxes with two decimal places. Display the total property tax with a dollar sign and two decimal places.

    e. Save the solution and then start the application. Test the application using 105000 as the assessed value. The total property tax should be $1,079.40.

    f. Now test the application using 121920 as the assessed value. Notice that the total of the taxes differs by a penny from the total property tax. If you add together the taxes, the total is 1253.33; however, the total property tax appears as $1,253.34. The "penny off" problem occurs because the ToString method rounds the various taxes before they are displayed. However, the tax amounts are not rounded when they are used to calculate the total tax. Stop the application.

g. You can fix the "penny off" problem using the Math.Round method. The method's syntax is **Math.Round**(*number, decimalPlaces*). In the syntax, *number* is the number to be rounded, and *decimalPlaces* indicates the number of decimal places to include in the rounding. For example, `Math.Round(4.658, 2)` evaluates to 4.66. Use the Math.Round method to fix the "penny off" problem.

h. Save the solution and then start the application. Test the application using 121920 as the assessed value. This time, the total property tax appears as $1,253.33. Close the Code Editor window and then close the solution.

12. In this exercise, you experiment with the TryParse method using different data types and values.

FIGURE THIS OUT

a. Open the FigureThisOut Solution (FigureThisOut Solution.sln) file contained in the ClearlyVB2010\Chap06\FigureThisOut Solution folder. Open the Code Editor window and review the code.

b. Start the application. Enter the number 34 in the Number box and then click the Convert button. The three TryParse methods in the button's Click event procedure convert the number 34 to text. The procedure then displays the text in the three label controls.

c. Enter the values listed in Figure 6-16, one at a time, clicking the Convert button after each entry. On a piece of paper, record the result of each TryParse method's conversion.

d. Close the Code Editor window and then close the solution.

Values
12.55
$5.67
−4.23
(4.23)
1,457.99
7%
7.88−
1 345 (notice the space after the number 1)
 33 (the number 33 preceded and followed by a space)
122a
an empty text box

Figure 6-16 Information for Exercise 12

13. Open the SwatTheBugs Solution (SwatTheBugs Solution.sln) file contained in the ClearlyVB2010\Chap06\SwatTheBugs Solution folder. Review the existing code. Start and then test the application. Notice that the code is not working correctly. Locate and correct any errors.

SWAT THE BUGS

CHAPTER 7

What's Wrong with It? (Syntax and Logic Errors)

After studying Chapter 7, you should be able to:

- ◎ Locate syntax errors using the Error List window
- ◎ Locate a logic error by stepping through the code
- ◎ Locate logic errors by using breakpoints
- ◎ Fix syntax and logic errors

There's a Bug in My Soup!

Congratulations on mastering the concepts of variables and named constants in Chapter 6. As you now know, you can use both types of memory locations to control the data type of numbers used in calculations. Both types of memory locations also make your code more self-documenting and easier to understand. In addition, you can use variables to store the values of processing items, which do not appear in a user interface. The only downside to variables and named constants is that their use requires additional lines of code. You may have noticed that you entered several more lines of code in Chapter 6's applications than you did in Chapter 5's applications. The amount of code you need to enter will increase as you learn new concepts throughout this book. As the amount of code increases, so does the likelihood for errors. Now would be a good time to start learning ways of finding and correcting the errors. An error in a program's code is referred to as a **bug**. The process of locating and correcting any bugs in a program is called **debugging**. Program bugs typically are caused by either syntax errors or logic errors. (You'll learn about another type of error, called a run time error, in Chapter 12.) Syntax errors are the easiest to find, so we'll tackle those first.

Finding Syntax Errors

The Ch07-Debugging video demonstrates all of the steps contained in this chapter. You may find it helpful to view the steps before you perform them.

As you learned in Chapter 4, the set of rules you must follow when using a programming language is called the language's syntax. A **syntax error** occurs when you break one of the language's rules. Most syntax errors are a result of typing errors that occur when entering instructions, such as typing `Me.Clse()` instead of `Me.Close()`. The Code Editor detects most syntax errors as you enter the instructions. However, if you are not paying close attention to your computer screen, you may not notice the errors. In the next set of steps, you will observe what happens when you try to start an application that contains a syntax error.

To begin debugging the Total Sales Calculator application:

1. Start Visual Studio 2010 or Visual Basic 2010 Express and permanently display the Solution Explorer window. Open the **Total Sales Solution** (**Total Sales Solution.sln**) file contained in the ClearlyVB2010\Chap07\Total Sales Solution folder. If the designer window is not open, double-click **frmMain.vb** in the Solution Explorer window. The application calculates and displays the total of the sales amounts entered by the user.

2. Auto-hide the Solution Explorer window and then open the Code Editor window. Figure 7-1 shows the code entered in the btnCalc control's Click event procedure. The jagged blue lines alert you that three lines of code contain a syntax error.

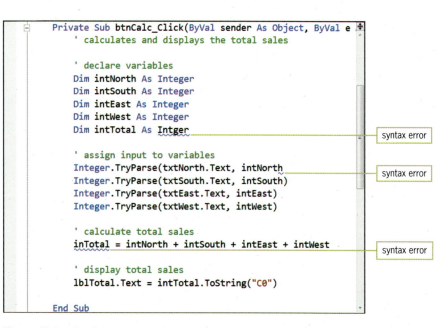

```
    Private Sub btnCalc_Click(ByVal sender As Object, ByVal e
        ' calculates and displays the total sales

        ' declare variables
        Dim intNorth As Integer
        Dim intSouth As Integer
        Dim intEast As Integer
        Dim intWest As Integer
        Dim intTotal As Intger ────────────────── syntax error

        ' assign input to variables
        Integer.TryParse(txtNorth.Text, intNorth ──── syntax error
        Integer.TryParse(txtSouth.Text, intSouth)
        Integer.TryParse(txtEast.Text, intEast)
        Integer.TryParse(txtWest.Text, intWest)

        ' calculate total sales
        inTotal = intNorth + intSouth + intEast + intWest ── syntax error

        ' display total sales
        lblTotal.Text = intTotal.ToString("C0")

    End Sub
```

Figure 7-1   btnCalc control's Click event procedure

3. Start the application. If the dialog box shown in Figure 7-2 appears, click the **No** button.

Microsoft Visual Studio

ⓘ There were build errors. Would you like to continue and run the last successful build?

[Yes] [No]

☐ Do not show this dialog again

Figure 7-2   Dialog box

4. The Error List window shown in Figure 7-3 opens at the bottom of the IDE, and the Code Editor displays a red rectangle next to each error in the code. The Error List window indicates that the code contains three errors, and it provides a description of each error and the location of each error in the code. The red rectangles indicate that the Code Editor has some suggestions for fixing the errors.

```
        Dim intWest As Integer
        Dim intTotal As Intger

        ' assign input to variables              ──── red rectangles
        Integer.TryParse(txtNorth.Text, intNorth
        Integer.TryParse(txtSouth.Text, intSouth)
        Integer.TryParse(txtEast.Text, intEast)
        Integer.TryParse(txtWest.Text, intWest)

        ' calculate total sales
        inTotal = intNorth + intSouth + intEast + intWest  ── red rectangle
```

150 %   Error List window

Error List

🔴 3 Errors   ⚠ 0 Warnings   ⓘ 0 Messages

	Description	File	Line	Column	Project
🔴 1	Type 'Intger' is not defined.	frmMain.vb	19	25	Total Sales Project
🔴 2	')' expected.	frmMain.vb	22	48	Total Sales Project
🔴 3	'inTotal' is not declared. It may be inaccessible due to its protection level.	frmMain.vb	28	9	Total Sales Project

Ready   Ln 1   Col 1   Ch 1   INS

Figure 7-3   Error List window

Important note: You can change the size of the Error List window by positioning your mouse pointer on the window's top border until the mouse pointer becomes a vertical line with an arrow at the top and bottom. Then press and hold down the left mouse button while you drag the border either up or down.

5. Double-click the **first error message** in the Error List window. The Code Editor opens the Error Correction window shown in Figure 7-4.

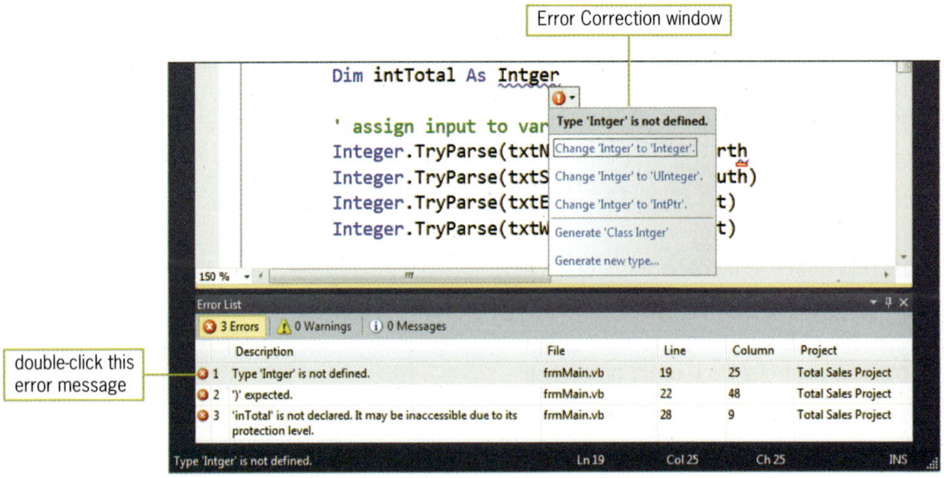

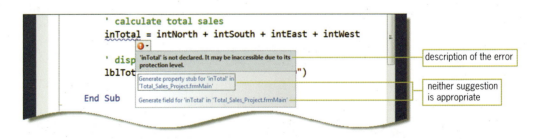

Figure 7-4   List of suggestions for fixing the error

6. The first error is nothing more than a typing error: the programmer meant to type `Integer`. You can type the missing e yourself. Or, you can simply click the appropriate suggestion in the Error Correction window. Click **Change 'Intger' to 'Integer'.** in the list. The Code Editor changes `Intger` to `Integer` in the Dim statement and removes the error from the Error List window.

7. Double-click the **first error message** in the Error List window. Move the scroll bar in the Error Correction window all the way to the right. The window indicates that the missing parenthesis will be inserted at the end of the assignment statement that contains the syntax error. Click the **Insert the missing ')'.** suggestion to insert the missing parenthesis. The Code Editor removes the error from the Error List window.

8. Only one error message remains in the Error List window. The error's description indicates that the Code Editor does not recognize the name `inTotal`. Double-click the **remaining error message** in the Error List window. See Figure 7-5.

Figure 7-5   Error Correction window for the last error message

Neither of the suggestions listed in the Error Correction window in Figure 7-5 is appropriate for fixing the error. Therefore, you will need to come up with your own solution to the problem. You do this by studying the line of code that contains the error. First, notice that the unrecognized name appears on the left side of an assignment statement. This tells you that the name belongs to something that can store information—either a control or a variable. It doesn't refer to the Text property, so it's most likely the name of a variable. Looking at the beginning of the procedure, where the variables are declared, you will notice that the procedure declares a variable named `intTotal`. Obviously, the programmer mistyped the variable's name.

To finish debugging the Total Sales Calculator application:

1. Change `inTotal` to **intTotal** in the assignment statement and then move the insertion point to another line in the Code Editor window. When you move the insertion point, the Code Editor removes the error message from the Error List window.

2. Close the Error List window. Save the solution and then start the application. Test the application using **2000** as the North sales, **3000** as the South sales, **1200** as the East sales, and **1800** as the West sales. Click the **Calculate** button. The total sales are $8,000. See Figure 7-6.

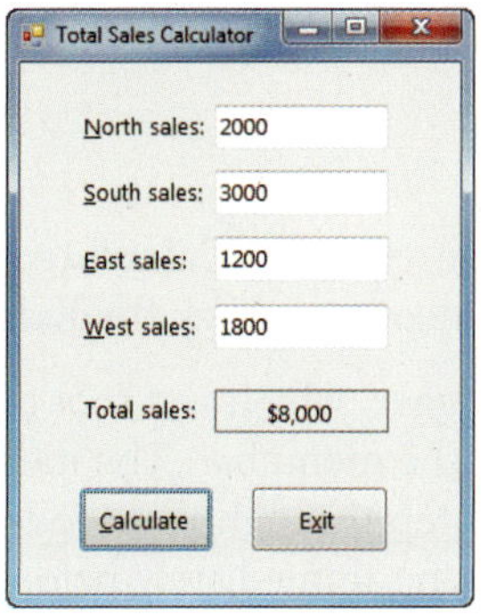

Figure 7-6   Sample run of the Total Sales Calculator application

3. Click the **Exit** button. Close the Code Editor window and then close the solution.

Locating Logic Errors

Unlike syntax errors, logic errors are much more difficult to find, because they do not trigger an error message from the Code Editor. A **logic error** can occur for a variety of reasons, such as forgetting to enter an instruction or entering the instructions in the wrong order. Some logic errors occur as a result of calculation statements that are correct syntactically but incorrect mathematically. For example, consider the statement `dblRadiusSquared = dblRadius + dblRadius`, which is supposed to calculate the square of the number stored in the `dblRadius` variable. The statement's syntax is correct, but it is incorrect mathematically because you square a number by multiplying it by itself, not by adding it to itself. In the remainder of this chapter, you will debug two applications that contain logic errors.

To debug the Discount Calculator application:

1. Open the **Discount Solution** (**Discount Solution.sln**) file contained in the ClearlyVB2010\Chap07\Discount Solution folder. If the designer window is not open, double-click **frmMain.vb** in the Solution Explorer window. The application calculates and displays three discount amounts, which are based on the price entered by the user. (The image in the picture box was downloaded from the Microsoft Office site at *http://office.microsoft.com/en-us/images/*.)

2. Open the Code Editor window. Figure 7-7 shows the code entered in the btnCalc control's Click event procedure.

```
Private Sub btnCalc_Click(ByVal sender As Object,
    ' calculates and displays a 10%, 20%, and
    ' 30% discount on an item's price

    ' declare variables
    Dim decPrice As Decimal
    Dim decDiscount10 As Decimal
    Dim decDiscount20 As Decimal
    Dim decDiscount30 As Decimal

    ' calculate discounts
    decDiscount10 = decPrice * 0.1
    decDiscount20 = decPrice * 0.2
    decDiscount30 = decPrice * 0.3

    ' display discounts
    lbl10.Text = decDiscount10.ToString("N2")
    lbl20.Text = decDiscount20.ToString("N2")
    lbl30.Text = decDiscount30.ToString("N2")
End Sub
```

Figure 7-7 btnCalc control's Click event procedure

3. Start the application. Type **100** in the Price box and then click the **Calculate** button. The interface shows that each discount is 0.00, which is incorrect. Click the **Exit** button.

4. You'll use the Debug menu to run the Visual Basic debugger, which is a tool that helps you locate the logic errors in your code. Click **Debug** on the menu bar. The menu's Step Into option will start your application and allow you to step through your code. It does this by executing the code one statement at a time, pausing immediately before each statement is executed. Click **Step Into**. Type **100** in the Price box and then click the **Calculate** button. The debugger highlights the first instruction to be executed. In this case, it highlights the btnCalc_Click procedure header. In addition, an arrow points to the instruction, as shown in Figure 7-8, and the code's execution is paused. (If the interface still appears on the screen, click the Code Editor window's title bar.)

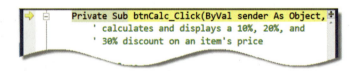

Figure 7-8 Result of using the Debug menu's Step Into option

5. You can use either the Debug menu's Step Into option or the F8 key on your keyboard to tell the computer to execute the highlighted instruction. Press the **F8** key. After the computer processes the procedure header, the debugger highlights the next statement to be processed—in this case, the decDiscount10 = decPrice * 0.1 statement—and then pauses execution of the code. (The Dim statements are skipped over because they are not considered executable by the debugger.)

6. While the execution of a procedure's code is paused, you can view the contents of controls and variables that appear in the highlighted statement, as well as in the statements above it in the procedure. Before you view the contents of a control or variable, however, you should consider the value you expect to find. Before the decDiscount10 = decPrice * 0.1 statement is processed, the decDiscount10 variable should contain its initial value, 0. (Recall that the Dim statement initializes numeric

variables to 0.) Place your mouse pointer on `decDiscount10` in the highlighted statement. The variable's name (`decDiscount10`) and current value (0D) appear in a small box, as shown in Figure 7-9. The letter D indicates that the data type of the value—in this case, 0—is Decimal. At this point, the `decDiscount10` variable's value is correct.

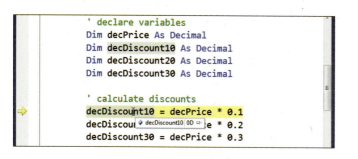

Figure 7-9   Value stored in `decDiscount10` before the highlighted statement is executed

7. Now consider the value you expect the `decPrice` variable to contain. Before the highlighted statement is processed, the `decPrice` variable should contain the number 100, which is the value you entered in the Price box. Place your mouse pointer on `decPrice` in the highlighted statement. As Figure 7-10 shows, the `decPrice` variable contains 0D, which is its initial value. Consider why the variable's value is incorrect. In this case, the value is incorrect because no statement above the highlighted statement assigns the Price box's value to the `decPrice` variable. In other words, a statement is missing from the procedure.

Figure 7-10   Value stored in `decPrice` before the highlighted statement is executed

8. Click **Debug** on the menu bar and then click **Stop Debugging** to stop the debugger. Click the **blank line** below the last Dim statement and then press **Enter** to insert another blank line. Now, enter the following comment and TryParse method:

   ' assign price to a variable
   Decimal.TryParse(txtPrice.Text, decPrice)

9. Save the solution. Click **Debug** on the menu bar and then click **Step Into**. Type **100** in the Price box and then click the **Calculate** button. Press **F8** to process the procedure header. The debugger highlights the TryParse method and then pauses execution of the code.

10. Before the TryParse method is processed, the txtPrice control's Text property should contain 100, which is the value you entered in the control. Place your mouse pointer on `txtPrice.Text` in the TryParse method. The box shows that the Text property contains the expected value. The 100 is enclosed in quotation marks because it is considered a string. As you learned in Chapter 6, a string is text enclosed in double quotation marks.

11. The `decPrice` variable should contain its initial value, 0D. Place your mouse pointer on `decPrice` in the TryParse method. The box shows that the variable contains the expected value.

12. Press **F8** to process the TryParse method. The debugger highlights the `decDiscount10 = decPrice * 0.1` statement before pausing execution of the code. Place your mouse pointer on `decPrice` in the TryParse method, as shown in Figure 7-11.

Notice that after the method is processed by the computer, the `decPrice` variable contains the number 100D, which is correct.

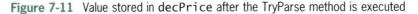

```
                    ' assign price to a variable
                    Decimal.TryParse(txtPrice.Text, decPrice)
                                                      decPrice 100D

                    ' calculate discounts
                    decDiscount10 = decPrice * 0.1
                    decDiscount20 = decPrice * 0.2
                    decDiscount30 = decPrice * 0.3
```

Figure 7-11   Value stored in `decPrice` after the TryParse method is executed

13. Before the highlighted statement is processed, the `decDiscount10` variable should contain its initial value, and the `decPrice` variable should contain the value assigned to it by the TryParse method. Place your mouse pointer on `decDiscount10` in the highlighted statement. The box shows that the variable contains 0D, which is correct. Place your mouse pointer on `decPrice` in the highlighted statement. The box shows that the variable contains 100D, which also is correct.

14. After the highlighted statement is processed, the `decPrice` variable should still contain 100D. However, the `decDiscount10` variable should contain 10D, which is 10% of 100. Press **F8** to execute the highlighted statement, and then place your mouse pointer on `decDiscount10` in the statement. The box shows that the variable contains the expected value. On your own, verify that the `decPrice` variable in the statement contains the appropriate value.

15. To continue program execution without the debugger, click **Debug** on the menu bar and then click **Continue**. This time, the correct discount amounts appear in the interface. See Figure 7-12.

Figure 7-12   Sample run of the Discount Calculator application

16. Click the **Exit** button. Close the Code Editor window and then close the solution.

I've Reached My Breaking Point

Stepping through code one line at a time is not the only way to search for logic errors. You also can use a breakpoint to pause execution at a specific line in the code. You will learn how to set a breakpoint in the next set of steps.

To begin debugging the Hours Worked application:

1. Open the **Hours Worked Solution (Hours Worked Solution.sln)** file contained in the ClearlyVB2010\Chap07\Hours Worked Solution folder. If the designer window is not open, double-click **frmMain.vb** in the Solution Explorer window. The application calculates and displays the total number of hours worked in four weeks. (The image in the picture box was downloaded from the Microsoft Office site at *http://office.microsoft.com/en-us/images/*.)

2. Open the Code Editor window. Figure 7-13 shows the code entered in the btnCalculate control's Click event procedure.

```
Private Sub btnCalculate_Click(ByVal sender As Object, ByV
    ' calculates and displays the total number
    ' of hours worked during 4 weeks

    ' declare variables
    Dim dblWeek1 As Double
    Dim dblWeek2 As Double
    Dim dblWeek3 As Double
    Dim dblWeek4 As Double
    Dim dblTotal As Double

    ' assign input to variables
    Double.TryParse(txtWeek1.Text, dblWeek1)
    Double.TryParse(txtWeek2.Text, dblWeek2)
    Double.TryParse(txtWeek3.Text, dblWeek2)
    Double.TryParse(txtWeek4.Text, dblWeek4)

    ' calculate total hours worked
    dblTotal = dblWeek1 + dblWeek2 + dblWeek3 + dblWeek4

    ' display total hours worked
    lblTotal.Text = dblTotal
End Sub
```

Figure 7-13   btnCalculate control's Click event procedure

3. Start the application. Type **1** in the Week 1 box, press **Tab**, type **2** in the Week 2 box, press **Tab**, type **3** in the Week 3 box, press **Tab**, type **4** in the Week 4 box, and then click the **Calculate** button. The interface shows that the total number of hours is 8, which is incorrect; it should be 10. Click the **Exit** button.

The statement that calculates the total number of hours worked is not giving the correct result. Rather than having the computer pause before processing each line of code in the procedure, you will have it pause only before processing the calculation statement. You do this by setting a breakpoint on the statement.

To finish debugging the Hours Worked application:

1. Right-click the **calculation statement**, point to **Breakpoint**, and then click **Insert Breakpoint**. (You also can set a breakpoint by clicking the statement and then using the Toggle Breakpoint option on the Debug menu. Or, you can simply click in the gray margin next to the statement.) The debugger highlights the statement and places a circle next to it, as shown in Figure 7-14.

```
    ' calculate total hours worked
    dblTotal = dblWeek1 + dblWeek2 + dblWeek3 + dblWeek4
```

Figure 7-14   Breakpoint set in the procedure

2. Start the application. Type the numbers **1**, **2**, **3**, and **4** in the Week 1, Week 2, Week 3, and Week 4 boxes, respectively. Click the **Calculate** button. The computer begins processing the code contained in the button's Click event procedure. It stops processing when it reaches the breakpoint statement, which it highlights. The highlighting indicates

that the statement is the next one to be processed. Notice that a yellow arrow now appears in the red dot next to the breakpoint. See Figure 7-15.

```
' calculate total hours worked
dblTotal = dblWeek1 + dblWeek2 + dblWeek3 + dblWeek4
```

Figure 7-15   Result of the computer reaching the breakpoint

3. Before viewing the values contained in each variable in the highlighted statement, consider the values you expect to find. Before the calculation statement is processed, the `dblTotal` variable should contain its initial value (0). Place your mouse pointer on `dblTotal` in the highlighted statement. The box shows that the variable's value is 0.0, which is correct. (You can verify the variable's initial value by placing your mouse pointer on `dblTotal` in its declaration statement.) Don't be concerned that 0.0 appears rather than 0. The .0 indicates that the value's data type is Double.

4. The other four variables should contain the numbers 1 through 4, which are the values you entered in the text boxes. On your own, view the values contained in the `dblWeek1`, `dblWeek2`, `dblWeek3`, and `dblWeek4` variables. Notice that two of the variables (`dblWeek1` and `dblWeek4`) contain the correct values (1.0 and 4.0). The `dblWeek2` variable, however, contains 3.0 rather than 2.0, and the `dblWeek3` variable contains its initial value (0.0) rather than the number 3.0.

5. Two of the TryParse methods are responsible for assigning the text box values to the `dblWeek2` and `dblWeek3` variables. Looking closely at the four TryParse methods in the procedure, you will notice that the third one is incorrect. After converting the contents of the txtWeek3 control to a number, the method should assign the number to the `dblWeek3` variable rather than to the `dblWeek2` variable. Click **Debug** on the menu bar and then click **Stop Debugging**.

6. Change `dblWeek2` in the third TryParse method to **dblWeek3**.

7. Now you can remove the breakpoint. Right-click the **statement containing the breakpoint**, point to **Breakpoint**, and then click **Delete Breakpoint**. (Or, you can simply click the breakpoint circle.)

8. Save the solution and then start the application. Type the numbers **1**, **2**, **3**, and **4** in the Week 1, Week 2, Week 3, and Week 4 boxes, respectively. Click the **Calculate** button. The interface shows that the total number of hours is 10, which is correct. See Figure 7-16.

Figure 7-16   Sample run of the Hours Worked application

9. On your own, test the application using other values for the hours worked in each week. When you are finished testing, click the **Exit** button. Close the Code Editor window and then close the solution.

Mini-Quiz 7-1

See Appendix B for the answers.

1. When entered in a procedure, which of the following statements will result in a syntax error?

   a. `Me.Clse()`

   b. `Integer.TryPars(txtHours.Text, intHours)`

   c. `Dim decRate as Decimel`

   d. all of the above

2. To step through each line of executable code, click Debug on the menu bar and then click _____ .

3. When a breakpoint is set, the computer stops processing the code immediately _____ it processes the breakpoint statement.

   a. after

   b. before

Summary

- In most cases, program errors (bugs) are caused by either syntax errors or logic errors. The Code Editor helps you locate and fix the syntax errors in your code. However, it cannot locate any logic errors in your code.

- Any syntax errors in an application's code are listed in the Error List window when you start the application.

- You can locate logic errors by stepping through the code entered in the Code Editor window. You also can set a breakpoint.

- You can step through the code in the Code Editor window using either the Step Into option on the Debug menu or the F8 key on your keyboard.

- You can set a breakpoint by right-clicking the desired line of code, pointing to Breakpoint, and then clicking Insert Breakpoint. You also can click the line of code and then use the Toggle Breakpoint option on the Debug menu. In addition, you can click in the gray margin next to the line of code.

- To remove a breakpoint, right-click the line of code containing the breakpoint, point to Breakpoint, and then click Delete Breakpoint. You also can simply click the breakpoint circle in the margin.

- The letter D at the end of a value indicates that the value's data type is Decimal.

- The .0 at the end of a number indicates that the number's data type is Double.

- Before viewing the value stored in a control or variable, you first should consider the value you expect to find.

Key Terms

Bug—an error in a program's code

Debugging—the process of locating and correcting any bugs in a program

Logic error—an error that can occur for a variety of reasons, such as forgetting to enter an instruction, entering the instructions in the wrong order, or entering a calculation statement that is incorrect mathematically

Syntax error—an error that occurs when a statement breaks one of a programming language's rules

Review Questions

1. The process of locating and fixing any errors in a program is called _____ .

   a. bug-proofing   c. debugging
   b. bug-eliminating   d. error removal

2. While stepping through code, the debugger highlights the statement that _____ .

   a. was just executed   c. contains the error
   b. will be executed next   d. none of the above

3. Logic errors are listed in the Error List window.

   a. True   b. False

4. While stepping through the code in the Code Editor window, you can view the contents of controls and variables that appear in the highlighted statement only.

   a. True   b. False

5. Which key is used to step through code?

   a. F5   c. F7
   b. F6   d. F8

6. The letter D after a number indicates that the number's data type is _____ .

   a. Decimal   b. Double

7. You use _____ to pause program execution at a specific line in the code.

   a. a breakpoint
   b. the Error List window
   c. the Step Into option on the Debug menu
   d. the Stop Debugging option on the Debug menu

Exercises

1. Open the Commission Calculator Solution (Commission Calculator Solution.sln) file contained in the ClearlyVB2010\Chap07\Commission Calculator Solution folder. Use what you learned in the chapter to debug the application. When you are finished debugging the application, close the Code Editor window and then close the solution. (See Appendix B for the answer.)

2. Open the New Pay Solution (New Pay Solution.sln) file contained in the ClearlyVB2010\Chap07\New Pay Solution folder. Use what you learned in the chapter to debug the application. When you are finished debugging the application, close the Code Editor window and then close the solution. (See Appendix B for the answer.)

3. Open the Hawkins Solution (Hawkins Solution.sln) file contained in the ClearlyVB2010\Chap07\Hawkins Solution folder. Use what you learned in the chapter to debug the application. When you are finished debugging the application, close the Code Editor window and then close the solution.

4. Open the Allenton Solution (Allenton Solution.sln) file contained in the ClearlyVB2010\Chap07\Allenton Solution folder. Use what you learned in the chapter to debug the application. When you are finished debugging the application, close the Code Editor window and then close the solution.

5. Open the Martins Solution (Martins Solution.sln) file contained in the ClearlyVB2010\Chap07\Martins Solution folder. Use what you learned in the chapter to debug the application. When you are finished debugging the application, close the Code Editor window and then close the solution.

6. Open the Average Score Solution (Average Score Solution.sln) file contained in the ClearlyVB2010\Chap07\Average Score Solution folder. Use what you learned in the chapter to debug the application. When you are finished debugging the application, close the Code Editor window and then close the solution.

7. Open the Beachwood Solution (Beachwood Solution.sln) file contained in the ClearlyVB2010\Chap07\Beachwood Solution folder. Use what you learned in the chapter to debug the application. When you are finished debugging the application, close the Code Editor window and then close the solution.

8. Open the Framington Solution (Framington Solution.sln) file contained in the ClearlyVB2010\Chap07\Framington Solution folder. Use what you learned in the chapter to debug the application. When you are finished debugging the application, close the Code Editor window and then close the solution.

CHAPTER 8

Decisions, Decisions, Decisions (Selection Structure)

After studying Chapter 8, you should be able to:

- ◎ Show the selection structure in both pseudocode and a flowchart
- ◎ Write If...Then...Else statements
- ◎ Include comparison operators in a selection structure's condition
- ◎ Add a check box to an interface

Someone Might Need to Make a Decision

As you learned in Chapter 1, all computer programs are written using one or more of three basic control structures: sequence, selection, and repetition. The procedures you coded in the previous chapters used the sequence structure only. When one of the procedures was invoked during run time, the computer processed the procedure's instructions sequentially—in other words, in the order the instructions appeared in the procedure. Every procedure you write will contain the sequence structure.

Many times, however, a procedure will need the computer to make a decision before selecting the next instruction to process. A procedure that calculates an employee's gross pay, for example, typically has the computer determine whether the number of hours the employee worked is greater than 40. The computer then would select either an instruction that computes regular pay only or an instruction that computes regular pay plus overtime pay. Procedures that need the computer to make a decision require the use of the selection structure (also called the decision structure). The **selection structure** indicates that a decision (based on some condition) needs to be made, followed by an appropriate action derived from that decision. But how does a programmer determine whether a problem's solution requires a selection structure? The answer to this question is by studying the problem specification.

The first problem specification you will examine in this chapter involves Rob, the mechanical man from Chapter 1. The problem specification and an illustration of the problem are shown in Figure 8-1. To solve the problem, you need to get Rob from his hallway into his bedroom. You do this by directing him to take two steps forward, open the bedroom door, and then take one step forward. The correct algorithm using the commands that Rob can understand is included in Figure 8-1. The algorithm uses only the sequence structure, because no decisions need to be made to get Rob from his initial location in the hallway to his ending location in the bedroom.

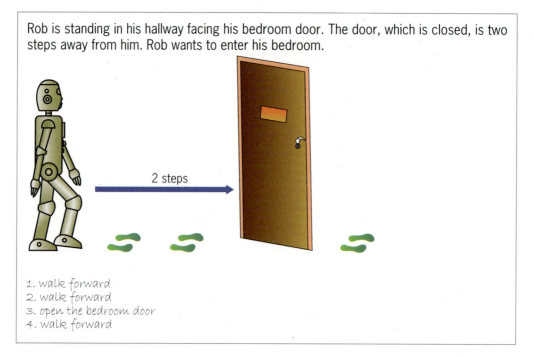

Rob is standing in his hallway facing his bedroom door. The door, which is closed, is two steps away from him. Rob wants to enter his bedroom.

2 steps

1. walk forward
2. walk forward
3. open the bedroom door
4. walk forward

Figure 8-1   A problem that requires the sequence structure only

Now let's make a slight change to the problem specification shown in Figure 8-1. This time, Rob's bedroom door may or may not be closed. What changes will need to be made to the original algorithm shown in Figure 8-1 as a result of this minor modification? The first two instructions in the original algorithm position Rob in front of his bedroom door; Rob will still need to follow those instructions. The third instruction tells Rob to open the bedroom door. That instruction was correct for the original problem specification, which states that the bedroom door is closed. However, in the modified problem specification, the status of the bedroom door is not known: it could be closed or it could already be open. As a result, Rob will need to make a decision and then take the appropriate action based on the result. More specifically, Rob will need to determine whether the bedroom door is closed, and then open the door only if it needs to be opened. The last instruction in the original algorithm positions Rob one step inside his bedroom; Rob will still need to follow that instruction.

Figure 8-2 shows the modified problem specification along with the modified algorithm. The selection structure begins with the if the bedroom door is closed, do this: line, and it ends with the end if line. The the bedroom door is closed portion of the selection structure is called the **condition**. A selection structure's condition must be phrased so that it evaluates to a Boolean value: either True or False. In this case, either the bedroom door is closed (True) or it's not closed (False). If the door is closed, Rob needs to follow the open the bedroom door instruction before walking into his bedroom. If the door is not closed, Rob can simply walk into his bedroom. The selection structure in Figure 8-2 is referred to as a **single-alternative selection structure**, because it requires a special action to be taken only when its condition evaluates to True. In this case, the special action is to open the bedroom door. The open the bedroom door instruction is indented within the selection structure to indicate that it should be followed only when the door is closed.

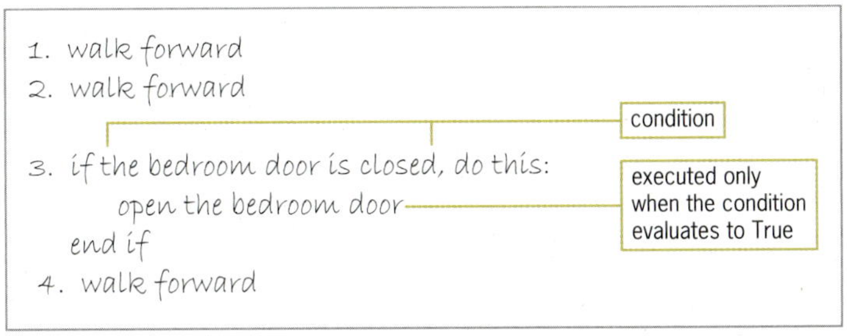

Figure 8-2   A problem that requires the sequence structure and a single-alternative selection structure

Figure 8-3 shows another problem specification and illustration involving Rob, along with the correct algorithm. As the algorithm indicates, the problem's solution does not require Rob to make any decisions in order to accomplish his tasks. He needs simply to lift the Trash container's lid, drop the bag of trash in the container, and then put the lid back on the container.

Rob is holding a bag of trash in his right hand. He is directly in front of two containers: one marked Trash and the other marked Recycle. A lid is on each container. Rob needs to lift the Trash container's lid, drop the bag of trash in the container, and then put the lid back on the container.

1. lift the Trash container's lid with your left hand
2. drop the bag of trash in the Trash container
3. put the lid back on the Trash container with your left hand

Figure 8-3   Another problem that requires the sequence structure only

Now we'll make a slight change to the problem specification from Figure 8-3. In the modified specification, the contents of the bag that Rob is holding are not certain: The bag might contain trash or it might contain recyclables. How will this change affect the original algorithm shown in Figure 8-3? The three instructions in the original algorithm pertain to the Trash container only. Those instructions were correct for the original problem specification, which states that Rob is holding a bag of trash. However, in the modified problem specification, the contents of the bag that Rob is holding are not certain. As a result, Rob will need to make a decision about the contents of the bag and then take the appropriate action based on the result. If the bag contains trash, Rob should follow the three instructions in the original algorithm. If the bag does not contain trash, it means the bag contains recyclables. In that case, Rob should lift the Recycle container's lid before dropping the bag into the container and then replacing the lid.

Figure 8-4 shows the modified problem specification and two versions of a correct algorithm. Notice that, unlike the algorithm in Figure 8-2, the algorithms in Figure 8-4 require Rob to perform one set of instructions when the condition evaluates to True, but a different set of instructions when the condition evaluates to False. The instructions to follow when the condition evaluates to True are called the **true path**. The instructions to follow when the condition evaluates to False are called the **false path**. Notice that the instructions to follow are indented within their respective paths. Selection structures that contain instructions in both paths, like the ones in Figure 8-4, are referred to as **dual-alternative selection structures**.

Rob is holding either a bag of trash or a bag of recyclables in his right hand. He is directly in front of two containers: one marked Trash and the other marked Recycle. A lid is on each container. Rob needs to lift the lid from the appropriate container, drop the bag in the container, and then put the lid back on the container.

Version 1

condition

if the bag contains trash, do this:
    lift the Trash container's lid with your left hand ⎤
    drop the bag of trash in the Trash container   ⎬ true path
    put the lid back on the Trash container with your left hand ⎦
otherwise, do this:
    lift the Recycle container's lid with your left hand ⎤
    drop the bag of recyclables in the Recycle container   ⎬ false path
    put the lid back on the Recycle container with your left hand ⎦
end if

Version 2

if the bag contains recyclables, do this:
    lift the Recycle container's lid with your left hand
    drop the bag of recyclables in the Recycle container
    put the lid back on the Recycle container with your left hand
otherwise, do this:
    lift the Trash container's lid with your left hand
    drop the bag of trash in the Trash container
    put the lid back on the Trash container with your left hand
end if

Figure 8-4 A problem that requires the sequence structure and a dual-alternative selection structure

Mini-Quiz 8-1

See Appendix B for the answers.

1. Rob is sitting in a chair in his living room. Next to the chair is a table. On top of the table is Rob's cell phone. Your task is to direct Rob to pick up his cell phone. Does the solution to this problem require a decision? If so, what decision needs to be made?

2. Rob is sitting in a chair in his living room. Next to the chair is a table. On top of the table is Rob's cell phone. Your task is to direct Rob to pick up his cell phone, but only when the phone rings. Does the solution to this problem require a decision? If so, what decision needs to be made?

3. Rob is holding a red ball and is facing two boxes. One of the boxes is red and the other is yellow. Your task is to direct Rob to drop the red ball into the red box. Does the solution to this problem require a decision? If so, what decision needs to be made?

4. Rob is holding either a red ball or a yellow ball. He is facing two boxes. One of the boxes is red and the other is yellow. Your task is to direct Rob to drop the ball he is carrying into the appropriate box. Does the solution to this problem require a decision? If so, what decision needs to be made?

Going Beyond Rob's Problems

Figure 8-5 shows a problem specification that doesn't involve Rob, the mechanical man. It also shows a correct algorithm for the problem. Because no decisions need to be made to solve the problem, the algorithm uses only the sequence structure.

Mary is paid a 2% bonus on her annual sales. She wants a program that both calculates and displays the amount of her bonus.

Output: bonus

Input: annual sales

Algorithm:
1. enter the annual sales
2. calculate the bonus by multiplying the annual sales by 2%
3. display the bonus

Figure 8-5 Bonus problem specification and algorithm

Consider how you would need to change the algorithm shown in Figure 8-5 if Mary is paid a 2% bonus only when she sells at least $3000 in product; otherwise, she is paid a 1.5% bonus. The modified problem specification and its algorithm are shown in Figure 8-6. Unlike the original algorithm, the modified algorithm needs to make a decision about Mary's sales amount before the bonus is calculated. Based on the result of that decision, the algorithm will assign either 2% or 1.5% as the bonus rate.

Mary is paid a 2% bonus on her annual sales when the sales are at least $3000; otherwise, she is paid a 1.5% bonus. She wants a program that both calculates and displays the amount of her bonus.

Output: bonus

Processing: bonus rate

Input: annual sales

Algorithm:
1. enter the annual sales
2. if the annual sales are at least 3000, do this:
      assign 2% as the bonus rate
   otherwise, do this:
      assign 1.5% as the bonus rate
   end if
3. calculate the bonus by multiplying the annual sales by the bonus rate
4. display the bonus

For more experience in examining problem specifications, see the Problem Specifications section in the Ch8WantMore.pdf file.

Figure 8-6 Modified bonus problem specification and its algorithm

In the next set of steps, you will begin coding the algorithm shown in Figure 8-6.

To begin coding the Bonus Calculator application:

1. Start Visual Studio 2010 or Visual Basic 2010 Express and permanently display the Solution Explorer window. Open the **Bonus Solution** (**Bonus Solution.sln**) file contained in the ClearlyVB2010\Chap08\Bonus Solution folder. If the designer window is not open, double-click **frmMain.vb** in the Solution Explorer window. The application's interface is shown in Figure 8-7.

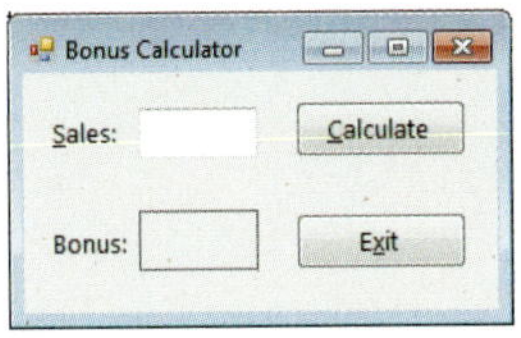

Figure 8-7   Bonus Calculator application's interface

2. Auto-hide the Solution Explorer window and then open the Code Editor window, which contains the code for the btnExit control's Click event procedure.

3. Open the btnCalc control's Click event procedure. Type the following comment and then press **Enter** twice:

   ' calculates and displays a bonus amount

4. First, you will enter the variable declaration statements. The procedure will use three Decimal variables for the input, processing, and output items. Enter the following three Dim statements. Press **Enter** twice after typing the last Dim statement.

   Dim decSales As Decimal
   Dim decRate As Decimal
   Dim decBonus As Decimal

5. The first step in the algorithm is to enter the annual sales. The user will enter the amount in the txtSales control in the interface. The procedure will need to convert the user's entry to a number, storing the result in the decSales variable. Enter the following comment and TryParse method. Press **Enter** twice after typing the method.

   ' assign sales to a variable
   Decimal.TryParse(txtSales.Text, decSales)

6. Save the solution.

The If...Then...Else Statement

Step 2 in the algorithm from Figure 8-6 is a selection structure. Visual Basic provides the **If...Then...Else statement** for coding single-alternative and dual-alternative selection structures. The statement's syntax is shown in Figure 8-8. The square brackets in the syntax indicate that the Else portion, referred to as the Else clause, is optional. Boldfaced items in a statement's syntax are required. In this case, the keywords If, Then, and End If are required. The Else keyword is necessary only in a dual-alternative selection structure. Italicized items in a statement's syntax indicate where the programmer must supply information. In the If...Then...Else statement, the programmer must supply the *condition* that the computer needs to evaluate before further processing can occur. The condition must be a Boolean expression, which is an expression that results in a Boolean value (True or False). Besides providing the condition, the programmer must provide the statements to be processed in the If...Then...Else statement's true path and (optionally) in its false path. The set of statements contained in each path is referred to as a **statement block**.

The expressions in most conditions are formed using comparison operators. A listing of the most commonly used comparison operators is included in Figure 8-8 along with examples of using comparison operators in the If...Then...Else statement's condition. The operators are called **comparison operators** because they are used to compare values. The selection structure in Example 1 directs the computer to perform one set of tasks when the condition evaluates to True, but a different set of tasks when the condition evaluates to False. Example 2's selection structure, on the other hand, directs the computer to perform the one task only when the condition evaluates to True. Notice that the expression contained in each example's condition evaluates to a Boolean value. All expressions containing a comparison operator will result in an answer of either True or False only.

If...Then...Else statement

Syntax

If condition **Then**

       statement block to be processed when the condition evaluates to True

[Else

       statement block to be processed when the condition evaluates to False]

End If

Comparison operator	Operation
=	equal to
>	greater than
>=	greater than or equal to
<	less than
<=	less than or equal to
<>	not equal to

Example 1

```
Dim intAge As Integer
Dim decDiscount As Decimal
Integer.TryParse(txtAge.Text, intAge)
If intAge >= 65 Then
    decDiscount = .15
    lblMessage.Text = "Senior Discount"
Else
    decDiscount = .1
    lblMessage.Text = "Regular Discount"
End If
```

dual-alternative selection structure

If the `intAge` variable contains a number that is greater than or equal to 65, the instructions in the true path assign .15 to the `decDiscount` variable and assign the string "Senior Discount" to the lblMessage control's Text property; otherwise, the instructions in the false path assign .1 to the `decDiscount` variable and assign the string "Regular Discount" to the lblMessage control's Text property.

Example 2

```
Dim decOwed As Decimal
Dim decPaid As Decimal
Dim decDifference As Decimal
Decimal.TryParse(txtOwed.Text, decOwed)
Decimal.TryParse(txtPaid.Text, decPaid)
decDifference = decPaid - decOwed
If decDifference < 0 Then
    lblMessage.Text = "You still owe money"
End If
lblDifference.Text = decDifference.ToString("C2")
```

single-alternative selection structure

If the `decDifference` variable contains a number that is less than zero, the instruction in the true path assigns the string "You still owe money" to the lblMessage control's Text property.

Figure 8-8 If...Then...Else statement and comparison operators

Keep in mind that comparison operators are evaluated after any arithmetic operators in an expression. When processing the expression 7 > 3 + 5, for example, the computer first adds the number 3 to the number 5, giving 8. It then compares the number 7 to the number 8. Because 7 is not greater than 8, the expression evaluates to False.

To complete the btnCalc control's Click event procedure:

1. According to Step 2 in the algorithm from Figure 8-6, the selection structure's condition needs to compare the sales amount with the number 3000. The "at least 3000" in the algorithm means that the smallest amount that qualifies for the 2% bonus is $3000. Therefore, the correct comparison operator to use in the condition is the >= (greater than or equal to) operator. Enter the following comment and If clause. When you press Enter after typing the If clause, the Code Editor automatically enters the End If clause for you. It also automatically indents the line between the If and End If clauses.

   ' determine bonus rate
   If decSales >= 3000 Then

2. If the value stored in the decSales variable is greater than or equal to 3000, the condition will evaluate to True. In that case, the bonus rate should be 2%. You will assign the bonus rate, converted to its decimal equivalent, to the decRate variable. Enter the following assignment statement:

   decRate = .02

3. If the value stored in the decSales variable is not greater than or equal to 3000, the condition will evaluate to False. In that case, the bonus rate should be 1.5%, or .015. Enter the following Else clause and assignment statement:

   Else
       decRate = .015

4. If necessary, delete the blank line above the End If clause.

5. Steps 3 and 4 in the algorithm are to calculate and then display the bonus. Click **immediately after the letter f** in the End If clause and then press **Enter** twice to insert two blank lines. Enter the following comment and assignment statements:

   ' calculate and display the bonus
   decBonus = decSales * decRate
   lblBonus.Text = decBonus.ToString("C2")

Figure 8-9 shows the code entered in the btnCalc control's Click event procedure, and Figure 8-10 shows a desk-check table for the program. On your own, desk-check the program using other sales amounts.

```
Private Sub btnCalc_Click(ByVal sender As Object,
ByVal e As System.EventArgs) Handles btnCalc.Click
    ' calculates and displays a bonus amount

    Dim decSales As Decimal
    Dim decRate As Decimal
    Dim decBonus As Decimal

    ' assign sales to a variable
    Decimal.TryParse(txtSales.Text, decSales)

    ' determine bonus rate
    If decSales >= 3000 Then
        decRate = 0.02
    Else
        decRate = 0.015
    End If

    ' calculate and display the bonus
    decBonus = decSales * decRate
    lblBonus.Text = decBonus.ToString("C2")

End Sub
```

Figure 8-9　btnCalc control's Click event procedure

decSales	decRate	decBonus (rounded to two decimal places)
~~3500.75~~	~~.02~~	~~70.02~~
500.25	.015	7.50

Figure 8-10　Desk-check table for the Bonus Calculator program

To test the Bonus Calculator application:

1. Save the solution and then start the application. Use the sales amounts shown in Figure 8-10, as well as your own sales amounts, to test the application.

2. When you are finished testing the application, click the **Exit** button. Close the Code Editor window and then close the solution.

Examining Another Problem Specification

Figure 8-11 shows another problem specification whose solution requires a selection structure. The figure also includes a correct algorithm (in flowchart form) for the problem. In this case, the algorithm needs to determine whether the customer is an employee. Recall from Chapter 2 that the oval in a flowchart is the start/stop symbol, the rectangle is the process symbol, and the parallelogram is the input/output symbol. The diamond in a flowchart is called the **decision symbol**, because it is used to represent the condition (decision) in both the selection and repetition structures. In Figure 8-11's flowchart, the diamond represents the condition in a selection structure. (You will learn how to use the diamond to represent a repetition structure's condition in Chapter 12.) Inside the diamond is a question whose answer is either True or False. Each diamond also has one flowline entering the symbol and two flowlines leaving the symbol. The two flowlines leading out of the diamond should be marked so that anyone reading the flowchart can distinguish the true path from the false path. You mark the flowline leading to the true path with a T (for True), and you mark the flowline leading to the false path with an F (for False). You also can mark the flowlines leading out of the diamond with a Y and an N (for Yes and No).

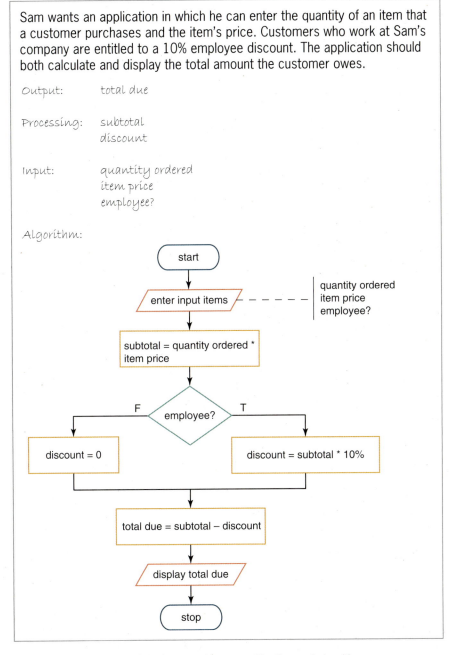

Sam wants an application in which he can enter the quantity of an item that a customer purchases and the item's price. Customers who work at Sam's company are entitled to a 10% employee discount. The application should both calculate and display the total amount the customer owes.

Output: total due

Processing: subtotal
               discount

Input: quantity ordered
               item price
               employee?

Algorithm:

Figure 8-11 Total Due Calculator problem specification and algorithm

Before coding the algorithm shown in Figure 8-11, you will add a check box to the application's interface. In Windows applications, **check boxes** are used to offer the user one or more independent and nonexclusive items from which to choose. The user can select a check box by clicking it. To deselect a check box, the user simply clicks the check box again. Each check box in an interface should be labeled to make its purpose obvious. You enter the label using sentence capitalization in the check box's Text property. Each check box also should have a unique access key. During run time, you can determine whether a check box is selected or unselected by looking at the value in its Checked property. If the property contains the Boolean value True, the check box is selected. If it contains the Boolean value False, the check box is not selected.

To open the Total Due Calculator application and then complete the user interface:

1. Open the **Total Due Solution** (**Total Due Solution.sln**) file contained in the ClearlyVB2010\Chap08\Total Due Solution folder. If the designer window is not open, double-click **frmMain.vb** in the Solution Explorer window. The application's partially completed interface appears on the screen. The user will enter the quantity ordered and the item's price in the two text boxes. The employee information will be entered using a check box, which you will add to the interface in the next step.

2. Use the CheckBox tool in the toolbox to add a check box control to the form. Position the check box as shown in Figure 8-12. The three-character ID used when naming check boxes is chk. Change the check box's name to **chkEmployee**. Change its Text property to **&Employee**.

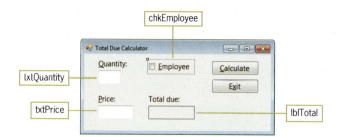

Figure 8-12 Check box included in the interface

3. If the customer is an employee, the user will need to select the check box; otherwise, the check box should be unselected. Lock the controls on the form. Click **View** on the menu bar and then click **Tab Order**. Use the information shown in Figure 8-13 to set the tab order.

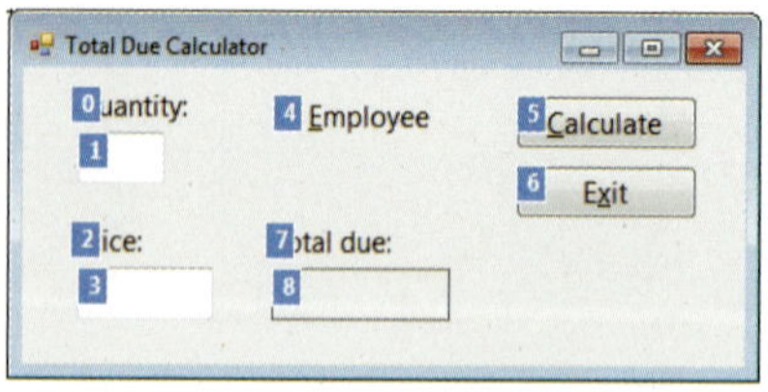

Figure 8-13 Correct TabIndex values for the interface

4. Press **Esc** to remove the TabIndex boxes from the form, and then save the solution.

Now that the interface is complete, you can begin coding the algorithm shown earlier in Figure 8-11.

To code the Total Due Calculator application:

1. Open the Code Editor window, which contains the code for the btnExit control's Click event procedure. It also contains the partially completed Click event procedure for the btnCalc control, as shown in Figure 8-14. Notice that the procedure declares a named constant for the 10% discount rate. It also declares five variables to store the quantity

ordered, item price, subtotal, discount, and total due. In addition, it assigns the quantity and price information to two of the variables. The assignment statement in the procedure displays the total due in the lblTotal control.

```
Private Sub btnCalc_Click(ByVal sender As Object, ByVal e As
    ' calculates and displays the total amount due

    Const decDISC_RATE As Decimal = 0.1
    Dim intQuantity As Integer
    Dim decPrice As Decimal
    Dim decSubtotal As Decimal
    Dim decDiscount As Decimal
    Dim decTotal As Decimal

    ' assign quantity and price to variables
    Integer.TryParse(txtQuantity.Text, intQuantity)
    Decimal.TryParse(txtPrice.Text, decPrice)

    ' calculate subtotal, discount, and total due

    ' display total due
    lblTotal.Text = decTotal.ToString("C2")
End Sub
```

Figure 8-14 Partially completed Click event procedure for the btnCalc control

2. Missing from the btnCalc control's Click event procedure are the instructions to calculate the subtotal, discount, and total due. According to the first processing symbol shown earlier in Figure 8-11, you calculate the subtotal by multiplying the quantity ordered by the item price. Click the **blank line** below the ' calculate subtotal, discount, and total due comment, and then enter the following assignment statement:

    decSubtotal = intQuantity * decPrice

3. The next symbol in the flowchart is a diamond that represents the condition in a selection structure. The selection structure's condition should determine whether the customer is an employee. Recall that the user indicates an employee by selecting the Employee check box. If the check box is not selected, it means that the customer is not an employee. You can use a check box's Checked property to determine its status: If the check box is selected, its Checked property contains the Boolean value True; otherwise, it contains the Boolean value False. Enter the following If clause:

    If chkEmployee.Checked = True Then

4. Next, you need to code the selection structure's true path. According to the flowchart, a customer who is an employee should receive a 10% discount. Enter the following assignment statement, which completes the selection structure's true path:

    decDiscount = decSubtotal * decDISC_RATE

5. Now you need to code the selection structure's false path. According to the flowchart, a customer who is not an employee should not receive a discount. Enter the following Else clause and assignment statement, which completes the selection structure's false path:

    Else
        decDiscount = 0

6. If necessary, delete the blank line above the End If clause.

7. The next symbol to code is the processing symbol located after the selection structure. The symbol tells you to calculate the total due by subtracting the discount from the

subtotal. Click **immediately after the letter f** in the End If clause and then press **Enter**. Enter the following assignment statement:

decTotal = decSubtotal – decDiscount

8. The procedure already contains the code pertaining to the last parallelogram in the flowchart. Therefore, you have finished coding the procedure. Save the solution.

Figure 8-15 shows the code entered in the btnCalc control's Click event procedure, and Figure 8-16 shows a desk-check table for the program. On your own, desk-check the program using other values for the input items.

```
Private Sub btnCalc_Click(ByVal sender As Object,
ByVal e As System.EventArgs) Handles btnCalc.Click
    ' calculates and displays the total amount due

    Const decDISC_RATE As Decimal = 0.1
    Dim intQuantity As Integer
    Dim decPrice As Decimal
    Dim decSubtotal As Decimal
    Dim decDiscount As Decimal
    Dim decTotal As Decimal

    ' assign quantity and price to variables
    Integer.TryParse(txtQuantity.Text, intQuantity)
    Decimal.TryParse(txtPrice.Text, decPrice)

    ' calculate subtotal, discount, and total due
    decSubtotal = intQuantity * decPrice
    If chkEmployee.Checked = True Then
        decDiscount = decSubtotal * decDISC_RATE
    Else
        decDiscount = 0
    End If
    decTotal = decSubtotal - decDiscount

    ' display total due
    lblTotal.Text = decTotal.ToString("C2")
End Sub
```

Figure 8-15 Completed Click event procedure for the btnCalc control

decDISC_RATE	intQuantity	decPrice	chkEmployee.Checked
~~0.1~~	~~10~~	~~2.50~~	~~True~~
0.1	10	2.50	False

decSubtotal	decDiscount	decTotal
~~25.00~~	~~2.50~~	~~22.50~~
25.00	0	25.00

Figure 8-16 Desk-check table for the Total Due Calculator program

To test the Total Due Calculator application:

1. Start the application. Use the quantity, price, and check box information shown in Figure 8-16, as well as your own data, to test the application.

2. When you are finished testing the application, click the **Exit** button. Close the Code Editor window and then close the solution.

Hey, That's Not the Way I Would Have Done It

There always are several ways of solving a problem. Figure 8-17, for example, shows a different way of solving the problem from the previous section. Notice that this version of the solution does not use any processing items. Also notice that, unlike the selection structure shown earlier in Figure 8-11, the selection structure in Figure 8-17 contains an instruction in its true path only. The instruction multiplies the total due by 90%, because that is the amount the employee would owe after receiving the 10% discount.

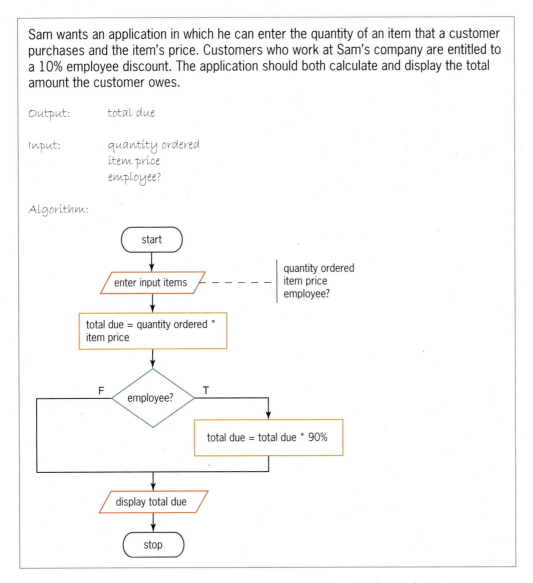

Sam wants an application in which he can enter the quantity of an item that a customer purchases and the item's price. Customers who work at Sam's company are entitled to a 10% employee discount. The application should both calculate and display the total amount the customer owes.

Output: total due

Input: quantity ordered
            item price
            employee?

Algorithm:

Figure 8-17 Total Due Calculator problem specification along with a different algorithm

To code this version of the Total Due Calculator application and then test the code:

1. Open the **Total Due Solution** (**Total Due Solution.sln**) file contained in the ClearlyVB2010\Chap08\Total Due Solution—Version 2 folder. If the designer window is not open, double-click **frmMain.vb** in the Solution Explorer window.

2. Open the Code Editor window, which contains the code for the btnExit control's Click event procedure. Open the code template for the btnCalc control's Click event procedure. Type the following comment and then press **Enter** twice:

   ' calculates and displays the total amount due

3. Now enter the remaining comments and code shown in Figure 8-18.

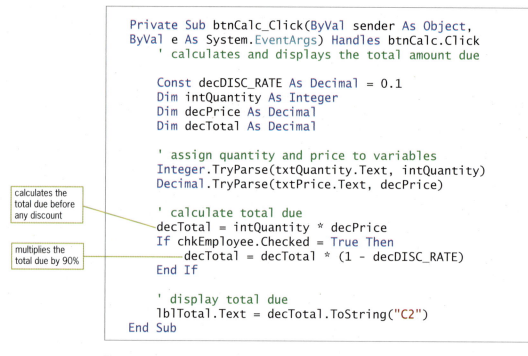

```vb
Private Sub btnCalc_Click(ByVal sender As Object,
ByVal e As System.EventArgs) Handles btnCalc.Click
    ' calculates and displays the total amount due

    Const decDISC_RATE As Decimal = 0.1
    Dim intQuantity As Integer
    Dim decPrice As Decimal
    Dim decTotal As Decimal

    ' assign quantity and price to variables
    Integer.TryParse(txtQuantity.Text, intQuantity)
    Decimal.TryParse(txtPrice.Text, decPrice)

    ' calculate total due
    decTotal = intQuantity * decPrice
    If chkEmployee.Checked = True Then
        decTotal = decTotal * (1 - decDISC_RATE)
    End If

    ' display total due
    lblTotal.Text = decTotal.ToString("C2")
End Sub
```

calculates the total due before any discount

multiplies the total due by 90%

Figure 8-18 Code corresponding to Figure 8-17's algorithm

4. Save the solution and then start the application. Use the quantity, price, and check box information shown earlier in Figure 8-16, as well as your own data, to test the application.

5. When you are finished testing the application, click the **Exit** button. Close the Code Editor window and then close the solution.

Figure 8-19 shows still a different way of solving the Total Due Calculator problem, and Figure 8-20 shows the corresponding code.

Sam wants an application in which he can enter the quantity of an item that a customer purchases and the item's price. Customers who work at Sam's company are entitled to a 10% employee discount. The application should both calculate and display the total amount the customer owes.

Output: total due

Processing: discount

Input: quantity ordered
             item price
             employee?

Algorithm:
1. enter the quantity ordered, item price, and employee? items
2. calculate the total due by multiplying the quantity ordered by the item price
3. if employee?, do this:
        calculate the discount by multiplying the total due by 10%
        subtract the discount from the total due
   end if
4. display the total due

Figure 8-19 A different way of solving the Total Due Calculator problem

```vb
Private Sub btnCalc_Click(ByVal sender As Object,
ByVal e As System.EventArgs) Handles btnCalc.Click
    ' calculates and displays the total amount due

    Const decDISC_RATE As Decimal = 0.1
    Dim intQuantity As Integer
    Dim decPrice As Decimal
    Dim decTotal As Decimal

    ' assign quantity and price to variables
    Integer.TryParse(txtQuantity.Text, intQuantity)
    Decimal.TryParse(txtPrice.Text, decPrice)

    ' calculate total due
    decTotal = intQuantity * decPrice
    If chkEmployee.Checked = True Then
        Dim decDiscount As Decimal          block-level variable
        decDiscount = decTotal * decDISC_RATE
        decTotal = decTotal - decDiscount
    End If

    ' display total due
    lblTotal.Text = decTotal.ToString("C2")
End Sub
```

Figure 8-20 Code corresponding to Figure 8-19's algorithm

Study closely the instructions in the selection structure's true path in Figure 8-20. The first instruction, `Dim decDiscount As Decimal`, declares a variable named `decDiscount`. Like the variables declared at the beginning of a procedure, variables declared within a statement block in a selection structure remain in memory until the procedure ends. However, unlike variables declared at the beginning of a procedure, variables declared within a statement block have block scope rather than procedure scope. A variable that has procedure scope can be used anywhere within the procedure, whereas a variable that has **block scope** can be used only within the statement block in which it is declared, and only after its declaration statement. In this case, for example, the `intQuantity`, `decPrice`, and `decTotal` variables (and also the `decDISC_RATE` named constant) can be used anywhere within the btnCalc control's Click event procedure, but the `decDiscount` variable can be used only within the If...Then...Else statement's true path.

You may be wondering why the `decDiscount` variable was not declared at the beginning of the procedure, along with the other variables. Although there is nothing wrong with declaring all variables at the beginning of a procedure, the `decDiscount` variable is necessary only when the discount needs to be calculated, so many programmers prefer to create the variable only if it is necessary to do so. This is because fewer unintentional errors occur in applications when the variables are declared using the minimum scope needed. In this case, the minimum scope for the `decDiscount` variable is block scope, because only the selection structure's true path uses the variable. A variable declared within a statement block is called a **block-level variable**.

To code this version of the Total Due Calculator application and then test the code:

1. Open the **Total Due Solution** (**Total Due Solution.sln**) file contained in the ClearlyVB2010\Chap08\Total Due Solution—Version 3 folder. If the designer window is not open, double-click **frmMain.vb** in the Solution Explorer window.

2. Open the Code Editor window, which contains the code for the btnExit control's Click event procedure. Open the code template for the btnCalc control's Click event procedure. Type the following comment and then press **Enter** twice:

    ' calculates and displays the total amount due

3. Now enter the remaining comments and code shown earlier in Figure 8-20.

4. Save the solution and then start the application. Use the quantity, price, and check box information shown earlier in Figure 8-16, as well as your own data, to test the application.

5. When you are finished testing the application, click the **Exit** button. Close the Code Editor window and then close the solution.

Mini-Quiz 8-2

For more examples of selection structures, see the Selection Structure section in the Ch8WantMore.pdf file.

See Appendix B for the answers.

1. Write an If...Then...Else statement that displays the string "Overtime pay" in the lblMsg control when the number of hours contained in the `decHours` variable is greater than 40.

2. Modify the If...Then...Else statement from Question 1 so that it displays the string "Regular pay only" when the selection structure's condition evaluates to False.

3. What is the scope of a variable declared in a selection structure's false path?

   a. the entire application

   b. the procedure containing the selection structure

   c. the entire selection structure

   d. only the selection structure's false path

It's time to view the Ch08-Selection Structure video.

Summary

- The selection structure is one of the three basic control structures used in programs. It is used when you need the computer to make a decision and then take an appropriate action.

- Studying the problem specification will help you determine whether a solution requires a selection structure.

- You should indent the instructions in a selection structure's true path and also in its false path. The set of instructions in each path is called a statement block.

- You can use the If…Then…Else statement to code the selection structure in Visual Basic. The statement's condition must contain an expression that evaluates to a Boolean value, either True or False. You will find comparison operators in most conditions.

- An expression containing a comparison operator will always evaluate to either True or False.

- In a flowchart, the selection structure's condition is represented by a diamond, which is called the decision symbol. The diamond should contain a question or comparison that evaluates to either True or False only. The two flowlines leading out of the diamond should be marked to indicate the true path and the false path.

- The three-character ID for naming check boxes is chk. When a check box is selected, its Checked property contains the Boolean value True; otherwise, its Checked property contains the Boolean value False.

- There are many ways to solve the same problem.

- A block-level variable has block scope, which means it can be used only within the statement block in which it is declared, and only after its declaration statement.

Key Terms

Block scope—the scope of a variable declared within a statement block; a variable with block scope can be used only within the statement block in which it is declared, and only after its declaration statement

Block-level variable—a variable declared within a statement block; the variable has block scope

Check boxes—controls used to offer the user one or more independent and nonexclusive choices

Comparison operators—operators used to compare values in an expression

Condition—specifies the decision you are making and must be phrased so that it evaluates to a Boolean value (either True or False)

Decision symbol—the diamond in a flowchart; used to represent the condition in selection and repetition structures

Dual-alternative selection structures—selection structures that require the computer to perform one set of actions when the structure's condition evaluates to True, but a different set of actions when the structure's condition evaluates to False

False path—contains the instructions to be processed when a selection structure's condition evaluates to False

If...Then...Else statement—used to code the single-alternative and dual-alternative forms of the selection structure in Visual Basic

Selection structure—one of the three basic control structures; directs the computer to make a decision based on some condition and then select the appropriate action; also called the decision structure

Single-alternative selection structure—a selection structure that requires the computer to perform a special set of actions only when the structure's condition evaluates to True

Statement block—in a selection structure, the set of statements in the true path and the set of statements in the false path

True path—contains the instructions to be processed when a selection structure's condition evaluates to True

Review Questions

1. Which of the following conditions evaluates to True when the `intPopulation` variable contains the number 56000?

   a. `If intPopulation = 56000 Then`

   b. `If intPopulation <> 0 Then`

   c. `If intPopulation > 1 Then`

   d. all of the above

2. Which of the following conditions evaluates to True when the chkShipping check box is not selected?

   a. `If chkShipping.Check = False Then`

   b. `If chkShipping.Checked = False Then`

   c. `If chkShipping.Checked = No Then`

   d. `If chkShipping.Check = No Then`

3. Which of the following has block scope?

   a. a variable declared at the beginning of a procedure

   b. a variable declared within a selection structure's true path

   c. a variable declared within a selection structure's false path

   d. both b and c

4. Which of the following symbols is used to represent the selection structure's condition in a flowchart?

   a. diamond

   b. oval

   c. parallelogram

   d. rectangle

5. If the `decRate` variable contains the number .25, the condition `decRate > 1` will evaluate to _____ .

   a. False

   b. No

   c. True

   d. Yes

6. If the `intNum1` and `intNum2` variables contain the numbers 10 and 7, respectively, the condition `intNum1 + 40 - 1 <= intNum2 ^ 2` evaluates to _____ .

   a. False

   b. No

   c. True

   d. Yes

7. Which of the following is the "not equal to" comparison operator in Visual Basic?

a. ≠

b. ><

c. Not =

d. <>

Exercises

1. Open the AddSub Solution (AddSub Solution.sln) file contained in the ClearlyVB2010\ Chap08\AddSub Solution folder. The interface provides text boxes for the user to enter two integers. If the Subtraction check box is selected, the application should subtract the second integer from the first integer; otherwise, it should add both integers. List the output and input items, as well as any processing items, and then create an appropriate algorithm. Code the btnCalc control's Click event procedure. Save the solution and then start and test the application. Close the Code Editor window and then close the solution. (See Appendix B for the answer.)

   TRY THIS

2. Open the New Pay Solution (New Pay Solution.sln) file contained in the ClearlyVB2010\Chap08\New Pay Solution folder. The application calculates and displays the amount of an employee's new weekly pay. Figure 8-21 shows the output, processing, and input items; it also shows the algorithm. Code the algorithm using Decimal variables for everything but the pay code. Format the new weekly pay with a dollar sign and two decimal places. Save the solution. Desk-check the program twice, first using 1 as the pay code and 200 as the current weekly pay, and then using 3 as the pay code and 200 as the current weekly pay. Start and then test the application. Close the Code Editor window and then close the solution. (See Appendix B for the answer.)

   TRY THIS

   Output: new weekly pay

   Processing: raise rate
                  weekly raise

   Input: pay code
                  current weekly pay

   Algorithm:
   1. enter the pay code and current weekly pay
   2. if the pay code is 1, do this:
           assign .03 as the raise rate
      otherwise, do this:
           assign .05 as the raise rate
      end if
   3. calculate the weekly raise by multiplying the current weekly
      pay by the raise rate
   4. calculate the new weekly pay by adding the weekly raise to
      the current weekly pay
   5. display the new weekly pay

   Figure 8-21 Information for Exercise 2

3. In this exercise, you modify one of the Total Due applications completed in the chapter. Use Windows to make a copy of the Total Due Solution folder. Save the copy in the ClearlyVB2010\Chap08 folder. Rename the copy Modified Total Due Solution. Open the Total Due Solution (Total Due Solution.sln) file contained in the Modified Total Due Solution folder. Currently, the selection structure in the btnCalc control's Click event procedure determines whether the check box is selected. Modify the selection structure so

   MODIFY THIS

that it determines whether the check box is not selected. Save the solution and then start and test the application. Close the Code Editor window and then close the solution.

INTRODUCTORY 4. Computer Haven offers programming seminars to companies. The price per person depends on the number of people the company registers. If the company registers more than 10 people, the price per person is $80; otherwise, the price per person is $100. Computer Haven wants an application that calculates the total amount a company owes. Display the total amount with a dollar sign and no decimal places.

   a. List the output and input items, as well as any processing items, and then create an appropriate algorithm.

   b. Create a Visual Basic Windows application. Use the following names for the solution and project, respectively: Seminar Solution and Seminar Project. Save the application in the ClearlyVB2010\Chap08 folder. Change the name of the form file on your disk to frmMain.vb. If necessary, change the form's name to frmMain.

   c. Create a suitable interface. Include an Exit button. Code the Exit button's Click event procedure and the problem's algorithm. Save the solution. Desk-check the program using your own sample data.

   d. Start and then test the application. Close the Code Editor window and then close the solution.

INTRODUCTORY 5. Tea Time Company wants an application that allows the clerk to enter the number of pounds of tea ordered, the price per pound, and whether the customer should be charged a $15 shipping fee. Use a check box for the shipping information. The application should calculate the total due.

   a. List the output and input items, as well as any processing items, and then create an appropriate algorithm.

   b. Create a Visual Basic Windows application. Use the following names for the solution and project, respectively: Tea Time Solution and Tea Time Project. Save the application in the ClearlyVB2010\Chap08 folder. Change the name of the form file on your disk to frmMain.vb. If necessary, change the form's name to frmMain.

   c. Create a suitable interface. Include an Exit button. Code the Exit button's Click event procedure and the problem's algorithm. Save the solution. Desk-check the program using your own sample data.

   d. Start and then test the application. Close the Code Editor window and then close the solution.

INTERMEDIATE 6. Marcy's Department Store is having a BoGoHo (Buy One, Get One Half Off) sale. The store manager wants an application that allows the store clerk to enter the prices of two items. The application should both calculate and display the total owed. The half-off should always be taken on the item having the lowest price. For example, if one item costs $24.99 and the second item costs $12.50, the $12.50 item would be half-off. (In other words, the item would cost $6.25.) Create a Visual Basic Windows application. Use the following names for the solution and project, respectively: Marcy Solution and Marcy Project. Save the application in the ClearlyVB2010\Chap08 folder. Change the name of the form file on your disk to frmMain.vb. If necessary, change the form's name to frmMain. Create a suitable interface. Code the application. Save the solution and then start and test the application. Close the Code Editor window and then close the solution.

INTERMEDIATE 7. Allenton Water Department wants an application that calculates a customer's monthly water bill. The clerk will enter the current and previous meter readings. The application should calculate and display the number of gallons of water used and the total charge for the water. The charge for water is $7 per 1000 gallons, or .007 per gallon. Make the calculations only when the current meter reading is greater than or equal to the previous meter reading; otherwise, display N/A as both the number of gallons used and total charge. Create a Visual Basic Windows application. Use the following names for the solution and project, respectively: Allenton Solution and Allenton Project. Save the application in the ClearlyVB2010\Chap08 folder. Change the name of the form file on your disk to frmMain.vb. If necessary, change the form's name to frmMain. Create a suitable interface. Code the application. Save the solution and then start and test the application. Close the Code Editor window and then close the solution.

8. Triple County Electric wants an application that calculates a customer's monthly electric bill. The clerk will enter the total number of units used during the month. The application should calculate and display the total charge. The charge per unit is $0.13. However, there is a minimum charge of $20. (In other words, every customer must pay at least $20.) Create a Visual Basic Windows application. Use the following names for the solution and project, respectively: Triple County Solution and Triple County Project. Save the application in the ClearlyVB2010\Chap08 folder. Change the name of the form file on your disk to frmMain.vb. If necessary, change the form's name to frmMain. Create a suitable interface. Code the application. Save the solution and then start and test the application. Close the Code Editor window and then close the solution.

INTERMEDIATE

9. Open the Swap Solution (Swap Solution.sln) file contained in the ClearlyVB2010\Chap08\Swap Solution folder. Open the Code Editor window. The Swap button's Click event procedure assigns the values entered in the two text boxes to two variables. The procedure should determine if the value in the intNum1 variable is greater than the value in the intNum2 variable. If it is, the procedure should swap the values in both variables. In other words, the intNum1 variable should always contain a value that is less than or equal to the value in the intNum2 variable. Complete the procedure accordingly. Save the solution and then start and test the application. Close the Code Editor window and then close the solution.

INTERMEDIATE

10. In this exercise, you modify the application from Chapter 6's Exercise 10. If you did not complete Chapter 6's Exercise 10, you will need to do so before you can complete this exercise. Use Windows to copy the Sun Solution folder from the ClearlyVB2010\Chap06 folder to the ClearlyVB2010\Chap08 folder. Open the Sun Solution (Sun Solution.sln) file contained in the ClearlyVB2010\Chap08\Sun Solution folder. Modify the code so that it pays the employee time and one-half for any hours worked over 40. Save and then start the application. Test the application using 35.5 as the hours worked and 9.56 as the pay rate. The net pay will be $237.56. Now test the application using 44 as the hours worked and 9.56 as the pay rate. The net pay will be $307.83. Close the Code Editor window and then close the solution.

ADVANCED

11. Ned's Health Club wants an application that calculates and displays a member's monthly dues. Each member is charged a basic fee of $25 per month. However, there are additional monthly charges for golf ($10), racquetball ($5), and tennis ($20). The interface should include three check boxes for the additional charge information. Use a text box for the member's name and a label to display the monthly dues. Create a Visual Basic Windows application. Use the following names for the solution and project, respectively: Health Solution and Health Project. Save the application in the ClearlyVB2010\Chap08 folder. Change the name of the form file on your disk to frmMain.vb. If necessary, change the form's name to frmMain. Create the interface and then code the application. Save the solution and then start and test the application. Close the Code Editor window and then close the solution.

ADVANCED

12. Open the FigureThisOut Solution (FigureThisOut Solution.sln) file contained in the ClearlyVB2010\Chap08\FigureThisOut Solution folder. Start the application. Enter 2 as the first number and 5 as the second number, and then click the Display button. Enter 7 as the first number and 6 as the second number, and then click the Display button. Stop the application. Open the Code Editor window and study the btnDisplay control's Click

FIGURE THIS OUT

event procedure. What task is performed by the procedure? What is the purpose of the selection structure? What is the purpose of the block-level variable? Why is the variable necessary? Close the Code Editor window and then close the solution.

SWAT THE BUGS   13.   Open the SwatTheBugs Solution (SwatTheBugs Solution.sln) file contained in the ClearlyVB2010\Chap08\SwatTheBugs Solution folder. Open the Code Editor window and study the code. Start and then test the application. Notice that the code is not working correctly. Locate and correct any errors. Close the Code Editor window and then close the solution.

CHAPTER 9

Time to Leave the Nest (Nested Selection Structures)

After studying Chapter 9, you should be able to:

◎ Nest selection structures

◎ Include logical operators in a selection structure's condition

Nested Selection Structures

As you learned in Chapter 8, you use the selection structure to make a decision and then select the appropriate path—either the true path or the false path—based on the result. Both paths in a selection structure can include instructions that declare variables, perform calculations, and so on. In this chapter, you will learn that both paths also can include other selection structures. When either a selection structure's true path or its false path contains another selection structure, the inner selection structure is referred to as a **nested selection structure**, because it is contained (nested) within the outer selection structure.

Similar to the initial examples of selection structures in Chapter 8, the first examples of nested selection structures will involve Rob, the mechanical man. The first problem specification and its algorithm are shown in Figure 9-1. (The problem specification and algorithm are from Figure 8-4 in Chapter 8. Figure 8-3 shows an illustration of Rob and the containers.) The algorithm requires a selection structure, but not a nested one. This is because only one decision—whether Rob is holding a bag of trash—is necessary.

Figure 9-1 A problem that requires a dual-alternative selection structure

Now let's make a slight change to the problem specification in Figure 9-1. This time, the status of the lid on each container is not known: one or both of the lids could be on or off. Consider the changes you will need to make to the original algorithm in Figure 9-1. The first instruction in the original algorithm represents the selection structure's condition. The condition requires Rob to make a decision about the contents of the bag he is holding; Rob still will need to make this decision. The next three instructions tell Rob what to do when the condition is true, which is when the bag contains trash. The first instruction in the true path directs Rob to lift the Trash container's lid. That instruction was correct for the original problem specification, which states that the lid is on the container. However, in the modified problem specification, the status of the lid is not known. Therefore, Rob first will need to make a decision about the lid's status and then only lift the lid if it's on the container. The last two instructions in the true path direct Rob to drop the bag of trash in the Trash container and then put the lid back on the container; Rob still will need to follow both instructions. Now look at the false path of the selection structure in Figure 9-1. The first instruction in the false path directs Rob to lift the lid from the Recycle container. Here again, Rob first will need to determine whether it's necessary to do this. The last two instructions in the false path tell Rob to drop the bag of recyclables in the Recycle container and then put the lid back on the container; Rob still will need to follow both instructions.

Figure 9-2 shows the modified problem specification and algorithm. The modified algorithm contains an outer dual-alternative selection structure and two nested single-alternative selection structures. The outer selection structure begins with the *if the bag contains trash, do this:* line, and it ends with the last *end if* line. The *otherwise, do this:* line belongs to the outer selection structure and separates the structure's true path from its false path. Notice that the instructions in both paths are indented within the outer selection structure. Indenting in this manner clearly indicates the instructions to be followed when Rob is holding a bag of trash, as well as the ones to be followed when the bag does not contain trash.

One of the nested selection structures appears in the outer selection structure's true path, and the other appears in its false path. The nested selection structure in the true path begins with the *if the lid is on the Trash container, do this:* line, and it ends with the first *end if* line. The instruction between both lines is indented to indicate that it is part of the nested selection structure. The nested selection structure in the false path begins with the *if the lid is on the Recycle container, do this:* line, and it ends with the second *end if* line. Here again, the instruction between both lines is indented within the nested selection structure. For a nested selection structure to work correctly, it must be contained entirely within the outer selection structure. Each nested selection structure in Figure 9-2, for example, appears entirely within its corresponding path in the outer selection structure.

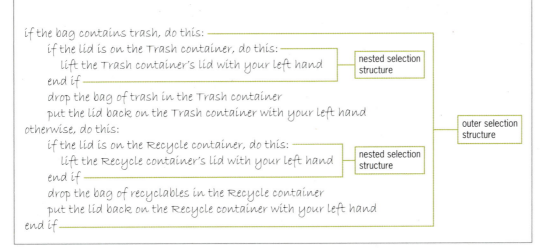

Figure 9-2   A problem that requires nested single-alternative selection structures

Figure 9-3 shows another problem specification and algorithm involving Rob. As the algorithm indicates, Rob needs to ask the store clerk whether the store accepts the Discovery card. Depending on the answer, Rob will use either his Discovery card or cash to pay for the items he is purchasing.

Rob is at a store's checkout counter. He would like to use his Discovery credit card to pay for the items he is purchasing, but he's not sure whether the store accepts the card. If the store doesn't accept the Discovery card, Rob will need to pay cash for the items.

1. ask the store clerk whether the store accepts the Discovery card

    | condition |

2. if the store accepts the Discovery card, do this:
       pay for your items using your Discovery card —— | true path |
    otherwise, do this:
       pay for your items using cash —— | false path |
    end if

Figure 9-3 Another problem that requires a dual-alternative selection structure

Here too, let's change Figure 9-3's problem specification. This time, Rob would like to use either his Discovery card or his Vita card, but he prefers to use his Discovery card. If the store does not take either card, Rob will need to pay cash for the items he is purchasing. Consider the changes you will need to make to the original algorithm in Figure 9-3. Rob still will need to ask the store clerk whether the store accepts the Discovery card; and if it does, he should use that card to pay for his items. Therefore, the first three lines in the original algorithm do not need to be changed. The next line in the algorithm is the *otherwise, do this:* line. The modified algorithm still will need this line to indicate that there are tasks to be performed when the store does not accept the Discovery card. The next line in the original algorithm tells Rob to use cash to pay for his items. That instruction was correct for the original problem specification, which gave Rob only two payment choices: either his Discovery card or cash. However, in the modified problem specification, Rob has three payment choices: his Discovery card, his Vita card, or cash. Before paying with cash, Rob needs to inquire whether the store accepts the Vita card; if it does, Rob should use his Vita card to pay for his items. Rob should pay with cash only when the store does not accept either credit card.

Figure 9-4 shows the modified problem specification and algorithm. The modified algorithm contains an outer dual-alternative selection structure and a nested dual-alternative selection structure. The outer selection structure begins with the *if the store accepts the Discovery card, do this:* line, and it ends with the last *end if* line. The first *otherwise, do this:* line belongs to the outer selection structure and separates the outer structure's true path from its false path. Notice that the instructions in the outer selection structure's true and false paths are indented. The nested selection structure, which appears in the outer selection structure's false path, begins with the *if the store accepts the Vita card, do this:* line, and it ends with the first *end if* line. The indented *otherwise, do this:* line belongs to the nested selection structure and separates the nested structure's true path from its false path. For clarity, the instructions in the nested selection structure's true and false paths are indented within the structure. Notice that the entire nested selection structure is contained in the outer selection structure's false path.

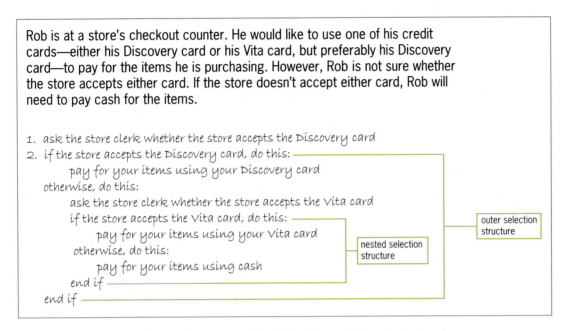

Rob is at a store's checkout counter. He would like to use one of his credit cards—either his Discovery card or his Vita card, but preferably his Discovery card—to pay for the items he is purchasing. However, Rob is not sure whether the store accepts either card. If the store doesn't accept either card, Rob will need to pay cash for the items.

1. ask the store clerk whether the store accepts the Discovery card
2. if the store accepts the Discovery card, do this:
        pay for your items using your Discovery card
   otherwise, do this:
        ask the store clerk whether the store accepts the Vita card
        if the store accepts the Vita card, do this:
             pay for your items using your Vita card
        otherwise, do this:
             pay for your items using cash
        end if
   end if

outer selection structure

nested selection structure

Figure 9-4   A problem that requires a nested dual-alternative selection structure

Mini-Quiz 9-1

See Appendix B for the answers.

1. Rob is sitting in a chair in his living room. Next to the chair is a table. On top of the table is Rob's cell phone. Your task is to direct Rob to answer his cell phone, but only when the phone rings. Does the solution to this problem require a nested selection structure? If so, what decision needs to be made by the nested selection structure's condition?

2. Rob is sitting in a chair in his living room. Next to the chair is a table. On top of the table is Rob's cell phone. Your task is to direct Rob to answer his cell phone, but only when the phone rings. If the caller is a telemarketer, Rob should hang up the phone. Does the solution to this problem require a nested selection structure? If so, what decision needs to be made by the nested selection structure's condition?

3. Rob is holding either a red ball or a yellow ball. He is facing two boxes: one red and the other yellow. Your task is to direct Rob to drop the ball he is carrying in the appropriate box, but only if the box is not already full. How many nested selection structures does this problem require? What decision needs to be made by each nested selection structure's condition?

Putting Rob's Problems Aside

Figure 9-5 shows a problem specification that doesn't involve Rob, the mechanical man. It also shows a correct algorithm for the problem. The algorithm requires only one selection structure. This is because only one decision needs to be made to solve the problem. In this case, the decision is whether the user wants to perform subtraction.

Jennifer wants an application that calculates and displays either the sum of the two integers she enters or the difference between both integers.

Output: answer

Input: first integer
          second integer
          subtraction?

Algorithm:
1. enter the first integer, second integer, and subtraction? items
2. if subtraction?, do this:
        calculate the answer by subtracting the second integer from the first integer
    otherwise, do this:
        calculate the answer by adding the second integer to the first integer
    end if
3. display the answer

Figure 9-5   Math problem specification and algorithm

Consider how you would need to change the algorithm in Figure 9-5 if, when performing subtraction, Jennifer wants the application to always subtract the smaller integer from the larger one. The modified problem specification and its algorithm are shown in Figure 9-6. Unlike the original algorithm, the modified algorithm needs to make two decisions. The first decision determines whether the user wants to perform subtraction; if she does, a second decision needs to be made. The second decision determines whether the first integer is greater than the second integer. You will code Figure 9-6's algorithm in the next set of steps.

Jennifer wants an application that calculates and displays either the sum of the two integers she enters or the difference between both integers. However, when calculating the difference, she wants the application to always subtract the smaller integer from the larger one.

Output: answer

Input: first integer
          second integer
          subtraction?

Algorithm:
1. enter the first integer, second integer, and subtraction? items
2. if subtraction?, do this: ———————————————————————   outer selection structure
        if the first integer is greater than the second integer, do this: ———
            calculate the answer by subtracting the second integer from the first integer
        otherwise, do this:
            calculate the answer by subtracting the first integer from the second integer
        end if ———————————————————————————————
    otherwise, do this: nested
        calculate the answer by adding the second integer to the first integer   selection
    end if ———————————————————————————————   structure
3. display the answer

For more experience in examining problem specifications, see the Problem Specifications section in the Ch9WantMore.pdf file.

Figure 9-6   Modified math problem specification and its algorithm

To code the Addition and Subtraction Calculator application:

1. Start Visual Studio 2010 or Visual Basic 2010 Express and permanently display the Solution Explorer window. Open the **AddSub Solution (AddSub Solution.sln)** file contained in the ClearlyVB2010\Chap09\AddSub Solution folder. If the designer window is not open, double-click **frmMain.vb** in the Solution Explorer window. The application's interface is shown in Figure 9-7.

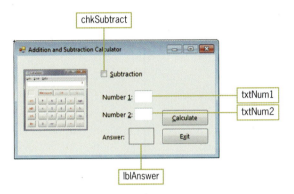

Figure 9-7   Addition and Subtraction Calculator application's interface

2. Auto-hide the Solution Explorer window and then open the Code Editor window, which contains the code for the btnExit control's Click event procedure. It also contains the partially completed code for the btnCalc control's Click event procedure.

3. The first step in the algorithm shown in Figure 9-6 is to enter the input items. The user will enter the first and second integers in the txtNum1 and txtNum2 controls, respectively, and use the Subtraction check box to indicate subtraction. The btnCalc control's Click event procedure already contains the code to declare the necessary variables, as well as to assign the integers to variables. The second step in the algorithm is an outer selection structure whose condition determines whether the user wants to perform subtraction. This can be determined using the Subtraction check box's Checked property. Click the **blank line** below the ' calculate and display the difference or sum comment in the btnCalc control's Click event procedure. Enter the following If clause:

    If chkSubtract.Checked = True Then

4. If the Subtraction check box is selected, a nested selection structure should determine whether the first integer is greater than the second integer. Enter the following If clause:

    If intNum1 > intNum2 Then

5. If the first integer is greater than the second integer, the nested selection structure's true path should calculate the answer by subtracting the second integer from the first integer. Enter the following assignment statement:

    intAnswer = intNum1 – intNum2

6. If the first integer is not greater than the second integer, the nested selection structure's false path should calculate the answer by subtracting the first integer from the second integer. Enter the following Else clause and assignment statement:

    Else
        intAnswer = intNum2 – intNum1

7. If necessary, delete the blank line above the nested selection structure's End If clause.

8. You have finished coding the nested selection structure and the true path of the outer selection structure. However, you still need to code the outer selection structure's false path. If the Subtraction check box is not selected, it means that the user wants addition.

Therefore, the outer selection structure's false path should add together both integers. Click **after the letter f** in the first End If clause and then press **Enter** to insert a blank line. Enter the following Else clause and assignment statement:

Else
    intAnswer = intNum2 + intNum1

9. If necessary, delete the blank line above the outer selection structure's End If clause. Figure 9-8 shows the code entered in the procedure.

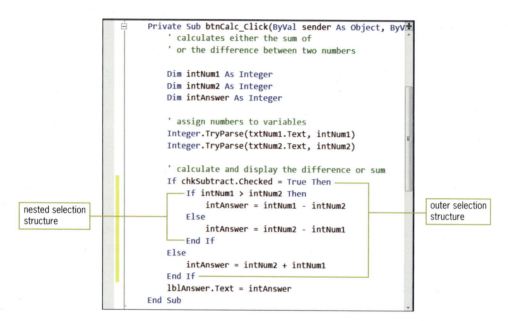

```
Private Sub btnCalc_Click(ByVal sender As Object, ByV
    ' calculates either the sum of
    ' or the difference between two numbers

    Dim intNum1 As Integer
    Dim intNum2 As Integer
    Dim intAnswer As Integer

    ' assign numbers to variables
    Integer.TryParse(txtNum1.Text, intNum1)
    Integer.TryParse(txtNum2.Text, intNum2)

    ' calculate and display the difference or sum
    If chkSubtract.Checked = True Then
        If intNum1 > intNum2 Then
            intAnswer = intNum1 - intNum2
        Else
            intAnswer = intNum2 - intNum1
        End If
    Else
        intAnswer = intNum2 + intNum1
    End If
    lblAnswer.Text = intAnswer
End Sub
```

nested selection structure

outer selection structure

Figure 9-8   btnCalc control's Click event procedure

To test the Addition and Subtraction Calculator application:

1. Save the solution and then start the application. Type **22** in the Number 1 box and type **12** in the Number 2 box. Click the **Calculate** button. The button's Click event procedure adds together both integers and then displays the sum (34) in the Answer box.

2. Click the **Subtraction** check box to select it, and then click the **Calculate** button. The button's Click event procedure subtracts the smaller integer (12) from the larger integer (22) and then displays the difference (10) in the Answer box.

3. Change the contents of the Number 1 box to **5** and then click the **Calculate** button. The button's Click event procedure subtracts the smaller integer (5) from the larger integer (12) and then displays the difference (7) in the Answer box. See Figure 9-9.

Figure 9-9   Difference shown in the interface

4. Click the **Exit** button to stop the application.

Let's Go to the Swap Meet

Jennifer thinks that the interface shown in Figure 9-9 might be misleading, because it looks as though the answer (7) is the result of subtracting the number 12 from the number 5. She has asked you to modify the application to make it obvious that the answer is the result of subtracting the smaller integer from the larger integer—in this case, subtracting 5 from 12. You can do this by **swapping** the contents of both text boxes when the smaller integer appears in the Number 1 text box. You swap the values by assigning the first integer (which the user enters in the Number 1 text box) to the Number 2 text box, and assigning the second integer (which the user enters in the Number 2 text box) to the Number 1 text box. But where do you enter the swapping instructions? Look carefully at the algorithm shown earlier in Figure 9-6. Locate the instructions that are followed when the user wants to perform subtraction; you will need to enter the swapping instructions somewhere in that location. In this case, the instructions in the nested selection structure are followed when the Subtraction check box is selected. Now consider where (in the nested selection structure) to enter the swapping instructions. If the nested selection structure's condition evaluates to True, it means that the Number 1 text box already contains the larger integer; so no swap is necessary in the nested selection structure's true path. However, if the nested selection structure's condition evaluates to False, it means that the number in the Number 1 text box is not larger than the number in the Number 2 text box; the numbers in both text boxes should be swapped at this point. Figure 9-10 shows the first modification to the algorithm from Figure 9-6.

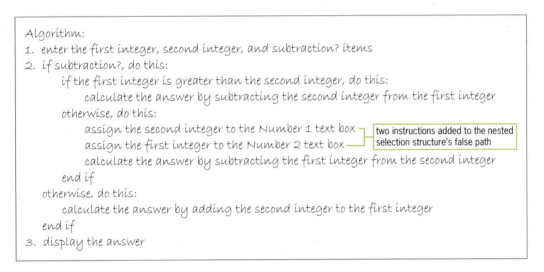

Figure 9-10 contents:

```
Algorithm:
1. enter the first integer, second integer, and subtraction? items
2. if subtraction?, do this:
       if the first integer is greater than the second integer, do this:
           calculate the answer by subtracting the second integer from the first integer
       otherwise, do this:
           assign the second integer to the Number 1 text box      ─┐ two instructions added to the nested
           assign the first integer to the Number 2 text box        ─┘ selection structure's false path
           calculate the answer by subtracting the first integer from the second integer
       end if
   otherwise, do this:
       calculate the answer by adding the second integer to the first integer
   end if
3. display the answer
```

Figure 9-10 First modification to the algorithm from Figure 9-6

When comparing two numbers, keep in mind that the first number can be greater than, less than, or equal to the second number. Study the comparison made in the nested selection structure's condition in Figure 9-10. If the condition evaluates to True, it means that the first integer (entered in the Number 1 text box) is the larger of the two integers, so the answer can be calculated by subtracting the second integer from the first integer. However, if the condition evaluates to False, it doesn't necessarily mean that the first integer (entered in the Number 1 text box) is less than the second integer (entered in the Number 2 text box); both integers could be equal. Therefore, the modified algorithm in Figure 9-10 will swap the text box values when the first integer is either less than or equal to the second integer. Although you could leave the algorithm as is, there is no reason to swap the text box values when both integers are equal. You can fix the algorithm by including the "equal to" comparison in the nested selection structure's condition, as shown in the final algorithm in Figure 9-11. In the final algorithm, the nested selection structure's condition determines whether the first integer is greater than or equal to the second integer. If the condition evaluates to True, the answer is calculated by subtracting the second integer from the first integer. If the condition evaluates to False, the text box values are swapped and the answer is calculated by subtracting the first integer from the second integer.

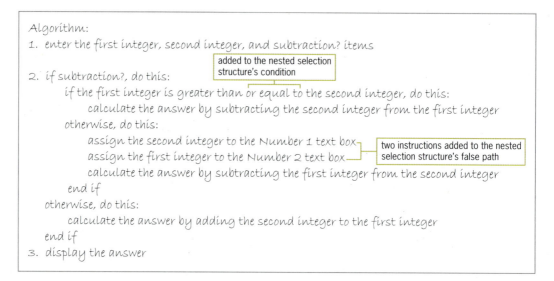

Figure 9-11 Final algorithm for the math problem

To modify the btnCalc control's Click event procedure and then test the code:

1. Change the nested selection structure's condition to **intNum1 >= intNum2**.

2. Click **after the letter e** in the nested selection structure's Else clause, and then press **Enter** to insert a blank line in the nested selection structure's false path. Enter the following assignment statements:

   txtNum1.Text = intNum2
   txtNum2.Text = intNum1

3. If necessary, delete the blank line above the last assignment statement in the nested selection structure's false path. See Figure 9-12.

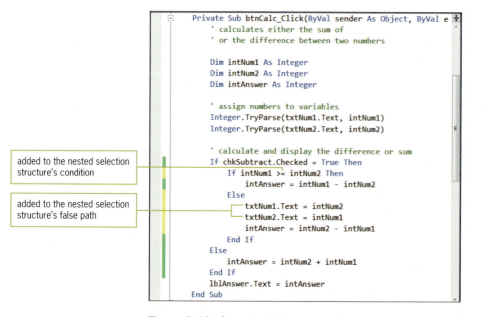

Figure 9-12 Completed Click event procedure for the btnCalc control

4. Save the solution and then start the application. Type **22** in the Number 1 box and type **12** in the Number 2 box. Click the **Calculate** button. The button's Click event procedure adds together both integers and then displays the sum (34) in the Answer box.

5. Click the **Subtraction** check box and then click the **Calculate** button. The button's Click event procedure subtracts the smaller integer (12) from the larger integer (22) and then displays the difference (10) in the Answer box.

6. Change the contents of the Number 1 box to **5** and then click the **Calculate** button. The button's Click event procedure swaps the values in the text boxes. It then subtracts the smaller integer (5) from the larger integer (12) and displays the difference (7) in the Answer box. See Figure 9-13.

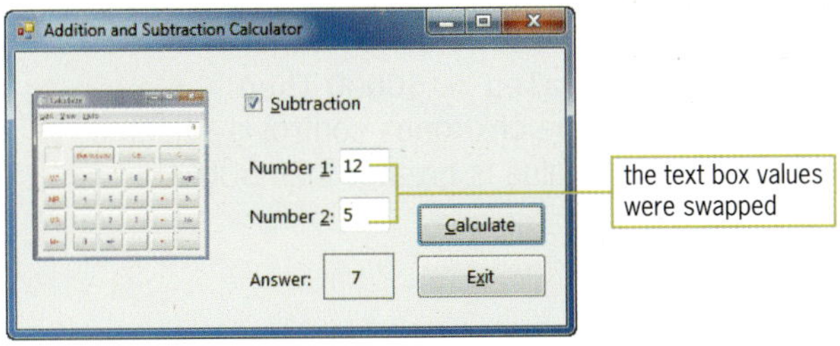

Figure 9-13 Interface showing that the values were swapped

7. Click the **Exit** button. Close the Code Editor window and then close the solution.

That's Way Too Logical for Me

In Chapter 8, you learned how to include comparison operators in an If…Then…Else statement's condition. You also can include logical operators in the condition. **Logical operators** let you combine two or more conditions, referred to as sub-conditions, into one compound condition. Logical operators are sometimes referred to as **Boolean operators**, because the compound condition in which they are contained always evaluates to a Boolean value (either True or False). Figure 9-14 lists two of the logical operators available in Visual Basic, along with their order of precedence. It also contains examples of using logical operators to create compound conditions. Notice that the compound condition in each example evaluates to either True or False only.

Logical operator	Operation	Precedence number
AndAlso	all sub-conditions must be true for the compound condition to evaluate to True	1
OrElse	only one of the sub-conditions needs to be true for the compound condition to evaluate to True	2

Example 1
`If intPopulation > 25000 AndAlso intPopulation <= 50000 Then`
The compound condition evaluates to True when the `intPopulation` variable's value is greater than 25000 but less than or equal to 50000; otherwise, it evaluates to False.

Example 2
`If chkBonus.Checked = True AndAlso decSales > 50000 Then`
The compound condition evaluates to True when the chkBonus control is selected and, at the same time, the `decSales` variable's value is greater than 50000; otherwise, it evaluates to False.

Example 3
`If intPayCode = 1 OrElse intPayCode = 2 Then`
The compound condition evaluates to True when the `intPayCode` variable contains either the number 1 or the number 2; otherwise, it evaluates to False.

Example 4
`If intRating = 5 OrElse decSales <= 2500 Then`
The compound condition evaluates to True when either (or both) of the following is true: the `intRating` variable's value is 5 or the `decSales` variable's value is less than or equal to 2500; otherwise, it evaluates to False.

Example 5
`If intCode = 1 OrElse intNum > 0 AndAlso intNum < 100 Then`
The compound condition evaluates to True when either (or both) of the following is true: the `intCode` variable contains the number 1 or the `intNum` variable's value is between 0 and 100; otherwise, it evaluates to False. (The AndAlso operator is evaluated before the OrElse operator, because it has a higher precedence.)

Figure 9-14 Logical operators and examples

Now, study the problem specification and algorithm shown in Figure 9-15. The selection structure in the algorithm makes a decision regarding the employee's hours. More specifically, it determines whether the hours are within the acceptable range. In this case, the acceptable range is greater than or equal to 0 but less than or equal to 40. Now compare the selection structure in the algorithm with the code shown in Figure 9-16. Notice that the *if the hours worked are greater than or equal to 0 but less than or equal to 40, do this:* line is coded as `If dblHours >= 0 AndAlso dblHours <= 40 Then` in Visual Basic.

ABC Company wants an application that displays an employee's gross pay. All employees earn $8.35 per hour. The payroll clerk will enter the number of hours worked, which should be greater than or equal to 0 but less than or equal to 40.

Output: gross pay

Input: hours worked

Algorithm:
1. enter the hours worked
2. if the hours worked are greater than or equal to 0 but less than or equal to 40, do this:
      calculate the gross pay by multiplying the hours worked by 8.35
      display the gross pay
   otherwise, do this:
      display an error message
   end if

Figure 9-15 Gross pay problem specification and algorithm

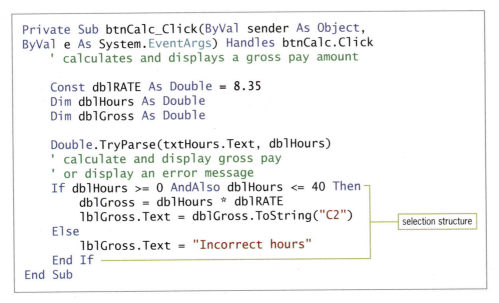

Figure 9-16 Code corresponding to Figure 9-15's algorithm

To complete the Gross Pay application's code:

1. Open the **Gross Pay Solution (Gross Pay Solution.sln)** file contained in the ClearlyVB2010\Chap09\Gross Pay Solution folder. If the designer window is not open, double-click **frmMain.vb** in the Solution Explorer window.

2. Open the Code Editor window, which contains the code for the btnExit control's Click event procedure. Click the **blank line** below the ' or display an error message comment in the btnCalc control's Click event procedure and then enter the following selection structure:

```
If dblHours >= 0 AndAlso dblHours <= 40 Then
    dblGross = dblHours * dblRATE
    lblGross.Text = dblGross.ToString("C2")
Else
```

         lblGross.Text = "Incorrect hours"
End If

3. Save the solution and then start the application. Type **20** in the Hours worked box and then click the **Calculate** button. Because the hours are within the acceptable range, the btnCalc control's Click event procedure calculates the gross pay and displays the result ($167.00) in the Gross pay box.

4. Change the hours entered in the Hours worked box to **45** and then click the **Calculate** button. In this case, the hours worked are not within the acceptable range, so the btnCalc control's Click event procedure displays the "Incorrect hours" message in the Gross pay box. See Figure 9-17.

For more examples of logical operators, see the Logical Operators section in the Ch9WantMore.pdf file.

Figure 9-17 Error message shown in the interface

5. Click the **Exit** button. Close the Code Editor window and then close the solution.

Summary of Operators

Figure 9-18 contains a listing of the arithmetic, comparison, and logical operators you have learned so far, along with their order of precedence. Notice that arithmetic operators are evaluated first, followed by comparison operators and then logical operators. As a result, the expression 12 > 0 AndAlso 12 < 10 * 2 evaluates to True, as shown in the figure.

	Operator	Operation	Precedence number
arithmetic operators	^	exponentiation (raises a number to a power)	1
	−	negation (reverses the sign of a number)	2
	*, /	multiplication and division	3
	\	integer division	4
	Mod	modulus	5
	+, −	addition and subtraction	6
comparison operators	=, >, >=, <, <=, <>	equal to, greater than, greater than or equal to, less than, less than or equal to, not equal to	7
logical operators	AndAlso	all sub-conditions must be true for the compound condition to evaluate to True	8
	OrElse	only one of the sub-conditions needs to be true for the compound condition to evaluate to True	9

	Evaluation steps	Result
example	Original expression	12 > 0 AndAlso 12 < 10 * 2
	10 * 2 is evaluated first	12 > 0 AndAlso 12 < 20
	12 > 0 is evaluated second	True AndAlso 12 < 20
	12 < 20 is evaluated third	True AndAlso True
	True AndAlso True is evaluated last	True

Figure 9-18 Listing of arithmetic, comparison, and logical operators

Mini-Quiz 9-2

See Appendix B for the answers.

1. Which of the following conditions determines whether the number in the `intNum` variable is less than 0 or greater than 1000?

    a. `intNum < 0 AndAlso intNum > 1000`

    b. `intNum < 0 OrElse intNum > 1000`

    c. `intNum < 0 AndAlso > 1000`

    d. `intNum < 0 OrElse > 1000`

2. Which of the following conditions determines whether the number in the `dblPrice` variable is greater than 15.45 but less than 25.75?

    a. `dblPrice < 15.45 AndAlso dblPrice > 25.75`

    b. `dblPrice > 15.45 OrElse < 25.75`

    c. `dblPrice > 15.45 AndAlso dblPrice < 25.75`

    d. `dblPrice > 15.45 OrElse dblPrice < 25.75`

3. Which of the following conditions determines whether both check boxes are selected?

    a. `chkDiscount.Checked = True AndAlso chkCoupon.Checked = True`

    b. `chkDiscount.Checked = True OrElse chkCoupon.Checked = True`

    c. `chkDiscount.Selected = True AndAlso chkCoupon.Selected = True`

    d. `chkDiscount.Selected = True OrElse chkCoupon.Selected = True`

    It's time to view the Ch09-Nested Selection Structure video.

4. The expression 6 + 3 > 7 AndAlso 8 < 4 will evaluate to _____ .

    a. True   b. False

Summary

- Both paths in a selection structure can include other selection structures, called nested selection structures.

- When two numbers are compared, the first number can be greater than, less than, or equal to the second number.

- Logical operators are used to combine two or more sub-conditions into one compound condition. The compound condition will always evaluate to either True or False only.

- When a compound condition contains the AndAlso logical operator, all of the sub-conditions must be true for the compound condition to evaluate to True. When a compound condition contains the OrElse logical operator, only one of the sub-conditions needs to be true for the compound condition to evaluate to True.

- The AndAlso operator has a higher precedence than the OrElse operator.

- Arithmetic operators in an expression are evaluated first, followed by comparison operators and then logical operators.

Key Terms

Boolean operators—another term for logical operators

Logical operators—operators used to combine two or more sub-conditions into one compound condition; examples are the AndAlso and OrElse operators; also called Boolean operators

Nested selection structure—a selection structure that is wholly contained (nested) within either the true or false path of another selection structure

Swapping—exchanging or switching two values

Review Questions

Use the code shown in Figure 9-19 to answer Review Questions 1 and 2.

```
If intNum <= 100 Then
        intNum = intNum * 2
Else
        If intNum > 500 Then
                intNum = intNum * 3
        End If
End If
```

Figure 9-19 Code for Review Questions 1 and 2

1. The intNum variable contains the number 1000 before the code in Figure 9-19 is processed. What value will be in the variable after the code is processed?

    a. 0

    b. 1000

    c. 2000

    d. 3000

2. The intNum variable contains the number 200 before the code in Figure 9-19 is processed. What value will be in the variable after the code is processed?

    a. 0

    b. 200

    c. 400

    d. 600

3. Which of the following expressions evaluates to True?

    a. 7 > 4 AndAlso 6 <> 3

    b. 9 + 3 < 20 OrElse 8 > 9

    c. 67 Mod 2 = 1

    d. all of the above

4. If the intUnits and dblPrice variables contain the numbers 5 and 12.45, respectively, the intUnits > 0 AndAlso intUnits < 10 OrElse dblPrice > 25 expression evaluates to _____ .

    a. True

    b. False

5. If the intUnits and dblPrice variables contain the numbers 5 and 12.45, respectively, the intUnits > 0 AndAlso dblPrice > 0 AndAlso dblPrice < 10 expression evaluates to _____ .

    a. True

    b. False

6. Which of the operators in the expression 6 + 7 * 3 > 25 − 2 is evaluated first?

   a. +
              c. >

   b. *
              d. −

7. The expression in Review Question 6 evaluates to _____ .

   a. True
              b. False

Exercises

1. Open the Total Due Solution (Total Due Solution.sln) file contained in the ClearlyVB2010\Chap09\Total Due Solution folder. Modify the btnCalc control's Click event procedure so that it calculates a 10% discount not only for employees, but for any customer whose quantity ordered is at least 10. Save the solution and then start and test the application. Close the Code Editor window and then close the solution. (See Appendix B for the answer.) **TRY THIS**

2. Open the Total Due Solution (Total Due Solution.sln) file contained in the ClearlyVB2010\Chap09\Total Due Solution—Version 2 folder. Sam's company now gives a 12% discount to employees. Non-employees ordering more than 20 items receive a 5% discount. Modify the btnCalc control's Click event procedure. Save the solution and then start and test the application. Close the Code Editor window and then close the solution. (See Appendix B for the answer.) **TRY THIS**

3. In this exercise, you modify the Gross Pay application coded in the chapter. Use Windows to make a copy of the Gross Pay Solution folder. Save the copy in the ClearlyVB2010\Chap09 folder. Rename the copy Modified Gross Pay Solution. Open the Gross Pay Solution (Gross Pay Solution.sln) file contained in the Modified Gross Pay Solution folder. The selection structure's condition in the Calculate button's Click event procedure determines whether the hours worked are in the acceptable range. Modify the condition so that it determines whether the hours worked are not in the acceptable range. Then make the appropriate modifications to the instructions within the selection structure. Save the solution and then start and test the application. Close the Code Editor window and then close the solution. **MODIFY THIS**

4. Professor Jones wants an application that both calculates and displays a student's average score on two tests. Open the Jones Solution (Jones Solution.sln) file contained in the ClearlyVB2010\Chap09\Jones Solution folder. Code the btnCalc control's Click event procedure. The procedure should verify that each score is valid. A valid score is one that is greater than or equal to zero. The procedure should display an appropriate message in the lblMessage control when one or more scores are not valid; otherwise, it should calculate and display the average score. Format the average score using the "N1" format. Save the solution and then start and test the application. Close the Code Editor window and then close the solution. **INTRODUCTORY**

5. Geriatric Medical Supplies pays each salesperson a 3% bonus on his or her annual sales. In addition, any salesperson who has been with the company for more than 10 years receives an additional bonus. The additional bonus is $100 for each year the employee has been with the company. The company wants an application that both calculates and displays a salesperson's total bonus. Include a dollar sign and two decimal places in the total bonus amount. **INTRODUCTORY**

   a. List the output and input items, as well as any processing items, and then create an appropriate algorithm. The algorithm should verify that the sales amount entered by the user is not less than zero. If it is less than zero, an appropriate error message should be displayed.

    b. Create a Visual Basic Windows application. Use the following names for the solution and project, respectively: Geriatric Solution and Geriatric Project. Save the application in the ClearlyVB2010\Chap09 folder. Change the name of the form file on your disk to frmMain.vb. If necessary, change the form's name to frmMain.

    c. Create a suitable interface. Include an Exit button. Code the Exit button's Click event procedure and the problem's algorithm. Save the solution. Desk-check the program using your own sample data.

    d. Start and then test the application. Close the Code Editor window and then close the solution.

INTERMEDIATE 6. Small Loans Inc wants an application that displays the maximum amount a customer can borrow. Use the following rules to determine the amount. Customers whose annual salary is at least $35000 can borrow up to 25% of their salary, but only if they have been employed at their current job for at least 5 years. If they have been employed less than 5 years, they can borrow only a maximum of 20% of their salary. Customers who earn less than $35000 per year can borrow up to 5% of their salary. Create a Visual Basic Windows application. Use the following names for the solution and project, respectively: Loans Solution and Loans Project. Save the application in the ClearlyVB2010\Chap09 folder. Change the name of the form file on your disk to frmMain.vb. If necessary, change the form's name to frmMain. Create a suitable interface. Code the application. Save the solution and then start and test the application. Close the Code Editor window and then close the solution.

INTERMEDIATE 7. Open the Total Due Solution (Total Due Solution.sln) file contained in the ClearlyVB2010\Chap09\Total Due Solution—Version 3 folder. Sam's company now gives a 15% discount to employees. Non-employees ordering more than 10 items receive an 8% discount. Modify the btnCalc control's Click event procedure. Save the solution and then start and test the application. Close the Code Editor window and then close the solution.

INTERMEDIATE 8. Westmoreland Water Department wants an application that calculates a customer's monthly water bill. The clerk will enter the current and previous meter readings. The application should calculate and display the number of gallons of water used and the total charge for the water. The charge for water is $6 per 1000 gallons, or .006 per gallon. However, there is a minimum charge of $15.65. (In other words, every customer must pay at least $15.65.) The application should determine whether the current meter reading is greater than or equal to the previous meter reading; if it's not, the application should display N/A as both the number of gallons used and total charge. Create a Visual Basic Windows application. Use the following names for the solution and project, respectively: Westmoreland Solution and Westmoreland Project. Save the application in the ClearlyVB2010\Chap09 folder. Change the name of the form file on your disk to frmMain.vb. If necessary, change the form's name to frmMain. Create a suitable interface. Code the application. Save the solution and then start and test the application. Close the Code Editor window and then close the solution.

ADVANCED 9. Kraton Supply wants an application that both calculates and displays the amount of a salesperson's bonus. The clerk will enter the salesperson's code and sales amount. The bonus rates are shown in Figure 9-20. Create a Visual Basic Windows application. Use the following names for the solution and project, respectively: Kraton Solution and Kraton Project. Save the application in the ClearlyVB2010\Chap09 folder. Change the name of the form file on your disk to frmMain.vb. If necessary, change the form's name to frmMain. Create a suitable interface and then code the application. Save the solution and then start and test the application. Close the Code Editor window and then close the solution.

Bonus code	Bonus rate
1	2%
2	3%
3	2%
4	3%
All other codes	1%

Figure 9-20 Information for Exercise 9

10. In this exercise, you modify the application from Chapter 8's Exercise 11. If you did not complete Chapter 8's Exercise 11, you will need to do so before you can complete this exercise. Use Windows to copy the Health Solution folder from the ClearlyVB2010\Chap08 folder to the ClearlyVB2010\Chap09 folder. Open the Health Solution (Health Solution.sln) file contained in the ClearlyVB2010\Chap09\Health Solution folder. Modify the code so that it gives club members a 10% discount on their monthly dues when they sign up for all three of the additional activities (golf, racquetball, and tennis). Save the solution and then start and test the application. Close the Code Editor window and then close the solution.

ADVANCED

11. Johnson Supply wants an application that displays the total price of an order. The price of each item ordered is based on the number of units ordered and the customer's status (either wholesaler or retailer). Use a check box to indicate that the customer is a wholesaler. The price per unit is shown in Figure 9-21. Create a Visual Basic Windows application. Use the following names for the solution and project, respectively: Johnson Solution and Johnson Project. Save the application in the ClearlyVB2010\Chap09 folder. Change the name of the form file on your disk to frmMain.vb. If necessary, change the form's name to frmMain. Create the interface and then code the application. Save the solution and then start and test the application. Close the Code Editor window and then close the solution.

ADVANCED

Wholesaler		**Retailer**	
Number of units	Price per unit ($)	Number of units	Price per unit ($)
1 – 4	10	1 – 3	15
5 and over	9	4 – 8	14
		9 and over	12

Figure 9-21 Information for Exercise 11

12. Open the FigureThisOut Solution (FigureThisOut Solution.sln) file contained in the ClearlyVB2010\Chap09\FigureThisOut Solution folder. Open the Code Editor window and study the btnDisplay control's Click event procedure. What task is performed by the procedure? What are the rules for charging the various fees? In other words, who is charged $10? Who is charged $5, and who is charged $20? You will test the application to verify that your answers are correct. Start the application. Enter 21 as the age and then click the Display Fee button. Select the Member check box and then click the Display Fee button. Now enter 66 as the age and then click the Display Fee button. Close the Code Editor window and then close the solution.

FIGURE THIS OUT

13. Open the SwatTheBugs Solution (SwatTheBugs Solution.sln) file contained in the ClearlyVB2010\Chap09\SwatTheBugs Solution folder. The application should calculate an 8% bonus on a salesperson's sales. However, a salesperson having a sales code of 5 receives an additional $150 bonus when the sales are at least $10000; otherwise, he or she receives an additional $125 bonus. Open the Code Editor window and study the code. Start and then test the application. Notice that the code is not working correctly. Locate and correct any errors. Close the Code Editor window and then close the solution.

SWAT THE BUGS

So Many Paths . . . So Little Time (Multiple-Alternative Selection Structures)

After studying Chapter 10, you should be able to:

- ◎ Code a multiple-alternative selection structure using If/ElseIf/Else
- ◎ Declare a variable using the String data type
- ◎ Convert a string to uppercase or lowercase
- ◎ Code a multiple-alternative selection structure using Select Case
- ◎ Include a radio button in an interface

Which Way Should I Go?

At times, you may need to create a selection structure that can choose from several alternatives. Such selection structures are referred to as either **multiple-alternative selection structures** or **extended selection structures**. Figure 10-1 contains a problem specification that requires a multiple-alternative selection structure. The figure also contains an appropriate algorithm. The multiple-alternative selection structure is in Step 2 in the algorithm.

George wants an application that displays a message based on a department code that he enters. The valid department codes and their corresponding messages are shown below. If the department code is not valid, the application should display the message "Invalid code".

Department code	Message
1	Payroll
2	Personnel
3	IT

Output: message

Input: code

Algorithm:
1. enter the code
2. if the code is: do this:
    1   display "Payroll"
    2   display "Personnel"
    3   display "IT"
    Invalid   display "Invalid code"
end if

multiple-alternative selection structure

Figure 10-1   Department code problem specification and algorithm

Figure 10-2 shows two ways of coding the multiple-alternative selection structure from Figure 10-1. Version 1 uses nested If...Then...Else statements, which you learned about in Chapter 9. Version 2 uses another form of the If...Then...Else statement, called **If/ElseIf/Else**. Although both versions of the code produce the same result, Version 2 is a much more convenient way of coding a multiple-alternative selection structure.

Version 1—nested If ... Then ... Else statements

```
If intCode = 1 Then
    lblName.Text = "Payroll"
Else
    If intCode = 2 Then
        lblName.Text = "Personnel"
    Else
        If intCode = 3 Then
            lblName.Text = "IT"
        Else
            lblName.Text = "Invalid code"
        End If
    End If
End If
```

requires three End If clauses

Version 2—If/ElseIf/Else form of the If...Then...Else statement

```
If intCode = 1 Then
    lblName.Text = "Payroll"
ElseIf intCode = 2 Then
    lblName.Text = "Personnel"
ElseIf intCode = 3 Then
    lblName.Text = "IT"
Else
    lblName.Text = "Invalid code"
End If
```

requires one End If clause

Figure 10-2   Two versions of the code for the multiple-alternative selection structure

Figure 10-3 shows another problem specification that requires a multiple-alternative selection structure. In this case, the selection structure must determine the membership type before it can display the correct fee. As the problem specification indicates, the fee for a Single membership is $40, and the fee for a Family membership is $50. The fees for the Single Senior and Couple Senior memberships are $30 and $35, respectively. Figure 10-3 also includes an appropriate algorithm in flowchart form. Recall that the oval in a flowchart is the start/stop symbol, the parallelogram is the input/output symbol, the diamond is the decision symbol, and the rectangle is the process symbol.

Fitness For Good health club wants an application that displays a member's monthly fee, which is based on a code entered by the user. The code corresponds to the membership type, as shown below. If the user enters an invalid code, display the number 0 as the monthly fee.

Code	Membership type	Monthly fee
S	Single	40
F	Family	50
S65	Single Senior	30
C65	Couple Senior	35

Output: fee

Input: code

Algorithm:

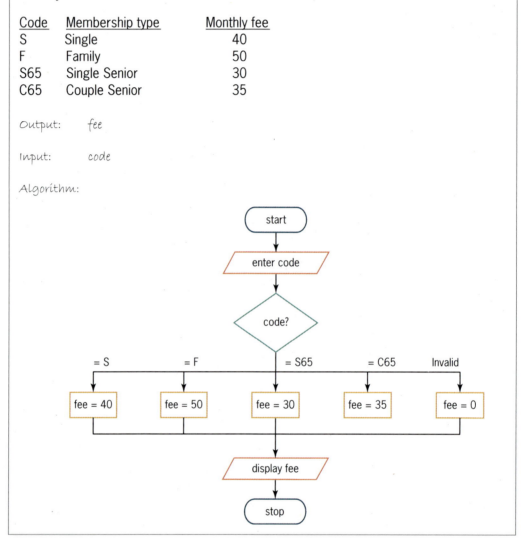

Figure 10-3   Fitness For Good problem specification and algorithm

Coding the Fitness For Good Application

In this section, you will begin coding the algorithm shown in Figure 10-3. First, however, you need to open the Fitness For Good application.

To open the Fitness For Good application:

1. Start Visual Studio 2010 or Visual Basic 2010 Express and permanently display the Solution Explorer window. Open the **Fitness Solution (Fitness Solution.sln)** file contained in the ClearlyVB2010\Chap10\Fitness Solution-If folder. If the designer window is not open, double-click **frmMain.vb** in the Solution Explorer window. The application's interface is shown in Figure 10-4.

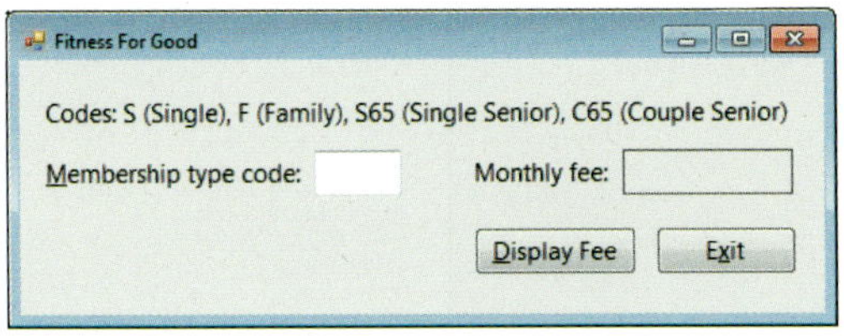

Figure 10-4 Fitness For Good application's interface

2. Open the Code Editor window, which contains the code for the btnExit control's Click event procedure. It also contains the partially completed code for the btnDisplay control's Click event procedure.

The btnDisplay control's Click event procedure will use an Integer variable named `intFee` to store the monthly fee. The procedure also will use a variable to store the code that represents the membership type: S, F, S65, or C65. You can't declare the variable using any of the data types you learned about in Chapter 6, which are the Integer, Decimal, and Double data types. This is because variables declared with those data types can store numbers only, and each code contains a letter. Instead, you declare the variable using a data type called String. Memory locations declared using the **String data type** can store alphanumeric text, which is text that may contain letters, numbers, or special characters. Examples of alphanumeric text include the membership codes F and S65, as well as the phone number 111-2222. The three-character ID used when naming String variables (and String named constants) is str. You will name the variable `strCode`.

To begin coding the algorithm shown in Figure 10-3:

1. Click the **blank line** below the last Const statement in the btnDisplay control's Click event procedure. Enter the following Dim statements. Press **Enter** twice after typing the second Dim statement.

   Dim intFee As Integer
   Dim strCode As String

2. Now you will use the flowchart from Figure 10-3 to code the procedure. The first symbol below the Start oval is the "enter code" parallelogram. The user will enter the code in the txtCode control. You will assign the control's Text property to the `strCode` variable. Recall that the value stored in the Text property is treated as alphanumeric text; therefore, you can simply assign the value to the variable. Enter the following comment and assignment statement. Press **Enter** twice after typing the assignment statement.

   ' assign code to a variable
   strCode = txtCode.text

3. The diamond and rectangles in the flowchart represent a multiple-alternative selection structure that uses the code to determine the appropriate fee. Enter the comment and multiple-alternative selection structure shown in Figure 10-5. Be sure to type the codes using uppercase letters.

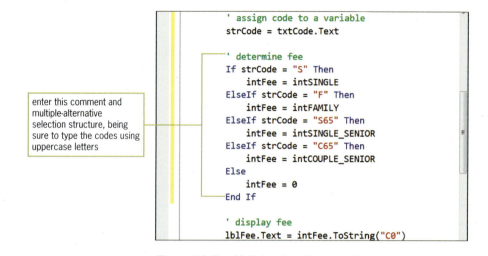

enter this comment and multiple-alternative selection structure, being sure to type the codes using uppercase letters

```
' assign code to a variable
strCode = txtCode.Text

' determine fee
If strCode = "S" Then
    intFee = intSINGLE
ElseIf strCode = "F" Then
    intFee = intFAMILY
ElseIf strCode = "S65" Then
    intFee = intSINGLE_SENIOR
ElseIf strCode = "C65" Then
    intFee = intCOUPLE_SENIOR
Else
    intFee = 0
End If

' display fee
lblFee.Text = intFee.ToString("C0")
```

Figure 10-5   Multiple-alternative selection structure entered in the procedure

4. Save the solution and then start the application. Test the application's code by displaying the Single Senior membership fee, which should be $30. Type **S65** (be sure to type an uppercase letter S) as the code and then click the **Display Fee** button. The correct fee appears in the Monthly fee box.

5. Now display the Couple Senior membership fee, which should be $35. Change the code to **C65** (be sure to type an uppercase letter C) and then click the **Display Fee** button. The correct fee appears in the Monthly fee box.

6. Next, display the fee for a Family membership. Change the code to the uppercase letter **F** and then click the **Display Fee** button. The correct amount ($50) appears as the monthly fee.

7. Finally, display the Single membership fee, which should be $40. Change the code to a lowercase letter **s** and then click the **Display Fee** button. The Monthly fee box shows $0, which is incorrect. You will learn how to fix this problem in the next section.

8. Click the **Exit** button.

Don't Be So Sensitive

As is true in most programming languages, string comparisons in Visual Basic are case sensitive. This means that the uppercase version of a letter is not the same as its lowercase counterpart. So, although a human being recognizes S and s as simply two different ways of writing the same letter, a computer does not make this connection between both letters. To a computer, an S is entirely different from an s, and both characters have no relation to each other. This is because each character on the computer keyboard is stored in the computer's internal memory using a different Unicode value. Unicode is the universal coding scheme for characters. It assigns a unique numeric value to each character used in the written languages of the world. (For more information, see The Unicode Standard at *www.unicode.org*.) As a result, the strCode = "S" condition in the multiple-alternative selection structure evaluates to False when the strCode variable contains the lowercase letter s; therefore, the selection structure assigns the number 0 to the intFee variable.

Before using a string in a comparison, you can convert it to either uppercase or lowercase and then use the converted string in the comparison. You use the **ToUpper method** to convert a string to uppercase, and the **ToLower method** to convert a string to lowercase. Figure 10-6 shows the syntax of both methods and includes examples of using the methods. In each syntax, *string* typically is either the name of a String variable or the Text property of an object. Both methods temporarily convert the *string* to the specified case. However, you also can use the methods to permanently convert the contents of a String variable to uppercase or lowercase; the same is true for the value stored in a control's Text property. You do this using an assignment statement, as illustrated in Example 3. When using the ToUpper method in a comparison, be sure that everything you are comparing is uppercase. In other words, the clause `If txtCode.Text.ToUpper = "f" Then` will not work correctly: the condition will always evaluate to False, because the uppercase version of a letter will never be equal to its lowercase counterpart. Likewise, when using the ToLower method in a comparison, be sure that everything you are comparing is lowercase. The ToUpper and ToLower methods affect only characters that represent letters of the alphabet, as these are the only characters that have uppercase and lowercase forms.

Converting a string to uppercase or lowercase

<u>Syntax</u>
string.**ToUpper**
string.**ToLower**

<u>Example 1</u>
`If txtCode.Text.ToUpper = "F" Then`
compares the uppercase version of the string stored in the txtCode's Text property with the uppercase string "F"

<u>Example 2</u>
`If txtCity.Text.ToLower = "reno" Then`
compares the lowercase version of the string stored in the txtCity's Text property with the lowercase string "reno"

<u>Example 3</u>
`strName = strName.ToUpper`
`txtState.Text = txtState.Text.ToLower`
changes the contents of the `strName` variable to uppercase, and changes the contents of the txtState's Text property to lowercase

---

Figure 10-6   Syntax and examples of the ToUpper and ToLower methods

To fix the code shown earlier in Figure 10-5, you will use the ToUpper method to convert the user input to uppercase. One way to accomplish this is by appending the ToUpper method to the end of the statement that assigns the code to the `strCode` variable, like this: `strCode = txtCode.Text.ToUpper`. When processing the statement, the computer first makes a temporary copy of the string stored in the txtCode control's Text property. It then converts the copy to uppercase and stores the result in the `strCode` variable. Finally, it removes the copy from its internal memory.

You also can convert the user input to uppercase in the selection structure. You would do this by appending the ToUpper method to the `strCode` variable in each of the four conditions, like this: `strCode.ToUpper`. However, keep in mind that each time a condition in the selection structure is evaluated, the computer will have to make a temporary copy of the user input, convert the copy to uppercase, and then compare the copy to the membership code. It's easier for the programmer, and more efficient for the computer, to convert the user input to uppercase in the statement that assigns the input to the `strCode` variable.

To fix the string comparison problem encountered in the previous set of steps:

1. Change the `strCode = txtCode.Text` statement to **strCode = txtCode.Text.ToUpper**.

2. Save the solution and then start the application. First, display the Single membership fee, which should be $40. Type **s** as the code and then click the **Display Fee** button. The correct fee appears in the Monthly fee box.

3. Next, display the Couple Senior membership fee. Change the code to **c65** and then click the **Display Fee** button. The correct fee ($35) appears in the Monthly fee box.

4. Now you will test the application using an invalid code; the Monthly fee box should show $0. Change the code to **x** and then click the **Display Fee** button. The correct amount appears in the Monthly fee box.

5. Click the **Exit** button. Close the Code Editor window and then close the solution.

Figure 10-7 shows the code entered in the btnDisplay control's Click event procedure.

```vb
Private Sub btnDisplay_Click(ByVal sender As Object,
ByVal e As System.EventArgs) Handles btnDisplay.Click
    ' displays a monthly membership fee

    Const intSINGLE As Integer = 40
    Const intFAMILY As Integer = 50
    Const intSINGLE_SENIOR As Integer = 30
    Const intCOUPLE_SENIOR As Integer = 35
    Dim intFee As Integer
    Dim strCode As String

    ' assign code to a variable
    strCode = txtCode.Text.ToUpper

    ' determine fee
    If strCode = "S" Then
        intFee = intSINGLE
    ElseIf strCode = "F" Then
        intFee = intFAMILY
    ElseIf strCode = "S65" Then
        intFee = intSINGLE_SENIOR
    ElseIf strCode = "C65" Then
        intFee = intCOUPLE_SENIOR
    Else
        intFee = 0
    End If

    ' display fee
    lblFee.Text = intFee.ToString("C0")
End Sub
```

For more examples of using the If... Then... Else statement to code a multiple-alternative selection structure, see the If...Then...Else Multiple-Alternative Selection Structure section in the Ch10WantMore.pdf file.

Figure 10-7 btnDisplay control's Click event procedure

Mini-Quiz 10-1

See Appendix B for the answers.

1. Write a multiple-alternative selection structure that determines the appropriate discount rate based on a promotion code entered by the user. The user's entry is stored in the `intPromoCode` variable. The valid promotion codes are 1, 2, 3, and 4. The corresponding discount rates are 2%, 5%, 10%, and 25%, respectively. Assign the discount rate (converted to its decimal form) to the `decRate` variable. If the user enters an invalid promotion code, assign the number 0 to the `decRate` variable. Use the If/ElseIf/Else form of the If…Then…Else statement.

2. Write a statement that assigns the contents of the txtId control, in uppercase, to the `strId` variable.

3. Write a multiple-alternative selection structure that displays both the first name and last name corresponding to an ID entered by the user. The ID is stored in the `strId` variable from Question 2. Display the first name in the lblFirst control. Display the last name in the lblLast control. The valid IDs are 12A, 45B, 67X, and 78Y. The corresponding names are Jerry Jones, Mark Smith, Jill Batist, and Cheryl Sworski. If the user enters an invalid ID, assign a question mark to both the lblFirst and lblLast controls. Use the If/ElseIf/Else form of the If…Then…Else statement.

What's the Next Case on the Docket?

The If…Then…Else statement is not the only statement you can use to code a multiple-alternative selection structure in Visual Basic; you also can use the **Select Case statement**. Figure 10-8 shows the Select Case statement's syntax. It also shows how to use the statement to code a multiple-alternative selection structure that displays a message corresponding to a letter grade. The Select Case statement begins with the keywords `Select Case`, followed by a *selectorExpression*. The selectorExpression can contain any combination of variables, constants, methods, operators, or properties. In the example in Figure 10-8, the selectorExpression is a String variable named `strGrade`. The Select Case statement ends with the End Select clause. Between the Select Case and End Select clauses are the individual Case clauses. Each Case clause represents a different path that the computer can follow. It is customary to indent each Case clause, as well as the instructions within each Case clause, as shown in the figure. You can have as many Case clauses as necessary in a Select Case statement. However, if the Select Case statement includes a Case Else clause, the Case Else clause must be the last clause in the statement.

Each of the individual Case clauses, except the Case Else clause, must contain an *expressionList*, which can include one or more expressions. To include more than one expression in an expressionList, you separate each expression with a comma, as in the expressionList `Case "D"`, `"F"`. The selectorExpression needs to match only one of the expressions listed in an expressionList. The data type of the expressions must be compatible with the data type of the selectorExpression. If the selectorExpression is numeric, the expressions in the Case clauses should be numeric. Likewise, if the selectorExpression is a string, the expressions should be strings. In the example in Figure 10-8, the selectorExpression (`strGrade`) is a string and so are the expressions: "A", "B", "C", "D", and "F".

Select Case statement

Syntax
Select Case *selectorExpression*
      Case *expressionList1*
          instructions for the first Case
      [**Case** *expressionList2*
          instructions for the second Case]
      [**Case** *expressionListN*
          instructions for the Nth case]
      [**Case Else**
          instructions for when the selectorExpression does not match
          any of the expressionLists]
End Select

Example
```
Dim strGrade As String = txtGrade.Text.ToUpper
Select Case strGrade
    Case "A"
        lblMsg.Text = "Excellent"
    Case "B"
        lblMsg.Text = "Above Average"
    Case "C"
        lblMsg.Text = "Average"
    Case "D", "F"
        lblMsg.Text = "Below Average"
    Case Else
        lblMsg.Text = "Error"
End Select
```

Figure 10-8   Syntax and an example of the Select Case statement

When processing the Select Case statement, the computer first compares the value of the selectorExpression with the values listed in expressionList1. If a match is found, the computer processes the instructions for the first Case, stopping when it reaches either another Case clause or the End Select clause; it then skips to the instruction following the End Select clause. If a match is not found in expressionList1, the computer skips to the second Case clause, where it compares the selectorExpression with the values listed in expressionList2. If a match is found, the computer processes the instructions for the second Case clause and then skips to the instruction following the End Select clause. If a match is not found, the computer skips to the third Case clause, and so on. If the selectorExpression does not match any of the values listed in any of the expressionLists, the computer processes the instructions listed in the Case Else clause (if there is one) and then skips to the instruction following the End Select clause. Keep in mind that if the selectorExpression matches a value in more than one Case clause, only the instructions in the first match are processed.

Using Select Case in the Fitness For Good Application

In this section, you will code the Fitness For Good application using the Select Case statement.

To code the Fitness For Good application using the Select Case statement:

1. Open the **Fitness Solution** (**Fitness Solution.sln**) file contained in the ClearlyVB2010\ Chap10\Fitness Solution-Select Case folder. If the designer window is not open, double-click **frmMain.vb** in the Solution Explorer window. The application's interface (shown earlier in Figure 10-4) appears on the screen.

2. Open the Code Editor window. In the btnDisplay control's Click event procedure, enter the Select Case statement shown in Figure 10-9.

```vb
Private Sub btnDisplay_Click(ByVal sender As Object,
ByVal e As System.EventArgs) Handles btnDisplay.Click
    ' displays a monthly membership fee

    Const intSINGLE As Integer = 40
    Const intFAMILY As Integer = 50
    Const intSINGLE_SENIOR As Integer = 30
    Const intCOUPLE_SENIOR As Integer = 35
    Dim intFee As Integer
    Dim strCode As String

    ' assign code to a variable
    strCode = txtCode.Text.ToUpper

    ' determine fee
    Select Case strCode
        Case "S"
            intFee = intSINGLE
        Case "F"
            intFee = intFAMILY
        Case "S65"
            intFee = intSINGLE_SENIOR
        Case "C65"
            intFee = intCOUPLE_SENIOR
        Case Else
            intFee = 0
    End Select

    ' display fee
    lblFee.Text = intFee.ToString("C0")
End Sub
```

enter this Select Case statement

Figure 10-9   btnDisplay control's Click event procedure

3. Save the solution and then start the application.

4. Type **f** as the code and then click the **Display Fee** button. The `strCode = txtCode.Text.ToUpper` statement in the button's Click event procedure assigns the uppercase letter F to the `strCode` variable. The Select Case statement is processed next. When processing the statement, the computer first compares the contents of the `strCode` variable (F) with the first Case clause's expressionList: `"S"`. F does not equal S, so the computer skips to the second Case clause, where it compares the contents of the `strCode` variable with that case's expressionList: `"F"`. F equals F, so the computer processes the `intFee = intFAMILY` assignment statement in the second Case clause. It then skips to the instruction following the End Select clause. The instruction displays the contents of the `intFee` variable (converted to Currency with zero decimal places) in the lblFee control; in this case, it displays $50.

5. On your own, test the application using the following codes: **S**, **s65**, **C65**, and **x**. The monthly fees should be $40, $30, $35, and $0, respectively.

6. Click the **Exit** button. Close the Code Editor window and then close the solution.

Specifying a Range of Values in a Case Clause's ExpressionList

You also can specify a range of values in a Case clause's expressionList, such as the values 1 through 5 or values greater than 10. You do this using either the keyword To or the keyword Is. You use the To keyword when you know both the upper and lower bounds of the range, and you use the Is keyword when you know only one end of the range (either the upper or lower end). The ABC Corporation's price chart can be used to illustrate this concept. The price chart is shown in Figure 10-10. Notice that the price of an item depends on the number of items ordered. For example, the price for 1 to 5 items is $25 each. Therefore, you could write the first Case clause in a Select Case statement as follows: `Case 1, 2, 3, 4, 5`. However, a more convenient way of writing that range of numbers is to use the keyword To, as shown in the example in Figure 10-10. To use the To keyword, you must follow this syntax: **Case** *smallest value in the range* **To** *largest value in the range*. The expression 1 To 5 in the first Case clause, for example, specifies the range of numbers from 1 to 5, inclusive. The expression 6 To 10 in the second Case clause specifies the range of numbers from 6 through 10. Notice that both Case clauses state both the lower (1 and 6) and upper (5 and 10) ends of each range.

The third Case clause in the example in Figure 10-10 contains the Is keyword rather than the To keyword. Recall that you use the Is keyword when you know only one end of the range of values—either the upper end or the lower end. In this case you know only the lower end of the range, 10. You always use the Is keyword in combination with one of the following comparison operators: =, <, <=, >, >=, <>. The `Case Is > 10` clause specifies all numbers greater than the number 10. Because `intQuantity` is an Integer variable, you also can write this Case clause as `Case Is >= 11`. The Case Else clause in the example is processed only when the `intQuantity` variable contains a value that is not included in any of the previous Case clauses—more specifically, a zero or a negative number.

ABC Corporation Price Chart

Quantity ordered	Price per item
1–5	$ 25
6–10	$ 23
More than 10	$ 20

Example
```
Select Case intQuantity
    Case 1 To 5
        intPrice = 25
    Case 6 To 10
        intPrice = 23
    Case Is > 10
        intPrice = 20
    Case Else
        intPrice = 0
End Select
```

Figure 10-10 Example of using the To and Is keywords in a Case clause

Coding the ABC Corporation Application

In this section, you will code the ABC Corporation application using ranges of values in a Select
Case statement.

To code and then test the ABC Corporation application:

1. Open the **ABC Solution** (**ABC Solution.sln**) file contained in the ClearlyVB2010\Chap10\
    ABC Solution folder. If the designer window is not open, double-click **frmMain.vb** in
    the Solution Explorer window. The application's interface is shown in Figure 10-11.

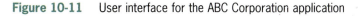

Figure 10-11   User interface for the ABC Corporation application

2. Open the Code Editor window. In the btnDisplayPrice control's Click event procedure,
    enter the Select Case statement shown in Figure 10-12.

```vb
Private Sub btnDisplayPrice_Click(ByVal sender As Object,
ByVal e As System.EventArgs) Handles btnDisplayPrice.Click
    ' displays the price per item

    Dim intQuantity As Integer
    Dim intPrice As Integer

    ' assign quantity ordered to a variable
    Integer.TryParse(txtQuantity.Text, intQuantity)

    ' determine the price per item and
    ' then display the price
    Select Case intQuantity
        Case 1 To 5
            intPrice = 25
        Case 6 To 10
            intPrice = 23
        Case Is > 10
            intPrice = 20
        Case Else
            intPrice = 0
    End Select
    lblPrice.Text = intPrice.ToString("C2")
End Sub
```
enter this Select
Case statement

Figure 10-12   btnDisplayPrice control's Click event procedure

3. Save the solution and then start the application.

For more examples of using the Select Case statement to code a multiple-alternative selection structure, see the Select Case Multiple-Alternative Selection Structure section in the Ch10Want-More.pdf file.

4. Type **4** in the Quantity ordered box and then click the **Display Price** button. The `Integer.TryParse(txtQuantity.Text, intQuantity)` statement in the button's Click event procedure assigns the number 4 to the `intQuantity` variable. The Select Case statement is processed next. When processing the statement, the computer first compares the contents of the `intQuantity` variable (4) with the first Case clause's expressionList: the range 1 To 5. The number 4 is included in that range, so the computer assigns the number 25 to the `intPrice` variable. It then skips to the instruction following the End Select clause. The instruction displays the contents of the `intPrice` variable (converted to Currency with two decimal places) in the lblPrice control; in this case, it displays $25.00.

5. On your own, test the application using the following numbers: **10**, **-3**, **12**, and **x**. The prices should be $23.00, $0.00, $20.00, and $0.00, respectively.

6. Click the **Exit** button. Close the Code Editor window and then close the solution.

Using Radio Buttons

The If/ElseIf/Else and Case forms of the selection structure are often used when coding interfaces that contain radio buttons. You create a radio button using the RadioButton tool in the toolbox. **Radio buttons** allow you to limit the user to only one choice from a group of two or more related but mutually exclusive choices. Figure 10-13 shows a sample run of the Gentry Supplies application, which uses radio buttons in its interface. Notice that each radio button is labeled so the user knows its purpose. You enter the label using sentence capitalization in the radio button's Text property. Each radio button also has a unique access key that allows the user to select the button using the keyboard. The three-character ID for a radio button's name is rad.

GroupBox1 control   GroupBox2 control

Gentry Supplies

State
- ○ Alabama
- ⦿ Georgia
- ○ Louisiana
- ○ North Carolina

Delivery
- ○ Standard
- ⦿ Overnight
- ○ Two-day

Shipping charge:

$45.00

[Display Shipping Charge] [Exit]

Figure 10-13   Sample run of the Gentry Supplies application

Two groups of radio buttons appear in the Gentry Supplies interface: one group contains the four state radio buttons and the other contains the three delivery radio buttons. To include two groups of radio buttons in an interface, at least one of the groups must be placed within a container control, such as a **group box**. Otherwise, the radio buttons are considered to be in the same group and only one can be selected at any one time. You create a group box using the GroupBox tool, which is located in the Containers section of the toolbox. In this case, the radio buttons pertaining to the state choice are contained in the GroupBox1 control, and the radio buttons pertaining to the delivery choice are contained in the GroupBox2 control. Placing each group of radio buttons in a separate group box allows the user to select one button from each group.

Keep in mind that the minimum number of radio buttons in a group is two, because the only way to deselect a radio button is to select another radio button. The recommended maximum number of radio buttons in a group is seven. It is customary in Windows applications to have one of the radio buttons in each group already selected when the user interface first appears. The selected button is called the **default radio button** and is either the radio button that represents the user's most likely choice or the first radio button in the group. You designate a radio button as the default radio button by setting the button's Checked property to the Boolean value True. When you set the Checked property to True in the Properties window, a colored dot appears inside the button's circle to indicate that the button is selected.

Coding the Gentry Supplies Application

In this section, you will code the Gentry Supplies application. When the user clicks the Display Shipping Charge button in the application's interface, the button's Click event procedure should display the appropriate shipping charge. The shipping charges are listed in Figure 10-14.

Gentry Supplies Shipping Chart

State	Standard delivery charge
Alabama	20
Georgia	35
Louisiana	30
North Carolina	28
Overnight delivery	add $10 to the standard delivery charge
Two-day delivery	add $5 to the standard delivery charge

Figure 10-14   Gentry Supplies shipping chart

To code and then test the Gentry Supplies application:

1. Open the **Gentry Supplies Solution** (**Gentry Supplies Solution.sln**) file contained in the ClearlyVB2010\Chap10\Gentry Supplies Solution folder. If the designer window is not open, double-click **frmMain.vb** in the Solution Explorer window.

2. Open the Code Editor window. In the btnDisplay control's Click event procedure, enter the two selection structures shown in Figure 10-15. Notice that the code uses the Checked property to determine the radio button selected in both groups of radio buttons.

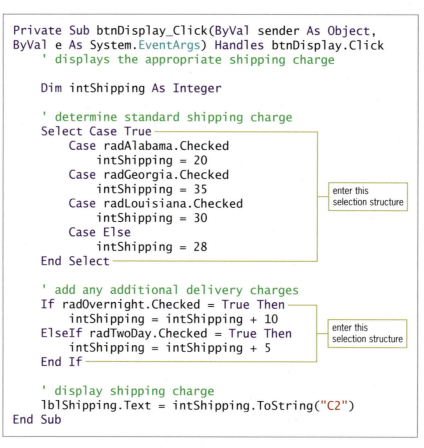

```
Private Sub btnDisplay_Click(ByVal sender As Object,
ByVal e As System.EventArgs) Handles btnDisplay.Click
    ' displays the appropriate shipping charge

    Dim intShipping As Integer

    ' determine standard shipping charge
    Select Case True
        Case radAlabama.Checked
            intShipping = 20
        Case radGeorgia.Checked
            intShipping = 35
        Case radLouisiana.Checked
            intShipping = 30
        Case Else
            intShipping = 28
    End Select

    ' add any additional delivery charges
    If radOvernight.Checked = True Then
        intShipping = intShipping + 10
    ElseIf radTwoDay.Checked = True Then
        intShipping = intShipping + 5
    End If

    ' display shipping charge
    lblShipping.Text = intShipping.ToString("C2")
End Sub
```

enter this selection structure

enter this selection structure

Figure 10-15 Selection structures entered in the procedure

To learn how to add a group box and radio button to a form, view the Ch10-Group Box and Radio Button video.

3. Save the solution and then start the application. Click the **Georgia** radio button and then click the **Overnight** radio button. Click the **Display Shipping Charge** button. The button's Click event procedure displays $45.00 in the Shipping charge box, as shown earlier in Figure 10-13.

4. On your own, display the shipping charge for a two-day delivery to Alabama, a standard delivery to North Carolina, an overnight delivery to North Carolina, and an overnight delivery to Louisiana. The shipping charges should be $25.00, $28.00, $38.00, and $40.00, respectively.

5. Click the **Exit** button. Close the Code Editor window and then close the solution.

Mini-Quiz 10-2

See Appendix B for the answers.

1. Rewrite Question 1 from Mini-Quiz 10-1 using the Select Case statement.

2. Rewrite Question 3 from Mini-Quiz 10-1 using the Select Case statement.

3. Which of the following Case clauses specifies integers from 10 through 20, inclusive?

   a. `Case Is 10 To 20`

   b. `Case Is >= 10 AndAlso <= 20`

   c. `Case 20 To 10`

   d. none of the above

4. A form contains three radio buttons: January, February, and March. The radio buttons are named radJanuary, radFebruary, and radMarch. Write a multiple-alternative selection structure that displays the name of the birthstone corresponding to the selected radio button. The birthstones for the three months are Garnet, Amethyst, and Aquamarine. Display the birthstone's name in the lblBirthstone control. Use the Select Case statement.

Summary

- The solutions to some problems require a multiple-alternative (or extended) selection structure.

- You can code a multiple-alternative selection structure using either the If … Then … Else statement or the Select Case statement.

- String comparisons in Visual Basic are case sensitive.

- Each character on the computer keyboard is associated with a unique Unicode value.

- Before using a string in a comparison, you can convert it (temporarily) to either uppercase or lowercase using the ToUpper or ToLower methods, respectively.

- The data type of the expressions in a Select Case statement must be compatible with the data type of the statement's selectorExpression.

- You can use the To or Is keywords to specify a range of values in a Select Case statement. You use the To keyword when you know both the upper and lower bounds of the range. You use the Is keyword when you know only one end of the range (either the upper or lower end).

- You can use radio buttons to limit the user to one choice from a group of two or more related but mutually exclusive choices.

- To include two groups of radio buttons in an interface, at least one of the groups must be placed within a container control, such as a group box.

- It is customary to have one radio button in each group of radio buttons selected when the user interface first appears.

- The Boolean value stored in a radio button's Checked property determines whether the radio button is selected (True) or unselected (False).

Key Terms

Default radio button—the radio button that is automatically selected when an interface first appears

Extended selection structures—another name for multiple-alternative selection structures

Group box—a control that is used to contain other controls; created using the GroupBox tool, which is located in the Containers section of the toolbox

If/ElseIf/Else—a form of the If … Then … Else statement; provides a convenient way of coding a multiple-alternative selection structure

Multiple-alternative selection structures—selection structures that contain several alternatives; also called extended selection structures

Radio buttons—used in an interface to limit the user to only one choice from a group of two or more related but mutually exclusive choices

Select Case statement—like the If...Then..Else statement, this statement can be used to code a multiple-alternative selection structure

String data type—the data type used for memory locations that store alphanumeric text

ToLower method—temporarily converts a string to lowercase

ToUpper method—temporarily converts a string to uppercase

Review Questions

1. Which of the following calculates a 5% discount when the units sold are from 1 through 100, a 7% discount when the units sold are from 101 through 200, and a 10% discount when the units sold are over 200? If the number of units sold is less than or equal to 0, the discount should be 0. The number of units sold is stored in the `intUnits` variable. Each unit costs $100.

   a.
   ```
   intTotal = intUnits * 100
   If intUnits <= 0 Then
         decDiscount = 0
   ElseIf intUnits < 101 Then
         decDiscount = intTotal * .05
   ElseIf intUnits < 201 Then
         decDiscount = intTotal * .07
   Else
         decDiscount = intTotal * .1
   End If
   ```

   b.
   ```
   intTotal = intUnits * 100
   Select Case intUnits
      Case 1 To 100
         decDiscount = intTotal * .05
      Case 101 To 200
         decDiscount = intTotal * .07
      Case > 200
         decDiscount = intTotal * .1
      Case Else
         decDiscount = 0
   End Case
   ```

   c.
   ```
   intTotal = intUnits * 100
   Select Case intUnits
      Case < 1
         decDiscount = 0
      Case 1 To 100
         decDiscount = intTotal * .05
      Case 101 To 200
         decDiscount = intTotal * .07
      Case Else
         decDiscount = intTotal * .1
   End Case
   ```

   d. all of the above

2. Which of the following assigns the contents of the txtState control, in uppercase, to the strState variable?

   a. `If strState = txtState.Text.ToUpper Then`

   b. `strState.ToUpper = txtState.Text`

   c. `strState = txtState.Text.ToUpper`

   d. all of the above

3. Which of the following Case clauses will be processed when the intNum variable contains one of the following integers: 5, 6, 7, 8, or 9?

   a. `Case >= 5 AndAlso <= 9`   c. `Case 9 To 5`

   b. `Case 5 To 9`   d. all of the above

4. Which of the following determines whether the radAddition radio button is selected?

   a. `If radAddition.Checked = True Then`

   b. `If radAddition.Checked = Yes Then`

   c. `If radAddition.Selected = On`

   d. `If radAddition.Selected = True`

5. What is the minimum number of radio buttons in a group?

   a. one   c. three

   b. two   d. there is no minimum

6. Which of the following data types is appropriate for a variable that will store alphanumeric text?

   a. Alpha   c. String

   b. AlphaNum   d. Text

7. The Case Other clause must be the last clause in a Select Case statement.

   a. True   b. False

Exercises

1. Open the Department Solution (Department Solution.sln) file contained in the ClearlyVB2010\Chap10\Department Solution folder. Replace the selection structure in the btnDisplay control's Click event procedure with a Select Case statement. Save the solution and then start and test the application. Close the Code Editor window and then close the solution. (See Appendix B for the answer.)

TRY THIS

2. Open the Total Due Solution (Total Due Solution.sln) file contained in the ClearlyVB2010\Chap10\Total Due Solution folder. Change the outer If...Then...Else statement in the btnCalc control's Click event procedure to a Select Case statement. Save the solution and then start and test the application. Close the Code Editor window and then close the solution. (See Appendix B for the answer.)

TRY THIS

3. In this exercise, you modify one of the Fitness For Good applications coded in the chapter. Use Windows to make a copy of the Fitness Solution-Select Case folder. Save the copy in the ClearlyVB2010\Chap10 folder. Rename the copy Modified Fitness Solution-Select Case. Open the Fitness Solution (Fitness Solution.sln) file contained in the Modified Fitness Solution-Select Case folder. The health club has added an additional membership type. The monthly fee for the new Child membership type is $5. Make the appropriate modifications to both the interface and the code. Save the

MODIFY THIS

solution and then start and test the application. Close the Code Editor window and then close the solution.

4. The owner of Harry's Car Sales pays each salesperson a commission based on his or her monthly sales. The sales ranges and corresponding commission rates are shown in Figure 10-16.

Monthly sales ($)	Commission rate
0–19,999.99	4%
20,000–29,999.99	5%
30,000–39,999.99	6%
40,000–49,999.99	7%
50,000 or more	9%
Less than 0	0%

Figure 10-16 Sales and commission rate information for Exercise 4

a. Open the Harry Car Solution (Harry Car Solution.sln) file contained in the ClearlyVB2010\Chap10\Harry Car Solution folder. Code the btnCalc control's Click event procedure so that it both calculates and displays a salesperson's commission. Use the If/ElseIf/Else form of the If...Then...Else statement. Save the solution and then start and test the application. Close the Code Editor window and then close the solution.

b. Use Windows to make a copy of the Harry Car Solution folder. Save the copy in the ClearlyVB2010\Chap10 folder. Rename the copy Modified Harry Car Solution. Open the Harry Car Solution (Harry Car Solution.sln) file contained in the Modified Harry Car Solution folder. Change the selection structure in the btnCalc control's Click event procedure to a Select Case statement. Save the solution and then start and test the application. Close the Code Editor window and then close the solution.

5. The owner of Concerts For All wants an application that displays the price of a concert ticket. The ticket price is based on the seat location. Box seats are $75, pavilion seats are $30, and lawn seats are $21. However, the owner sometimes offers a 10% discount on the ticket price. Use radio buttons for the seat locations, and use a check box for the 10% discount.

a. List the output and input items, as well as any processing items, and then create an appropriate algorithm using a flowchart.

b. Create a Visual Basic Windows application. Use the following names for the solution and project, respectively: Concerts Solution and Concerts Project. Save the application in the ClearlyVB2010\Chap10 folder. Change the name of the form file on your disk to frmMain.vb. If necessary, change the form's name to frmMain.

c. Create a suitable interface. Include an Exit button. Code the Exit button's Click event procedure and the problem's algorithm.

d. Save the solution and then start and test the application. Close the Code Editor window and then close the solution.

6. Create a Visual Basic Windows application. Use the following names for the solution and project, respectively: Songs Solution and Songs Project. Save the application in the ClearlyVB2010\Chap10 folder. Change the name of the form file on your disk to frmMain.vb. If necessary, change the form's name to frmMain. Create the interface shown in Figure 10-17. The four radio buttons contain song titles. The Artist Name

button's Click event procedure should display the name of the artist associated with the selected radio button. The names of the artists are Andrea Bocelli, Michael Jackson, Beyonce, and Josh Groban. Code the application. Save the solution and then start and test the application. Close the Code Editor window and then close the solution.

Figure 10-17   User interface for Exercise 6

INTERMEDIATE

7. Create a Visual Basic Windows application. Use the following names for the solution and project, respectively: Currency Solution and Currency Project. Save the application in the ClearlyVB2010\Chap10 folder. Change the name of the form file on your disk to frmMain.vb. If necessary, change the form's name to frmMain. The application's interface should provide a text box for the user to enter the number of U.S. dollars, and radio buttons for the seven currencies listed in Figure 10-18. The application should convert the U.S. dollars to the selected currency and then display the result (formatted to three decimal places). Use the exchange rates included in Figure 10-18. Save the solution and then start and test the application. Close the Code Editor window and then

Currency	Exchange rate
Canada Dollar	1.01615
Eurozone Euro	.638490
India Rupee	40.1798
Japan Yen	104.390
Mexico Peso	10.4613
South Africa Rand	7.60310
United Kingdom Pound	.504285

Figure 10-18   Currency and exchange rates for Exercise 7

close the solution.

INTERMEDIATE

8. Open the Bonus Solution (Bonus Solution.sln) file contained in the ClearlyVB2010\ Chap10\Bonus Solution folder. Figure 10-19 shows the flowchart for the btnCalc control's Click event procedure, which should display either a bonus amount or an error message. Format the bonus amount with a dollar sign and two decimal places. Code the procedure. Save the solution and then start and test the application. Close the Code Editor window and then close the solution.

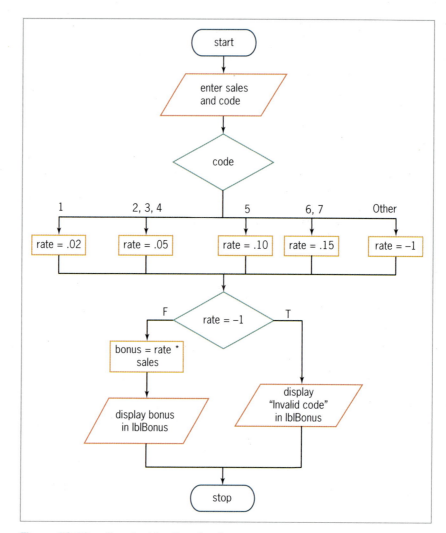

Figure 10-19   Flowchart for Exercise 8

INTERMEDIATE   9.   Create a Visual Basic Windows application. Use the following names for the solution and project, respectively: State Capital Solution and State Capital Project. Save the application in the ClearlyVB2010\Chap10 folder. Change the name of the form file on your disk to frmMain.vb. If necessary, change the form's name to frmMain. Create the interface shown in Figure 10-20. If the selected capital corresponds to the selected state, the Am I Right? button's Click event should display the message "Correct" in the Result box; otherwise, it should display the message "Try again". Code the application. Save the solution and then start and test the application. Close the Code Editor window and then close the solution.

Figure 10-20   User interface for Exercise 9

10. In this exercise, you create an application for Willow Health Club. The application
displays the number of daily calories needed to maintain a member's current weight.
The formulas for calculating the number of daily calories are shown in Figure 10-21.

Gender	Activity level	Total daily calories formula
Female	Moderately active	weight * 12 calories per pound
Female	Relatively inactive	weight * 10 calories per pound
Male	Moderately active	weight * 15 calories per pound
Male	Relatively inactive	weight * 13 calories per pound

Figure 10-21   Formulas for Exercise 10

a. List the output and input items, as well as any processing items, and then create an
appropriate algorithm using pseudocode.

b. Create a Visual Basic Windows application. Use the following names for the solution
and project, respectively: Willow Solution and Willow Project. Save the application
in the ClearlyVB2010\Chap10 folder. Change the name of the form file on your disk
to frmMain.vb. If necessary, change the form's name to frmMain.

c. Create a suitable interface. Include an Exit button. Code the Exit button's Click event
procedure and the problem's algorithm.

d. Save the solution and then start and test the application. Close the Code Editor
window and then close the solution.

11. Shopper Stoppers wants an application that displays the number of reward points a
customer earns each month. The reward points are based on the customer's
membership type and total monthly purchase amount, as shown in Figure 10-22.

Membership type	Total monthly purchase ($)	Reward points
Basic	Less than 100	5% of the total monthly purchase
	100 and over	7% of the total monthly purchase
Standard	Less than 150	6% of the total monthly purchase
	150–299.99	8% of the total monthly purchase
	300 and over	10% of the total monthly purchase
Premium	Less than 200	7% of the total monthly purchase
	200 and over	15% of the total monthly purchase

Figure 10-22 Reward points for Exercise 11

a. List the output and input items, as well as any processing items, and then create an appropriate algorithm using pseudocode.

b. Create a Visual Basic Windows application. Use the following names for the solution and project, respectively: Shopper Solution and Shopper Project. Save the application in the ClearlyVB2010\Chap10 folder. Change the name of the form file on your disk to frmMain.vb. If necessary, change the form's name to frmMain.

c. Create a suitable interface. Include an Exit button. Code the Exit button's Click event procedure and the problem's algorithm. Display the reward points as whole numbers.

d. Save the solution and then start and test the application. Close the Code Editor window and then close the solution.

FIGURE THIS OUT ▶ 12. Open the FigureThisOut Solution (FigureThisOut Solution.sln) file contained in the ClearlyVB2010\Chap10\FigureThisOut Solution folder. Open the Code Editor window and study the btnDisplay control's Click event procedure. What task is performed by the procedure? What are the rules for charging the various rates? Test the application to verify that your answers are correct. Close the Code Editor window and then close the solution.

SWAT THE BUGS ▶ 13. Open the SwatTheBugs Solution (SwatTheBugs Solution.sln) file contained in the ClearlyVB2010\Chap10\SwatTheBugs Solution folder. The application should display a shipping charge that is based on the total price entered by the user. If the total price is less than $1, the shipping charge is $0. If the total price is greater than or equal to $1 but less than $100, the shipping charge is $5. If the total price is greater than or equal to $100 but less than $501, the shipping charge is $10. If the total price is greater than or equal to $501 but less than $1001, the shipping charge is $12. If the total price is greater than or equal to $1001, the shipping charge is $14. Start the application. Test the application using the following total prices: 100, 501, 1500, 500.75, 30, and 1000.33. You will notice that the application does not display the correct shipping charge for some of these total prices. Open the Code Editor window and study the code. Locate and correct the errors in the code. Close the Code Editor window and then close the solution.

CHAPTER 11

Testing, Testing . . . 1, 2, 3 (Selecting Test Data)

After studying Chapter 11, you should be able to:

- ◎ Select appropriate test data for an application
- ◎ Prevent the entry of unwanted characters in a text box
- ◎ Create a message box with the MessageBox.Show method
- ◎ Trim leading and trailing spaces from a string

Will Your Application Pass the Test?

As you learned in Chapter 2, the last step in the problem-solving process is to rigorously test the program before releasing it to the user. You test the program using a computer along with a set of sample data that includes both valid and invalid data. Valid data is data that the program is expecting the user to enter. You test with valid data to ensure that the program produces the correct results. Invalid data, on the other hand, is data that the program is not expecting the user to enter. Invalid data typically is the result of the user making a typing error, entering the data in an incorrect format, or neglecting to make a required entry. You test with invalid data to ensure that the program does not display erroneous results or end abruptly because of an input error. Figure 11-1 lists some guidelines for selecting appropriate test data for an application. (Additional guidelines will be added to the list in subsequent chapters.) You will use these guidelines to test several applications in this chapter. As you will notice when working through this chapter, testing is an iterative process.

Testing guidelines

1. Test the application without entering any data.
2. If the application's code expects a text box to contain a number, use both valid and invalid values for the text box. Typically, the test data should include the number 0, positive and negative integers, positive and negative non-integers, and alphanumeric text.
3. If the application's code contains a selection structure, use values that will test each path. If a condition contains a range of values, the test data should include the lowest and highest values in the range, as well as a value within the range. If a condition compares strings, include uppercase text and lowercase text in the test data.

Figure 11-1 Guidelines for selecting an application's test data

The Only Cookies-Version 1 Application

Figure 11-2 shows the interface for the Only Cookies-Version 1 application. The interface provides a text box for entering the number of pounds of cookies ordered; the number of pounds may contain a decimal place. Each pound of cookies costs $5. When the user clicks the Calculate button, the button's Click event procedure calculates and displays the total price of the order. The Click event procedure is shown in Figure 11-3. Notice that the procedure uses an Integer named constant for the pound price, and two Decimal variables for the pounds ordered and the total price.

txtOrdered control (may contain a number with a decimal place)

Figure 11-2 Interface for the Only Cookies-Version 1 application

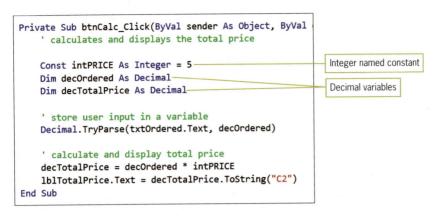

```
Private Sub btnCalc_Click(ByVal sender As Object, ByVal
    ' calculates and displays the total price

    Const intPRICE As Integer = 5
    Dim decOrdered As Decimal
    Dim decTotalPrice As Decimal

    ' store user input in a variable
    Decimal.TryParse(txtOrdered.Text, decOrdered)

    ' calculate and display total price
    decTotalPrice = decOrdered * intPRICE
    lblTotalPrice.Text = decTotalPrice.ToString("C2")
End Sub
```

Integer named constant

Decimal variables

Figure 11-3   Calculate button's Click event procedure in the Only Cookies-Version 1 application

Before testing the application, you will use the guidelines from Figure 11-1, as well as the interface and code shown in Figures 11-2 and 11-3, to create a set of test data. You will record the test data and the expected results in a testing chart. The first guideline is to test the application without entering any data. As the interface and code indicate, only one item of data is entered by the user in this application: the number of pounds of cookies ordered. If the user clicks the Calculate button without entering a value in the Pounds ordered box, the procedure should display $0.00 in the Total price box. (The "C2" in the last assignment statement formats the total price with a dollar sign and two decimal places.) In the testing chart, you record *No data entered* and *$0.00*, as shown in Figure 11-4.

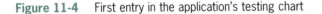

Test data	Expected result
No data entered	$0.00

Figure 11-4   First entry in the application's testing chart

According to the second guideline in Figure 11-1, you should test the application by entering both valid and invalid values in the Pounds ordered text box. As the guideline indicates, typical values used for testing include the number 0, positive and negative integers and non-integers, and alphanumeric text. Begin by making a list of valid values that the user might enter as the number of pounds ordered. For example, the user might enter the number 0, the positive integers 10 and 25, or the positive non-integer 4.5. The expected results are $0.00, $50.00, $125.00, and $22.50, respectively. (Recall that the price per pound is $5.) If the user wants to calculate a refund, he or she also might enter a negative number, such as the negative integer −3 or the negative non-integer −6.5. The expected results using these values are ($15.00) and ($32.50), respectively. You record the test data and the expected results in the testing chart, as shown in Figure 11-5.

Test data	Expected result
No data entered	$0.00
Valid values	
0	$0.00
10	$50.00
25	$125.00
4.5	$22.50
-3	($15.00)
-6.5	($32.50)

Figure 11-5 Valid values entered in the application's testing chart

Now consider values that the user might enter by mistake. In the current application, the user might inadvertently enter the letter x, the # symbol, or 3O (the number 3 followed by the uppercase letter O). If the user enters an invalid value, the application should display $0.00 in the Total price box. Figure 11-6 shows the invalid values and their expected results entered in the testing chart. Notice that the test data contains the number 0, positive and negative integers and non-integers, and alphanumeric text.

Test data	Expected result
No data entered	$0.00
Valid values	
0	$0.00
10	$50.00
25	$125.00
4.5	$22.50
-3	($15.00)
-6.5	($32.50)
Invalid values	
x, #, 3O	$0.00

Figure 11-6 Testing chart for the Only Cookies-Version 1 application

The third guideline in Figure 11-1 pertains to selection structures. You can skip the third guideline because the application's code does not contain a selection structure. In the following set of steps, you will test the application using the test data and expected results listed in Figure 11-6.

To test the Only Cookies-Version 1 application:

1. Start Visual Studio 2010 or Visual Basic 2010 Express and permanently display the Solution Explorer window. Open the **Only Cookies Solution (Only Cookies Solution.sln)** file contained in the ClearlyVB2010\Chap11\Only Cookies Solution-Version 1 folder. If the designer window is not open, double-click **frmMain.vb** in the Solution Explorer window.

2. Start the application. First, you will test the application without entering any data. Click the **Calculate** button. The Total price box shows the expected result, $0.00.

3. Type **0** in the Pounds ordered box and then click the **Calculate** button. Here again, the Total price box shows the expected result, $0.00.

4. Change the number of pounds ordered to **10** and then click the **Calculate** button. $50.00 appears in the Total price box, which is correct.

5. On your own, test the application using the following valid values: **25, 4.5, −3,** and **−6.5**. The total prices should agree with the corresponding results listed in Figure 11-6.

6. Change the number of pounds ordered to **x** and then click the **Calculate** button. The TryParse method in the button's Click event procedure cannot convert the letter x to the Decimal data type, so it assigns the number 0 to the decOrdered variable. The next statement in the procedure calculates the total price and assigns the result (0) to the decTotalPrice variable. The last assignment statement in the procedure formats the total price with a dollar sign and two decimal places, and then displays the expected result—$0.00—in the Total price box.

7. On your own, test the application using the following two invalid values: # and **3O** (be sure to type the uppercase letter O rather than the number 0). The results should agree with the ones listed in Figure 11-6.

8. Click the **Exit** button. Close the Code Editor window and then close the solution.

The Only Cookies-Version 2 Application

Figure 11-7 shows the interface for the Only Cookies-Version 2 application. Except for the title bar text, the interface is identical to the one in the Only Cookies-Version 1 application. However, in this version of the application, the number of pounds entered in the Pounds ordered text box must be an integer. Each pound of cookies still costs $5. Figure 11-8 shows the Calculate button's Click event procedure, which calculates and displays the total price of the order. Notice that in this version of the application, the Click event procedure uses Integer variables (rather than Decimal variables) for the pounds ordered and total price.

Figure 11-7 Interface for the Only Cookies-Version 2 application

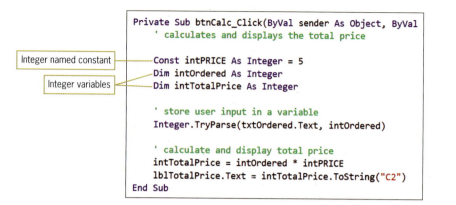

```
Private Sub btnCalc_Click(ByVal sender As Object, ByVal
    ' calculates and displays the total price

    Const intPRICE As Integer = 5
    Dim intOrdered As Integer
    Dim intTotalPrice As Integer

    ' store user input in a variable
    Integer.TryParse(txtOrdered.Text, intOrdered)

    ' calculate and display total price
    intTotalPrice = intOrdered * intPRICE
    lblTotalPrice.Text = intTotalPrice.ToString("C2")
End Sub
```

Integer named constant

Integer variables

Figure 11-8 Calculate button's Click event procedure in the Only Cookies-Version 2 application

Figure 11-9 shows the testing chart for the Only Cookies-Version 2 application. Comparing this testing chart with the one shown earlier in Figure 11-6, you will notice that the two non-integer values (4.5 and −6.5) now appear in the Invalid values section. This is because the Only Cookies-Version 2 application expects the user to enter an integer in the Pounds ordered text box.

Test data	Expected result
No data entered	$0.00
Valid values	
0	$0.00
10	$50.00
25	$125.00
−3	($15.00)
Invalid values	
X, #, 3O	$0.00
4.5	$0.00
−6.5	$0.00

Figure 11-9 Testing chart for the Only Cookies-Version 2 application

To test the Only Cookies-Version 2 application:

1. Open the **Only Cookies Solution (Only Cookies Solution.sln)** file contained in the ClearlyVB2010\Chap11\Only Cookies Solution-Version 2 folder. If the designer window is not open, double-click **frmMain.vb** in the Solution Explorer window.

2. Start the application. First, you will test the application without entering any data. Click the **Calculate** button. The Total price box shows the expected result, $0.00.

3. On your own, test the application using the following values: **0, 10, 25, −3, x, #,** and **3O** (be sure to type the uppercase letter O rather than the number 0). The total prices should agree with the corresponding results listed in Figure 11-9.

4. Change the number of pounds ordered to **4.5** and then click the **Calculate** button. The TryParse method in the button's Click event procedure cannot convert the non-integer 4.5 to the Integer data type, so it assigns the number 0 to the `intOrdered` variable. When the `intOrdered` variable contains the number 0, the total price will be 0. Because of this, the procedure displays $0.00 in the Total price box. See Figure 11-10. Although the total price agrees with the expected result, it is very misleading because it indicates that the cookies are free of charge. You will learn one way to fix this problem in the next section.

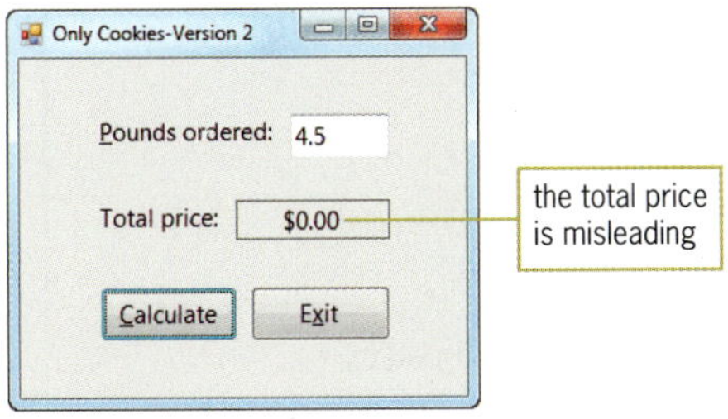

Figure 11-10 Result of entering a non-integer in the text box

5. Change the number of pounds ordered to **−6.5** and then click the **Calculate** button. $0.00 appears in the Total price box. Here again, the total price is misleading. Click the **Exit** button.

Stop! This Is a Restricted Area!

The Only Cookies-Version 2 application expects the user to enter the number of pounds as an integer. The number of pounds should not contain any letters, periods, or special characters. Unfortunately, you can't stop the user from trying to enter an inappropriate character into a text box. However, you can prevent the text box from accepting the character; you do this by coding the text box's KeyPress event procedure. A control's **KeyPress event** occurs each time the user presses a key while the control has the focus. When the KeyPress event occurs, a character corresponding to the pressed key is sent to the KeyPress event's e parameter, which appears between the parentheses in the event's procedure header. For example, when the user presses the period while entering data into a text box, the text box's KeyPress event occurs and a period is sent to the event's e parameter. Similarly, when the Shift key along with a letter is pressed, the uppercase version of the letter is sent to the e parameter.

To prevent a text box from accepting an inappropriate character, you first use the e parameter's **KeyChar property** to determine the pressed key. (KeyChar stands for "key character.") You then use the e parameter's **Handled property** to cancel the pressed key if it is an inappropriate one. Figure 11-11 shows examples of using the KeyChar and Handled properties in the KeyPress event procedure. Notice that you refer to the Backspace key on a computer keyboard using the **ControlChars.Back constant**. The Backspace key is necessary for editing the text box entry.

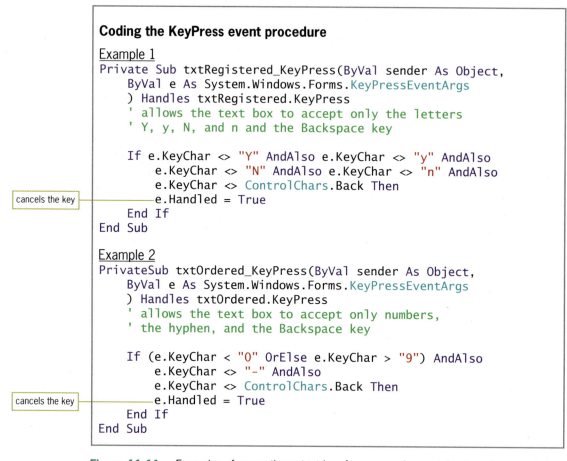

Coding the KeyPress event procedure

<u>Example 1</u>
```
Private Sub txtRegistered_KeyPress(ByVal sender As Object,
    ByVal e As System.Windows.Forms.KeyPressEventArgs
    ) Handles txtRegistered.KeyPress
    ' allows the text box to accept only the letters
    ' Y, y, N, and n and the Backspace key

    If e.KeyChar <> "Y" AndAlso e.KeyChar <> "y" AndAlso
        e.KeyChar <> "N" AndAlso e.KeyChar <> "n" AndAlso
        e.KeyChar <> ControlChars.Back Then
        e.Handled = True
    End If
End Sub
```

cancels the key →

<u>Example 2</u>
```
PrivateSub txtOrdered_KeyPress(ByVal sender As Object,
    ByVal e As System.Windows.Forms.KeyPressEventArgs
    ) Handles txtOrdered.KeyPress
    ' allows the text box to accept only numbers,
    ' the hyphen, and the Backspace key

    If (e.KeyChar < "0" OrElse e.KeyChar > "9") AndAlso
        e.KeyChar <> "-" AndAlso
        e.KeyChar <> ControlChars.Back Then
        e.Handled = True
    End If
End Sub
```

cancels the key →

Figure 11-11   Examples of preventing a text box from accepting certain characters

In the next set of steps, you will modify the Only Cookies-Version 2 application by entering code in the txtOrdered control's KeyPress event procedure. The code will prevent the text box from accepting any character other than a number, the hyphen, and the Backspace key. Whenever you make a change to an application's code, you should retest the application using the test data listed in the testing chart. Figure 11-12 shows the testing chart for the modified Only Cookies-Version 2 application.

Test data	Expected result
No data entered	$0.00
Valid values	
0	$0.00
10	$50.00
25	$125.00
-3	($15.00)
Invalid values	
x, #, 30, 4.5, -6.5	not allowed in the text box

Figure 11-12   Testing chart for the modified Only Cookies-Version 2 application

To modify and then test the Only Cookies-Version 2 application:

1. Open the Code Editor window and then open the code template for the txtOrdered control's KeyPress event procedure. Enter the comments and five lines of code shown in Example 2 in Figure 11-11.

2. Save the solution and then start the application. On your own, test the application without entering any data, and then test it using the following values: **0**, **10**, **25**, and **–3**.

3. Now test the application using the following values: **x**, **#**, **3O** (be sure to type the uppercase letter O rather than the number 0), **4.5**, and **–6.5**. You will not be able to enter the letter x, the # symbol, the uppercase letter O, or the period.

4. Click the **Exit** button. Close the Code Editor window and then close the solution.

For more examples of applications that require numeric data, see the Numeric Data Testing section in the Ch11WantMore.pdf file.

Mini-Quiz 11-1

See Appendix B for the answers

1. What is the first guideline for selecting test data?

2. If the txtSales control contains the number 345.78, what number will the `Integer.TryParse(txtSales.Text, intSales)` statement assign to the `intSales` variable?

3. When the user types the number 9 in a text box, the 9 is sent to the KeyPress event's _____ parameter.

The Shady Hollow Hotel-Version 1 Application

Figure 11-13 shows the interface for the Shady Hollow Hotel-Version 1 application, which displays the daily rate for a room at the hotel. The interface uses radio buttons for the room type selection: Standard, Deluxe, or Suite. The daily rate for a Standard room is $90. The daily rate for a Deluxe room is $115, and the daily rate for a Suite is $130. Figure 11-14 shows the code entered in the Display Rate button's Click event procedure.

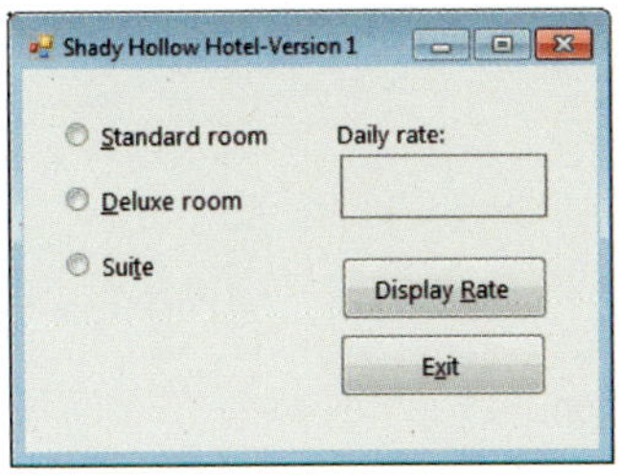

Figure 11-13   Interface for the Shady Hollow Hotel-Version 1 application

```
Private Sub btnDisplay_Click(ByVal sender As Objec
    ' displays a room's daily rate

    Dim intDailyRate As Integer

    Select Case True
        Case radStandard.Checked
            intDailyRate = 90
        Case radDeluxe.Checked
            intDailyRate = 115
        Case Else
            intDailyRate = 130
    End Select

    ' display daily rate
    lblDaily.Text = intDailyRate.ToString("C0")
End Sub
```

you need to test each path in this selection structure

Figure 11-14   Display Rate button's Click event procedure in the Shady Hollow Hotel-Version 1 application

Before testing the Shady Hollow Hotel-Version 1 application, you will use the guidelines, interface, and code from Figures 11-1, 11-13, and 11-14, respectively, to create a set of test data. The first guideline is to test the application without entering any data. If no radio buttons are selected, the Daily rate box should show $0. The second guideline pertains to numbers entered in a text box; you can skip this guideline because the application does not use any text boxes. The third guideline covers selection structures. The application's code contains one selection structure, which is located in the Display Rate button's Click event procedure. According to the third guideline, you need to test each path in the selection structure. The first path's condition (radStandard.Checked) will evaluate to True when the Standard room radio button is selected. When this condition evaluates to True, $90 should appear in the Daily rate box. The second path's condition (radDeluxe.Checked) will evaluate to True when the Deluxe room radio button is selected; when this condition is True, $115 should appear in the Daily rate box. The third path, which is the Case Else path, is processed when the conditions in the other two paths evaluate to False. When the Case Else path is processed, $130 should appear in the Daily rate box. Figure 11-15 shows the application's testing chart.

Test data	Expected result
No data entered	$0
Standard room radio button selected	$90
Deluxe room radio button selected	$115
Suite radio button selected	$130

Figure 11-15   Testing chart for the Shady Hollow Hotel-Version 1 application

To test the Shady Hollow Hotel-Version 1 application:

1. Open the **Shady Hollow Solution (Shady Hollow Solution.sln)** file contained in the ClearlyVB2010\Chap11\Shady Hollow Solution-Version 1 folder. If the designer window is not open, double-click **frmMain.vb** in the Solution Explorer window.

2. Start the application. First, you will test the application without entering any data. Click the **Display Rate** button. The Daily rate box shows $130, which is the daily rate for a Suite. The $130 rate is not correct, because the Suite radio button is not selected in the interface. Click the **Exit** button.

3. Open the Code Editor window. Locate the btnDisplay control's Click event procedure. Notice that the Suite rate is assigned in the Case Else clause, which is processed when the Standard room and Deluxe room radio buttons are not selected. In other words, it's processed when the Suite radio button is selected (which is correct) and also when no radio button is selected (which is incorrect). You can fix the problem by changing the Case Else clause to `Case radSuite.Checked`; doing this tells the computer to display $130 only when the Suite radio button is selected. Another way to fix the problem is by designating one of the radio buttons as the default radio button. As you learned in Chapter 10, designating a default radio button ensures that a radio button is automatically selected when the interface first appears.

4. Close the Code Editor window. Click the **Standard room** radio button and then set its Checked property to **True**. This makes the Standard room radio button the default radio button.

5. Save the solution and then start the application. Click the **Display Rate** button. The Daily rate box shows $90, which is the correct Standard room rate.

6. Click the **Deluxe room** radio button and then click the **Display Rate** button. The Daily rate box shows $115, which is correct.

7. Click the **Suite** radio button and then click the **Display Rate** button. The Daily rate box shows the correct rate, $130.

8. Click the **Standard room** radio button and then click the **Display Rate** button. The correct rate appears in the Daily rate box.

9. Click the **Exit** button. Close the solution.

Figure 11-16 shows the modified testing chart for the Shady Hollow Hotel-Version 1 application.

Test data	Expected result
No data entered	$90 (Standard room is the default radio button)
Standard room radio button selected	$90
Deluxe room radio button selected	$115
Suite radio button selected	$130

Figure 11-16   Modified testing chart for the Shady Hollow Hotel-Version 1 application

The Shady Hollow Hotel-Version 2 Application

The Shady Hollow Hotel is being renovated and now offers only two types of rooms: Standard and Deluxe. The daily rate for a Standard room is $90; the daily rate for a Deluxe room is $115. Figure 11-17 shows the interface for the Shady Hollow Hotel-Version 2 application. The interface uses a text box for the room type selection—either S for Standard or D for Deluxe. When the user clicks the Display Rate button, its Click event procedure displays the daily rate in the Daily rate box. The Click event procedure is shown in Figure 11-18.

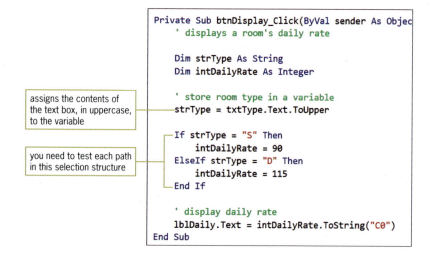

Figure 11-17 Interface for the Shady Hollow Hotel-Version 2 application

```
Private Sub btnDisplay_Click(ByVal sender As Objec
    ' displays a room's daily rate

    Dim strType As String
    Dim intDailyRate As Integer

    ' store room type in a variable
    strType = txtType.Text.ToUpper

    If strType = "S" Then
        intDailyRate = 90
    ElseIf strType = "D" Then
        intDailyRate = 115
    End If

    ' display daily rate
    lblDaily.Text = intDailyRate.ToString("C0")
End Sub
```

assigns the contents of the text box, in uppercase, to the variable → (points to `strType = txtType.Text.ToUpper`)

you need to test each path in this selection structure → (points to the If...ElseIf...End If structure)

Figure 11-18 Display Rate button's Click event procedure in the Shady Hollow Hotel-Version 2 application

Before testing the Shady Hollow Hotel-Version 2 application, you will create a set of test data. Recall that the first guideline in Figure 11-1 is to test the application without entering any data. This application requires the user to enter only one item of data: the room type. If the user clicks the Display Rate button without entering the room type, the procedure should display $0 in the Daily rate box. The second guideline in Figure 11-1 pertains to numbers entered in a text box. In this application, the user will be entering a string (rather than a number) in the txtType control; therefore, you can skip the second guideline. The third guideline covers selection structures. The only selection structure in the application's code is located in the Display Rate button's Click event procedure. According to the third guideline, you need to test each path in the selection structure. If a path's condition compares strings, you should include uppercase and lowercase text in the test data. Begin by making a list of valid values that the user might enter as the room type. In this case, the user might enter any of the following letters: S, s, D, or d; the expected results are $90, $90, $115, and $115, respectively. Now consider values that the user might enter by mistake. In the current application, the user might inadvertently enter the letter a, the $, or even the number 9. If the user enters an invalid value, the application should display $0 in the Daily rate box. Figure 11-19 shows the application's testing chart.

Test data	Expected result
No data entered	$0
valid values	
S, s	$90
D, d	$115
Invalid values	
a, $, 9	$0

Figure 11-19   Testing chart for the Shady Hollow Hotel-Version 2 application

To test the Shady Hollow Hotel-Version 2 application:

1. Open the **Shady Hollow Solution (Shady Hollow Solution.sln)** file contained in the ClearlyVB2010\Chap11\Shady Hollow Solution-Version 2 folder. If the designer window is not open, double-click **frmMain.vb** in the Solution Explorer window.

2. Start the application. First, you will test the application without entering any data. Click the **Display Rate** button. The expected result, $0, appears in the Daily rate box.

3. On your own, test the application using the following values: **S**, **a**, **D**, **$**, **s**, **d**, and **9**. The results should be $90, $0, $115, $0, $90, $115, and $0, respectively.

4. Click the **Exit** button.

I Need to Tell You Something

As you observed in the previous set of steps, $0 appears in the Daily rate box when the room type is either missing or invalid. In situations such as this, many programmers also display a message alerting the user of the input error. You can display the message either in a label control in the interface or in a message box; most programmers use a message box. You create a message box using the **MessageBox.Show method**. The basic syntax of the method is shown in Figure 11-20 along with an example of using the method. You enter the message in the method's *message* argument. Typically, the message is entered using sentence capitalization. The text in the *titleBarText* argument appears in the form's title bar. In most cases, the *titleBarText* is the name of the application and is entered using book title capitalization. The `MessageBoxButtons.OK` and `MessageBoxIcon.Information` arguments display an OK button and an Information icon in the message box, as shown in Figure 11-21. The user closes the message box by clicking the OK button.

```
MessageBox.Show method

Basic syntax
MessageBox.Show(message, titleBarText,
        MessageBoxButtons.OK,
        MessageBoxIcon.Information)

Example
MessageBox.Show("The message appears here",
        "The titleBarText appears here",
        MessageBoxButtons.OK,
        MessageBoxIcon.Information)
```

Figure 11-20   Basic syntax and an example of the MessageBox.Show method

Information icon

Figure 11-21   Message box created by the example in Figure 11-20

To modify the Shady Hollow Hotel-Version 2 application:

1. Open the Code Editor window.

2. Locate the btnDisplay control's Click event procedure. Modify the If...Then...Else statement as indicated in Figure 11-22.

```
If strType = "S" Then
        intDailyRate = 90
ElseIf strType = "D" Then
        intDailyRate = 115
Else
        MessageBox.Show("Please enter a valid room type.",
                        "Shady Hollow Hotel",
                        MessageBoxButtons.OK,
                        MessageBoxIcon.Information)
End If
```

enter these five lines of code

Figure 11-22   Modified If...Then...Else statement

As mentioned earlier, you should retest the application whenever you make a change to its code. Figure 11-23 shows the modified testing chart for the Shady Hollow Hotel-Version 2 application.

Test data	Expected result
No data entered	message, $0
Valid values	
S, s	$90
D, d	$115
Invalid values	
a, $, 9	message, $0

Figure 11-23   Modified testing chart for the Shady Hollow Hotel-Version 2 application

To test the modified Shady Hollow Hotel-Version 2 application:

1. Save the solution and then start the application. Click the **Display Rate** button. A message box appears on the screen, as shown in Figure 11-24.

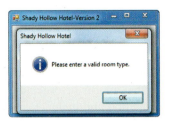

Figure 11-24 Message box

2. Click the **OK** button to close the message box. The Daily rate box shows $0, which is correct.

3. On your own, test the application using the valid and invalid values shown in Figure 11-23. The results should agree with the ones listed in the figure.

4. Click the **Exit** button.

Just When You Thought It Was Safe

When you are satisfied that an application is functioning correctly, you can release it to the user. However, keep this fact in mind: No matter how thoroughly you test an application, chances are it still will contain some errors, called **bugs**. This is because it's almost impossible to create a set of test data that covers every possible scenario the application will encounter. Typically, the number of bugs is directly related to the size and complexity of the application. In other words, large and complex applications usually have more errors than do small and simple ones. Because of this, most large and complex applications are beta tested by volunteers before being sold in the marketplace. Beta testers are encouraged to use the application as often as possible, because some bugs surface only after months of use. When a beta tester finds a bug in the application, he or she submits a bug report to the programmer. Although you tested the Shady Hollow Hotel-Version 2 application, which is small and very simple, even *it* contains a minor bug.

To locate the bug in the Shady Hollow Hotel-Version 2 application:

1. Start the application. When entering data in a text box, it is not uncommon for a user to inadvertently include a space character at the end of the entry. Type **d** and then press the **Spacebar** on your keyboard. Click the **Display Rate** button. The message "Please enter a valid room type." appears in a message box. At this point, the user most certainly is thinking, "But I did enter a valid room type: the letter d." It's doubtful that the user remembers pressing the Spacebar, because it's usually done unconsciously.

2. Click the **OK** button to close the message box. $0 appears in the Daily rate box, as shown in Figure 11-25. The interface adds to the user's confusion, because it appears that the daily rate for a Deluxe room is $0. (It's not obvious that a space character follows the letter d in the text box.)

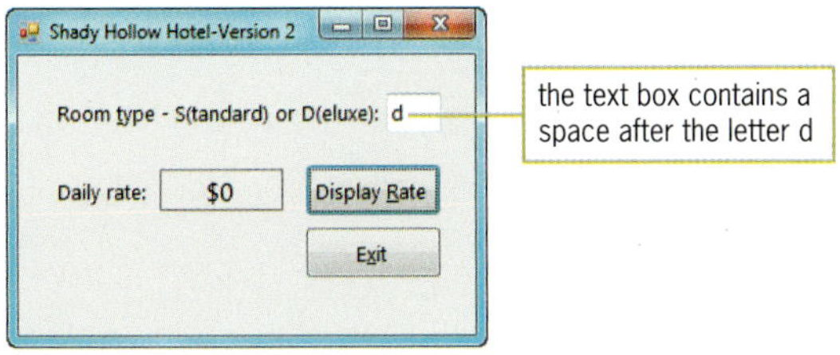

Figure 11-25 Result of including a space after the room type

3. Click the **Exit** button.

There are several ways to fix the bug in the application. For example, you can change the txtType control's **MaxLength property** to 1; doing this limits the text box entry to one character only. You also can use the txtType control's KeyPress event to prevent the text box from accepting the space character. You learned about the KeyPress event earlier in this chapter. In addition, you can use the **Trim method** to remove any spaces that appear before and after the room type. Figure 11-26 shows the basic syntax of the Trim method and includes examples of using the method. In the syntax, *string* typically is either the Text property of a control or the name of a String variable. When the computer processes the Trim method, it makes a temporary copy of the *string* in memory and then performs the necessary trimming on the copy only. In other words, the method does not remove any spaces from the original string. To remove the spaces from the original string, you must assign the result of the Trim method to the string, as shown in Example 2.

Trim method

Basic syntax
string.**Trim**

Example 1
strName = txtName.Text.Trim
assigns the contents of the txtName control, excluding any leading and trailing spaces, to the strName variable

Example 2
txtCity.Text = txtCity.Text.Trim
removes any leading and trailing spaces from the txtCity control

---

Figure 11-26 Basic syntax and examples of the Trim method

To include the Trim method in the Shady Hollow Hotel-Version 2 application:

1. Locate the statement that assigns the contents of the txtType control to the strType variable. Change txtType.Text.ToUpper to **txtType.Text.ToUpper.Trim**.

2. Save the solution and then start the application. Type **d** and then press the **Spacebar** on your keyboard. Click the **Display Rate** button. The daily rate for a Deluxe room, $115, appears in the Daily rate box.

3. Click the **Exit** button.

Figure 11-27 shows the final testing chart for the Shady Hollow Hotel-Version 2 application.

Test data	Expected result
No data entered	message, $0
Valid values	
S, s, one or more spaces before and/or after these letters	$90
D, d, one or more spaces before and/or after these letters	$115
Invalid values	
a, $, 9, one or more spaces	message, $0

Figure 11-27 Final testing chart for the Shady Hollow Hotel-Version 2 application

To retest the Shady Hollow Hotel-Version 2 application:

1. Start the application. On your own, test the application using the test data shown in Figure 11-27.

2. Click the **Exit** button. Close the Code Editor window and then close the solution.

It's time to view the Ch11-Testing video.

Mini-Quiz 11-2

See Appendix B for the answers.

1. Write a MessageBox.Show method that displays a message box with the "You win!" message, the "Game Over" text in its title bar, an OK button, and an Information icon.

2. Write the statement to remove any leading and/or trailing spaces from the txtState control.

3. Write a statement that first removes any leading and/or trailing spaces from the strDept variable and then changes the contents of the variable to uppercase.

For more examples of applications that require string data, see the String Data Testing section in the Ch11WantMore.pdf file.

Summary

- You should thoroughly test a program, using both valid and invalid data, before releasing the program to the user.

- The guidelines for selecting test data are listed in Figure 11-1 in the chapter.

- You can use a testing chart to record the test data and the expected results.

- You can prevent a text box from accepting a character by coding the text box's KeyPress event procedure. The KeyPress event occurs each time a key is pressed when the text box has the focus. A character corresponding to the pressed key is sent to the event's **e** parameter. You use the **e** parameter's KeyChar property to determine the pressed key. You cancel the key by setting the **e** parameter's Handled property to True.

- Whenever you make a change to an application's code, you should retest the application using the data listed in its testing chart.

- You can use the MessageBox.Show method to display a message while an application is running.

- The Trim method makes a temporary copy of a string. It then performs the necessary trimming on the copy only.

Key Terms

Bugs—the errors in an application's code

ControlChars.Back constant—the Visual Basic constant that represents the Backspace key on a computer keyboard

Handled property—a property of the KeyPress event procedure's **e** parameter; used to cancel the key pressed by the user

KeyChar property—a property of the KeyPress event procedure's **e** parameter; stores the character associated with the key pressed by the user

KeyPress event—occurs each time the user presses a key while the control has the focus

MaxLength property—the text box property that specifies the maximum number of characters that the user can enter in the text box

MessageBox.Show method—displays a message box that contains a message, title bar text, a button, and an icon; allows the application to communicate with the user during run time

Trim method—removes spaces from both the beginning and end of a string

Review Questions

1. Which of the following refers to the Backspace key on a computer keyboard?

    a. `Control.Back`

    b. `Control.Backspace`

    c. `ControlKey.Back`

    d. none of the above

2. Which of the following statements can be used in a text box's KeyPress event to cancel the key pressed by the user?

    a. `e.Cancel = True`

    b. `e.Handled = True`

    c. `e.KeyChar = True`

    d. none of the above

3. Which of the following determines whether the user pressed the $ key?

    a. `If ControlChars.DollarSign = True Then`

    b. `If e.KeyChar = Chars.DollarSign Then`

    c. `If e.KeyChar = "$" Then`

    d. `If KeyChar.ControlChars = "$" Then`

4. Which of the following creates a message box that displays an OK button, an Information icon, "Hatfield Sales" in the title bar, and the "Please enter a sales amount" message?

    a. ```
        MessageBox.Show("Please enter a sales amount",
            "Hatfield Sales", MessageBoxButtons.OK,
            MessageBoxIcon.Information)
        ```

    b.  ```
        MessageBox.Display("Hatfield Sales",
            "Please enter a sales amount",
            MessageBox.OKButton,
            MessageBox.InformationIcon)
        ```

    c. ```
        Message.Show("Please enter a sales amount",
            "Hatfield Sales", MessageButtons.OK,
            MessageIcon.Information)
        ```

    d.  ```
        MessageBox.Show("Hatfield Sales",
            "Please enter a sales amount",
            MessageBoxButtons.OK,
            MessageBoxIcon.Information)
        ```

5. If a condition contains a range of values, the test data should include which of the following?

    a. the lowest value in the range

    b. the highest value in the range

    c. a value within the range

    d. all of the above

6. Which of the following statements removes any leading and trailing spaces from the `strCity` variable?

    a. `strCity = Trim(strCity)`

    b. `strCity = strCity.Trim`

    c. `strCity = strCity.Text.Trim`

    d. none of the above

7. Which of the following determines whether the user pressed a key that is not a number or the Backspace key?

   a. `If (e.KeyChar < "0" AndAlso e.KeyChar > "9") OrElse`
           `e.KeyChar <> ControlChars.Back Then`

   b. `If e.KeyChar < "0" AndAlso e.KeyChar > "9" OrElse`
           `e.KeyChar <> ControlChars.Back Then`

   c. `If (e.KeyChar < "0" OrElse e.KeyChar > "9") AndAlso`
           `e.KeyChar <> ControlChars.Back Then`

   d. `If e.KeyChar < "0" OrElse e.KeyChar > "9" AndAlso`
           `e.KeyChar <> ControlChars.Back Then`

Exercises

1. Open the Shady Hollow Solution (Shady Hollow Solution.sln) file contained in the ClearlyVB2010\Chap11\Shady Hollow Solution-Version 3 folder. Open the Code Editor window and review the existing code. Use the guidelines from Figure 11-1, as well as the application's interface and code, to create a testing chart for the application. Start and then test the application. Close the Code Editor window and then close the solution. (See Appendix B for the answer.)
TRY THIS

2. Open the Bonus Solution (Bonus Solution.sln) file contained in the ClearlyVB2010\Chap11\Bonus Solution folder. Open the Code Editor window and review the existing code. Use the guidelines from Figure 11-1, as well as the application's interface and code, to create a testing chart for the application. Start and then test the application. Close the Code Editor window and then close the solution. (See Appendix B for the answer.)
TRY THIS

3. Open the Shady Hollow Solution (Shady Hollow Solution.sln) file contained in the ClearlyVB2010\Chap11\Shady Hollow Solution-Version 4 folder. Change the txtType control's MaxLength property to 1. The txtType control should accept only the Backspace key and the letters S, s, D, and d. Make the appropriate modifications to the code. Save the solution and then start and test the application. Close the Code Editor window and then close the solution.
MODIFY THIS

4. Open the Department Solution (Department Solution.sln) file contained in the ClearlyVB2010\Chap11\Department Solution folder. Change the text box's MaxLength property to 1. Change its CharacterCasing property to Upper. Open the Code Editor window. The text box should accept only the Backspace key and the letters A, a, B, and b. If the user clicks the Display button without entering a code, the selection structure should display the text "Not available" in the lblName control. It also should display a message box that contains the "Please enter a code" message, the text "Department Codes" in the title bar, an OK button, and an Information icon. Make the appropriate modifications to the code. Save the solution and then start and test the application. Close the Code Editor window and then close the solution.
INTRODUCTORY

5. Open the Sales Tax Solution (Sales Tax Solution.sln) file contained in the ClearlyVB2010\Chap11\Sales Tax Solution folder. Open the Code Editor window and review the existing code. The text box should accept only numbers, the period, and the Backspace key; make the appropriate modifications to the code. Use the guidelines from Figure 11-1, as well as the application's interface and code, to create a testing chart for the application. Save the solution and then start and test the application. Close the Code Editor window and then close the solution.
INTRODUCTORY

6. Open the Gross Pay Solution (Gross Pay Solution.sln) file contained in the ClearlyVB2010\Chap11\Gross Pay Solution folder. Open the Code Editor window and review the existing code. Both text boxes should accept only numbers, the period, and the Backspace key; make the appropriate modifications to the code. Use the guidelines from Figure 11-1, as well as the application's interface and code, to create a testing chart
INTERMEDIATE

for the application. Save the solution and then start and test the application. Close the Code Editor window and then close the solution.

INTERMEDIATE

7. Open the ABC Solution (ABC Solution.sln) file contained in the ClearlyVB2010\Chap11\ABC Solution folder. Open the Code Editor window and review the existing code. Modify the code so that the text box accepts only numbers and the Backspace key. Use the guidelines from Figure 11-1, as well as the application's interface and code, to create a testing chart for the application. Save the solution and then start and test the application. Make any needed changes to the code and testing chart. Save the solution and then start and test the application again. Close the Code Editor window and then close the solution.

ADVANCED

8. Open the Average Solution (Average Solution.sln) file contained in the ClearlyVB2010\Chap11\Average Solution folder. Open the Code Editor window and review the existing code. Start and then test the application, using the testing information included in the btnCalc control's Click event procedure. Notice that the code does not always produce the expected result. Make the necessary changes to the code. (Hint: You can determine whether a text box is empty by comparing its Text property to the String.Empty constant.) Save the solution and then start and test the application again. Close the Code Editor window and then close the solution.

ADVANCED

9. Open the Total Due Solution (Total Due Solution.sln) file contained in the ClearlyVB2010\Chap11\Total Due Solution folder. Open the Code Editor window and review the existing code. Create a testing chart for the application. Start and then test the application. Make any needed changes to the application's code. Save the solution and then start and test the application again. Close the Code Editor window and then close the solution.

FIGURE THIS OUT

10. Open the FigureThisOut Solution (FigureThisOut Solution.sln) file contained in the ClearlyVB2010\Chap11\FigureThisOut Solution folder. Open the Code Editor window and study the existing code. Start the application. Enter the number 1,200 (be sure to type the comma) in both text boxes and then click the Calculate button. The answers, which should be the same, appear in the two label controls. Why are the answers different? How can you fix the problem? Make the necessary changes to the code. Save the solution and then start and test the application. Close the Code Editor window and then close the solution.

SWAT THE BUGS

11. Open the SwatTheBugs Solution (SwatTheBugs Solution.sln) file contained in the ClearlyVB2010\Chap11\SwatTheBugs Solution folder. Create a testing chart. Start and then test the application. Be sure to verify that the KeyPress procedure works correctly. Locate and correct the errors in the code. Save the solution and then start and test the application. Close the Code Editor window and then close the solution.

CHAPTER 12

How Long Can This Go On? (Pretest Loops)

After studying Chapter 12, you should be able to:

◎ Write a looping condition and its opposing loop exit condition

◎ Show a pretest loop in both pseudocode and a flowchart

◎ Write a pretest loop using the Do…Loop statement

◎ Utilize counter and accumulator variables

◎ Refresh the screen

◎ Delay program execution

◎ Display a dialog box using the InputBox function

◎ Abbreviate assignment statements using the arithmetic assignment operators

Over and Over Again

Recall that all computer programs are written using one or more of three basic control structures: sequence, selection, and repetition. You learned about the sequence and selection structures in previous chapters. This chapter provides an introduction to the repetition structure. Programmers use the **repetition structure**, referred to more simply as a **loop**, when they need the computer to repeatedly process one or more program instructions. If and for how long the instructions are repeated are determined by the loop's condition. Like the condition in a selection structure, the condition in a loop must evaluate to either True or False. The condition is evaluated with each repetition (or iteration) of the loop and can be phrased in one of two ways: It can specify either the requirement for repeating the instructions or the requirement for *not* repeating them. The requirement for repeating the instructions is referred to as the **looping condition**, because it indicates when the computer should continue "looping" through the instructions. The requirement for *not* repeating the instructions is referred to as the **loop exit condition**, because it tells the computer when to exit (or stop) the loop. An example may help illustrate the difference between the looping condition and the loop exit condition. You've probably heard the old adage "Make hay while the sun shines." The "while the sun shines" is the looping condition, because it tells you when to continue making hay. The adage also could be phrased as "Make hay until the sun stops shining." In this case, the "until the sun stops shining" is the loop exit condition, because it indicates when you should stop making hay. Every looping condition has an opposing loop exit condition; in other words, one is the opposite of the other. See Figure 12-1.

Figure 12-1   Example of a looping condition and a loop exit condition

A repetition structure can be either a pretest loop or a posttest loop. In a **pretest loop**, the loop condition is evaluated *before* the instructions within the loop are processed. In a **posttest loop**, the evaluation occurs *after* the instructions within the loop are processed. Depending on the result of the evaluation, the instructions in a pretest loop may never be processed. The instructions in a posttest loop, however, will always be processed at least once. Of the two types of loops, the pretest loop is the most commonly used. You will learn about pretest loops in this chapter and in Chapter 14; posttest loops are covered in Chapter 13.

The programmer determines whether a problem's solution requires a loop by studying the problem specification. The first problem specification you will examine in this chapter involves Rob, the mechanical man from Chapter 1. The problem specification and an illustration of the problem are shown in Figure 12-2. The figure also includes the correct algorithm using the commands that Rob can understand. The algorithm uses only the sequence structure, because no decisions need to be made and no instructions need to be repeated.

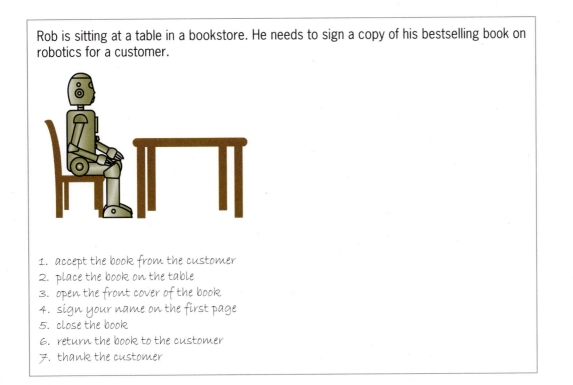

Rob is sitting at a table in a bookstore. He needs to sign a copy of his bestselling book on robotics for a customer.

1. accept the book from the customer
2. place the book on the table
3. open the front cover of the book
4. sign your name on the first page
5. close the book
6. return the book to the customer
7. thank the customer

Figure 12-2   First problem using Rob

Now let's change the problem specification slightly. Rob is still sitting at a table in the bookstore; but this time, he's there for a book signing. The store has just opened and there's already a long line of customers. Rob doesn't want to disappoint his fans, so he plans on staying until every book is signed. Consider how this change will affect the original algorithm shown in Figure 12-2. The original algorithm contains the instructions for signing only one customer's book. In the modified algorithm, Rob will need to repeat the same instructions for every customer standing in line. Figure 12-3 shows the modified problem specification along with two versions of the modified algorithm. The repetition structure in Version 1 begins with *repeat while there are customers in line:*. The repetition structure in Version 2 begins with *repeat until there are no more customers in line:*. The condition in Version 1 is phrased as a looping condition, because it tells Rob when to continue repeating the loop instructions. The condition in Version 2 is phrased as a loop exit condition, because it tells Rob when to stop repeating the loop instructions. Both repetition structures end with *end repeat*. The instructions between the first and last lines in both repetition structures are indented to indicate that they are part of the loop and, therefore, need to be followed for each customer standing in line.

Rob is sitting at a table in a bookstore, attending his book signing. He needs to sign a copy of his bestselling book on robotics for each customer standing in line.

Version 1   looping condition

repeat while there are customers in line:
    accept the book from the customer
    place the book on the table
    open the front cover of the book
    sign your name on the first page
    close the book
    return the book to the customer
    thank the customer
end repeat

Version 2   loop exit condition

repeat until there are no more customers in line:
    accept the book from the customer
    place the book on the table
    open the front cover of the book
    sign your name on the first page
    close the book
    return the book to the customer
    thank the customer
end repeat

Figure 12-3   Second problem using Rob

Figure 12-4 shows another problem specification and algorithm involving Rob. To solve the problem, you need to get Rob from his hallway into his bedroom. Notice that the algorithm contains both the sequence and selection structures. The first instruction positions Rob directly in front of his bedroom door. The second instruction determines whether the bedroom door is closed and then takes the appropriate action based on the result. The last instruction walks Rob into his bedroom.

Rob is standing in his hallway facing his bedroom door. The door, which may or may not be closed, is one step away from Rob. Rob wants to enter his bedroom.

1. walk forward
2. if the bedroom door is closed, do this:
       open the bedroom door
   end if
3. walk forward

Figure 12-4   Third problem using Rob

Figure 12-5 shows a modified version of the previous problem specification. In the modified version, Rob is 10 steps away from the door. How could you rewrite the original algorithm to reflect this minor change? One way is by adding nine more walk forward instructions to the original algorithm; however, that would be quite cumbersome to write. Imagine if Rob were 500 steps from the door! A better way to modify the original algorithm is by adding a repetition structure to it, as shown in the modified algorithm in Figure 12-5. The repetition structure directs Rob to walk forward 10 times.

Rob is standing in his hallway facing his bedroom door. The door, which may or may not be closed, is 10 steps away from Rob. Rob wants to enter his bedroom.

1. repeat 10 times:
       walk forward
   end repeat
2. if the bedroom door is closed, do this:
       open the bedroom door
   end if
3. walk forward

Figure 12-5   Fourth problem using Rob

Figure 12-6 shows a modified version of the previous problem specification. In this version, the number of steps between Rob and the door is unknown. He might be 10 steps away or 500 steps away; or, Rob might already be directly in front of the door. How will this affect the algorithm shown in Figure 12-5? The repetition structure in the algorithm will need to be changed because the number of steps between Rob and the door is no longer known. Rather than telling Rob to repeat the walk forward instruction 10 times, the repetition structure will need to tell him to repeat the instruction either until he is directly in front of the bedroom door (loop exit condition) or while he is not directly in front of the bedroom door (looping condition). Once Rob is positioned correctly, he still will need to follow the second and third instructions in the algorithm. Two versions of the modified algorithm are included in Figure 12-6.

Rob is standing in his hallway facing his bedroom door. The door, which may or may not be closed, is an unknown number of steps away from Rob. Rob wants to enter his bedroom.

Version 1 | loop exit condition |

1. repeat until you are directly in front of the bedroom door:
       walk forward
   end repeat
2. if the bedroom door is closed, do this:
       open the bedroom door
   end if
3. walk forward

Version 2 | looping condition |

1. repeat while you are not directly in front of the bedroom door:
       walk forward
   end repeat
2. if the bedroom door is closed, do this:
       open the bedroom door
   end if
3. walk forward

Figure 12-6   Fifth problem using Rob

Both repetition structures in Figure 12-6 end when Rob is standing directly in front of his bedroom door. If Rob is 10 steps away from the door, both repetition structures direct him to walk forward 10 times before determining whether the door is closed. Similarly, if Rob is 500 steps away from the door, both repetition structures direct him to walk forward 500 times. If Rob is directly in front of the bedroom door, the walk forward instruction in both repetition structures is bypassed.

Mini-Quiz 12-1

See Appendix B for the answers.

1. Rob is sitting in a chair that is next to a table in his living room. On top of the table is Rob's cell phone. Your task is to direct Rob to pick up his cell phone. Does the solution to this problem require a repetition structure? If so, what needs to be repeated?

2. Rob is sitting in a chair in his living room. At the other end of the room is a table. On top of the table is Rob's cell phone. Your task is to direct Rob to pick up his cell phone, but only when the phone rings. Does the solution to this problem require a repetition structure? If so, what needs to be repeated?

3. Rob wants to pick all of the flowers in his garden. Write an appropriate looping condition and its opposing loop exit condition.

The Do...Loop Statement

Before solving real-world problems that require a repetition structure, you will learn about the Do...Loop statement. You can use the **Do...Loop statement** to code both a pretest loop and a posttest loop in Visual Basic. As mentioned earlier, this chapter covers pretest loops. Figure 12-7 shows the syntax of the Do...Loop statement when used to code a pretest loop. The statement begins with the Do clause and ends with the Loop clause. Between both clauses, you enter the instructions you want the computer to repeat. The instructions between the Do and Loop clauses are referred to as the **loop body**.

The {While | Until} portion of the syntax indicates that you can select only one of the keywords appearing within the braces. You do not type the braces or the pipe symbol (|) when entering the Do...Loop statement. You follow the keyword with a *condition*, which can be phrased as either a looping condition or a loop exit condition. You use the While keyword in a looping condition to specify that the loop body should be processed *while* (in other words, as long as) the condition is true. You use the Until keyword in a loop exit condition to specify that the loop body should be processed *until* the condition becomes true, at which time the loop should stop. Like the condition in an If...Then...Else statement, the condition in a Do...Loop statement can contain variables, constants, properties, methods, and operators; it also must evaluate to a Boolean value. The condition is evaluated with each repetition of the loop and determines whether the computer processes the loop body. Also included in Figure 12-7 are two examples of pretest loops. In Example 1, the condition is phrased as a looping condition. In Example 2, the condition is phrased as a loop exit condition. Both examples produce the same result, which is to display the numbers 1, 2, and 3 in message boxes.

```
Do...Loop statement

Syntax for coding a pretest loop
Do {While | Until} condition
        loop body instructions, which will be processed either
        while the condition is true or until the condition becomes true
Loop

Example 1
intNumber = 1              ┌──── looping condition
                       ┌───┤
                   ┌───┘
Do While intNumber <= 3
    MessageBox.Show(intNumber)
    intNumber = intNumber + 1
Loop

Example 2
intNumber = 1              ┌──── loop exit condition
                       ┌───┤
                   ┌───┘
Do Until intNumber > 3
    MessageBox.Show(intNumber)
    intNumber = intNumber + 1
Loop
```

Figure 12-7   Syntax and examples of the Do...Loop statement for a pretest loop

Counter Variables

Both examples in Figure 12-7 begin by assigning the number 1 to an Integer variable named intNumber. The intNumber variable is called a **counter variable**, because it is used to count something. Repetition structures use counter variables to count such things as the number of employees paid in a week or the number of positive numbers entered by the user. The repetition structures in Figure 12-7 use the intNumber counter variable to keep track of the number of times the loop instructions are processed. Counter variables are always numeric variables and are typically assigned a beginning value of either 0 or 1, depending on the value required by the application. Assigning a beginning value to a variable is referred to as **initializing**. The initialization task is performed before the loop is processed, because it needs to be performed only once. In both examples in Figure 12-7, the initialization task is performed by the intNumber = 1 assignment statement. Counter variables also must be updated. **Updating**, often referred to as **incrementing**, means adding a number to the value stored in the counter variable. The number can be positive or negative, integer or non-integer. A counter variable is always incremented by a constant value, usually the number 1. The assignment statement that updates a counter variable is placed within the loop body, because the update task must be performed each time the loop instructions are processed. In both examples in Figure 12-7, the counter variable is updated by the intNumber = intNumber + 1 statement within the loop. Figure 12-8 shows the code from Example 1 in Figure 12-7 and describes the way the computer processes the code. Notice that the loop ends when the intNumber variable contains the number 4.

Code from Example 1 in Figure 12-7
```
intNumber = 1
Do While intNumber <= 3
    MessageBox.Show(intNumber)
    intNumber = intNumber + 1
Loop
```

Processing steps

1. The computer initializes the `intNumber` variable to 1.
2. The computer processes the Do clause, which checks whether the `intNumber` variable's value is less than or equal to 3. It is.
3. The loop instructions display the `intNumber` variable's value (1) and then update the value by adding 1 to it, giving 2.
4. The computer processes the Loop clause, which returns processing to the Do clause (the beginning of the loop).
5. The computer processes the Do clause, which checks whether the `intNumber` variable's value is less than or equal to 3. It is.
6. The loop instructions display the `intNumber` variable's value (2) and then update the value by adding 1 to it, giving 3.
7. The computer processes the Loop clause, which returns processing to the Do clause.
8. The Do clause checks whether the `intNumber` variable's value is less than or equal to 3. It is.
9. The loop instructions display the `intNumber` variable's value (3) and then update the value by adding 1 to it, giving 4.
10. The computer processes the Loop clause, which returns processing to the Do clause.
11. The computer processes the Do clause, which checks whether the `intNumber` variable's value is less than or equal to 3. It isn't, so the computer stops processing the Do...Loop statement. Processing continues with the statement following the Loop clause.

For more examples of using the Do...Loop statement to code a pretest loop, see the Do...Loop Pretest section in the Ch12WantMore.pdf file.

Figure 12-8 Code and processing steps for Example 1 in Figure 12-7

My Dream Car-Version 1 Application

Figure 12-9 shows the interface for the My Dream Car-Version 1 application. You will use a repetition structure to make the I WANT THIS CAR! message blink several times when the user clicks the Click Me button.

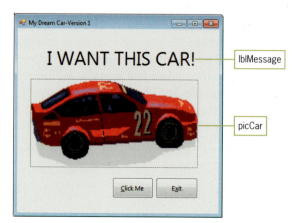

Figure 12-9 Interface for the My Dream Car-Version 1 application

You make a control blink using code that changes the control's Visible property while the application is running. The way the property is changed depends on its initial setting. If the Visible property is set to True in the Properties window, the code will need to set the property to False and then back to True for each blink. On the other hand, if the Visible property's initial setting is False, the code must switch the property to True and then back to False for each blink. In the My Dream Car-Version 1 application, the lblMessage control's Visible property is set to False in the Properties window. Therefore, to make the control blink once, the code will need to set the Visible property twice: first to True and then to False. Similarly, to make the control blink twice, the code needs to set the Visible property four times: first to True, then to False, then to True, and finally to False. The Click Me button's Click event procedure will make the control blink 10 times, so it will need to set the Visible property 20 times, alternating between the True and False settings. You will use a counter variable to keep track of the number of times the Visible property is set.

Switching the Visible property isn't all that is necessary to make a control blink. Because the computer will process the switching instructions so rapidly, you won't even notice that the control is blinking. You can solve this problem by refreshing the interface and then delaying program execution each time you change the Visible property's setting. You refresh the interface using the form's Refresh method. The method's syntax is **Me.Refresh()**, where Me refers to the current form. The **Refresh method** ensures that the computer processes any previous lines of code that affect the form's appearance. You can delay program execution using the **Sleep method** in the following syntax: **System.Threading.Thread.Sleep(***milliseconds***)**. The *milliseconds* argument is the number of milliseconds to suspend the program. A millisecond is 1/1000 of a second; in other words, there are 1000 milliseconds in a second.

Figure 12-10 shows the algorithm (in pseudocode and flowchart form) for the Click Me button's Click event procedure. Recall that the diamond in a flowchart is called the decision symbol, because it is used to represent the condition (decision) in both the selection and repetition structures. The first diamond in Figure 12-10 represents the condition in a repetition structure, and the second diamond represents the condition in a selection structure. Inside each diamond is a question whose answer is either True or False. The answer to the question in the first diamond determines whether the instructions within the loop are processed. Notice that the first diamond has one flowline entering the symbol and two flowlines leaving the symbol. The two flowlines leading out of the diamond should be marked so that anyone reading the flowchart can distinguish the true path from the false path. You mark the flowline leading to the true path with a T and the flowline leading to the false path with an F. You also can mark the flowlines leading out of the diamond with a Y and an N (for Yes and No). In the flowchart in Figure 12-10, the flowline entering the first diamond, along with the diamond and the symbols and flowlines within the true path, form a circle or loop. It is this loop, or circle, that distinguishes the repetition structure from the selection structure in a flowchart.

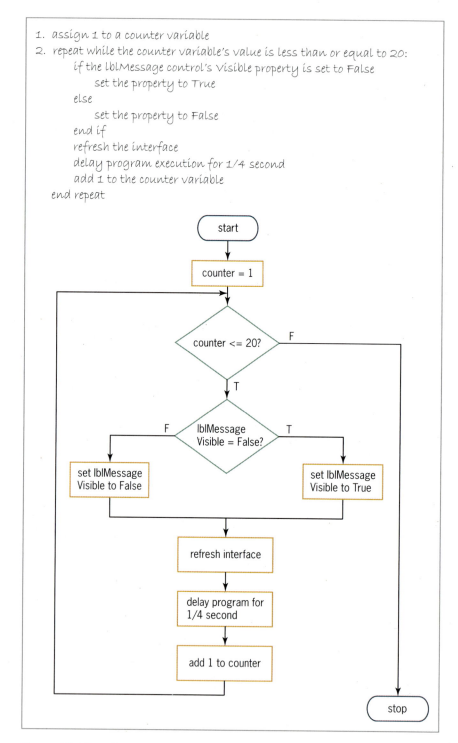

1. assign 1 to a counter variable
2. repeat while the counter variable's value is less than or equal to 20:
       if the lblMessage control's Visible property is set to False
           set the property to True
       else
           set the property to False
       end if
       refresh the interface
       delay program execution for 1/4 second
       add 1 to the counter variable
   end repeat

For more examples of flow-charts, see the Flow-chart section in the Ch12WantMore.pdf file.

Before you begin coding the My Dream Car-Version 1 application, you may want to view the Ch12-My Dream Car video. The video demonstrates the steps contained in this section and also shows a different way of coding the application. It also shows you how to stop an infinite (endless) loop.

Figure 12-10   Algorithm (pseudocode and flowchart) for the Click Me button's Click event procedure

To code and then test the My Dream Car-Version 1 application:

1. Start Visual Studio 2010 or Visual Basic 2010 Express and permanently display the Solution Explorer window. Open the **Car Solution** (**Car Solution.sln**) file contained in the ClearlyVB2010\Chap12\Car Solution-Version 1 folder. If the designer window is not open, double-click **frmMain.vb** in the Solution Explorer window.

2. Open the Code Editor window, which contains the code for the btnExit control's Click event procedure.

3. Open the code template for the btnClickMe control's Click event procedure. Type the following comment and then press **Enter** twice:

   ' blinks the message in the lblMessage control

4. First, you will declare a counter variable that the computer can use to keep track of the number of times it processes the loop instructions. Enter the following comment and Dim statement. Press **Enter** twice after typing the Dim statement.

   ' declare counter variable
   Dim intCount As Integer

5. The first step in the algorithm assigns the number 1 to the counter variable. Enter the following comment and assignment statement:

   ' begin counting
   intCount = 1

6. The second step in the algorithm is a repetition structure that repeats its instructions while the counter variable's value is less than or equal to 20. Type the following Do clause and then press **Enter**. When you press Enter, the Code Editor automatically enters the Loop clause for you. It also automatically indents the current line.

   Do While intCount <= 20

7. The first instruction in the loop is a selection structure whose condition determines whether the lblMessage control's Visible property contains the Boolean value, False. Enter the following If clause:

   If lblMessage.Visible = False Then

8. If the Visible property contains False, the selection structure's true path should assign True to the property; otherwise, its false path should assign False. Enter the following three lines of code, but don't press Enter after typing the last line:

   lblMessage.Visible = True
   Else
   lblMessage.Visible = False

9. The remaining loop instructions refresh the interface, delay program execution for a quarter of a second, and update the counter variable. Enter the comment and three lines of code indicated in Figure 12-11.

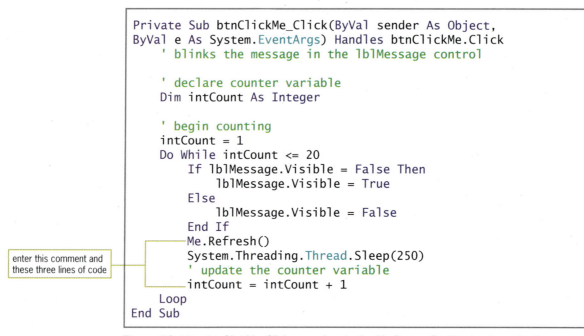

```
Private Sub btnClickMe_Click(ByVal sender As Object,
ByVal e As System.EventArgs) Handles btnClickMe.Click
    ' blinks the message in the lblMessage control

    ' declare counter variable
    Dim intCount As Integer

    ' begin counting
    intCount = 1
    Do While intCount <= 20
        If lblMessage.Visible = False Then
            lblMessage.Visible = True
        Else
            lblMessage.Visible = False
        End If
        Me.Refresh()
        System.Threading.Thread.Sleep(250)
        ' update the counter variable
        intCount = intCount + 1
    Loop
End Sub
```

enter this comment and these three lines of code

Figure 12-11   btnClickMe_Click procedure in the My Dream Car-Version 1 application

10. Save the solution and then start the application. Click the **Click Me** button. The message in the lblMessage control blinks 10 times. Click the **Exit** button. Close the Code Editor window and then close the solution.

My Dream Car-Version 2 Application

Except for the title bar text, the interface for the My Dream Car-Version 2 application appears identical to the one shown earlier in Figure 12-9. However, in this version of the application, the lblMessage control's Visible property is set to True in the Properties window, and the picCar control's Visible property is set to False. When the user clicks the Click Me button, the button's Click event procedure will position the picCar control off the left edge of the form. This can be accomplished by setting the control's Left property to a negative number; you will use −400. Next, the procedure will set the picCar control's Visible property to True and then slowly drag the control to the center of the form. You can drag the control by including, in a loop, an instruction that increments the control's Left property value; in this case, you will increment the value by 25. You will include the Refresh and Sleep methods within the loop to prevent the computer from processing the dragging instructions too rapidly. The loop will stop when the Left property value is greater than 20. Why 20? Currently, the picCar control is centered horizontally on the form. If you check its Location property, you will notice that its X value, which determines the location of its left border on the form, is set to 27 (your property value may differ slightly). The algorithm for the Click Me button's Click event procedure is shown in Figure 12-12.

> 1. position the picCar control off the left edge of the form by setting its Left property to -400
> 2. set the picCar control's Visible property to True
> 3. repeat until the value in the picCar control's Left property is greater than 20:
>   reposition the picCar control by adding 25 to its Left property
>   refresh the interface
>   delay program execution for 1/4 second
>   end repeat

Figure 12-12   Algorithm for the Click Me button's Click event procedure

To code and then test the My Dream Car-Version 2 application:

1. Open the **Car Solution** (**Car Solution.sln**) file contained in the ClearlyVB2010\Chap12\Car Solution-Version 2 folder. If the designer window is not open, double-click **frmMain.vb** in the Solution Explorer window.

2. Open the Code Editor window, which contains the code for the btnExit control's Click event procedure.

3. Open the code template for the btnClickMe control's Click event procedure. Type the following comment and then press **Enter** twice:

   ' drags the picCar control to the center of the form

4. The first two steps in the algorithm position the picCar control off the left edge of the form and then set the control's Visible property to True. Enter the following comments and assignment statements. Press **Enter** twice after typing the last assignment statement.

   ' position picCar off the left edge of the form
   picCar.Left = −400
   ' show picCar
   picCar.Visible = True

5. The third step in the algorithm is a repetition structure that repeats its instructions until the value in the picCar control's Left property is greater than 20. Enter the following Do clause:

   Do Until picCar.Left > 20

6. The first instruction in the loop repositions the picCar control by adding 25 to its Left property. The remaining loop instructions refresh the interface and delay program execution for a quarter of a second. Enter the comment and three lines of code indicated in Figure 12-13.

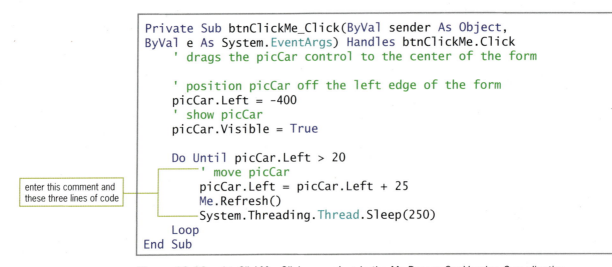

```
Private Sub btnClickMe_Click(ByVal sender As Object,
ByVal e As System.EventArgs) Handles btnClickMe.Click
    ' drags the picCar control to the center of the form

    ' position picCar off the left edge of the form
    picCar.Left = -400
    ' show picCar
    picCar.Visible = True

    Do Until picCar.Left > 20
        ' move picCar
        picCar.Left = picCar.Left + 25
        Me.Refresh()
        System.Threading.Thread.Sleep(250)
    Loop
End Sub
```

enter this comment and these three lines of code

Figure 12-13   btnClickMe_Click procedure in the My Dream Car-Version 2 application

7. Save the solution and then start the application. Click the **Click Me** button. The car image is dragged from the left edge of the form to the center of the form. Click the **Exit** button. Close the Code Editor window and then close the solution.

Mini-Quiz 12-2

See Appendix B for the answers.

1. Write a Visual Basic Do clause that tells the computer to process the loop instructions as long as the value in the `intQuantity` variable is greater than the number 0. Use the `While` keyword to create a looping condition.

2. Rewrite the Do clause from Question 1 using the `Until` keyword to create a loop exit condition.

3. Write an assignment statement that increments the `intNumEmployees` variable by 1.

4. Write a statement that tells the computer to pause program execution for 1 second.

The Sales Express Application-Counter and Accumulator Variables

Figure 12-14 shows another problem specification whose solution requires a repetition structure. It also shows a correct algorithm for the problem. In addition to a counter variable, which is used to keep track of the number of sales amounts entered by the sales manager, the algorithm also uses an accumulator variable. An **accumulator variable** is a numeric variable used for accumulating (adding together) something. Repetition structures use accumulator variables to tally information such as the total dollar amount of a week's payroll. The loop in Figure 12-14 uses the accumulator variable to total the sales amounts entered by the user. Like counter variables, accumulator variables are initialized before the loop is processed. In most cases, an accumulator variable is initialized to 0. Also like counter variables, accumulator variables are updated within the loop. However, unlike counter variables, accumulator variables are incremented by an amount that varies (rather than by a constant value). In the Sales Express algorithm, the accumulator variable is incremented by the sales amount entered by the sales manager. The algorithm uses the values in the accumulator and counter variables to calculate the average sales amount.

The sales manager at Sales Express wants an application that allows him to enter the amount of each salesperson's sales, one at a time. After all of the sales amounts have been entered, the application should calculate the average sales amount and then display the result on the screen.

Output: average sales amount

Processing: sales counter variable (start at 0)
               sales accumulator variable (start at 0)

Input: sales amount (for each salesperson)

Algorithm:
1. initialize the sales counter and sales accumulator variables to 0
2. enter a sales amount
3. repeat until there are no more sales amounts to enter:
      add the sales amount to the sales accumulator variable
      add 1 to the sales counter variable
      enter a sales amount
   end repeat
4. calculate the average sales amount by dividing the sales accumulator variable by the sales counter variable
5. display the average sales amount

Figure 12-14   Problem specification and algorithm for the Sales Express application

Notice that enter a sales amount appears twice in the algorithm: immediately above the loop and also within the loop. The enter a sales amount entry above the loop is referred to as the **priming read**, because it is used to prime (prepare or set up) the loop. The priming read initializes the loop condition by providing its first value. In this case, the priming read gets only the first salesperson's sales amount from the user. Because the loop in Figure 12-14 is a pretest loop, the first sales amount determines whether the instructions in the loop body are processed at all. If the loop body instructions are processed, the enter a sales amount instruction in the loop body gets the remaining sales amounts (if any) from the user. The enter a sales amount instruction in the loop body is referred to as the **update read**, because it allows the user to update the value of the input item (in this case, the sales amount) that controls the loop's condition. The update read is often an exact copy of the priming read.

Keep in mind that if you don't include the update read in the loop body, there will be no way to enter a value that will stop the loop after it has been processed the first time. This is because the priming read is processed only once and gets only the first sales amount from the user. A loop that has no way to end is called an **infinite loop** or an **endless loop**. You can stop a program that has an endless loop by clicking Debug on the menu bar and then clicking Stop Debugging.

To begin coding the Sales Express application:

1. Open the **Sales Express Solution (Sales Express Solution.sln)** file contained in the ClearlyVB2010\Chap12\Sales Express Solution folder. If the designer window is not open, double-click **frmMain.vb** in the Solution Explorer window. The application's interface is shown in Figure 12-15.

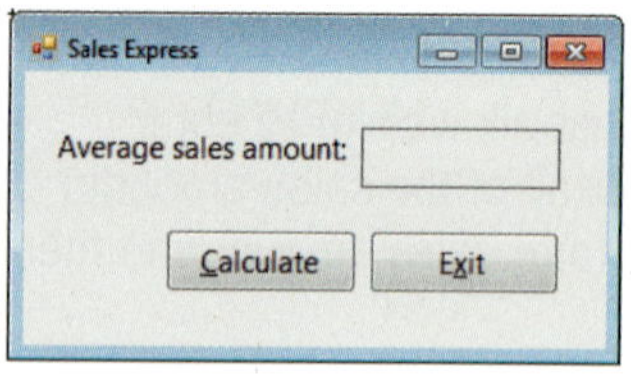

Figure 12-15 Sales Express application's interface

2. Open the Code Editor window, which contains the code for the btnExit control's Click event procedure.

3. Open the code template for the btnCalc control's Click event procedure. Type the following comment and then press **Enter** twice:

   ' calculates and displays the average sales amount

4. First, you will declare the necessary variables. The procedure requires four variables for the output, processing, and input items. Enter the following declaration statements and comments. Press **Enter** twice after typing the last declaration statement.

   Dim intNumSales As Integer   ' counter
   Dim decTotalSales As Decimal ' accumulator
   Dim decSales As Decimal
   Dim decAverage As Decimal

5. The first step in the algorithm is to initialize the counter and accumulator variables to 0. Both variables are initialized to 0 in their respective declaration statements, so the first step in the algorithm has already been coded. However, for clarity, some programmers enter assignment statements that document the initialization step. Enter the following assignment statements and then save the solution:

   intNumSales = 0
   decTotalSales = 0

The InputBox Function

The second step in the Sales Express algorithm is to enter the sales amount. You may have noticed that the Sales Express interface does not provide a text box for the user to enter the sales amount. Rather than using a text box, the application will use an input dialog box. You display an input dialog box using Visual Basic's **InputBox function**. An example of an input dialog box is shown in Figure 12-16. The input dialog box contains a message, an OK button, a Cancel button, and an input area where the user can enter information. The message in the dialog box should prompt the user to enter the appropriate information in the input area. The user closes the dialog box by clicking the OK button, Cancel button, or Close button. The value returned by the InputBox function depends on the button the user chooses. If the user clicks the OK button, the InputBox function returns the value contained in the input area of the dialog box; the return value is always treated as a string. If the user clicks either the Cancel button in the dialog box or the Close button on the dialog box's title bar, the InputBox function returns an empty string. The empty string is represented by the **String.Empty constant** in Visual Basic.

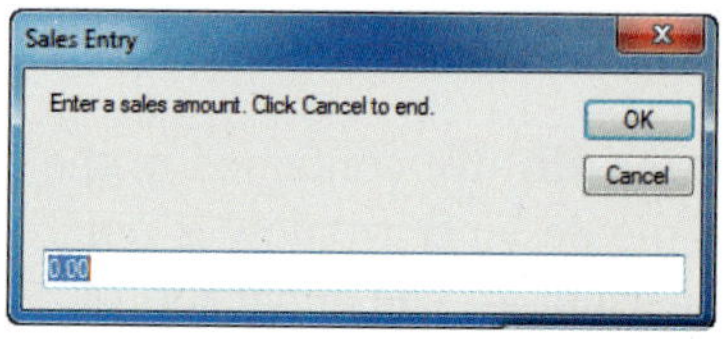

Figure 12-16 Example of an input dialog box created by the InputBox function

Figure 12-17 shows the basic syntax of the InputBox function. The *prompt* argument contains the message to display inside the dialog box. The optional *title* and *defaultResponse* arguments control the text that appears in the dialog box's title bar and input area, respectively. If you omit the title argument, the project name appears in the title bar. If you omit the defaultResponse argument, a blank input area appears when the dialog box opens. In the dialog box shown in Figure 12-16, "Enter a sales amount. Click Cancel to end." is the prompt, "Sales Entry" is the title, and "0.00" is the defaultResponse. When entering the InputBox function in the Code Editor window, the prompt, title, and defaultResponse arguments must be enclosed in quotation marks, unless that information is stored in a String named constant or a String variable. The Windows standard is to use sentence capitalization for the prompt, but book title capitalization for the title. The capitalization (if any) you use for the defaultResponse depends on the text itself. In most cases, you assign the value returned by the InputBox function to a String variable, as indicated in the first three examples in Figure 12-17. However, you also can store the value in a numeric variable by first converting the value to the appropriate numeric data type, as shown in Example 4 in the figure.

InputBox Function

Syntax
InputBox(*prompt*[, *title*][, *defaultResponse*])

Example 1
```
strName = InputBox("First name:", "Name Entry")
```
Displays an input dialog box that shows First name: as the prompt, Name Entry in the title bar, and an empty input area. When the user closes the dialog box, the assignment statement assigns the user's response to a String variable named strName.

Example 2
```
strState = InputBox("State name:", "State", "Alaska")
```
Displays an input dialog box that shows State name: as the prompt, State in the title bar, and Alaska in the input area. When the user closes the dialog box, the assignment statement assigns the user's response to a String variable named strState.

Example 3
```
Const strPROMPT As String =
    "Enter a sales amount. Click Cancel to end."
Const strTITLE As String = "Sales Entry"
strInputSales = InputBox(strPROMPT, strTITLE, "0.00")
```
Displays the input dialog box shown in Figure 12-16. When the user closes the dialog box, the assignment statement assigns the user's response to a String variable named strInputSales.

Example 4
```
Integer.TryParse(InputBox("How old are you?",
                "Discount Verification"), intAge)
```
Displays an input dialog box that shows How old are you? as the prompt, Discount Verification in the title bar, and an empty input area. When the user closes the dialog box, the TryParse method converts the user's response from String to Integer and then stores the result in an Integer variable named intAge.

Figure 12-17   Syntax and examples of the InputBox function

To continue coding the Sales Express application:

1. First, you will create named constants for the InputBox function's prompt and title arguments. Click the **blank line** above the first Dim statement and then press **Enter** to insert a blank line. Enter the following Const statements:

   Const strPROMPT As String =
       "Enter a sales amount. Click Cancel to end."
   Const strTITLE As String = "Sales Entry"

2. Now you will create a String variable to store the value returned by the InputBox function. Enter the following Dim statement:

   Dim strInputSales As String

3. Next, you will enter the InputBox function in the procedure. Click the **blank line** below the decTotalSales = 0 statement and then enter the following comment and assignment statement:

   ' get the first sales amount
   strInputSales = InputBox(strPROMPT, strTITLE, "0.00")

4. The third step in the algorithm is a loop that repeats its instructions until there are no more sales amounts to enter. The user indicates that he or she has finished entering data by clicking the Cancel button in the dialog box. Recall that when the Cancel button is clicked, the InputBox function returns the empty string. Enter the following Do clause:

   Do Until strInputSales = String.Empty

5. The first instruction in the loop increments the accumulator variable by the sales amount. Before you can do this, you need to convert the sales amount stored in the strInputSales variable to the Decimal data type. Enter the following TryParse method and assignment statement:

   Decimal.TryParse(strInputSales, decSales)
   decTotalSales = decTotalSales + decSales

6. The next instruction in the loop increments the counter variable by 1. Enter the following assignment statement:

   intNumSales = intNumSales + 1

7. The last instruction in the loop is to enter another sales amount. Enter the following comment and assignment statement, but don't press Enter after typing the assignment statement:

   ' get another sales amount
   strInputSales =
       InputBox(strPROMPT, strTITLE, "0.00")

8. The fourth and fifth steps in the algorithm calculate and display the average sales amount. As the algorithm indicates, both tasks are performed after the loop has finished processing. Click **after the letter p** in the Loop clause and then press **Enter** twice to insert two blank lines. Enter the following assignment statements:

   decAverage = decTotalSales / intNumSales
   lblAverage.Text = decAverage.ToString("C2")

Figure 12-18 shows a preliminary testing chart for the Sales Express application. At times, you may not be sure of the expected result when testing with an invalid value. In those cases, you can wait until after testing the application to complete the Expected result entry. However, after determining the result, you should study the code to understand why it generated that result.

Test data	Expected result
No data entered	$0.00
Valid values	
0	$0.00
25.67	$25.67
100, 75.50, 30.25	$68.58
-5	($5.00)
78.56, -4	$37.28
Invalid values	
Empty input area	
X, $5	

Figure 12-18 Preliminary testing chart for the Sales Express application

To begin testing the Sales Express application:

1. Save the solution and then start the application. Click the **Calculate** button. The input dialog box shown earlier in Figure 12-16 opens.

2. Click the **Cancel** button in the dialog box. After a few seconds, the screen appears as shown in Figure 12-19.

help box

```
    ' get the first sales amount
    strInputSales = InputBox(strPROMPT, st
    Do Until strInputSales = String.Empty
        Decimal.TryParse(strInputSales, de
        decTotalSales = decTotalSales + de
        intNumSales = intNumSales + 1
        ' get another sales amount
        strInputSales = InputBox(strPROMPT
    Loop

    decAverage = decTotalSales / intNumSales
    lblAverage.Text = decAverage.ToString("C2")
```

DivideByZeroException was unhandled

Attempted to divide by zero.

Troubleshooting tips:
Make sure the value of the denominator is not zero before performing a division operation.
Get general help for this exception.

Search for more Help Online...

Actions:
View Detail...
Copy exception detail to the clipboard

Figure 12-19 Result of the run time error caused by dividing by zero

When you click the Calculate button and then click the Cancel button, a run time error occurs. A **run time error** is an error that occurs while an application is running. Notice that an arrow points to the statement where the error was encountered, and the statement is highlighted. In addition, a help box opens; the help box provides information pertaining to the error. In this case, the run time error was encountered when the computer tried to process the decAverage = decTotalSales / intNumSales statement. The help box indicates that the statement is attempting to divide by zero.

To continue testing the Sales Express application:

1. Place your mouse pointer on intNumSales in the highlighted statement. The variable contains the number 0, because no sales amounts were entered.

2. Click **Debug** on the menu bar and then click **Stop Debugging**.

3. Before using a variable as the divisor in an expression, you always should verify that the variable does not contain the number 0 because, as in mathematics, division by zero is not possible. Click the **blank line** below the Loop clause and then press **Enter** to insert a blank line. Enter the selection structure shown in Figure 12-20. (You will need to move the calculation statement to the selection structure's true path.)

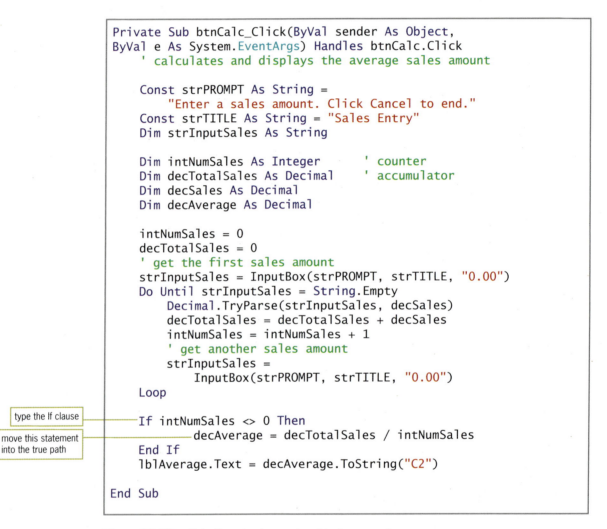

```
Private Sub btnCalc_Click(ByVal sender As Object,
ByVal e As System.EventArgs) Handles btnCalc.Click
    ' calculates and displays the average sales amount

    Const strPROMPT As String =
        "Enter a sales amount. Click Cancel to end."
    Const strTITLE As String = "Sales Entry"
    Dim strInputSales As String

    Dim intNumSales As Integer        ' counter
    Dim decTotalSales As Decimal      ' accumulator
    Dim decSales As Decimal
    Dim decAverage As Decimal

    intNumSales = 0
    decTotalSales = 0
    ' get the first sales amount
    strInputSales = InputBox(strPROMPT, strTITLE, "0.00")
    Do Until strInputSales = String.Empty
        Decimal.TryParse(strInputSales, decSales)
        decTotalSales = decTotalSales + decSales
        intNumSales = intNumSales + 1
        ' get another sales amount
        strInputSales =
            InputBox(strPROMPT, strTITLE, "0.00")
    Loop

    If intNumSales <> 0 Then
        decAverage = decTotalSales / intNumSales
    End If
    lblAverage.Text = decAverage.ToString("C2")

End Sub
```

type the If clause

move this statement into the true path

Figure 12-20   Selection structure entered in the procedure

4. Save the solution and then start the application. Click the **Calculate** button and then click the **Cancel** button in the dialog box. The Average sales amount box shows $0.00, which is correct.

5. Click the **Calculate** button. Type **25.67** in the dialog box and then press **Enter** to select the OK button. Now click the **Cancel** button to indicate that you have no more sales amounts to enter. The Average sales amount box shows $25.67, which is correct.

6. Click the **Calculate** button. Type the following three sales amounts, pressing **Enter** after typing each one: **100**, **75.50**, and **30.25**. Click the **Cancel** button. The Average sales amount box shows $68.58, which is correct.

7. Click the **Calculate** button. Type **−5** and then press **Enter**. Click the **Cancel** button. The Average sales amount box shows ($5.00), which is the expected result.

8. Click the **Calculate** button. Type the following two sales amounts, pressing **Enter** after typing each one: **78.56** and **−4**. Click the **Cancel** button. The average sales amount is $37.28, which is correct.

9. Now you will test the application with the invalid values listed in the testing chart (shown earlier in Figure 12-18). Click the **Calculate** button. Press the **Backspace** key to delete the 0.00 in the dialog box and then press **Enter**. Because the input area does not contain a value, the InputBox function returns the empty string. As a result, the loop ends and the procedure displays $0.00 as the average sales amount.

10. Click the **Calculate** button. Type the following values, pressing **Enter** after typing each one: **x** and **$5**. Click the **Cancel** button. $0.00 appears in the Average sales amount box. Why $0.00? The TryParse method converts the letter x to the number 0 and then stores the 0 in the decSales variable. The variable's value is then added to the accumulator variable, giving 0. Next, the counter variable is incremented by 1, giving 1. The InputBox function within the loop prompts you to enter another sales amount. Because the TryParse method does not recognize the $, it converts your $5 entry to the number 0 and stores the 0 in the decSales variable. The variable's value is added to the accumulator variable, giving 0. Next, the counter variable is incremented by 1, giving 2. The InputBox function within the loop prompts you to enter another sales amount. When you click the Cancel button, the loop ends and the average sales amount is calculated by dividing the accumulator variable's value (0) by the counter variable's value (2); the result is 0. The formatted result appears in the lblAverage control. The $0.00 is an acceptable value to display when the user enters a letter or a special character along with a number.

11. Click the **Exit** button. Close the Code Editor window and then close the solution.

Figure 12-21 shows the final testing chart for the Sales Express application.

Test data	Expected result
No data entered	$0.00
Valid values	
0	$0.00
25.67	$25.67
100, 75.50, 30.25	$68.58
−5	($5.00)
78.56, −4	$37.28
Invalid values	
Empty input area	$0.00
x, $5	$0.00

Figure 12-21 Final testing chart for the Sales Express application

Can I Abbreviate That Assignment Statement?

In addition to the arithmetic operators listed in Figure 5-5 in Chapter 5, Visual Basic also provides several arithmetic assignment operators. The **arithmetic assignment operators** allow you to abbreviate an assignment statement that contains an arithmetic operator, as long as the assignment statement has the following format, in which *variableName* is the name of the same variable: *variableName* = *variableName arithmeticOperator value*. For example, you can use the addition assignment operator (+=) to abbreviate the statement intAge = intAge + 1 as follows: intAge += 1. Both statements tell the computer to add the number 1 to the contents of the `intAge` variable and then store the result in the `intAge` variable. Figure 12-22 shows the syntax of a Visual Basic statement that uses an arithmetic assignment operator. The figure also lists the most commonly used arithmetic assignment operators, and it includes examples of using arithmetic assignment operators to abbreviate assignment statements. Notice that each arithmetic assignment operator consists of an arithmetic operator followed immediately by the assignment operator (=). The arithmetic assignment operators do not contain a space. In other words, the multiplication assignment operator is *=, not * =. (It's easy to abbreviate an assignment statement. Simply remove the variable name that appears on the left side of the assignment operator in the statement, and then put the assignment operator immediately after the arithmetic operator.)

Arithmetic assignment operators

Syntax
variableName arithmeticAssignmentOperator value

Operator	Purpose
+=	addition assignment
-=	subtraction assignment
*=	multiplication assignment
/=	division assignment

Example 1
Original statement: `intAge = intAge + 1`
Abbreviated statement: `intAge += 1`
Both statements add 1 to the number stored in the `intAge` variable and then assign the result to the variable.

Example 2
Original statement: `decPrice = decPrice - decDiscount`
Abbreviated statement: `decPrice -= decDiscount`
Both statements subtract the number stored in the `decDiscount` variable from the number stored in the `decPrice` variable and then assign the result to the `decPrice` variable.

Example 3
Original statement: `dblSales = dblSales * 1.05`
Abbreviated statement: `dblSales *= 1.05`
Both statements multiply the number stored in the `dblSales` variable by 1.05 and then assign the result to the variable.

Example 4
Original statement: `decPrice = decPrice / 2`
Abbreviated statement: `decPrice /= 2`
Both statements divide the number stored in the `decPrice` variable by 2 and then assign the result to the variable.

Figure 12-22   Syntax and examples of using the arithmetic assignment operators

To use the addition assignment operator in the Sales Express application:

1. Use Windows to make a copy of the Sales Express Solution folder. Save the copy in the ClearlyVB2010\Chap12 folder. Rename the copy **Sales Express Solution-Arithmetic Assignment**.

2. Open the **Sales Express Solution (Sales Express Solution.sln)** file contained in the Sales Express Solution-Arithmetic Assignment folder. Double-click **frmMain.vb** in the Solution Explorer window.

3. Open the Code Editor window. In the btnCalc control's Click event procedure, change the statement that updates the accumulator variable to **decTotalSales += decSales**. Also change the statement that updates the counter variable to **intNumSales += 1**.

4. Save the solution and then start the application. Test the application using the testing chart shown earlier in Figure 12-21.

5. Click the **Exit** button. Close the Code Editor window and then close the solution.

Mini-Quiz 12-3

See Appendix B for the answers.

1. Write an assignment statement that increments the `intTotalNum` variable by the contents of the `intNum` variable.

2. The empty string in Visual Basic is represented by which named constant?

3. Write a statement that assigns the InputBox function's return value to the `strItem` variable. The text "Item Name" should appear in the dialog box's title bar. The "Enter the item:" message should appear inside the dialog box. The input area should be empty.

4. Use the appropriate arithmetic assignment operator to abbreviate the following assignment statement: `intNum = intNum * 3`.

Summary

- You use a repetition structure, also called a loop, to repeatedly process one or more program instructions either while the looping condition is true or until the loop exit condition has been met. A loop's condition must result in an answer of true or false only.

- A repetition structure can be either a pretest loop or a posttest loop. Pretest loops are more commonly used. The condition in a pretest loop is evaluated before the loop instructions are processed. The condition in a posttest loop is evaluated after the loop instructions are processed.

- You can use the Do…Loop statement to code a pretest loop in Visual Basic. The `While` keyword in the statement's condition indicates that the loop instructions should be processed *while* (as long as) the condition is true. The `Until` keyword in the statement's condition indicates that the loop instructions should be processed *until* the condition becomes true.

- Counter and accumulator variables must be initialized and updated. The initialization is done outside of the loop that uses the counter or accumulator, and the updating is done within the loop. Counter variables are updated by a constant value, whereas accumulator variables are usually updated by an amount that varies.

- In a flowchart, the loop condition is represented by the decision symbol, which is a diamond.

- You can use the Refresh method to refresh (redraw) the form. The method's syntax is **Me.Refresh()**.

- You can use the Sleep method to delay program execution. The method's syntax is **System.Threading.Thread.Sleep(***milliseconds***)**.

- The priming read appears above the loop that it controls. The priming read gets only the first value from the user. The update read appears within the loop and gets any remaining values from the user. Neglecting to enter the update read will result in an infinite (endless) loop. You can stop a program that has an infinite loop by clicking Debug on the menu bar and then clicking Stop Debugging.

- The InputBox function displays an input dialog box that contains a message, an OK button, a Cancel button, and an input area. The function's return value is always treated as a string.

- If a run time error occurs, you can stop the application by clicking Debug on the menu bar and then clicking Stop Debugging.

- Before using a variable as the divisor in an expression, you first should verify that the variable does not contain the number 0. Dividing by 0 is mathematically impossible and will cause a run time error to occur.

- You can use an arithmetic assignment operator to abbreviate an assignment statement that has the following format, in which *variableName* is the name of the same variable: *variableName = variableName arithmeticOperator value*.

Key Terms

Accumulator variable—a numeric variable used for accumulating (adding together) something

Arithmetic assignment operators—composed of an arithmetic operator followed by the assignment operator; can be used to abbreviate assignment statements that have a specific format

Counter variable—a numeric variable used for counting something

Do...Loop statement—a Visual Basic statement that can be used to code both pretest loops and posttest loops

Endless loop—a loop whose instructions are processed indefinitely; also called an infinite loop

Incrementing—another name for updating

Infinite loop—another name for an endless loop

Initializing—the process of assigning a beginning value to a memory location, such as a counter or accumulator variable

InputBox function—a Visual Basic function that displays an input dialog box containing a message, OK and Cancel buttons, and an input area

Loop—another name for the repetition structure

Loop body—the instructions within a loop

Loop exit condition—the requirement that must be met for the computer to stop processing the loop body instructions

Looping condition—the requirement that must be met for the computer to continue processing the loop body instructions

Posttest loop— a loop whose condition is evaluated *after* the instructions in its loop body are processed

Pretest loop—a loop whose condition is evaluated *before* the instructions in its loop body are processed

Priming read—the input instruction that appears above the loop that it controls; used to get the first input item from the user

Refresh method—used to refresh (redraw) a form

Repetition structure—the control structure used to repeatedly process one or more program instructions either while a looping condition is true or until a loop exit condition becomes true; also called a loop

Run time error—an error that occurs while an application is running

Sleep method—used to delay program execution

String.Empty constant—the value that represents the empty string in Visual Basic

Update read—the input instruction that appears within a loop and is associated with the priming read

Updating—the process of adding a number to the value stored in a counter or accumulator variable; also called incrementing

Review Questions

1. Which of the following Do clauses will stop the loop only when the `intAge` variable's value is less than the number 0?

   a. `Do While intAge >= 0`   c. `Do Until intAge >= 0`

   b. `Do Until intAge <= 0`   d. both a and b

2. How many times will the computer process the MessageBox.Show method in the following code?

   ```
   intCounter = 0
   Do While intCounter > 3
       MessageBox.Show("Hello")
       intCounter = intCounter + 1
   Loop
   ```

   a. 0   c. 3

   b. 1   d. 4

3. What does the InputBox function return when the user clicks the Cancel button in the dialog box?

   a. the number 0   c. an error message

   b. the empty string   d. none of the above

4. Which of the following statements displays a dialog box that prompts the user for the name of a city, and then assigns the user's response to the `strCity` variable?

   a. `InputBox("Enter the city name:",`
      `"City", strCity)`

   b. `InputBox("Enter the city name:", strCity)`

   c. `strCity =`
      `InputBox("Enter the city name:", "City")`

   d. none of the above

5. How many times will the computer process the MessageBox.Show method in the following code?

```
intCounter = 0
Do Until intCounter > 3
    MessageBox.Show("Hello")
    intCounter = intCounter + 1
Loop
```

    a. 0   c. 3

    b. 1   d. 4

6. Which of the following statements decreases the intNum variable's value by 5?

    a. intNum = intNum − 5   c. intNum = intNum + −5

    b. intNum −= 5   d. all of the above

7. How can you stop a program that has an endless loop?

    a. click File on the menu bar and then click Stop

    b. click Debug on the menu bar and then click Exit

    c. click Debug on the menu bar and then click Stop Debugging

    d. none of the above

Exercises

TRY THIS

1. In this exercise, you modify the My Dream Car-Version 1 application coded in the chapter. (See Appendix B for the answer.)

    a. Use Windows to make a copy of the Car Solution-Version 1 folder. Save the copy in the ClearlyVB2010\Chap12 folder. Rename the copy Car Solution-Version 3. Open the Car Solution (Car Solution.sln) file contained in the Car Solution-Version 3 folder. Change Version 1 in the title bar to Version 3.

    b. Open the Code Editor window. Change the Do clause so that it uses the Until keyword rather than the While keyword. Save the solution and then start and test the application.

    c. Rather than having the counter variable count up from 1, have it count down from 20. Make the appropriate modifications to the code. Save the solution and then start and test the application. Close the Code Editor window and then close the solution.

TRY THIS

2. Open the Sales Tax Solution (Sales Tax Solution.sln) file contained in the ClearlyVB2010\Chap12\Sales Tax Solution folder. The Calculate Sales Tax button's Click event procedure should allow the user to enter zero or more sales amounts. After a sales amount is entered, the procedure should display the amount of a 6% sales tax. Display the sales tax in a message box before asking the user to enter another sales amount. Code the procedure. Save the solution and then start and test the application. Close the Code Editor window and then close the solution.

MODIFY THIS

3. In this exercise, you modify the Sales Express application coded in the chapter. Use Windows to make a copy of the Sales Express Solution folder. Save the copy in the ClearlyVB2010\Chap12 folder. Rename the copy Modified Sales Express Solution. Open the Sales Express Solution (Sales Express Solution.sln) file contained in the Modified Sales Express Solution folder. Open the Code Editor window. Change the Do clause so that it uses the While keyword rather than the Until keyword. If the counter variable contains the number 0, display a message informing the user that no sales amounts were entered. Display the message in a message box. After displaying the average sales

amount, change the lblAverage control's BorderStyle property to BorderStyle.None, blink the text in the control five times, and then change the BorderStyle property back to BorderStyle.FixedSingle. Save the solution and then start and test the application. Close the Code Editor window and then close the solution.

4. Open the Average Score Solution (Average Score Solution.sln) file contained in the ClearlyVB2010\Chap12\Average Score Solution folder. The Calculate button's Click event procedure should allow the user to enter five test scores. It then should both calculate and display the average test score. Code the procedure. Save the solution and then start and test the application. Close the Code Editor window and then close the solution.

INTRODUCTORY

5. Open the Weekly Pay Solution (Weekly Pay Solution.sln) file contained in the ClearlyVB2010\Chap12\Weekly Pay Solution folder. The Calculate button's Click event procedure should allow the user to enter zero or more weekly pay amounts. It then should display the number of amounts entered and the sum of the amounts entered. After displaying the sum, the procedure should change the lblSum control's ForeColor property from `Color.Black` to `Color.Red` and back again; it should do this several times. Code the procedure. Save the solution and then start and test the application. Close the Code Editor window and then close the solution.

INTRODUCTORY

6. Open the Temperature Solution (Temperature Solution.sln) file contained in the ClearlyVB2010\Chap12\Temperature Solution folder. The Calculate button's Click event procedure should allow the user to enter zero or more temperatures. It then should display the number of temperatures entered and the average temperature. Include one decimal place in the average temperature. Code the procedure. Save the solution and then start and test the application. Close the Code Editor window and then close the solution.

INTRODUCTORY

7. Effective January 1st of each year, Gabriela receives a 5% raise on her previous year's salary. She wants a program that both calculates and displays the amount of her raises for the next 3 years. Display the raise amounts in message boxes. Display her total salary for the 3 years in a label control.

INTERMEDIATE

   a. List the output and input items, as well as any processing items, and then create an appropriate algorithm using pseudocode.
   b. Create a Visual Basic Windows application. Use the following names for the solution and project, respectively: Raise Solution and Raise Project. Save the application in the ClearlyVB2010\Chap12 folder. Change the name of the form file on your disk to frmMain.vb. If necessary, change the form's name to frmMain.
   c. Create a suitable interface. Include a text box for entering the initial salary amount. Also include an Exit button. Code the Exit button's Click event procedure and the problem's algorithm.
   d. Save the solution and then start and test the application. (Hint: For an annual salary of 10000, the raise amounts are $500.00, $525.00, and $551.25. The total salary is $33,101.25.) Close the Code Editor window and then close the solution.

8. Open the Sum Even Solution (Sum Even Solution.sln) file contained in the ClearlyVB2010\Chap12\Sum Even Solution folder. The interface provides text boxes for the user to enter two numbers, which should be integers. Code the application so each text box accepts only numbers and the Backspace key. The Display button's Click event procedure should display the sum of the even numbers between the two integers entered by the user. If the user's entry is even, it should be included in the sum. For example, if the user enters the integers 2 and 7, the procedure should display 12 (2 + 4 + 6). If the user enters the integers 2 and 8, the procedure should display 20 (2 + 4 + 6 + 8). Code the Display button's Click event procedure. Save the solution and then start and test the application. Close the Code Editor window and then close the solution.

INTERMEDIATE

9. Open the Colfax Solution (Colfax Solution.sln) file contained in the ClearlyVB2010\Chap12\Colfax Solution folder. Code the Add button's Click event procedure so that it adds the amounts entered by the user to an accumulator variable and then displays the

INTERMEDIATE

variable's value in the lblSales control. Use an arithmetic assignment operator to update the accumulator. Display the total sales with a dollar sign and two decimal places. Save the solution and then start and test the application. Close the Code Editor window and then close the solution.

ADVANCED 10. In this exercise, you create an application for Premium Paper. The application allows the sales manager to enter the company's income and expense amounts. The number of income and expense amounts may vary each time the application is started. For example, the user may enter five income amounts and three expense amounts. Or, he or she may enter 20 income amounts and 30 expense amounts. The application should calculate and display the company's total income, total expenses, and profit (or loss). Use the InputBox function to get the individual income and expense amounts. If the company experienced a loss, display the amount of the loss using a red font; otherwise, display the profit using a black font. (Hint: Change the label control's ForeColor property to either Color.Red or Color.Black.)

    a. List the output and input items, as well as any processing items, and then create an appropriate algorithm using pseudocode.

    b. Create a Visual Basic Windows application. Use the following names for the solution and project, respectively: Premium Solution and Premium Project. Save the application in the ClearlyVB2010\Chap12 folder. Change the name of the form file on your disk to frmMain.vb. If necessary, change the form's name to frmMain.

    c. Create a suitable interface. Use label controls to display the total income, total expenses, and profit (loss) amounts.

    d. Code the application. Keep in mind that the income and expense amounts may contain decimal places. Display the calculated amounts with a dollar sign and two decimal places.

    e. Save the solution and then start and test the application. Close the Code Editor window and then close the solution.

ADVANCED 11. In this exercise, you modify the Sales Express application coded in the chapter. Use Windows to make a copy of the Sales Express Solution folder. Save the copy in the ClearlyVB2010\Chap12 folder. Rename the copy Advanced Sales Express Solution. Open the Sales Express Solution (Sales Express Solution.sln) file contained in the Advanced Sales Express Solution folder. Open the Code Editor window. If the user enters a sales amount that is not greater than 0, do not include the sales amount in the average; instead, use a message box to display an appropriate message to the user. In addition to displaying the average sales amount, the application also should display the number of sales amounts entered. Make the appropriate modifications to the application's interface and code. Save the solution and then start and test the application. Close the Code Editor window and then close the solution.

FIGURE THIS OUT 12. Open the FigureThisOut Solution (FigureThisOut Solution.sln) file contained in the ClearlyVB2010\Chap12\FigureThisOut Solution folder. Open the Code Editor window and study the existing code. List the steps the computer follows when processing the Calculate button's code. (You can use the processing steps shown in Figure 12-8 as a guide.) Start and then test the application. Close the Code Editor window and then close the solution.

SWAT THE BUGS 13. Open the SwatTheBugs Solution (SwatTheBugs Solution.sln) file contained in the ClearlyVB2010\Chap12\SwatTheBugs Solution folder. The application should drag the picture box up and then down again on the form. Start the application and then click the Up and Down button. Notice that the application is not working correctly. Click the Exit button. Locate and correct the errors in the code. Save the solution and then start and test the application again. Close the Code Editor window and then close the solution.

Do It, Then Ask Permission (Posttest Loops)

After studying Chapter 13, you should be able to:

◎ Show a posttest loop in both pseudocode and a flowchart

◎ Write a posttest loop using the Do…Loop statement

Testing After the Fact

As you learned in Chapter 12, a repetition structure can be either a pretest loop or a posttest loop. The difference between both types of loops pertains to when the loop condition is evaluated. The condition in a pretest loop is evaluated *before* the instructions within the loop are processed. The condition in a **posttest loop**, on the other hand, is evaluated *after* the instructions within the loop are processed. Depending on the result of the evaluation, the instructions in a pretest loop may never be processed. The instructions in a posttest loop, however, will always be processed at least once. Although most programmers use pretest loops, it is essential to understand the way posttest loops work because you may encounter a posttest loop in another programmer's code that you are either modifying or debugging. You also may encounter a situation where a posttest loop is the better choice of loops.

The problem specification and algorithms shown in Figure 13-1 will help clarify the difference between pretest and posttest loops. Algorithm 1 contains a pretest loop, and Algorithm 2 contains a posttest loop. The purpose of the loop in each algorithm is to position Rob (the mechanical man) directly in front of his bedroom door. Compare the first and last lines in the pretest loop with the first and last lines in the posttest loop. More specifically, notice the location of the loop condition: *until you are directly in front of the bedroom door*. In the pretest loop, the condition appears in the first line; this indicates that Rob should evaluate it *before* he follows the instructions in the loop. In the posttest loop, the condition appears in the last line, indicating that Rob should evaluate it only *after* following the instructions in the loop. The pretest loop in Algorithm 1 will work when Rob is zero or more steps away from his bedroom door. The posttest loop in Algorithm 2, however, will work only when Rob is at least one step away from the bedroom door.

Rob is standing in his hallway facing his bedroom door. The door, which may or may not be closed, is an unknown number of steps away from Rob. Rob wants to enter his bedroom.

Algorithm 1 – pretest loop

works when Rob is zero or more steps away from the door

1. repeat until you are directly in front of the bedroom door:
       walk forward
   end repeat
2. if the bedroom door is closed, do this:
       open the bedroom door
   end if
3. walk forward

Algorithm 2 – posttest loop

works only when Rob is at least one step away from the door

1. repeat:
       walk forward
   end repeat until you are directly in front of the bedroom door
2. if the bedroom door is closed, do this:
       open the bedroom door
   end if
3. walk forward

Figure 13-1   Rob algorithms containing pretest and posttest loops

To understand why the loops in Figure 13-1 are not interchangeable, you will test them. For the first test, Rob is one step away from the door. In the pretest loop in Algorithm 1, the loop condition tells Rob to check his current location. Rob is not directly in front of his bedroom door, so he is told to *walk forward* and then the loop condition is evaluated again. Rob is now positioned correctly in front of the door, so the loop ends and Rob continues to Step 2 in the algorithm. In the posttest loop in Algorithm 2, Rob is told to *walk forward*, which places him directly in front of his bedroom door. Next, the loop condition tells Rob to check whether he is positioned correctly; he is, so the loop ends and Rob continues to Step 2 in the algorithm. Notice that, when Rob is one step away from the door, the pretest and posttest loops produce the same result; both position Rob in front of the door.

For the second test, Rob is directly in front of his bedroom door. The condition in the pretest loop in Algorithm 1 tells Rob to check his current location. Rob is already positioned correctly, so the *walk forward* instruction is bypassed and the loop ends. In the posttest loop in Algorithm 2, Rob is told to *walk forward* before evaluating his current location. But if Rob walks forward, he will bump into the door. Obviously, the posttest loop in Algorithm 2 does not work correctly when Rob starts out directly in front of his bedroom door. You can fix this problem by adding a selection structure to the algorithm, as shown in Figure 13-2.

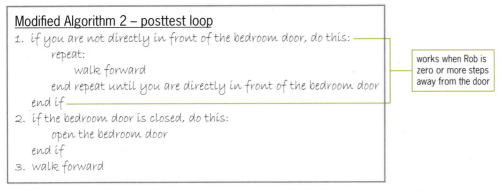

Figure 13-2   Selection structure added to Algorithm 2 from Figure 13-1

The posttest loop in Figure 13-2 is identical to the posttest loop in Figure 13-1, except it is processed only when Rob is not directly in front of his bedroom door. First, test the algorithm with Rob one step away from the door. The algorithm begins with a selection structure whose condition tells Rob to check his current location. Rob is not directly in front of his bedroom door, so the posttest loop instructs him to *walk forward*. The loop condition is evaluated next. At this point, Rob is positioned correctly; therefore, the loop and selection structure end and Rob continues to Step 2 in the algorithm. For the second test, Rob is directly in front of his bedroom door. Here again, the condition in the selection structure tells Rob to check his current location. In this case, Rob is already in front of his bedroom door, so the entire posttest loop is bypassed and Rob continues to Step 2 in the algorithm. Although the modified algorithm works correctly, most programmers prefer to use a pretest loop (rather than a posttest loop with a selection structure) because it is easier to write and understand. Posttest loops should be used only when their instructions must be processed at least once.

More on the Do...Loop Statement

In Chapter 12, you learned how to use the Do...Loop statement to code a pretest loop. The statement also is used to code a posttest loop; the syntax for doing this is shown in Figure 13-3. Comparing the statement's posttest syntax with its pretest syntax (shown in Figure 12-7 in Chapter 12), you will notice one difference: the location of the {While | Until} *condition* section. In the pretest syntax, that section is part of the Do clause and indicates that the condition is evaluated *before* the loop instructions are processed. In the posttest syntax, on the other hand, it's part of the Loop clause, indicating that the condition is evaluated *after* the loop instructions are processed. In the posttest syntax, the only purpose of the Do clause is to mark the beginning of the loop. Figure 13-3 also shows how to write the pretest loops from Figure 12-7 as posttest loops. Like the pretest loops, both posttest loops display the numbers 1, 2, and 3 in message boxes. Notice that the loop's condition can be phrased as either a looping condition or a loop exit condition.

Do...Loop statement

Syntax for coding a posttest loop
Do
loop body instructions, which will be processed either
while the condition is true or until the condition becomes true
Loop {While | Until} condition

Example 1
```
intNumber = 1
Do
    MessageBox.Show(intNumber)
    intNumber = intNumber + 1
Loop While intNumber <= 3
```
looping condition

Example 2
```
intNumber = 1
Do
    MessageBox.Show(intNumber)
    intNumber = intNumber + 1
Loop Until intNumber > 3
```
loop exit condition

Figure 13-3 Syntax and examples of the Do...Loop statement for a posttest loop

Pseudocode and Flowchart Containing a Posttest Loop

Figure 13-4 shows the pseudocode and flowchart for Example 2 in Figure 13-3. Not surprisingly, the diamond that represents the loop's condition in a flowchart appears at the bottom of a posttest loop. (Recall that it appears at the top of a pretest loop.) The loop in the figure is formed by all of the symbols and flowlines in the loop's false path.

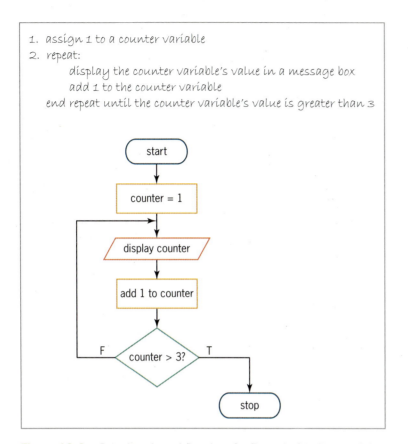

1. assign 1 to a counter variable
2. repeat:
       display the counter variable's value in a message box
       add 1 to the counter variable
   end repeat until the counter variable's value is greater than 3

Figure 13-4   Pseudocode and flowchart for Example 2 in Figure 13-3

The Bouncing Robot Application

The Bouncing Robot application, which you will finish coding in this section, illustrates the difference between a pretest loop and a posttest loop. The application bounces a robot up and down on the form. The number of times the robot bounces is entered in a text box.

To code and then test the Bouncing Robot application:

1. Start Visual Studio 2010 or Visual Basic 2010 Express and permanently display the Solution Explorer window. Open the **Bouncing Robot Solution** (**Bouncing Robot Solution.sln**) file contained in the ClearlyVB2010\Chap13\Bouncing Robot Solution folder. If the designer window is not open, double-click **frmMain.vb** in the Solution Explorer window.

2. Open the Code Editor window. Locate the btnPretest control's Click event procedure and examine its code.

3. The btnPretest control's Click event procedure will use a pretest loop to repeat the loop instructions while the value in the counter variable (intCounter) is less than the value in the intBounces variable. Change the Do clause to the following:

    Do While intCounter < intBounces

4. Next, locate the btnPosttest control's Click event procedure and examine its code.

5. The btnPosttest control's Click event procedure will use a posttest loop to repeat the loop instructions while the value in the counter variable (intCounter) is less than the value in the intBounces variable. Change the Loop clause to the following:

    Loop While intCounter < intBounces

6. Save the solution and then start the application.

7. First, you will test the Pretest Loop button's code. Type **4** in the Number of bounces box and then click the **Pretest Loop** button. The robot bounces up and down four times. Change the number of bounces to **2** and then click the **Pretest Loop** button. The robot bounces up and down two times. Change the number of bounces to **0** and then click the **Pretest Loop** button. This time, the robot does not bounce.

8. Now you will test the Posttest Loop button's code. Change the number of bounces to **4** and then click the **Posttest Loop** button. The robot bounces up and down four times. Change the number of bounces to **2** and then click the **Posttest Loop** button. The robot bounces up and down two times. Change the number of bounces to **0** and then click the **Posttest Loop** button. The robot bounces up and down one time; this is because the loop's condition is not evaluated until *after* the loop instructions are processed the first time.

9. Click the **Exit** button.

You can fix the problem in the Posttest Loop button's code by placing the posttest loop in a selection structure. The selection structure's condition will determine whether the `intBounces` variable contains a number other than 0. The posttest loop will be processed only when the selection structure's condition evaluates to True; otherwise, the loop will be skipped over.

To modify the Posttest Loop button's code:

1. Modify the btnPosttest control's Click event procedure by adding the selection structure shown in Figure 13-5.

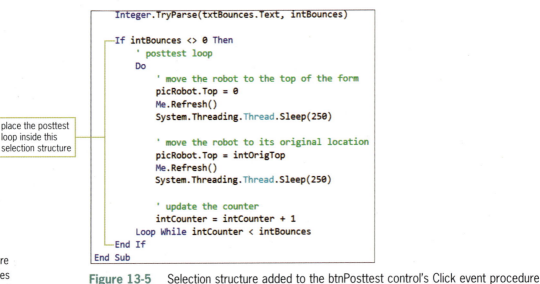

place the posttest loop inside this selection structure

```
Integer.TryParse(txtBounces.Text, intBounces)

If intBounces <> 0 Then
    ' posttest loop
    Do
        ' move the robot to the top of the form
        picRobot.Top = 0
        Me.Refresh()
        System.Threading.Thread.Sleep(250)

        ' move the robot to its original location
        picRobot.Top = intOrigTop
        Me.Refresh()
        System.Threading.Thread.Sleep(250)

        ' update the counter
        intCounter = intCounter + 1
    Loop While intCounter < intBounces
End If
End Sub
```

Figure 13-5 Selection structure added to the btnPosttest control's Click event procedure

For more examples of using the Do...Loop statement to code a posttest loop, see the Do...Loop Posttest section in the Ch13WantMore.pdf file.

2. Save the solution and then start the application. Test the Posttest Loop button's code using the numbers **4**, **2**, and **0**. The robot should bounce up and down four times, two times, and zero times, respectively.

3. Click the **Exit** button. Close the Code Editor window and then close the solution.

Mini-Quiz 13-1

See Appendix B for the answers.

1. Write a Visual Basic Loop clause that processes the loop instructions as long as the value in the `intQuantity` variable is greater than the number 0. Use the `While` keyword.

2. Rewrite the Loop clause from Question 1 using the `Until` keyword.

It's time to view the Ch13-Stepping Through a Loop video.

Summary

- The instructions in a posttest loop will always be processed at least once.

- You use the Do…Loop statement to code a posttest loop in Visual Basic. The Do clause simply marks the beginning of the loop. The Loop clause contains either the `While` keyword or the `Until` keyword, followed by the loop condition. The condition can be phrased as either a looping condition or a loop exit condition.

Key Term

Posttest loop—a loop whose condition is evaluated *after* the instructions in its loop body are processed

Review Questions

1. Which of the following Loop clauses will stop the loop only when the `intAge` variable's value is less than the number 0?

   a. `Loop While intAge >= 0`   c. `Loop Until intAge >= 0`

   b. `Loop Until intAge <= 0`   d. none of the above

2. How many times will the computer process the MessageBox.Show method in the following code?
   ```
   intCounter = 0
   Do
        MessageBox.Show("Hello")
        intCounter = intCounter + 1
   Loop While intCounter > 3
   ```

   a. 0   c. 3

   b. 1   d. 4

3. What is the value in the `intCounter` variable when the loop in Review Question 2 ends?

   a. 0   c. 3

   b. 1   d. 4

4. How many times will the computer process the MessageBox.Show method in the following code?

```
intCounter = 0
Do
    MessageBox.Show("Hello")
    intCounter += 1
Loop Until intCounter > 3
```

a. 0   c. 3

b. 1   d. 4

5. The instructions in a pretest loop will always be processed at least once.

a. True   b. False

6. The condition in a posttest loop can be phrased as either a looping condition or a loop exit condition.

a. True   b. False

Exercises

TRY THIS

1. Figure 13-6 shows the first four processing steps for the code in Example 1 in Figure 13-3. Complete the remaining steps. (See Appendix B for the answer.)

Processing steps
1. The computer initializes the intNumber variable to 1.
2. The computer processes the Do clause, which marks the beginning of the loop.
3. The loop instructions display the intNumber variable's value (1) and then update the value by adding 1 to it, giving 2.
4. The computer processes the Loop clause, which checks whether the intNumber variable's value is less than or equal to 3. It is, so processing returns to the Do clause.
5.
6.
7.
8.
9.
10.

Figure 13-6   Processing steps for Example 1 in Figure 13-3

TRY THIS

2. Open the Car Solution (Car Solution.sln) file contained in the ClearlyVB2010\Chap13\ Car Solution-Version 1 folder. Change the pretest loop in the btnClickMe control's Click event procedure to a posttest loop that uses the Until keyword. Save the solution and then start and test the application. Close the Code Editor window and then close the solution. (See Appendix B for the answer.)

MODIFY THIS

3. In this exercise, you modify the Bouncing Robot application coded in the chapter. Use Windows to make a copy of the Bouncing Robot Solution folder. Save the copy in the ClearlyVB2010\Chap13 folder. Rename the copy Modified Bouncing Robot Solution. Open the Bouncing Robot Solution (Bouncing Robot Solution.sln) file contained in the

Modified Bouncing Robot Solution folder. Open the designer and Code Editor windows. Currently, the pretest loop starts counting at 0 and stops when it reaches the number of bounces entered by the user. Modify the code so that it starts counting with the number of bounces entered by the user and stops when it reaches 0. Save the solution and then start the application. Test the Pretest Loop button's code. Close the Code Editor window and then close the solution.

4. Open the Average Score Solution (Average Score Solution.sln) file contained in the ClearlyVB2010\Chap13\Average Score Solution folder. The Calculate button's Click event procedure should use a posttest loop to allow the user to enter five test scores. It then should both calculate and display the average test score. If the average test score is greater than 80, the procedure should use a posttest loop to blink the lblAverage control six times. Code the procedure. Save the solution and then start and test the application. Close the Code Editor window and then close the solution.

INTRODUCTORY

5. Open the Temperature Solution (Temperature Solution.sln) file contained in the ClearlyVB2010\Chap13\Temperature Solution folder. The Calculate button's Click event procedure should use a posttest loop to allow the user to enter zero or more temperatures. It then should display the number of temperatures entered and the average temperature. Code the procedure. Save the solution and then start and test the application. Close the Code Editor window and then close the solution.

INTRODUCTORY

6. Effective January 1st of each year, Gabriela receives a 5% raise on her previous year's salary. She wants a program that both calculates and displays the amount of her raises for the next 3 years. Display the raise amounts in message boxes. Display her total salary for the 3 years in a label control.

INTERMEDIATE

   a. List the output and input items, as well as any processing items, and then create an appropriate algorithm using a flowchart and a posttest loop.
   b. Create a Visual Basic Windows application. Use the following names for the solution and project, respectively: Raise Solution and Raise Project. Save the application in the ClearlyVB2010\Chap13 folder. Change the name of the form file on your disk to frmMain.vb. If necessary, change the form's name to frmMain.
   c. Create a suitable interface. Include a text box for entering the initial salary amount. Also include an Exit button. Code the Exit button's Click event procedure and the problem's algorithm.
   d. Save the solution and then start and test the application. (Hint: For an annual salary of 10000, the raise amounts are $500.00, $525.00, and $551.25. The total salary is $33,101.25.) Close the Code Editor window and then close the solution.

7. Open the Sum Even Solution (Sum Even Solution.sln) file contained in the ClearlyVB2010\Chap13\Sum Even Solution folder. The interface provides text boxes for the user to enter two numbers, which should be integers. Code the application so each text box accepts only numbers and the Backspace key. The Display button's Click event procedure should display the sum of the even numbers between the two integers entered by the user. If the user's entry is even, it should be included in the sum. For example, if the user enters the integers 2 and 7, the procedure should display 12 (2 + 4 + 6). If the user enters the integers 2 and 8, the procedure should display 20 (2 + 4 + 6 + 8). Code the Display button's Click event procedure using a posttest loop. Save the solution and then start and test the application. Close the Code Editor window and then close the solution.

INTERMEDIATE

8. Open the Sales Express Solution (Sales Express Solution.sln) file contained in the ClearlyVB2010\Chap13\Sales Express Solution folder. Change the pretest loop in the btnCalc control's Click event procedure to a posttest loop. Save the solution and then start and test the application. Close the Code Editor window and then close the solution.

ADVANCED

9. Open the FigureThisOut Solution (FigureThisOut Solution.sln) file contained in the ClearlyVB2010\Chap13\FigureThisOut Solution folder. Open the Code Editor window and study the existing code. Start the application. Click the Display button and then click the Exit button. Change the `intCount = 1` statement to `intCount = 0`. What additional changes will need to be made to the code as a result of starting the counter at 0 rather than at 1? Make the necessary changes. Save the solution and then start and test the application. Close the Code Editor window and then close the solution.

10. Open the SwatTheBugs Solution (SwatTheBugs Solution.sln) file contained in the ClearlyVB2010\Chap13\SwatTheBugs Solution folder. Start the application and then test it by trying to enter three commission amounts. Notice that the application is not working correctly. Click the Exit button. Locate and correct the errors in the code. Save the solution and then start and test the application again. Close the Code Editor window and then close the solution.

CHAPTER 14

Let Me Count the Ways (Counter-Controlled Loops)

After studying Chapter 14, you should be able to:

◎ Code a counter-controlled pretest loop using the For...Next statement

◎ Play an audio file while an application is running

◎ Calculate a periodic payment using the Financial.Pmt method

◎ Concatenate strings

When Will It Stop?

A loop whose instructions you want processed a precise number of times is often referred to as a **counter-controlled loop**, because it uses a counter variable to keep track of the number of times the loop instructions are processed. A counter-controlled loop can be either a pretest loop or a posttest loop. You code a posttest counter-controlled loop using the Do...Loop statement. A pretest counter-controlled loop, on the other hand, can be coded using either the Do...Loop statement or the For...Next statement. However, the **For...Next statement** provides a more convenient way to code that type of loop, because it takes care of initializing and updating the counter variable, as well as evaluating the loop condition.

Figure 14-1 shows the For...Next statement's syntax and includes an example of using the statement. You enter the loop body, which contains the instructions you want the computer to repeat, between the statement's For and Next clauses. Notice that *counterVariableName* appears in both clauses. *CounterVariableName* is the name of a numeric variable that the computer can use to keep track of (in other words, count) the number of times it processes the loop body. Although, technically, you do not need to specify the name of the counter variable in the Next clause, doing so is highly recommended because it makes your code more self-documenting.

You can use the optional As *dataType* portion of the For clause to declare the counter variable. When you declare a variable in the For clause, the variable has block scope and can be used only within the For...Next loop. The variable is removed from the computer's internal memory when the loop ends. (You learned about block scope in Chapter 8.) Alternatively, you can declare the counter variable in a Dim statement, as long as the Dim statement appears somewhere above the For...Next statement in the procedure. As you know, a variable declared in a Dim statement at the beginning of a procedure has procedure scope and can be used within the entire procedure. When deciding where to declare the counter variable, keep in mind that if a variable is needed only by the For...Next loop, then it is a better programming practice to declare the variable in the For clause. As mentioned in Chapter 8, fewer unintentional errors occur in applications when the variables are declared using the minimum scope needed. Block variables have a smaller scope than do procedure-level variables. You should declare the counter variable in a Dim statement only when its value is required by statements outside the For...Next loop in the procedure.

The *startValue*, *endValue*, and *stepValue* items in the For clause control the number of times the loop body is processed. The three items must be numeric and can be either positive or negative, integer or non-integer. The startValue and endValue tell the computer where to begin and end counting, respectively. The stepValue tells the computer how much to count by—in other words, how much to add to the counter variable each time the loop is processed. If you omit the stepValue, a stepValue of positive 1 is used. The example in Figure 14-1 uses the For...Next statement to display (in message boxes) integers from 10 (the startValue) through 13 (the endValue) in increments of 1 (the stepValue). In addition to the syntax and example of the For...Next statement, Figure 14-1 also shows the tasks performed by the computer when processing the statement.

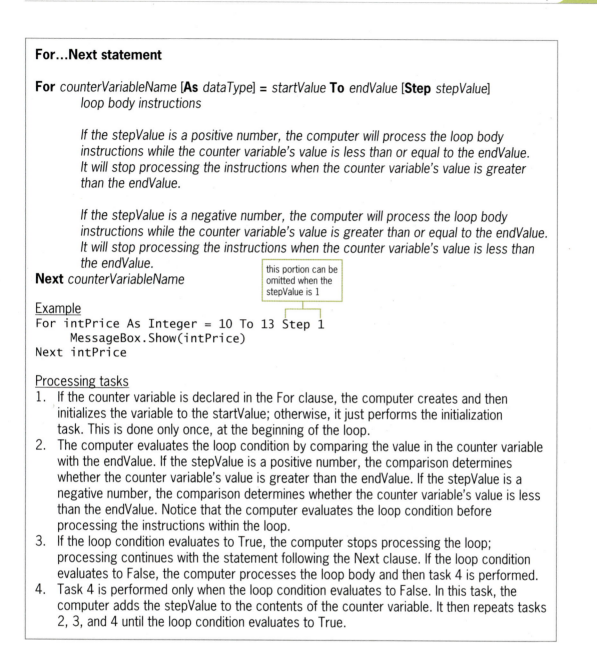

For...Next statement

For *counterVariableName* [**As** *dataType*] = *startValue* **To** *endValue* [**Step** *stepValue*]
    loop body instructions

      *If the stepValue is a positive number, the computer will process the loop body
      instructions while the counter variable's value is less than or equal to the endValue.
      It will stop processing the instructions when the counter variable's value is greater
      than the endValue.*

      *If the stepValue is a negative number, the computer will process the loop body
      instructions while the counter variable's value is greater than or equal to the endValue.
      It will stop processing the instructions when the counter variable's value is less than
      the endValue.*

Next *counterVariableName*

> this portion can be omitted when the stepValue is 1

Example
```
For intPrice As Integer = 10 To 13 Step 1
    MessageBox.Show(intPrice)
Next intPrice
```

Processing tasks
1. If the counter variable is declared in the For clause, the computer creates and then initializes the variable to the startValue; otherwise, it just performs the initialization task. This is done only once, at the beginning of the loop.
2. The computer evaluates the loop condition by comparing the value in the counter variable with the endValue. If the stepValue is a positive number, the comparison determines whether the counter variable's value is greater than the endValue. If the stepValue is a negative number, the comparison determines whether the counter variable's value is less than the endValue. Notice that the computer evaluates the loop condition before processing the instructions within the loop.
3. If the loop condition evaluates to True, the computer stops processing the loop; processing continues with the statement following the Next clause. If the loop condition evaluates to False, the computer processes the loop body and then task 4 is performed.
4. Task 4 is performed only when the loop condition evaluates to False. In this task, the computer adds the stepValue to the contents of the counter variable. It then repeats tasks 2, 3, and 4 until the loop condition evaluates to True.

Figure 14-1   Syntax, example, and processing tasks for the For...Next statement

Figure 14-2 describes the steps the computer follows when processing the code in Figure 14-1's example. As Step 2 indicates, the loop's condition is evaluated *before* the loop body is processed. This is because the loop created by the For...Next statement is a pretest loop. The instruction in the loop body is processed four times and displays the numbers 10, 11, 12, and 13 (one at a time) in message boxes. Notice that the `intPrice` variable contains the number 14 when the For...Next statement ends. The number 14 is the first integer that is greater than the loop's endValue of 13.

Processing steps

1. The computer creates the `intPrice` variable and initializes it to 10.
2. The computer checks whether the `intPrice` variable's value is greater than 13. It's not, so the computer displays the number 10 in a message box and then adds 1 to the variable's value, giving 11.
3. The computer again checks whether the `intPrice` variable's value is greater than 13. It's not, so the computer displays the number 11 in a message box and then adds 1 to the variable's value, giving 12.
4. The computer again checks whether the `intPrice` variable's value is greater than 13. It's not, so the computer displays the number 12 in a message box and then adds 1 to the variable's value, giving 13.
5. The computer again checks whether the `intPrice` variable's value is greater than 13. It's not, so the computer displays the number 13 in a message box and then adds 1 to the variable's value, giving 14.
6. The computer again checks whether the `intPrice` variable's value is greater than 13. It is, so the computer stops processing the loop body. Processing continues with the statement following the Next clause.

 For more examples of using the For...Next statement to code a counter-controlled loop, see the For...Next section in the Ch14WantMore.pdf file.

Figure 14-2 Processing steps for the example in Figure 14-1

Spaceship-Version 1 Application

Figure 14-3 shows the interface for the Spaceship-Version 1 application. (The spaceship image is from the Microsoft Office Clip Art collection, which is available at *http://office.microsoft.com*.) In the Go button's Click event procedure, you will include a For...Next statement that displays the numbers 1, 2, and 3 in the lblCountToBlastOff control.

 Before you begin coding the Spaceship-Version 1 application, you may want to view the Ch14-Spaceship video. The video demonstrates the steps contained in the following section. It also demonstrates the steps for coding the Spaceship-Version 2 application.

Figure 14-3 Interface for the Spaceship-Version 1 application

To code and then test the Spaceship-Version 1 application:

1. Start Visual Studio 2010 or Visual Basic 2010 Express and permanently display the Solution Explorer window. Open the **Spaceship Solution** (**Spaceship Solution.sln**) file contained in the ClearlyVB2010\Chap14\Spaceship Solution-Version 1 folder. If the designer window is not open, double-click **frmMain.vb** in the Solution Explorer window.

2. Open the Code Editor window. Locate the btnGo control's Click event procedure. The procedure positions the spaceship at the bottom of the form. It then removes the border from the lblCountToBlastOff control, sets the control's Visible property to True, and

displays the "Blast Off!" message in the control. The procedure then pauses program execution for a short time before hiding the control. The loop in the procedure drags the spaceship to the top of the form.

3. Start the application and then click the **Go** button. The "Blast Off!" message appears in the label control and then the spaceship is dragged to the top of the form. Click the **Exit** button.

4. Click the **blank line** below the ' count up from 1 to 3, pausing execution after each number comment. Type the following For clause and then press **Enter**. When you press Enter, the Code Editor automatically enters the Next clause for you.

For intCount As Integer = 1 To 3

5. Change the Next clause to **Next intCount**.

6. The first instruction in the loop will display the counter variable's value in the lblCountToBlastOff control. Click the **blank line** below the For clause and then enter the following assignment statement:

lblCountToBlastOff.Text = intCount

7. Now you will refresh the screen and then pause program execution for half of a second, allowing the user to view the current number in the lblCountToBlastOff control. Enter the additional statements shown in Figure 14-4.

```vb
Private Sub btnGo_Click(ByVal sender As Object, ByVal e As
System.EventArgs) Handles btnGo.Click
    ' drags the spaceship from the bottom to the top of the form

    ' position the spaceship at the bottom of the form
    picSpaceship.Top = 355
    ' remove the border from the label control
    ' then show the control
    lblCountToBlastOff.BorderStyle = BorderStyle.None
    lblCountToBlastOff.Visible = True

    ' count up from 1 to 3, pausing execution after each number
    For intCount As Integer = 1 To 3
        lblCountToBlastOff.Text = intCount
        Me.Refresh()                              ⎱ enter these two
        System.Threading.Thread.Sleep(500)        ⎰ statements
    Next intCount

    ' display the "Blast Off!" message, then pause execution
    lblCountToBlastOff.Text = "Blast Off!"
    Me.Refresh()
    System.Threading.Thread.Sleep(500)

    ' hide the label control
    lblCountToBlastOff.Visible = False

    ' drag the spaceship to the top of the form
    Do While picSpaceship.Top > 0
        picSpaceship.Top = picSpaceship.Top - 100
        Me.Refresh()
        System.Threading.Thread.Sleep(100)
    Loop
End Sub
```

Figure 14-4 Go button's Click event procedure in the Spaceship-Version 1 application

8. Save the solution and then start the application. Click the **Go** button. The numbers 1, 2, and 3 appear (one at a time) in the label control, followed by the "Blast Off!" message. The spaceship is then dragged to the top of the form.

9. Click the **Exit** button. Close the Code Editor window and then close the solution.

Spaceship-Version 2 Application

In this version of the Spaceship application, the For...Next statement in the Go button's Click event procedure will display the numbers 3, 2, and 1 in the lblCountToBlastOff control.

To code and then test the Spaceship-Version 2 application:

1. Open the **Spaceship Solution (Spaceship Solution.sln)** file contained in the ClearlyVB2010\Chap14\Spaceship Solution-Version 2 folder. If the designer window is not open, double-click **frmMain.vb** in the Solution Explorer window. Except for the title bar text, the interface is identical to the one shown earlier in Figure 14-3.

2. Open the Code Editor window. Locate the btnGo control's Click event procedure. Except for the For...Next loop and the fifth comment, the procedure contains the same code shown in Figure 14-4.

3. Click the **blank line** below the fifth comment and then enter the For...Next statement shown in Figure 14-5. Because the startValue is greater than the endValue, the stepValue is a negative number.

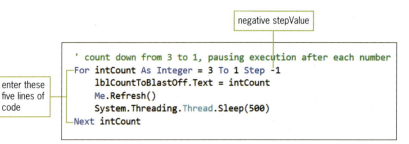

negative stepValue

enter these five lines of code

```
' count down from 3 to 1, pausing execution after each number
For intCount As Integer = 3 To 1 Step -1
    lblCountToBlastOff.Text = intCount
    Me.Refresh()
    System.Threading.Thread.Sleep(500)
Next intCount
```

Figure 14-5 For...Next statement entered in the Go button's Click event procedure in the Spaceship-Version 2 application

4. Save the solution and then start the application. Click the **Go** button. The numbers 3, 2, and 1 appear (one at a time) in the label control, followed by the "Blast Off!" message. The spaceship is then dragged to the top of the form. Click the **Exit** button.

Mini-Quiz 14-1

See Appendix B for the answers.

1. Write a Visual Basic For clause that creates a counter variable named `intX` and initializes it to 10. While the loop is processing, the counter variable should have values of 10, 12, 14, 16, 18, and 20. The loop should stop when the variable's value is 22.

2. Rewrite the For clause from Question 1 so that it initializes the counter variable to 30 and stops the loop when the variable's value is less than 0.

3. If the startValue in a For clause is greater than the endValue, the stepValue must be a _____ number for the For...Next loop to be processed.

   a. negative   b. positive

Hey, Turn That Noise Down!

You can make the Spaceship-Version 2 application more exciting by having it play the Rising Zap sound immediately before the spaceship blasts off. The Rising Zap sound is stored in an audio file named j0388399.wav; the file is contained in the current project's bin\Debug folder. (The audio file is from the Microsoft Office Clip Art collection, which is available at *http://office.microsoft.com*.) To have an application play an audio file while it is running, you use the syntax **My.Computer.Audio.Play(***fileName***)**, in which *fileName* is the name of the audio file you want to play. If the audio file is not in the project's bin\Debug folder, you will need to include the path to the file in the *fileName* argument. The My keyword in the syntax refers to Visual Basic's **My feature**, which exposes a set of commonly used objects to the programmer. One of the objects exposed by the My feature is the My.Computer object. Not surprisingly, the My.Computer object refers to your computer. The My.Computer object provides access to other objects, such as your computer's Audio object. To have the Audio object play an audio file, you use its Play method.

To modify and then test the Go button's Click event procedure:

1. Click the **blank line** above the ' drag the spaceship to the top of the form comment in the btnGo control's Click event procedure. Press **Enter** to insert another blank line and then enter the following comment and statement:

    ' play an audio file
    My.Computer.Audio.Play("j0388399.wav")

2. Save the solution and then start the application. Click the **Go** button. The numbers 3, 2, and 1 appear (one at a time) in the label control, followed by the "Blast Off!" message. The Rising Zap sound begins playing as the spaceship starts its journey to the top of the form.

3. Click the **Exit** button. Close the Code Editor window and then close the solution.

The Monthly Payment Calculator Application

Figure 14-6 shows the interface for the Monthly Payment Calculator application, which calculates and displays the monthly payments on a loan. The interface provides text boxes for the user to enter the principal and term. The principal is the amount of the loan, and the term is the number of years the borrower has to pay off the loan. The application will calculate the monthly payments using annual interest rates of 4% through 7%. Figure 14-7 shows the application's output, processing, and input items, along with its algorithm.

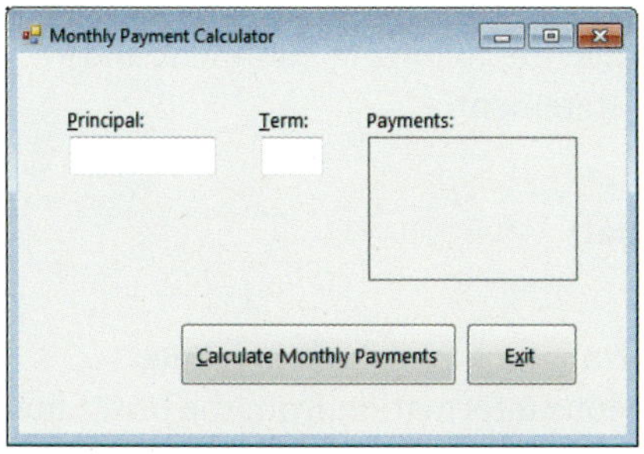

Figure 14-6   Interface for the Monthly Payment Calculator application

```
Output:       monthly payment (for each annual interest rate)

Processing:   annual interest rate (counter that counts from 4% through 7%
                                    in increments of 1%)

Input:        principal
              term (in years)

Algorithm:
1. enter the principal and term
2. remove any previous monthly payments from the Payments box
3. repeat for annual interest rates from 4% through 7% in increments of 1%:
       calculate the current monthly payment using the principal, term, and
       current annual interest rate
       display the current annual interest rate and the current monthly payment
   end repeat
```

Figure 14-7   Output, processing, input, and algorithm for the Monthly Payment Calculator application

To begin coding the Monthly Payment Calculator application:

1. Open the **Monthly Payment Solution (Monthly Payment Solution.sln)** file contained in the ClearlyVB2010\Chap14\Monthly Payment Solution folder. If the designer window is not open, double-click **frmMain.vb** in the Solution Explorer window.

2. Open the Code Editor window and then open the code template for the btnCalc control's Click event procedure. Type the following comment and then press **Enter** twice:

   ' calculates and displays monthly payment amounts

3. First, you will declare the necessary variables. The procedure will use Decimal variables to store the principal and monthly payment amounts, and an Integer variable to store the term. Because the counter variable that will keep track of the annual interest rates will be declared in a For...Next statement, you will not need a Dim statement for it. Enter the following three Dim statements. Press **Enter** twice after typing the last Dim statement.

   Dim decPrincipal As Decimal
   Dim decPayment As Decimal
   Dim intTerm As Integer

4. Now you can store the input items in variables. Enter the following comment and statements. Press **Enter** twice after typing the last statement.

   ' assign input to variables
   Decimal.TryParse(txtPrincipal.Text, decPrincipal)
   Integer.TryParse(txtTerm.Text, intTerm)

5. Before displaying the rates and payments in the Payments box, which is named lblPayments, the procedure should remove any previous information from the box. Enter the following comment and assignment statement. Press **Enter** twice after typing the assignment statement.

   ' clear label control
   lblPayments.Text = String.Empty

6. The next step in the algorithm is a counter-controlled loop whose instructions you want processed from 4% through 7% in increments of 1%. Enter the following comment and For clause:

' calculate and display the monthly payments
For decRate As Decimal = .04 to .07 Step .01

7. Change the Next clause to **Next decRate** and then save the solution.

The Financial.Pmt Method

According to the application's algorithm, the first instruction in the loop should calculate the monthly payment using the principal, term, and current annual interest rate. The mathematical formula for calculating a periodic payment on a loan is rather complex, so Visual Basic provides a method that performs the calculation for you; the method is called the **Financial.Pmt method**. (Pmt stands for Payment.) Figure 14-8 shows the method's basic syntax and lists the meaning of each argument. The *Rate* and *NPer* (number of periods) arguments must be expressed using the same units. If Rate is a monthly interest rate, then NPer must specify the number of monthly payments. Likewise, if Rate is an annual interest rate, then NPer must specify the number of annual payments.

Also included in Figure 14-8 are examples of using the Financial.Pmt method. Example 1 calculates the annual payment for a loan of $9000 for 3 years at 5% interest. As the example indicates, the annual payment rounded to the nearest cent is −3304.88. This means that if you borrow $9000 for 3 years at 5% interest, you will need to make three annual payments of $3304.88 to pay off the loan. Notice that the Financial.Pmt method returns a negative number. You can change the negative number to a positive number by preceding the method with the negation operator, like this: `−Financial.Pmt(.05, 3, 9000)`. As you learned in Chapter 5, the purpose of the negation operator is to reverse the sign of a number. A negative number preceded by the negation operator becomes a positive number, and vice versa.

The Financial.Pmt method shown in Example 2 in Figure 14-8 calculates the monthly payment for a loan of $12000 for 5 years at 6% interest. In this example, the Rate and NPer arguments are expressed in monthly terms rather than in annual terms. You change an annual rate to a monthly rate by dividing the annual rate by 12. You change the term from years to months by multiplying the number of years by 12. The monthly payment for the loan in Example 2, rounded to the nearest cent and expressed as a positive number, is 231.99. (The Financial.Pmt method also can be used to calculate a periodic payment on an investment rather than on a loan. You learn how to do this in Exercise 9 at the end of the chapter.)

Financial.Pmt method

Syntax
Financial.Pmt(_Rate_, _NPer_, _PV_**)**

Argument	Meaning
Rate	interest rate per period
NPer	total number of payment periods (the term)
_PV_	present value of the loan (the loan amount)

Example 1
```
Financial.Pmt(.05, 3, 9000)
```
Calculates the annual payment for a loan of $9000 for 3 years at 5% interest. _Rate_ is .05, _NPer_ is 3, and _PV_ is 9000. The annual payment (rounded to the nearest cent) is −3304.88.

Example 2
```
-Financial.Pmt(.06 / 12, 5 * 12, 12000)
```
Calculates the monthly payment for a loan of $12000 for 5 years at 6% interest. _Rate_ is .06 / 12, _NPer_ is 5 * 12, and _PV_ is 12000. The monthly payment (rounded to the nearest cent and expressed as a positive number) is 231.99.

Figure 14-8   Basic syntax and examples of the Financial.Pmt method

To continue coding the btnCalc control's Click event procedure:

1. Click the **blank line** above the Next decRate clause.

2. You will use the expressions decRate / 12 and intTerm * 12 as the Financial.Pmt method's Rate and NPer arguments, respectively. It is necessary to divide the annual interest rate by 12 to get a monthly rate, because you want to display monthly payments rather than annual payments. Similarly, you need to multiply the number of years by 12 to get the number of monthly payments. The method's PV argument will be decPrincipal. Enter the following assignment statement, being sure to type the hyphen before the Financial.Pmt method:

    decPayment =
        −Financial.Pmt(decRate / 12, intTerm * 12, decPrincipal)

The next instruction in the loop should display both the current annual interest rate and the current monthly payment in the interface. Before you can write the code to accomplish this task, you need to learn about string concatenation.

But They Said There Were No Strings Attached

You use the **concatenation operator**, which is the ampersand (**&**), to concatenate (connect or link together) strings. When concatenating strings, you must be sure to include a space before and after the ampersand; otherwise, the Code Editor will not recognize the ampersand as the concatenation operator. Figure 14-9 shows the syntax you use when concatenating strings. It also includes examples of string concatenation. The **ControlChars.NewLine constant** in the last example represents the Enter key on your keyboard and is used to advance the insertion point to the next line in a control, file, or printout.

String concatenation

Syntax
string **&** *string* [**&** *string*...]

Variables	Contents
strFirst	Lucretia
strLast	Jackson
intAge	30

Concatenated string	Result
strFirst & strLast	LucretiaJackson
strFirst & " " & strLast	Lucretia Jackson
strLast & ", " & strFirst	Jackson, Lucretia
"She is " & intAge.ToString & "!"	She is 30!
"Hi" & ControlChars.NewLine & strFirst	Hi Lucretia

Figure 14-9   Syntax and examples of concatenating strings

In the btnCalc control's Click event procedure, you will use the concatenation operator to concatenate the following five strings: the Text property of the lblPayments control, the contents of the **decRate** variable formatted to Percent with zero decimal places, the string " -> " (a space, a hyphen, a greater than sign, and a space), the contents of the **decPayment** variable formatted to Currency with two decimal places, and the ControlChars.NewLine constant.

To continue coding the btnCalc control's Click event procedure:

1. Enter the additional three lines of code indicated in Figure 14-10.

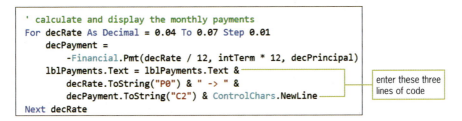

```
' calculate and display the monthly payments
For decRate As Decimal = 0.04 To 0.07 Step 0.01
    decPayment =
        -Financial.Pmt(decRate / 12, intTerm * 12, decPrincipal)
    lblPayments.Text = lblPayments.Text &
        decRate.ToString("P0") & " -> " &
        decPayment.ToString("C2") & ControlChars.NewLine
Next decRate
```

enter these three lines of code

Figure 14-10   Additional code entered in the Click event procedure

2. The instructions in the For...Next loop in Figure 14-10 will be processed four times, using rates of 4%, 5%, 6%, and 7%. Save the solution and then start the application. First, display the monthly payments for a loan of $12000 for 5 years. Type **12000** in the Principal box and then type **5** in the Term box. Click the **Calculate Monthly Payments** button. The four rates and monthly payments appear in the Payments box. See Figure 14-11.

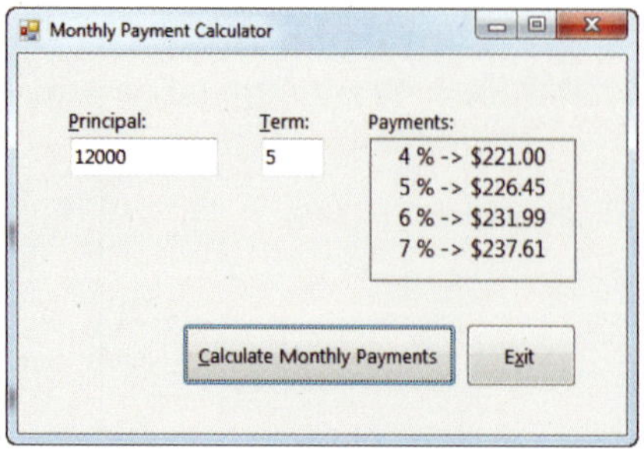

Figure 14-11 Rates and monthly payments shown in the interface

3. Remove the entries from the Principal and Term boxes and then click the **Calculate Monthly Payments** button; doing this results in a run time error, also referred to as an exception. The Code Editor highlights the statement where the error was encountered. In addition, a help box opens and provides information pertaining to the error. In this case, the Code Editor highlights the statement containing the Financial.Pmt method, and the help box indicates that the NPer argument does not contain a valid value.

4. Position your mouse pointer on `intTerm` in the highlighted statement, as shown in Figure 14-12. The variable contains the number 0, because no term was entered in the Term box.

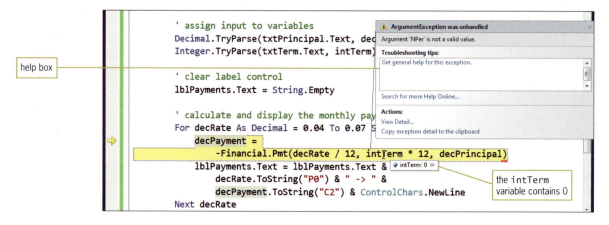

Figure 14-12 Result of the run time error caused by an invalid NPer value

5. Click **Debug** on the menu bar and then click **Stop Debugging**.

As mentioned earlier, the Financial.Pmt method contains a complex mathematical formula for calculating a periodic payment. The term appears in the divisor portion of the formula; therefore, its value cannot be 0, because division by zero is not mathematically possible.

To complete the btnCalc control's Click event procedure and then test the code:

1. Click the **blank line** above the ' calculate and display the monthly payments comment, and then press **Enter** to insert another blank line. Enter the following comment:

   ' determine whether the term is valid

2. Enter the selection structure shown in Figure 14-13. You will need to move the comment and the For...Next statement into the selection structure's false path.

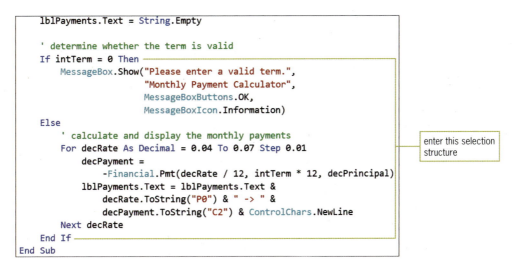

```
lblPayments.Text = String.Empty

' determine whether the term is valid
If intTerm = 0 Then
    MessageBox.Show("Please enter a valid term.",
                    "Monthly Payment Calculator",
                    MessageBoxButtons.OK,
                    MessageBoxIcon.Information)
Else
    ' calculate and display the monthly payments
    For decRate As Decimal = 0.04 To 0.07 Step 0.01
        decPayment =
            -Financial.Pmt(decRate / 12, intTerm * 12, decPrincipal)
        lblPayments.Text = lblPayments.Text &
            decRate.ToString("P0") & " -> " &
            decPayment.ToString("C2") & ControlChars.NewLine
    Next decRate
End If
End Sub
```

enter this selection structure

Figure 14-13   Selection structure entered in the procedure

3. Save the solution and then start the application. Click the **Calculate Monthly Payments** button. The message "Please enter a valid term." appears in a message box. Click the **OK** button to close the message box.

4. Type **12000** in the Principal box and then type **5** in the Term box. Click the **Calculate Monthly Payments** button. The Payments box lists the rates and monthly payments shown earlier in Figure 14-11.

5. Click the **Exit** button. Close the Code Editor window and then close the solution.

The code entered in the btnCalc control's Click event procedure is shown in Figure 14-14.

```vb
Private Sub btnCalc_Click(ByVal sender As Object,
ByVal e As System.EventArgs) Handles btnCalc.Click
    ' calculates and displays monthly payment amounts

    Dim decPrincipal As Decimal
    Dim decPayment As Decimal
    Dim intTerm As Integer

    ' assign input to variables
    Decimal.TryParse(txtPrincipal.Text, decPrincipal)
    Integer.TryParse(txtTerm.Text, intTerm)

    ' clear label control
    lblPayments.Text = String.Empty

    ' determine whether the term is valid
    If intTerm = 0 Then
      MessageBox.Show("Please enter a valid term.",
                    "Monthly Payment Calculator",
                    MessageBoxButtons.OK,
                    MessageBoxIcon.Information)
    Else
        ' calculate and display the monthly payments
        For decRate As Decimal = 0.04 To 0.07 Step 0.01
            decPayment =
                -Financial.Pmt(decRate / 12, intTerm * 12, decPrincipal)
            lblPayments.Text = lblPayments.Text &
                decRate.ToString("P0") & " -> " &
                decPayment.ToString("C2") & ControlChars.NewLine
        Next decRate
    End If
End Sub
```

Figure 14-14 btnCalc control's Click event procedure

Mini-Quiz 14-2

See Appendix B for the answers.

1. Write a Visual Basic statement that will play an audio file named Giggle.wav.

2. For the Financial.Pmt method to display an annual payment, you will need to _____ .

   a. divide the annual interest rate by 12
   b. multiply the annual interest rate by 12
   c. use the annual interest rate

3. Write an assignment statement that concatenates the message "My favorite city is " with the contents of the strCity variable, and then assigns the result to the lblCity control.

Summary

- The For...Next statement provides a convenient way to code a counter-controlled loop. The loop is a pretest loop, because its condition is evaluated *before* the instructions in the loop are processed.

- A variable declared in a For clause has block scope and can be used only within the For...Next loop.

- The For...Next statement's counter variable must be numeric. Its startValue, endValue, and stepValue can be positive or negative numbers, integers or non-integers. If the stepValue is a positive number, the loop condition checks whether the value in the counter variable is greater than the endValue. If the stepValue is a negative number, the loop condition checks whether the value in the counter variable is less than the endValue.

- To have an application play an audio file during run time, you use the syntax **My.Computer. Audio.Play**(*fileName*).

- You can use the Financial.Pmt method to calculate a periodic payment on either a loan or an investment.

- You concatenate strings using the concatenation operator, which is the ampersand (&). The concatenation operator must be both preceded and followed by a space.

- The Enter key on your keyboard is represented by the ControlChars.NewLine constant. You can use the constant to advance the insertion point to the next line in a control, file, or printout.

Key Terms

&—the concatenation operator in Visual Basic

Concatenation operator—the ampersand (&); used to concatenate strings; must be both preceded and followed by a space character

ControlChars.NewLine constant—a Visual Basic constant that represents the Enter key on your keyboard; creates a new line

Counter-controlled loop—a loop whose processing is controlled by a counter; the loop body will be processed a precise number of times

Financial.Pmt method—calculates and returns a periodic payment on either a loan or an investment

For...Next statement—used to code a pretest counter-controlled loop

My feature—the Visual Basic feature that exposes a set of commonly-used objects (such as the Computer object) to the programmer

Review Questions

1. A For...Next statement contains the following For clause: `For intX As Integer = 2 To 11 Step 2`. What value will cause the For...Next loop to stop?

   a. 11

   b. 12

   c. 13

   d. none of the above

2. How many times will the MessageBox.Show method in the following code be processed?
```
For intCount As Integer = 4 To 11 Step 3
    MessageBox.Show("Hello")
Next intCount
```

   a. 3   c. 5

   b. 4   d. none of the above

3. What value will cause the For...Next loop in Review Question 2 to stop?

   a. 11   c. 13

   b. 12   d. 14

4. Which of the following calculates an annual payment on a $50000 loan? The term is 10 years and the annual interest rate is 3%.

   a. `-Financial.Pmt(.03 / 12, 10, 50000)`

   b. `-Financial.Pmt(.03 / 12, 10 * 12, 50000)`

   c. `-Financial.Pmt(.03, 10 * 12, 50000)`

   d. `-Financial.Pmt(.03, 10, 50000)`

5. Which of the following calculates a monthly payment on a $50000 loan? The term is 10 years and the annual interest rate is 3%.

   a. `-Financial.Pmt(.03 / 12, 10, 50000)`

   b. `-Financial.Pmt(.03 / 12, 10 * 12, 50000)`

   c. `-Financial.Pmt(.03, 10 * 12, 50000)`

   d. `-Financial.Pmt(.03, 10, 50000)`

6. The **strCity** and **strState** variables contain the strings "Boston" and "MA", respectively. Which of the following assigns the string "Boston, MA" (the city, a comma, a space, and the state) to the lblAddress control's Text property?

   a. `lblAddress.Text = "strCity" & ", " & "strState"`

   b. `lblAddress.Text = strCity $ ", " $ strState`

   c. `lblAddress.Text = strCity & ", " & strState`

   d. `lblAddress.Text = "strCity, " & "strState"`

7. Which of the following will play the MySong.wav file stored in the current project's bin\Debug folder?

   a. `My.Computer.Audio.Play("MySong.wav")`

   b. `My.Computer.AudioPlay("MySong.wav")`

   c. `My.Computer.PlayAudio("MySong.wav")`

   d. `MyComputer.AudioPlay("MySong.wav")`

8. Which of the following advances the insertion point to the next line in a control?

   a. `Control.Chars.Advance`   c. `Control.Chars.NewLine`

   b. `ControlChars.Advance`   d. `ControlChars.NewLine`

Exercises

1. List the processing steps for the following code. Use Figure 14-2 as a guide. (See Appendix B for the answer.)

TRY THIS

```
For decX As Decimal = 6.5 To 8.5
    MessageBox.Show(decX.ToString("N1"))
Next decX
```

2. Open the OddEven Solution (OddEven Solution.sln) file contained in the ClearlyVB2010\Chap14\OddEven Solution folder. The interface provides text boxes for the user to enter two integers. The application should display all of the odd numbers from the first integer through the second integer, as well as all of the even numbers in that range. (See Appendix B for the answer.)

TRY THIS

   a. Code the application using the For...Next statement. If the integer in the txtNum1 control is greater than the integer in the txtNum2 control, the stepValue should be a negative number 1; otherwise, it should be a positive number 1.
   b. Save the solution and then start the application. Test the application using the integers 6 and 25. The application should display the following odd numbers: 7, 9, 11, 13, 15, 17, 19, 21, 23, and 25. It also should display the following even numbers: 6, 8, 10, 12, 14, 16, 18, 20, 22, and 24.
   c. Now test the application using the integers 25 and 6. The application should display the following odd numbers: 25, 23, 21, 19, 17, 15, 13, 11, 9, and 7. It also should display the following even numbers: 24, 22, 20, 18, 16, 14, 12, 10, 8, and 6. Close the Code Editor window and then close the solution.

3. Open the Car Solution (Car Solution.sln) file contained in the ClearlyVB2010\Chap14\Car Solution-Version 1 folder. Change the Do...Loop statement in the btnClickMe control's Click event procedure to a For...Next statement. Save the solution and then start and test the application. Close the Code Editor window and then close the solution.

MODIFY THIS

4. Open the New Salary Solution (New Salary Solution.sln) file contained in the ClearlyVB2010\Chap14\New Salary Solution folder. The interface provides a text box for the user to enter his or her current salary. The Calculate button's Click event procedure should calculate the new salary amounts using rates of 2% through 6% in increments of .5%. The procedure should display the rates and salary amounts in the lblNewSalary control. Code the procedure using the For...Next statement. Save the solution and then start and test the application. Close the Code Editor window and then close the solution.

INTRODUCTORY

5. Open the Quarterly Payment Solution (Quarterly Payment Solution.sln) file contained in the ClearlyVB2010\Chap14\Quarterly Payment Solution folder. The interface provides text boxes for the user to enter the principal and the rate (as a decimal number). Both text boxes should accept only numbers, the period, and the Backspace key. The Calculate Quarterly Payments button should calculate the quarterly payments using the principal and rate entered by the user, and terms of 2, 3, 4, and 5 years. If the rate is entered as an integer (which means it's greater than or equal to 1), convert the integer to its decimal equivalent by dividing it by 100. Display the terms and quarterly payments in the lblPayments control. Code the appropriate event procedures. Use the For...Next statement to calculate the quarterly payments. Save the solution and then start and test the application. Close the Code Editor window and then close the solution.

INTRODUCTORY

6. Open the Bouncing Robot Solution (Bouncing Robot Solution.sln) file contained in the ClearlyVB2010\Chap14\Bouncing Robot Solution folder. The Bounce button's Click event procedure should use the For...Next statement to bounce the robot up and down

INTRODUCTORY

10 times. Code the procedure. Save the solution and then start and test the application. Close the Code Editor window and then close the solution.

INTERMEDIATE 7. In this exercise, you create an application that multiplies the number entered in a text box by the numbers 1 through 9. It displays the multiplication table in a label control. A sample run of the application is shown in Figure 14-15.

a. List the output and input items, as well as any processing items, and then create an appropriate algorithm using pseudocode.
b. Create a Visual Basic Windows application. Use the following names for the solution and project, respectively: Multiplication Solution and Multiplication Project. Save the application in the ClearlyVB2010\Chap14 folder. Change the name of the form file on your disk to frmMain.vb. If necessary, change the form's name to frmMain.
c. Create the interface shown in Figure 14-15. Code the Display Table button's Click event procedure.
d. Save the solution and then start and test the application. Close the Code Editor window and then close the solution.

Figure 14-15 Sample run of the application from Exercise 7

INTERMEDIATE 8. In this exercise, you modify the Spaceship-Version 1 application coded in the chapter. Use Windows to make a copy of the Spaceship Solution-Version 1 folder. Save the copy in the ClearlyVB2010\Chap14 folder. Rename the copy Modified Spaceship Solution-Version 1. Open the Spaceship Solution (Spaceship Solution.sln) file contained in the Modified Spaceship Solution-Version 1 folder. Open the designer window. Modify the Go button's Click event procedure so that it uses a For…Next statement (rather than a Do…Loop statement) to drag the spaceship to the top of the form. Save the solution and then start and test the application. Close the Code Editor window and then close the solution.

INTERMEDIATE 9. In this exercise, you learn how to use the Financial.Pmt method to calculate a periodic payment on an investment (rather than on a loan).

a. Open the Investment Solution (Investment Solution.sln) file contained in the ClearlyVB2010\Chap14\Investment Solution folder. The application should calculate the amount you need to save each month to accumulate $40000 at the end of 20 years, assuming a 6% annual interest rate. You can calculate this amount using the syntax **Financial.Pmt(***Rate*, *NPer*, *PV*, *FV***)**. The *Rate* argument is the interest rate per period, and the *NPer* argument is the total number of payment periods. The *PV* argument is the present value of the investment, which is 0 (zero). The *FV* argument is the future value of the investment. The future value is the amount you want to accumulate.
b. Open the Code Editor window. Code the btnCalc control's Click event procedure. Display the monthly amount as a positive number. Save the solution and then start and test the application. (The answer should be $86.57.)

c. Modify the application to allow you to enter any future value. Use the InputBox function. Save the solution and then start and test the application. Close the Code Editor window and then close the solution.

10. In this exercise, you create an application that displays a monthly payment on a loan of $3000 for 1 year at 7% interest. The application also should display the amount applied to the loan's principal each month, and the amount that represents interest. The application will use the Financial.Pmt method, which you learned about in the chapter, to calculate the monthly payment. It also will use the Financial.PPmt method to calculate the portion of the payment applied to the principal each month. The method's syntax is **Financial.PPmt(**Rate, Per, NPer, PV**)**, where Rate is the interest rate, NPer is the number of payment periods, and PV is the present value of the loan. The Per argument is the payment period in which you are interested and must be from 1 through NPer.

a. List the output and input items, as well as any processing items, and then create an appropriate algorithm using pseudocode.
b. Create a Visual Basic Windows application. Use the following names for the solution and project, respectively: Principal and Interest Solution, and Principal and Interest Project. Save the application in the ClearlyVB2010\Chap14 folder. Change the name of the form file on your disk to frmMain.vb. If necessary, change the form's name to frmMain.
c. Create the interface shown in Figure 14-16. Set the text box's Multiline and ReadOnly properties to True.
d. Code the application using a For...Next statement to keep track of the Financial.PPmt method's Per argument. The Per values will be from 1 through 12.
e. Save the solution and then start and test the application. (Hint: The monthly payment should be $259.58. In the first month, 242.08 is applied to the principal, and 17.50 is interest.) Close the Code Editor window and then close the solution.

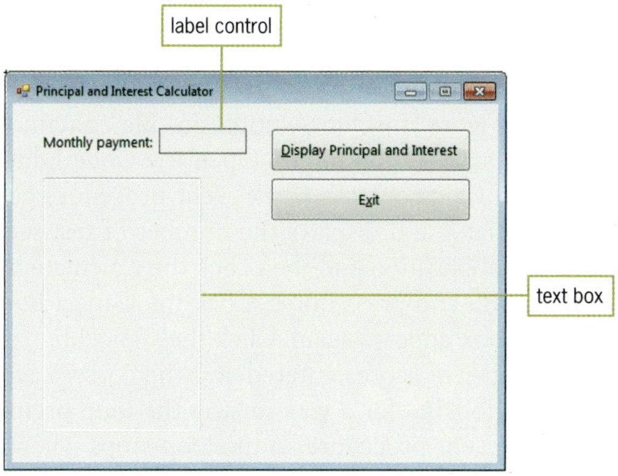

Figure 14-16   Interface for Exercise 10

11. In this exercise, you create an application for the accountant at Sonheim Manufacturing Company. The application will display an asset's annual depreciation schedule. The accountant will enter the asset's cost, useful life (in years), and salvage value (which is the asset's value at the end of its useful life). The application should use the double-declining balance method to calculate the annual depreciation amounts; you can calculate the amounts using the Financial.DDB method. The method's syntax is **Financial.DDB(**cost, salvage, life, period**)**, where period is the period for which you want the depreciation amount calculated.

a. List the output and input items, as well as any processing items, and then create an appropriate algorithm using pseudocode.

b. Create a Visual Basic Windows application. Use the following names for the solution and project, respectively: Sonheim Solution and Sonheim Project. Save the application in the ClearlyVB2010\Chap14 folder. Change the name of the form file on your disk to frmMain.vb. If necessary, change the form's name to frmMain.

c. Create the interface shown in Figure 14-17. Set the txtSchedule control's Multiline and ReadOnly properties to True, and its ScrollBars property to Vertical.

d. Code the application using a For...Next statement to keep track of the Financial.DDB method's *period* argument. The *period* values will be from 1 through the value in the *life* argument. The cost, salvage, and life text boxes should accept numbers and the Backspace key. The cost and salvage text boxes also should accept the period.

e. Save the solution and then start the application. Enter 1000, 100, and 4 as the cost, salvage, and life values, respectively. Click the Display Schedule button. The annual depreciation amounts for the four years should be 500.00, 250.00, 125.00, and 25.00. Close the Code Editor window and then close the solution.

Figure 14-17   Interface for Exercise 11

FIGURE THIS OUT   12. Open the FigureThisOut Solution (FigureThisOut Solution.sln) file contained in the ClearlyVB2010\Chap14\FigureThisOut Solution folder. Open the Code Editor window and study the existing code. The btnCalc control's Click event procedure gets four test scores from the user and then calculates and displays the number of test scores entered and the average test score. Start the application and then click the Calculate button. Type 100 and press Enter, and then type 85 and press Enter. Click the Cancel button. Notice that the InputBox function's dialog box appears again. Click the Cancel button. Does the application display the correct number of scores entered and the correct average? Research the For...Next statement, looking for a way to stop the loop prematurely. Modify the btnCalc control's Click event procedure so the loop stops when the user clicks the Cancel button. Save the solution and then start and test the application. Close the Code Editor window and then close the solution.

SWAT THE BUGS   13. Open the SwatTheBugs Solution (SwatTheBugs Solution.sln) file contained in the ClearlyVB2010\Chap14\SwatTheBugs Solution folder. Start and then test the application. Notice that the application is not working correctly. Click the Exit button. Locate and correct the errors in the code. Save the solution and then start and test the application again. Close the Code Editor window and then close the solution.

CHAPTER 15

I'm on the Inside; You're on the Outside (Nested Loops)

After studying Chapter 15, you should be able to:

◎ Nest repetition structures

◎ Utilize a text box's Multiline, ReadOnly, and ScrollBars properties

One Loop Within Another Loop

Like selection structures, repetition structures can be nested. In other words, you can place one loop (called the nested or inner loop) within another loop (called the outer loop). Both loops can be either pretest loops or posttest loops. Or, one can be a pretest loop and the other a posttest loop. A programmer determines whether a problem's solution requires a nested loop by studying the problem specification. Figure 15-1 shows one of the problem specifications and algorithms from Chapter 12. The algorithm requires a repetition structure because the instructions for signing a book need to be repeated while there are customers in line. However, the algorithm does not require a nested repetition structure. This is because all of the instructions within the repetition structure should be followed only once per customer.

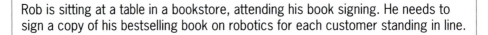

Rob is sitting at a table in a bookstore, attending his book signing. He needs to sign a copy of his bestselling book on robotics for each customer standing in line.

repeat while there are customers in line:
——accept the book from the customer
place the book on the table
open the front cover of the book
sign your name on the first page
close the book
return the book to the customer
——thank the customer
end repeat

follow these instructions for each customer

Figure 15-1   Problem specification and algorithm for signing one book for each customer

Now consider the possibility that a customer may have more than one book for Rob to sign. It's even possible that a customer, not knowing about the book signing in advance, has left his or her book at home and is standing in line for the sole purpose of meeting Rob. What changes will need to be made to the algorithm shown in Figure 15-1? The current instructions within the loop still must be repeated for each customer. In addition, however, all but the last instruction in the loop (the thank the customer instruction) must be repeated for each of the customer's books. You will need to use a nested loop to include this additional task in the algorithm. Rob will thank the customer only after all of the customer's books have been signed, so the thank the customer instruction should not be part of the nested loop.

Figure 15-2 shows the modified algorithm, which contains an outer loop and a nested loop. The outer loop begins with repeat while there are customers in line: and it ends with the last end repeat. The nested loop begins with repeat for each of the customer's books: and it ends with the first end repeat. All of the instructions will be followed for each customer; however, six instructions also will be followed for each book the customer wants signed.

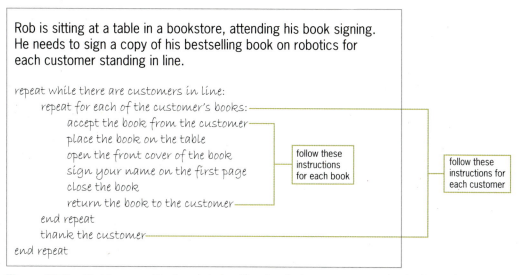

Figure 15-2   Problem specification and algorithm for signing zero or more books for each customer

Clock Application

A clock uses nested repetition structures to keep track of the time. For simplicity, consider a clock's minute and second hands only. The second hand on a clock moves one position, clockwise, for every second that has elapsed. After the second hand moves 60 positions, the minute hand moves one position, also clockwise. The second hand then begins its journey around the clock again. Figure 15-3 shows the logic used by a clock's minute and second hands. The outer loop controls the minute hand, while the inner (nested) loop controls the second hand. Notice that the entire nested loop is contained within the outer loop; this must be true for the loop to be nested and for it to work correctly.

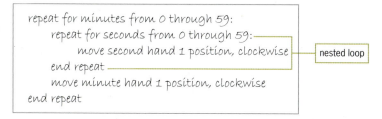

Figure 15-3   Logic used by a clock's minute and second hands

Figure 15-4 shows the interface for the Clock application. (The clock image is from the Microsoft Office Clip Art collection.) In the Start button's Click event procedure, you will have an outer loop display the number of minutes, and a nested loop display the number of seconds. For simplicity in watching the minutes and seconds tick away, you will display minute values from 0 through 2, and display second values from 0 through 5.

Figure 15-4 Clock application's user interface

To code and then test the Clock application:

1. Start Visual Studio 2010 or Visual Basic 2010 Express and permanently display the Solution Explorer window. Open the **Clock Solution** (**Clock Solution.sln**) file contained in the ClearlyVB2010\Chap15\Clock Solution folder. If the designer window is not open, double-click **frmMain.vb** in the Solution Explorer window.

2. Open the Code Editor window and then open the code template for the btnStart control's Click event procedure. Enter the following comments. Press **Enter** twice after typing the last comment.

   ' displays minutes (from 0 through 2 only)
   ' and seconds (from 0 through 5 only)

3. Now enter the outer and nested loops shown in Figure 15-5. The Refresh and Sleep methods are required so that you can view each of the minute and second values in the interface.

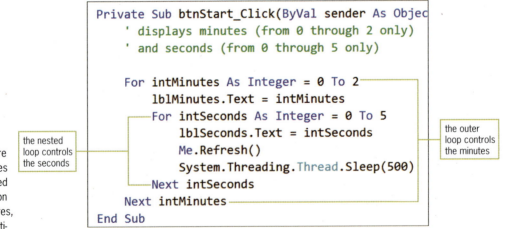

```
Private Sub btnStart_Click(ByVal sender As Objec
    ' displays minutes (from 0 through 2 only)
    ' and seconds (from 0 through 5 only)

    For intMinutes As Integer = 0 To 2
        lblMinutes.Text = intMinutes
        For intSeconds As Integer = 0 To 5
            lblSeconds.Text = intSeconds
            Me.Refresh()
            System.Threading.Thread.Sleep(500)
        Next intSeconds
    Next intMinutes
End Sub
```

the nested loop controls the seconds

the outer loop controls the minutes

Figure 15-5 Start button's Click event procedure

For more examples of nested repetition structures, see the Nested Repetition Structures section in the Ch15WantMore.pdf file.

Before coding the next application, it may be helpful to view the Ch15Nested Loops video.

4. Save the solution and then start the application. Click the **Start** button. The number 0 appears in the lblMinutes control, and the numbers 0 through 5 appear (one at a time) in the lblSeconds control. Notice that the number of minutes is increased by 1 when the number of seconds changes from 5 to 0. When the procedure ends, the lblMinutes and lblSeconds controls contain the numbers 2 and 5, respectively. (If you want to end the procedure prematurely, click Debug on the menu bar and then click Stop Debugging.)

5. Click the **Exit** button. Close the Code Editor window and then close the solution.

Revisiting the Monthly Payment Calculator Application

Figure 15-6 shows the output, processing, and input items for the Monthly Payment Calculator application from Chapter 14. It also shows the application's algorithm. Recall that the application calculates and displays the monthly payments on a loan. The payments are calculated using the principal and term entered by the user, along with a loop that varies the annual interest rates from 4% through 7%.

Output: monthly payment (for each annual interest rate)

Processing: annual interest rate (counter that counts from 4% through 7%
                        in increments of 1%)

Input: principal
             term (in years)

Algorithm:
1. enter the principal and term
2. remove any previous monthly payments from the Payments box
3. repeat for annual interest rates from 4% through 7% in increments of 1%:
       calculate the current monthly payment using the principal, term, and
       current annual interest rate
       display the current annual interest rate and the current monthly payment
   end repeat

Figure 15-6   Planning information for the Monthly Payment Calculator application from Chapter 14

Now let's say you are asked to modify the application so that, rather than having the user enter the term, it automatically uses terms of 2 through 5 years. What changes would need to be made to the algorithm shown in Figure 15-6? Obviously, you would change the first step in the algorithm to enter the principal. The algorithm's second step clears the contents of the Payments box and would still be necessary. The repetition structure in Step 3 in the algorithm contains the instructions to calculate and display the monthly payments. Currently, the instructions are repeated for annual interest rates from 4% through 7%. In the modified algorithm, those instructions also will need to be repeated for terms from 2 through 5 years. You can accomplish this task by including an additional loop in the algorithm. You can either nest the term loop within the rate loop, or nest the rate loop within the term loop. But how do you determine the nested loop? If you want to display the monthly payments by term within rate— for example, display the payments for 2 through 5 years using a 4% rate, followed by the payments for 2 through 5 years using a 5% rate, and so on—you would nest the term loop within the rate loop. However, if you want to display the monthly payments by rate within term—for example, display the 2-year payments for 4% through 7%, followed by the 3-year payments for 4% through 7%, and so on—you would nest the rate loop within the term loop. Figure 15-7 shows the planning information for the modified Monthly Payment Calculator application. The algorithm will display the monthly payments by rate within term.

> Output: monthly payment (for each annual interest rate and term)
>
> Processing: annual interest rate (counter that counts from 4% through 7%
>   in increments of 1%)
>   term (counter that counts from 2 years through 5 years in
>   increments of 1 year)
>
> Input: principal
>
> Algorithm:
> 1. enter the principal
> 2. remove any previous monthly payments from the Payments box
> 3. repeat for terms from 2 years through 5 years in increments of 1 year:
>   display the current term in the Payments box
>
>   repeat for annual interest rates from 4% through 7% in increments of 1%:
>   calculate the current monthly payment using the principal, current
>   term, and current annual interest rate
>   display the current annual interest rate and the current monthly payment
>   end repeat
>
>   display a blank line in the Payments box to separate the current term's
>   information from the next term's information
>   end repeat

Figure 15-7   Planning information for the modified Monthly Payment Calculator application

To open the Monthly Payment Calculator application:

1. Open the **Monthly Payment Solution** (**Monthly Payment Solution.sln**) file contained in the ClearlyVB2010\Chap15\Monthly Payment Solution-Version 1 folder. If the designer window is not open, double-click **frmMain.vb** in the Solution Explorer window. The application's user interface is shown in Figure 15-8. The user will enter the principal in the txtPrincipal control. When the user clicks the Calculate Monthly Payments button, the payments will appear in the txtPayments control.

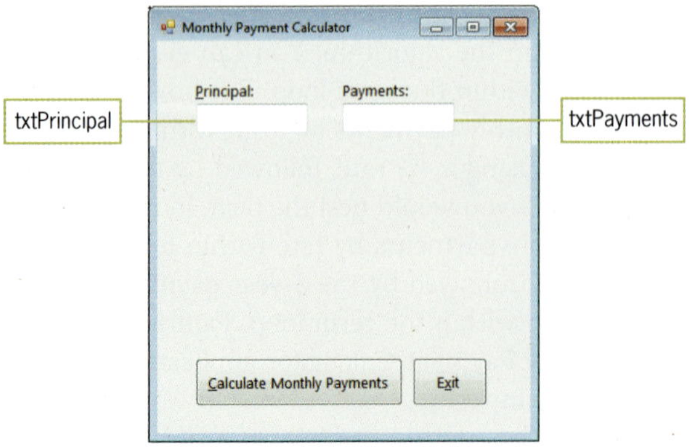

Figure 15-8   User interface for the Monthly Payment Calculator application

You may be wondering why the interface uses a text box rather than a label control to display the monthly payments. Although you can display a great deal of information in both types of controls, a text box can have scroll bars, which allow you to view any information not currently showing in the control. However, for a text box to include scroll bars, its ScrollBars and Multiline properties must be set appropriately. The **ScrollBars property** indicates whether the text box has no scroll bars (the default), a horizontal scroll bar, a vertical scroll bar, or both horizontal and vertical scroll bars. A text box's **Multiline property** specifies whether the text box can accept and display multiple lines of text. For a text box to contain scroll bars, its Multiline property must be set to True.

To set the txtPayments control's Multiline and ScrollBars properties:

1. Click the **txtPayments** control. Change the control's Multiline property to **True**.

2. Now change the txtPayments control's ScrollBars property to **Vertical**. A vertical scroll bar appears on the right side of the text box.

As you know, users cannot edit the contents of a label control during run time, but they can edit the contents of a text box. In this application, however, the user should not be allowed to change the payments displayed in the txtPayments control. You can prevent the user from editing the contents of a text box by setting the text box's **ReadOnly property** to True.

To set the txtPayments control's ReadOnly property and then size the control:

1. Change the txtPayments control's ReadOnly property to **True**. Notice that the text box is now colored gray rather than white.

2. Change the txtPayments control's Size property to **130, 195**.

Now that the interface is complete, you can code the Click event procedure for the Calculate Monthly Payments button.

To code and then test the btnCalc control's Click event procedure:

1. Open the Code Editor window and then open the code template for the btnCalc control's Click event procedure. Enter the following comments. Press **Enter** twice after typing the last comment.

   ```
   ' calculates and displays monthly payment amounts
   ' using terms of 2 through 5 years and rates
   ' of 4% through 7%
   ```

2. First, you will declare Decimal variables to store the principal and monthly payment amounts. Because the counter variables that will keep track of the annual interest rates and terms will be declared in For…Next statements, you will not need Dim statements for them. Enter the following two Dim statements. Press **Enter** twice after typing the last Dim statement.

   ```
   Dim decPrincipal As Decimal
   Dim decPayment As Decimal
   ```

3. Next, you will assign the principal to a variable. Enter the following comment and TryParse method. Press **Enter** twice after typing the TryParse method.

   ```
   ' assign principal to a variable
   Decimal.TryParse(txtPrincipal.Text, decPrincipal)
   ```

4. Now you will enter a statement to remove any previous payments from the Payments box. Enter the following comment and assignment statement. Press **Enter** twice after typing the assignment statement.

   ```
   ' clear the Payments box
   txtPayments.Text = String.Empty
   ```

5. Step 3 in the algorithm begins with a counter-controlled loop whose instructions should be processed for values from 2 through 5 in increments of 1. You will use the For...Next statement to code the loop. Enter the following comment and For clause:

    ' calculate and display the monthly payments
    For intTerm As Integer = 2 To 5

6. Change the Next clause to **Next intTerm**.

7. The first instruction in the outer loop displays the term in the txtPayments control. Click the **blank line** below the For clause and then enter the following two lines of code:

    txtPayments.Text = txtPayments.Text &
    **   "Term: " & intTerm & ControlChars.NewLine**

8. The next instruction in the outer loop is another counter-controlled loop. The instructions in the nested loop should be processed for values from 4% through 7% in increments of 1%. Here again, you will use the For...Next statement to code the loop. Enter the following For clause:

    For decRate As Decimal = .04 To .07 Step .01

9. Change the nested Next clause to **Next decRate**.

10. The two instructions in the nested loop should calculate and display the monthly payment amounts along with their corresponding annual interest rate. Click the **blank line** below the nested For clause and then enter the assignment statements shown in Figure 15-9; doing this completes the nested loop.

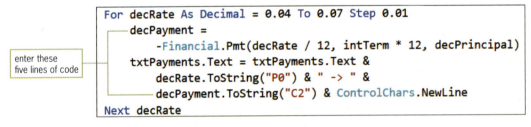

```
For decRate As Decimal = 0.04 To 0.07 Step 0.01
    decPayment =
        -Financial.Pmt(decRate / 12, intTerm * 12, decPrincipal)
    txtPayments.Text = txtPayments.Text &
        decRate.ToString("P0") & " -> " &
        decPayment.ToString("C2") & ControlChars.NewLine
Next decRate
```

enter these five lines of code

Figure 15-9   Additional code entered in the nested loop

11. The last instruction in the outer loop displays a blank line in the Payments box. The blank line will separate the current term's information from the previous term's information. Click **after the last e** in the Next decRate clause and then press **Enter** to insert a blank line below the clause. Type the following line of code and then click **any other line** in the Code Editor window:

    txtPayments.Text = txtPayments.Text & ControlChars.NewLine

12. Save the solution and then start the application. Type **12000** in the Principal box and then click the **Calculate Monthly Payments** button. The terms, rates, and monthly payments appear in the interface, as shown in Figure 15-10.

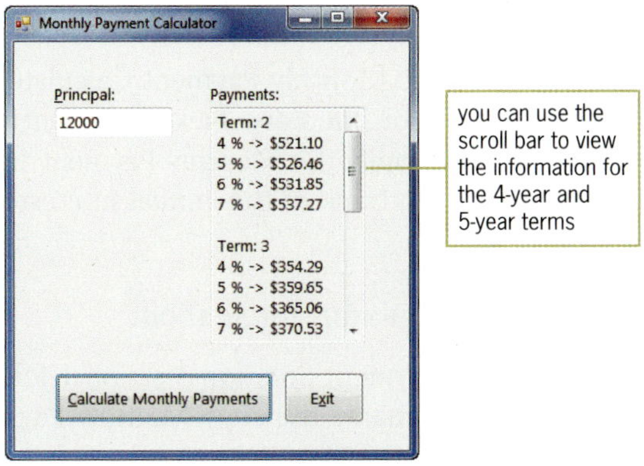

Figure 15-10 Interface showing the terms, rates, and monthly payments

13. Use the scroll bar to view the monthly payments for the 4-year and 5-year terms.

14. Delete the contents of the Principal box and then click the **Calculate Monthly Payments** button. A monthly payment of $0.00 appears for each rate within each term.

15. Click the **Exit** button. Close the Code Editor window and then close the solution.

The code entered in the btnCalc control's Click event procedure is shown in Figure 15-11.

```vb
Private Sub btnCalc_Click(ByVal sender As Object,
ByVal e As System.EventArgs) Handles btnCalc.Click
    ' calculates and displays monthly payment amounts
    ' using terms of 2 through 5 years and rates
    ' of 4% through 7%

    Dim decPrincipal As Decimal
    Dim decPayment As Decimal

    ' assign principal to a variable
    Decimal.TryParse(txtPrincipal.Text, decPrincipal)

    ' clear the Payments box
    txtPayments.Text = String.Empty

    ' calculate and display the monthly payments
    For intTerm As Integer = 2 To 5
        txtPayments.Text = txtPayments.Text &
            "Term: " & intTerm & ControlChars.NewLine
        For decRate As Decimal = 0.04 To 0.07 Step 0.01
            decPayment =
                -Financial.Pmt(decRate / 12, intTerm * 12, decPrincipal)
            txtPayments.Text = txtPayments.Text &
                decRate.ToString("P0") & " -> " &
                decPayment.ToString("C2") & ControlChars.NewLine
        Next decRate
        txtPayments.Text = txtPayments.Text & ControlChars.NewLine
    Next intTerm
End Sub
```

Figure 15-11 Click event procedure for the btnCalc control

But I Want to Do It a Different Way

Rather than using two For...Next statements to code the Monthly Payment Calculator application, you also can use two Do...Loop statements or one For...Next statement and one Do...Loop statement. In the next set of steps, you will modify the Monthly Payment Calculator application so that it uses a Do...Loop statement to keep track of the annual interest rates.

To modify and then test the Monthly Payment Calculator application:

1. Use Windows to make a copy of the Monthly Payment Solution-Version 1 folder. Save the copy in the ClearlyVB2010\Chap15 folder. Rename the copy Monthly Payment Solution-Version 2.

2. Open the **Monthly Payment Solution** (**Monthly Payment Solution.sln**) file contained in the Monthly Payment Solution-Version 2 folder. Double-click **frmMain.vb** in the Solution Explorer window.

3. Open the Code Editor window and then locate the btnCalc control's Click event procedure. Modify the procedure's code as shown in Figure 15-12. The changes are shaded in the figure. Notice that when you use the Do...Loop statement (rather than the For...Next statement) to keep track of the annual interest rates, you must include instructions to declare, initialize, and update the **decRate** variable.

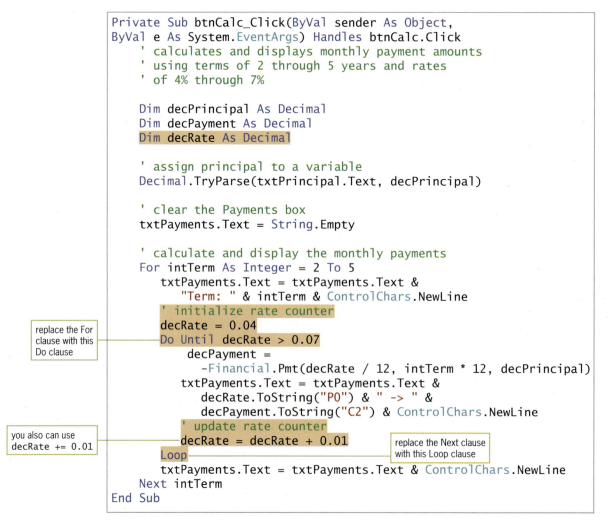

```vb
Private Sub btnCalc_Click(ByVal sender As Object,
ByVal e As System.EventArgs) Handles btnCalc.Click
    ' calculates and displays monthly payment amounts
    ' using terms of 2 through 5 years and rates
    ' of 4% through 7%

    Dim decPrincipal As Decimal
    Dim decPayment As Decimal
    Dim decRate As Decimal

    ' assign principal to a variable
    Decimal.TryParse(txtPrincipal.Text, decPrincipal)

    ' clear the Payments box
    txtPayments.Text = String.Empty

    ' calculate and display the monthly payments
    For intTerm As Integer = 2 To 5
        txtPayments.Text = txtPayments.Text &
            "Term: " & intTerm & ControlChars.NewLine
        ' initialize rate counter
        decRate = 0.04
        Do Until decRate > 0.07
            decPayment =
                -Financial.Pmt(decRate / 12, intTerm * 12, decPrincipal)
            txtPayments.Text = txtPayments.Text &
                decRate.ToString("P0") & " -> " &
                decPayment.ToString("C2") & ControlChars.NewLine
        ' update rate counter
            decRate = decRate + 0.01
        Loop
        txtPayments.Text = txtPayments.Text & ControlChars.NewLine
    Next intTerm
End Sub
```

replace the For clause with this Do clause

you also can use decRate += 0.01

replace the Next clause with this Loop clause

Figure 15-12   Modified Click event procedure for the btnCalc control

4. Save the solution and then start the application. Type **12000** in the Principal box and then click the **Calculate Monthly Payments** button. The terms, rates, and monthly payments appear in the interface, as shown earlier in Figure 15-10.

5. Click the **Exit** button. Close the Code Editor window and then close the solution.

Mini-Quiz 15-1

See Appendix B for the answers.

1. Write the code to display the following pattern using two pretest loops along with the letter X. Use the Do...Loop statement for the outer loop. Use the For...Next statement for the nested loop. Display the pattern in the lblPattern control.

    XXXX
    XXXX
    XXXX

2. Rewrite the code from Question 1 using a For...Next statement for the outer loop and a Do...Loop statement for the nested loop.

3. For a text box to display scroll bars, which of the following properties must be set to True?

    a. DisplayBars   c. Scrollable
    b. Multiline   d. ScrollBars

Summary

- Repetition structures can be nested, which means you can place one loop within another loop.

- For a nested loop to work correctly, it must be contained entirely within the outer loop.

- When a text box's Multiline property is set to True, it can accept and display multiple lines of text.

- A text box's ScrollBars property determines whether scroll bars appear on the control. However, for the ScrollBars property to take effect, the text box's Multiline property must be set to True.

- You can prevent the user from editing the contents of a text box by setting the text box's ReadOnly property to True.

Key Terms

Multiline property—the text box property that specifies whether the text box can accept and display multiple lines of text

ReadOnly property—the text box property that specifies whether the contents of the text box can be edited by the user during run time

ScrollBars property—the text box property that indicates whether scroll bars appear on the control; used in conjunction with the Multiline property

Review Questions

1. Which of the following will *not* display four asterisks on each of three lines in the lblMsg control?

   a. ```
   lblMsg.Text = "****" &
       ControlChars.NewLine & "****" &
       ControlChars.NewLine & "****"
   ```

   b. ```
   For intCounter As Integer = 1 To 3
       lblMsg.Text = lblMsg.Text &
           "****" & ControlChars.NewLine
   Next intCounter
   ```

   c. ```
   For intX As Integer = 1 To 4
       For intY As Integer = 1 To 3
           lblMsg.Text = lblMsg.Text & "*"
       Next intY
       lblMsg.Text = lblMsg.Text &
           ControlChars.NewLine
   Next intX
   ```

   d. ```
   For intX As Integer = 1 To 3
       For intY As Integer = 1 To 4
           lblMsg.Text = lblMsg.Text & "*"
       Next intY
       lblMsg.Text = lblMsg.Text &
           ControlChars.NewLine
   Next intX
   ```

2. How many times will the MessageBox.Show method in the following code be processed?
   ```
   For intX As Integer = 4 To 11 Step 3
       For intY As Integer = 1 To 3
           MessageBox.Show("Hello")
       Next intY
   Next intX
   ```

   a. 9   c. 11

   b. 10   d. none of the above

3. What value will cause the nested loop in Review Question 2 to stop?

   a. 0   c. 3

   b. 1   d. none of the above

4. Which of the following will *not* display the number 123 on each of two lines in the lblMsg control? (The intY variable was declared with the statement Dim intY As Integer.)

   a. ```
   For intX As Integer = 1 To 2
       intY = 1
       Do
           lblMsg.Text = lblMsg.Text & intY
           intY = intY + 1
       Loop Until intY > 3
       lblMsg.Text = lblMsg.Text & ControlChars.NewLine
   Next intX
   ```
   ```

b.
```
intY = 1
Do Until intY > 2
    For intX As Integer = 1 To 3
        lblMsg.Text = lblMsg.Text & intX
        intY = intY + 1
    Next intX
    lblMsg.Text = lblMsg.Text & ControlChars.NewLine
Loop
```

c.
```
For intX As Integer = 1 To 2
    intY = 1
    Do Until intY > 3
        lblMsg.Text = lblMsg.Text & intY
        intY = intY + 1
    Loop
    lblMsg.Text = lblMsg.Text & ControlChars.NewLine
Next intX
```

d.
```
intY = 1
Do Until intY > 2
    For intX As Integer = 1 To 3
        lblMsg.Text = lblMsg.Text & intX
    Next intX
    intY = intY + 1
    lblMsg.Text = lblMsg.Text & ControlChars.NewLine
Loop
```

5. How can you prevent the user from editing the contents of a text box during run time?

   a. set the text box's Editable property to False

   b. set the text box's Changeable property to False

   c. set the text box's ReadOnly property to True

   d. set the text box's WriteOnly property to False

6. What will the following code display in the lblSum control?
```
Dim intSum As Integer
Dim intY As Integer
Do While intY < 3
    For intX As Integer = 1 to 4
        intSum += intX
    Next intX
    intY += 1
Loop
lblSum.Text = intSum
```

   a. 5   c. 15

   b. 8   d. 30

7. Which of the following properties determines whether a text box contains a scroll bar?

   a. Scrollable   c. Scroller

   b. ScrollBars   d. none of the above

Exercises

TRY THIS   1. In this exercise, you modify the Clock application coded in the chapter. Use Windows to make a copy of the Clock Solution folder. Save the copy in the ClearlyVB2010\ Chap15 folder. Rename the copy Clock Solution-TRY THIS 1. Open the Clock Solution (Clock Solution.sln) file contained in the Clock Solution-TRY THIS 1 folder. Open the designer window. Change the For...Next statements in the Start button's Click event procedure to Do...Loop statements. Use the `Until` keyword in the Do clause. Save the solution and then start and test the application. Close the Code Editor window and then close the solution. (See Appendix B for the answer.)

TRY THIS   2. In this exercise, you modify the Clock application coded in the chapter. Use Windows to make a copy of the Clock Solution folder. Save the copy in the ClearlyVB2010\Chap15 folder. Rename the copy Clock Solution-TRY THIS 2. Open the Clock Solution (Clock Solution.sln) file contained in the Clock Solution-TRY THIS 2 folder. Open the designer window. Change the nested For...Next statement in the Start button's Click event procedure to a posttest loop. Use the `While` keyword in the Loop clause. Save the solution and then start and test the application. Close the Code Editor window and then close the solution. (See Appendix B for the answer.)

MODIFY THIS   3. In this exercise, you modify one of the Monthly Payment Calculator applications coded in the chapter. Use Windows to make a copy of the Monthly Payment Solution-Version 1 folder. Save the copy in the ClearlyVB2010\Chap15 folder. Rename the copy Modified Monthly Payment Solution-Version 1. Open the Monthly Payment Solution (Monthly Payment Solution.sln) file contained in the Modified Monthly Payment Solution-Version 1 folder. Open the designer window. Currently, the Click event procedure for the Calculate Monthly Payments button displays the payments by rate within term. Modify the procedure's code so that it displays the payments by term within rate. Save the solution and then start and test the application. Close the Code Editor window and then close the solution.

INTRODUCTORY   4. In this exercise, you modify one of the Monthly Payment Calculator applications coded in the chapter. Use Windows to make a copy of the Monthly Payment Solution-Version 2 folder. Save the copy in the ClearlyVB2010\Chap15 folder. Rename the copy Modified Monthly Payment Solution-Version 2. Open the Monthly Payment Solution (Monthly Payment Solution.sln) file contained in the Modified Monthly Payment Solution-Version 2 folder. Open the designer window. Currently, the Click event procedure for the Calculate Monthly Payments button uses a For...Next statement to keep track of the terms. Change the For...Next statement to a Do...Loop statement. Save the solution and then start and test the application. Close the Code Editor window and then close the solution.

INTRODUCTORY   5. Open the Discount Solution (Discount Solution.sln) file contained in the ClearlyVB2010\Chap15\Discount Solution folder. The Display button's Click event procedure should display discount amounts in the txtDiscounts control. Display the discount amounts using sales amounts of $10 through $15 in increments of $1, and rates from 5% through 10% in increments of 1%. Display the discount amounts by rate within sales. (In other words, display the six discount amounts for the $10 sales, then the six discount amounts for the $11 sales, and so on.) Code the procedure. Save the solution and then start and test the application. Close the Code Editor window and then close the solution.

6. Open the Commission Solution (Commission Solution.sln) file contained in the ClearlyVB2010\Chap15\Commission Solution folder. The Display button's Click event procedure should display commission amounts in the txtCommission control. Display the commission amounts using sales amounts of $10000 through $13000 in increments of $1000, and rates from 2% through 5% in increments of 1%. Display the commission amounts by sales amount within rate. (In other words, display the four commission amounts for the 2% rate, then the four commission amounts for the 3% rate, and so on.) Code the procedure. Save the solution and then start and test the application. Close the Code Editor window and then close the solution.

INTRODUCTORY

7. In this exercise, you code an application that displays a bar chart. The bar chart depicts the ratings for five hotels. Open the Hotel Solution (Hotel Solution.sln) file contained in the ClearlyVB2010\Chap15\Hotel Solution folder. The Create Bar Chart button's Click event procedure should allow the user to enter the hotel rating for each of five hotels. The rating can be from 1 through 6 only. Use the InputBox function to get each rating. If the user enters an invalid rating, the procedure should display an appropriate message in a message box and then ask the user for the hotel's rating again. (In other words, the procedure should not accept an invalid rating.) Use each hotel's rating to display the appropriate number of asterisks in the bar chart. Figure 15-13 shows a sample run of the application after the user enters the following ratings: 4, 6, 3, 8, 6, and 2. Save the solution and then start and test the application. Close the Code Editor window and then close the solution.

INTERMEDIATE

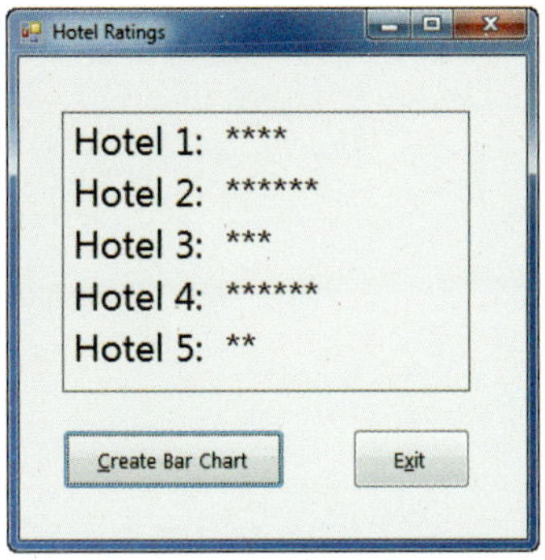

Figure 15-13 Sample run of the application from Exercise 7

8. In this exercise, you modify the Clock application coded in the chapter. Use Windows to make a copy of the Clock Solution folder. Save the copy in the ClearlyVB2010\Chap15 folder. Rename the copy Modified Clock Solution. Open the Clock Solution (Clock Solution.sln) file contained in the Modified Clock Solution folder. Open the designer window. Currently, the interface and code display the number of minutes and seconds. Modify the interface and code to also display the number of hours. Use hour values of 0 through 3 (rather than 0 through 23). Save the solution and then start and test the application. Close the Code Editor window and then close the solution.

INTERMEDIATE

INTERMEDIATE   9. Open the TwoToTenAsterisks Solution (TwoToTenAsterisks Solution.sln) file contained in the ClearlyVB2010\Chap15\TwoToTenAsterisks Solution folder. The Display Asterisks button should display the pattern of asterisks shown below. The pattern contains 2 asterisks, 4 asterisks, 6 asterisks, 8 asterisks, and 10 asterisks. Display the pattern in the lblAsterisks control. Use a For…Next statement for the outer loop, and a Do…Loop statement for the nested loop. Save the solution and then start and test the application. Close the Code Editor window and then close the solution.

```
**
****
******
********
**********
```

ADVANCED   10. Open the Cartwright Solution (Cartwright Solution.sln) file contained in the ClearlyVB2010\Chap15\Cartwright Solution folder. The Display Totals button's Click event procedure should allow the user to enter the salesperson ID for any number of salespeople. It also should allow the user to enter any number of sales amounts for each salesperson. Use the InputBox function to get the salesperson's ID and sales amounts. Total a salesperson's sales before moving on to the next salesperson. Display each salesperson's ID and total sales in the txtTotalSales control. When the user has finished entering data, display the company's total sales in the txtTotalSales control. Code the procedure. Save the solution and then start and test the application. Close the Code Editor window and then close the solution. Figure 15-14 shows a sample run of the application after the user enters the IDs and sales amounts shown here:

ID	Sales amounts
AB2	300.35, 200.50, and 250.75
BN4	45.67 and 350.05
CR7	100.23, 67.45, and 35.85

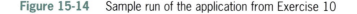

Figure 15-14   Sample run of the application from Exercise 10

ADVANCED   11. Open the Table Solution (Table Solution.sln) file contained in the ClearlyVB2010\Chap15\Table Solution folder. The Display Table button's Click event procedure should display a table consisting of three rows and seven columns, as shown in Figure 15-15. The first column contains the numbers 1 through 3. The second and subsequent columns contain the result of multiplying the number in the first column by the numbers 0 through 5. Code the procedure. Save the solution and then start and test the application. Close the Code Editor window and then close the solution.

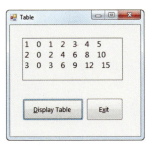

Figure 15-15   Sample run of the application from Exercise 11

12. Open the FigureThisOut Solution (FigureThisOut Solution.sln) file contained in the ClearlyVB2010\Chap15\FigureThisOut Solution folder. Open the Code Editor window and study the existing code. List the steps the computer takes when processing the code contained in the btnDisplay control's Click event procedure. What will the procedure display? Start and then test the application. Close the Code Editor window and then close the solution.

FIGURE THIS OUT

13. Open the SwatTheBugs Solution (SwatTheBugs Solution.sln) file contained in the ClearlyVB2010\Chap15\SwatTheBugs Solution folder. Open the Code Editor window and study the existing code. Start and then test the application. Notice that the application is not working correctly. To stop the application, click Debug on the menu bar and then click Stop Debugging. Locate and correct the errors in the code. Save the solution and then start and test the application again. Close the Code Editor window and then close the solution.

SWAT THE BUGS

I Hear You Are Breaking Up (Sub Procedures)

After studying Chapter 16, you should be able to:

◎ Create a Sub procedure

◎ Call a Sub procedure

◎ Pass data *by value* to a procedure

◎ Pass data *by reference* to a procedure

What's the Proper Procedure?

All of the procedures you have coded so far have been event procedures. Recall that an event procedure is a set of Visual Basic instructions that are processed when a specific event (such as the Click event) occurs. The Code Editor provides a code template for every event procedure. The code template contains the procedure's header and footer. As you know, an event procedure's header begins with the keywords `Private Sub`. The `Private` keyword indicates that the procedure can be used only within the current Code Editor window. The `Sub` keyword is an abbreviation of the term "Sub procedure," which is a block of code that performs a specific task. An event procedure always ends with the keywords `End Sub`. Figure 16-1 shows a sample Click event procedure for an Exit button.

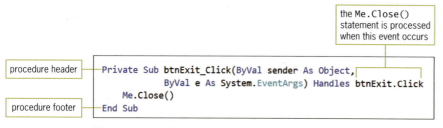

Figure 16-1   Sample Click event procedure for an Exit button

Event procedures are not the only Sub procedures available in Visual Basic; you also can create your own Sub procedures. The Sub procedures you create are called independent Sub procedures, because they are independent of any object and event. An **independent Sub procedure** is processed only when you call (invoke) it from code. But why would you want to create your own Sub procedure? First, you can use an independent Sub procedure to avoid duplicating code when different sections of a program need to perform the same task. Rather than entering the same code in each of those sections, you can enter the code in an independent Sub procedure and then have each section call the procedure to perform its task when needed. Second, consider an event procedure that must perform many tasks. To keep the event procedure's code from getting unwieldy and difficult to understand, you can assign some of the tasks to one or more independent Sub procedures. Doing this makes the event procedure easer to code, because it allows the programmer to concentrate on one small piece of the code at a time. And finally, independent Sub procedures are used extensively in large and complex programs, which typically are written by a team of programmers. The programming team will break up the program into small and manageable tasks, and then assign some of the tasks to different team members to be coded as independent procedures. Doing this allows more than one programmer to work on the program at the same time, decreasing the time it takes to write the program.

Figure 16-2 shows the syntax for creating an independent Sub procedure in Visual Basic. It also includes an example of an independent Sub procedure, as well as the steps for entering an independent Sub procedure in the Code Editor window. Some programmers enter independent procedures above the first event procedure, while others enter them below the last event procedure. Still others enter them either immediately above or immediately below the procedure from which they are called. In this book, the independent procedures will usually be entered above the first event procedure in the Code Editor window.

As the syntax in Figure 16-2 shows, independent Sub procedures have both a procedure header and a procedure footer. In most cases, the procedure header begins with the keywords `Private Sub` followed by the procedure name. The rules for naming an independent Sub procedure are the same as those for naming variables; however, procedure names are usually entered using Pascal case. When using Pascal case, you capitalize the first letter in the name and the first letter of each subsequent word in the name. The procedure's name should indicate the task the procedure performs. It is a common practice to begin the name with a verb. For example, a good name for a Sub procedure that clears the contents of the label controls in an interface is ClearLabels.

Following the procedure name in the procedure header is a set of parentheses that contains an optional *parameterList*. The *parameterList* lists the data type and name of one or more memory locations, called parameters. The **parameters** store the information passed to the procedure when it is invoked. The parameters in a procedure header have procedure scope, which means they can be used only by the procedure. If the procedure does not require any information to be passed to it, as is the case with the ClearLabels procedure in Figure 16-2, an empty set of parentheses follows the procedure name in the procedure header. You will learn more about parameters later in this chapter. An independent Sub procedure ends with its procedure footer, which is always End Sub. Between the procedure header and procedure footer, you enter the instructions to be processed when the procedure is invoked.

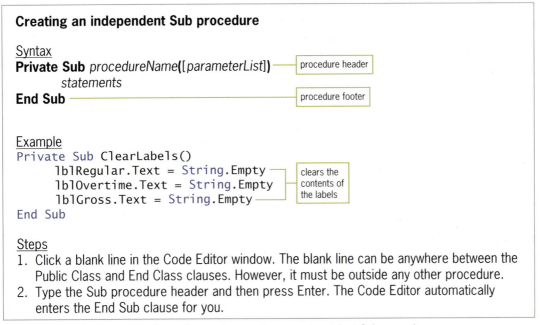

Creating an independent Sub procedure

Syntax
Private Sub *procedureName*(**[***parameterList***]**) ——— procedure header
    statements
End Sub ——————————————————— procedure footer

Example
Private Sub ClearLabels()
    lblRegular.Text = String.Empty
    lblOvertime.Text = String.Empty — clears the contents of the labels
    lblGross.Text = String.Empty
End Sub

Steps
1. Click a blank line in the Code Editor window. The blank line can be anywhere between the Public Class and End Class clauses. However, it must be outside any other procedure.
2. Type the Sub procedure header and then press Enter. The Code Editor automatically enters the End Sub clause for you.

Figure 16-2   Syntax, example, and steps for creating an independent Sub procedure

You can invoke an independent Sub procedure using the **Call statement**. Figure 16-3 shows the statement's syntax and includes an example of using the statement to invoke the ClearLabels procedure from Figure 16-2. In the syntax, *procedureName* is the name of the procedure you are calling (invoking), and *argumentList* (which is optional) is a comma-separated list of items, called arguments. Each **argument** represents an item of information that is passed to the procedure when the procedure is invoked. If you have no information to pass to the procedure that you are calling, as is the case with the ClearLabels procedure, you include an empty set of parentheses after the procedure name in the Call statement. The ClearLabels procedure is used in the Weekly Pay application, which you view in the next section.

Call statement

Syntax
Call *procedureName*(**[***argumentList***]**)

Example
Call ClearLabels()

Figure 16-3   Syntax and an example of the Call statement

The Weekly Pay Application

The Weekly Pay application calculates and displays an employee's regular pay, overtime pay, and gross pay. Employees are paid on an hourly basis and receive time and one-half for the hours worked over 40.

To open and then test the Weekly Pay application:

1. Start Visual Studio 2010 or Visual Basic 2010 Express and permanently display the Solution Explorer window. Open the **Weekly Pay Solution (Weekly Pay Solution.sln)** file contained in the ClearlyVB2010\Chap16\Weekly Pay Solution folder. If the designer window is not open, double-click **frmMain.vb** in the Solution Explorer window.

2. Start the application. Type **41** in the Hours box and then type **9** in the Rate box. Click the **Calculate** button. The button's Click event procedure calculates and displays the regular pay, overtime pay, and gross pay. See Figure 16-4.

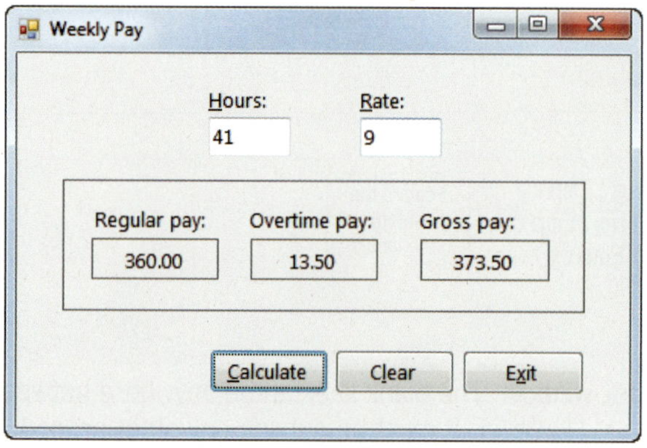

Figure 16-4   Pay amounts shown in the interface

3. Change the number of hours from 41 to **4**, but don't click the Calculate button yet. Notice that the interface still shows the pay amounts for 41 hours; this is because the amounts aren't updated until you click the Calculate button. Click the **Calculate** button to update the pay amounts and then click the **Exit** button.

To avoid confusion, it would be better to remove the pay amounts from the interface whenever a change is made to either the number of hours in the txtHours control or the rate of pay in the txtRate control. You can do this by entering the following three assignment statements in each text box's TextChanged event procedure: `lblRegular.Text = String.Empty`, `lblOvertime.Text = String.Empty`, and `lblGross.Text = String.Empty`. A text box's **TextChanged event** occurs whenever a change is made to the contents of the text box. You also can remove the pay amounts by entering the assignment statements in an independent Sub procedure and then entering the appropriate Call statement in both TextChanged event procedures. You will use the latter approach, because entering the assignment statements in an independent Sub procedure saves you from having to enter them more than once. In addition, if the application is modified—for example, if the user wants you to assign the string "N/A" rather than the empty string to the labels—you will need to make the change in only one place in the code.

To enter the ClearLabels Sub procedure and Call statements, and then test the code:

1. Open the Code Editor window. Click the **blank line** below the `Public Class frmMain` clause and then press **Enter** to insert another blank line. Enter the ClearLabels procedure shown in Figure 16-5.

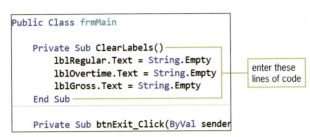

```
Public Class frmMain

    Private Sub ClearLabels()
        lblRegular.Text = String.Empty
        lblOvertime.Text = String.Empty
        lblGross.Text = String.Empty
    End Sub

    Private Sub btnExit_Click(ByVal sender
```

enter these lines of code

Figure 16-5   ClearLabels procedure

2. Open the code template for the txtHours control's TextChanged event procedure. Enter the following Call statement:

   Call ClearLabels()

3. Open the code template for the txtRate control's TextChanged event procedure. Enter the following Call statement:

   Call ClearLabels()

4. Save the solution and then start the application. Type **41** in the Hours box and then type **9** in the Rate box. Click the **Calculate** button. The pay amounts shown earlier in Figure 16-4 appear in the interface.

5. Change the number of hours from 41 to **4**. Changing the number of hours causes the txtHours control's TextChanged event to occur. As a result, the computer processes the `Call ClearLabels()` statement entered in the event procedure. When processing the statement, the computer temporarily leaves the event procedure to process the code contained in the ClearLabels procedure. The assignment statements in the ClearLabels procedure remove the pay amounts from the three label controls in the interface. After processing the assignment statements, the computer processes the ClearLabels procedure's End Sub clause, which ends the procedure. The computer then returns to the txtHours control's TextChanged event procedure and processes the line of code located below the Call statement. In this case, the line below the Call statement is End Sub, which ends the event procedure.

6. Click the **Calculate** button. Now change the rate of pay from 9 to **9.55**. Notice that the pay amounts are removed from the interface when you make a change to the rate. Click the **Calculate** button and then click the **Exit** button.

To complete the Weekly Pay application, you need to code the Clear button's Click event procedure. The procedure should remove the contents of both text boxes, as well as the pay amounts from the three label controls.

To code and then test the Clear button's Click event procedure:

1. Open the code template for the btnClear control's Click event procedure. Type the following comment and then press **Enter** twice:

   ' clear text boxes and label controls

2. First, you will remove the contents of the two text boxes. Enter the following assignment statements:

   txtHours.Text = String.Empty
   txtRate.Text = String.Empty

3. You can use the ClearLabels procedure to remove the pay amounts from the label controls. Enter the following Call statement:

   Call ClearLabels()

4. Save the solution and then start the application. Type **10** in the Hours box and then type **5** in the Rate box. Click the **Calculate** button. The values 50.00, 0.00, and 50.00 appear in the label controls.

5. Click the **Clear** button to remove the contents of the text boxes and label controls, and then click the **Exit** button. Close the Code Editor window and then close the solution.

Mini-Quiz 16-1

See Appendix B for the answers.

1. The items in the Call statement are referred to as _____ .

    a. arguments
    b. parameters

    c. passers
    d. none of the above

2. Where can you enter an independent Sub procedure in the Code Editor window?

    a. above the Public Class clause
    b. above the first event procedure

    c. below the End Class clause
    d. all of the above

3. When the contents of a text box change, the text box's _____ event occurs.

    a. ChangedText
    b. ModifiedText

    c. TextModified
    d. TextChanged

Send Me Something

As mentioned earlier, an independent Sub procedure can contain one or more parameters in its procedure header; each parameter stores an item of data. The data is passed to the procedure through the *argumentList* in the Call statement. The number of arguments in the Call statement's argumentList should agree with the number of parameters in the procedure's parameterList. In addition, the data type and position of each argument should agree with the data type and position of its corresponding parameter. For example, if the first parameter has a data type of String and the second a data type of Decimal, then the first argument in the Call statement should have the String data type and the second should have the Decimal data type. This is because, when the procedure is called, the computer stores the value of the first argument in the procedure's first parameter, the value of the second argument in the second parameter, and so on. An argument can be a constant, keyword, or variable; however, in most cases, it will be a variable.

Every variable has both a value and a unique address that represents its location in the computer's internal memory. Visual Basic allows you to pass either a copy of the variable's value or the variable's address to the receiving procedure. Passing a copy of the variable's value is referred to as **passing by value**. Passing a variable's address is referred to as **passing by reference**, and it gives the receiving procedure access to the variable in memory. The method you choose (*by value* or *by reference*) depends on whether you want to allow the receiving procedure to change the variable's contents.

Although the idea of passing information *by value* and *by reference* may sound confusing at first, it is a concept with which you already are familiar. To illustrate, Rob (the mechanical man) has a savings account at a local bank. During a conversation with his friend Jerome, Rob mentions the amount of money he has in his account. Sharing this information with Jerome is similar to passing a variable *by value*. Knowing Rob's account balance does not give Jerome access to Rob's bank account. It merely provides information that Jerome can use to compare to the balance in *his* savings account. Rob's savings account example also provides an illustration of passing information *by reference*. To deposit money to or withdraw money from the account, Rob must provide the bank teller with his account number. The account number represents the location of Rob's account at the bank and allows the teller to change the account balance. Giving the teller the bank account number is similar to passing a variable *by reference*. The account number allows the teller to change the contents of Rob's bank account, similar to the way a variable's address allows the receiving procedure to change the contents of the variable.

Just Give Me Its Value

To pass a variable *by value* in Visual Basic, you include the keyword `ByVal` before the name of its corresponding parameter in the receiving procedure's parameterList. When you pass a variable *by value*, the computer passes a copy of the variable's contents to the receiving procedure. When only a copy of the contents is passed, the receiving procedure is not given access to the variable in memory. Therefore, it cannot change the value stored inside the variable. It is appropriate to pass a variable *by value* when the receiving procedure needs to *know* the variable's contents, but it does not need to *change* the contents. Unless you specify otherwise, variables in Visual Basic are automatically passed *by value*. The Happy Birthday application, which you code in the next set of steps, passes two variables *by value* to an independent Sub procedure.

To code the Happy Birthday application:

1. Open the **Birthday Solution** (**Birthday Solution.sln**) file contained in the ClearlyVB2010\Chap16\Birthday Solution folder. If the designer window is not open, double-click **frmMain.vb** in the Solution Explorer window. When the user clicks the Display Message button, the button's Click event procedure will prompt the user to enter a first name and an age. It then will call an independent Sub procedure to display the two input items in a birthday message, like this one: "Happy 18th Birthday, Rob!".

2. Open the Code Editor window. Locate the btnDisplay control's Click event procedure. The code prompts the user to enter the first name and age (in years), and it stores the values in the `strName` and `strAge` variables, respectively.

3. The btnDisplay control's Click event procedure will call an independent Sub procedure named ShowMsg to display the birthday message. The ShowMsg procedure will need to know the person's name and age, but it will not need to change either of those values. Therefore, the event procedure will pass the ShowMsg procedure a copy of the values stored in the `strName` and `strAge` variables; in other words, the variables will be passed *by value*. The ShowMsg procedure will need two parameters to store the values passed to it. Because both values are strings, the parameters must have the String data type. Click the **blank line** below the `Public Class frmMain` clause and then press **Enter** to insert another blank line. Enter the ShowMsg procedure shown in Figure 16-6.

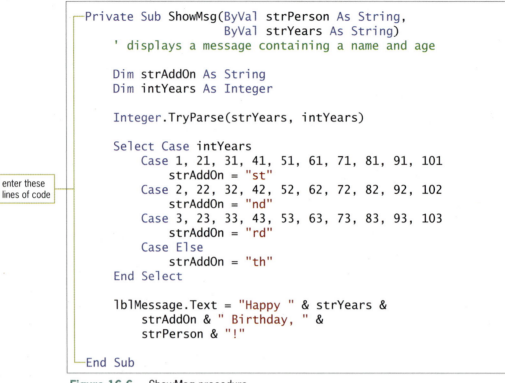

```
Private Sub ShowMsg(ByVal strPerson As String,
                    ByVal strYears As String)
    ' displays a message containing a name and age

    Dim strAddOn As String
    Dim intYears As Integer

    Integer.TryParse(strYears, intYears)

    Select Case intYears
        Case 1, 21, 31, 41, 51, 61, 71, 81, 91, 101
            strAddOn = "st"
        Case 2, 22, 32, 42, 52, 62, 72, 82, 92, 102
            strAddOn = "nd"
        Case 3, 23, 33, 43, 53, 63, 73, 83, 93, 103
            strAddOn = "rd"
        Case Else
            strAddOn = "th"
    End Select

    lblMessage.Text = "Happy " & strYears &
        strAddOn & " Birthday, " &
        strPerson & "!"

End Sub
```

enter these lines of code

Figure 16-6 ShowMsg procedure

4. Next, you will enter the Call statement. Click the **blank line** above the End Sub clause in the btnDisplay control's Click event procedure and then enter the following Call statement:

Call ShowMsg(strName, strAge)

Figure 16-7 shows the procedure header and Call statement. Notice that the number, data type, and sequence of the arguments in the Call statement match the number, data type, and sequence of the parameters in the procedure header. Also notice that the names of the arguments do not need to be identical to the names of the corresponding parameters. In fact, to avoid confusion, it usually is better to use different names for the arguments and parameters.

```
Private Sub ShowMsg(ByVal strPerson As String,
                    ByVal strYears As String)        parameters

                    arguments

Call ShowMsg(strName, strAge)
```

Figure 16-7 ShowMsg procedure header and Call statement

Before testing the application, you will desk-check it using Rob as the name and 18 as the age. When the user clicks the Display Message button, the button's Click event procedure creates the strName and strAge variables. Next, the two InputBox functions prompt the user to enter the name and age. The functions store the name (Rob) and age (18) in the strName and strAge variables, respectively. Figure 16-8 shows the desk-check table before the Call statement is processed.

strName	strAge
Rob	18

Figure 16-8 Desk-check table before the Call statement is processed

Next, the Call statement invokes the ShowMsg procedure, passing it the `strName` and `strAge` variables *by value*. You can tell that the variables are passed *by value* because the keyword `ByVal` appears before each variable's corresponding parameter in the ShowMsg procedure header. Passing both variables *by value* means that only a copy of each variable's contents—in this case, the string "Rob" and the string "18"—is passed to the procedure. At this point, the computer temporarily leaves the btnDisplay control's Click event procedure to process the ShowMsg procedure; the procedure header is processed first.

The parameterList in the ShowMsg procedure header tells the computer to create two procedure-level String variables named `strPerson` and `strYears`. The computer stores the information passed to the procedure in those variables. In this case, it stores the string "Rob" in the `strPerson` variable and the string "18" in the `strYears` variable. Figure 16-9 shows the desk-check table after the computer processes the Call statement and ShowMsg procedure header.

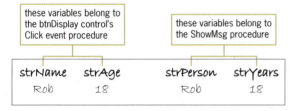

Figure 16-9 Desk-check table after the Call statement and procedure header are processed

Next, the computer processes the statements contained within the ShowMsg procedure. The Dim statements create and initialize the `strAddOn` and `intYears` variables. The TryParse method then converts the string stored in the `strYears` variable to an integer and stores the result in the `intYears` variable. Because the `intYears` variable contains the number 18, the `Case Else` clause in the Select Case statement assigns "th" to the `strAddOn` variable. Figure 16-10 shows the desk-check table after the Select Case statement is processed.

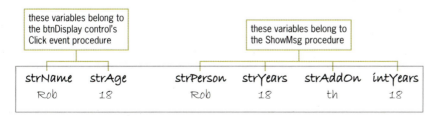

Figure 16-10 Desk-check table after the Select Case statement is processed

The last assignment statement in the ShowMsg procedure uses the values stored in the `strPerson`, `strYears`, and `strAddOn` variables to display the appropriate message. In this case, the statement displays the "Happy 18th Birthday, Rob!" message. The ShowMsg procedure's **End Sub** clause is processed next. At this point, the computer removes the

ShowMsg procedure's variables from internal memory, as illustrated in Figure 16-11. (Recall that a procedure-level variable is removed from the computer's memory when the procedure in which it is declared ends.)

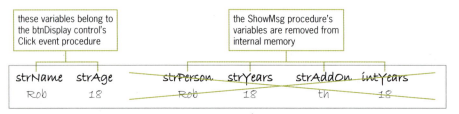

Figure 16-11   Desk-check table after the ShowMsg procedure ends

After the ShowMsg procedure ends, the computer returns to the line of code located below the Call statement in the btnDisplay control's Click event procedure. In this case, it returns to the End Sub clause, which marks the end of the event procedure. When the event procedure ends, the computer removes the strName and strAge variables from internal memory.

To test the Happy Birthday application:

1.   Save the solution and then start the application.

2.   Click the **Display Message** button. Type **Rob** and press **Enter**, and then type **18** and press **Enter**. The birthday message appears in the interface, as shown in Figure 16-12. Click the **Exit** button. Close the Code Editor window and then close the solution.

Figure 16-12   Birthday message shown in the interface

Where Do You Live?

Instead of passing a copy of a variable's value to a procedure, you can pass the variable's address. In other words, you can pass the variable's location in the computer's internal memory. As you learned earlier, passing a variable's address is referred to as passing *by reference*, and it gives the receiving procedure access to the variable being passed. You pass a variable *by reference* when you want the receiving procedure to change the contents of the variable. To pass a variable *by reference* in Visual Basic, you include the keyword ByRef before the name of its corresponding parameter in the receiving procedure's parameterList. The ByRef keyword tells the computer to pass the variable's address rather than a copy of its contents. The Total Due Calculator application, which you code in this section, provides an example of passing a variable *by reference*. The application's interface and planning information are shown in Figures 16-13 and 16-14, respectively.

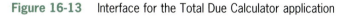

Figure 16-13 Interface for the Total Due Calculator application

```
Output:   subtotal
          discount
          total due


Input:    quantity
          price
          coupon?
          coupon code


Algorithm:
1. enter the quantity, price, and coupon? items
2. calculate the subtotal by multiplying the quantity by the price
3. if coupon?, do this:
        enter the coupon code

        if the coupon code is:    do this:
            A05                   assign 5 as the discount
            X25                   multiply the subtotal by 10% and assign the result
                                  as the discount
            NE4                   multiply the subtotal by 15% and assign the result
                                  as the discount
            Invalid               assign 0 as the discount and then display an
                                  appropriate message
        end if
    otherwise, do this:
        assign 0 as the discount
    end if
4. calculate the total due by subtracting the discount from the subtotal
5. display the subtotal, discount, and total due
```

Figure 16-14 Planning information for the Total Due Calculator application

Now let's say it is Friday afternoon and you are anxious to leave work early. Before you can do so, however, you need to code and test the Total Due Calculator application. You decide to recruit Sandy, one of your co-workers, to help you with the coding. More specifically, you ask Sandy to code Step 3 in the algorithm as an independent Sub procedure. Step 3's task is to assign the appropriate discount, so you and Sandy agree to name the procedure AssignDiscount. Both of you determine that the AssignDiscount procedure requires two items of information. First, it needs to know the value of the subtotal, because some of the discounts are based on that value. Second, it needs to know where to assign the discount. In other words, it needs to know the address of the variable that will store the discount.

To code the Total Due Calculator application:

1. Open the **Total Due Solution** (**Total Due Solution.sln**) file contained in the ClearlyVB2010\Chap16\Total Due Solution folder. If the designer window is not open, double-click **frmMain.vb** in the Solution Explorer window.

2. Open the Code Editor window. First, you will enter the Call statement. Locate the btnCalc control's Click event procedure. Click the **blank line** below the ' assigndiscount comment. The Click event procedure will need to pass a copy of the value stored in the decSubtotal variable. It also will need to pass the address of the decDiscount variable. Enter the following Call statement. (Don't be concerned about the jagged line that appears below the arguments in the Call statement. The jagged line will disappear when you enter the procedure's parameters in the next step.)

   Call AssignDiscount(decSubtotal, decDiscount)

3. Now you will enter the parameters in the AssignDiscount procedure header. The parameters will need to accept a Decimal value followed by the address of a Decimal variable. Click **between the parentheses** in the AssignDiscount procedure header and then type the following parameterList:

   ByVal decSub As Decimal, ByRef decDisc As Decimal

Figure 16-15 shows both the AssignDiscount procedure and the btnCalc control's Click event procedure.

```
Private Sub AssignDiscount(ByVal decSub As Decimal,
ByRef decDisc As Decimal)
    ' assigns the discount

    If chkCoupon.Checked = True Then
        Dim strCouponCode As String
        strCouponCode = InputBox("Coupon code:", "Coupon")
        Select Case strCouponCode.ToUpper
            Case "A05"
                decDisc = 5
            Case "X25"
                decDisc = 0.1 * decSub
            Case "NE4"
                decDisc = 0.15 * decSub
            Case Else
                decDisc = 0
                MessageBox.Show("Invalid coupon code",
                                "Total Due Calculator",
                            MessageBoxButtons.OK,
                            MessageBoxIcon.Information)
        End Select
    Else
        decDisc = 0
    End If
End Sub

Private Sub btnCalc_Click(ByVal sender As Object,
ByVal e As System.EventArgs) Handles btnCalc.Click
    ' displays the subtotal, discount, and total due
```

Figure 16-15 AssignDiscount and btnCalc_Click procedures *(continues)*

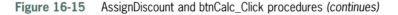

(continued)

```
        Dim intQuantity As Integer
        Dim decPrice As Decimal
        Dim decSubtotal As Decimal
        Dim decTotalDue As Decimal
        Dim decDiscount As Decimal

        Integer.TryParse(txtQuantity.Text, intQuantity)
        Decimal.TryParse(txtPrice.Text, decPrice)

        ' calculate subtotal
        decSubtotal = intQuantity * decPrice

        ' assign discount
        Call AssignDiscount(decSubtotal, decDiscount)

        ' calculate total due
        decTotalDue = decSubtotal - decDiscount

        ' display subtotal, discount, and total due
        lblSubtotal.Text = decSubtotal.ToString("N2")
        lblDiscount.Text = decDiscount.ToString("N2")
        lblTotalDue.Text = decTotalDue.ToString("N2")
    End Sub
```

Figure 16-15   AssignDiscount and btnCalc_Click procedures

Before testing the application, you will desk-check it using 4 as the quantity, 15 as the price, and X25 as the coupon code. In addition, the Coupon check box will be selected. When the user clicks the Calculate button, the btnCalc control's Click event procedure creates the variables declared in the five Dim statements. The two TryParse methods in the procedure convert the quantity and price to the appropriate data types and then store the results in the `intQuantity` and `decPrice` variables, respectively. Next, the `decSubtotal = intQuantity * decPrice` statement calculates the subtotal and stores the result (60) in the `decSubtotal` variable. Figure 16-16 shows the desk-check table before the Call statement is processed.

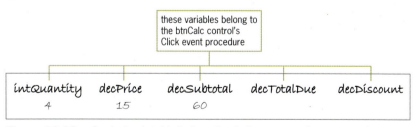

Figure 16-16   Desk-check table before the Call statement is processed

The computer processes the Call statement next. The Call statement invokes the AssignDiscount procedure, passing it two arguments. At this point, the computer temporarily leaves the Click event procedure to process the code contained in the AssignDiscount procedure; the procedure header is processed first. The `ByVal` keyword before the `decSub` parameter indicates that the parameter is receiving a value from the Call statement. In this case, it is receiving a copy of the number stored in the `decSubTotal` variable. As a result, the computer creates the `decSub` variable and then stores the number 60 in the variable. The `ByRef` keyword before the decDisc parameter indicates that the parameter is receiving the address of a variable. When you pass a variable's address to a procedure, the computer uses the address to locate the variable in its internal memory. It then assigns the parameter name to the memory location. In this case, the computer locates the decDiscount variable in memory and assigns the name decDisc to it. At this point, the memory location has two names: one assigned by the btnCalc control's Click event procedure and the other assigned by the AssignDiscount procedure, as indicated in Figure 16-17.

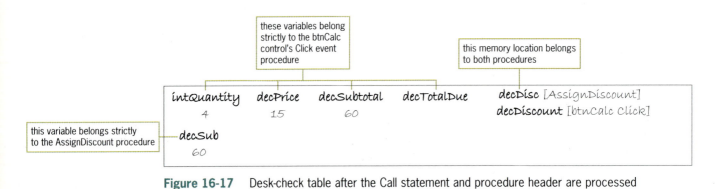

Figure 16-17   Desk-check table after the Call statement and procedure header are processed

Notice that four of the variables in Figure 16-17 belong strictly to the btnCalc control's Click event procedure, and one belongs strictly to the AssignDiscount procedure; one memory location, however, belongs to both procedures. Although both procedures can access the memory location, each procedure uses a different name to do so. The Click event procedure uses the name decDiscount, whereas the AssignDiscount procedure uses the name decDisc.

After processing the AssignDiscount procedure header, the computer processes the code contained in the procedure. For this desk-check, the Coupon check box is selected, so the computer follows the instructions in the selection structure's true path. The first instruction creates a variable named strCouponCode. Next, the statement containing the InputBox function prompts the user to enter the coupon code and stores the user's response (X25) in the strCouponCode variable. The Select Case statement is processed next. The instruction in the Case "X25" clause calculates the discount by multiplying the contents of the decSub variable (60) by 0.1. It then assigns the result (6) to the decDisc variable. Figure 16-18 shows the desk-check table after the Select Case statement is processed. Notice that when the value in the decDisc variable changes, the value in the decDiscount variable also changes. This happens because the names decDisc and decDiscount refer to the same location in the computer's internal memory.

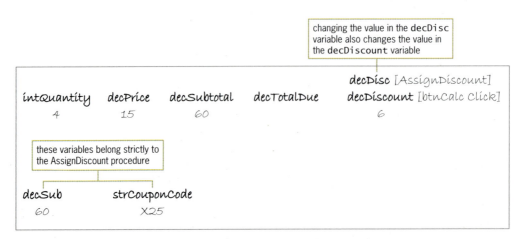

Figure 16-18   Desk-check table after the Select Case statement is processed

The AssignDiscount procedure's End Sub clause is processed next and ends the procedure. At this point, the computer removes the decSub and strCouponCode variables from memory. It also removes the decDisc name from the appropriate location in memory, as indicated in Figure 16-19. Notice that the decDiscount memory location now has only one name: the name assigned to it by the btnCalc control's Click event procedure.

Figure 16-19   Desk-check table after the AssignDiscount procedure ends

After the AssignDiscount procedure ends, the computer returns to the line of code below the Call statement in the btnCalc control's Click event procedure. In this case, it returns to the statement that calculates the total due. Figure 16-20 shows the desk-check table after the assignment statement is processed.

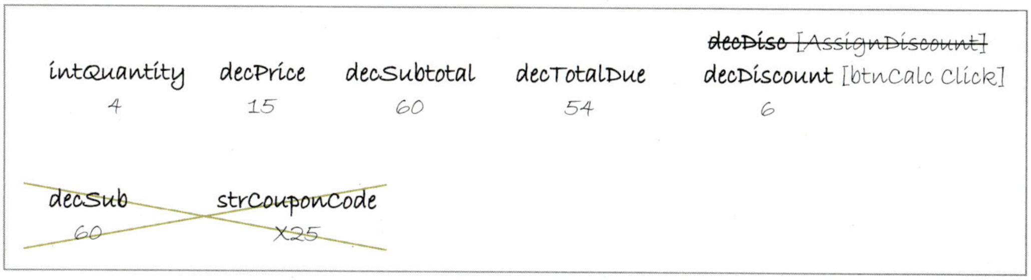

Figure 16-20   Desk-check table after the total due is calculated

The last three assignment statements in the Click event procedure display the contents of the decSubtotal, decDiscount, and decTotalDue variables (formatted with two decimal places) in the interface. Finally, the computer processes the Click event procedure's End Sub clause. When the Click event procedure ends, the computer removes the procedure's variables from memory.

To test the Total Due Calculator application:

1. Save the solution and then start the application. Type **4** in the Quantity box and then type **15** in the Price box. Click the **Coupon** check box to select it and then click the **Calculate** button.

2. Type **X25** as the coupon code and then press **Enter**. The correct subtotal, discount, and total due appear in the interface, as shown in Figure 16-21. Click the **Exit** button. Close the Code Editor window and then close the solution.

Figure 16-21   Calculated amounts shown in the interface

To review what you learned about Sub procedures, view the Ch16Sub video.

For more examples of Sub procedures, see the Sub Procedures section in the Ch16WantMore.pdf file.

Mini-Quiz 16-2

See Appendix B for the answers.

1. A procedure is passed a copy of the value stored in a String variable, followed by a copy of the value stored in an Integer variable. Which of the following is a valid header for the procedure?

    a. `Private Sub Display(ByRef strX As String,`
    `                        ByRef intY As Integer)`

    b. `Private Sub Display(ByVal strX As String,`
    `                        ByVal intY As Integer)`

    c. `Private Sub Display(strX As String,`
    `                        intY As Integer)`

    d. `Private Sub Display(ByVal intX As Integer,`
    `                        ByRef strY As String)`

2. Write a Call statement that invokes the Display procedure from Question 1. Pass the procedure a copy of the values stored in the `strName` and `intQuantity` variables.

3. In the receiving procedure's header, you use the keyword _____ to indicate that a variable is being passed *by reference*.

Summary

- You can create your own Sub procedures, called independent Sub procedures, in Visual Basic. Independent Sub procedures allow programmers to avoid duplicating code in different parts of a program. They also allow the programmer to concentrate on one small piece of a program at a time. In addition, they allow a team of programmers to work on large and complex programs.

- It is a common practice to begin a procedure name with a verb and to enter the name using Pascal case.

- You can use the Call statement to invoke an independent Sub procedure. The Call statement allows you to pass arguments to the procedure.

- When calling a procedure, the number of arguments listed in the Call statement's argumentList should agree with the number of parameters listed in the receiving procedure's parameterList. Also, the data type and position of each argument should agree with the data type and position of its corresponding parameter.

- You can pass information to an independent Sub procedure either *by value* or *by reference*. To pass a variable *by value*, you precede the variable's corresponding parameter with the keyword ByVal. To pass a variable *by reference*, you precede the variable's corresponding parameter with the keyword ByRef. The procedure header indicates whether a variable is being passed *by value* or *by reference*.

- When you pass a variable *by value*, only a copy of the variable's contents is passed. When you pass a variable *by reference*, the variable's address is passed.

- Variables that appear in the parameterList in a procedure header have procedure scope, which means they can be used only by the procedure.

Key Terms

Argument—an item listed within parentheses in a Call statement; represents information passed to the receiving procedure

Call statement—the statement used to invoke an independent Sub procedure in a Visual Basic program

Independent Sub procedure—a procedure that is not associated with any specific object or event and is processed only when invoked (called) from code

Parameters—the memory locations listed in a procedure header

Passing by reference—the process of passing a variable's address to a procedure

Passing by value—the process of passing a copy of a variable's value to a procedure

TextChanged event—occurs when a change is made to the Text property of its associated control

Review Questions

1. To determine whether a variable is being passed to a procedure *by value* or *by reference*, you will need to examine _____ .

   a. the Call statement

   b. the procedure header

   c. the statements entered in the procedure

   d. either a or b

2. Which of the following statements invokes the CalcArea Sub procedure, passing it two variables *by value*?

   a. `Call CalcArea(dblLength, dblWidth)`

   b. `Call CalcArea(ByVal dblLength, ByVal dblWidth)`

   c. `Call CalcArea ByVal(dblLength, dblWidth)`

   d. `Call ByVal CalcArea(dblLength, dblWidth)`

3. Which of the following is a valid header for a procedure that receives an integer followed by a number with a decimal place?

   a. `Private Sub CalcFee(intBase As Integer,`
      `                    decRate As Decimal)`

   b. `Private Sub CalcFee(ByRef intBase As Integer,`
      `                    ByRef decRate As Decimal)`

   c. `Private Sub CalcFee(ByVal intBase As Integer,`
      `                    ByVal decRate As Decimal)`

   d. `Private Sub CalcFee(ByValue intBase As Integer,`
      `                    ByValue decRate As Decimal)`

4. Which of the following statements invokes the CalcFee procedure from Review Question 3?

   a. `Call CalcFee(intX, decY)`

   b. `Call CalcFee(2, 3.5)`

   c. `Call CalcFee(intX, 25.45)`

   d. all of the above

5. Which of the following is false?

   a. The sequence of the arguments listed in the Call statement should agree with the sequence of the parameters listed in the receiving procedure's header.

   b. The data type of each argument in the Call statement should match the data type of its corresponding parameter in the procedure header.

   c. The name of each argument in the Call statement should be identical to the name of its corresponding parameter in the procedure header.

   d. When you pass information to a procedure *by value*, the procedure stores the value of each item it receives in a separate memory location.

6. The CalcEndInventory procedure is passed four Integer variables named `intBegin`, `intSales`, `intPurchases`, and `intEnding`. The procedure should calculate the ending inventory using the beginning inventory, sales, and purchase amounts passed to the procedure. The result should be stored in the `intEnding` variable. Which of the following procedure headers is correct?

   a. `Private Sub CalcEndInventory(ByVal intB As Integer,`
      `ByVal intS As Integer, ByVal intP As Integer,`
      `ByRef intFinal As Integer)`

   b. `Private Sub CalcEndInventory(ByVal intB As Integer,`
      `ByVal intS As Integer, ByVal intP As Integer,`
      `ByVal intFinal As Integer)`

   c. `Private Sub CalcEndInventory(ByRef intB As Integer,`
      `ByRef intS As Integer, ByRef intP As Integer,`
      `ByVal intFinal As Integer)`

   d. `Private Sub CalcEndInventory(ByRef intB As Integer,`
      `ByRef intS As Integer, ByRef intP As Integer,`
      `ByRef intFinal As Integer)`

7. The items listed between the parentheses in a procedure header are called _____ .

   a. arguments

   b. parameters

   c. receivers

   d. none of the above

Exercises

TRY THIS

1. Open the Bonus Solution (Bonus Solution.sln) file contained in the ClearlyVB2010\
    Chap16\Bonus Solution-TRY THIS 1 folder. The application should calculate and
    display a bonus amount, which is based on two sales amounts entered by the user.
    Use the algorithm shown in Figure 16-22 to code the btnCalc control's Click event
    procedure and the independent Sub procedure. Save the solution and then start
    and test the application. Close the Code Editor window and then close the solution.
    (See Appendix B for the answer.)

```
1. enter sale 1 and sale 2
2. calculate the sum by adding together sale 1 and sale 2
3. if the sum is greater than 1200, do this:
        calculate the bonus by multiplying the sum by 10%
   otherwise, do this:
        calculate the bonus by multiplying the sum by 8%
   end if
4. display the bonus
```

create an independent Sub procedure that will handle Steps 3 and 4

Figure 16-22   Algorithm for Exercise 1

TRY THIS

2. Open the Bonus Solution (Bonus Solution.sln) file contained in the ClearlyVB2010\Chap16\
    Bonus Solution-TRY THIS 2 folder. The application should calculate and display a bonus
    amount, which is based on two sales amounts entered by the user. Use the algorithm shown
    in Figure 16-23 to code the btnCalc control's Click event procedure and the independent Sub
    procedure. Save the solution and then start and test the application. Close the Code Editor
    window and then close the solution. (See Appendix B for the answer.)

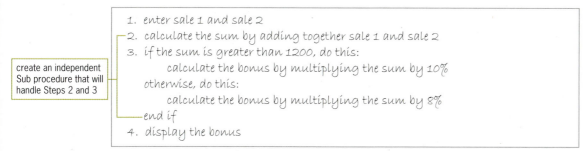

```
1. enter sale 1 and sale 2
2. calculate the sum by adding together sale 1 and sale 2
3. if the sum is greater than 1200, do this:
        calculate the bonus by multiplying the sum by 10%
   otherwise, do this:
        calculate the bonus by multiplying the sum by 8%
   end if
4. display the bonus
```

create an independent Sub procedure that will handle Steps 2 and 3

Figure 16-23   Algorithm for Exercise 2

MODIFY THIS

3. In this exercise, you modify the Total Due Calculator application coded in the chapter.
    Use Windows to make a copy of the Total Due Solution folder. Save the copy in the
    ClearlyVB2010\Chap16 folder. Rename the copy Total Due Solution-MODIFY THIS.
    Open the Total Due Solution (Total Due Solution.sln) file contained in the Total Due
    Solution-MODIFY THIS folder. Open the designer and Code Editor windows. Create
    an independent Sub procedure that clears the three payment amounts. Call the Sub
    procedure when a change is made to the contents of either text box. Also call the Sub
    procedure whenever the check box is clicked. Save the solution and then start and test
    the application. Close the Code Editor window and then close the solution.

INTRODUCTORY

4. Open the Grade Solution (Grade Solution.sln) file contained in the ClearlyVB2010\
    Chap16\Grade Solution folder. The application should display a letter grade, which is
    based on the average of three test scores. If the average is at least 90, the grade is A.
    If the average is at least 80 but less than 90, the grade is B. If the average is at least
    70 but less than 80, the grade is C. If the average is at least 60 but less than 70,
    the grade is D. If the average is below 60, the grade is F. Code the application, using an
    independent Sub procedure to both determine and display the letter grade. Save the

solution and then start and test the application. Close the Code Editor window and then close the solution.

INTRODUCTORY

5. In this exercise, you modify the Grade application from Exercise 4. Use Windows to make a copy of the Grade Solution folder. Save the copy in the ClearlyVB2010\Chap16 folder. Rename the copy Modified Grade Solution. Open the Grade Solution (Grade Solution.sln) file contained in the Modified Grade Solution folder. Open the designer and Code Editor windows. Currently, the independent Sub procedure both determines and displays the letter grade. Modify the code so that the Sub procedure determines but does not display the letter grade. The letter grade should be displayed by the btnDisplay control's Click event procedure. (Hint: If the Code Editor indicates that a String variable is being passed before it has been assigned a value, assign the `String.Empty` constant to the variable in the Dim statement.) Save the solution and then start and test the application. Close the Code Editor window and then close the solution.

INTERMEDIATE

6. Open the Temperature Solution (Temperature Solution.sln) file contained in the ClearlyVB2010\Chap16\Temperature Solution folder. Code the application so that it uses two independent Sub procedures: one to convert a temperature from Fahrenheit to Celsius, and the other to convert a temperature from Celsius to Fahrenheit. Save the solution and then start and test the application. Close the Code Editor window and then close the solution.

INTERMEDIATE

7. Open the Translator Solution (Translator Solution.sln) file contained in the ClearlyVB2010\Chap16\Translator Solution folder. Code the application so that it uses independent Sub procedures to translate the English words into French, Spanish, or Italian. (Hint: If the Code Editor indicates that a String variable is being passed before it has been assigned a value, assign the `String.Empty` constant to the variable in the Dim statement.) Save the solution and then start and test the application. Close the Code Editor window and then close the solution.

INTERMEDIATE

8. In this exercise, you modify the Happy Birthday application coded in the chapter. Use Windows to make a copy of the Birthday Solution folder. Save the copy in the ClearlyVB2010\Chap16 folder. Rename the copy Birthday Solution-Intermediate. Open the Birthday Solution (Birthday Solution.sln) file contained in the Birthday Solution-Intermediate folder. Open the designer window. The ShowMsg procedure should use another independent Sub procedure to assign the appropriate letters ("st", "nd", "rd", or "th"). Create the Sub procedure and then modify the ShowMsg procedure appropriately. Notice that an independent Sub procedure can call another independent Sub procedure. (Hint: If the Code Editor indicates that a String variable is being passed before it has been assigned a value, assign the `String.Empty` constant to the variable in the Dim statement.) Save the solution and then start and test the application. Close the Code Editor window and then close the solution.

INTERMEDIATE

9. In this exercise, you code an application that calculates a water bill. The clerk at the water department will enter the current meter reading and the previous meter reading in two text boxes. The application should calculate and display the number of gallons of water used and the total charge for the water. The charge for water is $2.05 per 1000 gallons, or .00205 per gallon. Use two independent Sub procedures: one to make the calculations and the other to display the results. Call both Sub procedures from the Calculate button's Click event procedure. Make the calculations only when the current meter reading is greater than or equal to the previous meter reading; otherwise, display an appropriate message in a message box.

   a. List the output and input items, as well as any processing items, and then create an appropriate algorithm using pseudocode.

   b. Create a Visual Basic Windows application. Use the following names for the solution and project, respectively: Water Bill Solution and Water Bill Project. Save the application in the ClearlyVB2010\Chap16 folder. Change the name of the form file on your disk to frmMain.vb. If necessary, change the form's name to frmMain.

c. Create the interface shown in Figure 16-24 and then code the application. Be sure to code each text box's KeyPress and TextChanged event procedures. Save the solution and then start and test the application. Close the Code Editor window and then close the solution.

Water Bill Calculator

Current reading: _____   Calculate

Previous reading: _____   Exit

Gallons used: _____

Total charge: _____

Figure 16-24   Interface for Exercise 9

10. Sharon Barrow, the billing supervisor at Cable Direct (a local cable company), has asked you to create an application that she can use to calculate and display a customer's bill. Create a Visual Basic Windows application. Use the following names for the solution and project, respectively: Cable Direct Solution and Cable Direct Project. Save the application in the ClearlyVB2010\Chap16 folder. Change the name of the form file on your disk to frmMain.vb. If necessary, change the form's name to frmMain. Create the interface shown in Figure 16-25 and then code the application. Use two independent Sub procedures: one to calculate the bill for a Residential customer, and the other to calculate the bill for a Business customer. The cable rates are shown in Figure 16-26. Also, clear the Total due box when a change is made to either text box, or when either radio button is clicked. Save the solution and then start and test the application. (Hint: The total due for a Business customer with three premium channels and 10 connections is $246.50.) Close the Code Editor window and then close the solution.

ADVANCED

Cable Direct

○ Business   Premium channels: Connections:

◉ Residential   _____   _____

Total due:

_____   Calculate Total Due   Exit

Figure 16-25   Interface for Exercise 10

Residential customers:
        Processing fee: $4.50
        Basic service fee: $30
        Premium channels: $5 per channel
Business customers (will have at least one connection):
        Processing fee: $16.50
        Basic service fee: $80 for the first 10 connections; $4 for each additional connection
        Premium channels: $50 per channel for any number of connections

Figure 16-26   Cable rates for Exercise 10

11. Employees at Harvey Industries are paid every Friday. All employees are paid on an hourly basis, with time and one-half paid for the hours worked over 40. The amount of Social Security and Medicare (or FICA) tax to deduct from an employee's weekly gross pay is calculated by multiplying the gross pay amount by 7.65%. The amount of federal

ADVANCED

withholding tax (FWT) to deduct from an employee's weekly gross pay is based on the employee's filing status—either single (including head of household) or married—and his or her weekly taxable wages. You calculate the weekly taxable wages by first multiplying the number of withholding allowances by $70.19 (the value of a withholding allowance in 2010), and then subtracting the result from the weekly gross pay. For example, if your weekly gross pay is $400 and you have two withholding allowances, your weekly taxable wages are $259.62. You use the weekly taxable wages, along with the filing status and the appropriate weekly federal withholding tax table, to determine the amount of FWT to withhold. The weekly tax tables for the year 2010 are shown in Figure 16-27.

a. Create a Visual Basic Windows application. Use the following names for the solution and project, respectively: Harvey Industries Solution and Harvey Industries Project. Save the application in the ClearlyVB2010\Chap16 folder. Change the name of the form file on your disk to frmMain.vb. If necessary, change the form's name to frmMain.

b. Create the interface shown in Figure 16-28 and then code the application. Use the Math.Round method, which you learned about in Chapter 6's Exercises 10 and 11. Use an independent Sub procedure to calculate the federal withholding tax.

c. Create a procedure that clears the contents of the Gross pay, FWT, FICA, and Net pay boxes. The four boxes should be cleared when a change is made to the Hours, Rate, or Allowances text boxes, or when one of the radio buttons is clicked.

d. Code the KeyPress event procedures for the Hours, Rate, and Allowances text boxes.

e. Save the solution and then start and test the application. Close the Code Editor window and then close the solution.

FWT Tables – Weekly Payroll Period

Single person (including head of household)

If the taxable wages are: The amount of income tax to withhold is:

Over	But not over	Base amount	Percentage	Of excess over
	$ 116	0		
$ 116	$ 200	0	10%	$ 116
$ 200	$ 693	$ 8.40 plus	15%	$ 200
$ 693	$1,302	$ 82.35 plus	25%	$ 693
$1,302	$1,624	$ 234.60 plus	27%	$1,302
$1,624	$1,687	$ 321.54 plus	30%	$1,624
$1,687	$3,344	$ 340.44 plus	28%	$1,687
$3,344	$7,225	$ 804.40 plus	33%	$3,344
$7,225		$2,085.13 plus	35%	$7,225

Married person

If the taxable wages are: The amount of income tax to withhold is:

Over	But not over	Base amount	Percentage	Of excess over
	$ 264	0		
$ 264	$ 471	0	10%	$ 264
$ 471	$1,457	$ 20.70 plus	15%	$ 471
$1,457	$1,809	$ 168.80 plus	25%	$1,457
$1,809	$2,386	$ 256.60 plus	27%	$1,809
$2,386	$2,789	$ 412.39 plus	25%	$2,386
$2,789	$4,173	$ 513.14 plus	28%	$2,789
$4,173	$7,335	$ 900.66 plus	33%	$4,173
$7,335		$1,944.12 plus	35%	$7,335

Figure 16-27 Weekly FWT tables for Exercise 11

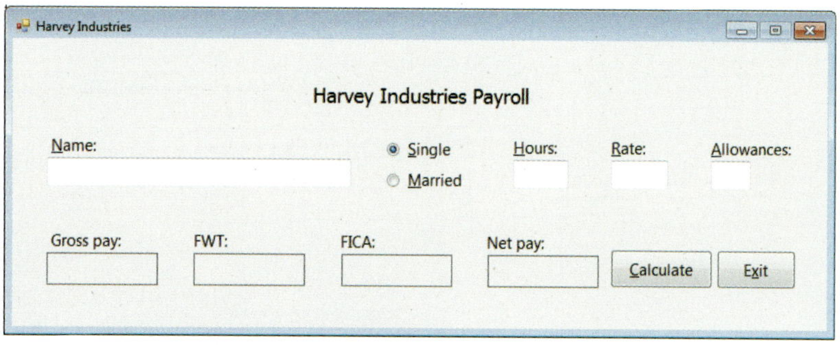

Figure 16-28   Interface for Exercise 11

12. Open the FigureThisOut Solution (FigureThisOut Solution.sln) file contained in the ClearlyVB2010\Chap16\FigureThisOut Solution folder. Open the Code Editor window and study the existing code. The first statement in the btnClear control's Click event procedure assigns the empty string to the txtSales control's Text property. As you learned in the chapter, when a change is made to the contents of a text box, the text box's TextChanged event occurs. In this case, the TextChanged event procedure calls the ClearLabels procedure to clear the contents of two label controls. Notice that the second statement in the btnClear control's Click event procedure also calls the ClearLabels procedure; your task is to determine whether the second statement is really necessary. Insert an apostrophe before the Call statement in the btnClear control's Click event procedure to make the statement a comment. Save the solution and then start and test the application. Why is it necessary for the btnClear control to call the ClearLabels procedure? Stop the application. Delete the apostrophe you inserted before the Call statement and then save the solution. Close the Code Editor window and then close the solution.

FIGURE THIS OUT

13. Open the SwatTheBugs Solution (SwatTheBugs Solution.sln) file contained in the ClearlyVB2010\Chap16\SwatTheBugs Solution folder. Open the Code Editor window and study the existing code. Start and then test the application. Notice that the application is not working correctly. Locate and correct the errors in the code. Save the solution and then start and test the application again. Close the Code Editor window and then close the solution.

SWAT THE BUGS

Talk to Me (Function Procedures)

After studying Chapter 17, you should be able to:

◎ Explain the difference between a Sub procedure and a Function procedure

◎ Create a Function procedure

◎ Invoke a Function procedure

What's the Answer?

In Chapter 16, you learned how to create independent Sub procedures. In this chapter, you will learn how to create Function procedures. The difference between both types of procedures is that a **Function procedure** returns a value after performing its assigned task, whereas a Sub procedure does not return a value. Function procedures are referred to more simply as **functions**. Figure 17-1 shows the syntax for creating a function in Visual Basic. The header and footer in a function are almost identical to the header and footer in a Sub procedure, except the function's header and footer contain the Function keyword rather than the Sub keyword. Also different from a Sub procedure header, a function's header includes the As *dataType* section. You use this section of the header to specify the data type of the value returned by the function. If the function returns a string, you enter As String at the end of the header. If the function returns a Double number, you enter As Double.

As is true with a Sub procedure, a function can receive information either *by value* or *by reference*. The information it receives is listed in the parameterList in the header. Between the function's header and footer, you enter the instructions to process when the function is invoked. In most cases, the **Return statement** is the last statement within a function. The statement's syntax is Return *expression*, where *expression* represents the one and only value that will be returned to the statement invoking the function. The data type of the *expression* must agree with the data type specified in the As *dataType* section.

In addition to the syntax, Figure 17-1 also includes two examples of a function, as well as the steps for entering a function in the Code Editor window. As with Sub procedures, you can enter your functions above the first event procedure, below the last event procedure, or immediately above or below the procedure from which they are invoked. In this book, you will enter the functions above the first event procedure. Like Sub procedure names, function names are entered using Pascal case and typically begin with a verb. The name should indicate the task the function performs. For example, a good name for a function that returns a new price is GetNewPrice.

Creating a Function procedure

specifies the data type of the return value

Syntax

function header → **Private Function** *procedureName*(**[***parameterList***]**) **As** *dataType*
      statements
      Return *expression*
function footer → **End Function**

Example 1

returns the dblNew variable's value to the statement that called the function

```
Private Function GetNewPrice(ByVal dblPrice As Double) As Double
    Dim dblNew As Double
    dblNew = dblPrice * 1.05
    Return dblNew
End Function
```

Example 2

calculates the new price and then returns it to the statement that called the function

```
Private Function GetNewPrice(ByVal dblPrice As Double) As Double
    Return dblPrice * 1.05
End Function
```

Steps

1. Click a blank line in the Code Editor window. The blank line can be anywhere between the Public Class and End Class clauses. However, it must be outside any other procedure.
2. Type the Function procedure header and then press Enter. The Code Editor automatically enters the End Function clause for you.

Figure 17-1   Syntax, example, and steps for creating a Function procedure

You can invoke a function from one or more places in an application's code. You invoke a function that you create in exactly the same way as you invoke one of Visual Basic's built-in functions, such as the InputBox function. You do this by including the function's name and arguments (if any) in a statement. The number, data type, and position of the arguments should agree with the number, data type, and position of the function's parameters. In most cases, the statement that invokes a function assigns the function's return value to a variable. However, it also may use the return value in a calculation or simply display the return value. Figure 17-2 shows examples of invoking the GetNewPrice function from Figure 17-1. The `GetNewPrice (dblCurrentPrice)` entry in each example invokes the function, passing it the value stored in the `dblCurrentPrice` variable. In Example 1, the function's return value is assigned to a variable. Example 2 uses the return value in a calculation, and Example 3 displays the return value in a label control. The GetNewPrice function is used in the Price Calculator application, which you view in the next section.

Invoking a Function procedure

Example 1 – assign the return value to a variable
```
dblNewPrice = GetNewPrice(dblCurrentPrice)
```

Example 2 – use the return value in a calculation
```
dblTotalDue = intQuantity * GetNewPrice(dblCurrentPrice)
```
the assignment statement multiplies the value in the `intQuantity` variable by the function's return value and then assigns the result to the `dblTotalDue` variable

Example 3 – display the return value
```
lblNewPrice.Text =
    GetNewPrice(dblCurrentPrice).ToString("C2")
```

Figure 17-2   Examples of invoking the GetNewPrice function

Price Calculator Application

Figure 17-3 shows the Price Calculator application's user interface. The interface provides a text box for the user to enter the current price of an item. When the user clicks the Calculate button, the button's Click event procedure will use the GetNewPrice function to calculate and return the new price, which will be 5% more than the current price. The Click event procedure will then display the function's return value in the interface.

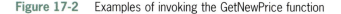

Figure 17-3   Interface for the Price Calculator application

To code the Price Calculator application:

1. Start Visual Studio 2010 or Visual Basic 2010 Express and permanently display the Solution Explorer window. Open the **Price Calculator Solution (Price Calculator Solution.sln)** file contained in the ClearlyVB2010\Chap17\Price Calculator Solution folder. If the designer window is not open, double-click **frmMain.vb** in the Solution Explorer window.

2. Open the Code Editor window. First, you will enter the GetNewPrice function. Click the **blank line** below the `Public Class frmMain` clause and then press **Enter** to insert another blank line. Enter the GetNewPrice function shown in Figure 17-4.

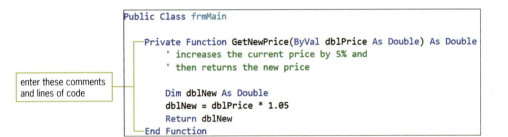

```
Public Class frmMain

    Private Function GetNewPrice(ByVal dblPrice As Double) As Double
        ' increases the current price by 5% and
        ' then returns the new price

        Dim dblNew As Double
        dblNew = dblPrice * 1.05
        Return dblNew
    End Function
```

enter these comments and lines of code

Figure 17-4   GetNewPrice function

3. In the btnCalc control's Click event procedure, you will enter a statement that invokes the GetNewPrice function and assigns the function's return value to the `dblNewPrice` variable. The statement will need to pass the function a copy of the current price stored in the `dblCurrentPrice` variable. Click the **blank line** below the `' get the new price` comment in the btnCalc control's Click event procedure and then enter the following assignment statement:

dblNewPrice = GetNewPrice(dblCurrentPrice)

Figure 17-5 shows the GetNewPrice function and the btnCalc control's Click event procedure.

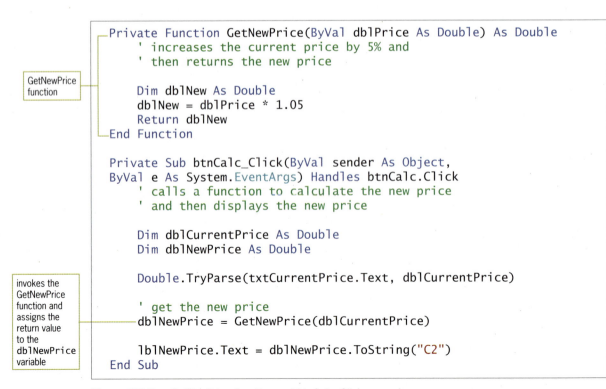

```
    Private Function GetNewPrice(ByVal dblPrice As Double) As Double
        ' increases the current price by 5% and
        ' then returns the new price

        Dim dblNew As Double
        dblNew = dblPrice * 1.05
        Return dblNew
    End Function

    Private Sub btnCalc_Click(ByVal sender As Object,
    ByVal e As System.EventArgs) Handles btnCalc.Click
        ' calls a function to calculate the new price
        ' and then displays the new price

        Dim dblCurrentPrice As Double
        Dim dblNewPrice As Double

        Double.TryParse(txtCurrentPrice.Text, dblCurrentPrice)

        ' get the new price
        dblNewPrice = GetNewPrice(dblCurrentPrice)

        lblNewPrice.Text = dblNewPrice.ToString("C2")
    End Sub
```

GetNewPrice function

invokes the GetNewPrice function and assigns the return value to the dblNewPrice variable

Figure 17-5   GetNewPrice function and btnCalc_Click procedure

Before testing the application, you will desk-check it using $10.99 as the current price. When the user clicks the Calculate button, the button's Click event procedure creates the `dblCurrentPrice` and `dblNewPrice` variables. Next, the TryParse method converts the contents of the `txtCurrentPrice` control to the Double data type and stores the result in the `dblCurrentPrice` variable. Figure 17-6 shows the desk-check table before the GetNewPrice function is invoked.

dblCurrentPrice	dblNewPrice
10.99	

Figure 17-6   Desk-check table before the GetNewPrice function is invoked

The `dblNewPrice = GetNewPrice(dblCurrentPrice)` statement is processed next. The statement invokes the GetNewPrice function, passing it the `dblCurrentPrice` variable *by value*. You can tell that the variable is passed *by value* because the keyword `ByVal` appears before its corresponding parameter in the function header. Recall that passing a variable *by value* means that only a copy of the variable's contents—in this case, the Double number 10.99—is passed to the function. At this point, the computer temporarily leaves the Click event procedure to process the GetNewPrice function; the function header is processed first.

The parameterList in the GetNewPrice function header tells the computer to create a procedure-level Double variable named `dblPrice`. The computer stores the information passed to the procedure—in this case, the Double number 10.99—in that variable. Next, the computer processes the code contained within the function. The Dim statement creates another procedure-level Double variable; this one is named `dblNew`. The assignment statement calculates the new price by multiplying the contents of the `dblPrice` variable by 1.05. It stores the new price in the `dblNew` variable. Figure 17-7 shows the desk check table after the assignment statement is processed.

Figure 17-7   Desk-check table after the new price is assigned to the `dblNew` variable

Next, the `Return dblNew` statement returns the contents of the `dblNew` variable to the statement that invoked the function. In this case, the GetNewPrice function was invoked by a statement in the btnCalc control's Click event procedure. More specifically, it was invoked by the `dblNewPrice = GetNewPrice(dblCurrentPrice)` statement, which assigns the function's return value to the `dblNewPrice` variable. The `End Function` clause is processed next and ends the function. At this point, the computer removes the `dblPrice` and `dblNew` variables from its internal memory. Figure 17-8 shows the desk-check table after the function ends. Notice that the `dblNewPrice` variable now contains the new price.

Figure 17-8   Desk-check table after the GetNewPrice function ends

The last assignment statement in the Click event procedure displays the new price (formatted with a dollar sign and two decimal places) in the interface. Finally, the computer processes the event procedure's End Sub clause. When the Click event procedure ends, the computer removes the dblCurrentPrice and dblNewPrice variables from its internal memory.

To test the Price Calculator application:

1. Save the solution and then start the application. Type **10.99** in the Current price box and then click the **Calculate** button. $11.54 appears in the New price box, as shown in Figure 17-9.

2. Click the **Exit** button. Close the Code Editor window and then close the solution.

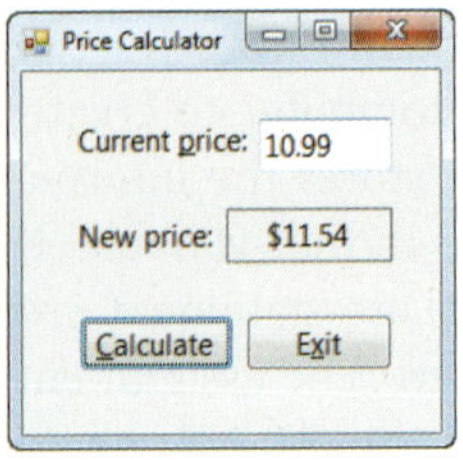

Figure 17-9   New price shown in the interface

Revisiting the Total Due Calculator Application

Figure 17-10 shows the interface for the Total Due Calculator application from Chapter 16. As you may remember, you coded the application using an independent Sub procedure to assign the discount amount. Figure 17-11 shows the code entered in both the AssignDiscount and btnCalc_Click procedures in Chapter 16. Notice that the Call statement in the event procedure passes two items of information to the AssignDiscount procedure: a copy of the value stored in the decSubtotal variable and the address of the decDiscount variable. You passed the decSubtotal variable's value because the AssignDiscount procedure required that information in two of the discount calculations. You passed the address of the decDiscount variable so that the AssignDiscount procedure could set the variable's value.

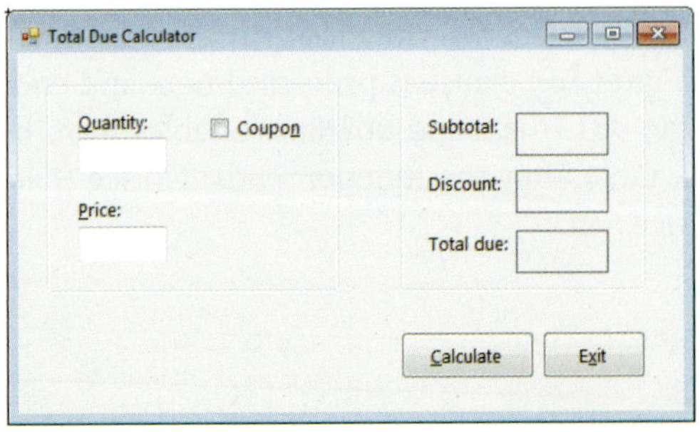

Figure 17-10   Interface for the Total Due Calculator application

```vb
Private Sub AssignDiscount(ByVal decSub As Decimal,          ┌─────────────┐
ByRef decDisc As Decimal)                                    │ AssignDiscount
    ' assigns the discount                                   │ Sub procedure
                                                             └─────────────┘
    If chkCoupon.Checked = True Then
        Dim strCouponCode As String
        strCouponCode = InputBox("Coupon code:", "Coupon")
        Select Case strCouponCode.ToUpper
            Case "A05"
                decDisc = 5
            Case "X25"
                decDisc = 0.1 * decSub
            Case "NE4"
                decDisc = 0.15 * decSub
            Case Else
                decDisc = 0
                MessageBox.Show("Invalid coupon code",
                                "Total Due Calculator",
                                MessageBoxButtons.OK,
                                MessageBoxIcon.Information)
        End Select
    Else
        decDisc = 0
    End If
End Sub

Private Sub btnCalc_Click(ByVal sender As Object,           ┌─────────────┐
ByVal e As System.EventArgs) Handles btnCalc.Click         │ btnCalc control's Click
    ' displays the subtotal, discount, and total due       │ event procedure
                                                           └─────────────┘
    Dim intQuantity As Integer
    Dim decPrice As Decimal
    Dim decSubtotal As Decimal
    Dim decTotalDue As Decimal
    Dim decDiscount As Decimal

    Integer.TryParse(txtQuantity.Text, intQuantity)
    Decimal.TryParse(txtPrice.Text, decPrice)

    ' calculate subtotal
    decSubtotal = intQuantity * decPrice

    ' assign discount                                       ┌─────────────┐
    Call AssignDiscount(decSubtotal, decDiscount)          │ Call statement
                                                           └─────────────┘
    ' calculate total due
    decTotalDue = decSubtotal - decDiscount

    ' display subtotal, discount, and total due
    lblSubtotal.Text = decSubtotal.ToString("N2")
    lblDiscount.Text = decDiscount.ToString("N2")
    lblTotalDue.Text = decTotalDue.ToString("N2")
End Sub
```

Figure 17-11   AssignDiscount Sub procedure and btnCalc control's Click event procedure

Instead of using an independent Sub procedure to assign the discount amount, you can use a function. Consider the changes you will need to make to the code shown in Figure 17-11 in order to use a function. You will make the changes in the following set of steps.

To modify the Total Due Calculator application's code to use a function:

1. Open the **Total Due Solution** (**Total Due Solution.sln**) file contained in the ClearlyVB2010\Chap17\Total Due Solution folder. If the designer window is not open, double-click **frmMain.vb** in the Solution Explorer window.

2. Open the Code Editor window. Locate the btnCalc control's Click event procedure. The Call statement will need to be replaced with a statement that invokes the AssignDiscount function (rather than the AssignDiscount Sub procedure). Like the independent Sub procedure, the function will need the statement to pass the value stored in the decSubtotal variable, because the value is used in two of the discount calculations. However, it will not need the statement to pass the address of the decDiscount variable, because the statement itself will store the discount amount in that variable. Replace the `Call AssignDiscount(decSubtotal, decDiscount)` statement with the following assignment statement, and then click **another line** within the procedure. (Don't be concerned about the jagged line that appears below a portion of the statement. It will disappear when you complete Step 4 below.)

   decDiscount = AssignDiscount(decSubtotal)

3. Now locate the AssignDiscount Sub procedure. Change the Sub keyword in the procedure header to **Function** and then click **another line** within the function. The Code Editor automatically changes the Sub keyword in the footer to the `Function` keyword. (Don't be concerned about the jagged line that appears below the function footer.)

4. Next, delete `, ByRef decDisc As Decimal` from the function header. (Be sure to delete the comma, but don't delete the ending parenthesis.) Now click **another line** within the function. A jagged line appears below each occurrence of decDisc in the function. The jagged line indicates that the decDisc variable has not been declared.

5. In order to use the decDisc variable, the function will need to declare it in a Dim statement. Click the **blank line** below the `' assigns the discount` comment and then press **Enter** to insert another blank line. Type the following Dim statement and then press **Enter**. When you press Enter, the Code Editor removes the jagged line below each occurrence of decDisc.

   Dim decDisc As Decimal

6. Recall that the data type of the function's return value is specified at the end of the function header. The AssignDiscount function returns a Decimal value. Click **after the)** in the function header, press the **Spacebar**, and then type **As Decimal**. Click **another line** within the function. (Notice that the jagged line from Step 3 no longer appears below the function footer.)

7. Finally, you need to tell the function to return the discount amount to the statement that invoked it. The discount amount is stored in the decDisc variable. Click **after the letter f** in the End If clause and then press **Enter** to insert a blank line. Enter the following Return statement:

   Return decDisc

Figure 17-12 shows the AssignDiscount function and the btnCalc control's Click event procedure. The modified lines of code are shaded in the figure.

```vbnet
Private Function AssignDiscount(ByVal decSub As Decimal) As Decimal        AssignDiscount
    ' assigns the discount                                                  function

    Dim decDisc As Decimal

    If chkCoupon.Checked = True Then
        Dim strCouponCode As String
        strCouponCode = InputBox("Coupon code:", "Coupon")
        Select Case strCouponCode.ToUpper
            Case "A05"
                decDisc = 5
            Case "X25"
                decDisc = 0.1 * decSub
            Case "NE4"
                decDisc = 0.15 * decSub
            Case Else
                decDisc = 0
                MessageBox.Show("Invalid coupon code",
                            "Total Due Calculator",
                            MessageBoxButtons.OK,
                            MessageBoxIcon.Information)
        End Select
    Else
        decDisc = 0
    End If
    Return decDisc

End Function

Private Sub btnCalc_Click(ByVal sender As Object, ByVal e As              btnCalc control's Click
System.EventArgs) Handles btnCalc.Click                                   event procedure
    ' displays the subtotal, discount, and total due

    Dim intQuantity As Integer
    Dim decPrice As Decimal
    Dim decSubtotal As Decimal
    Dim decTotalDue As Decimal
    Dim decDiscount As Decimal

    Integer.TryParse(txtQuantity.Text, intQuantity)
    Decimal.TryParse(txtPrice.Text, decPrice)

    ' calculate subtotal
    decSubtotal = intQuantity * decPrice

    ' assign discount                                                      invokes the function
    decDiscount = AssignDiscount(decSubtotal)                             and assigns its return
                                                                          value to a variable
    ' calculate total due
    decTotalDue = decSubtotal - decDiscount

    ' display subtotal, discount, and total due
    lblSubtotal.Text = decSubtotal.ToString("N2")
    lblDiscount.Text = decDiscount.ToString("N2")
    lblTotalDue.Text = decTotalDue.ToString("N2")
End Sub
```

Figure 17-12   AssignDiscount function and btnCalc control's Click event procedure

To test the modified Total Due Calculator application:

1. Save the solution and then start the application. Type **4** in the Quantity box and then type **15** in the Price box. Click the **Coupon** check box to select it and then click the **Calculate** button.

2. Type **X25** as the coupon code and then press **Enter**. The calculated amounts appear in the interface, as shown in Figure 17-13.

3. Click the **Exit** button. Close the Code Editor window and then close the solution.

Total Due Calculator		
Quantity: ☑ Coupon	Subtotal:	60.00
4	Discount:	6.00
Price:		
15	Total due:	54.00
	Calculate	Exit

Figure 17-13   Calculated amounts shown in the interface

Which Way Is Better?

Now that you've seen two different ways of assigning the discount in the Total Due Calculator application—one using an independent Sub procedure and the other using a function—you may be wondering whether one way is better than the other. Comparing the Sub procedure header in Figure 17-11 with the function header in Figure 17-12, you will notice that only the Sub procedure is passed a memory location *by reference*. This is because the Sub procedure is responsible for assigning a value to the memory location. After the computer processes the Sub procedure header, the memory location has two different names (`decDiscount` and `decDisc`) and can be accessed by two different procedures (the AssignDiscount Sub procedure and the btnCalc_Click event procedure). Allowing more than one procedure to change the contents of a memory location can lead to subtle errors that are difficult to find, especially in large applications. As you learned in Chapter 8, fewer unintentional errors occur in applications when memory locations have the minimum scope needed. Therefore, using a function to assign the discount is the better way to code the Total Due Calculator application. Most programmers pass a variable *by reference* only when a procedure needs to produce more than one result. For example, a procedure may need to return the number of hours an employee worked and also whether the hours are valid.

For more examples of functions, see the Function Procedures section in the Ch17WantMore.pdf file.

Mini-Quiz 17-1

To review what you learned about functions, view the Ch17Function video.

See Appendix B for the answers.

1. An event procedure invokes the GetBonus function using the statement `dblBonusAmount = GetBonus(dblSales)`. The function multiplies the sales amount passed to it by 3% and then returns the result. Which of the following is the appropriate function header for the GetBonus function?

    a. `Private Function GetBonus(ByVal dblSold As Double)`
    b. `Private Function GetBonus(ByRef dblSold As Double)`
    c. `Private Function GetBonus(ByVal dblSold As Double) As Double`
    d. `Private Function GetBonus(ByVal dblSold As Double, ByRef dblBonus As Double)`

2. Write a Visual Basic statement that instructs the GetIncome function to return the contents of the `decIncome` variable.

3. Write a Visual Basic statement that invokes the GetSales function, passing it two Decimal variables named `decSale1` and `decSale2`. The statement should multiply the function's return value by .08 and then assign the result to the `decTax` variable.

Summary

- You can create your own function procedures, called functions, in Visual Basic. Unlike a Sub procedure, a function returns a value after completing its task.

- Typically, the Return statement appears as the last statement in a function. A function returns only one value to the statement that invoked it.

- You invoke a function by including the function's name and arguments (if any) in a statement. The number of arguments listed in the statement should agree with the number of parameters listed in the function's parameterList. Also, the data type and position of each argument should agree with the data type and position of its corresponding parameter.

- The statement that invokes a function may assign the return value to a variable, use the return value in a calculation, or display the return value.

- Variables that appear in a function header's parameterList have procedure scope.

- In most cases, it is better to use a function rather than a Sub procedure that passes a variable *by reference*.

Key Terms

Function procedure—a procedure that returns a value after performing its assigned task; also referred to as a function

Functions—another term for Function procedures

Return statement—the Visual Basic statement that returns a function's value to the statement that invoked the function

Review Questions

1. Which of the following is false?

    a. A function can return one or more values to the statement that invoked it.

    b. A function can accept one or more items of data passed to it.

    c. The parameterList in a function header is optional.

    d. At times, a memory location inside the computer's internal memory may have more than one name.

2. Which of the following statements invokes the GetGross function and assigns its return value to the `decGrossPay` variable? The statement passes the contents of two Decimal variables to the function.

    a. `decGrossPay = Call GetGross(decHours, decRate)`

    b. `Call GetGross(decHours, decRate, decGrossPay)`

   c.   decGrossPay = GetGross(decHours, decRate)

   d.   decGrossPay = GetGross(ByVal decHours, ByVal decRate)

3.   When the GetExpenses function completes its processing, it should send the value stored in the decTotalExpenses variable to the statement that invoked the function. Which of the following statements accomplishes this task?

   a.   Return (ByVal decTotalExpenses)

   b.   Send ByVal(decTotalExpenses)

   c.   SendBack decTotalExpenses

   d.   Return decTotalExpenses

4.   Which of the following is false?

   a.   A function can receive information either *by value* or *by reference*.

   b.   When a function ends, any variables listed in the function's parameterList can be used by the statement that invoked the function.

   c.   The variables listed in a function's parameterList have procedure scope.

   d.   When a function ends, the computer removes the function's variables from its internal memory.

5.   A function named GetEnding is passed three Integer variables named intBegin, intSales, and intPurchases. The function's task is to calculate and return the ending inventory. Which of the following function headers is appropriate?

   a.   Private Function GetEnding(ByVal intB As Integer, ByVal intS As Integer, ByVal intP As Integer) As Integer

   b.   Private Function GetEnding(ByRef intB As Integer, ByRef intS As Integer, ByRef intP As Integer) As Integer

   c.   Private Function GetEnding(ByVal intB As Integer, ByVal intS As Integer, ByVal intP As Integer, ByRef intE) As Integer

   d.   Private Sub Function GetEnding(ByVal intB As Integer, ByVal intS As Integer, ByVal intP As Integer)

6.   Which of the following headers indicates that the procedure returns a Decimal number?

   a.   Private Function Calc() As Decimal

   b.   Private Sub Calc() As Decimal

   c.   Private Function Calc(Decimal)

   d.   both a and b

7.   The GetSqRoot function receives an integer and then returns the square root of the integer as a Double number. Which of the following statements is valid?

   a.   dblSqRoot = GetSqRoot(100)

   b.   dblAnswer = GetSqRoot(9) * 4

   c.   lblAnswer.Text = GetSqRoot(intX).ToString("N2")

   d.   all of the above

Exercises

1. Open the Bonus Solution (Bonus Solution.sln) file contained in the ClearlyVB2010\ Chap17\Bonus Solution-TRY THIS 1 folder. The application should calculate and display a bonus amount, which is based on two sales amounts entered by the user. Use the algorithm shown in Figure 17-14 to code the btnCalc control's Click event procedure and the GetBonus function. Save the solution and then start and test the application. Close the Code Editor window and then close the solution. (See Appendix B for the answer.)

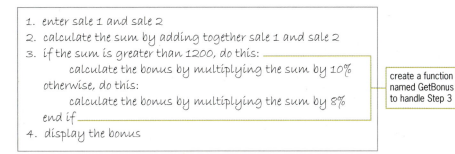

1. enter sale 1 and sale 2
2. calculate the sum by adding together sale 1 and sale 2
3. if the sum is greater than 1200, do this: ⎯⎯⎯⎯⎯⎯
      calculate the bonus by multiplying the sum by 10%
   otherwise, do this:
      calculate the bonus by multiplying the sum by 8%
   end if ⎯⎯⎯⎯⎯⎯
4. display the bonus

create a function named GetBonus to handle Step 3

Figure 17-14   Algorithm for Exercise 1

2. In this exercise, you modify the application from Exercise 1. Use Windows to make a copy of the Bonus Solution-TRY THIS 1 folder. Save the copy in the ClearlyVB2010\ Chap17 folder. Rename the copy Bonus Solution-TRY THIS 2. Open the Bonus Solution (Bonus Solution.sln) file contained in the Bonus Solution-TRY THIS 2 folder. Open the designer window and then change the form's Text property to Bonus Solution-TRY THIS 2. Open the Code Editor window. The btnCalc control's Click event procedure should use a function to add together the two sales amounts and then return the sum. Create the GetSum function and then modify the event procedure's code. Save the solution and then start and test the application. Close the Code Editor window and then close the solution. (See Appendix B for the answer.)

3. In this exercise, you modify the Price Calculator application coded in the chapter. Use Windows to make a copy of the Price Calculator Solution folder. Save the copy in the ClearlyVB2010\Chap17 folder. Rename the copy Price Calculator Solution-MODIFY THIS. Open the Price Calculator Solution (Price Calculator Solution.sln) file contained in the Price Calculator Solution-MODIFY THIS folder. Open the designer and Code Editor windows. Modify the code so that it uses an independent Sub procedure (rather than a function) to calculate the new price. Save the solution and then start and test the application. Close the Code Editor window and then close the solution.

4. Open the Grade Solution (Grade Solution.sln) file contained in the ClearlyVB2010\ Chap17\Grade Solution folder. The application should display a letter grade, which is based on the average of three test scores. If the average is at least 90, the grade is A. If the average is at least 80 but less than 90, the grade is B. If the average is at least 70 but less than 80, the grade is C. If the average is at least 60 but less than 70, the grade is D. If the average is below 60, the grade is F. Code the application, using a function to determine and return the letter grade. Save the solution and then start and test the application. Close the Code Editor window and then close the solution.

5. Open the Gross Pay Solution (Gross Pay Solution.sln) file contained in the ClearlyVB2010\Chap17\Gross Pay Solution folder. The application should display an employee's gross pay. Employees working more than 40 hours receive time and one-half for the hours over 40. Code the application, using a function to calculate and return the gross pay. Save the solution and then start and test the application. Close the Code Editor window and then close the solution.

INTERMEDIATE   6. Open the Temperature Solution (Temperature Solution.sln) file contained in the ClearlyVB2010\Chap17\Temperature Solution folder. Code the application so that it uses two functions: one to convert a temperature from Fahrenheit to Celsius, and the other to convert a temperature from Celsius to Fahrenheit. Save the solution and then start and test the application. Close the Code Editor window and then close the solution.

INTERMEDIATE   7. Open the Translator Solution (Translator Solution.sln) file contained in the ClearlyVB2010\Chap17\Translator Solution folder. Code the application so that it uses functions to translate the English words into French, Spanish, or Italian. Save the solution and then start and test the application. Close the Code Editor window and then close the solution.

INTERMEDIATE   8. Create a Visual Basic Windows application. Use the following names for the solution and project, respectively: Wallpaper Warehouse Solution and Wallpaper Warehouse Project. Save the application in the ClearlyVB2010\Chap17 folder. Change the name of the form file on your disk to frmMain.vb. If necessary, change the form's name to frmMain. Create the interface shown in Figure 17-15 and then code the application, which should calculate and display the number of single rolls of wallpaper required to cover a room. Use a function to calculate and return the number of single rolls. The text boxes should accept only numbers, the period, and the Backspace key. The Single rolls box should be cleared when a change is made to any of the four text boxes. Save the solution and then start and test the application. Close the Code Editor window and then close the solution.

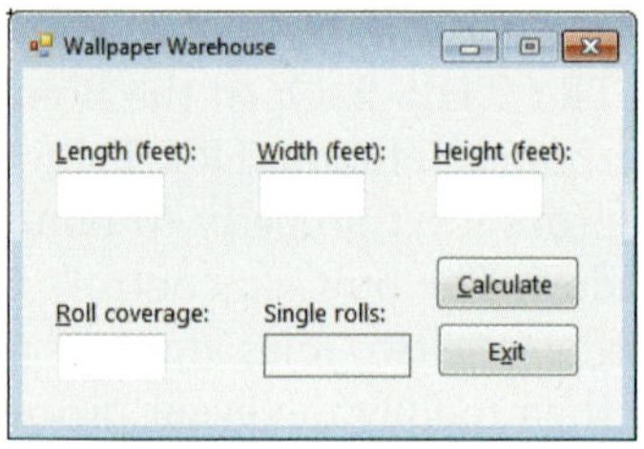

Figure 17-15   Interface for Exercise 8

INTERMEDIATE   9. In this exercise, you modify the application from Exercise 5. Use Windows to make a copy of the Gross Pay Solution folder. Save the copy in the ClearlyVB2010\Chap17 folder. Rename the copy Modified Gross Pay Solution. Open the Gross Pay Solution (Gross Pay Solution.sln) file contained in the Modified Gross Pay Solution folder. Open the designer window.

a. Change the form's Text property to Payroll Calculator. The application should display the federal and state tax amounts and the net pay. Add label controls for displaying the three amounts.

b. Open the Code Editor window. Create a function that calculates and returns the federal tax. Also create a function that calculates and returns the state tax. For simplicity, use a rate of 25% for the federal tax and a rate of 5% for the state tax. Calculate the taxes by multiplying the tax rate by the gross pay.

c. Modify the btnCalc control's Click event procedure to call both functions. The procedure also will need to calculate the net pay, as well as display the federal and state taxes and the net pay. Use the Math.Round method, which you learned about in Chapter 6's Exercises 10 and 11.

d. Modify both TextChanged event procedures to clear the contents of the three new label controls.

e. Save the solution and then start and test the application. Close the Code Editor window and then close the solution.

10. The Doughnut Shoppe sells four varieties of doughnuts: Glazed ($.65), Sugar ($.65), Chocolate ($.85), and Filled ($1.00). It also sells regular coffee ($1.80) and cappuccino ($2.50). The store manager wants an application that she can use to calculate and display a customer's subtotal, 3% sales tax, and total due.   ADVANCED

   a. Create a Visual Basic Windows application. Use the following names for the solution and project, respectively: Doughnut Shoppe Solution and Doughnut Shoppe Project. Save the application in the ClearlyVB2010\Chap17 folder. Change the name of the form file on your disk to frmMain.vb. If necessary, change the form's name to frmMain.

   b. Create the interface shown in Figure 17-16.

   c. Code the application. Use one function to calculate and return the cost of the doughnut. Use another function to calculate and return the cost of the coffee. Use a third function to calculate and return the 3% sales tax. Use a Sub procedure to clear the subtotal, sales tax, and total due amounts when a radio button is clicked.

   d. Save the solution and then start and test the application. Close the Code Editor window and then close the solution.

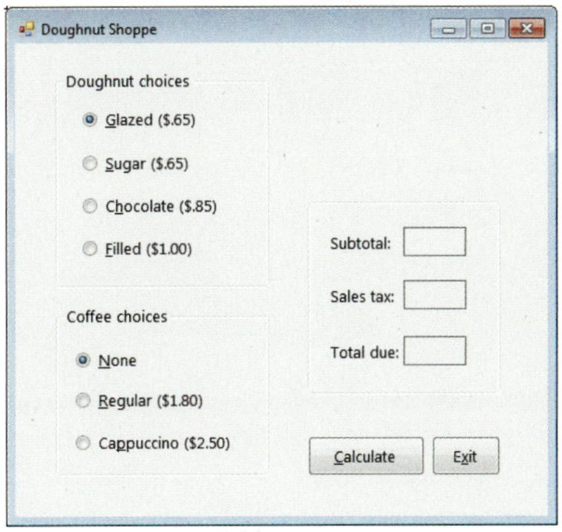

Figure 17-16   Interface for Exercise 10

11. In this exercise, you modify the Harvey Industries application created in Exercise 11 in Chapter 16. If you did not complete Chapter 16's Exercise 11, you will need to do so before you can complete this exercise. Use Windows to copy the Harvey Industries Solution folder from the ClearlyVB2010\Chap16 folder to the ClearlyVB2010\Chap17 folder. Open the Harvey Industries Solution (Harvey Industries Solution.sln) file contained in the ClearlyVB2010\Chap17\Harvey Industries Solution folder. Change the Sub procedure that calculates the federal withholding tax to a function. Also include two additional functions: one to calculate the gross pay and the other to calculate the FICA tax. Save the solution and then start and test the application. Close the Code Editor window and then close the solution.   ADVANCED

12. Open the FigureThisOut Solution (FigureThisOut Solution.sln) file contained in the ClearlyVB2010\Chap17\FigureThisOut Solution folder. Open the Code Editor window and study the existing code. Desk-check the code contained in both the function and Click event procedure. For the first desk-check, use A, 75, and 83 as the operation, first number, and second number, respectively; for the second desk-check, use M, 6, and 8. Save the solution and then start and test the application. Close the Code Editor window and then close the solution.   FIGURE THIS OUT

13. Open the SwatTheBugs Solution (SwatTheBugs Solution.sln) file contained in the ClearlyVB2010\Chap17\SwatTheBugs Solution folder. Open the Code Editor window and study the existing code. Start and then test the application. Notice that the application is not working correctly. Stop the application. Locate and correct the errors in the code. Save the solution and then start and test the application again. Close the Code Editor window and then close the solution.

A Ray of Sunshine (One-Dimensional Arrays)

After studying Chapter 18, you should be able to:

- ◎ Explain the purpose of an array
- ◎ Create a one-dimensional array
- ◎ Store data in a one-dimensional array
- ◎ Sort the contents of a one-dimensional array
- ◎ Search a one-dimensional array

Let's Join the Group

All of the applications you have coded since Chapter 6 have used simple variables. A **simple variable**, also called a **scalar variable**, is one that is unrelated to any other variable in memory. At times, however, you will encounter situations where some of the variables in an application *are* related to each other. In those cases, it is easier and more efficient to treat the related variables as a group. You already are familiar with the concept of grouping. The cutlery in one of your kitchen drawers is typically separated into groups, such as forks, knives, and spoons. You also probably have your CD (compact disc) collection grouped either by music type or artist. If your collection is grouped by artist, it will take only a few seconds to find all your Frank Sinatra CDs and, depending on the number of Frank Sinatra CDs you own, only a short time after that to locate a particular CD. When you group together related variables, the group is referred to as an array of variables or, more simply, an **array**. You might use an array of 12 String variables to store the names of the 12 months in a year. Or, you might use an array of 50 Decimal variables to store the sales amounts made in each of the 50 states. The most commonly used arrays in business applications are one-dimensional and two-dimensional. You will learn about one-dimensional arrays in this chapter and also in the next chapter. Two dimensional arrays are covered in Chapter 20.

Each variable in an array has the same name and data type. You distinguish one variable in a one-dimensional array from another variable in the array using a unique number, called a **subscript**. The subscript indicates the variable's position in the array and is assigned by the computer when the array is created in internal memory. The first variable in a one-dimensional array is assigned a subscript of 0, the second a subscript of 1, and so on. You refer to each variable in an array by the array's name and the variable's subscript, which is specified in a set of parentheses immediately following the array name. To refer to the first variable in a one-dimensional String array named `strFriends`, you use `strFriends(0)`—read "`strFriends` sub zero." Similarly, to refer to the third variable in the `strFriends` array, you use `strFriends(2)`. Figure 18-1 shows this naming convention using the storage bin illustration from Chapter 6. The `intAge`, `decRate`, and `strMonth` variables included in the figure are scalar variables.

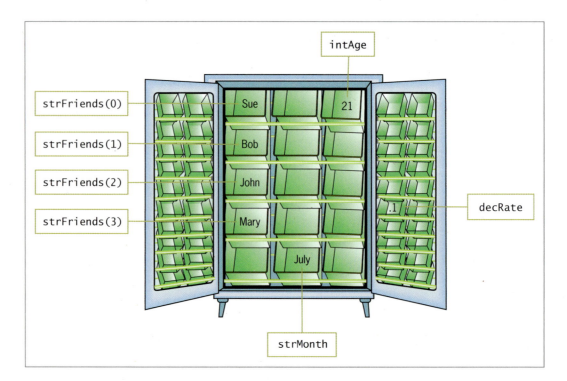

Figure 18-1   Illustration of the naming convention for the one-dimensional `strFriends` array

Figure 18-2 shows two versions of the syntax for declaring a procedure-level one-dimensional array in Visual Basic. The figure also includes examples of using both versions. In each syntax, *arrayName* is the name of the array and *dataType* is the type of data the array variables, referred to as **elements**, will store. In Version 1 of the syntax, *highestSubscript* is an integer that specifies the highest subscript in the array. When the array is created, it will contain one element more than the number specified in the highestSubscript argument; this is because the first element in a one-dimensional array has a subscript of 0. As a result, the `intNumbers` array declared in Example 1 will contain six elements with subscripts of 0, 1, 2, 3, 4, and 5. When you use Version 1 of the syntax, the computer automatically initializes each element in the array when the array is created. The elements in a numeric array are initialized to the number 0. The elements in a String array, on the other hand, are initialized using the keyword `Nothing`. The elements do not actually contain the word "Nothing"; rather, they contain no data at all.

Rather than having the computer use a default value to initialize each array element, you can use Version 2 of the syntax to specify each element's initial value when the array is declared. Assigning initial values to an array is often referred to as **populating the array**. You list the initial values in the *initialValues* section of the syntax, using commas to separate the values, and you enclose the list of values in braces ({}). Notice that Version 2's syntax does not include the highestSubscript argument; instead, an empty set of parentheses follows the array name. The computer automatically calculates the highest subscript based on the number of values listed in the initialValues section. Because the first subscript in a one-dimensional array is the number 0, the highest subscript is always one number less than the number of values listed in the initialValues section. The `Dim strFriends() As String = {"Sue", "Bob", "John", "Mary"}` statement in Example 2 in Figure 18-2, for instance, creates a four-element array with subscripts of 0, 1, 2, and 3. The computer assigns the string "Sue" to the `strFriends(0)` element, "Bob" to the `strFriends(1)` element, "John" to the `strFriends(2)` element, and "Mary" to the `strFriends(3)` element, as shown earlier in Figure 18-1.

Declaring a procedure-level one-dimensional array

Syntax—Version 1
Dim *arrayName*(*highestSubscript*) **As** *dataType*

Syntax—Version 2
Dim *arrayName*() **As** *dataType* = {*initialValues*}

Example 1—Version 1's syntax
```
Dim intNumbers(5) As Integer
```
declares and initializes (to 0) a six-element Integer array named `intNumbers`

Example 2—Version 2's syntax
```
Dim strFriends() As String = {"Sue", "Bob", "John", "Mary"}
```
declares and initializes a four-element String array named `strFriends`

Figure 18-2 Syntax versions and examples of declaring a procedure-level one-dimensional array

The variables (elements) in an array can be used just like any other variables: You can assign values to them, use them in calculations, display their contents, and so on. Figure 18-3 shows examples of statements that perform these tasks.

Using an element in a one-dimensional array

Example 1
```
Dim strCities() As String = {"Paris", "Rome", "Lisbon"}
strCities(0) = "Madrid"
```
assigns the string "Madrid" to the first element in the strCities array, replacing the string "Paris"

Example 2
```
Dim intSalaries() As Integer = {25000, 35000, 50000, 23000}
intSalaries(3) = intSalaries(3) + 2000
```
adds 2000 to the contents of the last element in the intSalaries array (23000) and then assigns the result (25000) to the element

Example 3
```
Dim decSales(10) As Decimal
Decimal.TryParse(txtSales.Text, decSales(2))
lblSales.Text = decSales(2).ToString("C2")
```
assigns the value returned by the TryParse method to the third element in the decSales array and then displays the value (formatted with a dollar sign and two decimal places) in the lblSales control

---

Figure 18-3   Examples of using an element in a one-dimensional array

The procedures you code in this chapter will demonstrate some of the ways one-dimensional arrays are used in an application. In most applications, the values stored in an array come from a file on the computer's disk and are assigned to the array after it is declared. However, so that you can follow the code and its results more easily, the applications in this chapter use the Dim statement to store the appropriate values in the array.

Mini-Quiz 18-1

See Appendix B for the answers.

1. Write a Visual Basic statement that declares a 20-element one-dimensional Integer array named intQuantities.

2. What is the highest subscript in the intQuantities array from Question 1?

3. Write a Visual Basic statement that assigns the number 7 to the fourth element in the intQuantities array.

My Friends Application

The My Friends application will store four names in a one-dimensional String array named strFriends. It then will display the contents of the array in three label controls named lblOriginal, lblAscending, and lblDescending. In the lblOriginal control, the names will appear in the same order as in the array. In the lblAscending and lblDescending controls, the names will appear in ascending and descending order, respectively.

To begin coding the My Friends application:

1. Start Visual Studio 2010 or Visual Basic 2010 Express and permanently display the Solution Explorer window. Open the **Friends Solution (Friends Solution.sln)** file contained in the ClearlyVB2010\Chap18\Friends Solution folder. If the designer window is not open, double-click **frmMain.vb** in the Solution Explorer window.

2. Open the Code Editor window and then open the code template for the btnDisplay control's Click event procedure. Type the following comments and then press **Enter** twice:

    ' displays names in original, ascending,
    ' and descending order

3. First, you will declare and initialize the strFriends array. Type the following declaration statement and then press **Enter** twice:

    Dim strFriends() As String =
    {"Sue", "Bob", "John", "Mary"}

4. Now you will clear the contents of the three label controls. Type the following comment and three assignment statements. Press **Enter** twice after typing the last assignment statement.

    ' clear label controls
    lblOriginal.Text = String.Empty
    lblAscending.Text = String.Empty
    lblDescending.Text = String.Empty

Next, you will display the contents of the array in the lblOriginal control. You can accomplish this task using a loop to access each element in the array, beginning with the element whose subscript is 0 and ending with the element whose subscript is 3. Because you want the loop instructions processed a precise number of times—in this case, from 0 to 3—you will code the loop using the For...Next statement. As you learned in Chapter 14, the For...Next statement provides a more convenient way to code a counter-controlled loop, because it takes care of initializing and updating the counter variable, as well as evaluating the loop condition.

Figure 18-4 shows two versions of the code for displaying the contents of the strFriends array in the lblOriginal control. Only the *endValue* in the For clause is different in each version. In Version 1, the endValue is 3 (the highest subscript in the array). In Version 2, the endValue is the expression strFriends.Length – 1. The expression uses the array's **Length property**, which contains an integer that represents the number of elements in the array; in this case, the Length property contains the number 4. To determine the highest subscript in the array, you simply subtract the number 1 from the value stored in the array's Length property, as shown in the expression. Although both versions of code in Figure 18-4 will work, Version 2's code is the preferred one for several reasons. First, if you use the Length property, you won't have to count the number of array elements yourself. Second, the Length property is essential when you don't know the exact number of array elements; this may be the case when the array values come from a file. Finally, if the number of array elements changes in the future, the Length property's value will automatically adjust.

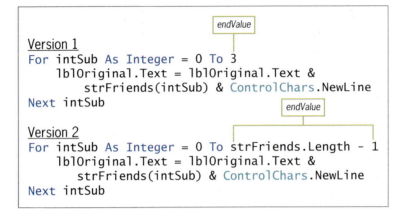

```
                              endValue
Version 1
For intSub As Integer = 0 To 3
    lblOriginal.Text = lblOriginal.Text &
        strFriends(intSub) & ControlChars.NewLine
Next intSub                   endValue

Version 2
For intSub As Integer = 0 To strFriends.Length - 1
    lblOriginal.Text = lblOriginal.Text &
        strFriends(intSub) & ControlChars.NewLine
Next intSub
```

Figure 18-4   Two versions of the code for displaying the array's contents

To continue coding the btnDisplay control's Click event procedure:

1. Enter the following comment and four lines of code:

    ' display array in original order
    For intSub As Integer = 0 To strFriends.Length – 1
    **   lblOriginal.Text = lblOriginal.Text &**
    **   strFriends(intSub) & ControlChars.NewLine**
    Next intSub

2. Save the solution and then start the application. Click the **Display** button. The names Sue, Bob, John, and Mary appear in the lblOriginal control, as shown in Figure 18-5. Click the **Exit** button.

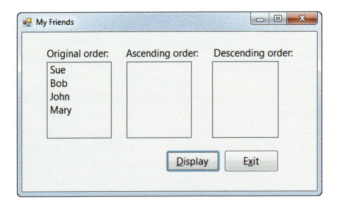

Figure 18-5   Array contents displayed in the Original order box

Before displaying the array values in the lblAscending and lblDescending controls, you need to arrange the values in the appropriate order. Arranging data in a specific order is called **sorting**. Visual Basic provides the **Array.Sort method** for sorting the values in a one-dimensional array in ascending order. When an array is sorted in ascending order, the first element in the array contains the smallest value and the last element contains the largest value. To sort the array values in descending order, you first use the Array.Sort method to sort the values in ascending order and then use the **Array.Reverse method** to reverse the order of the values. When an array is sorted in descending order, the first element in the array contains the largest value and the last element contains the smallest value. Figure 18-6 shows the syntax of both methods and includes examples of using the methods.

Array.Sort and Array.Reverse methods

Syntax
Array.Sort(_arrayName_**)**
Array.Reverse(_arrayName_**)**

Example 1
```
Dim intNums() As Integer = {1, 3, 10, 2, 4, 23}
Array.Sort(intNums)
```
sorts the values in the `intNums` array in ascending order as follows: 1, 2, 3, 4, 10, 23

Example 2
```
Dim intNums() As Integer = {1, 3, 10, 2, 4, 23}
Array.Reverse(intNums)
```
reverses the order of the values in the `intNums` array as follows: 23, 4, 2, 10, 3, 1

Example 3
```
Dim intNums() As Integer = {1, 3, 10, 2, 4, 23}
Array.Sort(intNums)
Array.Reverse(intNums)
```
sorts the values in the `intNums` array in descending order as follows: 23, 10, 4, 3, 2, 1

Figure 18-6   Syntax and examples of the Array.Sort and Array.Reverse methods

To complete the btnDisplay control's Click event procedure:

1. Insert two blank lines below the `Next intSub` clause. Enter the following comment and five lines of code:

   ' display array in ascending order
   Array.Sort(strFriends)
   For intSub As Integer = 0 To strFriends.Length − 1
      lblAscending.Text = lblAscending.Text &
        strFriends(intSub) & ControlChars.NewLine
   Next intSub

2. Insert two blank lines below the `Next intSub` clause from the previous step. Enter the following comment and six lines of code:

   ' display array in descending order
   Array.Sort(strFriends)
   Array.Reverse(strFriends)
   For intSub As Integer = 0 To strFriends.Length − 1
      lblDescending.Text = lblDescending.Text &
        strFriends(intSub) & ControlChars.NewLine
   Next intSub

Figure 18-7 shows the code entered in the btnDisplay control's Click event procedure.

```vb
Private Sub btnDisplay_Click(ByVal sender As Object,
ByVal e As System.EventArgs) Handles btnDisplay.Click
    ' displays names in original, ascending,
    ' and descending order

    Dim strFriends() As String =
        {"Sue", "Bob", "John", "Mary"}

    ' clear label controls
    lblOriginal.Text = String.Empty
    lblAscending.Text = String.Empty
    lblDescending.Text = String.Empty

    ' display array in original order
    For intSub As Integer = 0 To strFriends.Length - 1
        lblOriginal.Text = lblOriginal.Text &
            strFriends(intSub) & ControlChars.NewLine
    Next intSub

    ' display array in ascending order
    Array.Sort(strFriends)
    For intSub As Integer = 0 To strFriends.Length - 1
        lblAscending.Text = lblAscending.Text &
            strFriends(intSub) & ControlChars.NewLine
    Next intSub

    ' display array in descending order
    Array.Sort(strFriends)
    Array.Reverse(strFriends)
    For intSub As Integer = 0 To strFriends.Length - 1
        lblDescending.Text = lblDescending.Text &
            strFriends(intSub) & ControlChars.NewLine
    Next intSub
End Sub
```

Figure 18-7   btnDisplay control's Click event procedure

To test the btnDisplay control's Click event procedure:

1. Save the solution and then start the application. Click the **Display** button. See Figure 18-8.

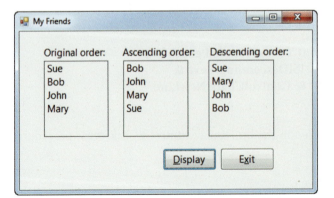

Figure 18-8   Array values displayed in the three label controls

The Array. Sort method is not the only way to sort the contents of an array. To learn more about sorting arrays, see the Sorting Routines section in the Ch18WantMore.pdf file.

2. Click the **Exit** button. Close the Code Editor window and then close the solution.

Salary Application

The Salary application will store six salary amounts in a one-dimensional Integer array named intSalaries. Each salary amount corresponds to a salary code; the valid codes are the numbers 1 through 6. Code 1's salary is stored in the intSalaries(0) element in the array, code 2's salary in the intSalaries(1) element, and so on. Notice that the code is one number more than the subscript of its corresponding salary in the array. After storing the salary amounts in the array, the application will prompt the user to enter a salary code. It then will display the amount associated with the code. Figure 18-9 shows the planning information for the application.

Output: salary amount

Processing: six-element one-dimensional array of salary amounts
               array subscript

Input: salary code (1 through 6)

Algorithm:
1. enter the salary code
2. calculate the subscript of the array element associated with the salary code
   by subtracting 1 from the salary code
3. use the array subscript to display (in a label control) the associated
   salary amount from the array

Figure 18-9   Planning information for the Salary application

To code and then test the Salary application:

1. Open the **Salary Solution** (**Salary Solution.sln**) file contained in the ClearlyVB2010\ Chap18\Salary Solution folder. If the designer window is not open, double-click **frmMain.vb** in the Solution Explorer window.

2. Open the Code Editor window and then open the code template for the btnDisplay control's Click event procedure. Type the following comment and then press **Enter** twice:

    ' displays the salary amount associated with a code

3. First, you will declare and initialize the intSalaries array. Enter the following array declaration statement:

    **Dim intSalaries() As Integer = {25000, 35000, 55000,
                    70000, 80200, 90500}**

4. Now you will declare the necessary variables. Enter the following declaration statements. Press **Enter** twice after typing the last declaration statement.

    **Dim intCode As Integer
    Dim intSub As Integer**

5. The first step in the algorithm is to enter the salary code. The user enters the code in the txtCode control. You will use the TryParse method to convert the code to the Integer data type, storing the result in the intCode variable. Enter the following TryParse method:

    Integer.TryParse(txtCode.Text, intCode)

6. Step 2 in the algorithm is to calculate the subscript of the array element associated with the salary code. You do this by subtracting the number 1 from the salary code. Enter the following comment and assignment statement. Press **Enter** twice after typing the assignment statement.

   ' calculate the appropriate subscript
   intSub = intCode − 1

7. The last step in the algorithm is to use the array subscript to display the appropriate salary amount from the array. Enter the following comment and assignment statement:

   ' display the salary amount from the array
   lblSalary.Text = intSalaries(intSub)

8. Save the solution and then start the application. Type **2** in the Code box and then click the **Display Salary** button. The salary amount stored in the `intSalaries(1)` element appears in the Salary box, as shown in Figure 18-10.

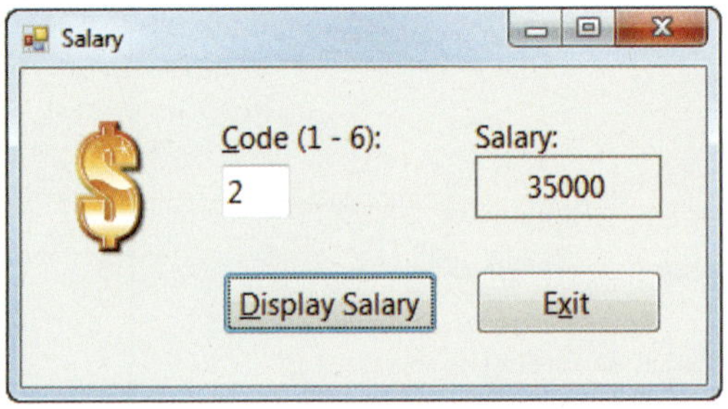

Figure 18-10   Interface showing the salary for code 2

9. Now you will observe the result of entering an invalid salary code. Replace the 2 in the Code box with **8** and then click the **Display Salary** button. A run time error occurs. As a result, the Code Editor highlights the `lblSalary.Text = intSalaries(intSub)` statement, which is the statement where the error was encountered; it also opens a help box. The help box indicates that the index (which is another term for subscript) is outside the bounds of the array.

10. Place your mouse pointer on `intSub` in the highlighted statement, as shown in Figure 18-11. The variable contains the number 7, which is one number less than the salary code you entered. The valid subscripts for the array, however, are the numbers 0 through 5 only.

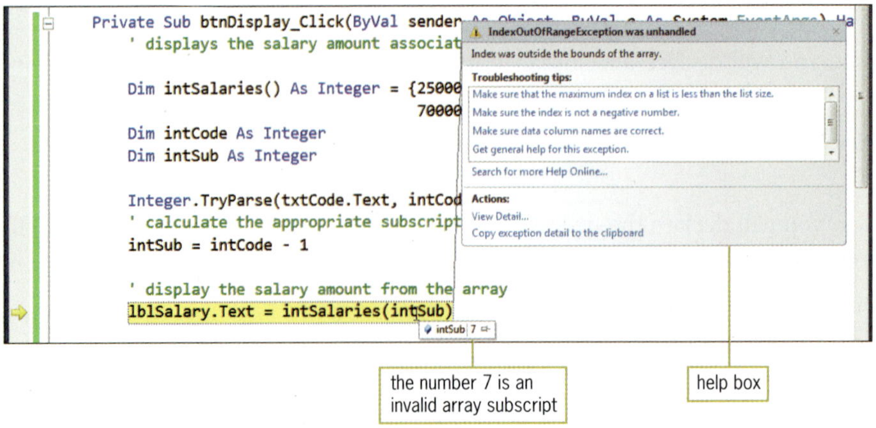

Figure 18-11   Result of the run time error caused by an invalid array subscript

11. Click **Debug** on the menu bar and then click **Stop Debugging**.

Before it attempts to access an array element, a procedure should verify that the subscript being used is valid. This can be accomplished using a selection structure whose condition verifies that the subscript is within an acceptable range for the array. The acceptable range is a number that is greater than or equal to 0 but less than the number of array elements. If the subscript is not in the acceptable range, the procedure should not try to access the element because doing so results in a run time error. Figure 18-12 shows the modified algorithm for the Salary application. Notice that Step 3 now validates the array subscript.

Output: salary amount

Processing: six-element one-dimensional array of salary amounts
               array subscript

Input: salary code (1 through 6)

Algorithm:
1. enter the salary code
2. calculate the subscript of the array element associated with the salary code
   by subtracting 1 from the salary code
3. if the array subscript is greater than or equal to 0 but less than the
   number of array elements, do this:
        use the array subscript to display (in a label control) the associated
        salary amount from the array
   otherwise, do this:
        clear the salary amount from the label control
        display a message informing the user that the salary code is invalid
        end if

Figure 18-12   Modified algorithm for the Salary application

To modify and then test the btnDisplay control's Click event procedure:

1. Enter the selection structure shown in Figure 18-13. (You will need to move the last comment and assignment statement, which you entered in Step 7 in the previous set of steps, into the selection structure's true path.)

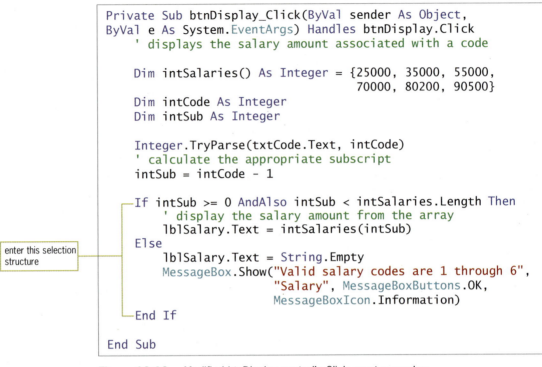

```
Private Sub btnDisplay_Click(ByVal sender As Object,
ByVal e As System.EventArgs) Handles btnDisplay.Click
    ' displays the salary amount associated with a code

    Dim intSalaries() As Integer = {25000, 35000, 55000,
                                    70000, 80200, 90500}
    Dim intCode As Integer
    Dim intSub As Integer

    Integer.TryParse(txtCode.Text, intCode)
    ' calculate the appropriate subscript
    intSub = intCode - 1

    If intSub >= 0 AndAlso intSub < intSalaries.Length Then
        ' display the salary amount from the array
        lblSalary.Text = intSalaries(intSub)
    Else
        lblSalary.Text = String.Empty
        MessageBox.Show("Valid salary codes are 1 through 6",
                        "Salary", MessageBoxButtons.OK,
                        MessageBoxIcon.Information)
    End If

End Sub
```

enter this selection structure

Figure 18-13   Modified btnDisplay control's Click event procedure

2. Save the solution and then start the application. Type **3** in the Code box and then click the **Display Salary** button. The number 55000 appears in the Salary box.

3. Replace the 3 in the Code box with **9** and then click the **Display Salary** button. The message "Valid salary codes are 1 through 6" appears in a message box. Close the message box. Notice that the Salary box is now empty.

4. On your own, test the application using salary codes of 2 through 6. Also test it by clicking the Display Salary button without entering any data.

5. When you are finished testing the application, click the **Exit** button. Close the Code Editor window and then close the solution.

States Application

The States application stores the names of nine states in a one-dimensional String array named strStates. The names are stored in the order each was visited by the user. For example, the user visited Hawaii first, followed by Colorado. Therefore, the strings "Hawaii" and "Colorado" are stored in the strStates(0) and strStates(1) elements, respectively. The application's interface provides a text box for the user to enter a state name. The application searches for the state name in the array, beginning with the first array element. It then displays a message indicating whether the state name was found. Sample messages include "Hawaii is number 1 in the list of states you visited" and "You did not visit Illinois". Figure 18-14 shows the planning information for the application.

Output: message

Processing: nine-element one-dimensional array of state names
                array subscript
                found

Input: state name to search for

Algorithm:
1. enter the state name to search for, and then convert the state name to uppercase
2. assign 0 to the array subscript
3. assign "N" to found
4. repeat until found = "Y" or the array subscript equals the number of
   array elements:
        If the contents of the current array element (converted to uppercase)
        is the same as the state name to search for, do this:
                assign "Y" to found
        otherwise, do this:
                add 1 to the array subscript
        end if
   end repeat
5. if found = "Y", do this:
        display the state name and visited rank in an appropriate message
   otherwise, do this:
        display the state name in an appropriate message
   end if

Figure 18-14   Planning information for the States application

To code the States application:

1. Open the **States Solution (States Solution.sln)** file contained in the ClearlyVB2010\
   Chap18\States Solution folder. If the designer window is not open, double-click
   frmMain.vb in the Solution Explorer window.

2. Open the Code Editor window and then locate the code template for the btnVisited
   control's Click event procedure. The procedure declares and initializes the strStates
   array.

3. First, you will declare the necessary variables: strSearchFor, intSub, and strFound. The
   strSearchFor variable will store the name of the state to search for in the array. The
   intSub variable will keep track of the array subscripts during the search. The strFound
   variable will keep track of whether the state name was found in the array. Click the **blank
   line** above the End Sub clause and then press **Enter**. Enter the following three declaration
   statements. Press **Enter** twice after typing the last declaration statement.

   Dim strSearchFor As String
   Dim intSub As Integer
   Dim strFound As String

4. Now you will convert the contents of the txtState control to uppercase and then assign
   the result to the strSearchFor variable. After doing this, the variable will contain the
   name of the state to search for in the array. Enter the following assignment statement:

   strSearchFor = txtState.Text.ToUpper

5. As mentioned earlier, the search should begin with the first array element. Enter the following assignment statement:

intSub = 0

6. Before the search begins, the procedure will assume that the state is not contained in the array. Enter the following assignment statement:

strFound = "N"

7. Step 4 in the algorithm is a loop that repeats its instructions until one of two conditions is true: either the state name has been found in the array or the subscript equals the number of array elements (which indicates there are no more elements to search). You will use the Do...Loop statement to code this loop. The For...Next statement is not appropriate in this case, because you don't know the exact number of times the loop instructions should be repeated. Enter the following Do clause:

Do Until strFound = "Y" OrElse intSub = strStates.Length

8. The first instruction in the loop is a selection structure that compares the contents of the current array element (converted to uppercase) with the state name stored in the strSearchFor variable. If both names match, the selection structure's true path will assign the string "Y" to the strFound variable to indicate that the name was located in the array. If both names do not match, the selection structure's false path will increment the array subscript by 1; this will allow the loop to search the next element in the array. Enter the following selection structure:

If strStates(intSub).ToUpper = strSearchFor Then
    strFound = "Y"
Else
    intSub = intSub + 1
End If

9. The value stored in the strFound variable indicates whether the state name was located in the array, and it determines the appropriate message to display. Insert two blank lines below the Loop clause and then enter the following selection structure:

If strFound = "Y" Then
    lblMessage.Text = strSearchFor & " is number " &
        intSub + 1 & " in the list of states you visited"
Else
    lblMessage.Text = "You did not visit " & strSearchFor
End If

Figure 18-15 shows the code entered in the btnVisited control's Click event procedure.

```
Private Sub btnVisited_Click(ByVal sender As Object,
ByVal e As System.EventArgs) Handles btnVisited.Click
    ' searches an array for the name of a state, and
    ' then displays an appropriate message

    Dim strStates() As String = {"Hawaii", "Colorado",
                                 "Florida", "California",
                                 "Georgia", "Idaho",
                                 "North Carolina", "Texas",
                                 "New York"}

    Dim strSearchFor As String
    Dim intSub As Integer
    Dim strFound As String

    strSearchFor = txtState.Text.ToUpper
    intSub = 0
    strFound = "N"
    Do Until strFound = "Y" OrElse intSub = strStates.Length
        If strStates(intSub).ToUpper = strSearchFor Then
            strFound = "Y"
        Else
            intSub = intSub + 1 ── you also can use intSub += 1
        End If
    Loop

    If strFound = "Y" Then
        lblMessage.Text = strSearchFor & " is number " &
            intSub + 1 & " in the list of states you visited"
    Else
        lblMessage.Text = "You did not visit " & strSearchFor
    End If
End Sub
```

Figure 18-15   btnVisited control's Click event procedure

To test the btnVisited control's Click event procedure:

1. Save the solution and then start the application. First, you will enter a state name that is contained in the array. Type **Texas** in the State box and then click the **Visited?** button. The appropriate message appears in the interface. See Figure 18-16.

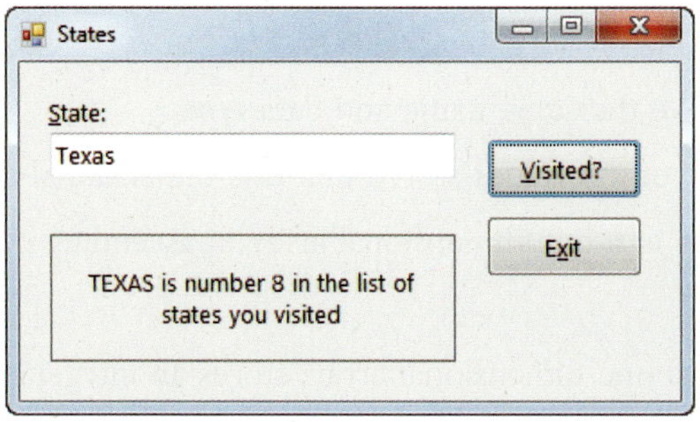

Figure 18-16   Interface showing the message for Texas

2. Now you will enter a state name that is not in the array. Replace Texas in the State box with **Louisiana** and then click the **Visited?** button. The "You did not visit LOUISIANA" message appears in the interface.

3. On your own, test the application using different state names. When you are finished testing the application, click the **Exit** button. Close the Code Editor window and then close the solution.

To review what you learned about one-dimensional arrays, view the Ch18One-Dimensional Arrays video.

Mini-Quiz 18-2

See Appendix B for the answers.

1. Write a Visual Basic statement that sorts the strStates array in ascending order.

2. The number of array elements is stored in an array's _____ property.

3. If the dblBonus array contains 10 elements, what will happen when the computer processes the dblBonus(10) = 35.67 statement?

Summary

- All of the variables in an array have the same name and data type.

- Each element in a one-dimensional array is identified by a unique integer, called a subscript. The subscript appears in parentheses after the array's name. The first subscript in a one-dimensional array is 0.

- When declaring a one-dimensional array, you provide either the highest subscript or the initial values.

- The number of elements in a one-dimensional array is one number more than its highest subscript.

- You refer to an element in a one-dimensional array using the array's name followed by the element's subscript.

- You can use an array variable just like any other variable.

- A one-dimensional array's Length property contains an integer that represents the number of elements in the array.

- The Array.Sort method sorts the elements in a one-dimensional array in ascending order. The Array.Reverse method reverses the order of the elements in a one-dimensional array.

Key Terms

Array—a group of related variables that have the same name and data type

Array.Reverse method—reverses the order of the values stored in a one-dimensional array

Array.Sort method—sorts the values stored in a one-dimensional array in ascending order

Elements—the variables in an array

Length property—one of the properties of a one-dimensional array; stores an integer that represents the number of array elements

Populating the array—refers to the process of initializing the elements in an array

Scalar variable—another name for a simple variable

Simple variable—a variable that is unrelated to any other variable in the computer's internal memory; also called a scalar variable

Sorting—the process of arranging data in a specific order

Subscript—a unique integer that identifies the position of an element in an array

Review Questions

1. Which of the following declares a four-element one-dimensional array named `strLetters`?

   a. `Dim strLetters(3) As String`

   b. `Dim strLetters() As String =`
      `"A", "B", "C", "D"`

   c. `Dim strLetters(3) As String =`
      `{"A", "B", "C", "D"}`

   d. both a and c

2. Which of the following assigns (to the lblCount control) the number of elements contained in the `intItems` array?

   a. `lblCount.Text = intItems.Len`

   b. `lblCount.Text = intItems.Length`

   c. `lblCount.Text = Length(intItems)`

   d. `lblCount.Text = intItems.NumElements`

3. The `intItems` array is declared using the `Dim intItems(20) As Integer` statement. The `intSub` variable keeps track of the array subscripts and is initialized to 0. Which of the following Do clauses tells the computer to process the loop instructions for each element in the array?

   a. `Do While intSub < 20`

   b. `Do While intSub > 20`

   c. `Do While intSub <= 20`

   d. `Do While intSub >= 20`

4. The `decSales` array is declared using the `Dim decSales(4) As Decimal` statement. Which of the following If clauses can be used to validate the array subscript stored in the `intX` variable?

   a. `If decSales(intX) >= 0 AndAlso`
      `decSales(intX) < 4 Then`

   b. `If decSales(intX) >= 0 AndAlso`
      `decSales(intX) <= 4 Then`

   c. `If intX >= 0 AndAlso intX < 4 Then`

   d. none of the above

5. The `decSales` array is declared using the `Dim decSales(4) As Decimal` statement. Which of the following loops will correctly add 100 to each element in the array?

   a.
   ```
   intX = 0
   Do While intX <= 4
       decSales(intX) = decSales(intX) + 100
       intX = intX + 1
   Loop
   ```

   b.
   ```
   For intSubscript As Integer = 0 To 4
       decSales(intSubscript) += 100
   Next intSubscript
   ```

   c.
   ```
   intX = 0
   Do
       decSales(intX) = decSales(intX) + 100
       intX = intX + 1
   Loop Until intX > 4
   ```

   d. all of the above

6. The `strCities` array is declared using the `Dim strCities(10) As String` statement. The `intSub` variable keeps track of the array subscripts and is initialized to 0. Which of the following Do clauses tells the computer to process the loop instructions for each element in the array?

   a. `Do While intSub < strCities.Length`

   b. `Do While intSub <= strCities.Length – 1`

   c. `Do Until intSub = strCities.Length`

   d. all of the above

7. The `strLetters` array is declared using the `Dim strLetters() As String = {"E", "A", "C", "G"}` statement. Which of the following will sort the array as follows: G, E, C, A?

   a. `Array.Sort(strLetters)`
       `Array.Reverse(strLetters)`

   b. `Array.Reverse(strLetters)`
       `Array.Sort(strLetters)`

   c. `Array.SortDescending(strLetters)`

   d. both a and b

Exercises

TRY THIS

1. Open the Party List Solution (Party List Solution.sln) file contained in the ClearlyVB2010\Chap18\Party List Solution folder. The interface provides a text box for the user to enter a name. When the user clicks the Verify Invitation button, the button's Click event procedure should display (in a message box) either the message "*NAME is invited.*" or "*NAME is not invited.*" In each message, *NAME* is the name entered by the user. Open the code template for the btnVerify control's Click event procedure. Declare an array containing the following names: Jacob, Karen, Gregory, Jerome, Susan, Michele, Heather, Jennifer, and George. Code the procedure using the `While` keyword in the Do clause. Save the solution and then start and test the application. Close the Code Editor window and then close the solution. (See Appendix B for the answer.)

TRY THIS

2. Open the Grades Solution (Grades Solution.sln) file contained in the ClearlyVB2010\Chap18\Grades Solution folder. The interface provides a text box for the user to enter a letter grade. When the user clicks the Count button, the button's Click event procedure should display (in a message box) the message "*Grade: number*", where *Grade* is the letter grade entered by the user, and *number* is the number of times the student earned the grade. Open the code template for the btnCount control's Click event procedure. Declare an array containing the following letter grades: A, B, C, A, B, A, F, A, D, B, and C. Code the procedure using the For…Next statement. Save the solution and then start and test the application. Close the Code Editor window and then close the solution. (See Appendix B for the answer.)

MODIFY THIS

3. In this exercise, you modify the application coded in Exercise 2. Use Windows to make a copy of the Grades Solution folder. Save the copy in the ClearlyVB2010\Chap18 folder. Rename the copy Grades Solution-MODIFY THIS. Open the Grades Solution (Grades Solution.sln) file contained in the Grades Solution-MODIFY THIS folder. Open the designer window. Change the For…Next statement in the Count button's Click event procedure to a Do…Loop statement. Save the solution and then start and test the application. Close the Code Editor window and then close the solution.

INTRODUCTORY

4. Open the Bonus Solution (Bonus Solution.sln) file contained in the Bonus Solution folder. Open the Code Editor window. The btnDisplay control's Click event procedure should display the total of the values stored in the `dblBonus` array, formatted with a

dollar sign and two decimal places. Code the procedure. Save the solution and then start and test the application. Close the Code Editor window and then close the solution.

5. Open the NumDays Solution (NumDays Solution.sln) file contained in the ClearlyVB2010\Chap18\NumDays Solution folder. Open the code template for the btnDisplay control's Click event procedure. Declare a 12-element one-dimensional array. Use the number of days in each month to initialize the array. (Use 28 for February.) The procedure should display (in the lblDays control) the number of days corresponding to the month number entered by the user. For example, if the user enters the number 1, the procedure should display 31 in the lblDays control, because there are 31 days in January. The procedure should display an appropriate message in a message box when the user enters an invalid month number. Code the procedure. Save the solution and then start and test the application. Close the Code Editor window and then close the solution.

INTRODUCTORY

6. Open the Update Prices (Update Prices Solution.sln) file contained in the ClearlyVB2010\Chap18\Update Prices Solution folder. The btnUpdate control's Click event procedure should display (in the lblOriginal control) each price stored in the dblPrices array. It then should increase each price by $2 and then display the updated array values in the lblIncreased control. Display the original and updated prices with two decimal places. Code the procedure. Save the solution and then start and test the application. Close the Code Editor window and then close the solution.

INTRODUCTORY

7. Open the Scores Solution (Scores Solution.sln) file contained in the ClearlyVB2010\Chap18\Scores Solution folder. Open the code template for the btnDisplay control's Click event procedure. Declare a 20-element one-dimensional array, using the following numbers to initialize the array: 88, 72, 99, 20, 66, 95, 99, 100, 72, 88, 78, 45, 57, 89, 85, 78, 75, 88, 72, and 88. The procedure should prompt the user to enter a score from 0 through 100. It then should display (in a message box) the number of students who earned that score. Save the solution and then start the application. How many students earned a score of 72? How many earned a score of 88? How many earned a score of 20? How many earned a score of 99? Close the Code Editor window and then close the solution.

INTRODUCTORY

8. In this exercise, you modify the application from Exercise 7. Use Windows to make a copy of the Scores Solution folder. Save the copy in the ClearlyVB2010\Chap18 folder. Rename the copy Scores Solution-Range. Open the Scores Solution (Scores Solution.sln) file contained in the Scores Solution-Range folder. Open the designer and Code Editor windows. The btnDisplay control's Click event procedure should prompt the user to enter a minimum score and a maximum score. It then should display (in a message box) the number of students who earned a score in that range. Save the solution and then start the application. How many students earned a score from 70 through 79, inclusive? How many earned a score from 65 through 85, inclusive? How many earned a score from 0 through 50, inclusive? Close the Code Editor window and then close the solution.

INTERMEDIATE

9. In this exercise, you modify the application you coded in Exercise 7. Use Windows to make a copy of the Scores Solution folder. Save the copy in the ClearlyVB2010\Chap18 folder. Rename the copy Scores Solution-Average. Open the Scores Solution (Scores Solution.sln) file contained in the Scores Solution-Average folder. Open the designer and Code Editor windows. Remove the existing code from the btnDisplay control's Click event procedure; however, leave the array declaration statement. Code the procedure so that it displays (in a message box) the average score in the array. Save the solution and then start and test the application. Close the Code Editor window and then close the solution.

INTERMEDIATE

10. JM Sales employs eight salespeople. The sales manager wants an application that allows him to enter a bonus rate. The application should use the rate, along with the eight sales

ADVANCED

amounts stored in an array, to calculate each salesperson's bonus amount. It also should calculate the total bonus paid to the salespeople. The application should display each salesperson's number (1 through 8) and bonus amount, as well as the total bonus paid, in the interface. Figure 18-17 shows a sample run of the application.

a. List the output and input items, as well as any processing items, and then create an appropriate algorithm using pseudocode.

b. Create a Visual Basic Windows application. Use the following names for the solution and project, respectively: JM Sales Solution and JM Sales Project. Save the application in the ClearlyVB2010\Chap18 folder. Change the name of the form file on your disk to frmMain.vb. If necessary, change the form's name to frmMain.

c. Create the interface shown in Figure 18-17. The txtReport control uses the Courier New font. The control's Multiline and ReadOnly properties are set to True, and its ScrollBars property is set to Vertical.

d. Code the application. The txtRate control should accept only numbers, the period, and the Backspace key. The contents of the txtReport control should be cleared when a change is made to the contents of the txtRate control. Use a one-dimensional array whose elements are initialized to the following sales amounts: 2400, 1500, 1600, 2790, 1000, 6300, 1300, and 2700.

e. Save the solution and then start the application. Enter .1 as the bonus rate and then click the Create Report button. The interface should appear as shown in Figure 18-17. Also test the application using your own data. Close the Code Editor window and then close the solution.

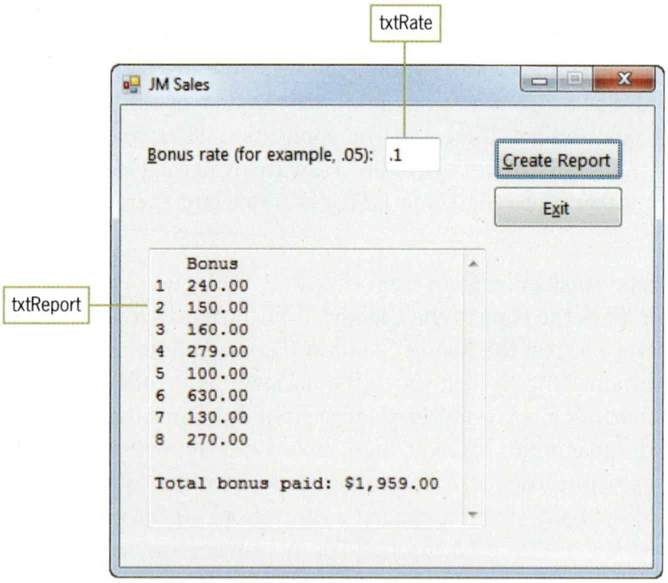

Figure 18-17   Sample run of the JM Sales application

ADVANCED   11.   In this exercise, you create an application that displays the highest and lowest values stored in an array.

a. Open the HighLow Solution (HighLow Solution.sln) file contained in the ClearlyVB2010\Chap18\HighLow Solution folder. Open the Code Editor window.

b. Locate the btnHighest control's Click event procedure. First, the procedure should sort the test scores to determine the highest score stored in the array. It then should count the number of students earning that score. Display the highest score, as well as the number of students earning that score, in the interface. Code the procedure. Save the solution and then start and test the application. Stop the application.

c. Locate the btnLowest control's Click event procedure. The procedure should determine the lowest score in the array without sorting the array. (Hint: Assign the first score to a variable and then compare the remaining array values with that score.) The procedure also should count the number of students earning that score. Display the lowest score, as well as the number of students earning that score, in the interface. Code the procedure. Save the solution and then start and test the application. Close the Code Editor window and then close the solution.

12. Open the FigureThisOut Solution (FigureThisOut Solution.sln) file contained in the ClearlyVB2010\Chap18\FigureThisOut Solution folder.

FIGURE THIS OUT

a. Open the Code Editor window and study the existing code. Start the application. Click the Find a Letter button. Type the letter a and press Enter. The message "A is in array element 0" appears in the interface. Test the application using the letters b, c, and d. The messages "B is in array element 1", "C is in array element 2", and "D is not in the array" will appear in the interface. Stop the application.

b. Change the Do clause to `Do Until strLetters(intSub) = strSearchFor OrElse intSub = strLetters.Length`. Save the solution and then start the application. Click the Find a Letter button. Type the letter a and press Enter. The message "A is in array element 0" appears in the interface. Test the application using the letters b and c. The messages "B is in array element 1" and "C is in array element 2" will appear in the interface.

c. Click the Find a Letter button and then type the letter d and press Enter. A run time error occurs. Read the error message. Click Debug on the menu bar and then click Stop Debugging. Why does a run time error occur when the Do clause is `Do Until strLetters(intSub) = strSearchFor OrElse intSub = strLetters.Length`, but not when it is `Do Until intSub = strLetters.Length OrElse strLetters(intSub) = strSearchFor`?

d. Change the Do clause to `Do Until intSub = strLetters.Length OrElse strLetters(intSub) = strSearchFor`. Save the solution and then start and test the application to verify that it is working correctly. Close the Code Editor window and then close the solution.

13. Open the SwatTheBugs Solution (SwatTheBugs Solution.sln) file contained in the ClearlyVB2010\Chap18\SwatTheBugs Solution folder. Open the Code Editor window and study the existing code. Start and then test the application. Notice that the application is not working correctly. Stop the application. Locate and correct the errors in the code. Save the solution and then start and test the application again. Close the Code Editor window and then close the solution.

SWAT THE BUGS

Parallel and Dynamic Universes (More on One-Dimensional Arrays)

After studying Chapter 19, you should be able to:

◎ Create parallel one-dimensional arrays

◎ Declare a class-level variable

◎ Declare a class-level one-dimensional array

◎ Utilize a dynamic one-dimensional array

We Share the Same Subscripts

In some applications, you may want to use an array to store items that are related but have different data types. For example, you may want to store employee IDs (which are strings) and their associated salary amounts (which are numbers) in an array. But how can you store the employee items in an array when all of the data in an array must have the same data type? One solution is to use two parallel one-dimensional arrays: a String array to store the IDs and an Integer array to store the salaries. **Parallel arrays** are two or more arrays whose elements are related by their position in the arrays. In other words, the elements are related by their subscripts. The strIds and intSalaries arrays illustrated in Figure 19-1 are parallel because each element in the strIds array corresponds to the element located in the same position in the intSalaries array. For example, employee A102's ID is stored in the first element in the strIds array, and his salary is stored in the first element in the intSalaries array. Likewise, employee C220's ID is stored in the strIds(1) element and her salary is stored in the intSalaries(1) element. The same relationship is true for the remaining elements in both arrays. To determine an employee's salary, you locate his or her ID in the strIds array and then view the corresponding element in the intSalaries array.

Figure 19-1   Illustration of two parallel one-dimensional arrays

You will use the strIds and intSalaries arrays in the Employee application, which you code in the next set of steps. The application's interface provides a text box for the user to enter the employee ID. The application will search for the ID in the strIds array, beginning with the first element in the array. If it finds the ID, it will display the corresponding salary from the intSalaries array; otherwise, it will display the "Invalid ID" message. Figure 19-2 shows the planning information for the application. Notice that the algorithm contains a loop. The loop instructions will be repeated either until the employee ID is located in the array or until the array subscript equals the number of array elements. When the array subscript equals the number of array elements, it indicates that there are no more elements to search.

Output: salary or "Invalid ID" message

Processing: five-element one-dimensional IDs array
               five-element one-dimensional salaries array
               array subscript
               found

Input: ID to search for

Algorithm:
1. enter the ID to search for and then convert it to uppercase
2. assign 0 to the array subscript
3. assign "N" to found
4. repeat until found = "Y" or the array subscript equals
   the number of elements in the IDs array:
        if the contents of the current IDs array element is
        the same as the ID to search for, do this:
             assign "Y" to found
        otherwise, do this:
             add 1 to the array subscript
        end if
   end repeat
5. if found = "Y", do this:
        display the corresponding salary from the salaries array
   otherwise, do this:
        display the "Invalid ID" message
   end if

Figure 19-2   Planning information for Employee application

To code the Employee application:

1. Start Visual Studio 2010 or Visual Basic 2010 Express and permanently display the Solution Explorer window. Open the **Employee Solution** (**Employee Solution.sln**) file contained in the ClearlyVB2010\Chap19\Employee Solution folder. If the designer window is not open, double-click **frmMain.vb** in the Solution Explorer window.

2. Open the Code Editor window. First, you will declare the two parallel arrays. Locate the code template for the btnDisplay control's Click event procedure. Click the **blank line** below the `' declare parallel arrays` comment. Enter the array declaration statements shown in Figure 19-3, and then position the insertion point as shown in the figure.

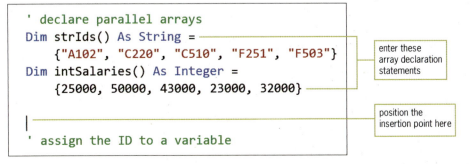

```
' declare parallel arrays
Dim strIds() As String =
    {"A102", "C220", "C510", "F251", "F503"}
Dim intSalaries() As Integer =
    {25000, 50000, 43000, 23000, 32000}


|
' assign the ID to a variable
```

enter these
array declaration
statements

position the
insertion point here

Figure 19-3   Parallel array declarations entered in the procedure

3. Now you will declare the remaining variables: strSearchFor, intSub, and strFound. The strSearchFor variable will store the ID to search for in the strIds array. The intSub variable will keep track of the array subscripts during the search. The strFound variable will keep track of whether the ID was found in the strIds array. Enter the following three declaration statements:

   Dim strSearchFor As String
   Dim intSub As Integer
   Dim strFound As String

4. The first step in the algorithm is to enter the ID and then convert it to uppercase. The user enters the ID in the txtId control. You will convert the contents of the control to uppercase and then store it in the strSearchFor variable. Click the **blank line** below the ' assign the ID to a variable comment and then enter the following assignment statement:

   strSearchFor = txtId.Text.Trim.ToUpper

5. As mentioned earlier, the search should begin with the first element in the strIds array. Click the **blank line** immediately below the ' or the end of the array is reached comment and then enter the following assignment statement:

   intSub = 0

6. Before the search begins, the procedure will assume that the ID is not contained in the strIds array. Enter the following assignment statement:

   strFound = "N"

7. Step 4 in the algorithm is a loop that repeats its instructions until one of two conditions is true: either the ID has been found in the strIds array or the subscript equals the number of array elements (which indicates there are no more elements to search). You will use the Do...Loop statement to code this loop. The For...Next statement is not appropriate in this case, because you don't know the exact number of times the loop instructions should be repeated. Enter the following Do clause:

   Do Until strFound = "Y" OrElse intSub = strIds.Length

8. The first instruction in the loop is a selection structure that compares the contents of the current element in the strIds array with the ID stored in the strSearchFor variable. If both IDs match, the selection structure's true path will assign "Y" to the strFound variable to indicate that the ID was located in the array. If both IDs do not match, the selection structure's false path will increment the array subscript by 1; this will allow the loop to search the next element in the strIds array. Enter the following selection structure:

   If strIds(intSub) = strSearchFor Then
   **   strFound = "Y"**
   Else
   **   intSub = intSub + 1**
   End If

9. The value stored in the strFound variable indicates whether the ID was located in the strIds array, and it determines the appropriate information to display. Click the **blank line** below the ' determine whether the ID was found comment and then enter the following selection structure:

   If strFound = "Y" Then
   **   lblSalary.Text =**
   **   intSalaries(intSub).ToString("C0")**
   Else
   **   lblSalary.Text = "Invalid ID"**
   End If

Figure 19-4 shows the code entered in the btnDisplay control's Click event procedure.

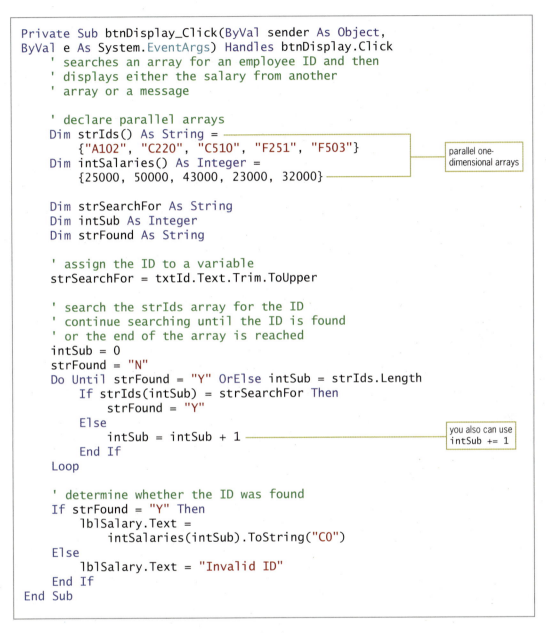

```
Private Sub btnDisplay_Click(ByVal sender As Object,
ByVal e As System.EventArgs) Handles btnDisplay.Click
    ' searches an array for an employee ID and then
    ' displays either the salary from another
    ' array or a message

    ' declare parallel arrays
    Dim strIds() As String =
        {"A102", "C220", "C510", "F251", "F503"}
    Dim intSalaries() As Integer =
        {25000, 50000, 43000, 23000, 32000}

    Dim strSearchFor As String
    Dim intSub As Integer
    Dim strFound As String

    ' assign the ID to a variable
    strSearchFor = txtId.Text.Trim.ToUpper

    ' search the strIds array for the ID
    ' continue searching until the ID is found
    ' or the end of the array is reached
    intSub = 0
    strFound = "N"
    Do Until strFound = "Y" OrElse intSub = strIds.Length
        If strIds(intSub) = strSearchFor Then
            strFound = "Y"
        Else
            intSub = intSub + 1
        End If
    Loop

    ' determine whether the ID was found
    If strFound = "Y" Then
        lblSalary.Text =
            intSalaries(intSub).ToString("C0")
    Else
        lblSalary.Text = "Invalid ID"
    End If
End Sub
```

parallel one-dimensional arrays

you also can use
intSub += 1

Figure 19-4 btnDisplay control's Click event procedure

To test the btnDisplay control's Click event procedure:

1. Save the solution and then start the application. First, you will enter a valid ID. Type **c510** in the Employee ID box. The ID appears in the strIds(2) element, and its corresponding salary amount (43000) appears in the intSalaries(2) element. Click the **Display Salary** button. The correct salary amount appears in the Salary box, as shown in Figure 19-5.

Figure 19-5   Salary amount displayed in the interface

2. Now you will enter an invalid ID. Change the employee ID to **c511** and then click the **Display Salary** button. The message "Invalid ID" appears in the Salary box.

3. Test the application several more times using valid and invalid IDs. When you are finished testing the application, click the **Exit** button. Close the Code Editor window and then close the solution.

Will You Share That with Me?

In the applications you have coded so far, the variables and arrays were declared in procedures. This is because the memory locations were needed only by the procedure that declared them. At times, however, two or more procedures in an application may need to use the same variable or array. In those cases, you can declare the memory locations in the form's Declarations section, which begins with the Public Class clause and ends with the End Class clause in the Code Editor window. Variables and arrays declared in a form's Declarations section have **class scope** and are referred to as **class-level variables** and **class-level arrays**, respectively. As you learned in Chapter 6, scope refers to the area where a memory location is recognized by an application's code. Class-level memory locations are recognized by every procedure contained in the form's Code Editor window.

You declare a class-level memory location using the `Private` keyword rather than the `Dim` keyword, which is used to declare a procedure-level memory location. For example, the `Private intNumber As Integer` statement declares a class-level variable named `intNumber`. Similarly, the `Private decSales(4) As Decimal` statement declares a class-level one-dimensional array named `decSales`. Class-level memory locations retain their values and remain in the computer's internal memory until the application ends.

You will use both a class-level array and a class-level variable in the Test Scores application, which you code in the next set of steps. Figures 19-6 and 19-7 show the application's user interface and planning information, respectively. Notice that each algorithm in Figure 19-7 uses a one-dimensional array of scores. The algorithm for the Enter Test Scores button fills the array with values. The algorithms for the Average Score and Highest Score buttons use the array values to determine the average score and highest score, respectively. For the array to be accessible by each button's Click event procedure, it will need to be declared as a class-level array. Rather than having each button's Click event procedure determine the highest subscript in the array, you will assign the highest subscript to a class-level variable that each procedure can use. As you learned in Chapter 18, you can determine the highest subscript in a one-dimensional array by subtracting 1 from the number of array elements. Recall that the number of elements in a one-dimensional array is stored in the array's Length property.

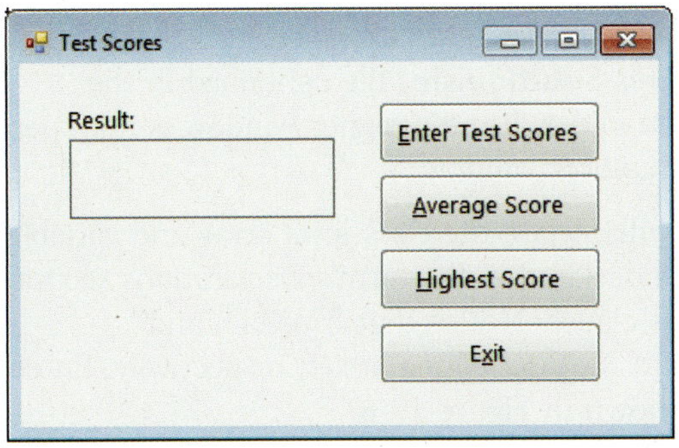

Figure 19-6   Interface for the Test Scores application

Output: average score or highest score

Processing: five-element one-dimensional scores array (class-level)
               highest subscript (class-level)
               array subscript
               total scores accumulator (start at 0)

Input: five scores

Algorithm for the Enter Test Scores button:
1. repeat for array subscripts from 0 through the highest
    subscript (in increments of 1):
         get a score from the user
         store the score in the current array element
    end repeat
2. remove the contents of the Result box

Algorithm for the Average Score button:
1. assign 0 to the total scores accumulator
2. repeat for array subscripts from 0 through the highest
    subscript (in increments of 1):
         add the contents of the current array element to the
         total scores accumulator
    end repeat
3. calculate the average score by dividing the total scores
    accumulator by the number of array elements
4. display the average score

Algorithm for the Highest Score button:
1. assign the contents of the first array element as the highest score
2. repeat for array subscripts from 1 through the highest
    subscript (in increments of 1):
         if the value stored in the current array element
         is greater than the highest score, do this:
              assign the contents of the current array
              element as the highest score
         end if
    end repeat
3. display the highest score

Figure 19-7   Planning information for the Test Scores application

To begin coding the Test Scores application:

1. Open the **Test Scores Solution (Test Scores Solution.sln)** file contained in the ClearlyVB2010\Chap19\Test Scores Solution folder. If the designer window is not open, double-click **frmMain.vb** in the Solution Explorer window.

2. Open the Code Editor window. First, you will declare the class-level array and variable. Recall that class-level memory locations are declared in the form's Declarations section. Click the **blank line** below the Public Class clause. Notice that frmMain and (Declarations) appear in the Class Name and Method Name boxes, respectively. Enter the comment and declaration statements shown in Figure 19-8.

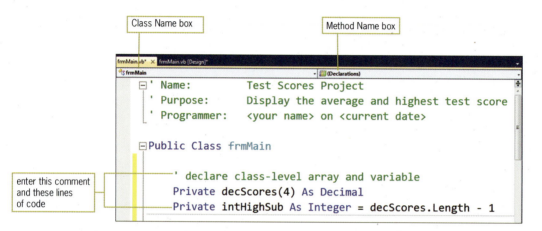

Figure 19-8 Class-level declarations entered in the form's Declarations section

The first algorithm you will code is for the Enter Test Scores button. The algorithm prompts the user to enter five test scores, and it stores each score in an element in the decScores array.

To code the btnEnter control's Click event procedure:

1. Locate the btnEnter control's Click event procedure. Click the **blank line** below the comment and then press **Enter**. The procedure will use the InputBox function to prompt the user to enter a test score. You will need to declare a String variable to store the user's response. Type the following declaration statement and then press **Enter** twice:

Dim strScore As String

2. The first step in the algorithm is a loop that repeats its instructions for array subscripts from 0 through the highest subscript. You can use either the Do...Loop statement or the For...Next statement to code the loop. In this case, because you know the exact number of times the loop instructions should be processed, you will use the For...Next statement. Enter the following For clause:

For intSub As Integer = 0 to intHighSub

3. Change the Next clause to **Next intSub**.

4. The first instruction in the loop gets a score from the user. Click the **blank line** below the For clause and then enter the following assignment statement:

strScore = InputBox("Score:", "Test Score")

5. The second instruction in the loop stores the score in the current array element. To accomplish this, you will need to use the TryParse method to convert the score to the Decimal data type. Type the following statement and then click **any other line** in the procedure:

Decimal.TryParse(strScore, decScores(intSub))

6. The last step in the algorithm is to remove the contents of the Result box. Insert two blank lines below the `Next intSub` clause. Type the following assignment statement and then click **any other line** in the procedure:

lblResult.Text = String.Empty

Figure 19-9 shows the code entered in the btnEnter control's Click event procedure.

```
Private Sub btnEnter_Click(ByVal sender As Object,
ByVal e As System.EventArgs) Handles btnEnter.Click
    ' gets test scores and stores them in
    ' the class-level array

    Dim strScore As String

    For intSub As Integer = 0 To intHighSub
        strScore = InputBox("Score:", "Test Score")
        Decimal.TryParse(strScore, decScores(intSub))
    Next intSub

    lblResult.Text = String.Empty
End Sub
```

Figure 19-9 btnEnter control's Click event procedure

You will code the Average Score button's algorithm next. The algorithm accumulates the values stored in the array. It then calculates the average value and displays it in the Result box in the interface.

To code the btnAverage control's Click event procedure:

1. Locate the code template for the btnAverage control's Click event procedure. Click the **blank line** below the comment and then press **Enter**. The procedure will use an accumulator variable to total the scores. It also will use a variable to store the average score. Enter the following declaration statements and comment. Press **Enter** twice after typing the second declaration statement.

   Dim decTotal As Decimal   ' accumulator
   Dim decAvg As Decimal

2. Step 1 in the algorithm is to assign the number 0 to the total scores accumulator. Enter the following comment and assignment statement:

   ' start accumulator at 0
   decTotal = 0

3. The second step in the algorithm is a loop that repeats its instructions for array subscripts from 0 through the highest subscript. Here again, because you know the exact number of times the loop instructions should be processed, you will code the loop using the For...Next statement. Enter the following comment and For clause:

   ' accumulate the scores
   For intSub As Integer = 0 To intHighSub

4. Change the Next clause to **Next intSub**.

5. The instruction in the loop should add the contents of the current array element to the total scores accumulator. You can accomplish this task using either the statement decTotal = decTotal + decScores(intSub) or the statement decTotal += decScores (intSub); both statements are equivalent. Click the **blank line** below the For clause. Type the following statement and then click **any other line** in the procedure:

   decTotal = decTotal + decScores(intSub)

6. Step 3 in the algorithm is to calculate the average score. You calculate the average score by dividing the value in the accumulator variable by the number of array elements. Insert two blank lines below the Next intSub clause and then enter the following comment and assignment statement:

   ' calculate and display the average score
   decAvg = decTotal / decScores.Length

7. The last step in the algorithm is to display the average score. Type the following assignment statement and then click **any other line** in the procedure:

   lblResult.Text = "Average: " &
       decAvg.ToString("N1")

Figure 19-10 shows the code entered in the btnAverage control's Click event procedure.

```
Private Sub btnAverage_Click(ByVal sender As Object,
ByVal e As System.EventArgs) Handles btnAverage.Click
    ' calculates and displays the average test score

    Dim decTotal As Decimal      ' accumulator
    Dim decAvg As Decimal

    ' start accumulator at 0
    decTotal = 0
    ' accumulate the scores
    For intSub As Integer = 0 To intHighSub
        decTotal = decTotal + decScores(intSub)
    Next intSub

    ' calculate and display the average score
    decAvg = decTotal / decScores.Length
    lblResult.Text = "Average: " &
        decAvg.ToString("N1")
End Sub
```

Figure 19-10   btnAverage control's Click event procedure

Finally, you will code the Highest Score button's algorithm. The algorithm finds the highest value stored in the array. It then displays the value in the Result box in the interface.

To code the btnHighest control's Click event procedure:

1. Locate the code template for the btnHighest control's Click event procedure. Click the **blank line** below the comment and then press **Enter**. The procedure will use a variable to keep track of the highest score. Type the following declaration statement and then press **Enter** twice:

   Dim decHighest As Decimal

2. When searching an array for the highest (or lowest) value, it's a common programming practice to assign the contents of the first array element to the variable that keeps track of the highest (or lowest) value. Enter the following comment and assignment statement:

   ' determine highest score
   decHighest = decScores(0)

3. Now you will use a loop to look at the second through the last element in the array. The loop will contain a selection structure that compares the value in each of those elements to the value stored in the **decHighest** variable. (You don't need to compare the first element's value, because that value is already assigned to the variable.) If the value stored in the current array element is greater than the value stored in the **decHighest** variable, the selection structure's true path should assign the array element's value to the variable. Enter the following loop and selection structure:

   For intSub As Integer = 1 To intHighSub
   ** If decScores(intSub) > decHighest Then**
   **   decHighest = decScores(intSub)**
   ** End If**
   Next intSub

4. Finally, you will display the highest score in the Result box. Insert two blank lines below the Next intSub clause. Type the following assignment statement and then click **any other line** in the procedure:

   ' display the highest score
   lblResult.Text = "Highest: " &
   **   decHighest.ToString("N1")**

Figure 19-11 shows the code entered in the btnHighest control's Click event procedure.

```
Private Sub btnHighest_Click(ByVal sender As Object,
ByVal e As System.EventArgs) Handles btnHighest.Click
    ' calculates and displays the highest test score

    Dim decHighest As Decimal

    ' determine highest score
    decHighest = decScores(0)
    For intSub As Integer = 1 To intHighSub
        If decScores(intSub) > decHighest Then
            decHighest = decScores(intSub)
        End If
    Next intSub

    ' display the highest score
    lblResult.Text = "Highest: " &
        decHighest.ToString("N1")
End Sub
```

Figure 19-11   btnHighest control's Click event procedure

To test the Test Scores application:

1. Save the solution and then start the application. First, you will enter five test scores. Click the **Enter Test Scores** button. Type the following five test scores, pressing **Enter** after typing each one: **80**, **75**, **90**, **63**, and **72**. The button's Click event procedure stores the scores in the decScores array.

2. Now you will display the average and highest scores. Click the **Average Score** button. The message "Average: 76.0" appears in the Result box. Click the **Highest Score** button. The message "Highest: 90.0" appears in the Result box.

3. Click the **Exit** button. Close the Code Editor window and then close the solution.

Mini-Quiz 19-1

See Appendix B for the answers.

1. The elements in parallel arrays are related by their subscripts and data type.

    a. True   b. False

2. The strState and strCapital arrays are parallel arrays. If Illinois is stored in the second element in the strState array, where is Springfield stored?

    a. strCapital(1)   b. strCapital(2)

3. Class-level variables are declared using the Private keyword.

    a. True   b. False

To learn more about class-level memory locations, see the Class-Level Memory Locations section in the Ch19WantMore.pdf file.

But I Don't Know How Many There Are

At times, you may not know the precise number of array elements needed to store an application's data. In those cases, you can use the ReDim statement to change the number of elements while the application is running. The **ReDim statement** allows you to make an array either larger or smaller; however, in most cases you will use it to increase the size of an array. Figure 19-12 shows the statement's syntax and includes examples of using the statement. The optional Preserve keyword in the syntax tells the computer to keep the current array values when the size of the array changes. For instance, the ReDim Preserve intNums(4) statement in Example 1 adds two elements to the end of the intNums array while preserving the values stored in the first three elements. The ReDim intNums(4) statement in Example 2 also adds two elements to the end of the intNums array; however, notice that the values stored in the first three elements are not saved. As Example 3 indicates, if you use the ReDim statement to reduce the size of an array, the values in the truncated elements are not saved. An array whose number of elements changes while an application is running is referred to as a **dynamic array**.

Redim statement

Syntax
ReDim [Preserve] *arrayName*(*highestSubscript*)

Example 1
```
Dim intNums() As Integer = {100, 120, 230}
ReDim Preserve intNums(4)
```

Result of Dim statement:

100
120
230

Result of ReDim statement:

100
120
230
0
0

Example 2
```
Dim intNums() As Integer = {100, 120, 230}
ReDim intNums(4)
```

Result of Dim statement:

100
120
230

Result of ReDim statement:

0
0
0
0
0

Example 3
```
Dim intNums() As Integer = {100, 120, 230}
ReDim intNums(1)
```

Result of Dim statement:

100
120
230

Result of ReDim statement:

100
120

Figure 19-12   Syntax and examples of the ReDim statement

You will use the ReDim statement in the ReDim application, which you finish coding in this section. The application allows the user to enter as many sales amounts as needed. It stores the sales amounts in a dynamic one-dimensional array and then displays the sales amounts in the interface.

To open the ReDim application:

1. Open the **ReDim Solution** (**ReDim Solution.sln**) file contained in the ClearlyVB2010\Chap19\ReDim Solution folder. If the designer window is not open, double-click **frmMain.vb** in the Solution Explorer window. The application's interface is shown in Figure 19-13.

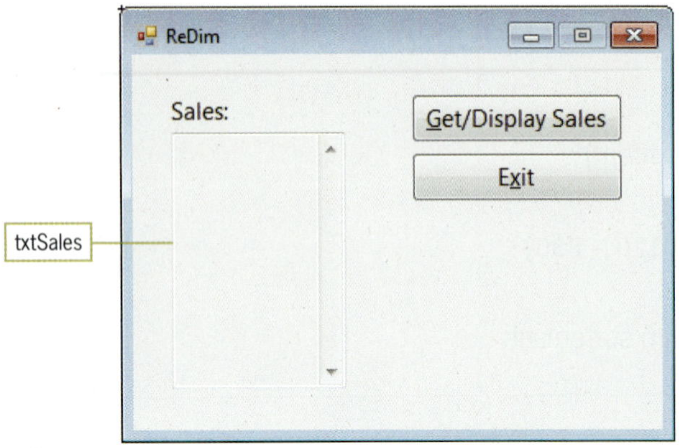

Figure 19-13 ReDim application's user interface

2. Open the Code Editor window and then locate the code template for the btnDisplay control's Click event procedure. Most of the procedure has already been coded for you. Notice that the procedure uses the InputBox function and a loop to get the sales amounts from the user. Keep in mind that the user may enter one amount, 10 amounts, or even 100 amounts. It's also possible that he or she may not enter any sales amounts.

The Click event procedure will store the sales amounts (if any) in an array named `decSales`. However, because the number of sales amounts the user will enter is unknown, the array will need to be declared as an empty array. An **empty array** is an array that contains no elements. You declare an empty array using an empty set of braces, like this: `Dim decSales() As Decimal = {}`.

To finish coding the btnDisplay control's Click event procedure:

1. Click the **blank line** below the `' declare array` comment and then enter the following declaration statement:

   Dim decSales() As Decimal = {}

2. The procedure uses the InputBox function to get a sales amount from the user, and it stores the user's response in the `strSales` variable. The procedure's loop is processed as long as the variable does not contain the empty string. Before you can store the user's input in the `decSales` array, you first need to add an element to the array. You can accomplish this task using the statement `ReDim Preserve decSales(intSub)`. The first time the statement is processed, the `intSub` variable will contain the number 0. As a result, the computer will change the size of the array to one element. Click the **blank line** below the `' add an element to the array` comment and then enter the following statement:

   ReDim Preserve decSales(intSub)

3. Now you will convert the sales amount stored in the `strSales` variable to the Decimal data type and then store it in the element added by the ReDim statement. Click the **blank line** below the `' store the sales amount in the array` comment and then enter the following statement:

   Decimal.TryParse(strSales, decSales(intSub))

4. Finally, you will update the array subscript by adding the number 1 to the contents of the `intSub` variable. You can accomplish this task using either the statement `intSub = intSub + 1` or the statement `intSub += 1`; both statements are equivalent. If the ReDim statement in the loop is processed a second time, the `intSub` variable will contain the

number 1. As a result, the computer will change the size of the array to two elements. Click the **blank line** below the ' update the subscript comment and then enter the following statement:

intSub += 1

Figure 19-14 shows the code contained in the btnDisplay control's Click event procedure. The code you entered is shaded in the figure.

```vb
Private Sub btnDisplay_Click(ByVal sender As Object,
ByVal e As System.EventArgs) Handles btnDisplay.Click
    ' displays the sales amounts stored in an array

    ' declare array
    Dim decSales() As Decimal = {}

    Const strPROMPT As String =
            "Enter a sales amount. Click Cancel to end."
    Dim strSales As String
    Dim intSub As Integer

    intSub = 0
    ' get a sales amount
    strSales = InputBox(strPROMPT, "ReDim")
    Do While strSales <> String.Empty
        ' add an element to the array
        ReDim Preserve decSales(intSub)

        ' store the sales amount in the array
        Decimal.TryParse(strSales, decSales(intSub))

        ' update the subscript
        intSub += 1

        ' get the next sales amount
        strSales = InputBox(strPROMPT, "ReDim")
    Loop

    ' display the sales amounts
    txtSales.Text = String.Empty
    For intX As Integer = 0 To decSales.Length - 1
        txtSales.Text = txtSales.Text &
            decSales(intX).ToString("N2") &
            ControlChars.NewLine
    Next intX
End Sub
```

Figure 19-14   Completed btnDisplay control's Click event procedure

To test the btnDisplay control's Click event procedure:

1. Save the solution and then start the application. First, you will enter two sales amounts. Click the **Get/Display Sales** button. Type **5000** and press **Enter**, and then type **7500** and press **Enter**. Click the **Cancel** button. The two sales amounts appear in the txtSales control. See Figure 19-15.

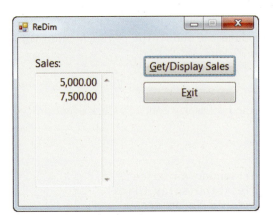

Figure 19-15   Interface showing the sales amounts stored in the array

To review what you learned about dynamic arrays, view the Ch19-ReDim video.

2. Now you will enter five sales amounts. Click the **Get/Display Sales** button. Enter the following five numbers, one at a time: **250.05**, **300**, **1000**, **25.67**, and **75**. Click the **Cancel** button. The five numbers appear in the txtSales control.

3. Click the **Exit** button. Close the Code Editor window and then close the solution.

Summary

- You can use parallel one-dimensional arrays to store related items of data that have different data types.

- Class-level memory locations are declared in the form's Declarations section, which begins with the Public Class clause and ends with the End Class clause in the Code Editor window. You use the `Private` keyword to declare a class-level memory location.

- Class-level memory locations are recognized by every procedure contained in the form's Code Editor window.

- You can use the ReDim statement to change the size of an array (in other words, the number of elements) while an application is running.

Key Terms

Class scope—the scope of a memory location declared in the form's Declarations section; refers to the fact that the memory location can be used by any procedure in the form's Code Editor window

Class-level arrays—arrays declared in the form's Declarations section; the arrays have class scope

Class-level variables—variables declared in the form's Declarations section; the variables have class scope

Dynamic array—an array whose number of elements changes during run time

Empty array—an array that contains no elements; declared using an empty set of braces

Parallel arrays—two or more arrays whose elements are related by their position (subscripts) in the arrays

ReDim statement—used to resize an array (in other words, change the number of its elements) during run time

Review Questions

1. The names of the 12 months are stored in the `strMonth` array. The bonus paid for each month is stored in a parallel array named `intBonus`. If the sixth element in the `strMonth` array contains the string "June", which of the following assigns the June bonus amount, which is 34000, to the appropriate element?

   a. `intBonus(5) = 34000`
   b. `intBonus(5) = "34000"`
   c. `intBonus(6) = 34000`
   d. `intBonus(7) = 34000`

2. Which of the following declares a class-level variable named `dblAmounts`?

   a. `Class dblAmounts As Double`
   b. `Dim dblAmounts As Class Double`
   c. `Private dblAmounts As Double`
   d. `Double dblAmounts As Class`

3. Class-level arrays are declared in _____.

   a. an event procedure
   b. a Sub procedure
   c. the form's Class section
   d. the form's Declarations section

4. If elements are added to an array during run time, the array is referred to as _____ array.

   a. an expanding
   b. a dynamic
   c. a parallel
   d. a run time

5. To save the current contents of an array when elements are added to the array, you use the _____ keyword in the ReDim statement.

   a. `Preserve`
   b. `Public`
   c. `Save`
   d. `Static`

6. If the elements in two arrays are related by their subscripts, the arrays are called _____ arrays.

   a. associated
   b. coupled
   c. dynamic
   d. parallel

7. Which of the following declares an empty array?

   a. `Dim strStates() As String = ()`
   b. `Dim strStates() As String = []`
   c. `Dim strStates() As String = {}`
   d. `Dim strStates() As String`

Exercises

1. Open the Price List Solution (Price List Solution.sln) file contained in the ClearlyVB2010\Chap19\Price List Solution folder. Open the designer window. The interface provides a text box for the user to enter a product ID. Open the Code Editor window and then open the code template for the btnDisplay control's Click event procedure. Declare a String array containing the following five product IDs: BX35, CR20, FE15, KW10, and MM67. The prices corresponding to the product IDs are as follows: 13, 10, 12, 24, and 4. Store the prices in a parallel Integer array. The procedure should display either the price associated with the product ID or the "Invalid product ID" message. Code the procedure. Save the solution and then start and test the application. Close the Code Editor window and then close the solution. (See Appendix B for the answer.)

TRY THIS

TRY THIS

2. Open the Temperature Solution (Temperature Solution.sln) file contained in the ClearlyVB2010\Chap19\Temperature Solution folder. Open the designer window. When the user clicks the Get Temperatures button, the button's Click event procedure should prompt the user to enter 10 temperatures. The procedure should store the temperatures in an Integer array. When the user clicks the Display High/Low button, the button's Click event procedure should display the highest and lowest temperature contained in the array. Code the application. Save the solution and then start and test the application. Close the Code Editor window and then close the solution. (See Appendix B for the answer.)

MODIFY THIS

3. In this exercise, you modify the Test Scores application coded in the chapter. Use Windows to make a copy of the Test Scores Solution folder. Save the copy in the ClearlyVB2010\Chap19 folder. Rename the copy Modified Test Scores Solution. Open the Test Scores Solution (Test Scores Solution.sln) file contained in the Modified Test Scores Solution folder. Open the designer and Code Editor windows. Modify the code to allow the user to enter as many test scores as needed. Save the solution and then start and test the application. Close the Code Editor window and then close the solution.

INTRODUCTORY

4. In this exercise, you code an application that displays a grade based on the number of points entered by the user. The grading scale is shown in Figure 19-16. Open the Carver Solution (Carver Solution.sln) file contained in the ClearlyVB2010\Chap19\Carver Solution folder. Open the Code Editor window and then open the code template for the btnDisplay control's Click event procedure. Store the minimum points in a five-element one-dimensional Integer array. Store the grades in a five-element one-dimensional String array. Both arrays should be parallel arrays. The procedure should display the grade corresponding to the number of points entered by the user. Code the procedure. Save the solution and then start and test the application. Close the Code Editor window and then close the solution.

Minimum points	Maximum points	Grade
0	299	F
300	349	D
350	399	C
400	449	B
450	500	A

Figure 19-16   Grading scale for Exercise 4

INTRODUCTORY

5. In this exercise, you code an application that displays a shipping charge based on the number of items ordered by a customer. The shipping charge information is shown in Figure 19-17. Open the Laury Solution (Laury Solution.sln) file contained in the ClearlyVB2010\Chap19\Laury Solution folder. Open the code template for the btnDisplay control's Click event procedure. Store the minimum order amounts in an Integer array. Store the shipping charge amounts in a different Integer array. Both arrays should be parallel arrays. The procedure should display the shipping charge corresponding to the number of items entered by the user. Code the procedure. Save the solution and then start and test the application. Close the Code Editor window and then close the solution.

Minimum order	Maximum order	Shipping charge
1	10	15
11	50	10
51	100	5
101	No maximum	0

Figure 19-17   Shipping charge information for Exercise 5

6. Open the Sales Tax Solution (Sales Tax Solution.sln) file contained in the ClearlyVB2010\Chap19\Sales Tax Solution folder. Open the Code Editor window. The btnCalc control's Click event procedure declares two parallel one-dimensional arrays. The procedure should multiply each element in the `decSales` array by 10%, storing the results in the `decTax` array. Finish coding the procedure. Save the solution and then start and test the application. Close the Code Editor window and then close the solution.

INTRODUCTORY

7. Open the Commission Solution (Commission Solution.sln) file contained in the ClearlyVB2010\Chap19\Commission Solution folder. Open the Code Editor window. The btnCalc control's Click event procedure declares three parallel one-dimensional arrays. The procedure should multiply each element in the `dblSales` array by its corresponding element in the `dblRate` array and then store the results in the `dblCommission` array. Finish coding the procedure. Save the solution and then start and test the application. Close the Code Editor window and then close the solution.

INTERMEDIATE

8. Open the Magazine Solution (Magazine Solution.sln) file contained in the ClearlyVB2010\Chap19\Magazine Solution folder. The interface provides a text box for the user to enter a salesperson's ID. When the user clicks the Display button, the button's Click event procedure should display the number of magazine subscriptions sold by the salesperson. Finish coding the procedure. Save the solution and then start and test the application. Close the Code Editor window and then close the solution.

INTERMEDIATE

9. In this exercise, you code an application that displays a name corresponding to a letter entered by the user. Open the Letter Solution (Letter Solution.sln) file contained in the ClearlyVB2010\Chap19\Letter Solution folder. The interface provides a text box for the user to enter a letter. The text box's MaxLength property is set to 1. Open the Code Editor window. Declare a class-level String array. Initialize the array using the letters A, B, C, G, and K. Open the code template for the btnFood control's Click event procedure. Declare a parallel String array and initialize it using the following values: Apple, Banana, Carrot, Grape, and Kiwi. Code the procedure so that it searches for the letter in the class-level array and then displays the corresponding food from the procedure-level array. Open the code template for the btnAnimal control's Click event procedure. Declare a parallel String array and initialize it using the following values: Antelope, Bear, Camel, Goat, and Kangaroo. Code the procedure so that it searches for the letter in the class-level array and then displays the corresponding animal from the procedure-level array. Save the solution and then start and test the application. Close the Code Editor window and then close the solution.

INTERMEDIATE

10. In this exercise, you create an application that allows the user to enter as many rainfall amounts as needed. The application's user interface is shown in Figure 19-18. Each time the user enters a rainfall amount in the text box and then clicks the Add to Total button, the amount should be added to the total rainfall amount, which then should be displayed in the interface. In other words, the application should keep a running total of the rainfall amounts. When the user clicks the Calculate Average button, the button's Click event procedure should calculate and display the average rainfall amount. When the user clicks the Start Over button, the button's Click event procedure should reset the counter and accumulator variables to 0 and also clear the total and average rainfall amounts from the labels.

ADVANCED

a. Create a Visual Basic Windows application. Use the following names for the solution and project, respectively: Rainfall Solution and Rainfall Project. Save the application in the ClearlyVB2010\Chap19 folder. Change the name of the form file on your disk to frmMain.vb. If necessary, change the form's name to frmMain.

b. Create the interface shown in Figure 19-18. Code the application. The text box should accept only numbers, the period, and the Backspace key. Display the average rainfall with two decimal places. Clear the Total rainfall and Average rainfall boxes when a change is made to the text box.

c. Save the solution and then start the application. Enter 3.5 in the Rainfall amount box and then click the Add to Total button. The number 3.5 appears in the Total rainfall box. Change the entry in the Rainfall amount box to 2 and then click the Add to Total button. The number 5.5 appears in the Total rainfall box. Change the entry in the Rainfall amount box to 1.5 and then click the Add to Total button. The number 7.0 appears in the Total rainfall box. Change the entry in the Rainfall amount box to 4 and then click the Add to Total button. The number 11.0 appears in the Total rainfall box. Click the Calculate Average button. The number 2.75 appears in the Average rainfall box.

d. Click the Start Over button. Change the entry in the Rainfall amount box to 3 and then click the Add to Total button. The number 3 appears in the Total rainfall box. Click the Calculate Average button. The number 3.00 appears in the Average rainfall box. Close the Code Editor window and then close the solution.

Figure 19-18 Interface for Exercise 10

ADVANCED 11. In this exercise, you create an application that displays the names of the students earning a specific grade.

a. Open the Grade Solution (Grade Solution.sln) file contained in the ClearlyVB2010\Chap19\Grade Solution folder. The interface provides a text box for the user to enter a letter grade. The text box's MaxLength property is set to 1.

b. Open the Code Editor window. The txtGrade control should accept only the following letters and the Backspace key: A, a, B, b, C, c, D, d, F, and f. The contents of the txtNames control should be cleared when the user changes the grade entered in the txtGrade control. Code the appropriate event procedures.

c. Locate the btnDisplay control's Click event procedure. Declare an empty String array named **strNamesFound**. The procedure should search the entire **strGrades** array for the letter grade entered by the user. When the letter grade is found in the array, the procedure should store the corresponding name from the **strNames** array in the **strNamesFound** array. After searching the **strGrades** array, the procedure should sort the contents of the **strNamesFound** array in ascending order and then display the result in the interface. Save the solution and then start and test the application. Close the Code Editor window and then close the solution.

12. Open the FigureThisOut Solution (FigureThisOut Solution.sln) file contained in the ClearlyVB2010\Chap19\FigureThisOut Solution folder. Open the Code Editor window and study the existing code. Start the application. Click the Calculate Average button. Why does a run time error occur? How can you fix the problem? Click Debug on the menu bar and then click Stop Debugging. Modify the code to prevent the run time error from occurring. Save the solution and then start and test the application. Close the Code Editor window and then close the solution.

FIGURE THIS OUT

13. Open the SwatTheBugs Solution (SwatTheBugs Solution.sln) file contained in the ClearlyVB2010\Chap19\SwatTheBugs Solution folder. Open the Code Editor window and study the existing code. Start and then test the application. Notice that the application is not working correctly. (The average sales should be $8,377.88.) Stop the application. Locate and correct the errors in the code. Save the solution and then start and test the application again. Close the Code Editor window and then close the solution.

SWAT THE BUGS

Table Tennis, Anyone? (Two-Dimensional Arrays)

After studying Chapter 20, you should be able to:

- ◎ Create a two-dimensional array
- ◎ Store data in a two-dimensional array
- ◎ Search a two-dimensional array
- ◎ Sum the values in a two-dimensional array

364

CHAPTER 20   Table Tennis, Anyone? (Two-Dimensional Arrays)

Let's Table That Idea for Now

As you learned in Chapter 18, the most commonly used arrays in business applications are one-dimensional and two-dimensional. You can visualize a one-dimensional array as a column of variables in memory, similar to the column of storage bins shown in Figure 18-1 in Chapter 18. A **two-dimensional array**, on the other hand, resembles a table in that the variables (elements) are in rows and columns. You can determine the number of elements in a two-dimensional array by multiplying the number of its rows by the number of its columns. An array that has four rows and three columns, for example, contains 12 elements.

Each element in a two-dimensional array is identified by a unique combination of two subscripts that the computer assigns to the element when the array is created. The subscripts specify the element's row and column positions in the array. Elements located in the first row in a two-dimensional array are assigned a row subscript of 0. Elements in the second row are assigned a row subscript of 1, and so on. Similarly, elements located in the first column in a two-dimensional array are assigned a column subscript of 0. Elements in the second column are assigned a column subscript of 1, and so on.

You refer to each element in a two-dimensional array by the array's name and the element's row and column subscripts, with the row subscript listed first and the column subscript listed second. The subscripts are separated by a comma and specified in a set of parentheses immediately following the array name. For example, to refer to the element located in the first row, first column in a two-dimensional array named strProducts, you use strProducts(0, 0)—read "strProducts sub zero comma zero." Similarly, to refer to the element located in the second row, third column, you use strProducts(1, 2). Notice that an element's subscripts are one number less than the row and column in which the element is located. This is because the row and column subscripts start at 0 rather than at 1. You will find that the last row subscript in a two-dimensional array is always one number less than the number of rows in the array. Likewise, the last column subscript is always one number less than the number of columns in the array. Figure 20-1 illustrates the elements contained in the two-dimensional strProducts array using the storage bin analogy.

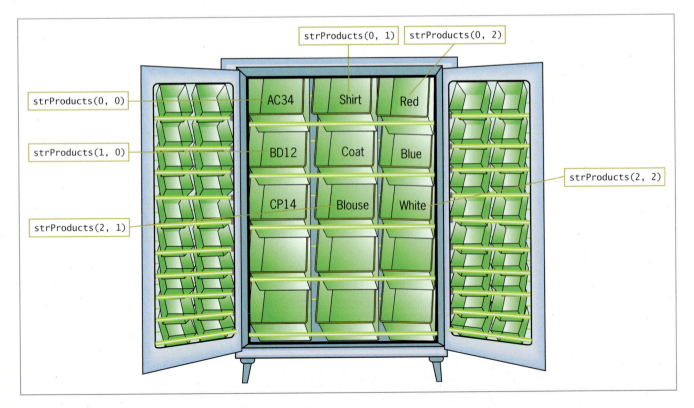

Figure 20-1   Illustration of the elements in the strProducts array

Figure 20-2 shows two versions of the syntax for declaring a two-dimensional array in Visual Basic. You use the Dim statement in a procedure to declare a procedure-level array. You use the Private statement in the form's Declarations section to declare a class-level array. In each version of the syntax, *arrayName* is the name of the array and *dataType* is the type of data the array elements will store. In Version 1's syntax, *highestRowSubscript* and *highestColumnSubscript* are integers that specify the highest row and column subscripts, respectively, in the array. When the array is created, it will contain one row more than the number specified in the highestRowSubscript argument and one column more than the number specified in the highestColumnSubscript argument. This is because the first row and column subscripts in a two-dimensional array are 0.

When you declare a two-dimensional array using the syntax shown in Version 1, the computer automatically initializes each element in the array when the array is created. You would use Version 2's syntax when you want to specify each element's initial value. You do this by including a separate *initialValues* section, enclosed in braces, for each row in the array. If the array has two rows, then the statement that declares and initializes the array should have two initialValues sections. If the array has five rows, then the declaration statement should have five initialValues sections. Within the individual initialValues sections, you enter one or more values separated by commas. The number of values to enter corresponds to the number of columns in the array. If the array contains 10 columns, then each individual initialValues section should contain 10 values. In addition to the set of braces enclosing each individual initialValues section, Version 2's syntax also requires all of the initialValues sections to be enclosed in a set of braces. When using Version 2's syntax, be sure to include a comma within the parentheses that follow the array's name. The comma indicates that the array is a two-dimensional array. (Recall that a comma is used to separate the row subscript from the column subscript in a two-dimensional array.) Also included in Figure 20-2 are examples of using both syntax versions.

Declaring a two-dimensional array

Syntax—Version 1
{**Dim** | **Private**} *arrayName*(*highestRowSubscript,* *highestColumnSubscript*) **As** *dataType*

Syntax—Version 2
{**Dim** | **Private**} *arrayName*(,) **As** *dataType* = {{*initialValues*},...{*initialValues*}}

Example 1—Version 1's syntax
```
Dim intScores(5, 3) As Integer
```
declares and initializes (to 0) a procedure-level array named `intScores`; the array has six rows and four columns

Example 2—Version 2's syntax
```
Private strProducts(,) As String =
        {{"AC34", "Shirt", "Red"},
         {"BD12", "Coat", "Blue"},
         {"CP14", "Blouse", "White"}}
```
declares and initializes a class-level array named `strProducts`; the array has three rows and three columns, as illustrated in Figure 20-1

Figure 20-2 Syntax versions and examples of declaring a two-dimensional array

The variables (elements) in a two-dimensional array can be used just like any other variables: You can assign values to them, use them in calculations, display their contents, and so on. Figure 20-3 shows examples of statements that perform these tasks. If you need to access each element in a two-dimensional array, you typically do so using an outer loop and a nested loop: one loop

366

CHAPTER 20   Table Tennis, Anyone? (Two-Dimensional Arrays)

for the row subscript and the other for the column subscript. If the outer loop controls the row subscript, as it does in Example 4, the array is filled with data, row by row. However, if the outer loop controls the column subscript, the array is filled with data, column by column.

Using an element in a two-dimensional array

Example 1
```
Dim intScores(5, 3) As Integer
intScores(0, 1) = 95
```
assigns the number 95 to the element located in the first row, second column in the `intScores` array

Example 2
```
Dim intSalaries(,) As Integer = {{25000, 35000},
                                 {50000, 23000},
                                 {75000, 45000},
                                 {36000, 24000}}
intSalaries(3, 0) = intSalaries(3, 0) + 2000
```
adds 2000 to the contents of the element located in the fourth row, first column in the `intSalaries` array and then assigns the result (38000) to the element

Example 3
```
Private decSales(10, 2) As Decimal
Decimal.TryParse(txtSales.Text, decSales(2, 1))
lblSales.Text = decSales(2, 1).ToString("C2")
```
assigns the value returned by the TryParse method to the element located in the third row, second column in the `decSales` array and then displays the value (formatted with a dollar sign and two decimal places) in the lblSales control

Example 4
```
Private intNumbers(5, 3) As Integer
For intRow As Integer = 0 To 5
    For intColumn As Integer = 0 To 3
        intNumbers(intRow, intColumn) = 0
    Next intColumn
Next intRow
```
assigns the number 0 to each element in the six-row, four-column `intNumbers` array

---

Figure 20-3   Examples of using an element in a two-dimensional array

The procedures you code in this chapter will demonstrate some of the ways two-dimensional arrays are used in an application. As mentioned in Chapter 18, the values stored in an array in most applications come from a file on the computer's disk and are assigned to the array after it is declared. However, so that you can follow the code and its results more easily, the applications in this chapter use the Dim statement to store the appropriate values in the array.

Mini-Quiz 20-1

See Appendix B for the answers.

1. Write a Dim statement that declares an Integer array named `intQuantities`. The array should have four rows and two columns.

2. What is the highest row subscript in the `intQuantities` array from Question 1?

3. Write a statement that assigns the number 7 to the element located in the third row, first column in the `intQuantities` array.

Revisiting the Employee Application

You coded the Employee application in Chapter 19. As you may remember, the application stores five employee IDs in a one-dimensional String array named strIds, and it stores the corresponding salaries in a parallel one-dimensional Integer array named intSalaries. The application searches for an ID (which is entered by the user) in the strIds array and then displays the corresponding salary from the intSalaries array. Instead of storing the employee information in parallel one-dimensional arrays, you can store it in a two-dimensional array, with the IDs in the first column and the corresponding salaries in the second column. However, to do this, you will need to treat the numeric salaries as strings. This is because the IDs are strings and all of the elements in an array must have the same data type. In this case, the application will search for the ID in the first column of the array. It will search the column, row by row, beginning with the first row. If it finds the ID, it will display the corresponding salary from the second column of the array; otherwise, it will display the "Invalid ID" message. Figure 20-4 shows the planning information for the application, using a two-dimensional array.

Output: salary or "Invalid ID" message

Processing: two-dimensional employee information array
                 row subscript
                 number of rows
                 found

Input: ID to search for

Algorithm:
1. enter the ID to search for and then convert it to uppercase
2. assign 0 to the array subscript
3. assign "N" to found
4. determine the number of rows in the array
5. repeat until found = "Y" or the row subscript equals
   the number of rows in the array:
         if the ID in the first column of the current row is
         the same as the ID to search for, do this:
               assign "Y" to found
         otherwise, do this:
               add 1 to the row subscript
         end if
   end repeat
6. if found = "Y", do this:
         display the corresponding salary, which is located in the
         second column of the current row
   otherwise, do this:
         display the "Invalid ID" message
   end if

Figure 20-4   Planning information for the Employee application, using a two-dimensional array

To code the Employee application:

1. Start Visual Studio 2010 or Visual Basic 2010 Express and permanently display the Solution Explorer window. Open the **Employee Solution (Employee Solution.sln)** file contained in the ClearlyVB2010\Chap20\Employee Solution folder. If the designer window is not open, double-click **frmMain.vb** in the Solution Explorer window.

368

CHAPTER 20 Table Tennis, Anyone? (Two-Dimensional Arrays)

2. Open the Code Editor window and then locate the code template for the btnDisplay control's Click event procedure. First, you will declare the two-dimensional array. Click the **blank line** below the ' declare the two-dimensional array comment and then enter the array declaration statement shown in Figure 20-5. Notice that each ID is stored in the first column of the array. The salary associated with the ID is stored in the corresponding row in the second column.

```
' declare the two-dimensional array
Dim strEmployInfo(,) As String = {{"A102", "25000"},
                                  {"C220", "50000"},
                                  {"C510", "43000"},
                                  {"F251", "23000"},
                                  {"F503", "32000"}}

' assign the ID to a variable
```

enter this array declaration statement

be sure to include the comma

Figure 20-5   Two-dimensional array declared in the procedure

3. Now you will declare the remaining variables: strSearchFor, intRow, intNumRows, and strFound. The strSearchFor variable will store the ID to search for in the array. The intRow variable will keep track of the row subscripts while the array is being searched. The intNumRows variable will store an integer that represents the number of rows in the array. The strFound variable will keep track of whether the ID was found in the first column of the array. Enter the following four declaration statements:

Dim strSearchFor As String
Dim intRow As Integer
Dim intNumRows As Integer
Dim strFound As String

4. The first step in the algorithm is to enter the ID and then convert it to uppercase. The user enters the ID in the txtId control. You will convert the contents of the control to uppercase and then store it in the strSearchFor variable. Click the **blank line** below the ' assign the ID to a variable comment and then enter the following assignment statement:

strSearchFor = txtId.Text.Trim.ToUpper

5. As mentioned earlier, the search will begin with the first row in the array. Click the **blank line** immediately below the ' row has been searched comment and then enter the following assignment statement:

intRow = 0

6. Before the search begins, the procedure will assume that the ID is not contained in the array. Enter the following assignment statement:

strFound = **"N"**

Before coding the fourth step in the algorithm, you will learn about an array's GetLowerBound and GetUpperBound methods.

The GetLowerBound and GetUpperBound Methods

Both an array's **GetLowerBound method** and **GetUpperBound method** return an integer that indicates the lowest subscript and highest subscript, respectively, in the specified dimension in the array. Figure 20-6 shows the syntax of both methods. In each syntax, *arrayName* is the name of the array, and *dimension* is an integer that specifies the dimension whose upper or lower bound you want to retrieve. In a one-dimensional array, the dimension argument will always be 0 (zero). In a two-dimensional array, the dimension argument will be either 0 or 1: The 0 represents the row dimension and the 1 represents the column dimension. Figure 20-6 also includes examples of using both methods.

GetLowerBound and GetUpperBound methods

Syntax—GetLowerBound method
arrayName.**GetLowerBound(***dimension***)**

Syntax—GetUpperBound method
arrayName.**GetUpperBound(***dimension***)**

Example 1 (one-dimensional array)
```
Dim strCities(20) As String
intLowSub = strCities.GetLowerBound(0)
intHighSub = strCities.GetUpperBound(0)
```
assigns the numbers 0 and 20 to the `intLowSub` and `intHighSub` variables, respectively

Example 2 (two-dimensional array)
```
Dim intScores(5, 3) As Integer
intLowColSub = intScores.GetLowerBound(1)
intHighRowSub = intScores.GetUpperBound(0)
```
assigns the numbers 0 and 5 to the `intLowColSub` and `intHighRowSub` variables, respectively

---

Figure 20-6 Syntax and examples of the GetLowerBound and GetUpperBound methods

You will use the GetUpperBound method to code the fourth step in the algorithm from Figure 20-4. The fourth step is to determine the number of rows in the array. To do this, you first use the GetUpperBound method to get the highest row subscript. You then increase that value by 1, because the number of rows in a two-dimensional array is always one number more than the highest row subscript.

To continue coding the btnDisplay control's Click event procedure:

1. The insertion point should be positioned below the `strFound = "N"` statement. Enter the following assignment statement:

   intNumRows = strEmployInfo.GetUpperBound(0) + 1

2. The fifth step in the algorithm is a pretest loop that repeats its instructions until one of two conditions is true: either the ID has been found in the first column of the array, or the row subscript equals the number of rows in the array (which indicates there are no more rows to search). You will code the loop using the Do...Loop statement (rather than the For...Next statement), because you don't know the exact number of times the loop instructions should be processed. Enter the following Do clause:

   Do Until strFound = "Y" OrElse intRow = intNumRows

3. The first instruction in the loop is a selection structure that compares the ID stored in the first column of the current row in the array with the ID stored in the `strSearchFor` variable. If both IDs match, the selection structure's true path will assign "Y" to the `strFound` variable to indicate that the ID was located in the array. If both IDs do not match, the selection structure's false path will increment the row subscript by 1; this will

370

CHAPTER 20 Table Tennis, Anyone? (Two-Dimensional Arrays)

allow the loop to search the next row in the array. Enter the following selection structure:

If strEmployInfo(intRow, 0) = strSearchFor Then
    strFound = "Y"
Else
    intRow = intRow + 1
End If

4. The value stored in the strFound variable indicates whether the ID was located in the array, and it determines the appropriate information to display. If the ID was found, the procedure should display the salary stored in the second column of the current row in the array; otherwise, it should display the "Invalid ID" message. Click the **blank line** below the ' determine whether the ID was found comment and then enter the following selection structure:

If strFound = "Y" Then
    lblSalary.Text = strEmployInfo(intRow, 1)
Else
    lblSalary.Text = "Invalid ID"
End If

5. Save the solution and then start the application. First, you will enter a valid ID. Type **c510** in the Employee ID box. The ID is contained in the strEmployInfo(2, 0) element, and its corresponding salary amount (43000) is contained in the strEmployInfo(2, 1) element. Click the **Display Salary** button. The correct salary amount appears in the Salary box, as shown in Figure 20-7. However, unlike the salary amount shown in Figure 19-5 in Chapter 19, the salary amount in Figure 20-7 is not formatted.

Figure 20-7   Unformatted salary amount shown in the interface

6. Click the **Exit** button.

In Chapter 19's Employee application, the salary amounts are stored in an Integer array. Because that application treats the salary amounts as numbers, it can use the ToString method to format the appropriate salary before displaying it in the Salary box. (The code for Chapter 19's Employee application is shown in Figure 19-4 in Chapter 19.) As you learned in Chapter 6, the ToString method can be used only with variables that have a numeric data type. In this chapter's Employee application, however, the salary amounts are treated as strings and stored in the second column of a String array. Before you can use the ToString method to format the appropriate salary, you first need to convert the salary to a number.

To complete and then test the btnDisplay control's Click event procedure:

1. Modify the second selection structure as indicated in Figure 20-8.

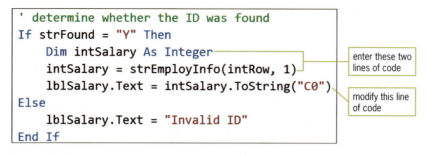

```
' determine whether the ID was found
If strFound = "Y" Then
    Dim intSalary As Integer
    intSalary = strEmployInfo(intRow, 1)
    lblSalary.Text = intSalary.ToString("C0")
Else
    lblSalary.Text = "Invalid ID"
End If
```

enter these two lines of code

modify this line of code

Figure 20-8   Modified selection structure

2. Save the solution and then start the application. Type **c510** in the Employee ID box and then click the **Display Salary** button. The formatted salary amount ($43,000) appears in the Salary box. See Figure 20-9.

Figure 20-9   Formatted salary amount shown in the interface

3. Now you will enter an invalid ID. Change the employee ID to **c511** and then click the **Display Salary** button. The message "Invalid ID" appears in the Salary box.

4. Test the application several more times using valid and invalid IDs. When you are finished testing the application, click the **Exit** button. Close the Code Editor window and then close the solution.

Figure 20-10 shows the code entered in the btnDisplay control's Click event procedure.

372

CHAPTER 20   Table Tennis, Anyone? (Two-Dimensional Arrays)

```vbnet
Private Sub btnDisplay_Click(ByVal sender As Object,
ByVal e As System.EventArgs) Handles btnDisplay.Click
    ' searches a two-dimensional array for an
    ' employee ID and then displays either the
    ' salary or a message

    ' declare the two-dimensional array
    Dim strEmployInfo(,) As String = {{"A102", "25000"},
                                      {"C220", "50000"},
                                      {"C510", "43000"},
                                      {"F251", "23000"},
                                      {"F503", "32000"}}
    Dim strSearchFor As String
    Dim intRow As Integer
    Dim intNumRows As Integer
    Dim strFound As String

    ' assign the ID to a variable
    strSearchFor = txtId.Text.Trim.ToUpper

    ' search for the ID in the first column of the array
    ' continue searching until the ID is found or each
    ' row has been searched
    intRow = 0
    strFound = "N"
    intNumRows = strEmployInfo.GetUpperBound(0) + 1
    Do Until strFound = "Y" OrElse intRow = intNumRows
        If strEmployInfo(intRow, 0) = strSearchFor Then
            strFound = "Y"
        Else
            intRow = intRow + 1          you also can use
        End If                           intRow += 1
    Loop

    ' determine whether the ID was found
    If strFound = "Y" Then
        Dim intSalary As Integer
        intSalary = strEmployInfo(intRow, 1)
        lblSalary.Text = intSalary.ToString("C0")
    Else
        lblSalary.Text = "Invalid ID"
    End If
End Sub
```

Figure 20-10   btnDisplay control's Click event procedure

Calendar Orders Application

The Calendar Orders application displays the total number of calendars ordered by three stores in each of six months. The number ordered each month by each store is stored in a three-row, six-column array. Each row in the two-dimensional array represents a store, and each column represents a month. To display the total number of calendars ordered, you will need to accumulate the values stored in the array.

To code the Calendar Orders application:

1. Open the **Orders Solution** (**Orders Solution.sln**) file contained in the ClearlyVB2010\Chap20\Orders Solution folder. If the designer window is not open, double-click **frmMain.vb** in the Solution Explorer window.

2. Open the Code Editor window and then locate the code template for the btnDisplay control's Click event procedure. First, you will declare the two-dimensional array. Click the **blank line** below the `' declare the two-dimensional array` comment. Enter the array declaration statement shown in Figure 20-11.

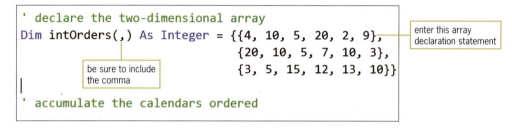

Figure 20-11   Array declaration entered in the procedure

3. The procedure will need an accumulator variable to total the orders. Enter the following declaration statement and comment:

   Dim intTotal As Integer   ' accumulator

4. The procedure will use two Integer variables to store the array's highest row and column subscripts. Enter the following declaration statements:

   Dim intHighRow As Integer = intOrders.GetUpperBound(0)
   Dim intHighCol As Integer = intOrders.GetUpperBound(1)

5. You will need to access all array elements in order to accumulate their values. As mentioned earlier, you access each element in an array using both an outer loop and a nested loop. You can access the elements either row by row or column by column; in this case, you will access them column by column. Click the **blank line** below the `' accumulate the calendars ordered` comment and then enter the following repetition structures:

   For intCol As Integer = 0 To intHighCol
       For intRow As Integer = 0 To intHighRow
           intTotal = intTotal + intOrders(intRow, intCol)
       Next intRow
   Next intCol

6. Finally, you will display the total number of calendars ordered. Click the **blank line** below the last comment in the procedure and then enter the following assignment statement:

   lblTotal.Text = intTotal.ToString("N0")

Figure 20-12 shows the code entered in the btnDisplay control's Click event procedure.

374

CHAPTER 20 ⎞ Table Tennis, Anyone? (Two-Dimensional Arrays)

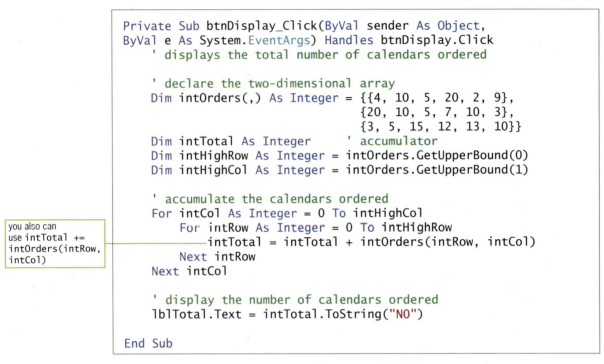

```
Private Sub btnDisplay_Click(ByVal sender As Object,
ByVal e As System.EventArgs) Handles btnDisplay.Click
    ' displays the total number of calendars ordered

    ' declare the two-dimensional array
    Dim intOrders(,) As Integer = {{4, 10, 5, 20, 2, 9},
                                   {20, 10, 5, 7, 10, 3},
                                   {3, 5, 15, 12, 13, 10}}
    Dim intTotal As Integer     ' accumulator
    Dim intHighRow As Integer = intOrders.GetUpperBound(0)
    Dim intHighCol As Integer = intOrders.GetUpperBound(1)

    ' accumulate the calendars ordered
    For intCol As Integer = 0 To intHighCol
        For intRow As Integer = 0 To intHighRow
            intTotal = intTotal + intOrders(intRow, intCol)
        Next intRow
    Next intCol

    ' display the number of calendars ordered
    lblTotal.Text = intTotal.ToString("N0")

End Sub
```

you also can use intTotal += intOrders(intRow, intCol)

Figure 20-12   Code entered in the btnDisplay control's Click event procedure

To test the Calendar Orders application:

1. Save the solution and then start the application. Click the **Display Total** button. The total number of calendars ordered appears in the Total ordered box, as shown in Figure 20-13.

Calendar Orders

Total ordered:

163

Display Total

Exit

Figure 20-13   Interface showing the total number of calendars ordered

To learn more about two-dimensional arrays, see the Two-Dimensional Arrays section in the Ch20WantMore.pdf file.

2. Click the **Exit** button. Close the Code Editor window and then close the solution.

Mini-Quiz 20-2

See Appendix B for the answers.

1. If the `decSales` array is a two-dimensional array, which of the following assigns the lowest column subscript to the `intLowCol` variable?

   a. `intLowCol = decSales.GetLowestSub(0)`
   b. `intLowCol = decSales.GetLowBound(1)`
   c. `intLowCol = decSales.GetLowerBound(0)`
   d. none of the above

2. Which of the following adds the number 20 to the value stored in the first row, second column of the `decSales` array?

   a. `decSales(0, 1) += 20`
   b. `decSales(1, 2) = decSales(1, 2) + 20`
   c. `decSales(1, 2) += 20`
   d. both b and c

 To review what you learned about two-dimensional arrays, view the Ch20-Two-Dimensional Arrays video.

Summary

- A two-dimensional array resembles a table in that the variables (elements) are in rows and columns.

- You can determine the number of elements in a two-dimensional array by multiplying the number of its rows by the number of its columns.

- Each element in a two-dimensional array is identified by a unique combination of two subscripts: a row subscript and a column subscript. The subscripts appear in parentheses after the array's name. You list the row subscript first, followed by a comma and the column subscript.

- The first row subscript in a two-dimensional array is 0. The first column subscript also is 0.

- When declaring a two-dimensional array, you provide either the highest row and column subscripts or the initial values.

- The number of rows in a two-dimensional array is one number more than its highest row subscript. Likewise, the number of columns is one number more than its highest column subscript.

- You refer to an element in a two-dimensional array using the array's name followed by the element's row and column subscripts, which are separated by a comma and enclosed in parentheses.

- You can use an array's GetLowerBound and GetUpperBound methods to determine the lowest subscript and highest subscript, respectively, in a specified dimension of an array.

- You use both an outer loop and a nested loop to access each element in a two-dimensional array. One loop controls the row subscript and the other loop controls the column subscript.

Key Terms

GetLowerBound method—returns an integer that represents the lowest subscript in a specified dimension of an array; the dimension is 0 for a one-dimensional array; for a two-dimensional array, the dimension is 0 for the row subscript, but 1 for the column subscript

GetUpperBound method—returns an integer that represents the highest subscript in a specified dimension of an array; the dimension is 0 for a one-dimensional array; for a two-dimensional array, the dimension is 0 for the row subscript, but 1 for the column subscript

376

CHAPTER 20 | Table Tennis, Anyone? (Two-Dimensional Arrays)

Two-dimensional array—an array made up of rows and columns; each element has the same name and data type and is identified by a unique combination of two subscripts: a row subscript and a column subscript

Review Questions

1. Which of the following declares a two-dimensional array that contains four rows and two columns?

    a. `Dim strLetters(3, 1) As String`

    b. `Private strLetters(3, 1) As String`

    c. ```
    Dim strLetters(,) =
        {{"A", "B"}, {"C", "D"},
         {"E", "F"}, {"G", "H"}}
    ```

    d. all of the above

2. Which of the following statements assigns the highest column subscript in the array to the `intHighCol` variable?

    a. `intHighCol = decSales.GetHighest(1)`

    b. `intHighCol = decSales.GetHighSub(1)`

    c. `intHighCol = decSales.GetUpperBound(1)`

    d. `intHighCol = decSales.GetUpperBound(0)`

3. Which of the following statements assigns the string "Hawaii" to the variable located in the third column, fifth row in the `strStates` array?

    a. `strStates(4, 2) = "Hawaii"`      c. `strStates(2, 4) = "Hawaii"`

    b. `strStates(5, 3) = "Hawaii"`      d. `strStates(3, 5) = "Hawaii"`

4. Which of the following assigns the number 0 to each element in the `intSums` array, which contains two rows and four columns?

    a. ```
    For intRow As Integer = 0 To 1
        For intCol As Integer = 0 To 3
            intSums(intRow, intCol) = 0
        Next intCol
    Next intRow
    ```

    b. ```
    Dim intRow As Integer
    Dim intCol As Integer
    Do While intRow < 2
        intCol = 0
        Do While intCol < 4
            intSums(intRow, intCol) = 0
            intCol = intCol + 1
        Loop
        intRow = intRow + 1
    Loop
    ```

    c. ```
    For intRow As Integer = 1 To 2
        For intCol As Integer = 1 To 4
            intSums(intRow - 1, intCol - 1) = 0
        Next intCol
    Next intRow
    ```

    d. all of the above

5. Which of the following increases by 100 the value stored in the element located in the first row, second column of the array?

a. `intNum(0, 1) = intNum(0, 1) + 100`

b. `intNum(1, 0) = intNum(1, 0) + 100`

c. `intNum(1, 2) = intNum(1, 2) + 100`

d. `intNum(2, 1) = intNum(2, 1) + 100`

6. How can you determine the number of elements in a two-dimensional array?

a. multiply the number of rows in the array by the number of columns

b. add the number of rows in the array to the number of columns and then multiply the result by 2

c. add the number 1 to the number returned by the array's GetUpperBound method

d. none of the above

7. To access the elements in a two-dimensional array, row by row, you use an outer loop to control the _____ subscript and the nested loop to control the _____ subscript.

a. column, row

b. row, column

Exercises

1. Open the Price List Solution (Price List Solution.sln) file contained in the ClearlyVB2010\Chap20\Price List Solution folder. Open the designer window. The interface provides a text box for the user to enter a product ID. Open the Code Editor window and then open the code template for the btnDisplay control's Click event procedure. Declare a two-dimensional String array that contains the following product IDs and prices: BX35, 13, CR20, 10, FE15, 12, KW10, 24, MM67, and 4. The procedure should display either the price associated with the product ID or the "Invalid product ID" message. Code the procedure. Save the solution and then start and test the application. Close the Code Editor window and then close the solution. (See Appendix B for the answer.)

   TRY THIS

2. Open the Inventory Solution (Inventory Solution.sln) file contained in the ClearlyVB2010\Chap20\Inventory Solution folder. Open the designer and Code Editor windows. Locate the btnDisplay control's Click event procedure. The procedure should add together the values stored in the `intInventory` array and then display the total in the lblTotal control. Code the procedure. Save the solution and then start and test the application. Close the Code Editor window and then close the solution. (See Appendix B for the answer.)

   TRY THIS

3. Open the Temperature Solution (Temperature Solution.sln) file contained in the ClearlyVB2010\Chap20\Temperature Solution folder. Open the designer and Code Editor windows. Make the following modifications to the code. When the user clicks the Get Temperatures button, the button's Click event procedure should prompt the user to enter the highest and lowest temperatures for seven days. Store the temperatures in a seven-row, two-column Integer array. The first column should contain the highest temperatures, and the second column should contain the lowest temperatures. When the user clicks the Display High/Low button, the button's Click event procedure should display the highest and lowest temperature contained in the array. Code the application. Save the solution and then start and test the application. Close the Code Editor window and then close the solution.

   MODIFY THIS

4. In this exercise, you code an application that displays a grade based on the number of points entered by the user. The grading scale is shown in Figure 20-14. Open the Carver Solution (Carver Solution.sln) file contained in the ClearlyVB2010\Chap20\Carver

   INTRODUCTORY

378

CHAPTER 20   Table Tennis, Anyone? (Two-Dimensional Arrays)

Solution folder. Open the Code Editor window and then open the code template for the btnDisplay control's Click event procedure. Store the minimum points and grades in a five-row, two-column array. The procedure should display the grade corresponding to the number of points entered by the user. Code the procedure. Save the solution and then start and test the application. Close the Code Editor window and then close the solution.

Minimum points	Maximum points	Grade
0	299	F
300	349	D
350	399	C
400	449	B
450	500	A

Figure 20-14   Grading scale for Exercise 4

INTRODUCTORY

5. In this exercise, you code an application that displays a shipping charge based on the number of items ordered by a customer. The shipping charge information is shown in Figure 20-15. Open the Laury Solution (Laury Solution.sln) file contained in the ClearlyVB2010\Chap20\Laury Solution folder. Open the code template for the btnDisplay control's Click event procedure. Store the minimum order amounts and shipping charges in a four-row, two-column array. The procedure should display the shipping charge corresponding to the number of items entered by the user. Code the procedure. Save the solution and then start and test the application. Close the Code Editor window and then close the solution.

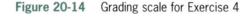

Minimum order	Maximum order	Shipping charge
1	10	15
11	50	10
51	100	5
101	No maximum	0

Figure 20-15   Shipping charge information for Exercise 5

INTRODUCTORY

6. Open the Sales Tax Solution (Sales Tax Solution.sln) file contained in the ClearlyVB2010\Chap20\Sales Tax Solution folder. Open the Code Editor window. The btnCalc control's Click event procedure declares a two-dimensional array. The procedure should multiply each element in the first column of the array by 10% and then store the results in the second column of the array. Finish coding the procedure. Save the solution and then start and test the application. Close the Code Editor window and then close the solution.

INTERMEDIATE

7. Open the Commission Solution (Commission Solution.sln) file contained in the ClearlyVB2010\Chap20\Commission Solution folder. Open the Code Editor window. The btnCalc control's Click event procedure declares a two-dimensional array. The procedure should multiply each element in the first column of the array by its corresponding element in the second column and then store the results in the third column. Finish coding the procedure. Save the solution and then start and test the application. Close the Code Editor window and then close the solution.

INTERMEDIATE

8. JM Sales employs 10 salespeople. The sales made by the salespeople during the months of January, February, and March are listed in Figure 20-16. The sales manager wants an

application that allows him to enter the current bonus rate. The application should display each salesperson's number (1 through 10), total sales amount, and total bonus amount. It also should display the total bonus paid to all salespeople. Figure 20-17 shows a sample run of the application.

a. Create a Visual Basic Windows application. Use the following names for the solution and project, respectively: JM Sales Solution and JM Sales Project. Save the application in the ClearlyVB2010\Chap20 folder. Change the name of the form file on your disk to frmMain.vb. If necessary, change the form's name to frmMain.

b. Create the interface shown in Figure 20-17. The txtReport control uses the Courier New font. Its Multiline and ReadOnly properties are set to True, and its ScrollBars property is set to Vertical.

c. Store the sales amounts in a two-dimensional Integer array that has 10 rows and three columns. The txtRate control should accept only numbers, the period, and the Backspace key. The contents of the txtReport control should be cleared when a change is made to the contents of the txtRate control. Code the application.

d. Save the solution and then start and test the application. Close the Code Editor window and then close the solution.

Salesperson	January	February	March
1	2400	3500	2000
2	1500	7000	1000
3	600	450	2100
4	790	240	500
5	1000	1000	1000
6	6300	7000	8000
7	1300	450	700
8	2700	5500	6000
9	4700	4800	4900
10	1200	1300	400

Figure 20-16   Sales amounts for Exercise 8

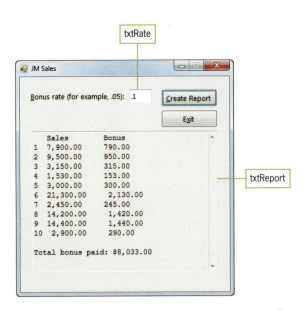

Figure 20-17   Sample run of the application from Exercise 8

380

CHAPTER 20   Table Tennis, Anyone? (Two-Dimensional Arrays)

INTERMEDIATE   9. In this exercise, you code an application that displays the number of times a specific value appears in a two-dimensional array. Open the Count Solution (Count Solution.sln) file contained in the ClearlyVB2010\Chap20\Count Solution folder. Open the Code Editor window. The btnDisplay control's Click event procedure should display the number of times each of the numbers from 1 through 9 appears in the `intNumbers` array. (Hint: Store the counts in a one-dimensional array.) Finish coding the procedure. Save the solution and then start and test the application. Close the Code Editor window and then close the solution.

ADVANCED   10. Conway Enterprises has both domestic and international sales operations. The company's sales manager wants an application that she can use to display the total domestic, total international, and total company sales made during a six-month period. The sales amounts are listed in Figure 20-18. Create a Visual Basic Windows application. Use the following names for the solution and project, respectively: Conway Solution and Conway Project. Save the application in the ClearlyVB2010\Chap20 folder. Change the name of the form file on your disk to frmMain.vb. If necessary, change the form's name to frmMain. Create the interface shown in Figure 20-19. Code the application using a six-row, two-column array to store the sales amounts. Save the solution and then start and test the application. Close the Code Editor window and then close the solution.

Month	Domestic	International
1	100,000	150,000
2	90,000	120,000
3	75,000	210,000
4	88,000	50,000
5	125,000	220,000
6	63,000	80,000

Figure 20-18   Sales amounts for Exercise 10

Figure 20-19   Interface for Exercise 10

ADVANCED   11. Each year, Sabrina Cantrell, the owner of Waterglen Horse Farms, enters four of her horses in five local horse races. She uses a table similar to the one shown in Figure 20-20 to keep track of her horses' performances in each race. In the table, a 1 indicates that the horse won the race, a 2 indicates second place, and a 3 indicates third place. A 0 indicates that the horse did not finish in the top three places. Sabrina wants an application that displays a summary of each horse's individual performance, as well as the performances of all the horses. For example, according to the table shown in Figure 20-20, horse 1 won one race, finished second in one race, finished third in one race, and didn't finish in the top three in two races. Overall, Sabrina's horses won four races, finished second in three races, finished third in three races, and didn't finish in the top three in 10 races. Create a Visual Basic Windows application. Use the following names for the solution and project, respectively: Waterglen Solution and Waterglen Project. Save the application in the ClearlyVB2010\Chap20 folder. Change the name of the form file on your disk to frmMain.vb. If necessary, change the form's name to frmMain. Create the interface shown in Figure 20-21. Code the application using a four-row, five-column array to store the race results. Save the solution and then start and test the application. Close the Code Editor window and then close the solution.

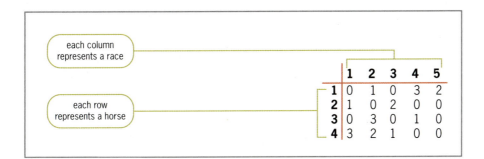

Figure 20-20   Horse race results for Exercise 11

Figure 20-21   Interface for Exercise 11

12. Open the FigureThisOut Solution (FigureThisOut Solution.sln) file contained in the ClearlyVB2010\Chap20\FigureThisOut Solution folder. Open the Code Editor window and then locate the btnCount control's Click event procedure. The procedure should display the number of array elements. Finish coding the procedure. Save the solution and then start and test the application. Close the Code Editor window and then close the solution.

FIGURE THIS OUT

13. Open the SwatTheBugs Solution (SwatTheBugs Solution.sln) file contained in the ClearlyVB2010\Chap20\SwatTheBugs Solution folder. Open the Code Editor window and study the existing code. Start and then test the application. Notice that the application is not working correctly. Click Debug on the menu bar and then click Stop Debugging. Locate and correct the errors in the code. Save the solution and then start and test the application again. Close the Code Editor window and then close the solution.

SWAT THE BUGS

Building Your Own Structure (Structures)

After studying Chapter 21, you should be able to:

- ◎ Create a structure
- ◎ Declare and use a structure variable
- ◎ Understand the advantages of using a structure
- ◎ Pass a structure variable to a procedure
- ◎ Create an array of structure variables

Putting the Pieces Together

The data types used in previous chapters, such as the Integer and Decimal data types, are built into the Visual Basic language. You also can create your own data types in Visual Basic; you do this using the **Structure statement**. Data types created by the Structure statement are referred to as **user-defined data types** or **structures**. Similar to an array, a structure allows the programmer to group related items into a single unit. However, unlike the items in an array, the items in a structure can have different data types.

Figure 21-1 shows the Structure statement's syntax. The structure's name is typically entered using Pascal case, which means you capitalize the first letter in the name and the first letter of each subsequent word in the name. Between the statement's Structure and End Structure clauses, you define the members included in the structure. The members can be variables, constants, or procedures. However, in most cases, the members will be variables. This is because most programmers use the Class statement (rather than the Structure statement) to create data types that contain procedures. (You will learn about the Class statement in Chapter 26.) In most applications, you enter the Structure statement in the form's Declarations section, which begins with the Public Class clause and ends with the End Class clause.

The variables defined in a structure are referred to as **member variables**. Each member variable's definition contains the keyword `Public` followed by the variable's name, which typically is entered using camel case. Following the variable's name is the keyword `As` and the variable's *dataType*. The dataType identifies the type of data the member variable will store and can be any of the standard data types available in Visual Basic; it also can be another structure (user-defined data type). The Employee structure shown in the example in Figure 21-1 contains four member variables: three String variables and one Double variable. The variables are related in that each is an attribute of an employee.

Structure statement

Syntax
Structure *structureName*
      Public *memberVariableName1* **As** *dataType*
      [**Public** *memberVariableNameN* **As** *dataType*]
End Structure

Example
```
Structure Employee
     Public strId As String
     Public strFirst As String
     Public strLast As String
     Public dblPay As Double
End Structure
```

Figure 21-1   Syntax and an example of the Structure statement

The Structure statement does not reserve any memory locations inside the computer. Rather, it merely provides a pattern for a data type that can be used when declaring a memory location. Variables declared using a structure as their data type are often referred to as **structure variables**. The syntax for declaring a structure variable is shown in Figure 21-2. You use the `Dim` keyword to declare a procedure-level structure variable, but the `Private` keyword to declare a class-level structure variable. (Recall that class-level memory locations are declared in the form's Declarations section.) Figure 21-2 also includes examples of declaring structure variables using the Employee structure from Figure 21-1.

Declaring a structure variable

<u>Syntax</u>
{**Dim** | **Private**} *structureVariableName* **As** *structureName*

<u>Example 1</u>
`Dim hourly As Employee`
declares a procedure-level Employee structure variable named `hourly`

<u>Example 2</u>
`Private salaried As Employee`
declares a class-level Employee structure variable named `salaried`

Figure 21-2   Syntax and an example of declaring a structure variable

Similar to the way the `Dim intAge As Integer` instruction declares an Integer variable named `intAge`, the `Dim hourly As Employee` instruction in Example 1 declares an Employee variable named `hourly`. However, unlike the `intAge` variable, the `hourly` variable contains four member variables. In code, you refer to the entire structure variable by its name—in this case, `hourly`. You refer to a member variable by preceding its name with the name of the structure variable in which it is defined. You use the **dot member access operator** (a period) to separate the structure variable's name from the member variable's name. For instance, to refer to the member variables within the `hourly` structure variable, you use `hourly.strId`, `hourly.strFirst`, `hourly.strLast`, and `hourly.dblPay`. Similarly, the names of the member variables within the `salaried` variable in Example 2 are `salaried.strId`, `salaried.strFirst`, `salaried.strLast`, and `salaried.dblPay`. The dot member access operator indicates that `strId`, `strFirst`, `strLast`, and `dblPay` are members of the `hourly` and `salaried` structure variables. Figure 21-3 uses the storage bin analogy from Chapter 6 to illustrate the `salaried` structure variable and its members.

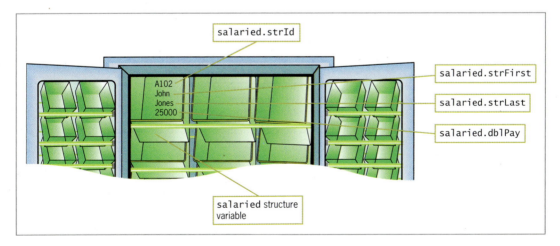

Figure 21-3   Illustration of the `salaried` structure variable

The member variables in a structure variable can be used just like any other variables. You can assign values to them, use them in calculations, display their contents, and so on. Figure 21-4 shows examples of statements that perform these tasks using the member variables contained in the `hourly` and `salaried` structure variables.

Using a member of a structure variable

Example 1
```
hourly.strLast = "Williamson"
```
assigns the string "Williamson" to the `hourly.strLast` member variable

Example 2
```
hourly.dblPay = hourly.dblPay * 1.05
```
multiplies the contents of the `hourly.dblPay` member variable by 1.05 and then assigns the result to the member variable; you also can write the statement as `hourly.dblPay *= 1.05`

Example 3
```
lblSalary.Text = salaried.dblPay.ToString("C2")
```
formats the value contained in the `salaried.dblPay` member variable and then displays the result in the lblSalary control

---

Figure 21-4　Examples of using a member of a structure variable

Programmers use structure variables when they need to pass a group of related items to a procedure for further processing, because it's easier to pass one structure variable rather than many individual variables. Programmers also use structure variables to store related items in an array, even when the members have different data types. In the next two sections, you will learn how to pass a structure variable to a procedure and also store a structure variable in an array.

Willow Pools Application

The sales manager at Willow Pools wants an application that determines the amount of water required to fill a rectangular pool. To perform this task, the application will need to calculate the volume of the pool. You calculate the volume by first multiplying the pool's length by its width and then multiplying the result by the pool's depth. Assuming the length, width, and depth are measured in feet, this gives you the volume in cubic feet. To determine the number of gallons of water, you multiply the number of cubic feet by 7.48, because there are 7.48 gallons in one cubic foot. Figure 21-5 shows a sample run of the Willow Pools application, and Figure 21-6 shows one way of coding the application without using a structure. Notice that the btnCalc control's Click event procedure calls the GetGallons function, passing it three variables *by value*. The GetGallons function uses the values to calculate the number of gallons required to fill the pool. The function returns the number of gallons as a Double number to the btnCalc control's Click event procedure, which assigns the value to the `dblGallons` variable.

Figure 21-5　Sample run of the Willow Pools application

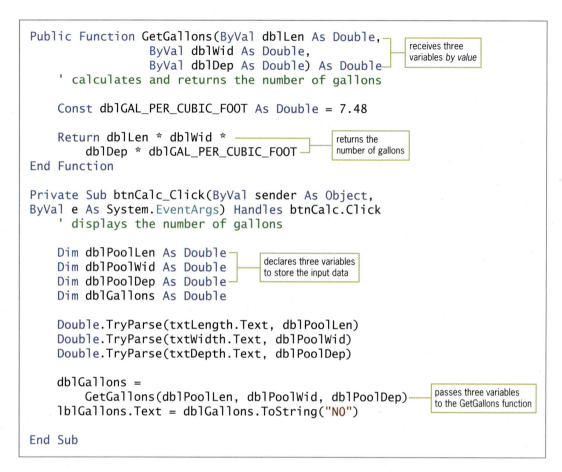

```
Public Function GetGallons(ByVal dblLen As Double,          receives three
                ByVal dblWid As Double,                     variables by value
                ByVal dblDep As Double) As Double
    ' calculates and returns the number of gallons

    Const dblGAL_PER_CUBIC_FOOT As Double = 7.48

    Return dblLen * dblWid *                    returns the
        dblDep * dblGAL_PER_CUBIC_FOOT          number of gallons
End Function

Private Sub btnCalc_Click(ByVal sender As Object,
ByVal e As System.EventArgs) Handles btnCalc.Click
    ' displays the number of gallons

    Dim dblPoolLen As Double              declares three variables
    Dim dblPoolWid As Double              to store the input data
    Dim dblPoolDep As Double
    Dim dblGallons As Double

    Double.TryParse(txtLength.Text, dblPoolLen)
    Double.TryParse(txtWidth.Text, dblPoolWid)
    Double.TryParse(txtDepth.Text, dblPoolDep)

    dblGallons =
        GetGallons(dblPoolLen, dblPoolWid, dblPoolDep)    passes three variables
    lblGallons.Text = dblGallons.ToString("N0")           to the GetGallons function

End Sub
```

Figure 21-6 Code for the Willow Pools application (without a structure)

A more convenient way of coding the Willow Pools application is to use a structure to group together the input items: length, width, and depth. It's logical to group the three items because they are related; each represents one of the three dimensions of a rectangular pool.

To begin modifying the Willow Pools application to use a structure:

1. Start Visual Studio 2010 or Visual Basic 2010 Express and permanently display the Solution Explorer window. Open the **Willow Pools Solution (Willow Pools Solution.sln)** file contained in the ClearlyVB2010\Chap21\Willow Pools Solution folder. If the designer window is not open, double-click **frmMain.vb** in the Solution Explorer window.

2. Open the Code Editor window, which contains the code from Figure 21-6. First, you will create the structure. Click the **blank line** below the `Public Class frmMain` clause. As the Class Name and Method Name boxes indicate, this is the Declarations section of the form. The input items represent the pool's dimensions, so Dimensions would be a descriptive name for the structure. The Dimensions structure will contain three member variables named `dblLength`, `dblWidth`, and `dblDepth`. Press **Enter** to insert another blank line and then enter the Structure statement shown in Figure 21-7.

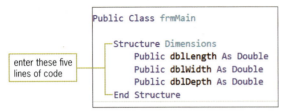

enter these five lines of code

```
Public Class frmMain

    Structure Dimensions
        Public dblLength As Double
        Public dblWidth As Double
        Public dblDepth As Double
    End Structure
```

Figure 21-7 Dimensions structure entered in the form's Declarations section

3. Locate the code template for the btnCalc control's Click event procedure. The procedure will use a structure variable (rather than three scalar variables) to store the input items. Replace the three Dim statements that declare the `dblPoolLen`, `dblPoolWid`, and `dblPoolDep` variables with the following Dim statement:

   Dim poolSize As Dimensions

4. Now you will store each input item in its corresponding member in the structure variable. In the first TryParse method, change `dblPoolLen` to **poolSize.dblLength**. In the second TryParse method, change `dblPoolWid` to **poolSize.dblWidth**. In the third TryParse method, change `dblPoolDep` to **poolSize.dblDepth**.

Next, consider the changes you will need to make to the statement that invokes the GetGallons function. Instead of passing three scalar variables to the function, you now need to pass only one variable: the structure variable. When you pass a structure variable to a procedure, all of its members are passed automatically. Although passing one structure variable rather than three scalar variables may not seem like a great advantage, consider the convenience of passing one structure variable rather than 10 scalar variables!

To continue modifying the btnCalc control's Click event procedure:

1. Replace the assignment statement that invokes the GetGallons function with the following statement. (Don't be concerned about the jagged line that appears below `GetGallons(poolSize)` in the statement. It will disappear when you modify the GetGallons function in the next step.)

   dblGallons = GetGallons(poolSize)

2. Locate the GetGallons function's code. The function will now receive a Dimensions structure variable rather than three Double variables. Like the Double variables, the structure variable will be passed *by value*. Replace the three parameters in the function header with the following parameter:

   ByVal pool As Dimensions

3. The function's Return statement will need to use the members of the structure variable (rather than the scalar variables) to calculate the number of gallons. Replace the Return statement with the following statement:

   Return pool.dblLength * pool.dblWidth *
       pool.dblDepth * dblGAL_PER_CUBIC_FOOT

Figure 21-8 shows the modified code, which uses a structure.

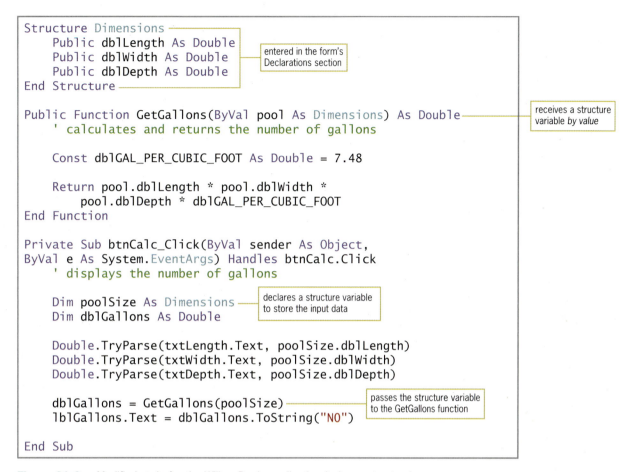

```
Structure Dimensions                          ┌─────────────────┐
    Public dblLength As Double                │ entered in the form's
    Public dblWidth As Double                 │ Declarations section
    Public dblDepth As Double                 └─────────────────┘
End Structure

Public Function GetGallons(ByVal pool As Dimensions) As Double ──┐ receives a structure
    ' calculates and returns the number of gallons                │ variable by value

    Const dblGAL_PER_CUBIC_FOOT As Double = 7.48

    Return pool.dblLength * pool.dblWidth *
        pool.dblDepth * dblGAL_PER_CUBIC_FOOT
End Function

Private Sub btnCalc_Click(ByVal sender As Object,
ByVal e As System.EventArgs) Handles btnCalc.Click
    ' displays the number of gallons

    Dim poolSize As Dimensions ──┐ declares a structure variable
    Dim dblGallons As Double      │ to store the input data

    Double.TryParse(txtLength.Text, poolSize.dblLength)
    Double.TryParse(txtWidth.Text, poolSize.dblWidth)
    Double.TryParse(txtDepth.Text, poolSize.dblDepth)

    dblGallons = GetGallons(poolSize) ──┐ passes the structure variable
    lblGallons.Text = dblGallons.ToString("N0")  │ to the GetGallons function

End Sub
```

Figure 21-8   Modified code for the Willow Pools application (using a structure)

To test the modified Willow Pools application:

1. Save the solution and then start the application. Type **100** in the Length box, **30** in the Width box, and **4** in the Depth box. Click the **Calculate** button. The number 89,760 appears in the Gallons box, as shown earlier in Figure 21-5.

2. Test the application several more times. When you are finished testing the application, click the **Exit** button. Close the Code Editor window and then close the solution.

Revisiting the Employee Application...Again!

As mentioned earlier, another advantage of using a structure is that a structure variable can be stored in an array, even when its members have different data types. The Employee application from the previous two chapters can be used to illustrate this concept. As you may remember, the application's interface provides a text box for the user to enter an employee ID. The application searches for the ID in an array. If it finds the ID, it displays the corresponding salary; otherwise, it displays the "Invalid ID" message. In Chapter 19, you stored the five employee IDs and corresponding salaries in two parallel one-dimensional arrays: a String array for the IDs and an Integer array for the salaries. In Chapter 20, you stored the employee information in a two-dimensional String array. Recall that, in order to do so, you had to treat the numeric salary amounts as strings. This is because the IDs are strings and all the elements in an array must have the same data type. Rather than using parallel one-dimensional arrays or a two-dimensional array, you also can use a one-dimensional array of structure variables. In the Employee application, the array will contain five structure variables, because there are five employees. Each structure variable will store an employee's ID and salary amount.

To use a structure in the Employee application:

1. Open the **Employee Solution (Employee Solution.sln)** file contained in the ClearlyVB2010\Chap21\Employee Solution folder. If the designer window is not open, double-click **frmMain.vb** in the Solution Explorer window.

2. Open the Code Editor window. First, you will create the structure. The IDs and salaries represent employee information, so EmployInfo would be a descriptive name for the structure. The EmployInfo structure will contain two member variables named `strId` and `intSalary`. Click the **blank line** below the `Public Class frmMain` clause and then press **Enter** to insert another blank line. Enter the Structure statement shown in Figure 21-9.

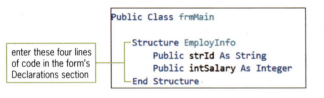

enter these four lines of code in the form's Declarations section

```
Public Class frmMain

    Structure EmployInfo
        Public strId As String
        Public intSalary As Integer
    End Structure
```

Figure 21-9   EmployInfo structure entered in the form's Declarations section

The btnDisplay control's Click event procedure will store each employee's ID and salary in an EmployInfo structure variable. If the company had only one employee, you could declare the structure variable using the statement `Dim employee As EmployInfo`. However, because there are five employees, you need five structure variables: one for each employee. You can reserve five structure variables by declaring a five-element, one-dimensional array, using the EmployInfo structure as the array's data type.

To begin coding the btnDisplay control's Click event procedure:

1. Locate the code template for the btnDisplay control's Click event procedure. Click the **blank line** below the `' declare an array of structure variables` comment. Type the following statement and then press **Enter** twice:

   Dim employees(4) As EmployInfo

2. Now you will declare the remaining variables: `strSearchFor`, `intSub`, and `strFound`. The `strSearchFor` variable will store the ID to search for in the array. The `intSub` variable will keep track of the array subscripts during the search. The `strFound` variable will keep track of whether the ID was found in the array. Enter the following three declaration statements:

   Dim strSearchFor As String
   Dim intSub As Integer
   Dim strFound As String

Next, you need to store the five IDs and salaries in the `employees` array. Keep in mind that each element in the array is a structure variable that contains two member variables: `strId` and `intSalary`. You refer to a member variable in an array using the syntax *arrayName*(*subscript*).*memberVariableName*. For example, `employees(0).strId` refers to the `strId` member contained in the first element in the `employees` array. Likewise, `employees(4).intSalary` refers to the `intSalary` member contained in the last element in the `employees` array. Figure 21-10 illustrates this naming convention.

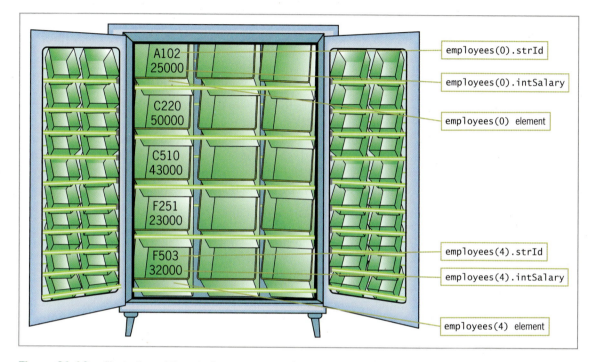

Figure 21-10   Illustration of the `employees` array of structure variables

To finish coding the btnDisplay control's Click event procedure:

1. Click the **blank line** below the `' assign the IDs and salaries to the array` comment and then enter the following 10 assignment statements:

   employees(0).strId = "A102"
   employees(0).intSalary = 25000
   employees(1).strId = "C220"
   employees(1).intSalary = 50000
   employees(2).strId = "C510"
   employees(2).intSalary = 43000
   employees(3).strId = "F251"
   employees(3).intSalary = 23000
   employees(4).strId = "F503"
   employees(4).intSalary = 32000

2. Now you will assign the employee ID entered by the user to a variable. Click the **blank line** below the `' assign the ID to a variable` comment and then enter the following statement:

   strSearchFor = txtId.Text.Trim.ToUpper

3. The search will begin with the first element in the array. Click the **blank line** immediately below the `' each row has been searched` comment and then enter the following assignment statement:

intSub = 0

4. Before the search begins, the procedure will assume that the ID is not contained in the array. Enter the following assignment statement:

strFound = "N"

5. Next, you will enter a loop that repeats its instructions until one of two conditions is true: either the ID has been found in the array or the subscript equals the number of array elements (which indicates there are no more elements to search). Enter the following Do clause:

Do Until strFound = "Y" OrElse intSub = employees.Length

6. Now you will use a selection structure to compare the contents of the `strId` member in the current array element with the ID stored in the `strSearchFor` variable. If both IDs match, the selection structure's true path will assign "Y" to the `strFound` variable to indicate that the ID was located in the array. If both IDs do not match, the selection structure's false path will increment the array subscript by 1; this will allow the loop to search the next element in the array. Enter the following selection structure:

If employees(intSub).strId = strSearchFor Then
    strFound = "Y"
Else
    intSub = intSub + 1
End If

7. The value stored in the `strFound` variable indicates whether the ID was located in the array, and it determines the appropriate information to display. Click the **blank line** below the `' determine whether the ID was found` comment and then enter the following selection structure:

If strFound = "Y" Then
    lblSalary.Text =
        employees(intSub).intSalary.ToString("C0")
Else
    lblSalary.Text = "Invalid ID"
End If

Figure 21-11 shows the code entered in the btnDisplay control's Click event procedure. The figure also includes the Structure statement entered in the form's Declarations section.

```vb
Structure EmployInfo
    Public strId As String
    Public intSalary As Integer
End Structure

Private Sub btnDisplay_Click(ByVal sender As Object,
ByVal e As System.EventArgs) Handles btnDisplay.Click
    ' searches for an employee ID in an array of
    ' structure variables and then displays either
    ' the salary or a message

    ' declare an array of structure variables
    Dim employees(4) As EmployInfo

    Dim strSearchFor As String
    Dim intSub As Integer
    Dim strFound As String

    ' assign the IDs and salaries to the array
    employees(0).strId = "A102"
    employees(0).intSalary = 25000
    employees(1).strId = "C220"
    employees(1).intSalary = 50000
    employees(2).strId = "C510"
    employees(2).intSalary = 43000
    employees(3).strId = "F251"
    employees(3).intSalary = 23000
    employees(4).strId = "F503"
    employees(4).intSalary = 32000

    ' assign the ID to a variable
    strSearchFor = txtId.Text.Trim.ToUpper

    ' search for the ID in the array
    ' continue searching until the ID is found or
    ' each row has been searched
    intSub = 0
    strFound = "N"
    Do Until strFound = "Y" OrElse intSub = employees.Length
        If employees(intSub).strId = strSearchFor Then
            strFound = "Y"
        Else
            intSub = intSub + 1
        End If
    Loop

    ' determine whether the ID was found
    If strFound = "Y" Then
        lblSalary.Text =
            employees(intSub).intSalary.ToString("C0")
    Else
        lblSalary.Text = "Invalid ID"
    End If
End Sub
```

Callout annotations:
- Structure statement
- declares an array of structure variables
- you also can use `intSub += 1`

Figure 21-11   Structure statement and btnDisplay control's Click event procedure

To test the Employee application:

1. Save the solution and then start the application. First, you will enter a valid ID. Type **f503** in the Employee ID box. The ID is stored in the `employees(4).strId` variable, and its corresponding salary amount (32000) is stored in the `employees(4).intSalary` variable. Click the **Display Salary** button. The correct salary amount appears in the Salary box, as shown in Figure 21-12.

Figure 21-12   Salary amount displayed in the interface

2. Now you will enter an invalid ID. Change the employee ID to **f502** and then click the **Display Salary** button. The message "Invalid ID" appears in the Salary box.

3. Test the application several more times using valid and invalid IDs. When you are finished testing the application, click the **Exit** button. Close the Code Editor window and then close the solution.

As you observed by coding the Employee application in this chapter and in the previous two chapters, there are many different ways of solving the same problem. Most times, the "best" way is simply a matter of personal preference.

To learn more about structures, see the Structures section in the Ch21WantMore.pdf file.

Mini-Quiz 21-1

See Appendix B for the answers.

1. The Structure statement is usually entered in the form's _____ section in the Code Editor window.

2. Write a Visual Basic statement that assigns the string "Maple" to the `strStreet` member of a structure variable named `address`.

3. An array of structure variables is declared using the statement `Dim inventory(4) As Product`. Write a Visual Basic statement that assigns the number 100 to the `intQuantity` member contained in the last array element.

To review what you learned about structures, view the Ch21-Structures video.

Summary

- You can use the Structure statement to create your own data types in Visual Basic. The Structure statement is usually entered in the form's Declarations section in the Code Editor window.

- After a structure is defined, you can use it to declare a structure variable. A structure variable contains one or more members, usually variables. You refer to the structure variable using its name. You refer to a member variable within a structure variable using the syntax *structureVariableName.memberVariableName.*

- The member variables in a structure variable can be used just like any other variables.

- A structure variable can be passed to a procedure or stored in an array.

- You can create a one-dimensional array of structure variables. To do this, you declare the array using the structure as the array's data type. You access a member variable in an array of structure variables using the syntax *arrayName(subscript).memberVariableName*.

Key Terms

Dot member access operator—a period; used to separate a structure variable's name from a member variable's name

Member variables—the variables contained in a structure

Structure statement—used to create user-defined data types, called structures, in Visual Basic

Structure variables—variables declared using a structure as the data type

Structures—data types created using the Structure statement; allow the programmer to group related items into one unit; also called user-defined data types

User-defined data types—data types created by the Structure statement; see Structures

Review Questions

1. Which of the following declares a Country structure variable named `england`?

    a. `Private england As Country`   c. `Dim Country As england`
    b. `Dim england As Country`   d. both a and b

2. Which of the following statements assigns the string "London" to the `strCity` member of the Country variable from Review Question 1?

    a. `england.strCity = "London"`
    b. `Country.strCity = "London"`
    c. `Country.england.strCity = "London"`
    d. `strCity.england = "London"`

3. An application uses a structure named Product. Which of the following creates a five-element, one-dimensional array of Product structure variables?

    a. `Dim items(5) As Product`   c. `Dim items As Product(5)`
    b. `Dim items(4) As Product`   d. `Dim items As Product(4)`

4. Regarding the `items` array from Review Question 3, which of the following assigns the number 23 to the `intPrice` member contained in the first array element?

    a. `items(0).intPrice = 23`   c. `Product.items(1).intPrice = 23`
    b. `intPrice(0) = 23`   d. `items.intPrice(0) = 23`

5. Regarding the `items` array from Review Question 3, which of the following increases by 100 the contents of the `intPrice` member located in the second array element?

    a. `intPrice(1) = intPrice(1) + 100`
    b. `items.intPrice(1) = items.intPrice(1) + 100`
    c. `Product.items(1).intPrice =`
         `Product.items(1).intPrice + 100`
    d. `items(1).intPrice = items(1).intPrice + 100`

6. The member variables in a structure can have different data types.

   a. True   b. False

7. An application uses the Music structure to declare a structure variable named **songs**. Which of the following displays the contents of the **strArtist** member variable in the lblArtist control?

   a. `lblArtist.Text = Music.songs.strArtist`

   b. `lblArtist.Text = Music.strArtist`

   c. `lblArtist.Text = songs.strArtist`

   d. none of the above

Exercises

TRY THIS 1. Open the Commission Solution (Commission Solution.sln) file contained in the ClearlyVB2010\Chap21\Commission Solution folder. Open the designer window. The interface provides three text boxes for the user to enter the sales for three regions. Open the Code Editor window. Declare a structure named SalesInfo. The structure should contain three Decimal member variables to store the three sales amounts. The btnCalc control's Click event procedure should store the contents of the text boxes in a SalesInfo structure variable. It then should use a function named GetCommission to sum the three sales amounts. The function also should calculate and return a 3% commission. Finally, the Click event procedure should display the commission (formatted with a dollar sign and two decimal places) in the lblComm control. Code the function and Click event procedure. Save the solution and then start and test the application. Close the Code Editor window and then close the solution. (See Appendix B for the answer.)

TRY THIS 2. Open the Price List Solution (Price List Solution.sln) file contained in the ClearlyVB2010\Chap21\Price List Solution folder. Open the designer window. The interface provides a text box for the user to enter a product ID. When the user clicks the Display Price button, the button's Click event procedure should display either the price associated with the product ID or the "Invalid product ID" message. (Display the message in a message box.) Open the Code Editor window. Declare a structure named Item. The structure should contain two members: a String variable for the product ID and an Integer variable for the price. Locate the code template for the btnDisplay control's Click event procedure. Declare a five-element array of Item structure variables; name the array **gifts**. Assign the following IDs and prices to the **gifts** array: BX35, 13, CR20, 10, FE15, 12, KW10, 24, MM67, and 4. Finish coding the procedure. Save the solution and then start and test the application. Close the Code Editor window and then close the solution. (See Appendix B for the answer.)

MODIFY THIS 3. In this exercise, you modify the application from TRY THIS Exercise 1. Use Windows to make a copy of the Commission Solution folder. Save the copy in the ClearlyVB2010\Chap21 folder. Rename the copy Modified Commission Solution. Open the Commission Solution (Commission Solution.sln) file contained in the Modified Commission Solution folder. Open the designer and Code Editor windows. The btnCalc control's Click event procedure should prompt the user to enter the commission rate. It then should pass the rate to the GetCommission function. Make the appropriate modifications to the code. Save the solution and then start and test the application. Close the Code Editor window and then close the solution.

INTRODUCTORY 4. Open the Test Scores Solution (Test Scores Solution.sln) file contained in the ClearlyVB2010\Chap21\Test Scores Solution folder. Open the Code Editor window. Create a structure that contains three member variables; each member variable will represent a test score. The test scores may contain a decimal place. The btnAverage control's Click event procedure should prompt the user to enter the three test scores. Each test score should be stored in a member of a structure variable. The procedure should pass the structure variable to a function that calculates and returns the average score. Finally, the procedure should display the average score (formatted with one decimal place) in the lblResult control. Code the procedure and function. Save the solution and then start and test the application. Close the Code Editor window and then close the solution.

5. Open the Colors Solution (Colors Solution.sln) file contained in the ClearlyVB2010\Chap21\Colors Solution folder. Open the Code Editor window. Create a structure that contains two member variables named strEnglish and strSpanish. The btnTranslate control's Click event procedure should use the structure to declare an array of structure variables. It then should store the values shown in Figure 21-13 in the array. The procedure should prompt the user to enter an English word. It then should display the English word and its corresponding Spanish word. If the English word is not in the array, display "N/A". Code the procedure. Save the solution and then start and test the application. Close the Code Editor window and then close the solution.

INTRODUCTORY

English	Spanish
Blue	Azul
Brown	Marron
Gray	Gris
Green	Verde
Orange	Anaranjado
Pink	Rosa
Purple	Morado
Red	Rojo
Yellow	Amarillo

Figure 21-13 Information for Exercise 5

6. In this exercise, you modify the application from Exercise 4. If you did not complete Exercise 4, you will need to do so before completing this exercise. Use Windows to make a copy of the Test Scores Solution folder. Save the copy in the ClearlyVB2010\Chap21 folder. Rename the copy Modified Test Scores Solution. Open the Test Scores Solution (Test Scores Solution.sln) file contained in the Modified Test Scores Solution folder. Open the designer and Code Editor windows. Modify the btnAverage control's Click event procedure so it uses a three-element array of structure variables. Each element will contain the test scores for one student. The procedure should prompt the user for a student's three test scores and then store the scores in one of the structure variables in the array. It then should use the function to determine the student's average score. Finally, it should display the student's number (1, 2, or 3) along with the average score (formatted with one decimal place) in the lblResult control. Save the solution and then start and test the application. Figure 21-14 shows a sample run of the application when the user enters the following scores: 100, 100, 100, 90, 85, 78, 73, 72, and 67. Close the Code Editor window and then close the solution.

INTERMEDIATE

Figure 21-14 Sample run of the application from Exercise 6

INTERMEDIATE   7. In this exercise, you modify the application from Exercise 5. If you did not complete Exercise 5, you will need to do so before completing this exercise. Use Windows to make a copy of the Colors Solution folder. Save the copy in the ClearlyVB2010\Chap21 folder. Rename the copy Modified Colors Solution. Open the Colors Solution (Colors Solution.sln) file contained in the Modified Colors Solution folder. Open the designer window. Add two radio buttons to the form. Use the following captions for the radio buttons: Translate to English and Translate to Spanish. Also, include the Spanish words in the Label3 control. Open the Code Editor window. If the Translate to English radio button is selected, the btnTranslate control's Click event procedure should display the English word associated with the Spanish word entered by the user. If the Translate to spanish radio button is selected, the procedure should display the Spanish word associated with the English word entered by the user. Modify the procedure's code. Save the solution and then start and test the application. Close the Code Editor window and then close the solution.

ADVANCED   8. In this exercise, you modify the Willow Pools application coded in the chapter. Use Windows to make a copy of the Willow Pools Solution folder. Save the copy in the ClearlyVB2010\Chap21 folder. Rename the copy Modified Willow Pools Solution. Open the Willow Pools Solution (Willow Pools Solution.sln) file contained in the Modified Willow Pools Solution folder. Currently, the application assumes that the entire pool has the same depth. Modify the interface and code so that the application displays the number of gallons for a pool whose depth may vary. The formula for calculating the volume for such a pool is *length * width * (shallow end's depth + deep end's depth) / 2*. Save the solution and then start and test the application. Close the Code Editor window and then close the solution.

FIGURE THIS OUT   9. Open the FigureThisOut Solution (FigureThisOut Solution.sln) file contained in the ClearlyVB2010\Chap21\FigureThisOut Solution folder. Open the Code Editor window and study the existing code. What members are defined in the Structure statement? What is the purpose of the `salesperson.decSales(0) = 2000` statement? Why does the procedure use `salesperson.decSales(0)` in the statement rather than `salesperson(0).decSales`? Start and then test the application. Close the Code Editor window and then close the solution.

SWAT THE BUGS   10. Open the SwatTheBugs Solution (SwatTheBugs Solution.sln) file contained in the ClearlyVB2010\Chap21\SwatTheBugs Solution folder. Open the Code Editor window and study the existing code. Correct the code to remove the jagged lines. Save the solution and then start and test the application. Notice that the application is not working correctly. Locate and correct the errors in the code. Save the solution and then start and test the application again. Close the Code Editor window and then close the solution.

I'm Saving for the Future (Sequential Access Files)

After studying Chapter 22, you should be able to:

◎ Open and close a sequential access file

◎ Write data to a sequential access file

◎ Send the focus to a text box

◎ Read data from a sequential access file

◎ Determine whether a sequential access file exists

◎ Test for the end of a sequential access file

Sequential Access Files

In addition to getting data from the keyboard and sending data to the computer screen, an application also can get data from and send data to a file on a disk. Getting data from a file is referred to as "reading from the file," and sending data to a file is referred to as "writing to the file." Files to which data is written are called **output files**, because the files store the output produced by an application. Files that are read by the computer are called **input files**, because an application uses the data in these files as input. Most input and output files are composed of lines of text that are both read and written sequentially. In other words, they are read and written in consecutive order, one line at a time, beginning with the first line in the file and ending with the last line in the file. Such files are referred to as **sequential access files**, because of the manner in which the lines of text are accessed. They also are called **text files**, because they are composed of lines of text. Examples of text stored in sequential access files include an employee list, a memo, and a sales report.

You will use a sequential access file in the Game Show Contestants application, which you code in the remaining sections of this chapter. Figure 22-1 shows the application's user interface. The interface provides a text box for entering a contestant's name. The Write to File button will write the name to a sequential access file. The Read from File button will read each name from the sequential access file and display each in the Contestants box. (The txtContestants control's Multiline and ReadOnly properties are set to True, and its ScrollBars property is set to Vertical.) You will code the Write to File button first.

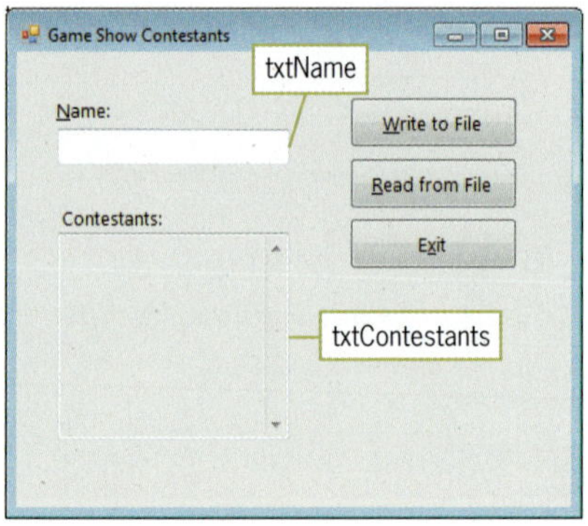

Figure 22-1   Interface for the Game Show Contestants application

Write Those Lines of Text

An item of data—such as the string "Yolanda"—is viewed differently by a human being and a computer. To a human being, the string represents a person's name; to a computer, it is merely a sequence of characters. Programmers refer to a sequence of characters as a **stream of characters**. In Visual Basic, you use a **StreamWriter object** to write a stream of characters to a sequential access file. Before you create the StreamWriter object, you first declare a variable to store the object in the computer's internal memory. Figure 22-2 shows the syntax and an example of declaring a StreamWriter variable. The IO in the syntax stands for Input/Output.

Declaring a StreamWriter variable

Syntax
{**Dim** | **Private**} *streamWriterVariableName* **As IO.StreamWriter**

Example
```
Dim outFile As IO.StreamWriter
```
declares a StreamWriter variable named `outFile`

Figure 22-2 Syntax and an example of declaring a StreamWriter variable

To begin coding the Write to File button's Click event procedure:

1. Start Visual Studio 2010 or Visual Basic 2010 Express and permanently display the Solution Explorer window. Open the **Contestant Solution (Contestant Solution.sln)** file contained in the ClearlyVB2010\Chap22\Contestant Solution folder. If the designer window is not open, double-click **frmMain.vb** in the Solution Explorer window.

2. Open the Code Editor window. Locate the code template for the btnWrite control's Click event procedure. Click the **blank line** below the `' declare a StreamWriter variable` comment and then enter the following declaration statement:

   Dim outFile As IO.StreamWriter

After declaring a StreamWriter variable, you can use the syntax shown in Figure 22-3 to create a StreamWriter object. As the figure indicates, creating a StreamWriter object involves opening a sequential access file using one of two methods: CreateText or AppendText. You use the **CreateText method** to open a sequential access file for output. When you open a file for output, the computer creates a new, empty file to which data can be written. If the file already exists, the computer erases the contents of the file before writing any data to it. You use the **AppendText method** to open a sequential access file for append. When a file is opened for append, new data is written after any existing data in the file. If the file does not exist, the computer creates the file for you. In addition to opening the file, both methods automatically create a StreamWriter object to represent the file in the application. You assign the StreamWriter object to a StreamWriter variable, which you use to refer to the file in code.

Also included in Figure 22-3 are examples of using the CreateText and AppendText methods. When processing the statement in Example 1, the computer searches for the pay.txt file in the Chap22 folder on the F drive. If the file exists, its contents are erased and the file is opened for output; otherwise, a new, empty file is created and opened for output. The statement creates a StreamWriter object and assigns it to the `outFile` variable. You should specify the folder path in the *fileName* argument only when you are sure that the folder path will not change. (Keep in mind that a USB drive may have a different letter designation on another computer.) Unlike the fileName argument in Example 1, the fileName argument in Example 2 does not contain a folder path. Therefore, the computer will search for the file in the default folder, which is the current project's bin\Debug folder. In this case, if the computer locates the report.txt file in the default folder, it opens the file for append. If it does not find the file, it creates a new, empty file and then opens the file for append. Like the statement in Example 1, the statement in Example 2 creates a StreamWriter object and assigns it to the `outFile` variable.

Creating a StreamWriter object

Syntax
IO.File._method_(_fileName_)

method   Description
CreateText   opens a sequential access file for output
AppendText   opens a sequential access file for append

Example 1
`outFile = IO.File.CreateText("F:\Chap22\pay.txt")`
opens the pay.txt file for output; creates a StreamWriter object and assigns it to the
`outFile` variable

Example 2
`outFile = IO.File.AppendText("report.txt")`
opens the report.txt file for append; creates a StreamWriter object and assigns it to the
`outFile` variable

Figure 22-3   Syntax and examples of creating a StreamWriter object by opening a file

When the user clicks the Write to File button in the Game Show Contestants interface, the
name entered in the Name box should be added to the end of the existing names in the file.
Therefore, you will need to open the sequential access file for append. A descriptive name for a
file that stores the names of contestants is contestants.txt. Although it is not a requirement, the
"txt" (short for "text") filename extension is commonly used when naming sequential access files;
this is because the files contain text.

To continue coding the btnWrite control's Click event procedure:

1. Click the **blank line** below the `' open the file for append` comment and then enter
   the following assignment statement:

   outFile = IO.File.AppendText("contestants.txt")

After opening a file for either output or append, you can begin writing data to it. You write data
to a sequential access file using either the **Write method** or the **WriteLine method**; however, in
most cases you will use the WriteLine method. The difference between both methods is that the
WriteLine method writes a newline character after the data. Figure 22-4 shows the syntax and
an example of both methods. As the figure indicates, when using the Write method, the next
character written to the file will appear immediately after the letter o in the string "Hello". When
using the WriteLine method, however, the next character written to the file will appear on the
line immediately below the string. You do not need to include the file's name in either method's
syntax, because the data will be written to the file associated with the StreamWriter variable.

Writing data to a sequential access file

Syntax
streamWriterVariableName.**Write**(*data*)
streamWriterVariableName.**WriteLine**(*data*)

Example 1
```
outFile.Write("Hello")
```

Result
Hello| ——— the next character will appear
immediately after the letter o

Example 2
```
outFile.WriteLine("Hello")
```

Result
Hello
| ——— the next character will
appear on the next line

Figure 22-4   Syntax and examples of writing data to a sequential access file

In the Game Show Contestants application, each contestant's name should appear on a separate line in the file, so you will use the WriteLine method to write each name to the file.

To continue coding the btnWrite control's Click event procedure:

1. Click the blank line below the `' write the name on a separate line in the file` comment and then enter the following statement:

   outFile.WriteLine(txtName.Text)

You should use the **Close method** to close an output sequential access file as soon as you are finished using it. This ensures that the data is saved and it makes the file available for use elsewhere in the application. The syntax to close an output sequential access file is *streamWriterVariableName*.**Close()**. Here again, notice that you use the StreamWriter variable to refer to the file in code.

To continue coding the btnWrite control's Click event procedure:

1. Click the **blank line** below the `' close the file` comment and then enter the following statement:

   outFile.Close()

To make it more convenient for the user to enter the next name, you will clear the current name from the Name box and then send the focus to the box. You can use a text box's **Focus method** to send the focus to the text box. The method's syntax is *textbox*.**Focus()**.

To complete the btnWrite control's Click event procedure:

1. Click the **blank line** below the `' clear the Name box and then set the focus` comment. Enter the following two statements:

   txtName.Text = String.Empty
   txtName.Focus()

Figure 22-5 shows the code entered in the Write to File button's Click event procedure.

```vb
Private Sub btnWrite_Click(ByVal sender As Object,
ByVal e As System.EventArgs) Handles btnWrite.Click
    ' writes a name to a sequential access file

    ' declare a StreamWriter variable
    Dim outFile As IO.StreamWriter

    ' open the file for append
    outFile = IO.File.AppendText("contestants.txt")

    ' write the name on a separate line in the file
    outFile.WriteLine(txtName.Text)

    ' close the file
    outFile.Close()

    ' clear the Name box and then set the focus
    txtName.Text = String.Empty
    txtName.Focus()

End Sub
```

Figure 22-5   Write to File button's Click event procedure

To test the btnWrite control's Click event procedure:

1. Save the solution and then start the application. Type **Hannah Jones** in the Name box and then click the **Write to File** button. Use the application to write the following four names to the file:

   Clark Smith
   Khalid Shaw
   Joe Mendez
   Charise Jackson

2. Click the **Exit** button.

3. Now you will open the contestants.txt file to verify its contents. Click **File** on the menu bar and then click **Open File**. Open the project's bin\Debug folder. Click **contestants.txt** in the list of filenames and then click the **Open** button. The contestants.txt window opens and shows the five names contained in the file. See Figure 22-6.

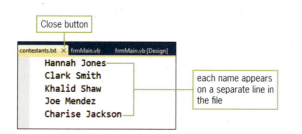

Figure 22-6   Names contained in the contestants.txt file

4. Close the contestants.txt window by clicking its **Close** button.

Mini-Quiz 22-1

See Appendix B for the answers.

1. Write the code to declare a variable that can be used to write data to a sequential access file. Name the variable `outFile`.

2. The AppendText method creates a _____ object.

3. Write a Visual Basic statement that sends the focus to the txtCity control.

Now Read Those Lines of Text

Next, you will code the Read from File button. In Visual Basic, you use a **StreamReader object** to read data from a sequential access file. Before creating the StreamReader object, you first declare a variable to store the object in the computer's internal memory. Figure 22-7 shows the syntax and an example of declaring a StreamReader variable. As mentioned earlier, the IO in the syntax stands for Input/Output.

Declaring a StreamReader variable

Syntax
{**Dim** | **Private**} *streamReaderVariableName* **As IO.StreamReader**

Example
```
Dim inFile As IO.StreamReader
```
declares a StreamReader variable named `inFile`

Figure 22-7   Syntax and an example of declaring a StreamReader variable

To begin coding the Read from File button's Click event procedure:

1. Locate the code template for the btnRead control's Click event procedure.

2. Click the **blank line** below the `' declare variables` comment and then enter the following declaration statement:

   Dim inFile As IO.StreamReader

After declaring a StreamReader variable, you can use the **OpenText method** to open a sequential access file for input; doing this automatically creates a StreamReader object. When a file is opened for input, the computer can read the lines of text stored in the file. Figure 22-8 shows the OpenText method's syntax along with an example of using the method. The *fileName* argument in the example does not include a folder path, so the computer will search for the report.txt file in the current project's bin\Debug folder. If the computer finds the file, it opens the file for input; otherwise, a run time error occurs and causes the application to end abruptly. You assign the StreamReader object created by the OpenText method to a StreamReader variable, which you use to refer to the file in code.

Creating a StreamReader object

Syntax
IO.File.OpenText(fileName**)**

Example
`inFile = IO.File.OpenText("report.txt")`
opens the report.txt file for input; creates a StreamReader object and assigns it to the `inFile` variable

---

Figure 22-8 Syntax and an example of creating a StreamReader object by opening a file

You can use the Exists method to avoid the run time error that occurs when the computer cannot locate the file you want opened for input. Figure 22-9 shows the method's syntax and includes an example of using the method. If the *fileName* argument does not include a folder path, the computer searches for the file in the current project's bin\Debug folder. The **Exists method** returns the Boolean value True if the file exists; otherwise, it returns the Boolean value False.

Determining whether a sequential access file exists

Syntax
IO.File.Exists(fileName**)**

Example
`If IO.File.Exists("report.txt") = True Then`
determines whether the report.txt file exists in the current project's bin\Debug folder; you also can write the If clause as `If IO.File.Exists("report.txt") Then`

Figure 22-9 Syntax and an example of the Exists method

To continue coding the btnRead control's Click event procedure:

1. Click the **blank line** below the `' determine whether the file exists` comment and then enter the following If clause:

   If IO.File.Exists("contestants.txt") = True Then

2. If the file exists, you will use the OpenText method to open the file. Enter the following comment and assignment statement. Press **Enter** twice after typing the assignment statement.

   ' open the file for input
   inFile = IO.File.OpenText("contestants.txt")

3. If the file does not exist, you will display an appropriate message. Enter the additional lines of code shown in Figure 22-10.

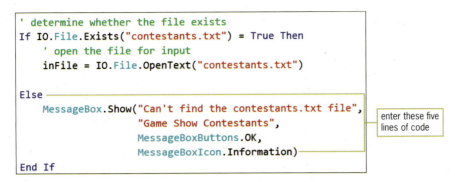

```
' determine whether the file exists
If IO.File.Exists("contestants.txt") = True Then
    ' open the file for input
    inFile = IO.File.OpenText("contestants.txt")

Else
    MessageBox.Show("Can't find the contestants.txt file",
                    "Game Show Contestants",
                    MessageBoxButtons.OK,
                    MessageBoxIcon.Information)
End If
```

enter these five lines of code

Figure 22-10   Code entered in the selection structure's false path

After opening a file for input, you can use the **ReadLine method** to read the file's contents, one line at a time. A **line** is defined as a sequence (stream) of characters followed by the newline character. The ReadLine method returns a string that contains only the sequence of characters in the current line; the string does not include the newline character at the end of the line. In most cases, you assign the string returned by the ReadLine method to a String variable. Figure 22-11 shows the ReadLine method's syntax and includes an example of using the method. The ReadLine method does not require you to provide the file's name, because it uses the file associated with the StreamReader variable.

ReadLine method

Syntax
streamReaderVariableName.**ReadLine**

Example
`strMessage = inFile.ReadLine`
reads a line of text from the sequential access file associated with the `inFile` variable and assigns the line, excluding the newline character, to the `strMessage` variable

---

Figure 22-11   Syntax and an example of the ReadLine method

In most cases, an application will need to read each line of text contained in a sequential access file, one line at a time. You can do this using a loop along with the Peek method. The **Peek method** "peeks" into the file to determine whether the file contains another character to read. If the file contains another character, the Peek method returns the character; otherwise, it returns the number −1 (a negative 1). The Peek method's syntax is shown in Figure 22-12 along with an example of using the method. The Do clause in the example tells the computer to process the loop instructions until the Peek method returns the number −1, which indicates that there are no more characters to read. In other words, the Do clause tells the computer to process the loop instructions until it reaches the end of the file.

Peek method

Syntax
streamReaderVariableName.**Peek**

Example
```
Do Until inFile.Peek = -1
    strLineOfText = inFile.ReadLine
    MessageBox.Show(strLineOfText)
Loop
```
reads each line of text from the sequential access file associated with the `inFile` variable, line by line; each line (excluding the newline character) is assigned to the `strLineOfText` variable and is then displayed in a message box

---

Figure 22-12   Syntax and an example of the Peek method

To continue coding the btnRead control's Click event procedure:

1. First, you will declare a variable to store the string returned by the ReadLine method. Click the **blank line** below the Dim statement. Each line in the contestants.txt file represents a name, so you will call the variable `strName`. Enter the following declaration statement:

   Dim strName As String

2. Click the **blank line** below the statement that opens the contestants.txt file for input. Enter the following comment and Do clause, being sure to type the minus sign before the number 1:

   ' process the loop instructions until the end of the file
   Do Until inFile.Peek = -1

3. Now you will tell the computer to read a line of text and assign it (excluding the newline character) to the `strName` variable. Enter the following comment and assignment statement:

   ' read a name
   strName = inFile.ReadLine

4. Next, you will display the name in the Contestants box. Enter the following comment and assignment statement:

   ' display the name
   txtContestants.Text = txtContestants.Text &
        strName & ControlChars.NewLine

5. If necessary, delete the blank line above the Loop clause.

Just as you do with an output sequential access file, you should use the Close method to close an input sequential access file as soon as you are finished using it. Doing this makes the file available for use elsewhere in the application. The syntax to close an input sequential access file is *streamReaderVariableName*.**Close()**. Notice that you use the StreamReader variable to refer to the file in code.

To finish coding the btnRead control's Click event procedure:

1. Click **after the letter p** in the Loop clause and then press **Enter** to insert a blank line.

2. Enter the following comment and statement:

   ' close the file
   inFile.Close()

Figure 22-13 shows the code entered in the Read from File button's Click event procedure.

```
Private Sub btnRead_Click(ByVal sender As Object,
ByVal e As System.EventArgs) Handles btnRead.Click
    ' reads names from a sequential access file
    ' and displays them in the interface

    ' declare variables
    Dim inFile As IO.StreamReader
    Dim strName As String

    ' clear previous names from the Contestants box
    txtContestants.Text = String.Empty

    ' determine whether the file exists
    If IO.File.Exists("contestants.txt") = True Then
        ' open the file for input
        inFile = IO.File.OpenText("contestants.txt")
        ' process the loop instructions until the end of the file
        Do Until inFile.Peek = -1
            ' read a name
            strName = inFile.ReadLine
            ' display the name
            txtContestants.Text = txtContestants.Text &
                strName & ControlChars.NewLine
        Loop
        ' close the file
        inFile.Close()

    Else
        MessageBox.Show("Can't find the contestants.txt file",
                    "Game Show Contestants",
                    MessageBoxButtons.OK,
                    MessageBoxIcon.Information)
    End If
End Sub
```

Figure 22-13   Read from File button's Click event procedure

To test the btnRead control's Click event procedure:

1. Save the solution and then start the application. Click the **Read from File** button. The five names contained in the contestants.txt file appear in the Contestants box, as shown in Figure 22-14.

Figure 22-14 Contents of the contestants.txt file listed in the Contestants box

2. On your own, add the following two names to the file:

Ginger Ozark
James Kartony

3. Click the **Read from File** button to display the seven names in the interface, and then click the **Exit** button.

To learn more about sequential access files, see the Sequential Access Files section in the Ch22WantMore.pdf file.

4. Next, you will modify the If clause in the btnRead control's Click event procedure. More specifically, you will change the Exists method's fileName argument from contestants.txt to Chap22\contestants.txt. Doing this will allow you to test the code entered in the selection structure's false path. Change `contestants.txt` in the If clause to **Chap22\contestants.txt**.

5. Save the solution and then start the application. Click the **Read from File** button. Because the contestants.txt file does not exist in the Chap22 folder, the Exists method in the If clause returns the Boolean value False. As a result, the instruction in the selection structure's false path is processed. The instruction displays the "Can't find the contestants.txt file" message in a message box. Close the message box and then click the **Exit** button.

To learn how to handle exceptions that occur when using sequential access files, view the Ch22-TryCatch video.

6. Change `Chap22\contestants.txt` in the If clause to **contestants.txt**. Save the solution and then start the application. Click the **Read from File** button to display the contents of the contestants.txt file in the Contestants box.

7. Click the **Exit** button. Close the Code Editor window and then close the solution.

Mini-Quiz 22-2

See Appendix B for the answers.

1. Write the code to declare a variable that can be used to read data from a sequential access file. Name the variable `inFile`.

2. The OpenText method creates a _____ object.

3. The string returned by the ReadLine method contains the newline character.

   a. True   b. False

Summary

- An application can write data to a sequential access file. It also can read data from the file. The data in a sequential access file is always accessed in consecutive order (sequentially) from the beginning of the file through the end of the file.

- You use a StreamWriter object to write a sequence (stream) of characters to a sequential access file. The StreamWriter object is created when you open a file for either output or append. You use a StreamReader object to read a sequence (stream) of characters from a sequential access file. The StreamReader object is created when you open a file for input.

- You can use either the Write method or the WriteLine method to write data to a sequential access file. You use the ReadLine method to read a line of text from a sequential access file. The ReadLine method returns a string that includes only the characters on the current line; it does not include the newline character at the end of the line.

- You should use the Close method to close a sequential access file as soon as you are finished using the file.

- You can use a text box's Focus method to send the focus to the text box.

- The Exists method returns a Boolean value that indicates whether a sequential access file exists.

- If a file contains another character to read, the Peek method returns the character; otherwise, it returns the number −1.

Key Terms

AppendText method—used with a StreamWriter variable to open a sequential access file for append

Close method—used with either a StreamWriter variable or a StreamReader variable to close a sequential access file

CreateText method—used with a StreamWriter variable to open a sequential access file for output

Exists method—used to determine whether a file exists

Focus method—moves the focus to a specified control during run time

Input files—files from which an application reads data

Line—a sequence (stream) of characters followed by the newline character

OpenText method—used with a StreamReader variable to open a sequential access file for input

Output files—files to which an application writes data

Peek method—used with a StreamReader variable to determine whether a file contains another character to read

ReadLine method—used with a StreamReader variable to read a line of text from a sequential access file

Sequential access files—files composed of lines of text that are both read and written sequentially; also called text files

Stream of characters—a sequence of characters

StreamReader object—used to read a sequence (stream) of characters from a sequential access file

StreamWriter object—used to write a sequence (stream) of characters to a sequential access file

Text files—another name for sequential access files

Write method—used with a StreamWriter variable to write data to a sequential access file; differs from the WriteLine method in that it does not write a newline character after the data

WriteLine method—used with a StreamWriter variable to write data to a sequential access file; differs from the Write method in that it writes a newline character after the data

Review Questions

1. Which of the following opens the cities.txt file and allows the computer to write new data to the end of the file's existing data?

    a. `outFile = IO.File.AddText("cities.txt")`

    b. `outFile = IO.File.AppendText("cities.txt")`

    c. `outFile = IO.File.InsertText("cities.txt")`

    d. `outFile = IO.File.OpenText("cities.txt")`

2. If the file to be opened exists, the _____ method erases the file's contents.

    a. AppendText   c. InsertText

    b. CreateText   d. OpenText

3. Which of the following reads a line of text from a sequential access file and assigns the line (excluding the newline character) to the `strLine` variable?

    a. `inFile.Read(strLine)`   c. `strLine = inFile.ReadLine`

    b. `inFile.ReadLine(strLine)`   d. `strLine = inFile.Read(line)`

4. What does the Peek method return when the end of the file is reached?

    a. −1   c. the last character in the file

    b. 0   d. the newline character

5. Which of the following can be used to determine whether the pay.txt file exists?

    a. `If IO.File.Exists("pay.txt") = True Then`

    b. `If IO.File("pay.txt").Exists = True Then`

    c. `If IO.Exists("pay.txt") = True Then`

    d. `If IO.Exists.File("pay.txt") = True Then`

6. Which of the following closes an input sequential access file named states.txt? The file is associated with a StreamReader variable named `inFile`.

    a. `StreamReader(inFile).Close()`   c. `inFile.Close()`

    b. `StreamReader.Close(inFile)`   d. `Close(inFile)`

7. Which of the following writes the contents of the `strFirst` and `strLast` variables on separate lines in the names.txt file? The file is associated with a StreamWriter object named `outFile`.

   a. `StreamWriter.WriteLine(strFirst)`
      `StreamWriter.Write(strLast)`

   b. `outFile.WriteLine(strFirst)`
      `outFile.WriteLine(strLast)`

   c. `outFile.Write(strFirst)`
      `outFile.Write(strLast)`

   d. `outFile("names.txt").WriteLine(strFirst)`
      `outFile("names.txt").WriteLine(strLast)`

Exercises

1. Open the Gross Pay Solution (Gross Pay Solution.sln) file contained in the ClearlyVB2010\Chap22\Gross Pay Solution folder. If necessary, open the designer window. The interface provides a text box for entering a gross pay amount. The Save button should write the gross pay amount to a sequential access file named gross.txt. Save the file in the project's bin\Debug folder. The Display button should read the gross pay amounts from the gross.txt file and display each (formatted with a dollar sign and two decimal places) in the interface. Open the Code Editor window. Code the Click event procedures for the btnSave and btnDisplay controls. Save the solution and then start the application. Write the following 10 gross pay amounts to the file: 600, 1250, 750.67, 350.75, 2000, 450, 125.89, 560, 1400, and 555.78. Click the Display button to display the gross pay amounts in the interface. Close the Code Editor window and then close the solution. (See Appendix B for the answer.) **TRY THIS**

2. Open the Name Solution (Name Solution.sln) file contained in the ClearlyVB2010\Chap22\Name Solution folder. If necessary, open the designer window. Open the names.txt file contained in the project's bin\Debug folder. The sequential access file contains five names. Close the names.txt window. The Display button's Click event procedure should read the five names contained in the names.txt file, storing each in a five-element one-dimensional array. The procedure should sort the array in ascending order and then display the contents of the array in the lblFriends control. Code the procedure. Save the solution and then start and test the application. Close the Code Editor window and then close the solution. If you need to recreate the names.txt file, open the file in a window in the IDE. Delete the contents of the file and then type the following five names, pressing Enter after typing each name: Jennifer, Zelda, Abby, Bruce, and Karen. (See Appendix B for the answer.) **TRY THIS**

3. Open the Salary Solution (Salary Solution.sln) file contained in the ClearlyVB2010\Chap22\Salary Solution folder. If necessary, open the designer window. Open the Code Editor window and study the existing code. The btnDisplay control's Click event procedure stores six salary amounts in a one-dimensional Integer array named `intSalaries`. Each salary amount corresponds to a salary code from 1 through 6. Code 1's salary is stored in the `intSalaries(0)` element in the array, code 2's salary is stored in the `intSalaries(1)` element, and so on. After storing the salary amounts in the array, the procedure prompts the user to enter a salary code. It then displays the amount associated with the code. Currently, the Dim statement assigns the six salary amounts to the array. Modify the procedure so that it reads the salary amounts from the salary.txt file and stores each in the array. The salary.txt file is contained in the project's bin\Debug folder. Save the solution and then start and test the application. Close the Code Editor window and then close the solution. **MODIFY THIS**

INTRODUCTORY   4. Open the CD Solution (CD Solution.sln) file contained in the ClearlyVB2010\Chap22\ CD Solution-Introductory folder. The interface provides a text box for entering the name of a CD. The Save CD button's Click event procedure should write the CD name to a sequential access file named cds.txt. Save the file in the project's bin\Debug folder. The Display CDs button's Click event procedure should read the CD names from the cds.txt file and display each in the interface. Open the Code Editor window and code both procedures. Save the solution and then start and test the application. Close the Code Editor window and then close the solution.

INTRODUCTORY   5. Open the Test Scores Solution (Test Scores Solution.sln) file contained in the ClearlyVB2010\Chap22\Test Scores Solution folder. Open the Code Editor window. The btnSave control's Click event procedure should allow the user to enter an unknown number of test scores, saving each score in a sequential access file. The btnCount control's Click event procedure should display (in a message box) the number of scores stored in the file. Code both procedures. Save the solution and then start and test the application. Close the Code Editor window and then close the solution.

INTERMEDIATE   6. Open the CD Solution (CD Solution.sln) file contained in the ClearlyVB2010\Chap22\ CD Solution-Intermediate folder. The interface allows the user to enter the name of a CD and the name of the artist associated with the CD. The Save Information button's Click event procedure should write the CD and artist names to a sequential access file named cdInfo.txt. Save the file in the project's bin\Debug folder. The CD and artist names should be written on separate lines in the file. In other words, the first CD name should be written on the first line in the file, and the first artist name should be written on the second line in the file. The Display Information button's Click event procedure should read the names from the cdInfo.txt file and display each in the interface. Display the CD names in the txtCds control. Display the artist names in the txtArtists control. Open the Code Editor window and code both procedures. Save the solution and then start and test the application. Close the Code Editor window and then close the solution.

INTERMEDIATE   7. In this exercise, you code an application that reads five numbers from a sequential access file and stores the numbers in a one-dimensional array. The application then increases each number by 1 and writes the numbers to the file. The application also displays the current contents of the sequential access file. Open the Numbers Solution (Numbers Solution.sln) file contained in the ClearlyVB2010\Chap22\Numbers Solution folder. Open the Code Editor window. Code the btnDisplay control's Click event procedure so it reads the five numbers stored in the numbers.txt file and displays the numbers in the lblNumbers control. The numbers.txt file is contained in the project's bin\Debug folder. Currently, the file contains the numbers 1 through 5. Code the btnUpdate control's Click event procedure so it reads the five numbers from the numbers.txt file and stores the numbers in an array. It then should increase each number in the array by 1 and write the array contents to an empty numbers.txt file. Save the solution and then start the application. Click the Display button. The numbers 1 through 5 appear in the interface. Click the Update button and then click the Display button. The numbers 2 through 6 appear in the interface. Close the Code Editor window and then close the solution. If you need to recreate the numbers.txt file, open the file in a window in the IDE. Delete the contents of the file and then type the numbers 1 through 5, pressing Enter after typing each number.

ADVANCED   8. During July and August of each year, the Political Awareness Organization (PAO) sends a questionnaire to the voters in its district. The questionnaire asks each voter for his or her political party (Democratic, Republican, or Independent) and age. From the returned questionnaires, the organization's secretary tabulates the number of Democrats, Republicans, and Independents in the district. The secretary wants an application that she can use to save each respondent's information (political party and age) to a sequential access file. The application also should calculate and display the number of voters in each political party. Create a new Visual Basic Windows application. Use the following names for the solution and project, respectively: PAO Solution and PAO Project. Save the application in the ClearlyVB2010\Chap22 folder. Change the name of the form file on your disk to frmMain.vb. If necessary, change the form's name to frmMain. Create the interface shown in Figure 22-15. The Party text box should accept only the Backspace key and the letters D, d, R, r, I, or i. The Age text box should accept only numbers and the Backspace key. Code the Click event procedures for the Write to File and Display Totals buttons. Save the solution and then start and test the application. Close the Code Editor window and then close the solution.

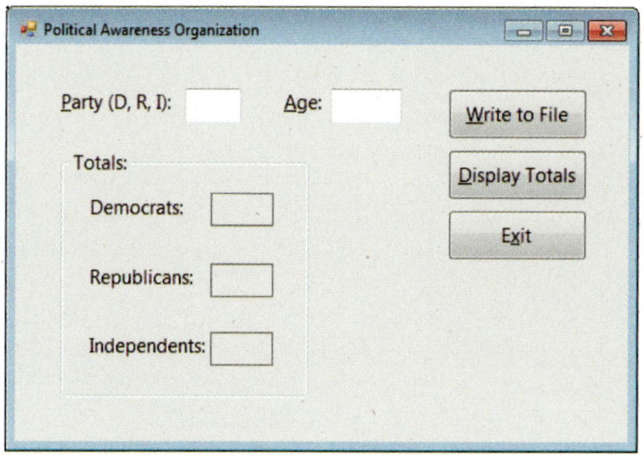

Figure 22-15   Interface for Exercise 8

9. Open the FigureThisOut Solution (FigureThisOut Solution.sln) file contained in the ClearlyVB2010\Chap22\FigureThisOut Solution folder. Open the Code Editor window and study the existing code. Why does the true path in the btnWrite control's Click event procedure use the CreateText method to open the sequential access file, while its false path uses the AppendText method? Start and test the application. Close the Code Editor window and then close the solution.

    FIGURE THIS OUT

10. Open the SwatTheBugs Solution (SwatTheBugs Solution.sln) file contained in the ClearlyVB2010\Chap22\SwatTheBugs Solution folder. Open the Code Editor window and study the existing code. Start the application. Test the application using Sue and 1000, and then using Pete and 5000. After a short time, the application ends with an error. Read the error message. Click Debug on the menu bar and then click Stop Debugging. Open the bonus.txt file. Notice that the file is empty. Close the bonus.txt window. Locate and correct the errors in the code. Save the solution and then start and test the application again. Close the Code Editor window and then close the solution.

    SWAT THE BUGS

The String Section (String Manipulation)

After studying Chapter 23, you should be able to:

- ◎ Determine the number of characters in a string
- ◎ Remove spaces from the beginning and end of a string
- ◎ Replace characters in a string
- ◎ Insert characters in a string
- ◎ Search a string
- ◎ Access characters in a string
- ◎ Remove characters located anywhere in a string
- ◎ Compare strings using pattern-matching

Working with Strings

Many times, an application will need to manipulate (process) string data in some way. For example, it may need to look at the first character in an inventory part number to determine the part's location in the warehouse. Or, it may need to search an address to determine the street name. In this chapter, you will learn several ways of manipulating strings in Visual Basic. You will begin by learning how to determine the number of characters in a string.

How Many Characters Are There?

If an application expects the user to enter a seven-digit phone number or a five-digit ZIP code, you should verify that the user entered the required number of characters. The number of characters contained in a string is stored in the string's **Length property**. Not surprisingly, the value stored in the property is an integer. Figure 23-1 shows the syntax of the Length property and includes examples of using the property. In the syntax, *string* can be a String variable, a String named constant, or the Text property of a control.

Length property

Syntax
string.**Length**

Purpose
stores an integer that represents the number of characters contained in the string

Example 1
```
strFullName = "Lee Thompson"
intNumChars = strFullName.Length
```
assigns the number 12 to the `intNumChars` variable

Example 2
```
intNumChars = txtZip.Text.Length
```
assigns the number of characters in the txtZip control's Text property to the `intNumChars` variable

Example 3
```
Do
        strZip = InputBox("5-digit ZIP code", "ZIP")
Loop Until strZip.Length = 5
```
continues prompting the user for a ZIP code until the user enters exactly five characters

---

Figure 23-1   Syntax and examples of the Length property

Get Rid of Those Spaces

When entering data in either a text box or an input box, it's not unusual for a user to inadvertently press the Spacebar either before or after typing the data. You can use the **Trim method** to remove (trim) these extraneous space characters. Figure 23-2 shows the method's syntax and includes an example of using the method. In the syntax, *string* can be a String variable, a String named constant, or the Text property of a control. When processing the Trim method, the computer first makes a temporary copy of the *string* in memory. It then performs the necessary trimming on the copy only. In other words, the Trim method does not remove any characters from the original *string*. The Trim method returns a string that excludes any leading or trailing spaces. (You learned about the Trim method in Chapter 11.)

Trim method

<u>Syntax</u>   <u>Purpose</u>
string.**Trim**   removes any spaces from both the beginning and end of a string

<u>Example</u>
strFullName = txtName.Text.Trim
assigns the contents of the txtName control's Text property, excluding any leading and trailing spaces, to the strFullName variable

---

Figure 23-2   Syntax and an example of the Trim method

You will use both the Length property and the Trim method in the Product ID application, which you code in the next section.

The Product ID Application

The Product ID application displays (in a label control) a listing of the product IDs entered by the user. Each product ID must contain exactly five characters.

To code and then test the Product ID application:

1. Start Visual Studio 2010 or Visual Basic 2010 Express and permanently display the Solution Explorer window. Open the **Product Solution (Product Solution.sln)** file contained in the ClearlyVB2010\Chap23\Product Solution folder. If the designer window is not open, double-click **frmMain.vb** in the Solution Explorer window. The interface provides a text box for entering the product ID.

2. Open the Code Editor window and locate the btnAdd control's Click event procedure. Before verifying the product ID's length, you will remove any leading and trailing spaces from the ID. Click the **blank line** below the ' remove any leading and trailing spaces comment and then enter the following assignment statement:

   strId = txtId.Text.Trim

3. Now you will determine whether the ID contains exactly five characters. Click the **blank line** below the ' verify length comment and then enter the following If clause:

   If strId.Length = 5 Then

4. If the ID contains exactly five characters, the selection structure's true path should display the ID in the lblListing control. Enter the following assignment statement:

   lblListing.Text = lblListing.Text &
   strId.ToUpper & ControlChars.NewLine

5. If the ID does not contain exactly five characters, the selection structure's false path should display an appropriate message. Enter the additional four lines of code indicated in Figure 23-3.

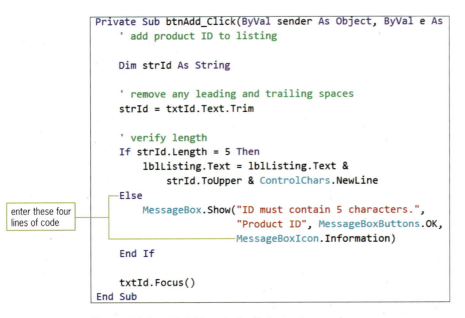

```
Private Sub btnAdd_Click(ByVal sender As Object, ByVal e As
    ' add product ID to listing

    Dim strId As String

    ' remove any leading and trailing spaces
    strId = txtId.Text.Trim

    ' verify length
    If strId.Length = 5 Then
        lblListing.Text = lblListing.Text &
            strId.ToUpper & ControlChars.NewLine
    Else
        MessageBox.Show("ID must contain 5 characters.",
                        "Product ID", MessageBoxButtons.OK,
                        MessageBoxIcon.Information)
    End If

    txtId.Focus()
End Sub
```

enter these four lines of code

Figure 23-3   btnAdd control's Click event procedure

6. Save the solution and then start the application. First, you will enter an ID that contains four characters. Type **abc2** as the product ID and then click the **Add to List** button. A message box opens and displays the "ID must contain 5 characters." message. Close the message box.

7. Now you will include two trailing spaces after the ID. Change the product ID to **abc23** and then press the **Spacebar** twice. Click the **Add to List** button. ABC23 appears in the listing of product IDs.

8. On your own, test the application using an ID that contains nine characters. Also test it using an ID that contains both leading and trailing spaces.

9. When you are finished testing the application, click the **Exit** button. Close the Code Editor window and then close the solution.

Let's Make a Substitution

Visual Basic provides the **Replace method** for replacing a sequence of characters in a string with another sequence of characters, such as replacing area code "(800)" with area code "(877)" in a phone number. Figure 23-4 shows the syntax of the Replace method and includes examples of using the method. In the syntax, *string* can be a String variable, a String named constant, or the Text property of a control. The *oldValue* argument is the sequence of characters that you want to replace in the *string*, and the *newValue* argument contains the replacement characters. When processing the Replace method, the computer makes a temporary copy of the *string* in memory and then replaces the characters in the copy only. The Replace method returns a string with *all* occurrences of oldValue replaced with newValue.

Replace method

Syntax   Purpose
string.**Replace(***oldValue*, *newValue***)**   replaces every occurrence of *oldValue* with *newValue*

Example 1
```
strPhone = "(800) 111-2222"
strPhone = strPhone.Replace("(800)", "(877)")
```
changes the contents of the `strPhone` variable to (877) 111-2222

Example 2
```
strWord = "latter"
strWord = strWord.Replace("t", "d")
```
changes the contents of the `strWord` variable to ladder

Figure 23-4   Syntax and examples of the Replace method

I Need to Fit This in Somewhere

Rather than replacing characters in a string, an application may need to insert characters in a string. You insert characters using the **Insert method**. Possible uses for the method include inserting an employee's middle initial within his or her name and inserting parentheses around the area code in a phone number. Figure 23-5 shows the Insert method's syntax along with examples of using the method. In the syntax, *string* can be a String variable, a String named constant, or the Text property of a control.

When processing the Insert method, the computer makes a temporary copy of the *string* in memory. It then performs the specified insertion on the copy only. In other words, the method does not affect the original *string*. The *startIndex* argument in the Insert method is an integer that specifies where in the string's copy you want the *value* inserted. The integer represents the character's index—in other words, its position in the string. The first character in a string has an index of 0; the second character has an index of 1, and so on. To insert the value beginning with the first character in the string, you use a startIndex of 0, as shown in Example 1 in Figure 23-5. To insert the value beginning with the fifth character in the string, you use a startIndex of 4, as shown in Example 2. The Insert method returns a string with the appropriate characters inserted.

Insert method

Syntax   Purpose
string.**Insert(***startIndex*, *value***)** inserts characters anywhere in a string

Example 1
```
strPhone   = "111-2222"
txtPhone.Text = strPhone.Insert(0, "(877) ")
```
changes the contents of the txtPhone control's Text property to (877) 111-2222

Example 2
```
strName   = "Rob Smith"
strFullName = strName.Insert(4, "T. ")
```
changes the contents of the `strFullName` variable to Rob T. Smith

Figure 23-5   Syntax and examples of the Insert method

You will use the Replace and Insert methods in the Phone Numbers application, which you code in the next section.

The Phone Numbers Application

The Phone Numbers application saves (in a sequential access file) the phone numbers entered by the user. Each phone number is entered using 12 characters in the following format: 111-222-3333. Before writing a phone number to the file, the application removes the hyphens and then verifies that the phone number contains 10 characters (the original 12 characters minus the two hyphens). The application also displays the phone numbers contained in the file, both with and without the hyphens.

To begin coding the Phone Numbers application:

1. Open the **Phone Solution** (**Phone Solution.sln**) file contained in the ClearlyVB2010\ Chap23\Phone Solution folder. If the designer window is not open, double-click **frmMain.vb** in the Solution Explorer window. The interface provides a text box for entering a phone number.

2. Open the Code Editor window and locate the txtPhone control's KeyPress event procedure. Notice that the text box will accept only numbers, the hyphen, and the Backspace key.

3. Locate the btnSave control's Click event procedure. Before saving the phone number to the sequential access file, the procedure will replace the hyphens with the empty string. Click the **blank line** below the ' remove the hyphens comment and then enter the following assignment statement:

    strPhone = txtPhone.Text.Replace("-", String.Empty)

4. Save the solution and then start the application. First, you will enter an invalid phone number. Type **111-2222** as the phone number and then click the **Save** button. A message box opens and displays the "Invalid phone number" message. Close the message box.

5. Next, you will enter two valid phone numbers. Type **111-222-3333** as the phone number and then click the **Save** button. Now type **222-333-4444** as the phone number and then click the **Save** button.

6. Click the **Display** button. The button's Click event procedure reads each phone number from the phoneNumbers.txt file and displays each in the lblFileContents control. See Figure 23-6. Notice that the phone numbers do not contain any hyphens.

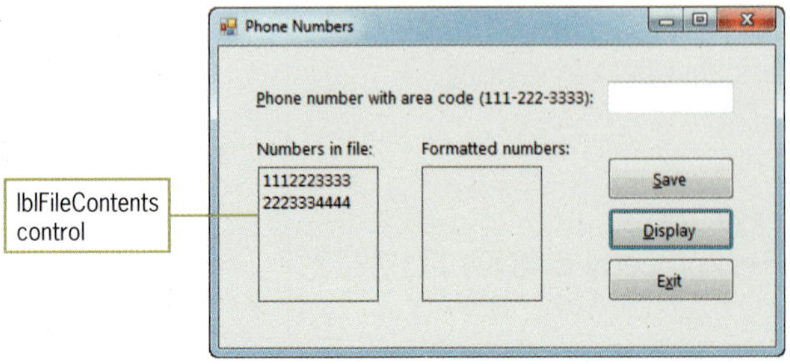

Figure 23-6   Contents of the file displayed in the lblFileContents control

7. Click the **Exit** button.

In addition to displaying the phone numbers contained in the phoneNumbers.txt file, the Display button also should insert the appropriate hyphens in each number and then display the formatted number in the lblFormattedNumbers control. You can insert the hyphens using the Insert methods shown in Figure 23-7.

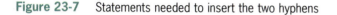

Original phone number: 1112223333

> insert the first hyphen in position 3

strPhone = strPhone.Insert("-", 3)   111-2223333
strPhone = strPhone.Insert("-", 7)   111-222-3333

> insert the second hyphen in position 7

Figure 23-7   Statements needed to insert the two hyphens

To finish coding the Phone Numbers application:

1. Locate the btnDisplay control's Click event procedure. Click the **blank line** below the `' display the phone number with hyphens` comment.

2. Enter the following lines of code:

   strPhone = strPhone.Insert(3, "-")
   strPhone = strPhone.Insert(7, "-")
   lblFormattedNumbers.Text =
       lblFormattedNumbers.Text &
       strPhone & ControlChars.NewLine

Figure 23-8 shows the code entered in the Click event procedures for the btnSave and btnDisplay controls.

```
Private Sub btnSave_Click(ByVal sender As Object,
ByVal e As System.EventArgs) Handles btnSave.Click
    ' saves the phone number to a sequential access file

    ' declare variables
    Dim strPhone As String
    Dim outFile As IO.StreamWriter

    ' remove the hyphens
    strPhone = txtPhone.Text.Replace("-", String.Empty)      Replace method

    ' verify the length
    If strPhone.Length = 10 Then
        outFile = IO.File.AppendText("phoneNumbers.txt")
        outFile.WriteLine(strPhone)
        outFile.Close()
    Else
        MessageBox.Show("Invalid phone number",
                        "Phone Numbers",
                        MessageBoxButtons.OK,
                        MessageBoxIcon.Information)
    End If
```

Figure 23-8   Click event procedures for the btnSave and btnDisplay controls *(continues)*

(continued)

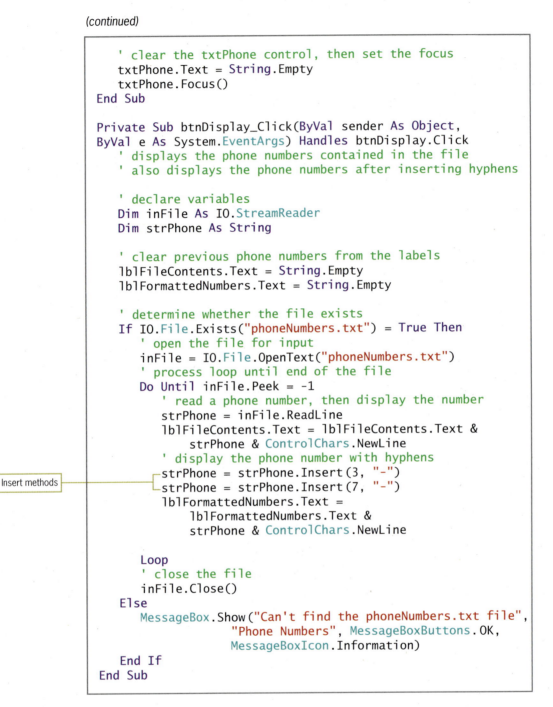

```
        ' clear the txtPhone control, then set the focus
        txtPhone.Text = String.Empty
        txtPhone.Focus()
    End Sub

    Private Sub btnDisplay_Click(ByVal sender As Object,
    ByVal e As System.EventArgs) Handles btnDisplay.Click
        ' displays the phone numbers contained in the file
        ' also displays the phone numbers after inserting hyphens

        ' declare variables
        Dim inFile As IO.StreamReader
        Dim strPhone As String

        ' clear previous phone numbers from the labels
        lblFileContents.Text = String.Empty
        lblFormattedNumbers.Text = String.Empty

        ' determine whether the file exists
        If IO.File.Exists("phoneNumbers.txt") = True Then
            ' open the file for input
            inFile = IO.File.OpenText("phoneNumbers.txt")
            ' process loop until end of the file
            Do Until inFile.Peek = -1
                ' read a phone number, then display the number
                strPhone = inFile.ReadLine
                lblFileContents.Text = lblFileContents.Text &
                    strPhone & ControlChars.NewLine
                ' display the phone number with hyphens
                strPhone = strPhone.Insert(3, "-")
                strPhone = strPhone.Insert(7, "-")
                lblFormattedNumbers.Text =
                    lblFormattedNumbers.Text &
                    strPhone & ControlChars.NewLine

            Loop
            ' close the file
            inFile.Close()
        Else
            MessageBox.Show("Can't find the phoneNumbers.txt file",
                    "Phone Numbers", MessageBoxButtons.OK,
                    MessageBoxIcon.Information)
        End If
    End Sub
```

Insert methods

Figure 23-8   Click event procedures for the btnSave and btnDisplay controls

To test the Phone Numbers application:

1. Save the solution and then start the application. Click the **Display** button. The button's Click event procedure displays the numbers both with and without hyphens. See Figure 23-9.

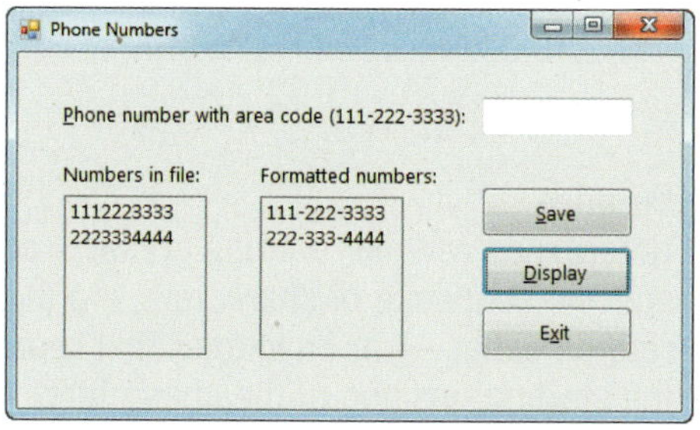

Figure 23-9 Numbers displayed both with and without hyphens

2. Click the **Exit** button. Close the Code Editor window and then close the solution.

Mini-Quiz 23-1

See Appendix B for the answers.

1. Write the Visual Basic statement to remove the leading and trailing spaces from the txtAddress control.

2. Write a Visual Basic statement that uses the Insert method to change the contents of the `strWord` variable from "men" to "women".

3. Write the Visual Basic statement that uses the Replace method to change the contents of the `strWord` variable from "dog" to "frog".

Where Does It Begin?

You can use the **IndexOf method** to search a string to determine whether it contains a specific sequence of characters. Possible uses for the method include determining whether the area code "(312)" appears in a phone number, and whether "Elm Street" appears in an address. Figure 23-10 shows the IndexOf method's syntax. In the syntax, *string* can be a String variable, a String named constant, or the Text property of a control. The *subString* argument represents the sequence of characters for which you are searching, and the optional *startIndex* argument represents the starting position for the search.

The IndexOf method performs a case-sensitive search, which means the case of the subString must match the case of the string in order for both to be considered equal. The IndexOf method returns an integer—either −1 if the subString is not contained in the string, or the character index that represents the starting position of the subString in the string. Unless you specify otherwise, the IndexOf method starts the search with the first character in the string. To specify a different starting location, you use the optional startIndex argument. For instance, to begin the search with the second character in the string, you use a startIndex of 1.

Also included in Figure 23-10 are examples of using the IndexOf method. Notice that two methods appear in the expression in Example 1: ToUpper and IndexOf. When an expression contains more than one method, the computer processes the methods from left to right. In this case, the computer will process the ToUpper method before it processes the IndexOf method.

IndexOf method

Syntax
string.**IndexOf**(*subString*[, *startIndex*])

Purpose
determines whether a string contains a specific sequence of characters and then returns either –1 or an integer that represents the starting position of the characters

Example 1
```
strMsg = "Visual Basic is fun!"
intIndex = strMsg.ToUpper.IndexOf("FUN")
```
character index 16

assigns the number 16 to the `intIndex` variable

Example 2
```
strMsg = "Visual Basic is fun!"
intIndex = strMsg.IndexOf("is", 7)
```
character index 13

assigns the number 13 to the `intIndex` variable

Example 3
```
strMsg = "Visual Basic is fun!"
intIndex = strMsg.IndexOf("S")
```
assigns the number –1 to the `intIndex` variable, because the `strMsg` variable does not contain an uppercase letter S

Figure 23-10 Syntax and examples of the IndexOf method

I Just Want a Part of It

In some applications, it is necessary to access one or more characters contained in a string. For instance, you may need to display only the string's first five characters, which identify an item's location in the warehouse. Visual Basic provides the **Substring method** for accessing any number of characters in a string. Figure 23-11 shows the method's syntax and includes examples of using the method. In the syntax, *string* can be a String variable, a String named constant, or the Text property of a control.

When processing the Substring method, the computer first makes a temporary copy of the *string* in memory. It then accesses the specified number of characters in the copy only. The *startIndex* argument in the syntax is the index of the first character you want to access in the string. As you already know, the first character in a string has an index of 0. The optional *numCharsToAccess* argument specifies the number of characters you want to access. The Substring method returns a string that contains the number of characters specified in the numCharsToAccess argument, beginning with the character whose index is startIndex. If you omit the numCharsToAccess argument, the Substring method returns all characters from the startIndex position through the end of the string.

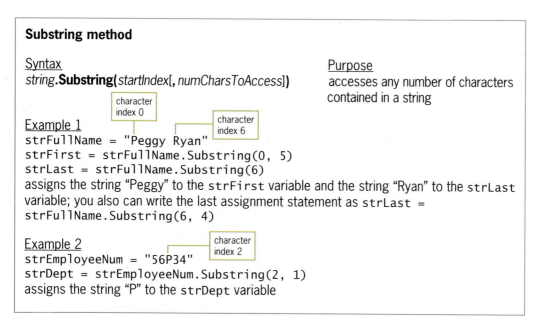

Figure 23-11   Syntax and examples of the Substring method

You will use the IndexOf and Substring methods in the Rearrange Name application, which you code in the next section.

The Rearrange Name Application

The Rearrange Name application's interface provides a text box for entering a person's first name followed by a space and the person's last name. The application rearranges the name so that the last name comes first, followed by a comma, a space, and the first name.

To code the Rearrange Name application:

1. Open the **Rearrange Name Solution** (**Rearrange Name Solution.sln**) file contained in the ClearlyVB2010\Chap23\Rearrange Name Solution folder. If the designer window is not open, double-click **frmMain.vb** in the Solution Explorer window.

2. Open the Code Editor window and locate the btnRearrange control's Click event procedure. The procedure assigns the name entered by the user, excluding any leading and trailing spaces, to the strName variable.

3. Before you can rearrange the name stored in the strName variable, you need to separate the first name from the last name. To do this, you first search for the space character that appears between the names. Click the **blank line** below the ' search for the space in the name comment and then enter the following assignment statement, being sure to include a space character between the quotation marks:

    intIndex = strName.IndexOf(" ")

4. If the value in the intIndex variable is not −1, it means that the IndexOf method found a space character in the strName variable. In that case, the selection structure's true path should continue rearranging the name; otherwise, its false path should display the "Invalid name format" message. Notice that the statement to display the message is already entered in the selection structure's false path. Change the If clause in the procedure to the following:

    If intIndex <> −1 Then

5. Now you will use the value stored in the `intIndex` variable to separate the first name from the last name. Click the **blank line** below the `' separate the first and last names` comment. All of the characters to the left of the space character represent the first name, and all of the characters to the right of the space character represent the last name. Enter the following assignment statements:

   strFirstName = strName.Substring(0, intIndex)
   strLastName = strName.Substring(intIndex + 1)

6. Finally, you will display the rearranged name in the interface. Click the **blank line** above the Else clause and then enter the following line of code, being sure to include a space character after the comma:

   lblRearrangedName.Text =
       strLastName & ", " & strFirstName

Figure 23-12 shows the code entered in the btnRearrange control's Click event procedure.

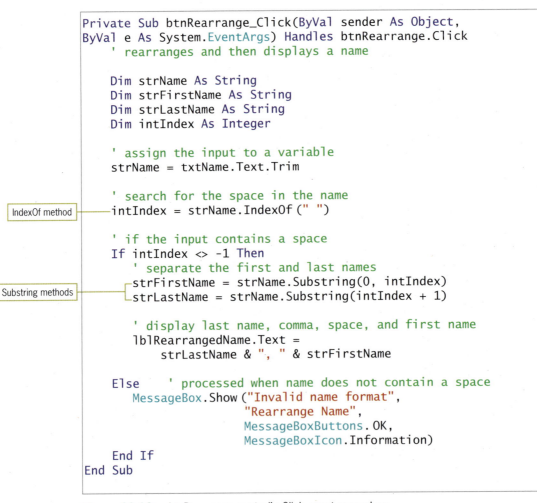

```
Private Sub btnRearrange_Click(ByVal sender As Object,
ByVal e As System.EventArgs) Handles btnRearrange.Click
    ' rearranges and then displays a name

    Dim strName As String
    Dim strFirstName As String
    Dim strLastName As String
    Dim intIndex As Integer

    ' assign the input to a variable
    strName = txtName.Text.Trim

    ' search for the space in the name
    intIndex = strName.IndexOf (" ")          [IndexOf method]

    ' if the input contains a space
    If intIndex <> -1 Then
        ' separate the first and last names
        strFirstName = strName.Substring(0, intIndex)     [Substring methods]
        strLastName = strName.Substring(intIndex + 1)

        ' display last name, comma, space, and first name
        lblRearrangedName.Text =
            strLastName & ", " & strFirstName

    Else      ' processed when name does not contain a space
        MessageBox.Show ("Invalid name format",
                        "Rearrange Name",
                        MessageBoxButtons.OK,
                        MessageBoxIcon.Information)
    End If
End Sub
```

Figure 23-12   btnRearrange control's Click event procedure

To test the Rearrange Name application's code:

1. Save the solution and then start the application. Type **Veronica Chowski** as the name and then click the **Rearrange Name** button. The button's Click event procedure rearranges the name and then displays it in the interface. See Figure 23-13.

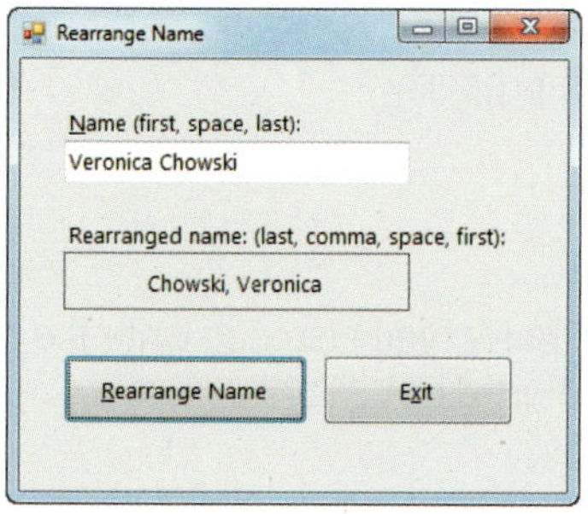

Figure 23-13   Rearranged name shown in the interface

2. Click the **Exit** button. Close the Code Editor window and then close the solution.

Throw Away Those Characters

You can use the **Remove method** to remove a specified number of characters located anywhere in a string. Figure 23-14 shows the method's syntax and includes examples of using the method. In the syntax, *string* can be a String variable, a String named constant, or the Text property of a control. When processing the Remove method, the computer first makes a temporary copy of the *string* in memory. It then performs the specified removal on the copy only. In other words, the Remove method does not remove any characters from the original *string*. The Remove method returns a string with the appropriate characters removed.

The Remove method's *startIndex* argument is the index of the first character you want removed from the string. The optional *numCharsToRemove* argument is the number of characters you want removed. To remove only the first character from a string, you use 0 as the startIndex and 1 as the numCharsToRemove. To remove the fourth through the eighth characters, you use 3 as the startIndex and 5 as the numCharsToRemove. If the numCharsToRemove argument is omitted, the Remove method removes all of the characters from the startIndex position through the end of the string, as shown in Example 2 in Figure 23-14.

Remove method

Syntax
string.**Remove**(*startIndex*[, *numCharsToRemove*])

Purpose
removes characters from anywhere in a string

Example 1
```
strName = "Joanne Cromwell"
txtLast.Text = strName.Remove(0, 7)
```
assigns the string "Cromwell" to the txtLast control's Text property

Example 2
```
strName = "Jerry Helperson"
txtFirst.Text = strName.Remove(5)
```
assigns the string "Jerry" to the txtFirst control's Text property; you also can write the last assignment statement as `txtFirst.Text = strName.Remove(5, 10)`

Example 3
```
strFirst = "John"
strFirst = strFirst.Remove(2, 1)
```
assigns the string "Jon" to the strFirst variable

Figure 23-14 Syntax and examples of the Remove method

You will use the Remove method in the Last Name application, which you code in the next section.

The Last Name Application

The Last Name application's interface provides a text box for entering a person's first name followed by a space and the person's last name. The application displays only the person's last name.

To code the Last Name application:

1. Open the **Last Name Solution** (**Last Name Solution.sln**) file contained in the ClearlyVB2010\Chap23\Last Name Solution folder. If the designer window is not open, double-click **frmMain.vb** in the Solution Explorer window.

2. Open the Code Editor window and locate the btnDisplay control's Click event procedure. The procedure assigns the name entered by the user, excluding any leading or trailing spaces, to the strName variable.

3. Before you can display only the last name stored in the strName variable, you need to separate the last name from the first name. To do this, you first search for the space character that appears between the names. Click the **blank line** below the ' search for the space in the name comment and then enter the following assignment statement, being sure to include a space character between the quotation marks:

intIndex = strName.IndexOf(" ")

4. If the value in the `intIndex` variable is −1, it means that the IndexOf method did not find a space character in the `strName` variable. In that case, the selection structure's true path should display the "Invalid name format" message. Notice that the procedure already contains the appropriate code.

5. However, if the value in the `intIndex` variable is not −1, the selection structure's false path should display only the person's last name. The last name begins with the character to the right of the space character. To display only the last name, you simply need to remove the first name and the space character. Click the **blank line** below the ' display the last name comment and then enter the following assignment statement:

lblLast.Text = strName.Remove(0, intIndex)

Figure 23-15 shows the code entered in the btnDisplay control's Click event procedure.

```
Private Sub btnDisplay_Click(ByVal sender As Object,
ByVal e As System.EventArgs) Handles btnDisplay.Click
    ' displays the last name

    Dim strName As String
    Dim intIndex As Integer

    ' assign the input to a variable
    strName = txtName.Text.Trim

    ' search for the space in the name
    intIndex = strName.IndexOf(" ")

    ' determine whether the name contains a space
    If intIndex = -1 Then
        MessageBox.Show("Invalid name format",
                        "Last Name",
                        MessageBoxButtons.OK,
                        MessageBoxIcon.Information)
    Else

            ' display the last name
            lblLast.Text = strName.Remove(0, intIndex)    Remove method
    End If
End Sub
```

Figure 23-15   btnDisplay control's Click event procedure

To test the Last Name application's code:

1. Save the solution and then start the application. Type **Susan Paransky** as the name and then click the **Display Last Name** button. The button's Click event procedure displays the last name in the interface, as shown in Figure 23-16.

Figure 23-16   Last name displayed in the interface

2. Click the **Exit** button. Close the Code Editor window and then close the solution.

Mini-Quiz 23-2

See Appendix B for the answers.

1. If the `strAddress` variable contains the string "34 Elmset Street", what value will the `strAddress.IndexOf("Elm")` method return?

2. If the `strAddress` variable contains the string "34 Elmset Street", what value will the `strAddress.IndexOf("Elm", 4)` method return?

3. The `strPartNum` variable contains the string "ABCD34G". Write the Visual Basic statement that assigns the string "CD34" from the `strPartNum` variable to the `strCode` variable. Use the Substring method.

4. The `strPartNum` variable contains the string "ABCD34G". Write the Visual Basic statement that assigns the string "AB34G" from the `strPartNum` variable to the `strCode` variable. Use the Remove method.

I Like This Operator

The **Like operator** allows you to use pattern-matching characters to determine whether one string is equal to another string. Figure 23-17 shows the Like operator's syntax. In the syntax, *string* can be a String variable, a String named constant, or the Text property of a control. *Pattern* is a String expression containing one or more of the pattern-matching characters listed in the figure. As the figure indicates, the question mark (?) character in a pattern represents one character only, whereas the asterisk (*) character represents zero or more characters. To represent a single digit in a pattern, you use the number sign (#) character. The last two pattern-matching characters listed in Figure 23-17 contain a *characterList*, which is simply a listing of characters. "[A9M]" is a characterList that contains three characters: A, 9, and M. You also can include a range of values in a characterList. You do this using a hyphen to separate the lowest value in the range from the highest value in the range. For example, to include all lowercase letters in a characterList, you use "[a-z]". To include both lowercase and uppercase letters in the characterList, you use "[a-zA-Z]".

The Like operator compares the *string* to the *pattern*; the comparison is case-sensitive. If the string matches the pattern, the Like operator returns the Boolean value True; otherwise, it returns the Boolean value False. Examples of using the Like operator are included in Figure 23-17.

Like operator

Syntax	Purpose
string **Like** *pattern*	uses pattern-matching characters to determine whether one string is equal to another string

Pattern-matching characters	Matches in string
?	any single character
*	zero or more characters
#	any single digit (0 through 9)
[*characterList*]	any single character in the characterList (for example, "[A5T]" matches A, 5, or T, whereas "[a-z]" matches any lowercase letter)
[!*characterList*]	any single character *not* in the characterList (for example, "[!A5T]" matches any character other than A, 5, or T, whereas "[!a-z]" matches any character that is not a lowercase letter)

Example 1
```
If strFirst.ToUpper Like "B?LL" Then
```
The condition evaluates to True when the string stored in the strFirst variable (converted to uppercase) begins with the letter B followed by one character and then the two letters LL; otherwise, it evaluates to False. Examples of strings that would make the condition evaluate to True include "Bill", "Ball", "bell", and "bull". Examples of strings for which the condition would evaluate to False include "BPL", "BLL", and "billy".

Example 2
```
If txtState.Text Like "K*" Then
```
The condition evaluates to True when the value in the txtState control's Text property begins with the letter K followed by zero or more characters; otherwise, it evaluates to False. Examples of strings that would make the condition evaluate to True include "KANSAS", "Ky", and "Kentucky". Examples of strings for which the condition would evaluate to False include "kansas" and "ky".

Example 3
```
Do While strId Like "###*"
```
The condition evaluates to True when the string stored in the strId variable begins with three digits followed by zero or more characters; otherwise, it evaluates to False. Examples of strings that would make the condition evaluate to True include "178" and "983Ab". Examples of strings for which the condition would evaluate to False include "X34" and "34Z5".

Example 4
```
If strFirst.ToUpper Like "T[OI]M" Then
```
The condition evaluates to True when the string stored in the strFirst variable (converted to uppercase) is either "TOM" or "TIM". When the variable does not contain "TOM" or "TIM"— for example, when it contains "TAM" or "Tommy"—the condition evaluates to False.

Example 5
```
If strLetter Like "[a-z]" Then
```
The condition evaluates to True when the string stored in the strLetter variable is one lowercase letter; otherwise, it evaluates to False.

Figure 23-17   Syntax and examples of the Like operator *(continues)*

(continued)

Example 6
```
For intIndex As Integer = 0 to strInput.Length - 1
        strChar = strInput.Substring(intIndex, 1)
        If strChar Like "[!a-zA-Z]" Then
                intNonLetter = intNonLetter + 1
        End If
Next intIndex
```
Compares each character contained in the strInput variable with the lowercase and uppercase letters of the alphabet, and counts the number of characters that are not letters.

Example 7
```
If strInput Like "*.*" Then
```
The condition evaluates to True when a period appears anywhere in the strInput variable; otherwise, it evaluates to False.

Figure 23-17   Syntax and examples of the Like operator

Modifying the Product Id Application

Earlier in this chapter, you coded the Product ID application, which displayed a listing of the product IDs entered by the user. As you may remember, each product ID contained exactly five characters. In the following set of steps, you will modify the application to ensure that the five characters are three letters followed by two numbers.

To modify the Product ID application's code:

1. Use Windows to make a copy of the Product Solution folder. Save the copy in the ClearlyVB2010\Chap23 folder. Rename the copy **Modified Product Solution**.

2. Open the **Product Solution (Product Solution.sln)** file contained in the Modified Product Solution folder. Double-click **frmMain.vb** in the Solution Explorer window to open the designer window.

3. Open the Code Editor window and locate the btnAdd control's Click event procedure. Insert a blank line below the ' remove any leading and trailing spaces comment and then type ' **and then convert to uppercase**.

4. Change the strId = txtId.Text.Trim statement to the following:

    strId = txtId.Text.Trim.ToUpper

5. Replace the ' verify length comment with the following comments:

    ' **verify that the ID contains 3 letters**
    ' **followed by 2 numbers**

6. Change the If clause to the following:

    If strId Like "[A-Z][A-Z][A-Z]##" Then

7. In the assignment statement below the If clause, change strId.ToUpper to **strId**.

8. Finally, in the selection structure's false path, change the message displayed by the MessageBox.Show method to **"Invalid product ID"**.

Figure 23-18 shows the modified Click event procedure. The modified comments and code are shaded in the figure.

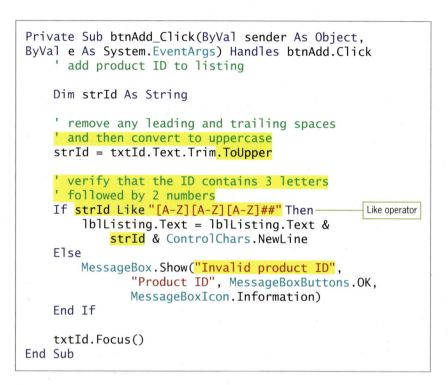

```
Private Sub btnAdd_Click(ByVal sender As Object,
ByVal e As System.EventArgs) Handles btnAdd.Click
    ' add product ID to listing

    Dim strId As String

    ' remove any leading and trailing spaces
    ' and then convert to uppercase
    strId = txtId.Text.Trim.ToUpper

    ' verify that the ID contains 3 letters
    ' followed by 2 numbers
    If strId Like "[A-Z][A-Z][A-Z]##" Then          Like operator
        lblListing.Text = lblListing.Text &
            strId & ControlChars.NewLine
    Else
        MessageBox.Show("Invalid product ID",
            "Product ID", MessageBoxButtons.OK,
            MessageBoxIcon.Information)
    End If

    txtId.Focus()
End Sub
```

Figure 23-18   Click event procedure for the btnAdd control

To test the modified Product ID application:

1. Save the solution and then start the application. First, you will enter an invalid ID. Type **abc2f** as the product ID and then click the **Add to List** button. A message box opens and displays the "Invalid product ID" message. Close the message box.

2. Now you will enter a valid ID. Change the product ID to **abc23** and then click the **Add to List** button. ABC23 appears in the listing of product IDs.

3. On your own, test the application using different valid and invalid IDs.

4. When you are finished testing the application, click the **Exit** button. Close the Code Editor window and then close the solution.

 To review what you learned about string manipulation, view the Ch23-String Manipulation video.

To learn more about other string manipulation techniques, see the String Manipulation Techniques section in the Ch23Want-More.pdf file.

Summary

- A string's Length property stores an integer that represents the number of characters contained in the string.

- Visual Basic provides methods that allow you to manipulate strings. Each method covered in this chapter is listed in the Key Terms section.

- The first character in a string has an index of 0.

Key Terms

IndexOf method—determines whether a string contains a specific sequence of characters; returns either −1 (if the string does not contain the sequence of characters) or an integer that represents the starting position of the characters; its syntax is *string***.IndexOf**(*subString*[, *startIndex*])

Insert method—inserts characters anywhere in a string; its syntax is *string***.Insert**(*startIndex*, *value*)

Length property—stores an integer that represents the number of characters contained in a string; its syntax is *string*.**Length**

Like operator—uses pattern-matching characters to determine whether one string is equal to another string; its syntax is *string* **Like** *pattern*

Remove method—removes characters from anywhere in a string; its syntax is *string*.**Remove**(*startindex*[, *numCharsToRemove*])

Replace method—replaces *all* occurrences of a sequence of characters in a string with another sequence of characters; its syntax is *string*.**Replace**(*oldValue*, *newValue*)

Substring method—accesses any number of characters contained in a string; its syntax is *string*.**Substring**(*startIndex*[, *numCharsToAccess*])

Trim method—removes any spaces from both the beginning and end of a string; its syntax is *string*.**Trim**

Review Questions

1. Which of the following changes the string stored in the `strName` variable from "Mary Smyth" to "Mark Smyth"?

   a. `strName = strName.Change("y", "k")`

   b. `strName = strName.Replace("y", "k")`

   c. `strName = strName.Replace(3, "k")`

   d. none of the above

2. Which of the following expressions evaluates to True when the `strPart` variable contains the string "123X45"?

   a. `strPart Like "999[A-Z]99"`   c. `strPart Like "###[A-Z]##"`

   b. `strPart Like "######"`   d. none of the above

3. Which of the following changes the contents of the `strCityState` variable from "Boise Idaho" to "Boise, Idaho"?

   a. `strCityState = strCityState.Insert(5, ",")`

   b. `strCityState = strCityState.Insert(6, ",")`

   c. `strCityState = strCityState.Insert(7, ",")`

   d. none of the above

4. If the `strMessage` variable contains the string "Today is Monday", which of the following assigns the number 9 to the `intNum` variable?

   a. `intNum = strMessage.Substring("M")`

   b. `intNum = strMessage.Substring("M", 1)`

   c. `intNum = strMessage.IndexOf("M")`

   d. `intNum = strMessage.IndexOf(0, "M")`

5. If the `strName` variable contains the string "John Jones", which of the following changes the contents of the variable to "John K. Jones"?

   a. `strName = strName.Replace(" ", " K. ")`

   b. `strName = strName.Insert(5, "K. ")`

   c. `strName= strName.Insert(4, " K.")`

   d. all of the above

6. Which of the following changes the contents of the `strWord` variable from "Bells" to "Bell"?

   a. `strWord = strWord.Trim(4)`   c. `strWord = strWord.Remove(4)`

   b. `strWord = strWord.Trim(5)`   d. `strWord = strWord.Remove(5, 1)`

7. Which of the following changes the contents of the `strZip` variable from 60521 to 60721?

   a. `strZip = strZip.Insert(2, "7")`   c. `strZip = strZip.Remove(2, 1)`
       `strZip = strZip.Remove(3, 1)`   `strZip = strZip.Insert(2, "7")`

   b. `strZip = strZip.Insert(3, "7")`   d. all of the above
       `strZip = strZip.Remove(2, 1)`

Exercises

1. The `strAmount` variable contains the string "3,123,560". Write the Visual Basic statement to change the contents of the variable to "3123560"; use the Replace method. Now that the `strAmount` variable contains the string "3123560", write the Visual Basic statements to change the variable's contents to "$3,123,560". (See Appendix B for the answer.)

TRY THIS

2. Open the Zip Solution (Zip Solution.sln) file contained in the ClearlyVB2010\Chap23 \Zip Solution folder. If necessary, open the designer window. The Display Shipping Charge button's Click event procedure should display the shipping charge associated with the ZIP code entered by user. To be valid, the ZIP code must contain exactly five digits; the first three digits must be either "605" or "606". The shipping charge for "605" ZIP codes is $25. The shipping charge for "606" ZIP codes is $30. Display an appropriate message if the ZIP code is invalid. Code the procedure. Save the solution and then start the application. Test the application using the following ZIP codes: 60677, 60511, 60344, and 7130. Close the Code Editor window and then close the solution. (See Appendix B for the answer.)

TRY THIS

3. In this exercise, you modify the Phone Numbers application from the chapter. Use Windows to make a copy of the Phone Solution folder. Save the copy in the ClearlyVB2010\Chap23 folder. Rename the copy Modified Phone Solution. Open the Phone Solution (Phone Solution.sln) file contained in the Modified Phone Solution folder. Open the designer and Code Editor windows. The btnSave control's Click event procedure should determine whether the user entered the phone number in the required format: three digits, a hyphen, three digits, a hyphen, and four digits. Display an appropriate message if the format is not correct. Modify the procedure appropriately. Save the solution and then start the application. Test the application using the following phone numbers: 1-234-567890 and 999-888-1111. Close the Code Editor window and then close the solution.

MODIFY THIS

4. Open the CityState Solution (CityState Solution.sln) file contained in the ClearlyVB2010\ Chap23\CityState Solution folder. The interface provides a text box for entering the name of a city, followed by a comma, a space, and a state name. The Display Message button's Click event procedure should display the message "*cityName* is located in *stateName*", where *cityName* and *stateName* are the names of the city and state entered by the user. Code the procedure. Save the solution and then start and test the application. Close the Code Editor window and then close the solution.

INTRODUCTORY

5. Open the First Name Solution (First Name Solution.sln) file contained in the ClearlyVB2010\Chap23\First Name Solution folder. The interface provides a text box for entering a person's last name followed by a comma, a space, and the person's first name. The Display First Name button's Click event procedure should display the

INTRODUCTORY

person's first name only. Code the procedure. Save the solution and then start and test the application. Close the Code Editor window and then close the solution.

INTRODUCTORY

6. The `strAmount` variable contains the string "3,123,560". Write the Visual Basic statements to change the contents of the variable to "3123560"; use the Remove method.

INTERMEDIATE

7. Open the Color Solution (Color Solution.sln) file contained in the ClearlyVB2010\ Chap23\Color Solution folder. The Display Color button's Click event procedure should display the color of the item whose item number is entered by the user. All item numbers contain exactly five characters. All items are available in four colors: blue, green, red, and white. The third character in the item number indicates the item's color, as follows: a B or b indicates Blue, a G or g indicates Green, an R or r indicates Red, and a W or w indicates White. If the item number does not contain exactly five characters, or if the third character is not one of the valid color characters, the procedure should display an appropriate message. Code the procedure. Save the solution and then start the application. Test the application using 12b45 as the item number. The procedure should display the word "Blue" in the lblColor control. Test the application using the following valid item numbers: 99G44, abr55, and 78w99. Now test the application using the following invalid item numbers: 12x and 23abc. Close the Code Editor window and then close the solution.

INTERMEDIATE

8. Open the Proper Case (Proper Case Solution.sln) file contained in the ClearlyVB2010\ Chap23\Proper Case Solution folder. The interface provides a text box for entering a person's first and last names. The Proper Case button's Click event procedure should display the first and last names in the proper case. In other words, the first and last names should begin with an uppercase letter and the remaining letters should be lowercase. Code the procedure. Save the solution and then start and test the application. Close the Code Editor window and then close the solution.

ADVANCED

9. Open the Jacobson Solution (Jacobson Solution.sln) file contained in the ClearlyVB2010\ Chap23\Jacobson Solution folder. The interface provides a text box for entering a password. The text box's CharacterCasing property is set to Upper. The password can contain five, six, or seven characters, but no space characters. The Display New Password button should create and display a new password using the following three rules: First, replace all vowels (A, E, I, O, and U) with the letter X. Second, replace all numbers with the letter Z. Third, reverse the characters in the password. Code the procedure. Save the solution and then start and test the application. Close the Code Editor window and then close the solution.

FIGURE THIS OUT

10. Open the FigureThisOut Solution (FigureThisOut Solution.sln) file contained in the ClearlyVB2010\Chap23\FigureThisOut Solution folder. Open the Code Editor window and study the existing code. Explain the condition in the If clause. Start the application. Test the application using the following valid ID: anyUser@hotmail.com. Now test it using the following invalid IDs: anyUser, j@, and @hotmail.com. Close the Code Editor window and then close the solution.

SWAT THE BUGS

11. Open the SwatTheBugs Solution (SwatTheBugs Solution.sln) file contained in the ClearlyVB2010\Chap23\SwatTheBugs Solution folder. Open the Code Editor window and study the existing code. Start and then test the application, using a sales amount of 100 and rates of 5 and .05. The commission should be $5.00. Notice that the application is not working correctly. Locate and correct the errors in the code. Save the solution and then start and test the application again. Close the Code Editor window and then close the solution.

I'm Suffering from Information Overload (Access Databases)

After studying Chapter 24, you should be able to:

◎ Define basic database terminology

◎ Connect an application to a Microsoft Access database

◎ Bind table and field objects to controls

◎ Customize a DataGridView control

◎ Handle exceptions using the Try...Catch statement

◎ Position the record pointer in a dataset

Keeping Good Records

In order to maintain accurate records, most businesses store information about their employees, customers, and inventory in computer databases. A **computer database** is an electronic file that contains an organized collection of related information. Many products exist for creating computer databases; such products are called database management systems (or DBMS). Some of the most popular database management systems are Microsoft Access, Microsoft SQL Server, and Oracle. You can use Visual Basic to access the data stored in databases created by these database management systems. As a result, companies can use Visual Basic to create a standard interface that allows employees to access information stored in a variety of database formats. Instead of learning each DBMS's user interface, the employee needs to know only one interface. The actual format of the database is unimportant and will be transparent to the user.

In this chapter, you will learn how to access the data stored in Microsoft Access databases. Databases created using Microsoft Access are relational databases. A **relational database** stores information in tables composed of columns and rows, similar to the format used in a spreadsheet. The databases are called relational because the information in the tables can be related in different ways. Each column in a table represents a field and each row represents a record. A **field** is a single item of information about a person, place, or thing—such as a name, a salary amount, a Social Security number, or a price. A **record** is a group of related fields that contain all of the necessary data about a specific person, place, or thing. The college you are attending keeps a student record on you. Examples of fields contained in your student record include your Social Security number, name, address, phone number, credits earned, and grades earned. A group of related records is called a **table**. Each record in a table pertains to the same topic and contains the same type of information. In other words, each record in a table contains the same fields.

A relational database can contain one or more tables. A one-table database would be a good choice for storing information about the college courses you have taken. An example of such a table is shown in Figure 24-1. Each record in the table contains four fields: an ID field that indicates the department name and course number, a course title field, a field listing the number of credit hours, and a grade field. Most tables have a **primary key**, which is a field that uniquely identifies each record. In the table shown in Figure 24-1, you could use either the ID field or the Title field as the primary key, because the data in those fields will be unique for each record.

ID	Title	CreditHours	Grade
CS100	Introduction to Computers	3	A
CS106	Windows Seminar	2	B
CS204	Visual Basic	3	B
EN100	English Composition	3	A
EN104	Speech	2	B

Figure 24-1   Example of a one-table relational database

You might use a two-table database to store information about a CD (compact disc) collection. You would store the general information about each CD (such as the CD's name and the artist's name) in one table and the information about the songs on each CD (such as their title and track number) in the other table. You then would use a common field—for example, a CD number—to relate the records contained in both tables. Figure 24-2 shows an example of a two-table database that stores CD information. The first table is referred to as the **parent table**, and the second table is referred to as the **child table**. The CD_Number field is the primary key in the parent table, because it uniquely identifies each record in the table. The CD_Number field in the child table is used solely to link the song title and track information to the appropriate CD in the parent table. In the child table, the CD_Number field is called the **foreign key**. (Parent and child tables also are referred to as master and detail tables, respectively.)

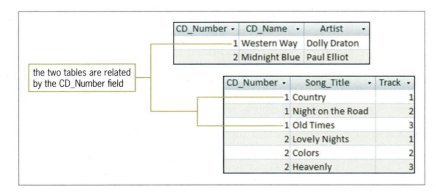

Figure 24-2   Example of a two-table relational database

Storing data in a relational database offers many advantages. The computer can retrieve data stored in a relational format both quickly and easily, and the data can be displayed in any order. The information in the CD database, for example, can be arranged by artist name, song title, and so on. You also can control the amount of information you want to view from a relational database. You can view all of the information in the CD database, only the information pertaining to a certain artist, or only the names of the songs contained on a specific CD.

Connecting...Connecting

Raye Industries stores information about its employees in a Microsoft Access database named Employees. The Employees database is stored in the Employees.accdb file, which is located in the ClearlyVB2010\Chap24\Access Databases folder. The .accdb filename extension stands for Access Database and indicates that the database was created using Microsoft Access. The Employees database contains one table, which is named tblEmploy. The seven fields and 14 records in the table are shown in Figure 24-3. The Emp_Number field is the primary key, because it uniquely identifies each record in the table. The Status field contains the employment status, which is either the letter F (for full-time) or the letter P (for part-time). The Code field identifies the employee's department: 1 for Accounting, 2 for Advertising, 3 for Personnel, and 4 for Inventory.

Emp_Number	Last_Name	First_Name	Hired	Rate	Status	Code
100	Benton	Jack	3/5/2001	$15.00	F	2
101	Jones	Carol	4/2/2001	$15.60	F	2
102	Ismal	Asaad	1/15/2002	$10.00	P	1
103	Rodriguez	Carl	5/6/2002	$12.00	P	3
104	Iovanelli	Rebecca	8/15/2002	$20.00	F	1
105	Nyugen	Thomas	10/20/2002	$11.00	P	3
106	Vine	Martha	2/5/2003	$9.50	P	2
107	Smith	Jefferson	5/14/2003	$17.50	F	2
108	Gerber	Sarah	9/24/2004	$21.00	F	3
109	Jones	Samuel	1/10/2005	$13.50	F	4
110	Smith	John	5/6/2005	$9.00	P	4
111	Krutchen	Jerry	5/7/2006	$9.00	P	4
112	Smithson	Jose	6/27/2009	$14.50	F	1
113	Johnson	Leshawn	7/20/2009	$10.00	P	4

field names

records

Figure 24-3   Data contained in the tblEmploy table

In order to access the data stored in a database, an application needs to be connected to the database. The Data Source Configuration Wizard in Visual Basic provides an easy way to connect an application to a database. The wizard also allows you to specify the data you want to access. The computer makes a copy of the specified data and stores the copy in its internal memory during run time. The copy of the data you want to access is called a **dataset**. In the following set of steps, you will connect the Raye Industries application to the Employees database.

Before completing Version 1 of the Raye Industries application, it may be helpful to view the Ch24-Database 1 video.

To connect the Raye Industries application to the Employees database:

1. Start Visual Studio 2010 or Visual Basic 2010 Express. If necessary, auto-hide the Properties window and permanently display the Solution Explorer window.

2. Open the **Raye Industries Solution** (**Raye Industries Solution.sln**) file contained in the ClearlyVB2010\Chap24\Raye Industries Solution-Version 1 folder. If the designer window is not open, double-click **frmMain.vb** in the Solution Explorer window.

3. If necessary, click **View** on the menu bar and then click either **Server Explorer** (Visual Studio) or **Database Explorer** (Visual Basic Express) to open the Server (Database) Explorer window. The window lists the available data connections.

4. Click **Data** on the menu bar and then click **Show Data Sources** to open the Data Sources window.

5. Click **Add New Data Source** in the Data Sources window to start the Data Source Configuration Wizard. If necessary, click **Database** on the Choose a Data Source Type screen.

6. Click the **Next** button to display the Choose a Database Model screen. If necessary, click **Dataset**.

7. Click the **Next** button to display the Choose Your Data Connection screen. Click the **New Connection** button to open the Add Connection dialog box. If Microsoft Access Database File (OLE DB) does not appear in the Data source box, click the **Change** button to open the Change Data Source dialog box, click **Microsoft Access Database File**, and then click the **OK** button to return to the Add Connection dialog box.

8. Click the **Browse** button in the Add Connection dialog box. Open the ClearlyVB2010\ Chap24\Access Databases folder and then click **Employees.accdb** in the list of filenames. Click the **Open** button. Figure 24-4 shows the completed Add Connection dialog box. (The dialog box in the figure was widened to show the entire entry in the Database file name box. It is not necessary for you to widen the dialog box.)

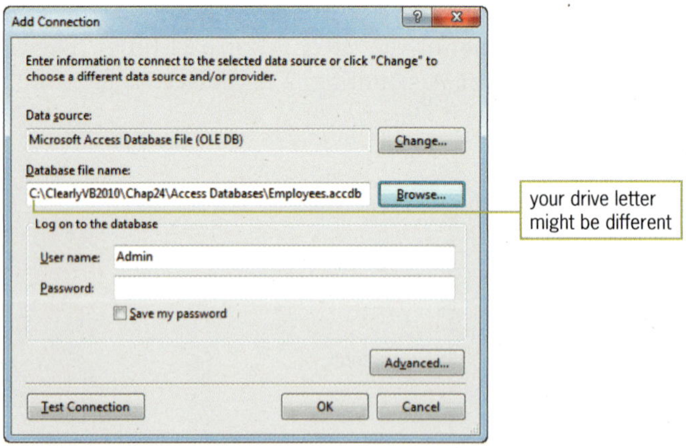

Figure 24-4   Completed Add Connection dialog box

9. Click the **Test Connection** button. The "Test connection succeeded." message appears in a message box. Close the message box.

10. Click the **OK** button to close the Add Connection dialog box. Employees.accdb appears in the Choose Your Data Connection screen. Click the **Next** button. The message box shown in Figure 24-5 opens. The message asks whether you want to include the database file in the current project. By including the file in the current project, you can more easily copy the application and its database to another computer.

Figure 24-5   Message regarding copying the database file

11. Click the **Yes** button to add the Employees.accdb file to the application's project folder. The Save the Connection String to the Application Configuration File screen appears next. The name of the connection string, EmployeesConnectionString, appears on the screen. If necessary, select the **Yes, save the connection as** check box.

12. Click the **Next** button to display the Choose Your Database Objects screen. Expand the Tables node and then expand the tblEmploy node. You use this screen to select the table and/or field objects to include in the dataset, which is automatically named EmployeesDataSet.

13. In this application, you need the dataset to include all of the fields. Click the **empty box** next to tblEmploy. Doing this selects the table and field check boxes, as shown in Figure 24-6.

Data Source Configuration Wizard

Choose Your Database Objects

Which database objects do you want in your dataset?

- ▲ ☑ Tables
    - ▲ ☑ tblEmploy
        - ☑ Emp_Number
        - ☑ Last_Name
        - ☑ First_Name
        - ☑ Hired
        - ☑ Rate
        - ☑ Status
        - ☑ Code
- ☐ Views

DataSet name:

EmployeesDataSet ——————————— `name of the dataset`

< Previous   Next >   Finish   Cancel

Figure 24-6   Objects selected in the Choose Your Database Objects screen

14. Click the **Finish** button. The computer adds the EmployeesDataSet to the Data Sources window. Expand the tblEmploy node in the Data Sources window. The dataset contains one table object and seven field objects.

15. Save the solution. Now you will preview the data contained in the dataset. Right-click **EmployeesDataSet** in the Data Sources window and then click **Preview Data** to open the Preview Data dialog box. Click the **Preview** button. The EmployeesDataSet contains the 14 records (rows) shown earlier in Figure 24-3. Each record is composed of seven fields (columns). Click the **Close** button to close the Preview Data dialog box.

16. Auto-hide the Solution Explorer window. If necessary, auto-hide the Server (Database) Explorer and Data Sources windows.

Let the Computer Do It

For the user to view the contents of a dataset while an application is running, you need to connect one or more objects in the dataset to one or more controls in the interface. Connecting an object to a control is called **binding**, and the connected controls are called **bound controls** (or data-aware controls). You can bind an object to a control that the computer creates for you; or, you can bind it to an existing control in the interface. In this section, you will have the computer create a DataGridView control and then bind the tblEmploy table object to it.

The **DataGridView control** is one of the most popular controls for displaying table data, because it allows you to view a great deal of information at the same time. The control displays the data in a row and column format, similar to a spreadsheet. Each row represents a record, and each column represents a field. The intersection of a row and column in a DataGridView control is called a **cell**. Like the PictureBox control, which you learned about in Chapter 3, the DataGridView control has a task list. The task list is shown in Figure 24-7. The first three check boxes on the task list allow you to specify whether the user can add, edit, or delete records while the application is running. The fourth check box allows you to specify whether the user can reorder the columns in the DataGridView control during run time.

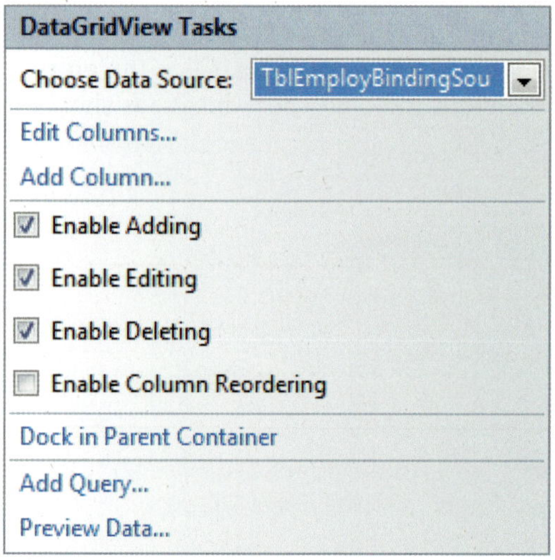

DataGridView Tasks

Choose Data Source: [TblEmployBindingSou ▼]

Edit Columns...
Add Column...
☑ Enable Adding
☑ Enable Editing
☑ Enable Deleting
☐ Enable Column Reordering
Dock in Parent Container
Add Query...
Preview Data...

Figure 24-7 DataGridView control's task list

To have the computer bind the tblEmploy object to a DataGridView control:

1. Temporarily display the Data Sources window and then click **tblEmploy** to select the object. The icon that appears before an object's name in the Data Sources window indicates the type of control the computer will create when you drag the object to the form. The ▦ icon indicates that a DataGridView control will be created when you drag the tblEmploy object to the form. (You can use the list arrow that appears next to an object's name to change the type of control the computer creates.)

2. Drag the tblEmploy object from the Data Sources window to the form and then release the mouse button. The computer adds a DataGridView control to the form and then binds the tblEmploy object to the control. See Figure 24-8.

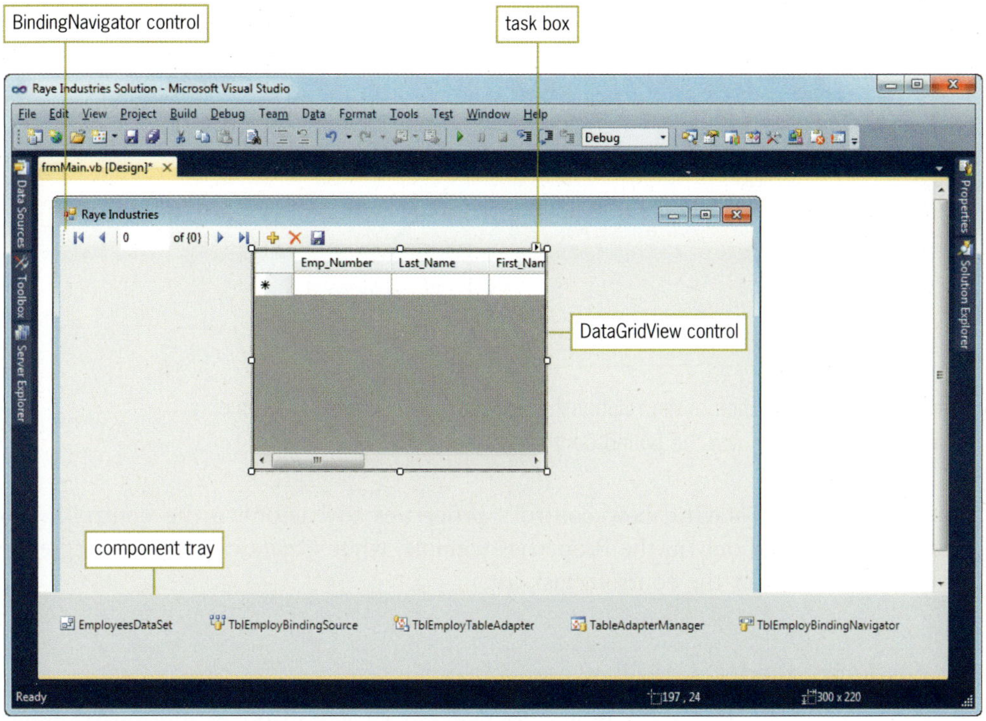

Figure 24-8   Result of dragging the tblEmploy object to the form

As Figure 24-8 shows, besides adding a DataGridView control to the form, the computer also adds a BindingNavigator control. While an application is running, you can use the **BindingNavigator control** to move from one record to the next in the dataset, as well as to add or delete a record and save any changes made to the dataset. The computer also places five objects in the component tray: a DataSet, BindingSource, TableAdapter, TableAdapterManager, and BindingNavigator. The **component tray** stores objects that do not appear in the user interface while an application is running. An exception to this is the BindingNavigator object, which appears as the BindingNavigator control during both design time and run time.

The **TableAdapter object** connects the database to the **DataSet object**, which stores the information you want to access from the database. The TableAdapter is responsible for retrieving the appropriate information from the database and storing it in the DataSet. It also can be used to save to the database any changes made to the data contained in the DataSet. However, in most cases, you will use the **TableAdapterManager object** to save the changes, because it can handle saving data to multiple tables in the DataSet. The **BindingSource object** provides the connection between the DataSet and the bound controls on the form. The TblEmployBindingSource in Figure 24-8 connects the EmployeesDataSet to two bound controls: a DataGridView control and a BindingNavigator control. The TblEmployBindingSource allows the DataGridView control to display the data contained in the EmployeesDataSet. It also allows the BindingNavigator control to access the records stored in the EmployeesDataSet. Figure 24-9 illustrates the relationships among the database, the objects in the component tray, and the bound controls on the form.

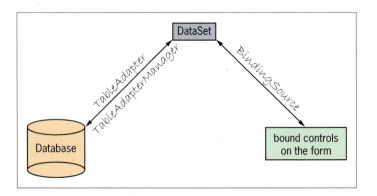

Figure 24-9   Illustration of the relationships among the database, the objects in the component tray, and the bound controls

You can use the DataGridView control's properties to customize the control. Some of the properties are listed only in the Properties window, while others can be set using either the Properties window or the control's task list.

To customize the DataGridView control:

1. Temporarily display the Properties window. Click **AutoSizeColumnsMode** in the Properties list and then set the property to **Fill**. The Fill setting automatically adjusts the column widths so that all of the columns exactly fill the display area of the control.

2. Click the **DataGridView** control and then click its **task box**. A list of tasks associated with the control appears. First, you will have the grid fill the interior of its parent container, which is the form. Click **Dock in Parent Container**.

3. Now you will change the header text for four of the columns. Click **Edit Columns** on the task list to open the Edit Columns dialog box. Emp_Number appears highlighted in the Selected Columns box. Click the **Alphabetical** button (see Figure 24-10) in the dialog box to display the property names in alphabetical order. Click **HeaderText** in the Bound Column Properties list. Type **Employee Number** and then press **Enter**. See Figure 24-10.

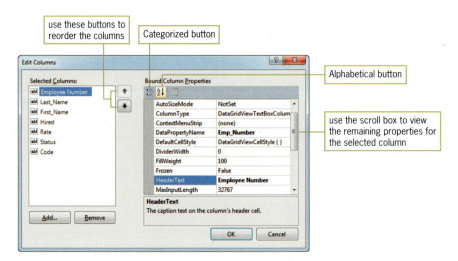

Figure 24-10   Edit Columns dialog box

4. Click **Last_Name** in the Selected Columns list and then change the HeaderText property to **Last Name**. On your own, change the First_Name column's HeaderText property to **First Name**. Also change the Rate column's HeaderText property to **Pay Rate**.

5. Now you will have the DataGridView control format the pay rates to show two decimal places. With Pay Rate selected in the Selected Columns list, click **DefaultCellStyle** in the Bound Column Properties list and then click the **...** (ellipsis) button to open the CellStyle Builder dialog box. Click **Format** in the Behavior section of the dialog box and then click the **...** (ellipsis) button to open the Format String Dialog box. Click **Numeric** in the Format type list and then verify that the number 2 appears in the Decimal places box. Click the **OK** button to close the Format String Dialog box. You are returned to the CellStyle Builder dialog box. The Format property now shows N2, which stands for Numeric format with two decimal places.

6. Next, you will have the DataGridView control align the pay rates in the Pay Rate column. Click **Alignment** in the Layout section of the dialog box and then set the property to **MiddleRight**. See Figure 24-11.

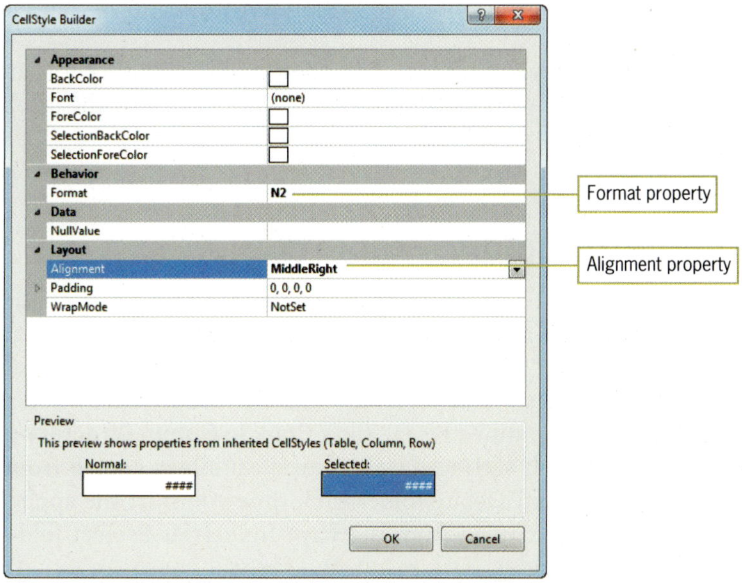

Figure 24-11   Completed CellStyle Builder dialog box

7. Click the **OK** button to close the CellStyle Builder dialog box and then click the **OK** button to close the Edit Columns dialog box.

8. Click the **DataGridView** control to close its task list.

9. Save the solution and then start the application. See Figure 24-12.

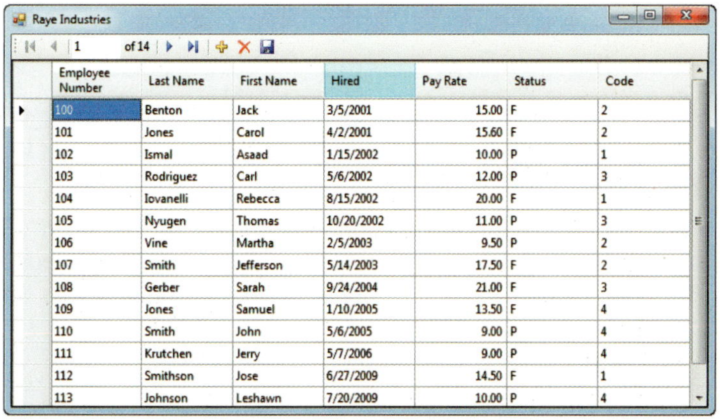

Figure 24-12   Records shown in the customized DataGridView control

10. You can use the arrow keys on your keyboard to move the highlight to a different cell. Press the **down arrow** key on your keyboard twice and then press the **right arrow** key three times.

11. The BindingNavigator control provides buttons for accessing the first, previous, next, and last records in the dataset. Click the **Move first** button ◄| and then click the **Move last** button |►. Click the **Move previous** button ◄ and then click the **Move next** button ►.

12. You also can use the BindingNavigator control to access a record by its record number. The first record in a dataset has a record number of 1; the second record has a record number of 2, and so on. Change the number in the Current position box (which is located to the right of the Move previous button) to **3** and then press **Enter** to move the highlight to the third record.

13. Click the **Close** button on the form's title bar to stop the application.

The BindingNavigator control also provides buttons for adding and deleting records and saving the changes made to the records. The way changes are saved is controlled by the database file's Copy to Output Directory property.

The Copy to Output Directory Property

When the Data Source Configuration Wizard connected the Raye Industries application to the Employees database, it added the database file (Employees.accdb) to the application's project folder. (You can verify this in the Solution Explorer window.) A database file contained in a project is referred to as a local database file. The way Visual Basic saves changes to a local database file is determined by the file's **Copy to Output Directory property**. When the property is set to its default setting, Copy always, the file is copied from the project folder to the project folder's bin\Debug folder each time you start the application. In this case, the Employees.accdb file is copied from the Raye Industries Project folder to the Raye Industries Project\bin\Debug folder. As a result, the file will appear in two different folders in the solution. When you click the Save Data button 🖫 on the BindingNavigator control, any changes made in the DataGridView control are recorded in the file stored in the bin\Debug folder; the file stored in the project folder is not changed. The next time you start the application, the file in the project folder is copied to the bin\Debug folder, overwriting the file that contains the changes. One way to fix this problem is to set the database file's Copy to Output Directory property to "Copy if newer." The "Copy if newer" setting tells the computer to compare the dates on both files to determine which file has the newer (more current) date. If the database file in the project folder has the newer date, the computer should copy it to the bin\Debug folder; otherwise, it shouldn't copy it.

To change the Employees.accdb file's Copy to Output Directory property:

1. Temporarily display the Solution Explorer window. Right-click **Employees.accdb** in the window and then click **Properties**. Change the Employees.accdb file's Copy to Output Directory property to **Copy if newer**.

2. Save the solution and then start the application. Click the **cell** located in Carl Rodriguez's Status field. When a cell is highlighted, you can modify its existing data by simply typing the new data. Type **F** and press **Enter** to change Carl's status to full-time.

3. Click the **Add new** button ✚ on the BindingNavigator control to add a new record to the end of the DataGridView control. Click the **cell** located in the Employee Number field in the new record. Type **999** as the employee number, press **Tab**, and then type **Kral** as the last name. Press **Tab** and then type **George** as the first name. On your own, enter **10/23/2009**, **12**, **F**, and **2** in the Hired, Pay Rate, Status, and Code fields, respectively. Press **Enter** after typing the number 2.

4. Click the **Save Data** button 💾 and then click the **Close** button on the form's title bar.

5. Start the application again. Drag the form's bottom border until all of the records are visible. Notice that the DataGridView control now contains the record you added, as well as the change you made to Carl Rodriguez's Status field. See Figure 24-13.

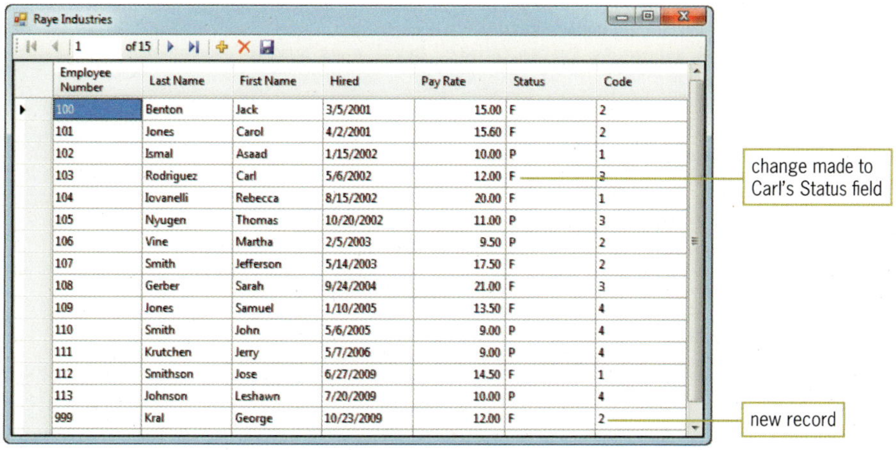

Figure 24-13   Changes to the dataset shown in the DataGridView control

6. Change Carl Rodriguez's Status field from F to **P**. Click the **Move last** button to move the highlight to the last record and then click the **Delete** button ✖ to delete the record. Click the **Save Data** button.

7. Click the **Close** button on the form's title bar. Start the application again to verify that your changes were saved, and then stop the application.

Mini-Quiz 24-1

See Appendix B for the answers.

1. In a table, a _____ is a single item of information about a person, place, or thing.

2. Which object connects a DataSet object to a bound control?

   a. BindingNavigator   c. BindingSource

   b. TableAdapter   d. TableAdapterManager

3. The process of connecting an object in a dataset to a control is called _____.

How Does Visual Basic Do It?

When a table or field object is dragged to the form, the computer adds the appropriate controls and objects to the application. It also enters two event procedures in the Code Editor window.

To view the code automatically entered in the Code Editor window:

1. Open the Code Editor window.

2. Locate the two procedures shown in Figure 24-14. Both procedures were automatically entered when the tblEmploy object was dragged to the form. (In your Code Editor window, the procedure headers and comments will appear on one line.)

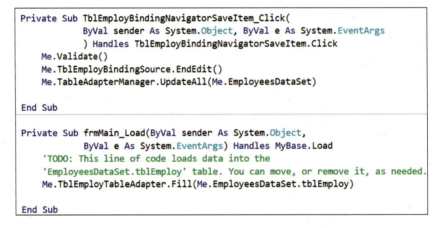

```
Private Sub TblEmployBindingNavigatorSaveItem_Click(
            ByVal sender As System.Object, ByVal e As System.EventArgs
            ) Handles TblEmployBindingNavigatorSaveItem.Click
    Me.Validate()
    Me.TblEmployBindingSource.EndEdit()
    Me.TableAdapterManager.UpdateAll(Me.EmployeesDataSet)

End Sub


Private Sub frmMain_Load(ByVal sender As System.Object,
            ByVal e As System.EventArgs) Handles MyBase.Load
        'TODO: This line of code loads data into the
        'EmployeesDataSet.tblEmploy' table. You can move, or remove it, as needed.
    Me.TblEmployTableAdapter.Fill(Me.EmployeesDataSet.tblEmploy)

End Sub
```

Figure 24-14   Code automatically entered in the Code Editor window

The first event procedure in Figure 24-14, TblEmployBindingNavigatorSaveItem_Click, is processed when you click the Save Data button on the BindingNavigator control. The procedure's code validates the changes made to the data before saving the data to the database. Two methods are involved in the save operation: the BindingSource object's EndEdit method and the TableAdapterManager's UpdateAll method. The EndEdit method applies any pending changes (such as new records, deleted records, or changed records) to the dataset. The UpdateAll method commits the dataset changes to the database. The second event procedure in Figure 24-14 is the form's Load event procedure. A form's **Load event** occurs when the application is started and the form is displayed the first time. Any code in the Load event procedure is processed before the form appears on the screen. The code in this Load event procedure uses the TableAdapter object's Fill method to retrieve the data from the database and store it in the DataSet object. In most applications, the code to fill a dataset belongs in the form's Load event procedure. However, as the comments in the Load event procedure indicate, you can either move or delete the code.

Because it is possible for an error to occur when saving data to a database, it is a good programming practice to add error handling code to the Save Data button's Click event procedure.

Thank You for Catching My Errors

As you learned in Chapter 14, an error that occurs while an application is running is called an exception. If you do not take deliberate steps in your code to handle the exceptions, Visual Basic handles them for you. Typically, it does this by displaying an error message and then abruptly terminating the application. You can prevent your application from behaving in such an unfriendly manner by taking control of the exception handling in your code; you can do this using the **Try...Catch statement**. Figure 24-15 shows the statement's basic syntax and includes examples of using the syntax. The basic syntax contains a Try block and a Catch block. Within the Try block, you place the code that could possibly generate an exception. When an exception occurs in the Try block's code, the computer processes the code contained in the Catch block; it then skips to the code following the End Try clause. A description of the exception that occurred is stored in the Message property of the Catch block's **ex** variable. You can access the description using the code **ex.Message**, as shown in Example 2 in the figure.

Try...Catch Statement

<u>Basic syntax</u>
Try
    one or more statements that might generate an exception
Catch ex As Exception
    one or more statements to execute when an exception occurs
End Try

<u>Example 1</u>
```
Private Sub btnDisplay_Click(ByVal sender As Object,
ByVal e As System.EventArgs) Handles btnDisplay.Click

    Dim inFile As IO.StreamReader
    Dim strLine As String

    Try
        inFile = IO.File.OpenText("names.txt")
        Do Until inFile.Peek = -1
            strLine = inFile.ReadLine
            MessageBox.Show(strLine)
        Loop
        inFile.Close()
    Catch ex As Exception
        MessageBox.Show("File error", "JK's",
            MessageBoxButtons.OK,
            MessageBoxIcon.Information)
    End Try
End Sub
```

<u>Example 2</u>
```
Private Sub TblSalesBindingNavigatorSaveItem_Click(
ByVal sender As System.Object, ByVal e As System.EventArgs
) Handles TblSalesBindingNavigatorSaveItem.Click
    Try
        Me.Validate()
        Me.TblSalesBindingSource.EndEdit()
        Me.TableAdapterManager.UpdateAll(Me.SalesDataSet)
    Catch ex As Exception
        MessageBox.Show(ex.Message, "Sales Data",
            MessageBoxButtons.OK,
            MessageBoxIcon.Information)
    End Try
End Sub
```

Figure 24-15   Syntax and examples of the Try...Catch statement

To include a Try...Catch statement in the Save Data button's Click event procedure:

1. Insert a blank line above the `Me.Validate` statement in the TblEmployBindingNavigatorSaveItem's Click event procedure. Type **Try** and then press **Enter**. The Code Editor automatically enters the `Catch ex As Exception` and `End Try` clauses for you.

2. Select (highlight) the three statements and the blank line that appear below the `End Try` clause. Press **Ctrl+x** to place the selected lines on the Clipboard. Click the **blank line** below the Try clause and then press **Ctrl+v**.

3. If the three statements in the Try block do not produce (throw) an exception, the Try block should display the "Changes saved" message; otherwise, the Catch block should display a description of the exception. Enter the two MessageBox.Show methods shaded in Figure 24-16.

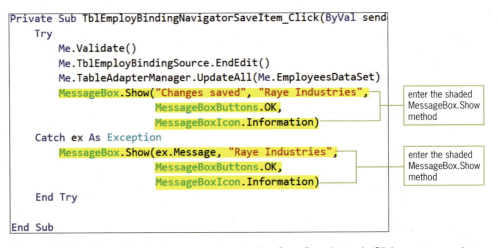

```
Private Sub TblEmployBindingNavigatorSaveItem_Click(ByVal send
    Try
        Me.Validate()
        Me.TblEmployBindingSource.EndEdit()
        Me.TableAdapterManager.UpdateAll(Me.EmployeesDataSet)
        MessageBox.Show("Changes saved", "Raye Industries",
                    MessageBoxButtons.OK,
                    MessageBoxIcon.Information)
    Catch ex As Exception
        MessageBox.Show(ex.Message, "Raye Industries",
                    MessageBoxButtons.OK,
                    MessageBoxIcon.Information)
    End Try

End Sub
```
enter the shaded MessageBox.Show method

enter the shaded MessageBox.Show method

Figure 24-16   Try...Catch statement entered in the Save Data button's Click event procedure

4. Save the solution and then start the application. The statement in the form's Load event procedure (shown earlier in Figure 24-14) retrieves the appropriate data from the Employees database and loads the data into the EmployeesDataSet. The data is displayed in the DataGridView control, which is bound to the tblEmploy table contained in the dataset.

5. Now you will change Jack Benton's Code field to 3. Click the **cell** located in the Code field in the first record. Type **3** and press **Enter**.

6. Click the **Save Data** button on the BindingNavigator control. The "Changes saved" message appears in a message box. Close the message box and then click the **Close** button on the form's title bar.

7. Start the application again. Change Jack Benton's Code field to **2** and then click the **Save Data** button. Close the "Changes saved" message box and then click the **Close** button on the form's title bar.

8. Close the Code Editor window and then close the solution.

I'll Use My Own Controls, Thank You

As mentioned earlier, you can bind an object in a dataset to an existing control on the form. The easiest way to do this is by dragging the object from the Data Sources window to the control. However, you also can click the control and then set one or more properties in the Properties window. The appropriate property (or properties) to set depends on the control you are binding. For example, you use the DataSource property to bind a DataGridView control. However, you use the DataBindings/Text property to bind label and text box controls.

Before completing Version 2 of the Raye Industries application, it may be helpful to view the Ch24-Database 2 video.

To bind objects to existing controls:

1. Open the **Raye Industries Solution** (**Raye Industries Solution.sln**) file contained in the ClearlyVB2010\Chap24\Raye Industries Solution-Version 2 folder. If the designer window is not open, double-click **frmMain.vb** in the Solution Explorer window. For your convenience, the application is already connected to the Employees.accdb database. You can verify the connection in the Server (Database) Explorer window.

2. Permanently display the Data Sources window. If necessary, expand the EmployeesDataSet and tblEmploy nodes. The dataset contains one table object and four field objects.

3. Click **Emp_Number** in the Data Sources window and then drag the field object to the lblNumber control, as shown in Figure 24-17. When you drag an object from the Data Sources window to an existing control, the computer does not create a new control; rather, it merely binds the object to the existing control.

Figure 24-17   Emp_Number field object being dragged to the lblNumber control

4. Release the mouse button. In addition to binding the Emp_Number object to the lblNumber control, the computer also adds the DataSet, BindingSource, TableAdapter, and TableAdapterManager objects to the component tray. It also enters (in the Code Editor window) the Load event procedure shown earlier in Figure 24-14. Recall that the procedure uses the TableAdapter object's Fill method to retrieve the data from the database and store it in the DataSet object. Notice that when you drag an object from the Data Sources window to an existing control, the computer does not add a BindingNavigator object to the component tray, nor does it add a BindingNavigator control to the form. (You can use the BindingNavigator tool in the toolbox to add a BindingNavigator control and object to the application. You then would set the BindingNavigator control's DataSource property to the name of the BindingSource object in the application—in this case, TblEmployBindingSource.)

5. On your own, drag the Last_Name, Status, and Code field objects to the lblLastName, lblStatus, and lblCode controls, respectively.

6. Auto-hide the Data Sources window and then open the Code Editor window. As mentioned earlier, the window contains the Load event procedure shown earlier in Figure 24-14. However, it does not contain the Save Data button's Click event procedure, because the form does not contain a BindingNavigator control.

7. Save the solution and then start the application. Only the first record in the dataset appears in the interface, as shown in Figure 24-18.

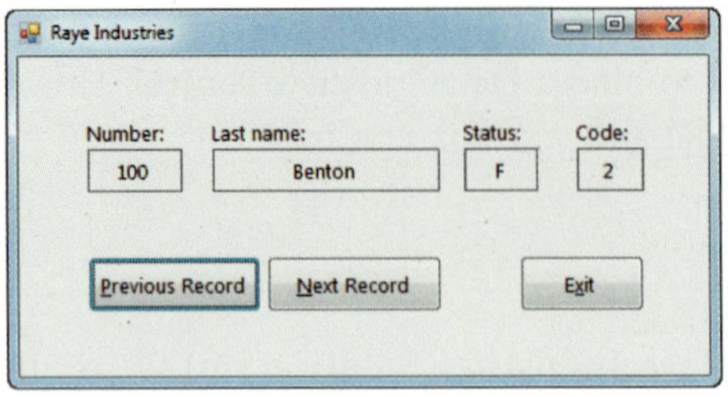

Figure 24-18 Interface showing the first record

8. Because the form does not contain a BindingNavigator control, which would allow you to move from one record to the next, you will need to code the interface's Next Record and Previous Record buttons. Click the **Exit** button.

Coding the Next Record and Previous Record Buttons

The BindingSource object uses an invisible record pointer to keep track of the current record in the dataset. It stores the position of the record pointer in its **Position property**. The first record is in position 0. The second record is in position 1, and so on. Figure 24-19 shows the Position property's syntax and includes examples of using the property. As Examples 2 and 3 indicate, you can use the Position property to move the record pointer to a specific record in the dataset.

BindingSource object's Position property

Syntax
bindingSourceName.**Position**

Example 1
`intRecordNum = TblEmployBindingSource.Position`
assigns the current record's position to the `intRecordNum` variable

Example 2
`TblEmployBindingSource.Position = 4`
moves the record pointer to the fifth record in the dataset

Example 3
`TblEmployBindingSource.Position =`
`      TblEmployBindingSource.Position + 1`
moves the record pointer to the next record in the dataset; you also can write the statement as
`TblEmployBindingSource.Position += 1`

Figure 24-19 Syntax and examples of the BindingSource object's Position property

Rather than using the Position property to position the record pointer in a dataset, you also can use the BindingSource object's Move methods. The **Move methods** move the record pointer to the first, last, next, or previous record in the dataset. Figure 24-20 shows each Move method's syntax and includes examples of using two of the methods.

```
BindingSource object's Move methods

Syntax
bindingSourceName.MoveFirst()
bindingSourceName.MoveLast()
bindingSourceName.MoveNext()
bindingSourceName.MovePrevious()

Example 1
TblEmployBindingSource.MoveFirst()
moves the record pointer to the first record in the dataset

Example 2
TblEmployBindingSource.MoveNext()
moves the record pointer to the next record in the dataset
```

Figure 24-20   Syntax and examples of the BindingSource object's Move methods

To code the Next Record and Previous Record buttons:

1. Open the code template for the btnNext control's Click event procedure. Type the following comment and then press **Enter** twice:

   ' moves the record pointer to the next record

2. Now enter the following line of code:

   TblEmployBindingSource.MoveNext()

3. Open the code template for the btnPrevious control's Click event procedure. Type the following comment and then press **Enter** twice:

   ' moves the record pointer to the previous record

4. Now enter the following line of code:

   TblEmployBindingSource.MovePrevious()

Figure 24-21 shows the Click event procedures for the btnNext and btnPrevious controls. (The procedure headers in your Code Editor window will be on one line.)

```vbnet
Private Sub btnNext_Click(ByVal sender As Object,
          ByVal e As System.EventArgs) Handles btnNext.Click
    ' moves the record pointer to the next record

    TblEmployBindingSource.MoveNext()

End Sub

Private Sub btnPrevious_Click(ByVal sender As Object,
          ByVal e As System.EventArgs) Handles btnPrevious.Click
    ' moves the record pointer to the previous record

    TblEmployBindingSource.MovePrevious()

End Sub
```

Figure 24-21   Click event procedures for the btnNext and btnPrevious controls

To test the Next Record and Previous Record buttons:

1. Save the solution and then start the application. Click the **Next Record** button to display the second record. Continue clicking the **Next Record** button until the last record appears in the interface.

2. Click the **Previous Record** button until the first record appears in the interface.

3. Click the **Exit** button. Close the Code Editor window and then close the solution.

Mini-Quiz 24-2

See Appendix B for the answers.

1. Write the Visual Basic statement to move the record pointer to the first record in the dataset. Use the appropriate Move method of the TblInventoryBindingSource object.

2. A description of the exception that occurred is stored in the Message property of the Catch block's _____ variable.

3. When you drag a field object to an existing control in the interface, Visual Basic replaces the existing control with a new control.

   a. True   b. False

To learn more about connecting an application to a database, see the Database section in the Ch24WantMore.pdf file.

Summary

- Databases created by Microsoft Access are relational databases. A relational database can contain one or more tables. Each table contains fields and records.

- You can display the data in a relational database in any order. You also can control the amount of information you want to view.

- Most tables contain a primary key that uniquely identifies each record.

- To access the data stored in a database, you first connect the application to the database. Doing this creates a dataset that contains objects, such as table objects and field objects.

- You display the information contained in a dataset by binding one or more of the dataset objects to one or more controls in the application's interface.

- The TableAdapter object connects a database to a DataSet object. A BindingSource object connects a DataSet object to the bound controls on a form.

- The DataGridView control displays data in a row and column format, similar to a spreadsheet.

- A database file's Copy to Output Directory property determines when and if the file is copied from the project folder to the project folder's bin\Debug folder each time the application is started.

- In most applications, the statement to fill a dataset is entered in the form's Load event procedure.

- You can use the Try...Catch statement to handle exceptions that occur while an application is running. A description of the exception is stored in the **ex** variable's Message property.

- The BindingSource object uses an invisible record pointer to keep track of the current record in a dataset. The location of the record pointer is stored in the BindingSource object's Position property. You can use the Position property, as well as the BindingSource object's Move methods, to move the record pointer in a dataset.

Key Terms

Binding—the process of connecting an object in a dataset to a control on a form

BindingNavigator control—can be used to move the record pointer from one record to another in a dataset, as well as to add, delete, and save records

BindingSource object—connects a DataSet object to the bound controls on a form

Bound controls—the controls connected to an object in a dataset

Cell—the intersection of a row and column in a DataGridView control

Child table—a table linked to a parent table

Component tray—a special area in the IDE; stores objects that do not appear in the user interface during run time

Computer database—an electronic file that contains an organized collection of related information

Copy to Output Directory property—a property of a database file; determines when and if the file is copied from the project folder to the project folder's bin\Debug folder

DataGridView control—displays table data in a row and column format

Dataset—a copy of the data (database fields and records) that can be accessed by an application

DataSet object—stores the information you want to access from a database

Field—a single item of information about a person, place, or thing

Foreign key—the field used to link a child table to a parent table

Load event—occurs when an application is started and the form is displayed the first time

Move methods—methods of a BindingSource object; used to move the record pointer to the first, last, next, or previous record in a dataset

Parent table—a table linked to a child table

Position property—a property of a BindingSource object; stores the position of the record pointer

Primary key—a field that uniquely identifies each record in a table

Record—a group of related fields that contain all of the necessary data about a specific person, place, or thing

Relational database—a database that stores information in tables composed of columns (fields) and rows (records)

Table—a group of related records

TableAdapter object—connects a database to a DataSet object

TableAdapterManager object—handles saving data to multiple tables in a dataset

Try...Catch statement—used for exception handling in a procedure

Review Questions

1. A group of related fields is called a _____.

   a. database
   b. record
   c. table
   d. none of the above

2. The _____ control contains buttons for moving from one record to another in a dataset.

   a. BindingNavigator
   b. BindingSource
   c. TableAdapter
   d. TableAdapterManager

3. The form's _____ event occurs before the form makes its initial appearance on the screen.

   a. Appearance
   b. Initial
   c. Load
   d. none of the above

4. If the current record is the second record in the dataset, which of the following statements will position the record pointer on the first record?

   a. `TblEmployBindingSource.Position = 0`
   b. `TblEmployBindingSource.Position =`
      `    TblEmployBindingSource.Position - 1`
   c. `TblEmployBindingSource.MoveFirst()`
   d. all of the above

5. If a procedure contains the `Catch ex As Exception` clause, you can use _____ to access the exception's description.

   a. `ex.Description`
   b. `ex.Exception`
   c. `ex.Message`
   d. none of the above

6. Which of the following statements retrieves data from the Friends database and stores it in the FriendsDataSet?

   a. `Me.FriendsDataSet.Fill(Friends.accdb)`
   b. `Me.TblNamesBindingSource.Fill(Me.FriendsDataSet)`
   c. `Me.TblNamesBindingNavigator.Fill(Me.FriendsDataSet.tblNames)`
   d. `Me.TblNamesTableAdapter.Fill(Me.FriendsDataSet.tblNames)`

7. Which of the following is true?

   a. Data stored in a relational database can be retrieved both quickly and easily by the computer.
   b. Data stored in a relational database can be displayed in any order.
   c. A relational database stores data in a column and row format.
   d. all of the above

Exercises

TRY THIS

1. Open the Morgan Solution (Morgan Solution.sln) file contained in the ClearlyVB2010\Chap24\Morgan Solution folder. If necessary, open the designer window. Connect the application to the Employees database. The database is stored in the Employees.accdb file, which is located in the ClearlyVB2010\Chap24\Access Databases folder. After

connecting the application to the database, click tblEmploy in the Data Sources window and then click the down arrow that appears next to tblEmploy. Click Details in the list. Drag the tblEmploy object to the form and then release the mouse button. Click Format on the menu bar, point to Center in Form, and then click Horizontally. Click Format on the menu bar, point to Center in Form, and then click Vertically. Add a Try...Catch statement to the Save Data button's Click event procedure. Change the database file's Copy to Output Directory property to "Copy if newer." Save the solution and then start and test the application. Close the Code Editor window and then close the solution. (See Appendix B for the answer.)

2. In this exercise, you modify one of the Raye Industries applications from the chapter. Use Windows to make a copy of the Raye Industries Solution-Version 2 folder. Save the copy in the ClearlyVB2010\Chap24 folder. Rename the copy Modified Raye Industries Solution-Version 2. Open the Raye Industries Solution (Raye Industries Solution.sln) file contained in the Modified Raye Industries Solution-Version 2 folder. Open the designer window. Modify the Click event procedures for the Previous Record and Next Record buttons to use the Position property rather than a Move method. Save the solution and then start and test the application. Close the Code Editor window and then close the solution.

MODIFY THIS

3. Open the Cartwright Solution (Cartwright Solution.sln) file contained in the ClearlyVB2010\Chap24\Cartwright Solution folder. Connect the application to the Items database. The database is stored in the Items.accdb file, which is contained in the ClearlyVB2010\Chap24\Access Databases folder. The database contains one table named tblItems. The table contains 10 records, each composed of three fields. The ItemNum and ItemName fields contain text; the Price field contains numbers. Display the records in a DataGridView control. Add a Try...Catch statement to the Save Data button's Click event procedure. Change the database file's Copy to Output Directory property appropriately. Save the solution and then start and test the application. Close the Code Editor window and then close the solution.

INTRODUCTORY

4. Sydney Industries records the item number, name, and price of each of its products in a database named Products. The Products database is stored in the Products.accdb file, which is contained in the ClearlyVB2010\Chap24\Access Databases folder. The database contains a table named tblProducts. The table contains 10 records, each composed of three fields. The ItemNum and ItemName fields contain text; the Price field contains numbers. Open the Sydney Solution (Sydney Solution.sln) file contained in the ClearlyVB2010\Chap24\Sydney Solution folder. Connect the application to the Products database. Bind the appropriate objects to the existing label controls. Open the Code Editor window. Code the Click event procedures for the Next Record and Previous Record buttons. Save the solution and then start and test the application. Close the Code Editor window and then close the solution.

INTRODUCTORY

5. Open the Playhouse Solution (Playhouse Solution.sln) file contained in the ClearlyVB2010\Chap24\Playhouse Solution folder. Connect the application to the Play database. The database is contained in the Play.accdb file, which is located in the ClearlyVB2010\Chap24\Access Databases folder. The Play database contains one table named tblReservations. The table contains 20 records. Each record has three fields: a numeric field named Seat and two text fields named Patron and Phone. Drag the field objects to the appropriate label controls in the interface. Code the Click event procedures for the First Record, Last Record, Previous Record, and Next Record buttons. Save the solution and then start and test the application. Close the Code Editor window and then close the solution.

INTERMEDIATE

6. In this exercise, you modify the application from Exercise 5. Use Windows to make a copy of the Playhouse Solution folder. Save the copy in the ClearlyVB2010\Chap24 folder. Rename the copy Modified Playhouse Solution. Open the Playhouse Solution

INTERMEDIATE

(Playhouse Solution.sln) file contained in the Modified Playhouse Solution folder. Open the designer window. Add another button to the interface. Name the button btnRecordNumber. Change the button's Text property to &Record Number. The button's Click event procedure should ask the user for a record number from 1 through 20. It then should move the record pointer to the specified record. Code the procedure. Save the solution and then start and test the application. Close the Code Editor window and then close the solution.

INTERMEDIATE

7. Open the Morgan Industries Solution (Morgan Industries Solution.sln) file contained in the Morgan Industries Solution-ListBox folder. Connect the application to the Employees database. The database is stored in the Employees.accdb file, which is located in the ClearlyVB2010\Chap24\Access Databases folder. Drag the Last_Name, Status, and Code field objects to the appropriate label controls. Set the lstNumber control's DataSource and DisplayMember properties to TblEmployBindingSource and Emp_Number, respectively. Code the Previous Record and Next Record buttons. Save the solution and then start and test the application. Close the solution.

FIGURE THIS OUT

8. Open the FigureThisOut Solution (FigureThisOut Solution.sln) file contained in the ClearlyVB2010\Chap24\FigureThisOut Solution folder. Open the Code Editor window. What tasks are performed by the form's Load event procedure? Start and then test the application. What does the application do? (Hint: Refer to Figure 24-2.) Close the Code Editor window and then close the solution.

SWAT THE BUGS

9. Open the SwatTheBugs Solution (SwatTheBugs Solution.sln) file contained in the ClearlyVB2010\Chap24\SwatTheBugs Solution folder. Open the Code Editor window. Correct the code to remove the jagged line and then save the solution. Start and then test the application. (The dataset contains nine records.) Notice that the application is not working correctly. Locate and correct the errors in the code. Save the solution and then start and test the application again. Close the Code Editor window and then close the solution.

The Missing "LINQ" (Querying a Database)

After studying Chapter 25, you should be able to:

◎ Query a dataset using LINQ

◎ Use the LINQ aggregate operators

Asking Questions

In Chapter 24, you learned how to use the Data Source Configuration Wizard to connect an application to a database, thereby creating a dataset. Recall that a dataset is a copy of the fields and records the application can access from the database. The dataset is stored in the computer's internal memory while the application is running. You also learned how to display the fields and records by binding table and field objects to controls in the interface. In Chapter 24, all of the records were displayed in the order they appeared in the database. In this chapter, you will learn how to display the records in a particular order, as well as how to display only records that meet specific criteria.

The examples in this chapter use the Employees database from Chapter 24. The database, which contains one table named tblEmploy, is shown in Figure 25-1. The table contains seven fields and 14 records. The Emp_Number field is the primary key, because it uniquely identifies each record in the table. The Status field contains the employment status, which is either the letter F (for full-time) or the letter P (for part-time). The Code field identifies the employee's department: 1 for Accounting, 2 for Advertising, 3 for Personnel, and 4 for Inventory.

Emp_Number ▾	Last_Name ▾	First_Name ▾	Hired ▾	Rate ▾	Status ▾	Code ▾
100	Benton	Jack	3/5/2001	$15.00	F	2
101	Jones	Carol	4/2/2001	$15.60	F	2
102	Ismal	Asaad	1/15/2002	$10.00	P	1
103	Rodriguez	Carl	5/6/2002	$12.00	P	3
104	Iovanelli	Rebecca	8/15/2002	$20.00	F	1
105	Nyugen	Thomas	10/20/2002	$11.00	P	3
106	Vine	Martha	2/5/2003	$9.50	P	2
107	Smith	Jefferson	5/14/2003	$17.50	F	2
108	Gerber	Sarah	9/24/2004	$21.00	F	3
109	Jones	Samuel	1/10/2005	$13.50	F	4
110	Smith	John	5/6/2005	$9.00	P	4
111	Krutchen	Jerry	5/7/2006	$9.00	P	4
112	Smithson	Jose	6/27/2009	$14.50	F	1
113	Johnson	Leshawn	7/20/2009	$10.00	P	4

field names ⟶ (points to header row)
records ⟶ (points to data rows)

Figure 25-1   Data contained in the tblEmploy table

You use a **query** to specify both the records to select in a dataset and the order in which to arrange the records. You can create a query in Visual Basic 2010 using a language feature called **Language Integrated Query** or, more simply, **LINQ**. Figure 25-2 shows the basic syntax of LINQ when used to select and arrange records in a dataset. The figure also includes examples of using the syntax. In the syntax, *variableName* and *elementName* can be any names you choose, as long as the name follows the naming rules for variables. In other words, there is nothing special about the `records` and `employee` names used in the examples. The Where and Order By clauses are optional parts of the syntax. You use the **Where clause**, which contains a *condition*, to limit the records you want to view. Similar to the condition in If...Then...Else and Do...Loop statements, the condition in a Where clause specifies a requirement that must be met for a record to be selected. The **Order By clause** is used to arrange (sort) the records in either ascending (the default) or descending order by one or more fields. Notice that the syntax does not require you to specify the data type of the variable in the Dim statement. Instead, the syntax allows the computer to infer the data type from the value being assigned to the variable.

The statement in Example 1 in Figure 25-2 selects all of the records in the dataset and assigns the records to the `records` variable. The statement in Example 2 performs the same task; however, the records are assigned in ascending order by the Code field. If you are sorting records in ascending order, you do not need to include the keyword `Ascending` in the Order By clause, because `Ascending` is the default. The statement in Example 3 assigns only the records for part-time employees to the `records` variable. The statement in Example 4 performs the same task; however, the records are assigned in descending order by the Code field. The statement in Example 5 uses the Like operator and the asterisk pattern-matching character to select only records whose First_Name field begins with the letter J. You learned about the Like operator and its pattern-matching characters in Chapter 23.

Using LINQ to select and arrange records in a dataset

Basic syntax
Dim *variableName* **= From** *elementName* **In** *dataset.table*
      [**Where** *condition*]
      [**Order By** *elementName.fieldName1* [**Ascending** | **Descending**]
         [**,** *elementName.fieldNameN* [**Ascending** | **Descending**]]]
      Select *elementName*

Example 1
```
Dim records = From employee In EmployeesDataSet.tblEmploy
              Select employee
```
selects all of the records in the dataset

Example 2
```
Dim records = From employee In EmployeesDataSet.tblEmploy
              Order By employee.Code
              Select employee
```
selects all of the records in the dataset and arranges them in ascending order by the Code field

Example 3
```
Dim records = From employee In EmployeesDataSet.tblEmploy
              Where employee.Status.ToUpper = "P"
              Select employee
```
selects only the part-time employee records in the dataset

Example 4
```
Dim records = From employee In EmployeesDataSet.tblEmploy
              Where employee.Status.ToUpper = "P"
              Order By employee.Code Descending
              Select employee
```
selects only the part-time employee records in the dataset and arranges them in descending order by the Code field

Example 5
```
Dim records = From employee In EmployeesDataSet.tblEmploy
              Where employee.First_Name.ToUpper Like "J*"
              Select employee
```
selects only the employee records in the dataset whose first name begins with the letter J

Figure 25-2 Basic LINQ syntax and examples for selecting and arranging records in a dataset

Revisiting the Raye Industries Application

You coded two versions of the Raye Industries application in Chapter 24. In this chapter, you will modify the second version of the application. The modified application will display records whose Last_Name field begins with one or more letters entered by the user. It also will both calculate and display the average pay rate.

To begin modifying the Raye Industries application:

1. Start Visual Studio 2010 or Visual Basic 2010 Express. Open the **Raye Industries Solution (Raye Industries Solution.sln)** file contained in the ClearlyVB2010\Chap25\Raye Industries Solution folder. If the designer window is not open, double-click **frmMain.vb** in the Solution Explorer window. The interface was modified to display the First_Name field. It also includes two new buttons: Find Record and Calculate Average. See Figure 25-3.

Figure 25-3   Modified user interface for the Raye Industries application

2. Open the Code Editor window and locate the btnFind control's Click event procedure. First, you will use the InputBox function to prompt the user to either enter one or more letters or leave the input area empty. Click the **blank line** below the `' get user input` comment. Enter the following assignment statement:

   strSearch = InputBox(strPROMPT,
                   "Find Last Name").ToUpper

3. Now you will enter the LINQ statement to select the appropriate records. Click the **blank line** below the `' select the appropriate records` comment and then enter the following LINQ statement:

   Dim records =
       From employee In EmployeesDataSet.tblEmploy
       Where employee.Last_Name.ToUpper Like strSearch & "*"
       Select employee

   Important note: If a jagged line appears below `records` in the LINQ statement, click Tools on the menu bar and then click Options. Expand the Projects and Solutions node and then click VB Defaults. Change Option Strict to Off and (if necessary) change Option Infer to On.

The LINQ statement merely selects the records and assigns them to the `records` variable. To actually view the records, you need to assign the variable's contents to the DataSource property of a BindingSource object. The syntax for doing this is shown in Figure 25-4 along with an example of using the syntax.

Assigning a LINQ variable's contents to a BindingSource object

<u>Basic syntax</u>
bindingSource.**DataSource** = *variableName*.**AsDataView**

<u>Example</u>
```
TblEmployBindingSource.DataSource = records.AsDataView
```
assigns the contents of the `records` variable to the
TblEmployBindingSource object

Figure 25-4   Syntax and an example of assigning a LINQ variable's contents to a BindingSource object

To complete the btnFind control's Click event procedure:

1. Click the **blank line** below the ' display the records comment and then enter the following assignment statement:

   TblEmployBindingSource.DataSource = records.AsDataView

Figure 25-5 shows the code entered in the Find Record button's Click event procedure.

```
Private Sub btnFind_Click(ByVal sender As Object,
ByVal e As System.EventArgs) Handles btnFind.Click
    ' displays records whose last name
    ' begins with the user's entry

    Const strPROMPT As String =
        "Enter one or more characters in the " &
        "last name. " &
        "Leave blank to retrieve all records."
    Dim strSearch As String

    ' get user input
    strSearch = InputBox(strPROMPT,
                        "Find Last Name").ToUpper

    ' select the appropriate records
    Dim records =
        From employee In EmployeesDataSet.tblEmploy
        Where employee.Last_Name.ToUpper Like strSearch & "*"
        Select employee

    ' display the records
    TblEmployBindingSource.DataSource = records.AsDataView

End Sub
```

Figure 25-5   Find Record button's Click event procedure

To test the btnFind control's Click event procedure:

1. Save the solution and then start the application. First, you will select all of the records whose Last_Name field begins with the letter i. Click the **Find Record** button. Type **i** in the Find Last Name dialog box and then press **Enter**. The first record that meets the criterion—the Asaad Ismal record—appears in the interface. Click the **Next Record** button to display Rebecca Iovanelli's record. Click the **Next Record** button again. Notice that Rebecca Iovanelli's record is the last record that meets the criterion.

2. Now you will have the LINQ statement select all of the records. Click the **Find Record** button and then click the **OK** button. Click the **Next Record** button repeatedly to verify that all 14 records have been retrieved.

3. Click the **Exit** button.

Mini-Quiz 25-1

See Appendix B for the answers.

1. Complete the Where clause in the following statement, which should select only records whose LastName field begins with an uppercase letter A:

   ```
   Dim records = From name In NamesDataSet.tblNames
                 Where _____
                 Select name
   ```

2. Complete the following statement, which should arrange the records in descending order by the LastName field:

   ```
   Dim records = From name In NamesDataSet.tblNames

                 _____
                 Select name
   ```

3. What does LINQ stand for?

4. In a LINQ statement, which clause is used to arrange the selected records in a particular order?

   a. Order   c. Sort

   b. Order By   d. Where

5. In a LINQ statement, which clause contains a condition?

   a. Order   c. Sort

   b. Order By   d. Where

One for All

In addition to using LINQ to sort and select the records in a dataset, you also can use it to perform arithmetic calculations on the fields in the records. The calculations are performed using the LINQ aggregate operators. The most commonly used aggregate operators are Average, Count, Max, Min, and Sum. An **aggregate operator** returns a single value from a group of values. The Sum operator, for example, returns the sum of the values in the group, whereas the Min operator returns the smallest value in the group. You include an aggregate operator in a LINQ statement using the syntax shown in Figure 25-6. The figure also includes examples of using the syntax. The statement in Example 1 calculates the average of the values contained in the Rate field, assigning the result to the dblAvgRate variable. The statement in Example 2 first selects only the part-time employee records. It then determines the highest value stored in the Rate field for those records. The statement assigns the result to the dblMaxRate variable. Example 3's statement counts the number of employees in the Advertising department (Code = 2) and assigns the result to the intCounter variable.

LINQ aggregate operators

Syntax
Dim *variableName* [**As** *dataType*] =
                   Aggregate *elementName* **In** *dataset.table*
                   [**Where** *condition*]
                   Select *elementName.fieldName*
                   Into *aggregateOperator*()

Example 1
```
Dim dblAvgRate As Double =
    Aggregate employee In EmployeesDataSet.tblEmploy
    Select employee.Rate Into Average()
```
calculates the average of the pay rates in the dataset and assigns the result to the
dblAvgRate variable

Example 2
```
Dim dblMaxRate As Double =
    Aggregate employee In EmployeesDataSet.tblEmploy
    Where employee.Status.ToUpper = "P"
    Select employee.Rate Into Max()
```
finds the highest pay rate for a part-time employee and assigns the result to the
dblMaxRate variable

Example 3
```
Dim intCounter As Integer =
    Aggregate employee In EmployeesDataSet.tblEmploy
    Where employee.Code = 2
    Select employee.Emp_Number Into Count()
```
counts the number of employees whose department code is 2 and assigns the result to the
intCounter variable

Figure 25-6   Syntax and examples of the LINQ aggregate operators

You will use the Average aggregate operator to code the Calculate Average button's Click event procedure.

To code the Calculate Average button's Click event procedure:

1. Locate the btnCalc control's Click event procedure. First, you will enter the LINQ statement to calculate the average pay rate for all employees. Click the **blank line** below the ' calculate average pay rate comment and then enter the following LINQ statement:

   Dim dblAvgRate As Double =
           Aggregate employee In EmployeesDataSet.tblEmploy
           Select employee.Rate Into Average()

2. Now you will display the average pay rate in a message box. Click the **blank line** below the ' display average pay rate comment and then enter the following lines of code:

   MessageBox.Show("Average pay rate for all employees: " &
                   dblAvgRate.ToString("C2"),
                   "Raye Industries",
                   MessageBoxButtons.OK,
                   MessageBoxIcon.Information)

Figure 25-7 shows the code entered in the Calculate Average button's Click event procedure.

```
Private Sub btnCalc_Click(ByVal sender As Object,
ByVal e As System.EventArgs) Handles btnCalc.Click
    ' displays the average pay rate

    ' calculate average pay rate
    Dim dblAvgRate As Double =
        Aggregate employee In EmployeesDataSet.tblEmploy
        Select employee.Rate Into Average()

    ' display average pay rate
    MessageBox.Show("Average pay rate for all employees: " &
                    dblAvgRate.ToString("C2"),
                    "Raye Industries",
                    MessageBoxButtons.OK,
                    MessageBoxIcon.Information)
End Sub
```

Figure 25-7   Calculate Average button's Click event procedure

To test the Calculate Average button's Click event procedure:

1. Save the solution and then start the application. Click the **Calculate Average** button. The average pay rate for all employees appears in a message box, as shown in Figure 25-8.

Figure 25-8   Average pay rate displayed in a message box

To learn more about LINQ, see the LINQ section in the Ch25WantMore.pdf file.

2. Close the message box and then click the **Exit** button. Close the Code Editor window and then close the solution.

Mini-Quiz 25-2

See Appendix B for the answers.

1. Complete the following statement, which should calculate the sum of the values stored in a numeric field named JanSales:
    ```
    Dim intTotal As Integer =
            Aggregate sales In SalesDataSet.tblSales
            Select _____
            Into Sum()
    ```

2. Complete the following statement, which should calculate the average of the values stored in a numeric field named PointsEarned:
    ```
    Dim dblAvg As Double =
            Aggregate points In PointsDataSet.tblPoints
            _____
            _____
    ```

To review what you learned about LINQ, view the Ch25-LINQ video.

3. Which of the LINQ aggregate operators returns the smallest value in the group?

Summary

- LINQ stands for Language Integrated Query. You can use LINQ to select and sort the records in a dataset. You also can use LINQ to perform calculations on the fields in the dataset.

- LINQ provides the Average, Sum, Count, Min, and Max aggregate operators for performing calculations.

Key Terms

Aggregate operator—an operator that returns a single value from a group of values; LINQ provides the Average, Count, Max, Min, and Sum aggregate operators

Language Integrated Query—LINQ; the query language built into Visual Basic 2010

LINQ—an acronym for Language Integrated Query

Order By clause—used in LINQ to arrange (sort) the records in a dataset

Query—specifies the records to select in a dataset and the order in which to arrange the records

Where clause—used in LINQ to limit the records you want to view in a dataset

Review Questions

1. Which of the following LINQ statements selects all of the records in the tblStates table?

   a. ```
       Dim records =
               From state In StatesDataSet.tblStates
               Select All state
       ```

   b.  ```
       Dim records =
               From state In StatesDataSet.tblStates
               Select state
       ```

   c. ```
       Dim records =
               Select state From StatesDataSet.tblStates
       ```

   d.  ```
       Dim records =
               From StatesDataSet.tblStates
               Select tblStates.state
       ```

2. The tblCities table contains a numeric field named Population. Which of the following LINQ statements selects all cities having a population that exceeds 15000?

   a. ```
       Dim records =
               From city In CitiesDataSet.tblCities
               Where Population > 15000 Select city
       ```

   b.  ```
       Dim records =
               From city In CitiesDataSet.tblCities
               Select city.Population > 15000
       ```

   c. ```
       Dim records =
               From city In CitiesDataSet.tblCities
               Where city.Population > 15000 Select city
       ```

   d.  ```
       Dim records =
               Select city.Population > 15000
               From tblCities
       ```

3. The tblCities table contains a numeric field named Population. Which of the following LINQ statements calculates the total population of all the cities in the table?

   a. `Dim intTotal As Integer =`
```
        Aggregate city In CitiesDataSet.tblCities
        Select city.Population
        Into Sum()
```

   b. `Dim intTotal As Integer =`
```
        Sum city In CitiesDataSet.tblCities
        Select city.Population
        Into total
```

   c. `Dim intTotal As Integer =`
```
        Aggregate CitiesDataSet.tblCities.city
        Select city.Population
        Into Sum()
```

   d. `Dim intTotal As Integer =`
```
        Sum city
        In CitiesDataSet.tblCities.population
```

4. Which clause is used in a LINQ statement to limit the records that will be selected?

   a. Limit   c. Select

   b. Order By   d. Where

5. Which of the following LINQ statements arranges the records in ascending order by the LastName field, with records having the same last name arranged in descending order by the FirstName field?

   a. `Dim records =`
```
        From name In NamesDataSet.tblNames
        Order By name.LastName Ascending,
        name.FirstName Descending
        Select name
```

   b. `Dim records =`
```
        From name In NamesDataSet.tblNames
        Order By name.LastName, name.FirstName Descending
        Select name
```

   c. `Dim records =`
```
        Select name From NamesDataSet.tblNames
        Order By name.FirstName Descending, name.LastName
```

   d. both a and b

6. Which of the following will select only records whose CityName field begins with an uppercase letter S?

   a. `Dim records =`
```
        From name In CitiesDataSet.tblCities
        Where name.CityName Like "S*"
        Select name
```

   b. `Dim records =`
```
        From CitiesDataSet.tblCities
        Select CityName Like "S*"
```

c. ```
Dim records = From tblCities
      Where tblCities.CityName Like "S*"
      Select name
```

d. ```
Dim records =
      From name In CitiesDataSet.tblCities
      Where tblCities.CityName Like "S*"
      Select name
```

7. Which of the following determines the number of records in the tblBooks table?

a. ```
Dim intNum As Integer =
      Aggregate book In BooksDataSet.tblBooks
      Select book.Title In Count()
```

b. ```
Dim intNum As Integer =
      Aggregate book In BooksDataSet.tblBooks
      Select book.Title Into Count()
```

c. ```
Dim intNum As Integer =
      Aggregate book In BooksDataSet.tblBooks
      Select book.Title Into Sum()
```

d. ```
Dim intNum As Integer =
      Aggregate book In BooksDataSet.tblBooks
      Select book.Title Into Number()
```

Exercises

1. Open the Magazine Solution (Magazine Solution.sln) file contained in the ClearlyVB2010\Chap25\Magazine Solution-TRY THIS 1 folder. If necessary, open the designer window. The application is connected to the Magazines database, which is stored in the Magazines.accdb file. The database contains a table named tblMagazine. The table has three fields; the Cost field is numeric, and the Code and MagName fields contain text. Start the application to view the records contained in the dataset. Stop the application and open the Code Editor window. Code the btnSort control's Click event procedure so that it displays the records in descending order by the Cost field. Code the btnDisplayCode control's Click event procedure so that it displays the record whose Code field contains PG24. Code the btnDisplayName control's Click event procedure so that it displays only the Java record. Save the solution and then start and test the application. Close the Code Editor window and then close the solution. (See Appendix B for the answer.)

▶ TRY THIS

2. Open the Magazine Solution (Magazine Solution.sln) file contained in the ClearlyVB2010\Chap25\Magazine Solution-TRY THIS 2 folder. If necessary, open the designer window. The application is connected to the Magazines database, which is stored in the Magazines.accdb file. The database contains a table named tblMagazine. The table has three fields; the Cost field is numeric, and the Code and MagName fields contain text. Start the application to view the records contained in the dataset. Stop the application and open the Code Editor window. Code the btnDisplayCost control's Click event procedure so that it displays records having a cost of at least $4. Code the btnDisplayName control's Click event procedure so that it displays only magazines whose name begins with the letter C (in either uppercase or lowercase). Code the btnAverage control's Click event procedure so that it displays the average cost of a magazine. Display the average in a message box. Save the solution and then start and test the application. Close the Code Editor window and then close the solution. (See Appendix B for the answer.)

▶ TRY THIS

MODIFY THIS ▶ 3. In this exercise, you modify the Raye Industries application from the chapter. Use Windows to make a copy of the Raye Industries Solution folder. Save the copy in the ClearlyVB2010\Chap25 folder. Rename the copy Raye Industries Solution-MODIFY THIS. Open the Raye Industries Solution (Raye Industries Solution.sln) file contained in the Raye Industries Solution-MODIFY THIS folder. Open the designer window. Open the Code Editor window and locate the btnCalc control's Click event procedure. Currently, the procedure displays the average pay rate for all employees. Modify the procedure so it displays three values in the message box: the average pay rate for part-time employees, the average pay rate for full-time employees, and the average pay rate for all employees. Save the solution and then start and test the application. Close the Code Editor window and then close the solution.

INTRODUCTORY ▶ 4. In this exercise, you code a different version of the Raye Industries application from the chapter. Open the Raye Industries Solution (Raye Industries Solution.sln) file contained in the ClearlyVB2010\Chap25\Raye Industries Solution-INTRODUCTORY folder. Open the Code Editor window. Code the btnDisplay control's Click event procedure so that it asks the user for the department code (1, 2, 3, or 4); use the InputBox function. The procedure should display only records matching that department code. If the user enters an invalid department code, display an appropriate message. If the user does not enter a department code, display all the records. Save the solution and then start and test the application. Close the Code Editor window and then close the solution.

INTRODUCTORY ▶ 5. Open the Addison Playhouse Solution (Addison Playhouse Solution.sln) file contained in the ClearlyVB2010\Chap25\Addison Playhouse Solution folder. The application is connected to a Microsoft Access database named Play. The Play database contains one table named tblReservations. The table has 20 records. Each record has three fields: a numeric field named Seat and two text fields named Patron and Phone. Code the btnDisplay control's Click event procedure so that it asks the user for one or more characters in the patron's name; use the InputBox function. The procedure should display only records whose names begin with those characters. If the user does not enter any characters in the InputBox function's input area, the procedure should display all the records. Save the solution and then start and test the application. Close the Code Editor window and then close the solution.

INTERMEDIATE ▶ 6. In this exercise, you modify the Raye Industries application from the chapter. Use Windows to make a copy of the Raye Industries Solution folder. Save the copy in the ClearlyVB2010\Chap25 folder. Rename the copy Raye Industries Solution-INTERMEDIATE. Open the Raye Industries Solution (Raye Industries Solution.sln) file contained in the Raye Industries Solution-INTERMEDIATE folder. Open the designer window. Open the Code Editor window and locate the btnFind control's Click event procedure. Modify the procedure's code so that it displays (in a message box) the number of employees found. Save the solution and then start and test the application. Close the Code Editor window and then close the solution.

ADVANCED ▶ 7. Open the Books Solution (Books Solution.sln) file contained in the Books Solution folder. The application is connected to a Microsoft Access database named Books. The Books database contains one table named tblBooks. The table has 11 records. Each record has five fields. The BookNumber, Price, and QuantityInStock fields contain numbers. The Title and Author fields contain text. The btnCalc control's Click event procedure should display (in a message box) the total value of the books in inventory. The total value is calculated by multiplying the quantity of each book by its price and then adding together the results. Code the procedure. Save the solution and then start and test the application. Close the Code Editor window and then close the solution.

8. In this exercise, you use a Microsoft Access database named Courses. The database is stored in the Courses.accdb file, which is located in the ClearlyVB2010\Chap25\Access Databases folder. The database contains one table named tblCourses. The table has 10 records, each having four fields: ID, Title, CreditHours, and Grade. The CreditHours field is numeric; the other fields contain text. Open the College Courses Solution (College Courses Solution.sln) file contained in the ClearlyVB2010\Chap25\College Courses Solution folder. Connect the application to the Courses database. Drag the table into the group box control and then dock the DataGridView control in its parent container. (In this case, the parent container is the group box control.) Use the DataGridView control's task list to disable Adding, Editing, and Deleting. Change the DataGridView control's AutoSizeColumnsMode property to Fill. Remove the BindingNavigator control from the form by deleting the BindingNavigator object from the component tray. Open the Code Editor window. Delete the Save Data button's Click event procedure. Code the Next Record and Previous Record buttons. Code the btnDisplay control's Click event procedure so it allows the user to display either all the records or only the records matching a specific grade. Code the btnCalc control's Click event procedure so it displays the student's GPA. An A grade is worth 4 points, a B is worth 3 points, and so on. Save the solution and then start and test the application. Close the Code Editor window and then close the solution.

ADVANCED

9. What task is performed by the following LINQ statement?

FIGURE THIS OUT

```
Dim decArea As Decimal =
    Aggregate rec In RectanglesDataSet.tblRectangles
    Select rec.Length * rec.Width
    Into Min()
```

10. Open the SwatTheBugs Solution (SwatTheBugs Solution.sln) file contained in the ClearlyVB2010\Chap25\SwatTheBugs Solution folder. Open the Code Editor window and study the existing code. Start and then test the application. Notice that the application is not working correctly. Locate and correct the errors in the code. Save the solution and then start and test the application again. Close the Code Editor window and then close the solution.

SWAT THE BUGS

I Love This Class (Creating a Class)

After studying Chapter 26, you should be able to:

- ◎ Explain the terminology used in object-oriented programming
- ◎ Create a class
- ◎ Instantiate an object
- ◎ Add Property procedures to a class
- ◎ Include data validation in a class
- ◎ Create a default constructor
- ◎ Include methods other than constructors in a class

That's a Real Classy Object

Visual Basic 2010 is an **object-oriented programming language**, which is a language that allows the programmer to use objects to accomplish a program's goal. An **object** is anything that can be seen, touched, or used. In other words, an object is nearly any *thing*. The objects used in an object-oriented program can take on many different forms. The text boxes, labels, and buttons included in most Windows applications are objects, and so are the application's named constants and variables. An object also can represent something found in real life, such as a credit card receipt or a paycheck.

Every object used in an object-oriented program is created from a **class**, which is a pattern that the computer uses to create the object. Using object-oriented programming (**OOP**) terminology, objects are **instantiated** (created) from a class, and each object is referred to as an **instance** of the class. A button control, for example, is an instance of the Button class. The button is instantiated when you drag the Button tool from the toolbox to the form. A String variable, on the other hand, is an instance of the String class and is instantiated the first time you refer to the variable in code. Keep in mind that the class itself is not an object. Only an instance of a class is an object.

Every object has **attributes**, which are the characteristics that describe the object. Attributes are also called properties. Included in the attributes of buttons and text boxes are the Name and Text properties. DataGridView controls have a DataSource property as well as an AutoSizeColumnsMode property. In addition to attributes, every object also has behaviors. An object's **behaviors** include methods and events. **Methods** are the operations (actions) that the object is capable of performing. For example, a button control can use its Focus method to send the focus to itself. **Events** are the actions to which an object can respond. A button control's Click event, for instance, allows the button to respond to a mouse click. A class contains—or, in OOP terms, it **encapsulates**—all of the attributes and behaviors of the object it instantiates. The term "encapsulate" means "to enclose in a capsule." In the context of OOP, the capsule is a class.

In previous chapters, you instantiated objects using classes that are built into Visual Basic, such as the TextBox and Label classes. You used the instantiated objects in a variety of ways in many different applications. In some applications, you used a text box to enter a name, while in other applications you used it to enter a sales tax rate. Similarly, you used label controls to identify text boxes and also to display the result of calculations. The ability to use an object for more than one purpose saves programming time and money—an advantage that contributes to the popularity of object-oriented programming.

Visual Basic also provides a way for you to define your own classes and then create instances (objects) from those classes. Like the classes built into Visual Basic, your classes must specify the attributes and behaviors of the objects they create. You define a class using the **Class statement**, which you enter in a class file. Figure 26-1 shows the statement's syntax and lists the steps for adding a class file to an open project. Although it is not a requirement, the convention is to use Pascal case for the class name. Recall that Pascal case means you capitalize the first letter in the name and the first letter in any subsequent words in the name. The names of Visual Basic classes (for example, String and TextBox) also follow this naming convention. Within the Class statement, you define the attributes and behaviors of the objects the class will create. In most cases, the attributes are represented by variables and Property procedures. You will learn about Property procedures later in this chapter. The behaviors are represented by methods, which can be Sub or Function procedures. (Some behaviors are represented by Event procedures; however, that topic is beyond the scope of this book.) Also included in Figure 26-1 is an example of a Class statement that defines a class named RectangularPool.

Class statement

Syntax
Public Class *className*
    attributes section
    behaviors section
End Class

Example
```
Public Class RectangularPool
        attributes
        behaviors
End Class
```

Adding a class file to an open project
1. Click Project on the menu bar and then click Add Class. The Add New Item dialog box opens with Class selected in the middle column of the dialog box.
2. Type the name of the class followed by a period and the letters vb in the Name box, and then click the Add button.

Figure 26-1   Class statement syntax, example, and steps

You will use the Class statement in the Willow Pools application, which you begin coding in the next section.

Revisiting the Willow Pools Application

You coded the Willow Pools application in Chapter 21. As you may remember, the application determines the amount of water required to fill a rectangular pool. To make this determination, the application first calculates the volume of the pool. Recall that you calculate the volume of a rectangular pool by multiplying the pool's length by its width and then multiplying the result by the pool's depth. Assuming the length, width, and depth are measured in feet, this gives you the volume in cubic feet. To determine the number of gallons of water, the application multiplies the number of cubic feet by 7.48, because there are 7.48 gallons in one cubic foot. In Chapter 21, you used a structure to group together the pool's length, width, and depth measurements. Recall that it's logical to group the three items because they are related; each represents one of the three dimensions of a rectangular pool. Most of the application's code from Chapter 21 is shown in Figure 26-2. However, unlike the code from Chapter 21, the code in Figure 26-2 uses the Decimal (rather than Double) data type. Also, the `txtLength.Focus()` statement was added to the btnCalc control's Click event procedure. In this chapter, you will modify the code to use a class rather than a structure.

```vb
Structure Dimensions
    Public decLength As Decimal
    Public decWidth As Decimal
    Public decDepth As Decimal
End Structure

Public Function GetGallons(ByVal pool As Dimensions) As Decimal
    ' calculates and returns the number of gallons

    Const decGAL_PER_CUBIC_FOOT As Decimal = 7.48

    Return pool.decLength * pool.decWidth *
        pool.decDepth * decGAL_PER_CUBIC_FOOT
End Function

Private Sub btnCalc_Click(ByVal sender As Object,
ByVal e As System.EventArgs) Handles btnCalc.Click
    ' displays the number of gallons

    Dim poolSize As Dimensions
    Dim decGallons As Decimal

    Decimal.TryParse(txtLength.Text, poolSize.decLength)
    Decimal.TryParse(txtWidth.Text, poolSize.decWidth)
    Decimal.TryParse(txtDepth.Text, poolSize.decDepth)

    decGallons = GetGallons(poolSize)
    lblGallons.Text = decGallons.ToString("N0")

    txtLength.Focus()
End Sub
```

entered in the form's Declarations section

receives a structure variable *by value*

declares a structure variable to store the input data

passes the structure variable to the GetGallons function

Figure 26-2   Code for the Willow Pools application using a structure

To begin creating a class in the Willow Pools application:

1. Start Visual Studio 2010 or Visual Basic 2010 Express. Open the **Willow Pools Solution** (**Willow Pools Solution.sln**) file contained in the ClearlyVB2010\Chap26\Willow Pools Solution folder. If the designer window is not open, double-click **frmMain.vb** in the Solution Explorer window.

2. If necessary, permanently display the Solution Explorer window.

3. First, you will use the Class statement to define a class named RectangularPool. As mentioned earlier, you enter a Class statement in a class file. Click **Project** on the menu bar and then click **Add Class**. The Add New Item dialog box opens with Class selected in the middle column of the dialog box. Change the filename in the Name box to **RectangularPool.vb** and then click the **Add** button. The RectangularPool.vb window opens and shows the code template for the Class statement. In addition, the RectangularPool.vb filename appears in the Solution Explorer window. See Figure 26-3.

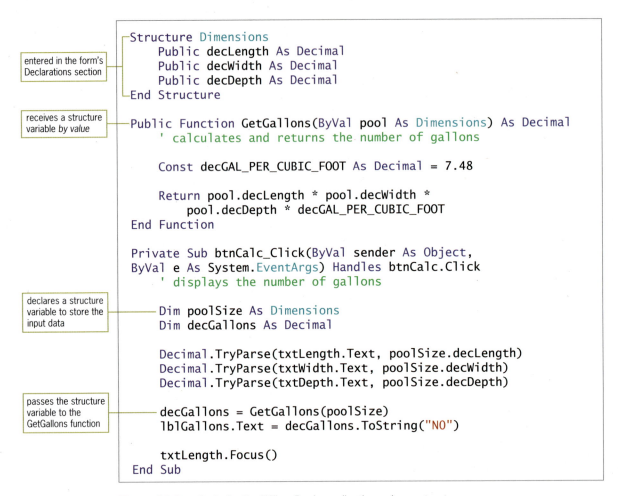

Figure 26-3   Class statement entered in the RectangularPool.vb window

In the context of OOP, a RectangularPool object has three attributes: a length, a width, and a depth. As mentioned earlier, the attributes are represented in the Class statement by variables and Property procedures. The variables appear first in the Class statement, followed by the Property procedures. In most cases, the variables are declared using the keyword `Private`. The `Private` keyword indicates that the variables can be used only within the class in which they are defined. When naming the Private variables in a class, many programmers use the underscore as the first character and then camel case for the remainder of the name. Following this naming convention, you will use the names `_decLength`, `_decWidth`, and `_decDepth` for the Private variables in the RectangularPool class.

To begin coding the RectangularPool class definition:

1. Auto-hide the Solution Explorer window and then click the **blank line** below the `Public Class RectangularPool` clause.

2. Enter the following three declaration statements. Press **Enter** twice after typing the last declaration statement.

    Private _decLength As Decimal
    Private _decWidth As Decimal
    Private _decDepth As Decimal

Who Owns That Property?

When an application instantiates an object, only the Public members of the object's class are visible (available) to the application; the application cannot access the Private members of the class. Using OOP terminology, the Public members are "exposed" to the application, whereas the Private members are "hidden" from the application. In this case, the `_decLength`, `_decWidth`, and `_decDepth` variables will be hidden from any application that contains an instance of the RectangularPool class. For an application to assign data to or retrieve data from a Private variable in a class, it must use a Public property. In other words, an application cannot directly refer to a Private variable in a class. Rather, it must refer to the variable indirectly, through the use of a Public property.

You create a Public property using a **Property procedure** whose procedure header begins with the keyword `Public`. A Public Property procedure creates a property that is visible to any application that contains an instance of the class. The basic syntax for creating a Public property is shown in Figure 26-4 along with examples of Public properties. You should use nouns and adjectives to name a property and enter the name using Pascal case, as in Length and AnnualSales. The property's *dataType* must match the data type of the Private variable associated with the property. Between a Property procedure's header and footer, you include a Get block of code and a Set block of code. The code contained in the **Get block** allows an application to retrieve the contents of the Private variable associated with the property. The code in the **Set block** allows an application to assign a value to the Private variable associated with the property.

Figure 26-4   Basic syntax and examples of a Public Property procedure

The Get block in a Property procedure contains the **Get statement**, which begins with the keyword `Get` and ends with the keywords `End Get`. Most times, you will enter only the `Return` *privateVariable* instruction within the Get statement. The instruction directs the computer to return the contents of the Private variable associated with the property. In Example 1 in Figure 26-4, the `Return _decLength` statement tells the computer to return the contents of the `_decLength` variable, which is the Private variable associated with the Length property. Similarly, the `Return _intAnnualSales` statement in Example 2 tells the computer to return the contents of the `_intAnnualSales` variable, which is the Private variable associated with the AnnualSales property.

The Set block in a Property procedure contains the **Set statement**, which begins with the keyword `Set` and ends with the keywords `End Set`. Following the `Set` keyword is a parameter enclosed in parentheses. The parameter begins with the keywords `ByVal value As`. The keywords are followed by a *dataType*, which must match the data type of the Private variable associated with the property. The value parameter temporarily stores the value that is passed to the Property procedure's Set statement by the application. You can enter one or more instructions within the Set statement. One of the instructions should assign the contents of the value parameter to the Private variable associated with the property. In Example 2 in Figure 26-4, the _intAnnualSales = value statement assigns the contents of the procedure's value parameter to the Private _intAnnualSales variable.

In the Set statement, you often will include instructions to validate the value received from the application before assigning it to the Private variable. The Set statement in Example 1 in Figure 26-4 includes a selection structure that determines whether the length measurement received from the application is valid. In this case, a valid length measurement is a decimal number that is greater than the number 0. If the length measurement is valid, the _decLength = value statement assigns the number stored in the value parameter to the Private _decLength variable. Otherwise, the _decLength = 0 instruction assigns a default value (in this case, 0) to the variable.

In the next set of steps, you will create a Public property for each Private variable in the RectangularPool class. Each Public property will allow an application indirect access to the Private variable associated with the property.

To enter a Property procedure for each Private variable in the RectangularPool class:

1. The insertion point should be positioned immediately above the End Class clause. First, you will enter a Public Property procedure for the Private _decLength variable. Enter the following procedure header and Get clause. When you press Enter after typing the Get clause, the Code Editor automatically enters the End Get clause, the Set statement, and the End Property clause.

   Public Property Length As Decimal
   Get

2. Recall that, in most cases, the Get statement simply returns the contents of the Private variable associated with the Property procedure. Type the following Return statement, but don't press Enter:

   Return _decLength

3. The Set statement should assign either the contents of its value parameter or a default value to the Private variable associated with the Property procedure. In this case, you will assign the number contained in the value parameter only when the number is greater than 0; otherwise, you will assign the number 0. Click the **blank line** above the End Set clause and then enter the following selection structure:

   If value > 0 Then
   **   _decLength = value**
   Else
   **   _decLength = 0**
   End If

4. Save the solution. Figure 26-5 shows the Length Property procedure associated with the _decLength variable.

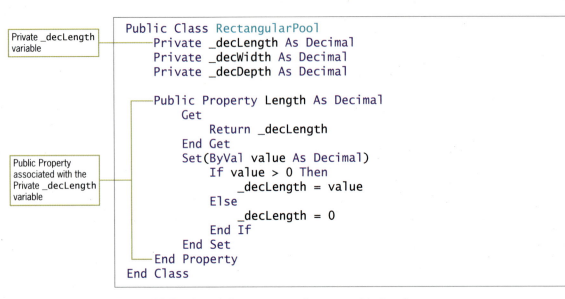

```
                          Public Class RectangularPool
Private _decLength            Private _decLength As Decimal
variable                     Private _decWidth As Decimal
                             Private _decDepth As Decimal

                             Public Property Length As Decimal
                                 Get
                                     Return _decLength
                                 End Get
Public Property                  Set(ByVal value As Decimal)
associated with the                  If value > 0 Then
Private _decLength                       _decLength = value
variable                             Else
                                         _decLength = 0
                                     End If
                                 End Set
                             End Property
                          End Class
```

Figure 26-5   Length Property procedure entered in the class

5. Now you will enter a Public Property procedure for the Private `_decWidth` variable. Insert two blank lines below the End Property clause. Enter the following Property procedure header and Get clause:

Public Property Width As Decimal
Get

6. Now type the following Return statement in the line below the Get clause, but don't press Enter:

Return _decWidth

7. Click the **blank line** above the End Set clause and then enter the following selection structure:

If value > 0 Then
    _decWidth = value
Else
    _decWidth = 0
End If

8. Finally, you will enter a Public Property procedure for the Private `_decDepth` variable. Insert two blank lines below the last End Property clause. On your own, enter the following Public Property procedure:

Public Property Depth As Decimal
    Get
        Return _decDepth
    End Get
    Set(ByVal value As Decimal)
        If value > 0 Then
            _decDepth = value
        Else
            _decDepth = 0
        End If
    End Set
End Property

9. Save the solution.

Mini-Quiz 26-1

See Appendix B for the answers.

1. OOP stands for _____.

2. Data validation code is entered in the _____ block of code in a Property procedure.
   a. Get
   b. Set

3. A Property procedure named City is associated with a Private variable named _strCity. Which of the following statements should be entered in the procedure's Get block of code?
   a. _strCity = value
   b. City = value
   c. Return _strCity
   d. Return City

Behave Yourself

Besides having attributes, objects also have behaviors. As you learned earlier, behaviors include the operations (actions) that the object is capable of performing. A RectangularPool object will have three behaviors. First, it will be able to initialize its Private variables when it is instantiated. Second, it will be able to calculate its volume. Third, it will be able to calculate the number of gallons of water required to fill it. The first behavior—initializing the Private variables—requires a constructor.

Constructive Behavior Is the Key to Success

A **constructor** is a class method, always named New, whose sole purpose is to initialize the class's Private variables. Constructors never return a value, so they are always Sub procedures rather than Function procedures. The syntax for creating a constructor is shown in Figure 26-6. Within the constructor you enter the initialization code for the class's Private variables. The initialization code will be processed each time an object is instantiated from the class. A class can have more than one constructor. Each constructor will have the same name (New) but its optional *parameterList* must be unique within the class. A constructor that has no parameters, like the constructor shown in Figure 26-6, is called the **default constructor**. A class can have only one default constructor.

Creating a constructor

Syntax
Public Sub New([*parameterList*]**)**
    instructions to initialize the class's Private variables
End Sub

Example (default constructor)
```
Public Sub New()
    _decLength = 0
    _decWidth = 0
    _decDepth = 0
End Sub
```

Figure 26-6   Syntax and an example of a constructor

To include a default constructor in the RectangularPool class:

1. Insert two blank lines below the Depth property's End Property clause.

2. Enter the following default constructor:

Public Sub New()
    ' default constructor
    _decLength = 0
    _decWidth = 0
    _decDepth = 0
End Sub

Methods Other than Constructors

A class also can contain methods other than constructors. Except for constructors, which must be Sub procedures, the other methods in a class can be either Sub procedures or Function procedures. Recall from Chapter 17 that the difference between both types of procedures is that a Function procedure returns a value after performing its assigned task, whereas a Sub procedure does not return a value. Figure 26-7 shows the syntax for a method that is not a constructor. The figure also includes two examples of a method that allows a RectangularPool object to calculate its volume. Like property names, method names should be entered using Pascal case. However, unlike property names, the first word in a method name should be a verb and any subsequent words should be nouns and adjectives. The method name used in the examples in Figure 26-7, GetVolume, follows this naming convention.

Creating a method that is not a constructor

Syntax
Public {Sub | Function} *methodName(*[*parameterList*]**) [As dataType]**
        instructions
End {Sub | Function}

Example 1 (coded as a Function procedure)
```
Public Function GetVolume() As Decimal
     Return _decLength * _decWidth * _decDepth
End Function
```

Example 2 (coded as a Sub procedure)
```
Public Sub GetVolume(ByRef decVol As Decimal)
     decVol = _decLength * _decWidth * _decDepth
End Sub
```

Figure 26-7 Syntax and examples of a method that is not a constructor

As mentioned earlier, a RectangularPool object should be able to calculate both its volume and the number of gallons of water required to fill it. For a RectangularPool object to perform these tasks, you will need to include two additional methods in the class: GetVolume and GetGallons. In this case, you will code both methods as Function procedures. Each Function procedure will return its calculated value to the application that invokes it.

To enter the GetVolume and GetGallons methods in the RectangularPool class definition:

1. First, you will enter the GetVolume function. Insert two blank lines below the default constructor's End Sub clause and then enter the following lines of code:

   Public Function GetVolume() As Decimal
      Return _decLength * _decWidth * _decDepth
   End Function

2. Next, you will enter the GetGallons function. Recall that you determine the number of gallons of water by multiplying the pool's volume by 7.48. You can use the class's GetVolume method to get the volume. Insert two blank lines below the End Function clause and then enter the following lines of code:

   Public Function GetGallons() As Decimal
      Dim decVol As Decimal
      decVol = GetVolume()
      Return decVol * 7.48
   End Function

3. Save the solution.

Figure 26-8 shows the RectangularPool class definition. For your convenience, line numbers are included in the figure. To display line numbers in the Code Editor window, click Tools on the menu bar, click Options, select the Show all settings check box, expand the Text Editor node, click Basic, select the Line numbers check box, and then click OK.

```
 1 Public Class RectangularPool
 2     Private _decLength As Decimal
 3     Private _decWidth As Decimal
 4     Private _decDepth As Decimal
 5
 6     Public Property Length As Decimal
 7         Get
 8             Return _decLength
 9         End Get
10         Set(ByVal value As Decimal)
11             If value > 0 Then
12                 _decLength = value
13             Else
14                 _decLength = 0
15             End If
16         End Set
17     End Property
18
19     Public Property Width As Decimal
20         Get
21             Return _decWidth
22         End Get
23         Set(ByVal value As Decimal)
24             If value > 0 Then
25                 _decWidth = value
26             Else
27                 _decWidth = 0
28             End If
29         End Set
30     End Property
31
```

Figure 26-8 RectangularPool class definition (*continues*)

(continued)

```
32    Public Property Depth As Decimal
33       Get
34          Return _decDepth
35       End Get
36       Set(ByVal value As Decimal)
37          If value > 0 Then
38             _decDepth = value
39          Else
40             _decDepth = 0
41          End If
42       End Set
43    End Property
44
45    Public Sub New()
46       ' default constructor
47       _decLength = 0
48       _decWidth = 0
49       _decDepth = 0
50    End Sub
51
52    Public Function GetVolume() As Decimal
53       Return _decLength * _decWidth * _decDepth
54    End Function
55
56    Public Function GetGallons() As Decimal
57       Dim decVol As Decimal
58       decVol = GetVolume()
59       Return decVol * 7.48
60    End Function
61 End Class
```

Figure 26-8   RectangularPool class definition

Using the Pattern to Create an Object

After you define a class, it then can be used to instantiate one or more objects. Figure 26-9 shows two versions of the basic syntax for instantiating an object. In both versions, *className* is the name of the class, and *variableName* is the name of a variable that will represent the object. The difference between both versions relates to when the object is actually created. The computer creates the object only when it processes the statement containing the New keyword. Recall that New is the name of a class's constructor. The New keyword invokes the constructor, which then creates the object and assigns initial values to the Private variables.

Also included in Figure 26-9 is an example of using each version of the syntax. In Example 1, the `Private pool As RectangularPool` instruction creates a variable that can store a RectangularPool object; however, it does not create the object. The object isn't created until the computer processes the `pool = New RectangularPool` statement, which uses the RectangularPool class to instantiate a RectangularPool object. In Example 2, the `Dim pool As New RectangularPool` instruction creates a variable named `pool`. It also instantiates a RectangularPool object and assigns it to the variable.

Instantiating an object from a class

Syntax—Version 1
{**Dim** | **Private**} *variableName* **As** *className*
variableName = **New** *className*

Syntax—Version 2
{**Dim** | **Private**} *variableName* **As New** *className*

Example 1—Version 1's syntax
```
Private pool As RectangularPool
pool = New RectangularPool
```
the Private instruction declares a RectangularPool variable named `pool`; the `New` keyword in the assignment statement instantiates a RectangularPool object and initializes its Private variables; the assignment statement then assigns the RectangularPool object to the `pool` variable

Example 2—Version 2's syntax
```
Dim pool As New RectangularPool
```
the `New` keyword in the instruction instantiates a RectangularPool object and initializes its Private variables; the instruction creates a RectangularPool variable named `pool` and then assigns the RectangularPool object to the variable

Figure 26-9   Syntax and examples of instantiating an object from a class

To modify the form's code to use a RectangularPool object rather than a structure:

1. If necessary, save the solution. Close the RectangularPool.vb window and then open the form's Code Editor window. The application will use the RectangularPool class rather than the Structure statement, so you will delete the Structure statement from the form's Declarations section. Click the **blank line** above the Structure statement. Press and hold down the **Shift** key as you click the **blank line** below the End Structure clause, and then release the Shift key. Press **Delete** to remove the Structure statement and the blank line from the Code Editor window.

2. You also will delete the GetGallons function, because the number of gallons will be calculated by the GetGallons method in the class. Click the **blank line** above the Public Function clause. Press and hold down the **Shift** key as you click the **blank line** below the End Function clause, and then release the Shift key. Press **Delete** to remove the GetGallons function and the blank line from the Code Editor window.

3. Next, you will instantiate a RectangularPool object in the btnCalc control's Click event procedure. Replace the `Dim poolSize As Dimensions` instruction with the following instruction:

   Dim pool As New RectangularPool

4. Now you will modify the three TryParse methods to use the object's Public properties. Select (highlight) `poolSize.decLength` in the first TryParse method. Type **pool.** (be sure to type the period) and then click the **Common** tab (if necessary). The properties and methods for a RectangularPool object appear in the IntelliSense list, as shown in Figure 26-10. The only method that does not appear in the list is the default constructor (New).

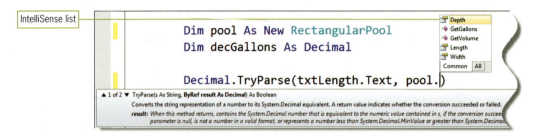

Figure 26-10 IntelliSense list showing a RectangularPool object's properties and methods

5. Click **Length** in the list and then press **Tab**. Click **another line** in the Code Editor window.

6. On your own, change `poolSize.decWidth` and `poolSize.decDepth` in the remaining TryParse methods to **pool.Width** and **pool.Depth**, respectively.

7. Next, you will use the class's GetGallons method to get the number of gallons. Change the `decGallons = GetGallons(poolSize)` statement to the following:

decGallons = pool.GetGallons

Figure 26-11 shows the modified Click event procedure. The changes you made to the procedure are shaded in the figure.

```
Private Sub btnCalc_Click(ByVal sender As Object,
ByVal e As System.EventArgs) Handles btnCalc.Click
    ' displays the number of gallons

    Dim pool As New RectangularPool
    Dim decGallons As Decimal

    Decimal.TryParse(txtLength.Text, pool.Length)
    Decimal.TryParse(txtWidth.Text, pool.Width)
    Decimal.TryParse(txtDepth.Text, pool.Depth)

    decGallons = pool.GetGallons
    lblGallons.Text = decGallons.ToString("N0")

    txtLength.Focus()
End Sub
```

Figure 26-11 Modified Click event procedure for the btnCalc control

To test the application's code:

1. Save the solution and then start the application. Type **100** in the Length box, **30** in the Width box, and **4** in the Depth box. Click the **Calculate** button. The number 89,760 appears in the Gallons box, as shown in Figure 26-12.

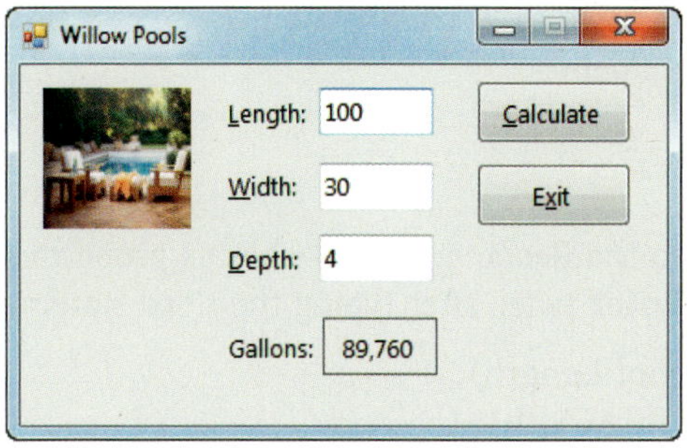

Figure 26-12   Number of gallons displayed in the interface

2. Click the **Exit** button. Close the Code Editor window and then close the solution.

At this point, the advantage of creating a class and instantiating objects—in other words, the advantage of object-oriented programming—may not be apparent. After all, modifying the Willow Pools application to include a class (rather than a structure) required many more lines of code. The real advantage of object-oriented programming is the ability to reuse a class in a different way or in a different application. In the next section, you will use the RectangularPool class in the Pool Supplies application.

Pool Supplies Application

Pool Supplies sells a water clarifier designed to combat a common problem in swimming pools: cloudy water. The company recommends one ounce of SoClear clarifier per 5000 gallons of water. The manager of Pool Supplies wants an application that calculates the number of gallons of water contained in a pool and the required number of ounces of clarifier. You can code this application using the RectangularPool class that you created earlier in this chapter. The RectangularPool.vb file is contained in the ClearlyVB2010\Chap26\Willow Pools Solution\ Willow Pools Project folder.

To code the Pool Supplies application:

1. Use Windows to copy the RectangularPool.vb file from the ClearlyVB2010\Chap26\ Willow Pools Solution\Willow Pools Project folder to the ClearlyVB2010\Chap26\Pool Supplies Solution\Pool Supplies Project folder.

2. Open the **Pool Supplies Solution (Pool Supplies Solution.sln)** file contained in the ClearlyVB2010\Chap26\Pool Supplies Solution folder. If the designer window is not open, double-click **frmMain.vb** in the Solution Explorer window. The user interface provides text boxes for the user to enter the pool's dimensions.

3. First, you will add the RectangularPool.vb file to the project. Click **Project** on the menu bar and then click **Add Existing Item** to open the Add Existing Item dialog box. Click **RectangularPool.vb** in the Pool Supplies Project folder and then click the **Add** button. Temporarily display the Solution Explorer window to verify that it contains the RectangularPool.vb filename.

4. Open the Code Editor window and locate the btnCalc control's Click event procedure. Click the **blank line** above the procedure's End Sub clause. First, you will instantiate a RectangularPool object. Enter the following declaration statement:

   Dim pool As New RectangularPool

5. Now you will declare variables to store the number of gallons of water and the number of ounces of clarifier. Enter the following two declaration statements. Press **Enter** twice after typing the second declaration statement.

   Dim decGallons As Decimal
   Dim decOunces As Decimal

6. Next, you will assign the input items to the RectangularPool object's properties. Enter the following three statements. Press **Enter** twice after typing the third statement.

   Decimal.TryParse(txtLength.Text, pool.Length)
   Decimal.TryParse(txtWidth.Text, pool.Width)
   Decimal.TryParse(txtDepth.Text, pool.Depth)

7. Now you will use the RectangularPool object's GetGallons method to get the number of gallons of water. Enter the following assignment statement:

   decGallons = pool.GetGallons

8. You calculate the number of ounces of clarifier by dividing the number of gallons of water by 5000. Type the following assignment statement and then press **Enter** twice:

   decOunces = decGallons / 5000

9. Finally, you will display the calculated amounts in the interface. Enter the following assignment statements:

   lblGallons.Text = decGallons.ToString("N0")
   lblClarifier.Text = decOunces.ToString("N1")

Figure 26-13 shows the code entered in the btnCalc control's Click event procedure.

```
Private Sub btnCalc_Click(ByVal sender As Object,
ByVal e As System.EventArgs) Handles btnCalc.Click
    ' calculates and displays the number of gallons
    ' in a pool and the number of ounces of
    ' clarifier needed

    Dim pool As New RectangularPool
    Dim decGallons As Decimal
    Dim decOunces As Decimal

    Decimal.TryParse(txtLength.Text, pool.Length)
    Decimal.TryParse(txtWidth.Text, pool.Width)
    Decimal.TryParse(txtDepth.Text, pool.Depth)

    decGallons = pool.GetGallons
    decOunces = decGallons / 5000

    lblGallons.Text = decGallons.ToString("N0")
    lblClarifier.Text = decOunces.ToString("N1")

End Sub
```

Figure 26-13   btnCalc control's Click event procedure

To test the Pool Supplies application's code:

1. Save the solution and then start the application. Type **100** in the Length box, **30** in the Width box, and **4** in the Depth box. Click the **Calculate** button. The interface shows that the pool contains 89,760 gallons of water and requires 18.0 ounces of clarifier. See Figure 26-14.

Pool Supplies

Length: 100   Calculate

Width: 30   Exit

Depth: 4

Gallons of water in pool: 89,760

Ounces of SoClear clarifier: 18.0

Figure 26-14   Calculated amounts shown in the interface

To learn about a new feature in Visual Basic 2010, called auto-implemented properties, view the Ch26-Auto-Implemented Properties video.

2. Click the **Exit** button. Close the Code Editor window and then close the solution.

Mini-Quiz 26-2

See Appendix B for the answers.

1. What is the name of the default constructor for a class named Animal?

2. Write a Dim statement that instantiates an Animal object and assigns the object to a variable named **dog**.

3. A Private variable in a class can be accessed directly by a Public method in the same class.
   a. True   b. False

To learn about overloading methods and inheritance, see the Overloading and Inheritance sections in the Ch26WantMore.pdf file.

Summary

- The objects used in an object-oriented program are instantiated (created) from classes. A class encapsulates (contains) the attributes that describe the object it creates. The class also contains the behaviors that allow the object to perform tasks and respond to actions.

- You use the Class statement to define a class. Class names are entered using Pascal case. You enter a class definition in a class file, which you can add to the current project using the Project menu.

- When naming the Private variables in a class, many programmers begin the name with the underscore character. Subsequent characters in the name are entered using camel case.

- When an object is instantiated in an application, the Public members of the class are exposed to the application. However, the Private members are hidden from the application.

- An application must use a Public property to either assign data to or retrieve data from a Private variable in a class. You create a Public property using a Property procedure. The names of the properties in a class should be entered using Pascal case and consist of nouns and adjectives.

- The Get block in a Property procedure allows an application to access the contents of the Private variable associated with the property. The Set block, on the other hand, allows an application to assign a value to the Private variable.

- A class can have one or more constructors. The purpose of a constructor is to initialize the class's Private variables.

- All constructors are Sub procedures that are named New. Each constructor must have a different *parameterList* (if any). A constructor that has no parameters is the default constructor. A class can contain only one default constructor.

- The names of the methods in a class should be entered using Pascal case. You should use a verb for the first word in the name, and nouns and adjectives for any subsequent words in the name.

Key Terms

Attributes—the characteristics that describe an object

Behaviors—an object's methods and events

Class—a pattern that the computer follows when instantiating (creating) an object

Class statement—the statement used to define a class in Visual Basic

Constructor—a method whose instructions are automatically processed each time the class is used to instantiate an object; its purpose is to initialize the class's Private variables; always a Sub procedure named New

Default constructor—a constructor that has no parameters; a class can have only one default constructor

Encapsulates—an OOP term that means "contains"

Events—the actions to which an object can respond

Get block—the section of a Property procedure that contains the Get statement

Get statement—appears in a Get block in a Property procedure; contains the code that allows an application to retrieve the contents of the Private variable associated with the property

Instance—an object created from a class

Instantiated—the process of creating an object from a class

Methods—the actions that an object is capable of performing

Object—anything that can be seen, touched, or used; an instance of a class

Object-oriented programming language—a programming language that allows the use of objects to accomplish a program's goal

OOP—an acronym for object-oriented programming

Property procedure—used to create a Public property that an application can use to access a Private variable in a class

Set block—the section of a Property procedure that contains the Set statement

Set statement—appears in a Set block in a Property procedure; contains the code that allows an application to assign a value to the Private variable associated with the property; may also contain validation code

Review Questions

1. Which of the following statements is false?

   a. An example of an attribute is the _intMinutes variable in a Time class.

   b. An example of a behavior is the SetTime method in a Time class.

   c. A class is considered an object.

   d. An object created from a class is referred to as an instance of the class.

2. An application can access the Private variables in a class _____.

   a. directly

   b. using Public properties created by Property procedures

   c. through Private procedures contained in the class

   d. none of the above

3. Which of the following instantiates an Animal object and assigns the object to the `cat` variable?

   a. `Dim cat As Animal`

   c. `Dim cat As Animal`
      `cat = New Animal`

   b. `Dim cat As New Animal`

   d. both b and c

4. An application instantiates an Animal object and assigns it to the `cat` variable. Which of the following assigns to the `strName` variable the value returned by the Animal class's GetName method?

   a. `strName = Animal.GetName`

   c. `strName = Animal.GetName.cat`

   b. `strName = cat.GetName`

   d. none of the above

5. A constructor must be _____.

   a. a Function procedure

   c. an Event procedure

   b. a Sub procedure

   d. either a Function procedure or a Sub procedure

6. To expose a method contained in a class, you declare the method using the keyword _____.

   a. `Expose`

   c. `Public`

   b. `Private`

   d. `Viewable`

7. The Return statement is entered in the _____ statement in a Property procedure.

   a. Get

   b. Set

Exercises

1. Open the Area Solution (Area Solution.sln) file contained in the ClearlyVB2010\Chap26\ Area Solution folder. If necessary, open the designer window. TRY THIS

   a. Use the Project menu to add a new class file named Square.vb to the project. The Square class should have one attribute: a side measurement (which may contain a decimal place). It also should have two behaviors: a default constructor that initializes the class's Private variable and a function that calculates and returns the area of the square. Code the Square class. Save the solution and then close the Square.vb window.

b. Open the form's Code Editor window. Use the comments entered in the btnCalc control's Click event procedure to code the procedure.

c. Save the solution and then start and test the application. Close the Code Editor window and then close the solution. (See Appendix B for the answer.)

MODIFY THIS   2. In this exercise, you modify the Square class from Exercise 1.

a. Use Windows to copy the Square.vb file from the ClearlyVB2010\Chap26\Area Solution\Area Project folder to the ClearlyVB2010\Chap26\Square Box Solution\ Square Box Project folder.

b. Open the Square Box Solution (Square Box Solution.sln) file contained in the Square Box Solution folder. If necessary, open the designer window.

c. Use the Project menu to add the Square.vb file to the project. Open the Square.vb file. Modify the Square class to include a method that calculates and returns the perimeter of a square. (To calculate the perimeter, you multiply the side measurement by 4.) Save the solution and then close the Square.vb window.

d. Open the form's Code Editor window. The btnDisplay control's Click event procedure should calculate and display both the area and the perimeter of a square. Code the procedure.

e. Save the solution and then start and test the application. Close the Code Editor window and then close the solution.

INTRODUCTORY   3. Open the Sweets Solution (Sweets Solution.sln) file contained in the ClearlyVB2010\ Chap26\Sweets Solution folder. If necessary, open the designer window.

a. Add a new class file named Salesperson.vb to the project. The Salesperson class should have two attributes: a salesperson's ID and a sales amount. The ID may contain letters; the sales amount may contain a decimal place. The class should have one behavior: the default constructor. Code the Salesperson class. Save the solution and then close the Salesperson.vb window.

b. Open the form's Code Editor window. The btnSave control's Click event procedure should save each salesperson's ID and sales amount to a sequential access file. Finish coding the procedure.

c. Save the solution and then start and test the application. Be sure to verify that the sales.txt file contains the IDs and sales amounts that you entered. Close the Code Editor window and then close the solution.

INTRODUCTORY   4. In this exercise, you modify both the RectangularPool class and the Willow Pools application from the chapter. Use Windows to make a copy of the Willow Pools Solution folder. Save the copy in the ClearlyVB2010\Chap26 folder. Rename the copy Willow Pools Solution-INTRODUCTORY. Open the Willow Pools Solution (Willow Pools Solution.sln) file contained in the Willow Pools Solution-INTRODUCTORY folder. Open the designer window. Open the RectangularPool.vb file. Change the GetGallons function to a Sub procedure. Save the solution and then close the RectangularPool.vb window. Open the form's Code Editor window and then modify the btnCalc control's Click event procedure. Save the solution and then start and test the application. Close the Code Editor window and then close the solution.

INTERMEDIATE   5. Open the Grade Solution (Grade Solution.sln) file contained in the ClearlyVB2010\ Chap26\Grade Solution folder. Add a new class file named CourseGrade to the project. The CourseGrade class should have three attributes: the scores for three tests. Each test score will be an integer. The class also should have two behaviors: the default constructor and a method that determines and returns the letter grade. The letter grade is based on the total score, as indicated in Figure 26-15. Code the CourseGrade class. Save the solution and then close the CourseGrade.vb window. Open the form's Code

Editor window. Code the btnDisplay control's Click event procedure. Each test score should be from 0 through 100 only. Save the solution and then start and test the application. Close the Code Editor window and then close the solution.

Total score	Grade
270 – 300	A
240 – 269	B
210 – 239	C
180 – 209	D
Less than 180	F

Figure 26-15 Information for Exercise 5

6. In this exercise, you modify the RectangularPool class from the chapter. Use Windows to make a copy of the Willow Pools Solution folder. Save the copy in the ClearlyVB2010\Chap26 folder. Rename the copy Willow Pools Solution-INTERMEDIATE. Open the Willow Pools Solution (Willow Pools Solution.sln) file contained in the Willow Pools Solution-INTERMEDIATE folder. Open the designer window. Open the RectangularPool.vb file. Change the GetVolume function to a Sub procedure. Save the solution and then start and test the application. Close the RectangularPool.vb window and then close the solution.

   INTERMEDIATE

7. Shelly Jones, the manager of Pennington Book Store, wants an application that calculates and displays the total amount a customer owes. The interface for this application is shown in Figure 26-16. A customer can purchase one or more books at either the same price or different prices. The application should keep a running total of the amount the customer owes, and display the total in the Total due box. For example, a customer might purchase two books at $6 and three books at $10. To calculate the total due, Shelly will need to enter 2 in the Quantity box and 6 in the Price box, and then click the Add to Sale button. The Total due box should display $12.00. To complete the order, Shelly will need to enter 3 in the Quantity box and 10 in the Price box, and then click the Add to Sale button. The Total due box should display $42.00. Before calculating the next customer's order, Shelly will need to click the New Order button.

   ADVANCED

   a. Create a Visual Basic Windows application. Use the following names for the solution and project, respectively: Pennington Solution and Pennington Project. Save the application in the ClearlyVB2010\Chap26 folder. Change the name of the form file on your disk to frmMain.vb. If necessary, change the form's name to frmMain.

   b. Create the interface shown in Figure 26-16.

   c. Add a class file named BookSale.vb to the project. The BookSale class should have three attributes: a quantity, a price, and a total due. It also should have two behaviors: the default constructor and a method that keeps a running total of the amount the customer owes. Code the BookSale class. Save the solution and then close the BookSale.vb window.

   d. Open the form's Code Editor window and code the application.

   e. Save the solution and then start and test the application. Close the Code Editor window and then close the solution.

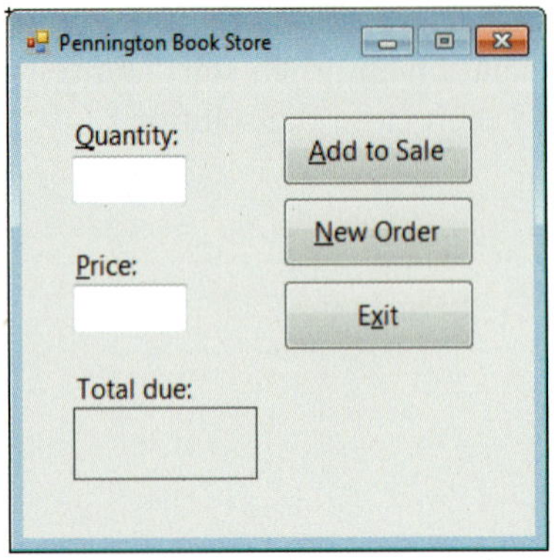

Figure 26-16   Interface for Exercise 7

FIGURE THIS OUT

8.   Open the FigureThisOut Solution (FigureThisOut Solution.sln) file contained in the ClearlyVB2010\Chap26\FigureThisOut Solution folder. Open the form's Code Editor window and the class's Code Editor window. Study the existing code. What is the difference between both constructors? Start and then test the application. Close the Code Editor windows and then close the solution.

SWAT THE BUGS

9.   Open the SwatTheBugs Solution (SwatTheBugs Solution.sln) file contained in the ClearlyVB2010\Chap26\SwatTheBugs Solution folder. Open the form's Code Editor window and the class's Code Editor window. Correct the btnCalc_Click procedure to remove the jagged lines. Save the solution and then start and test the application. Notice that the application is not working correctly. Locate and correct the errors in the code. Save the solution and then start and test the application again. Close the Code Editor windows and then close the solution.

CHAPTER 27

Getting "Web-ified" (Web Applications)

After studying Chapter 27, you should be able to:

- ◎ Define basic Web terminology
- ◎ Create a Web application
- ◎ Add Web pages to an application
- ◎ Customize a Web page
- ◎ Add static text to a Web page
- ◎ Format a Web page's static text
- ◎ View a Web page in full screen view
- ◎ Add controls (link button, image, text box, label, and button) to a Web page
- ◎ Start, close, and open a Web application
- ◎ Reposition a control on a Web page
- ◎ Code a control on a Web page
- ◎ Use a RequiredFieldValidator control

Web Applications

The Internet is the world's largest computer network, connecting millions of computers located all around the world. One of the most popular features of the Internet is the World Wide Web, often referred to simply as the Web. The Web consists of documents called **Web pages** that are stored on Web servers. A **Web server** is a computer that contains special software that "serves up" Web pages in response to requests from client computers. A **client computer** is a computer that requests information from a Web server. The information is requested and subsequently viewed through the use of a program called a Web browser or, more simply, a **browser**. Currently, the two most popular browsers are Microsoft Internet Explorer and Mozilla Firefox.

Many Web pages are static. A **static Web page** is a document whose purpose is merely to display information to the viewer. Static Web pages are not interactive. The only interaction that can occur between static Web pages and the viewer is through links that allow the viewer to "jump" from one Web page to another. Figures 27-1 and 27-2 show examples of static Web pages created for the Cottage Toy Store. The Web page in Figure 27-1 shows the store's name, address, and telephone number. The page also provides a link to the Web page shown in Figure 27-2. That page shows the store's business hours and provides a link for returning to the first Web page. You will create both Web pages in this chapter.

Figure 27-1   Example of a static Web page

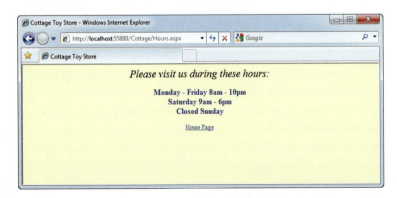

Figure 27-2   Another example of a static Web page

Although static Web pages provide a means for a store to list its location and hours, a company wanting to do business on the Web must be able to do more than just list information: It must be able to interact with customers through its Web site. The Web site should allow customers to submit inquiries, select items for purchase, and submit payment information. It also should allow the company to track customer inquiries and process customer orders. Tasks such as these can be accomplished using dynamic Web pages.

Unlike a static Web page, a **dynamic Web page** is interactive in that it can accept information from the user and also retrieve information for the user. Examples of dynamic Web pages that you might have already encountered include forms for purchasing merchandise online and for submitting online resumes. Figure 27-3 shows a dynamic Web page that you will create in this chapter. The Web page allows the user to enter the number of American dollars. When he or she clicks the Submit button, the button's Click event procedure will convert the number of dollars to the number of Mexican pesos and then display the result on the Web page.

Figure 27-3   Example of a dynamic Web page

The Web applications created in this chapter use a technology called ASP.NET 4.0. **ASP** stands for "active server page" and refers to the type of Web page created by the ASP technology. All ASP pages contain HTML (Hypertext Markup Language) tags that tell the client's browser how to render the page on the computer screen. For example, the instruction <h1>Hello</h1> uses the opening <h1> tag and its closing </h1> tag to display the word "Hello" as a heading on the Web page. Many ASP pages also contain ASP tags that specify the controls to include on the Web page. In addition to the HTML and ASP tags, dynamic ASP pages contain code that tells the objects on the Web page how to respond to the user's actions. In this chapter, you will write the appropriate code using the Visual Basic programming language.

When a client computer's browser sends a request for an ASP page, the Web server locates the page and then sends the appropriate HTML instructions to the client. The client's browser uses the instructions to render the Web page on the computer screen. If the Web page is a dynamic one, like the Currency Converter page shown in Figure 27-3, the user can interact with the page by entering data. In most cases, the user then clicks a button on the Web page to submit the data to the server for processing. When the server receives the data, it executes the Visual Basic code associated with the Web page. It then sends back the appropriate HTML, which now includes the result of processing the code and data, to the client for rendering in the browser window. Using the Currency Converter Web page as an example, the user first enters the number of American dollars and then clicks the Submit button, which submits the user's entry to the Web server. The server executes the Visual Basic code to convert the American dollars to Mexican pesos and then sends back the HTML, which now includes the number of pesos. Notice that the Web page's HTML is interpreted and executed by the client computer, whereas the program code is executed by the Web server. Figure 27-4 illustrates the relationship between the client computer and the Web server.

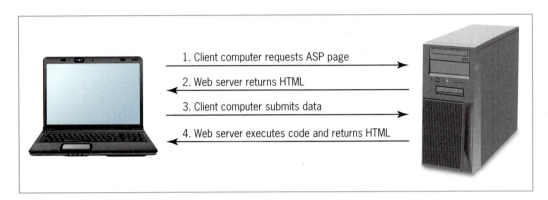

Figure 27-4 Illustration of the relationship between a client computer and a Web server

Mini-Quiz 27-1

See Appendix B for the answers.

1. ASP is an acronym for _____.

2. HTML is an acronym for _____.

3. The HTML instructions in a Web page are processed by the _____.

    a. client computer   b. Web server

Creating a Web Application

You create a Web application in Visual Basic using Visual Web Developer 2010, which is available either as a stand-alone product (called Visual Web Developer 2010 Express) or as part of Visual Studio 2010. You can download a free copy of Visual Web Developer 2010 Express from Microsoft's Web site. At the time of this writing, the address is *http://www.microsoft.com/express/Downloads/#2010-Visual-Web-Developer*. The following steps show you how to configure Visual Web Developer 2010 Express. You should perform these steps only if you are using Visual Web Developer 2010 Express.

To configure Visual Web Developer 2010 Express:

1. Click the **Start** button on the Windows 7 taskbar and then point to **All Programs**.

2. Click **Microsoft Visual Studio 2010 Express** and then click **Microsoft Visual Web Developer 2010 Express**.

3. Click **Tools** on the menu bar, and then click **Options** to open the Options dialog box. If necessary, select the **Show all settings** check box. Click the **Projects and Solutions** node. Use the information shown in Figure 27-5 to select and deselect the appropriate check boxes.

Figure 27-5   Options dialog box

4. Click the **OK** button to close the Options dialog box.

5. Click **Tools** on the menu bar and then point to **Settings**. If necessary, click **Expert Settings** to select it.

In the next set of steps, you begin creating the Cottage Toy Store Web application.

To begin creating the Cottage Toy Store Web application:

1. If necessary, start Visual Studio 2010 or Visual Web Developer 2010 Express.

2. If necessary, open the Solution Explorer and Properties windows, and auto-hide the Toolbox window.

3. Click **File** on the menu bar and then click **New Web Site** to open the New Web Site dialog box. If necessary, click **Visual Basic** in the Installed Templates list. Click **ASP.NET Empty Web Site** in the middle column of the dialog box.

4. If necessary, change the entry in the Web location box to **File System**. The File System selection allows you to store your Web application in any folder on either your computer or a network drive.

5. In this chapter, you will be instructed to store your Web applications in the F:\ClearlyVB2010\Chap27 folder; however, you can use any location. In the box that appears next to the Web location box, replace the existing text with **F:\ClearlyVB2010\Chap27\Cottage**. Figure 27-6 shows the completed New Web Site dialog box if you are using Visual Studio 2010. Your New Web Site dialog box will look slightly different if you are using Visual Web Developer 2010 Express.

Before you begin creating the Cottage Toy Store Web application, you may find it helpful to view the Ch27-Web video.

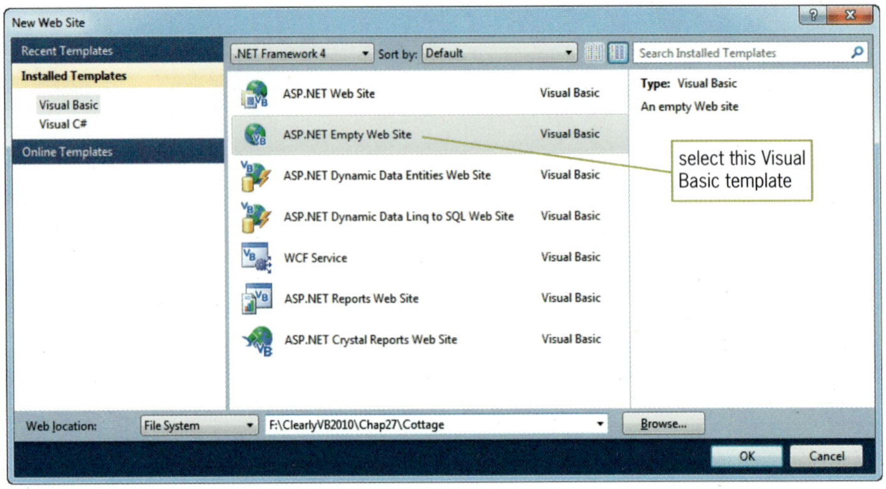

Figure 27-6   New Web Site dialog box

6. Click the **OK** button to close the New Web Site dialog box. The computer creates an empty Web application named Cottage.

Adding the Default.aspx Web Page to the Application

After creating an empty Web application, you need to add a Web page to it. The first Web page added to an application is usually named Default.aspx.

To add the Default.aspx Web page to the application:

1. Click **Website** on the menu bar and then click **Add New Item** to open the Add New Item dialog box. (If Website does not appear on the menu bar, click the Web application's location and name in the Solution Explorer window.)

2. If necessary, click **Visual Basic** in the Installed Templates list and then (if necessary) click **Web Form** in the middle column of the dialog box. Verify that the Place code in separate file check box is selected, and that the Select master page check box is not selected. As indicated in Figure 27-7, the Web page will be named Default.aspx.

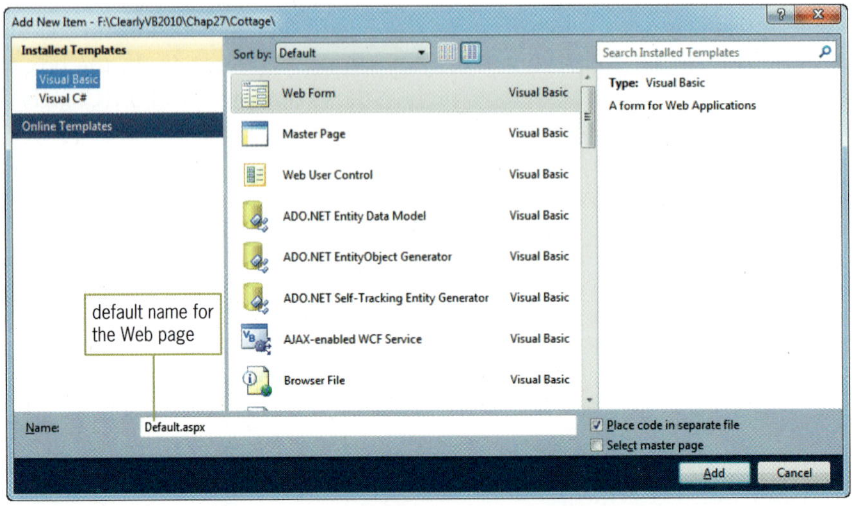

Figure 27-7   Add New Item dialog box

3. Click the **Add** button to display the Default.aspx page in the Document window. If necessary, click the **Design** tab that appears at the bottom of the IDE. When the Design tab is selected, the Web page appears in Design view in the Document window, as shown in Figure 27-8. You can use Design view to add text and controls to the Web page. If the Formatting toolbar does not appear on your screen, click **View** on the menu bar, point to **Toolbars**, and then click **Formatting**. If the div tag does not appear in the Document window, click either the **<div>** button at the bottom of the IDE or the **rectangle** below the body tag.

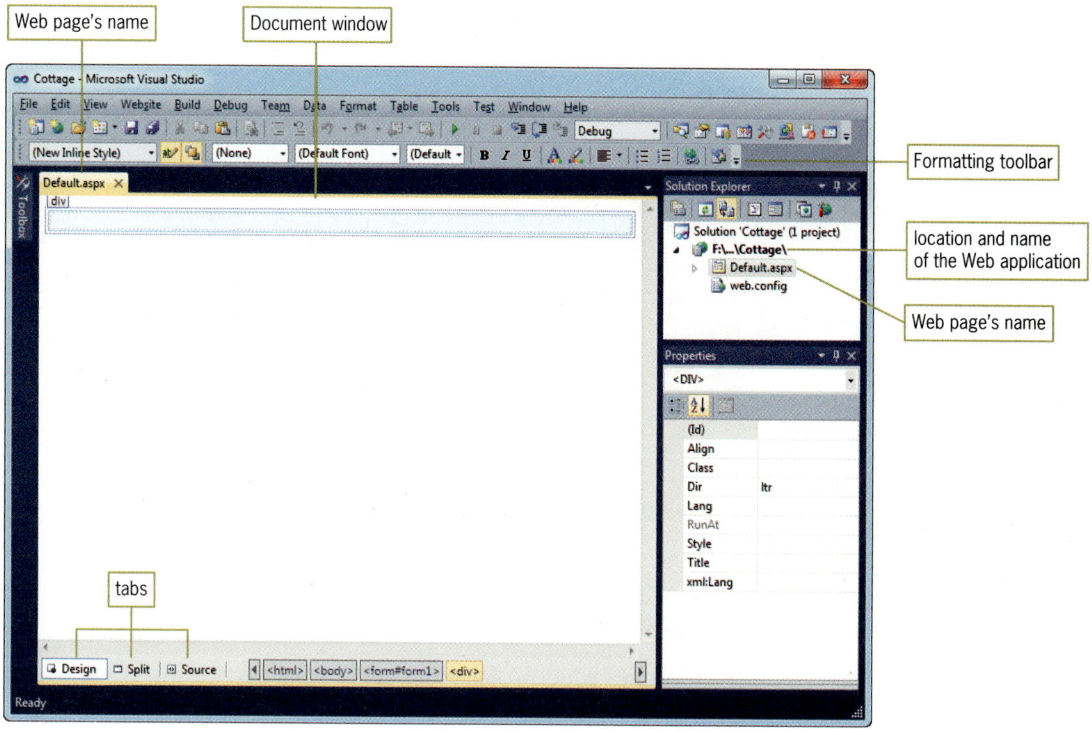

Figure 27-8   Default.aspx Web page shown in Design view

4. Click the **Source** tab to display the Web page in Source view. This view shows the HTML and ASP tags that tell a browser how to render the Web page. The tags are automatically generated for you as you are creating the Web page in Design view. Currently, the Web page contains only HTML tags.

5. Click the **Split** tab to split the Document window into two parts. The upper half displays the Web page in Source view, and the lower half displays it in Design view.

6. Click the **Design** tab to return to Design view, and then auto-hide the Solution Explorer window.

Customizing a Web Page

You can use the Properties window to customize a Web page. The properties appear in the Properties window when you select DOCUMENT in the window's Object box. A Web page's Title property, for example, determines the value that appears in the browser's title bar and also on the page's tab in the browser window. Its BgColor property controls the page's background color.

To change the Title and BgColor properties:

1. Click the **down arrow** button in the Properties window's Object box and then click **DOCUMENT** in the list. (If DOCUMENT does not appear in the Object box, click the Design tab.) The DOCUMENT object represents the Web page.

2. If necessary, click the **Alphabetical** button in the Properties window to display the properties in alphabetical order. Click **Title** in the Properties list. Type **Cottage Toy Store** in the Settings box and then press **Enter**.

3. Click **BgColor** in the Properties list and then click the **...** (ellipsis) button to open the More Colors dialog box. Click the **hexagon** indicated in Figure 27-9.

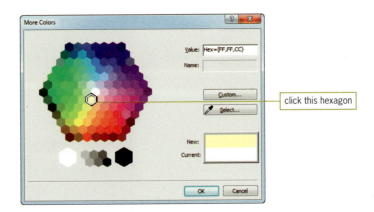

Figure 27-9   More Colors dialog box

4. Click the **OK** button to close the More Colors dialog box. The page's background color changes from white to a pale yellow.

5. Auto-hide the Properties window. Save the application by clicking either the **Save All** button on the Standard toolbar or the **Save All** option on the File menu.

Adding Static Text to a Web Page

All Web pages contain some text that the user is not allowed to edit, such as a company name or the caption that identifies a text box. Text that cannot be changed by the user is referred to as **static text**. You can add static text to a Web page by simply typing the text on the page itself. Or, you can use a label control that you dragged to the Web page from the Toolbox window. In the following set of steps, you will type the static text on the Web page.

To add static text to the Web page:

1. If necessary, click **inside the rectangle** that appears below the div tag at the top of the Document window. The div tag defines a division in a Web page. (If the div tag does not appear in the Document window, click the <div> button at the bottom of the IDE.)

2. Enter the following four lines of text. Press **Enter** twice after typing the last line.

   Cottage Toy Store
   123 Elm Street
   Bowling Green, KY 42101
   (111) 555-5555

3. Save the application.

You can use either the Format menu or the Formatting toolbar to format the static text on a Web page. Figure 27-10 indicates some of the tools available on the Formatting toolbar.

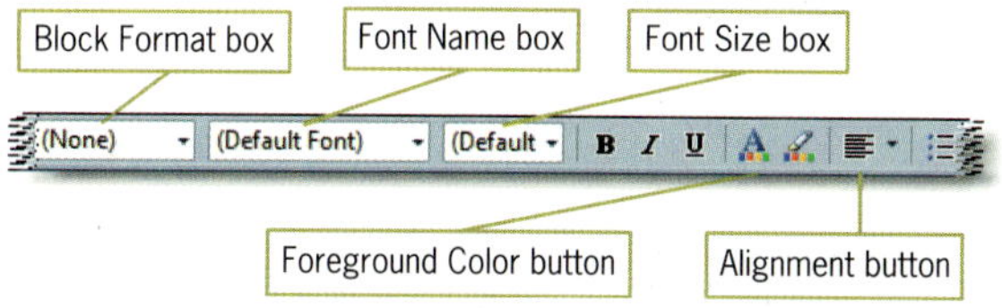

Figure 27-10 Formatting toolbar

To use the Formatting toolbar to format the static text:

1. Select (highlight) the Cottage Toy Store text on the Web page. Click the **down arrow** in the Block Format box on the Formatting toolbar. Click **Heading 1 <h1>**. (If the Formatting toolbar does not appear on your screen, click View on the menu bar, point to Toolbars, and then click Formatting.)

2. Select the address and phone number text on the Web page. Click the **down arrow** in the Block Format box and then click **Heading 2 <h2>**.

3. Now, you will use the Formatting toolbar's Alignment button to center all of the static text. Select all of the static text on the Web page and then click the **down arrow** on the Alignment button. See Figure 27-11.

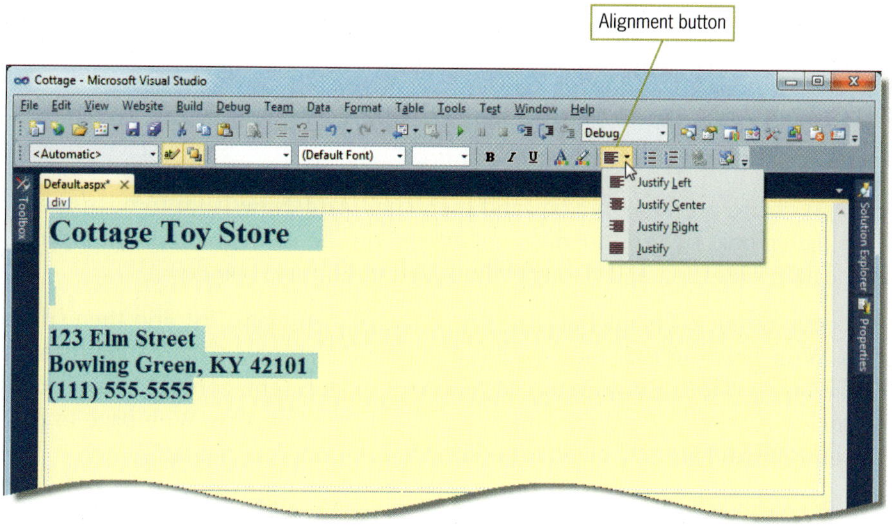

Figure 27-11 Result of clicking the Alignment button

4. Click **Justify Center**. The selected text appears centered, horizontally, on the Web page. Click **anywhere below the phone number** to deselect the text, and then save the application.

Viewing a Web Page in Full Screen View

While you are designing a Web page, you can periodically view the page in full screen view to determine how it will appear to the user. You do this using the Full Screen option on the View menu.

To view the Web page using the Full Screen option:

1. Click **View** on the menu bar and then click **Full Screen** on the menu. See Figure 27-12. Although not identical to viewing in a browser window, full screen view provides a quick and easy way to verify the placement of controls and text on the Web page.

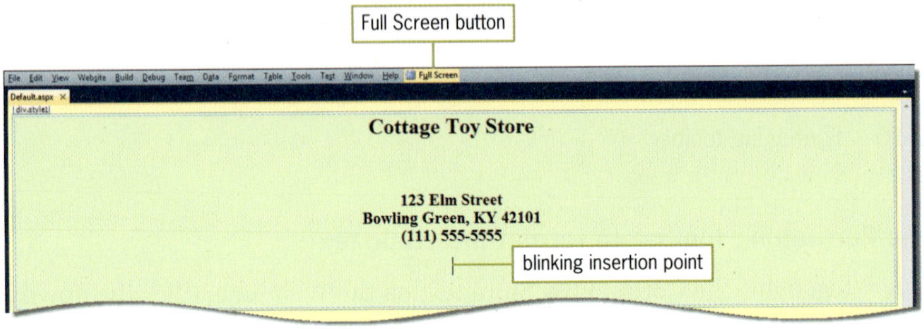

Figure 27-12   Default.aspx Web page displayed in full screen view

2. Click the **Full Screen** button to return to the standard view. (If you mistakenly clicked the window's Close button, click the Full Screen button, right-click Default.aspx in the Solution Explorer window, and then click View Designer.)

Adding Another Web Page to the Application

In the next set of steps, you will add a second Web page to the Cottage Toy Store application. The Web page will display the store's hours of operation.

To add another Web page to the application:

1. Click **Website** on the menu bar and then click **Add New Item** to open the Add New Item dialog box. (If Website does not appear on the menu bar, click the Web application's location and name in the Solution Explorer window.)

2. If necessary, click **Visual Basic** in the Installed Templates list and then (if necessary) click **Web Form** in the middle column of the dialog box. Change the filename in the Name box to **Hours** and then click the **Add** button. The computer appends the .aspx extension on the filename and then displays the Hours.aspx Web page in the Document window.

3. Temporarily display the Solution Explorer window. Notice that the window now contains the Hours.aspx filename.

4. Temporarily display the Properties window. Click the **down arrow** button in the Properties window's Object box and then click **DOCUMENT** in the list. (If DOCUMENT does not appear in the Object box, click the Design tab.) Change the Web page's Title property to **Cottage Toy Store**. Also change its BgColor property to the same color as the Default.aspx page. (If necessary, refer back to Figure 27-9.) Click the **OK** button to close the More Colors dialog box.

5. If necessary, click the **Design** tab and then click **inside the rectangle** that appears below the div tag at the top of the Document window. (If the div tag does not appear in the Document window, click either the <div> button at the bottom of the IDE or the rectangle below the body tag.) Type **Please visit us during these hours:** and press **Enter** twice.

6. Next, enter the following three lines of text. Press **Enter** twice after typing the last line.

   Monday – Friday 8am – 10pm
   Saturday 9am – 6pm
   Closed Sunday

7. Select the Please visit us during these hours: text. Click the **down arrow** in the Font Size box and then click **x-large (24pt)**. Also click the *I* (Italic) button on the Formatting toolbar.

8. Select the three lines of text that contain the store hours. Click the **down arrow** in the Font Size box and then click **large (18pt)**. Also click the **B** (Bold) button on the Formatting toolbar.

9. Now, you will change the color of the selected text. Click the **Foreground Color** button on the Formatting toolbar to open the More Colors dialog box. Click **any dark blue hexagon** and then click the **OK** button.

10. Select all of the static text on the Web page. Click the **down arrow** on the Alignment button and then click **Justify Center**.

11. Click the **blank line** below the store hours to deselect the text, and then save the application.

Adding a Link Button Control to a Web Page

In addition to customizing a Web page by changing its properties and formatting its static text, you also can add controls to the Web page. You do this using the tools provided in the Toolbox window. In the next set of steps, you will add a **link button control** to both Web pages. The link button control on the Default.aspx page will display the Hours.aspx page. The link button control on the Hours.aspx page will return the user to the Default.aspx page.

To add a link button control to both Web pages:

1. First, you will add a link button control to the Hours.aspx page. Permanently display the Toolbox window and then click the **LinkButton** tool. Drag your mouse pointer to the location shown in Figure 27-13 and then release the mouse button.

Figure 27-13   Link button control added to the Hours.aspx Web page

2. Temporarily display the Properties window. Change the control's Text property to **Home Page** and press **Enter**. Click **PostBackUrl** in the Properties list and then click the **...** (ellipsis) button to open the Select URL dialog box. Click **Default.aspx** in the Contents of folder list. See Figure 27-14.

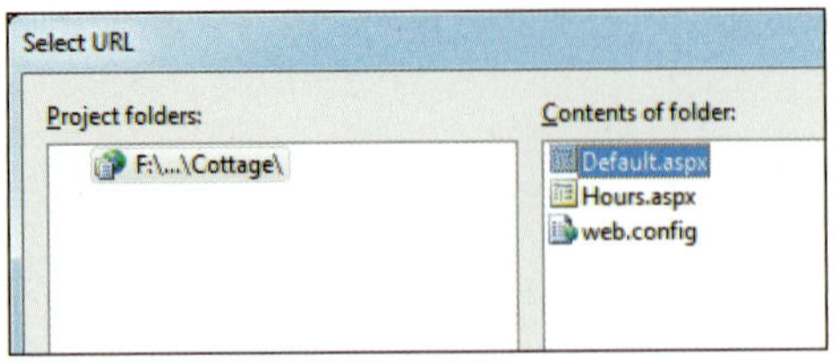

Figure 27-14   Select URL dialog box

3. Click the **OK** button to close the dialog box and then click the **Web page**.

4. Now, you will add a link button control to the Default.aspx page. Click the **Default.aspx** tab. Click the **LinkButton** tool. Drag your mouse pointer to the location shown in Figure 27-15 and then release the mouse button.

Figure 27-15   Link button control added to the Default.aspx Web page

5. Temporarily display the Properties window. Change the control's Text property to **Store Hours** and press **Enter**. Change its PostBackUrl property to **Hours.aspx**.

6. Click the **OK** button to close the Select URL dialog box and then click the **Web page**. Save the application.

Starting a Web Application

Typically, you start a Web application either by pressing Ctrl+F5 or by clicking the Start Without Debugging option on the Debug menu. The method you use—either the shortcut keys or the menu option—is a matter of personal preference. If you prefer to use a menu option, you might need to add the Start Without Debugging option to the Debug menu, because the option is not automatically included on the menu in either Visual Studio or Visual Web Developer Express. You can add the option to the menu by performing the next set of steps. If you prefer to use the Ctrl+F5 shortcut keys, you can skip the next set of steps.

To add the Start Without Debugging option to the Debug menu:

1. First, you will determine whether your Debug menu already contains the Start Without Debugging option. Click **Debug** on the menu bar. If the Debug menu contains the Start Without Debugging option, close the menu by clicking **Debug** again, and then skip the remaining steps in this set of steps.

2. If the Debug menu does not contain the Start Without Debugging option, close the menu by clicking **Debug** again. Click **Tools** on the menu bar and then click **Customize** to open the Customize dialog box.

3. Click the **Commands** tab. The Menu bar radio button should be selected. Click the **down arrow** in the Menu bar list box. Scroll down the list until you see Debug, and then click **Debug**.

4. Click the **Add Command** button to open the Add Command dialog box, and then click **Debug** in the Categories list. Scroll down the Commands list until you see Start Without Debugging, and then click **Start Without Debugging**. Click the **OK** button to close the Add Command dialog box.

5. Click the **Move Down** button three times. The completed Customize dialog box is shown in Figure 27-16. Click the **Close** button to close the Customize dialog box.

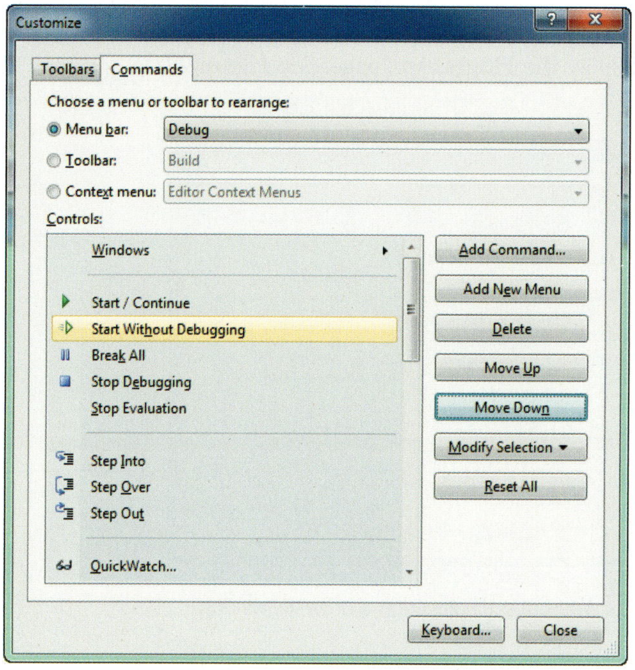

Figure 27-16   Customize dialog box

When you start a Web application in either Visual Studio 2010 or Visual Web Developer 2010 Express, the computer creates a temporary Web server that allows you to view your Web page in a browser. However, keep in mind that your Web page will need to be placed on an actual Web server for others to view it.

To start the Cottage Toy Store Web application:

1. Start the Web application either by pressing **Ctrl+F5** or by clicking the **Start Without Debugging** option on the Debug menu. Your browser requests the Default.aspx page from the server. The server locates the page and then sends the appropriate HTML instructions to your browser for rendering on the screen. Notice that the value in the page's Title property appears in the browser's title bar and on the page's tab in the browser window. See Figure 27-17.

the Title property's value appears here

Figure 27-17   Default.aspx Web page displayed in a browser window

2. Click **Store Hours** to display the Hours.aspx page. See Figure 27-18.

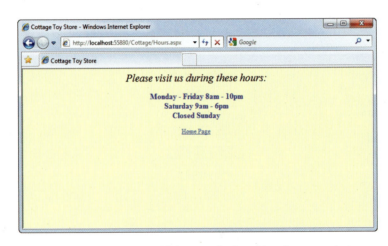

Figure 27-18   Hours.aspx Web page displayed in a browser window

3. Click **Home Page** to display the Default.aspx page, and then close the browser window.

Adding an Image to a Web Page

In the next set of steps, you will add an image to the Default.aspx page. The image is stored in the Small_house.jpg file, which is contained in the ClearlyVB2010\Chap27 folder. The image file was downloaded from the Stock.XCHNG site and was generously contributed by photographer Gerrit Schneider. (You can browse and optionally download other free images at *www.sxc.hu*. However, be sure to read the Web site's copyright policies before downloading any images.)

To add an image to the Web page:

1. First, you will need to add the image file to the application. Click **Website** on the menu bar and then click **Add Existing Item**. Open the ClearlyVB2010\Chap27 folder. Click the **down arrow** in the box that controls the file types and then click **All Files (*.*)** in the list. Click **Small_house.jpg** in the list of filenames and then click the **Add** button.

2. If necessary, insert a blank line below the Store Hours link button control. Click the **blank line** below the control and then press **Enter** to insert another blank line. Click the

Image tool in the toolbox. Drag your mouse pointer to the location shown in Figure 27-19 and then release the mouse button.

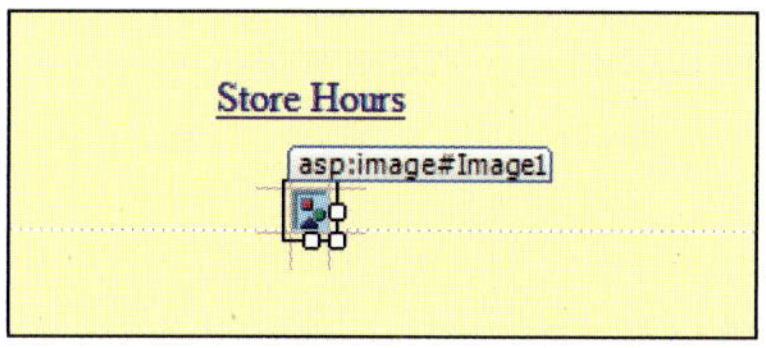

Figure 27-19   Image control added to the Default.aspx Web page

3. Temporarily display the Properties window. Click **ImageUrl** in the Properties list and then click the **...** (ellipsis) button to open the Select Image dialog box. Click **Small_house.jpg** in the Contents of folder section and then click the **OK** button.

4. Next, you will put a colored border around the image control and also change the border's width to 10 pixels. Change the image control's BorderStyle property to **Groove**, and then change its BorderWidth property to **10**. Press **Enter** after typing the number 10.

5. Now, you will change the color of the image's border to match the Web page's color. Click **BorderColor** in the Properties list and then click the **...** (ellipsis) button. When the More Colors dialog box opens, click the same hexagon as you did for the DOCUMENT's BgColor. (If necessary, refer back to Figure 27-9.) Click the **OK** button to close the dialog box and then click the **Web page**.

6. Auto-hide the toolbox. Save and then start the application. See Figure 27-20.

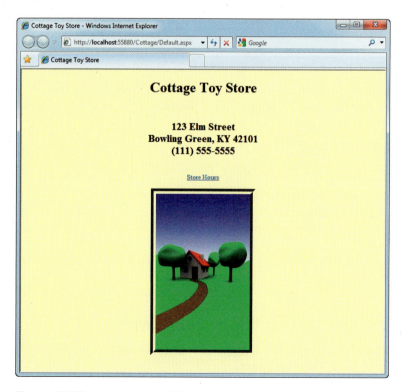

Figure 27-20   Default.aspx Web page

7. Verify that the browser window is not maximized. Place your mouse pointer on the window's right border and then drag the border to the left to make the window narrower. Notice that the text and image remain centered in the visible portion of the window. Now, drag the right border to the right to make the window wider. Here again, the text and image remain centered in the visible portion of the window.

8. Close the browser window.

Closing and Opening an Existing Web Application

You can use the File menu to close and also open an existing Web application.

To close and then open the Cottage Toy Store application:

1. Click **File** on the menu bar and then click **Close Solution** to close the application.

2. Now, you will open the application. Click **File** on the menu bar and then click **Open Web Site**. The Open Web Site dialog box appears. If necessary, click the **File System** button. Open the ClearlyVB2010\Chap27 folder. Click the **Cottage** folder and then click the **Open** button. (If you need to open the Web page in the Document window, right-click the Web page's name in the Solution Explorer window and then click View Designer.)

Repositioning a Control on a Web Page

At times, you may want to reposition a control on a Web page. In this section, you will move the image and link button controls to different locations on the Default.aspx Web page. First, however, you will create a new Web application and then copy the Cottage files to the application.

To create a new Web application and then copy files to the application:

1. Close the Cottage application. Use the New Web Site option on the File menu to create an empty Web application named **Cottage2**. Save the application in the ClearlyVB2010\Chap27 folder.

2. Close the Cottage2 application.

3. Use Windows to open the Cottage2 folder. Delete the web.config file.

4. Use Windows to open the Cottage folder. Select the folder's contents, which include six files (Default.aspx, Default.aspx.vb, Hours.aspx, Hours.aspx.vb, Small_house.jpg, and web.config). Copy the six files to the Cottage2 folder.

Now, you will open the Cottage2 application and move the two controls to different locations on the Default.aspx Web page.

To open the Cottage2 application and then move the controls:

1. Open the Cottage2 Web application. Right-click **Default.aspx** in the Solution Explorer window and then click **View Designer**.

2. First, you will move the image control from the bottom of the Web page to the top of the Web page. If necessary, click **immediately before the letter C** in the Cottage Toy Store heading. Press **Enter** to insert a blank line above the heading.

3. Click the **image control** on the Web page. Drag the image control to the blank line immediately above the heading, and then release the mouse button.

4. Next, you will move the link button control to the empty area below the store's name. Click the **link button control**. Drag the control to the empty area below the store's name, and then release the mouse button.

5. Save and then start the application. See Figure 27-21.

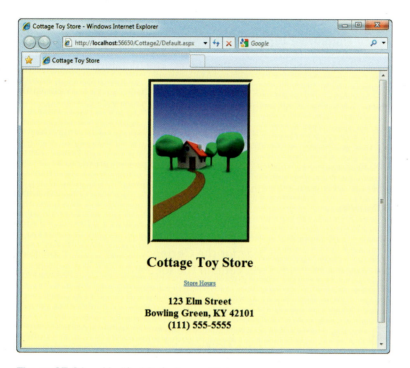

Figure 27-21   Modified Default.aspx Web page

6. Close the browser window and then close the application.

Mini-Quiz 27-2

See Appendix B for the answers.

1. A Web page's _____ property determines the value that appears on the page's tab in a browser window.

   a. Name
   b. Text
   c. Title
   d. Value

2. The _____ property specifies the image displayed in an image control on a Web page.

   a. Image
   b. ImageUrl
   c. Url
   d. Picture

3. A link button control's _____ property specifies the Web page that will appear when the control is clicked.

   a. PostBackUrl
   b. PostBack
   c. Url
   d. none of the above

Dynamic Web Pages

A dynamic Web page contains controls with which the user can interact. It also contains code that tells the controls how to respond to the user's actions. In the following sections, you will create the dynamic Web page shown earlier in Figure 27-3. Recall that the Web page allows the user to enter the number of American dollars. When the user clicks the page's Submit button, the button's Click event procedure will convert the dollars to Mexican pesos and then display the result.

To create the Currency Converter Web application:

1. If necessary, open the Solution Explorer, Properties, and Toolbox windows.

2. Use the New Web Site option on the File menu to create an empty Web application named **Currency**. Save the application in the ClearlyVB2010\Chap27 folder.

3. Use the Add New Item option on the Website menu to add a Web page named Default.aspx to the application. (If Website does not appear on the menu bar, click the Web application's location and name in the Solution Explorer window.)

4. If necessary, click the **Design** tab. Change the DOCUMENT object's Title property to **Currency Converter**.

Before you add any text or controls to a Web page, you should plan the page's layout. Figure 27-22 shows a sketch of the Web page for the Currency Converter application. The Web page will contain static text. It also will contain the following controls: an image, a text box, a label, and a button.

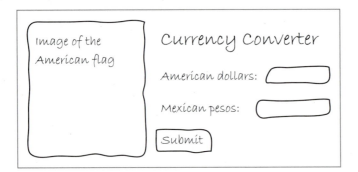

Figure 27-22 Sketch of the Currency Converter application's Web page

To begin creating the Web page:

1. Click **inside the rectangle** that appears below the div (or body) tag at the top of the Document window. Recall that the div tag defines a division in a Web page. All of the text in this division will use the Segoe UI font. If necessary, use the View menu to display the Formatting toolbar. Click the **down arrow** in the Font Name box and then scroll the list until you see Segoe UI. Click **Segoe UI** in the list.

2. Before dragging an image control to the Web page, you will add the American flag image file to the application. Click **Website** on the menu bar and then click **Add Existing Item**. Open the ClearlyVB2010\Chap27 folder. Click the **down arrow** in the box that controls the file types and then click **All Files (*.*)** in the list. Click **USflag.jpg** in the list of filenames and then click the **Add** button.

3. Drag an image control into the rectangle that appears below the div tag and then release the mouse button. Change the image control's ImageUrl property to **USflag.jpg** and then click the **OK** button to close the Select Image dialog box.

4. Click an **empty area** to the right of the flag to deselect the image control, and then press **Enter** twice.

5. Next, you will enter the Web page's static text. Press **Tab** twice. Type **Currency Converter** and then press **Enter** twice.

6. Press **Tab** twice. Type **American dollars:**, press the **Spacebar** twice, and then press **Enter** twice.

7. Press **Tab** twice. Type **Mexican pesos:**, press the **Spacebar** twice, and then press **Enter** twice.

8. Press **Tab** twice. Figure 27-23 shows the image control and static text on the Web page.

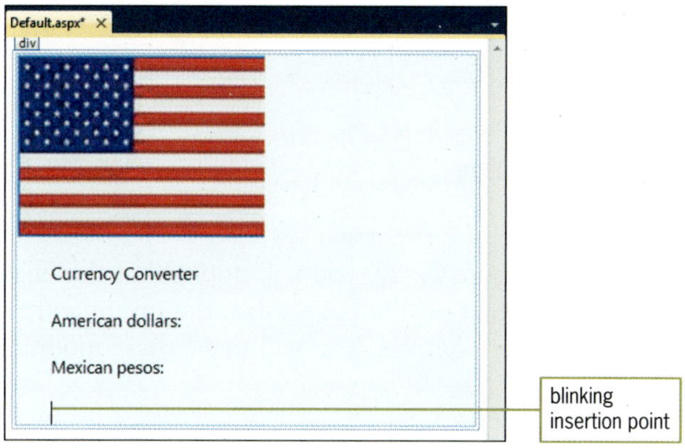

Figure 27-23   Image control and static text on the Web page

In addition to the image control and static text, the Web page will contain a text box, a label, and a button. You will add those controls next.

To add a text box, a label, and a button to the page:

1. Drag a text box control to the Web page. Position the control immediately after the two spaces that follow the "American dollars:" text, and then release the mouse button.

2. Unlike Windows controls, Web controls have an ID property rather than a Name property. Use the Properties window to set the TextBox1 control's ID property (which appears at the top of the Properties list) to **txtDollars**. Also set its Width property to **90px**.

3. Drag a label control to the Web page. Position the control immediately after the two spaces that follow the "Mexican pesos:" text, and then release the mouse button. Set the following properties for the Label1 control:

ID	**lblPesos**
BorderStyle	**Solid**
BorderWidth	**1px**
Text	**0**
Width	**90px**

4. Change the label control's BackColor property to a pale yellow.

5. Finally, drag a button control to the Web page. Position the control two blank lines below the letter M in the "Mexican pesos:" text, and then release the mouse button. Set the following properties for the Button1 control:

ID	**btnSubmit**
Text	**Submit**

6. Click a **blank area** on the Web page. See Figure 27-24.

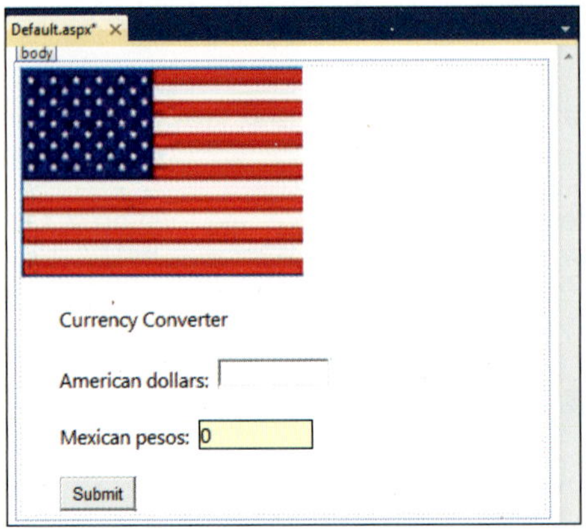

Figure 27-24   Current status of the Web page

Looking back at the sketch shown earlier in Figure 27-22, you will notice that the heading text (Currency Converter) is larger than the other text on the page. Also, the image control is positioned to the left of the static text and other controls. You will make these modifications in the next set of steps.

To complete the Web page's interface:

1. Auto-hide the Solution Explorer, Properties, and Toolbox windows.

2. Select (highlight) the Currency Converter text. Use the Font Size box on the Formatting toolbar to change the font size to **xx-large (36pt)**. (You also can use the Font option on the Format menu to change the font size.)

3. Click the **image control**. Click **Format** on the menu bar and then click **Position** to open the Position dialog box. See Figure 27-25.

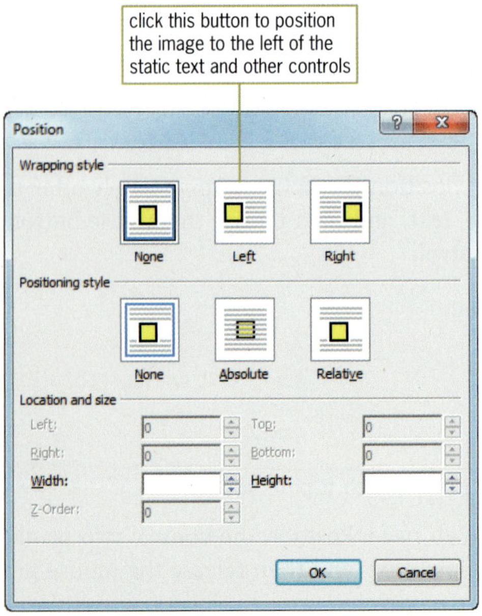

Figure 27-25   Position dialog box

4. The image control should appear on the left side of the static text and other controls. Click **Left** in the Wrapping style section, and then click the **OK** button.

5. Position your mouse pointer on the image control's lower-right sizing handle, as shown in Figure 27-26. Drag the sizing handle until the control is approximately the size shown in the figure. (The number of pixels may be different on your screen. Just be sure that all of the static text and other controls appear to the right of the image control.)

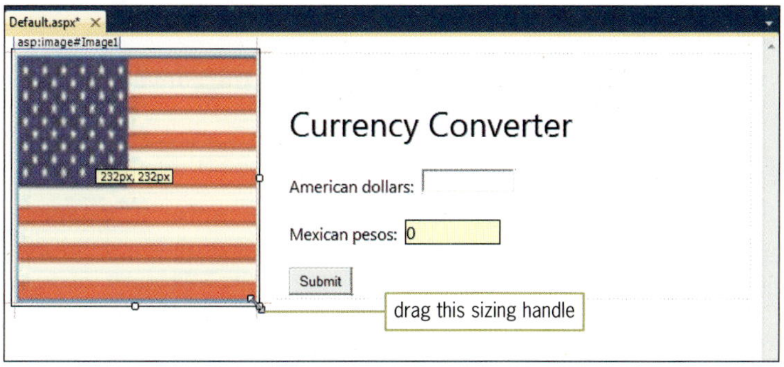

Figure 27-26 Size and position of the image control

6. Click an **empty area** on the Web page to deselect the image control. Save the application and then start it by pressing **Ctrl+F5**. The Web page appears in a browser window. Close the browser window.

Coding the Submit Button's Click Event Procedure

In the following set of steps, you will code the Submit button's Click event procedure so that it converts the number of American dollars to Mexican pesos and then displays the result on the Web page. At the time of this writing, an American dollar was equivalent to approximately 12.36 Mexican pesos. As you do when coding a control on a Windows form, you enter the code for a control on a Web page in the Code Editor window.

To code the Submit button's Click event procedure:

1. Right-click the **Web page** and then click **View Code** to open the Code Editor window. The Default.aspx.vb window opens. The .vb extension on the filename indicates that the file is a Visual Basic source file, which is a file that contains Visual Basic code. The file is referred to as the code-behind file, because it contains code that supports the Web page. Temporarily display the Solution Explorer window. See Figure 27-27.

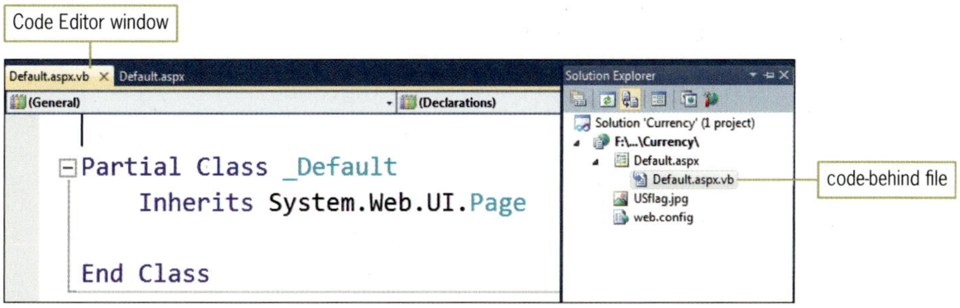

Figure 27-27 Code Editor and Solution Explorer windows

2. Enter the following comments above the Partial Class clause, except replace <your name> and <current date> with your name and the current date, respectively:

' Name: Currency
' Purpose: Convert dollars to pesos
' Programmer: <your name> on <current date>

3. Open the btnSubmit control's Click event procedure. Type the following comment and then press **Enter** twice:

' converts dollars to pesos

4. The procedure will use a Double named constant to store the conversion rate of 12.36. Enter the following Const statement:

Const dblPESO_RATE As Double = 12.36

5. The procedure will use two Double variables to store the number of American dollars and the number of Mexican pesos. Enter the following Dim statements. Press **Enter** twice after typing the second Dim statement.

Dim dblDollars As Double
Dim dblPesos As Double

6. Now, you will store the user's entry in the `dblDollars` variable. Enter the following TryParse method:

Double.TryParse(txtDollars.Text, dblDollars)

7. Next, you will convert the dollars to pesos and then store the result in the `dblPesos` variable. Enter the following assignment statement:

dblPesos = dblDollars * dblPESO_RATE

8. Finally, you will display the number of pesos in the lblPesos control. Enter the following assignment statement:

lblPesos.Text = dblPesos.ToString("N2")

Figure 27-28 shows the code entered in the btnSubmit control's Click event procedure.

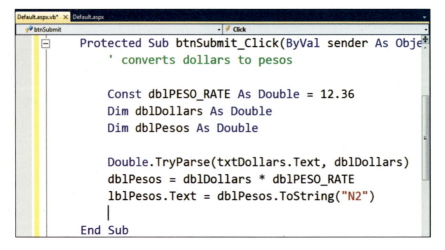

```
Default.aspx.vb*  ×  Default.aspx
btnSubmit                                        Click

    Protected Sub btnSubmit_Click(ByVal sender As Obje
        ' converts dollars to pesos

        Const dblPESO_RATE As Double = 12.36
        Dim dblDollars As Double
        Dim dblPesos As Double

        Double.TryParse(txtDollars.Text, dblDollars)
        dblPesos = dblDollars * dblPESO_RATE
        lblPesos.Text = dblPesos.ToString("N2")

    End Sub
```

Figure 27-28   btnSubmit control's Click event procedure

Now you will test the Currency Converter application to verify that it is working correctly.

To test the Currency Converter application:

1. Save and then start the application. Your browser requests the Default.aspx page from the server. The server locates the page and then sends the appropriate HTML instructions to your browser for rendering on the screen.

2. Click the **American dollars** box and then type **10**. Click the **Submit** button; doing this submits your entry to the server, along with a request for additional services. The server processes the code contained in the button's Click event procedure and then sends the appropriate HTML to the browser for rendering on the screen. See Figure 27-29.

Figure 27-29   Result of clicking the Submit button

3. Close the browser window and then close the Code Editor window.

Validating User Input

The Validation section of the toolbox provides several tools for validating user input. The tools are referred to as **validator tools**. The name, purpose, and important properties of each validator tool are listed in Figure 27-30. In the Currency Converter application, you will use a RequiredFieldValidator control to verify that the user entered the number of American dollars.

Name	Purpose	Properties
CompareValidator	compare an entry with a constant value or the property stored in a control	ControlToCompare ControlToValidate ErrorMessage Type ValueToCompare
CustomValidator	verify that an entry passes the specified validation logic	ClientValidationFunction ControlToValidate ErrorMessage
RangeValidator	verify that an entry is within the specified minimum and maximum values	ControlToValidate ErrorMessage MaximumValue MinimumValue Type
RegularExpressionValidator	verify that an entry matches a specific pattern	ControlToValidate ErrorMessage ValidationExpression
RequiredFieldValidator	verify that a control contains data	ControlToValidate ErrorMessage
ValidationSummary	display all of the validation error messages in a single location on a Web page	DisplayMode HeaderText

Figure 27-30   Validator tools

To verify that the user entered the number of American dollars:

1. If necessary, maximize the Visual Studio (Visual Web Developer) window.

2. Click **to the immediate right of the txtDollars control** and then press the **Spacebar** three times.

3. Temporarily display the Toolbox window. If necessary, expand the Validation section. Click the **RequiredFieldValidator** tool and then drag your mouse pointer to the Web page. Position your mouse pointer to the right of the txtDollars control and then release the mouse button.

4. Temporarily display the Properties window. Set the following properties for the RequiredFieldValidator1 control:

    ControlToValidate   **txtDollars**
    ErrorMessage   **Required entry**
    ForeColor   choose a red hexagon

5. Click an **empty area** of the Web page. Save the application and then start it by pressing **Ctrl+F5**.

6. Click the **Submit** button without entering a value in the txtDollars control. The RequiredFieldValidator control displays the "Required entry" message, as shown in Figure 27-31.

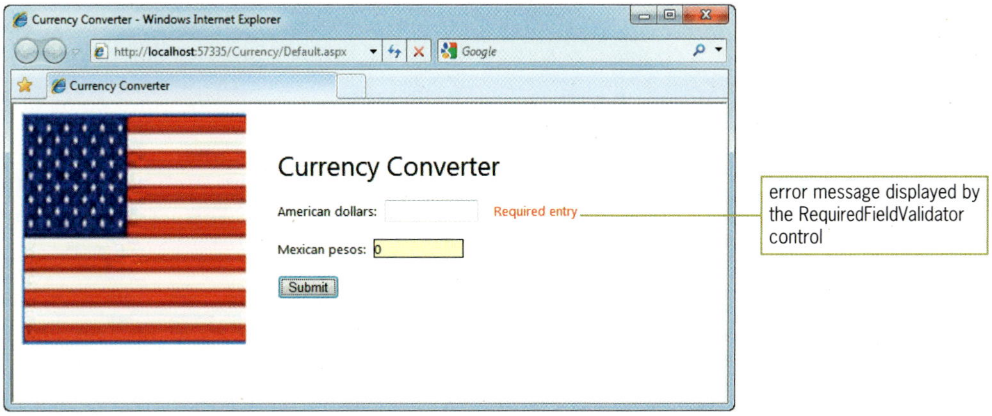

Figure 27-31   Result of clicking the Submit button when the American dollars box is empty

7. Click the **American dollars** box and then type **20**. Click the **Submit** button. The error message is removed from the Web page and the number 247.20 appears in the lblPesos control.

8. Close the browser window and then close the application.

Mini-Quiz 27-3

See Appendix B for the answers.

1. If you want text to appear to the left of the selected image control on a Web form, you would need to click the _____ button in the Position dialog box.

   a. Align
   b. AlignLeft

   c. Left
   d. Right

2. The Visual Basic code in a Web page is processed by the _____.

   a. client computer

   b. Web server

3. You can use a _____ control to verify that a control on a Web page contains data.

   a. RequiredFieldValidator
   b. RequiredField

   c. RequiredValidator
   d. none of the above

Summary

- The Web consists of Web pages that are stored on Web servers.

- A client computer uses a browser to request a Web page from a Web server. It also uses the browser to view the Web page.

- Web pages can be either static or dynamic (interactive).

- HTML tags tell the browser how to render a Web page on the computer screen. ASP tags specify the controls to include on a Web page.

- Dynamic Web pages contain code that is processed by the Web server.

- You use the New Web Site option on the File menu to create an empty Web application.

- You can use the Add New Item option on the Website menu to add a Web page to an application.

- You add a title to a Web page by setting the DOCUMENT object's Title property.

- The DOCUMENT object's BgColor property determines the background color of a Web page.

- You can add static text to a Web page by typing the text on the Web page; or, you can use a label control. You can format the static text using either the Format menu or the Formatting toolbar.

- You can display a Web page in full screen view using the Full Screen option on the View menu. You display a Web page in a browser window by starting the Web application.

- You use the LinkButton tool to add a link button control to a Web page. The control's PostBackUrl property specifies the Web page to display when the control is clicked.

- You can use an image control to display an image on a Web page. You specify the image in the control's ImageUrl property.

- To close a Web application, click File on the menu bar and then click Close Solution.

- To open an existing Web application, click File on the menu bar and then click Open Web Site.

- You can drag a control to reposition it on a Web page.

- You can use the Position option on the Format menu to wrap text around an image control.

- To have a control on a Web page respond to the user's action, you enter the appropriate code in the Code Editor window.

- The Validation section of the toolbox provides validator tools for validating the user input on a Web page.

Key Terms

ASP—stands for "active server page"

Browser—a program that allows a client computer to request and view Web pages

Client computer—a computer that requests information from a Web server

Dynamic Web page—an interactive document that can accept information from the user and also retrieve information for the user

Link button control—allows the user to "jump" from one Web page to another Web page

Static text—text that the user is not allowed to edit

Static Web page—a non-interactive document whose purpose is merely to display information to the viewer

Validator tools—the tools contained in the Validation section of the toolbox; used to validate user input on a Web page

Web pages—the documents stored on Web servers

Web server—a computer that contains special software that "serves up" Web pages in response to requests from client computers

Review Questions

1. A computer that requests an ASP page from a Web server is called a _____ computer.

    a. browser
    b. client

    c. requesting
    d. none of the above

2. A _____ is a program that uses HTML to render a Web page on the computer screen.

    a. browser
    b. client

    c. server
    d. none of the above

3. An online form used to purchase a product is an example of a _____ Web page.

    a. dynamic

    b. static

4. The first Web page in an empty Visual Basic Web application is automatically assigned the name _____.

    a. Default.aps
    b. Default1.vb

    c. WebForm1.aspx
    d. none of the above

5. The background color of a Web page is determined by the _____ property.

    a. BackColor
    b. BackgroundColor

    c. BgColor
    d. none of the above

6. In code, you refer to a control on a Web page using the control's _____ property.

    a. Caption
    b. ID

    c. Name
    d. Text

7. You can use a(n) _____ control to verify that an entry on a Web page is within a minimum and maximum value.

    a. MinMaxValidation
    b. MaxMinValidation

    c. EntryValidator
    d. RangeValidator

Exercises

1. In this exercise, you modify the Currency Converter application from the chapter. **MODIFY THIS**

    a. Create an empty Web application named CurrencyRangeValidator. Save the application in the ClearlyVB2010\Chap27 folder. Close the CurrencyRangeValidator application.
    b. Use Windows to open the CurrencyRangeValidator folder. Delete the web.config file.
    c. Use Windows to open the Currency folder. Select the folder's contents. Copy the selected contents to the CurrencyRangeValidator folder.
    d. Open the CurrencyRangeValidator Web site. Right-click Default.aspx in the Solution Explorer window and then click View Designer.
    e. Add a RangeValidator control to the Web page. Change the control's Type property to Double. The control should display an appropriate message when the number of American dollars is either less than 1 or greater than 100,000.
    f. Save the application and then start and test it. Close the browser window and then close the application.

INTRODUCTORY

2. Create an empty Web application named Johansen. Save the application in the ClearlyVB2010\Chap27 folder. Add a new Web page named Default.aspx to the application. Change the DOCUMENT object's Title property to Johansen Pet Supplies. Create a Web page similar to the one shown in Figure 27-32. The static text should be centered, horizontally, on the page. Save and then start the application. Close the browser window and then close the application.

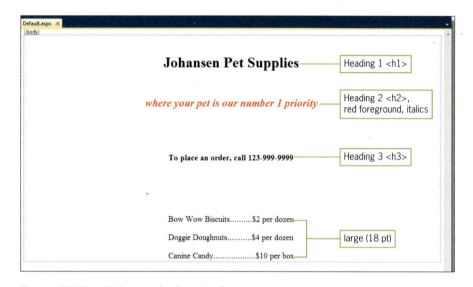

Figure 27-32   Web page for Exercise 2

INTRODUCTORY

3. Create an empty Web application named Winterland. Save the application in the ClearlyVB2010\Chap27 folder. Add a new Web page named Default.aspx to the application. Change the DOCUMENT object's Title property to Winterland Farms. Change the DOCUMENT object's BgColor property to a light blue. Create a Web page similar to the one shown in Figure 27-33. The winterland.jpg file is contained in the ClearlyVB2010\Chap27 folder. Save and then start the application. Close the browser window and then close the application.

Figure 27-33   Web page for Exercise 3

INTRODUCTORY

4. Create an empty Web application named Multiplication. Save the application in the ClearlyVB2010\Chap27 folder.

   a. Add a new Web page named Default.aspx to the application. Change the DOCUMENT object's Title property to Multiplication Calculator. Create a Web page similar to the one shown in Figure 27-34. The X image is contained in the ClearlyVB2010\Chap27\Times.jpg file.

b. Add two RequiredFieldValidator controls to the Web page. The controls should verify that their respective text box contains data.

c. Open the Code Editor window. Code the Submit button's Click event procedure so it multiplies the value entered in the txtMultiplier control by the value entered in the txtMultiplicand control and then displays the result in the lblProduct control.

d. Save the application and then start and test it. Close the browser window. Close the Code Editor window and then close the application.

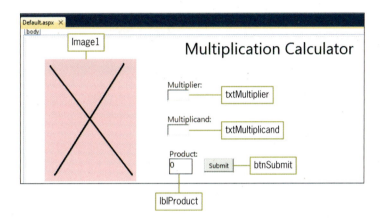

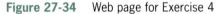

Figure 27-34   Web page for Exercise 4

5. In this exercise, you create an application that displays the result of converting British pounds to American dollars. Create an empty Web application named PoundsToDollars. Save the application in the ClearlyVB2010\Chap27 folder. Add a new Web page named Default.aspx to the application. Change the DOCUMENT object's Title property to Pounds to Dollars. Include a Submit button on the Web page. Also include an image control that displays the contents of the BritishFlag.jpg image file. The image file is contained in the ClearlyVB2010\Chap27 folder. Open the Code Editor window. Use comments to document the application's name and purpose, as well as your name and the current date. Code the Submit button's Click event procedure. Use 1.56 as the number of American dollars for each British pound. Save the application and then start and test it. Close the browser window. Close the Code Editor window and then close the application.

INTRODUCTORY

6. Create an empty Web application named Gutierrez. Save the application in the ClearlyVB2010\Chap27 folder. Add two new Web pages named Default.aspx and Message.aspx to the application. Change the DOCUMENT object's Title property to Gutierrez Heating and Cooling. Create Web pages similar to the ones shown in Figures 27-35 and 27-36. The static text and link button control on the Default.aspx page should be centered, horizontally, on the page. As you are creating the Web pages, periodically view them in full screen view. Save and then start the application. Close the browser window and then close the application.

INTERMEDIATE

Figure 27-35   Default.aspx Web page for Exercise 6

Figure 27-36   Message.aspx Web page for Exercise 6

ADVANCED

7. Create an empty Web application named ZipCode. Save the application in the
    ClearlyVB2010\Chap27 folder. Add a new Web page named Default.aspx to the
    application. Change the DOCUMENT object's Title property to ZIP Code Verifier.
    Create a Web page similar to the one shown in Figure 27-37. Use labels for the static
    text. Also, use the Segoe UI font for the static text and controls. Verify that the user
    entered the ZIP code and that the ZIP code is in the appropriate format. (Hint: Use a
    RegularExpressionValidator control to verify the format.) If the ZIP code is valid, the
    Submit button's Click event procedure should display the message "Your ZIP code is "
    followed by the ZIP code and a period. Save and then start the application. Test the
    application by clicking the Submit button without entering a ZIP code. Then test it
    using the following ZIP codes: 60611, 606123, 60611-3456, and 60611-5. Close the
    browser window. Close the Code Editor window and then close the application.

Figure 27-37   Web page for Exercise 7

Data Types

Data type	Stores	Memory required
Boolean	a logical value (True, False)	2 bytes
Char	one Unicode character	2 bytes
Date	date and time information Date range: January 1, 0001 to December 31, 9999 Time range: 0:00:00 (midnight) to 23:59:59	8 bytes
Decimal	a number with a decimal place Range with no decimal place: +/–79,228,162,514,264,337,593,543,950,335 Range with a decimal place: +/–7.9228162514264337593543950335	16 bytes
Double	a number with a decimal place Range: $+/-4.94065645841247 \times 10^{-324}$ to $+/-1.79769313486231 \times 10^{308}$	8 bytes
Integer	integer Range: –2,147,483,648 to 2,147,483,647	4 bytes
Long	integer Range: –9,223,372,036,854,775,808 to 9,223,372,036,854,775,807	8 bytes
Object	data of any type	4 bytes
Short	integer Range: –32,768 to 32,767	2 bytes
Single	a number with a decimal place Range: $+/-1.401298 \times 10^{-45}$ to $+/-3.402823 \times 10^{38}$	4 bytes
String	text; 0 to approximately 2 billion Unicode characters	

Answers to Mini-Quizzes and TRY THIS Exercises

Chapter 1

TRY THIS 1 (Chapter 1)

1. repeat 5 times:
       walk forward
2. jump over the box
3. repeat until you are directly in front of the chair:
       walk forward
4. repeat 2 times:
       turn to the right 90 degrees
5. sit down

TRY THIS 2 (Chapter 1)

repeat 25 times:
       read the student's answer and the correct answer
       if the student's answer is not the same as the correct answer, do this:
           mark the student's answer incorrect

Chapter 2

Mini-Quiz 2-1

1. Output: annual state income tax

   Input: yearly taxable wages
          state income tax rate

2. Output: savings

   Input: number of CDs purchased
          club CD price
          store CD price

3. Output: total amount saved

   Input: daily savings
          number of days

Mini-Quiz 2-2

1. Algorithm:
   1. enter the yearly taxable wages and state income tax rate
   2. calculate the annual state income tax by multiplying the yearly taxable wages by the state income tax rate
   3. display the annual state income tax

2.

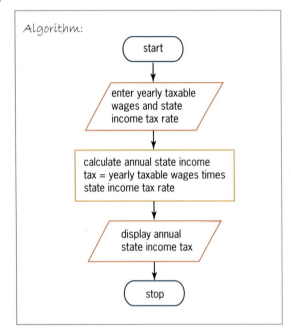

Algorithm:

start

enter yearly taxable wages and state income tax rate

calculate annual state income tax = yearly taxable wages times state income tax rate

display annual state income tax

stop

3. Algorithm:
   1. enter the number of CDs purchased, the club CD price, and the store CD price
   2. calculate the club cost by multiplying the number of CDs purchased by the club CD price
   3. calculate the store cost by multiplying the number of CDs purchased by the store CD price
   4. calculate the savings by subtracting the club cost from the store cost
   5. display the savings

Mini-Quiz 2-3

1. Desk-check table

yearly taxable wages	state income tax rate	annual state income tax
~~23000~~	~~.03~~	~~690~~
14000	.02	280

2. Desk-check table

number of CDs purchased	club CD price	store CD price	club cost	store cost	savings
~~20~~	~~10.50~~	~~14.99~~	~~210~~	~~299.80~~	~~89.80~~
5	9.99	11	49.95	55	5.05

TRY THIS 1 (Chapter 2)

Output: tip

Input: total bill
     liquor charge
     tip percentage

Algorithm:
1. enter the total bill, liquor charge, and tip percentage
2. calculate the tip by subtracting the liquor charge from the total bill, and then multiplying the remainder by the tip percentage
3. display the tip

Desk-check table

total bill	liquor charge	tip percentage	tip
~~85~~	~~20~~	~~.2~~	~~13~~
35	0	.15	5.25

TRY THIS 2 (Chapter 2)

Output: total cost of purchase

Processing: total cup cost
     total plate cost
     subtotal

Input: cup price
     plate price
     number of cups
     number of plates
     sales tax rate

Algorithm:
1. enter the cup price, plate price, number of cups, number of plates, and sales tax rate
2. calculate the total cup cost by multiplying the number of cups by the cup price
3. calculate the total plate cost by multiplying the number of plates by the plate price
4. calculate the subtotal by adding together the total cup cost and total plate cost
5. calculate the total cost of purchase by multiplying the subtotal by the sales tax rate, and then adding the result to the subtotal
6. display the total cost of purchase

Desk-check table

cup price	plate price	number of cups	number of plates	sales tax rate
~~.50~~	~~1~~	~~35~~	~~35~~	~~.02~~
.25	.75	20	10	.06

total cup cost	total plate cost	subtotal	total cost of purchase
~~17.50~~	~~35~~	~~52.50~~	~~53.55~~
5	7.50	12.50	13.25

Chapter 3

Mini-Quiz 3-1

1. label
2. Toolbox window
3. graphical user interface

Mini-Quiz 3-2

1. Image
2. Text
3. upper-left
4. PictureBox2
5. Start Debugging

TRY THIS 1 (Chapter 3)

Set the form's Font property to Segoe UI, 9pt. Set its StartPosition and Text properties to CenterScreen and Scottsville Library, respectively. Set the Label1 control's Text property to WELCOME!. Set the PictureBox1 control's Image and SizeMode properties to Book_opens.gif and StretchImage, respectively. Use the Format menu to center the label and picture box controls.

Chapter 4

Mini-Quiz 4-1

1. label
2. c. txtCity
3. btn

Mini-Quiz 4-2

1. 6
2. a. Alt+t
3. procedure header

TRY THIS 1 (Chapter 4)

Interface:

Tab order:

Code:

Chapter 5

Mini-Quiz 5-1

1. `Val(lblTotal.Text) + 100`

2. 0

3. 1

Mini-Quiz 5-2

1. `lblGross.Text = Val(txtHours.Text) * Val(txtRate.Text)`

2. `lblNewPrice.Text = Val(txtOldPrice.Text) + 5`

3. assignment operator

4. General Declarations section

TRY THIS 1 (Chapter 5)

```
' Name:          New Pay Project
' Purpose:       Display the new weekly pay
' Programmer:    <your name> on <current date>

Public Class frmMain

    Private Sub btnExit_Click(ByVal sender As Object,
                              ByVal e As System.EventArgs) Handles btnExit.Click
        Me.Close()

    End Sub

    Private Sub btnCalculate_Click(ByVal sender As Object,
                                   ByVal e As System.EventArgs) Handles btnCalculate.Click
        ' calculates and displays the new weekly pay

        lblNewPay.Text = Val(txtCurrentPay.Text) *
            Val(txtRaisePercentage.Text) + Val(txtCurrentPay.Text)
    End Sub
End Class
```

Chapter 6

Mini-Quiz 6-1

1. Integer

2. d. `dblPay.Rate`

3. `Dim dblHoursWorked As Double`

Mini-Quiz 6-2

1. `Decimal.TryParse(txtIncome.Text, decIncome)`

2. `Const intMINIMUM As Integer = 55`

3. `lblSales.Text = dblSales.ToString("C0")`

TRY THIS 1 (Chapter 6)

```
Private Sub btnCalculate_Click(ByVal sender As Object,
    ' calculates and displays the annual commission

    ' declare variables
    Dim decSales As Decimal
    Dim decRate As Decimal
    Dim decCommission As Decimal

    ' assign input to variables
    Decimal.TryParse(txtSales.Text, decSales)
    Decimal.TryParse(txtRate.Text, decRate)

    ' calculate and display the commission
    decCommission = decSales * decRate
    lblCommission.Text = decCommission.ToString("C2")

End Sub
```

TRY THIS 2 (Chapter 6)

```
Private Sub btnCalculate_Click(ByVal sender As Object,
    ' calculates and displays the new weekly pay

    ' declare named constant
    Const dblRATE As Double = 0.03

    ' declare variables
    Dim dblNewPay As Double
    Dim dblRaise As Double
    Dim dblCurrentPay As Double

    ' assign input to a variable
    Double.TryParse(txtCurrentPay.Text, dblCurrentPay)

    ' calculate raise and new pay
    dblRaise = dblCurrentPay * dblRATE
    dblNewPay = dblCurrentPay + dblRaise

    ' display new pay
    lblNewPay.Text = dblNewPay.ToString("C2")
End Sub
```

dblRATE	dblNewPay	dblRaise	dblCurrentPay
~~.03~~	~~206~~	~~6~~	~~200~~
.03	339.90	9.90	330

Chapter 7

Mini-Quiz 7-1

1. d. all of the above
2. Step Into
3. b. before

TRY THIS 1 (Chapter 7)

```
Private Sub btnCalculate_Click(ByVal sender As Object, ByVal e As
    ' calculates and displays the quarterly commission

    ' declare named constant
    Const decRATE As Decimal = 0.1

    ' declare variables
    Dim decSales1 As Decimal
    Dim decSales2 As Decimal
    Dim decSales3 As Decimal
    Dim decCommission As Decimal

    ' assign input to variables
    Decimal.TryParse(txtSales1.Text, decSales1)
    Decimal.TryParse(txtSales2.Text, decSales2)
    Decimal.TryParse(txtSales3.Text, decSales3)

    ' calculate and display commission
    decCommission = (decSales1 + decSales2 + decSales3) * decRATE
    lblCommission.Text = decCommission.ToString("C2")
End Sub
```

TRY THIS 2 (Chapter 7)

```
Private Sub btnCalculate_Click(ByVal sender As Object, B
    ' calculates and displays the new weekly pay
    ' using a raise rate of 3%

    ' declare named constant
    Const dblRATE As Double = 0.03

    ' declare variables
    Dim dblNewPay As Decimal
    Dim dblCurrentPay As Decimal

    ' assign input to a variable
    Double.TryParse(txtCurrentPay.Text, dblCurrentPay)

    ' calculate new pay
    dblNewPay = dblCurrentPay + dblRATE * dblCurrentPay

    ' display new pay
    lblNewPay.Text = dblNewPay.ToString("C2")
End Sub
```

Chapter 8

Mini-Quiz 8-1

1. The solution does not require a decision.

2. The solution requires a decision about whether the phone is ringing.

3. The solution does not require a decision.

4. The solution requires a decision about the color of the ball.

Mini-Quiz 8-2

1. ```
   If decHours > 40 Then
        lblMsg.Text = "Overtime pay"
   End If
   ```

2. ```
   If decHours > 40 Then
        lblMsg.Text = "Overtime pay"
   Else
        lblMsg.Text = "Regular pay only"
   End If
   ```

3. d. only the selection structure's false path

TRY THIS 1 (Chapter 8)

Output: answer

Input: first integer
        second integer
        subtraction?

Algorithm:
1. enter the first integer, second integer, and subtraction? items
2. if subtraction?, do this:
        calculate the answer by subtracting the second integer from the first integer
    otherwise, do this:
        calculate the answer by adding the second integer to the first integer
    end if
3. display the answer

```vb
Private Sub btnCalc_Click(ByVal sender As Object, ByVal e As System.Event
    ' calculates either the sum of or the difference between two numbers

    Dim intNum1 As Integer
    Dim intNum2 As Integer
    Dim intAnswer As Integer

    ' assign numbers to variables
    Integer.TryParse(txtNum1.Text, intNum1)
    Integer.TryParse(txtNum2.Text, intNum2)

    ' calculate and display the difference or sum
    If chkSubtract.Checked = True Then
        intAnswer = intNum1 - intNum2
    Else
        intAnswer = intNum1 + intNum2
    End If
    lblAnswer.Text = intAnswer
End Sub
```

TRY THIS 2 (Chapter 8)

intCode	decCurrentPay	decRate	decRaise	decNewPay
~~1~~	~~200~~	~~.03~~	~~6~~	~~206~~
3	200	.05	10	210

```vb
Private Sub btnCalculate_Click(ByVal sender As Object, ByVal
    ' calculates and displays the new weekly pay

    Dim intCode As Integer
    Dim decCurrentPay As Decimal
    Dim decRate As Decimal
    Dim decRaise As Decimal
    Dim decNewPay As Decimal

    ' assign input to variables
    Integer.TryParse(txtCode.Text, intCode)
    Decimal.TryParse(txtCurrentPay.Text, decCurrentPay)

    ' calculate raise and new pay
    If intCode = 1 Then
        decRate = 0.03
    Else
        decRate = 0.05
    End If
    decRaise = decCurrentPay * decRate
    decNewPay = decCurrentPay + decRaise

    ' display new pay
    lblNewPay.Text = decNewPay.ToString("C2")
End Sub
```

Chapter 9

Mini-Quiz 9-1

1. The solution does not require a nested selection structure.

2. The solution requires a nested selection structure whose condition determines whether the caller is a telemarketer.

3. The solution requires two nested selection structures. The condition in one of the nested selection structures should determine whether the red box is full. The condition in the other nested selection structure should determine whether the yellow box is full.

Mini-Quiz 9-2

1. b. `intNum < 0 OrElse intNum > 1000`

2. c. `dblPrice > 15.45 AndAlso dblPrice < 25.75`

3. a. `chkDiscount.Checked = True AndAlso chkCoupon.Checked = True`

4. b. False

TRY THIS 1 (Chapter 9)

To modify the btnCalc control's Click event procedure, change the selection structure's condition to `chkEmployee.Checked = True OrElse intQuantity >= 10`.

TRY THIS 2 (Chapter 9)

```
Private Sub btnCalc_Click(ByVal sender As Object,
ByVal e As System.EventArgs) Handles btnCalc.Click
    ' calculates and displays the total amount due

    Const decEMP_DISC_RATE As Decimal = 0.12
    Const decNON_EMP_DISC_RATE As Decimal = 0.05
    Dim intQuantity As Integer
    Dim decPrice As Decimal
    Dim decTotal As Decimal

    ' assign quantity and price to variables
    Integer.TryParse(txtQuantity.Text, intQuantity)
    Decimal.TryParse(txtPrice.Text, decPrice)

    ' calculate total due
    decTotal = intQuantity * decPrice
    If chkEmployee.Checked = True Then
        decTotal = decTotal * (1 - decEMP_DISC_RATE)
    Else
        If intQuantity > 20 Then
            decTotal = decTotal * (1 - decNON_EMP_DISC_RATE)
        End If
    End If

    ' display total due
    lblTotal.Text = decTotal.ToString("C2")
End Sub
```

Chapter 10

Mini-Quiz 10-1

1. ```
   If intPromoCode = 1 Then
       decRate = .02
   ElseIf intPromoCode = 2 Then
       decRate = .05
   ElseIf intPromoCode = 3 Then
       decRate = .1
   ElseIf intPromoCode = 4 Then
       decRate = .25
   Else
       decRate = 0
   End If
   ```

2. ```
   strId = txtId.Text.ToUpper
   ```

3.
```
If strId = "12A" Then
    lblFirst.Text = "Jerry"
    lblLast.Text = "Jones"
ElseIf strId = "45B" Then
    lblFirst.Text = "Mark"
    lblLast.Text = "Smith"
ElseIf strId = "67X" Then
    lblFirst.Text = "Jill"
    lblLast.Text = "Batist"
ElseIf strId = "78Y" Then
    lblFirst.Text = "Cheryl"
    lblLast.Text = "Sworski"
Else
    lblFirst.Text = "?"
    lblLast.Text = "?"
End If
```

Mini-Quiz 10-2

1.
```
Select Case intPromoCode
    Case 1
            decRate = .02
    Case 2
            decRate = .05
    Case 3
            decRate = .1
    Case 4
            decRate = .25
    Case Else
            decRate = 0
End Select
```

2.
```
Select Case strId
    Case "12A"
            lblFirst.Text = "Jerry"
            lblLast.Text = "Jones"
    Case "45B"
            lblFirst.Text = "Mark"
            lblLast.Text = "Smith"
    Case "67X"
            lblFirst.Text = "Jill"
            lblLast.Text = "Batist"
    Case "78Y"
            lblFirst.Text = "Cheryl"
            lblLast.Text = "Sworski"
    Case Else
            lblFirst.Text = "?"
            lblLast.Text = "?"
End Select
```

3. d. none of the above

```
4. Select Case True
       Case radJanuary.Checked
               lblBirthstone.Text = "Garnet"
       Case radFebruary.Checked
               lblBirthstone.Text = "Amethyst"
       Case Else
               lblBirthstone.Text = "Aquamarine"
   End Select
```

TRY THIS 1 (Chapter 10)

```vb
Private Sub btnDisplay_Click(ByVal sender As Ob
    ' displays the department name correspondin

    Dim intCode As Integer
    Integer.TryParse(txtCode.Text, intCode)

    Select Case intCode
        Case 1
            lblName.Text = "Payroll"
        Case 2
            lblName.Text = "Personnel"
        Case 3
            lblName.Text = "IT"
        Case Else
            lblName.Text = "Invalid code"
    End Select
End Sub
```

TRY THIS 2 (Chapter 10)

```vb
' calculate total due
decTotal = intQuantity * decPrice
Select Case chkEmployee.Checked
    Case True
        decTotal = decTotal * (1 - decEMP_DISC_RATE)
    Case Else
        If intQuantity > 20 Then
            decTotal = decTotal * (1 - decNON_EMP_DISC_RATE)
        End If
End Select
```

Chapter 11

Mini-Quiz 11-1

1. Test the application without entering any data.

2. 0

3. e

Mini-Quiz 11-2

1. `MessageBox.Show("You win!", "Game Over", MessageBoxButtons.OK, MessageBoxIcon.Information)`

2. `txtState.Text = txtState.Text.Trim`

3. `strDept = strDept.Trim.ToUpper`

TRY THIS 1 (Chapter 11)

Test data	Expected result
No data entered	$90 (Standard radio button is the default radio button)
Gold Club member check box not selected	
Standard room radio button selected	$90
Deluxe room radio button selected	$115
Suite radio button selected	$130
Gold Club member check box selected	
Standard room radio button selected	$80
Deluxe room radio button selected	$105
Suite radio button selected	$120

TRY THIS 2 (Chapter 11)

Some of the values listed in the first column in your testing chart may be different from those here. However, your values should include 0, a negative integer, a negative non-integer, a positive integer, a positive non-integer, and alphanumeric text. Your values should test each path in the selection structure. Recall that when a condition contains a range of values, the test data should include the lowest and highest values in the range, as well as a value within the range. Therefore, your values should include the numbers 100 and 5000 (which are the lowest and highest values in the first condition), as well as a number within that range. Your values also should include the number 5000.01 (which is the lowest value in the second condition), as well as another number that would make the second condition evaluate to True.

Test data	Expected result
No data entered	$0.00
Valid values:	
0	$0.00
100	$5.00
2500.75	$125.04
5000	$250.00
5000.01	$500.00
12000	$1,200.00
10	$0.00
−5	$0.00
−6.5	$0.00
Invalid values:	
x, $6, 3A	$0.00

Chapter 12

Mini-Quiz 12-1

1. The solution does not require a repetition structure.

2. The solution requires a repetition structure. The walk forward instruction will need to be repeated until Rob is directly in front of the table (or while Rob is not directly in front of the table).

3. repeat until there are no more flowers to pick (or repeat while there are flowers to pick).

Mini-Quiz 12-2

1. Do While intQuantity > 0

2. Do Until intQuantity <= 0

3. intNumEmployees = intNumEmployees + 1

4. System.Threading.Thread.Sleep(1000)

Mini-Quiz 12-3

1. intTotalNum = intTotalNum + intNum (or intTotalNum += intNum)

2. String.Empty

3. strItem = InputBox("Enter the item:", "Item Name")

4. intNum *= 3

TRY THIS 1 (Chapter 12)

Step b:

```
Private Sub btnClickMe_Click(ByVal sender As Object,
    ' blinks the message in the lblMessage control

    ' declare counter variable
    Dim intCount As Integer

    ' begin counting
    intCount = 1
    Do Until intCount > 20
        If lblMessage.Visible = False Then
            lblMessage.Visible = True
        Else
            lblMessage.Visible = False
        End If
        Me.Refresh()
        System.Threading.Thread.Sleep(250)
        ' update the counter variable
        intCount = intCount + 1
    Loop
End Sub
```

Step c:

```vb
Private Sub btnClickMe_Click(ByVal sender As Object,
    ' blinks the message in the lblMessage control

    ' declare counter variable
    Dim intCount As Integer

    ' begin counting
    intCount = 20
    Do Until intCount < 1
        If lblMessage.Visible = False Then
            lblMessage.Visible = True
        Else
            lblMessage.Visible = False
        End If
        Me.Refresh()
        System.Threading.Thread.Sleep(250)
        ' update the counter variable
        intCount = intCount - 1
    Loop
End Sub
```

TRY THIS 2 (Chapter 12)

```vb
Private Sub btnCalc_Click(ByVal sender As Object, ByVal e As System.EventArgs
    ' calculates and displays sales tax amounts

    Const strPROMPT As String = "Enter a sales amount. Click Cancel to end."
    Const strTITLE As String = "Sales Entry"
    Const decTAX_RATE As Decimal = 0.06
    Dim strInputSales As String
    Dim decSales As Decimal
    Dim decTax As Decimal

    ' get the first sales amount
    strInputSales = InputBox(strPROMPT, strTITLE, "0.00")
    Do Until strInputSales = String.Empty
        Decimal.TryParse(strInputSales, decSales)
        decTax = decSales * decTAX_RATE
        MessageBox.Show(decTax.ToString("C2"), "Sales Tax",
                        MessageBoxButtons.OK, MessageBoxIcon.Information)
        ' get another sales amount
        strInputSales = InputBox(strPROMPT, strTITLE, "0.00")
    Loop
End Sub
```

Chapter 13

Mini-Quiz 13-1

1. Loop While intQuantity > 0
2. Loop Until intQuantity <= 0

TRY THIS 1 (Chapter 13)

Processing steps

1. The computer initializes the intNumber variable to 1.

2. The computer processes the Do clause, which marks the beginning of the loop.

3. The loop instructions display the `intNumber` variable's value (1) and then update the value by adding 1 to it, giving 2.

4. The computer processes the Loop clause, which checks whether the `intNumber` variable's value is less than or equal to 3. It is, so processing returns to the Do clause.

5. The computer processes the Do clause, which marks the beginning of the loop.

6. The loop instructions display the `intNumber` variable's value (2) and then update the value by adding 1 to it, giving 3.

7. The computer processes the Loop clause, which checks whether the `intNumber` variable's value is less than or equal to 3. It is, so processing returns to the Do clause.

8. The computer processes the Do clause, which marks the beginning of the loop.

9. The loop instructions display the `intNumber` variable's value (3) and then update the value by adding 1 to it, giving 4.

10. The computer processes the Loop clause, which checks whether the `intNumber` variable's value is less than or equal to 3. It's not, so the loop ends.

TRY THIS 2 (Chapter 13)

Make the changes shaded in the following figure:

```
Private Sub btnClickMe_Click(ByVal sender As Object, E
    ' blinks the message in the lblMessage control

    ' declare counter variable
    Dim intCount As Integer

    ' begin counting
    intCount = 1
    Do
        If lblMessage.Visible = False Then
            lblMessage.Visible = True
        Else
            lblMessage.Visible = False
        End If
        Me.Refresh()
        System.Threading.Thread.Sleep(250)
        ' update the counter variable
        intCount = intCount + 1
    Loop Until intCount > 20
End Sub
```

Chapter 14

Mini-Quiz 14-1

1. `For intX As Integer = 10 To 20 Step 2`

2. `For intX As Integer = 30 To 0 Step –2`

3. a. negative

Mini-Quiz 14-2

1. `My.Computer.Audio.Play("Giggle.wav")`

2. c. use the annual interest rate

3. `lblCity.Text = "My favorite city is " & strCity`

TRY THIS 1 (Chapter 14)

Processing steps

1. The computer creates the **decX** variable and initializes it to 6.5.

2. The computer checks whether the **decX** variable's value is greater than 8.5. It's not, so the computer displays the number 6.5 in a message box and then adds 1 to the variable's value, giving 7.5.

3. The computer again checks whether the **decX** variable's value is greater than 8.5. It's not, so the computer displays the number 7.5 in a message box and then adds 1 to the variable's value, giving 8.5.

4. The computer again checks whether the **decX** variable's value is greater than 8.5. It's not, so the computer displays the number 8.5 in a message box and then adds 1 to the variable's value, giving 9.5.

5. The computer again checks whether the **decX** variable's value is greater than 8.5. It is, so the computer stops processing the loop body. Processing continues with the statement following the Next clause.

TRY THIS 2 (Chapter 14)

```
Private Sub btnDisplay_Click(ByVal sender As Object,
ByVal e As System.EventArgs) Handles btnDisplay.Click
    ' displays the odd and even numbers
    ' from one integer to another

    Dim intNum1 As Integer
    Dim intNum2 As Integer
    Dim intStep As Integer

    Integer.TryParse(txtNum1.Text, intNum1)
    Integer.TryParse(txtNum2.Text, intNum2)

    ' determine stepValue
    If intNum1 > intNum2 Then
        intStep = -1
    Else
        intStep = 1
    End If

    lblOdd.Text = String.Empty
    lblEven.Text = String.Empty

    For intNumber As Integer = intNum1 To intNum2 Step intStep
        If intNumber Mod 2 = 0 Then
            lblEven.Text = lblEven.Text &
                intNumber & ControlChars.NewLine
        Else
            lblOdd.Text = lblOdd.Text &
                intNumber & ControlChars.NewLine
        End If
    Next intNumber
End Sub
```

Chapter 15

Mini-Quiz 15-1

1.  ```
    Dim intOuter As Integer
    intOuter = 1
    Do While intOuter < 4
        For intNested As Integer = 1 To 4
            lblPattern.Text =
                lblPattern.Text & "X"
        Next intNested
        lblPattern.Text =
            lblPattern.Text & ControlChars.NewLine
        intOuter = intOuter + 1
    Loop
    ```

2.  ```
    Dim intNested As Integer
    For intOuter = 1 To 3
        intNested = 1
        Do While intNested < 5
            lblPattern.Text =
                lblPattern.Text & "X"
            intNested = intNested + 1
        Loop
        lblPattern.Text =
            lblPattern.Text & ControlChars.NewLine
    Next intOuter
    ```

3. b. Multiline

TRY THIS 1 (Chapter 15)

```
Private Sub btnStart_Click(ByVal sender As Object,
    ' displays minutes (from 0 through 2 only)
    ' and seconds (from 0 through 5 only)

    Dim intMinutes As Integer
    Dim intSeconds As Integer

    Do Until intMinutes > 2
        lblMinutes.Text = intMinutes
        Do Until intSeconds > 5
            lblSeconds.Text = intSeconds
            Me.Refresh()
            System.Threading.Thread.Sleep(500)
            intSeconds = intSeconds + 1
        Loop
        intMinutes = intMinutes + 1
        intSeconds = 0
    Loop

End Sub
```

TRY THIS 2 (Chapter 15)

```
Private Sub btnStart_Click(ByVal sender As Object,
    ' displays minutes (from 0 through 2 only)
    ' and seconds (from 0 through 5 only)

    Dim intSeconds As Integer

    For intMinutes As Integer = 0 To 2
        lblMinutes.Text = intMinutes
        Do
            lblSeconds.Text = intSeconds
            Me.Refresh()
            System.Threading.Thread.Sleep(500)
            intSeconds += 1
        Loop While intSeconds <= 5
        intSeconds = 0
    Next intMinutes
End Sub
```

Chapter 16

Mini-Quiz 16-1

1. a. arguments

2. b. above the first event procedure

3. d. TextChanged

Mini-Quiz 16-2

1. b. `Private Sub Display(ByVal strX As String,`
   `                     ByVal intY As Integer)`

2. `Call Display(strName, intQuantity)`

3. `ByRef`

TRY THIS 1 (Chapter 16)

```vb
Private Sub CalcAndDisplayBonus(ByVal decTotal As Decimal)
    ' calculates and displays the bonus

    Dim decBonus As Decimal

    If decTotal > 1200 Then
        decBonus = decTotal * 0.1
    Else
        decBonus = decTotal * 0.08
    End If
    lblBonus.Text = decBonus.ToString("C2")
End Sub

Private Sub btnCalc_Click(ByVal sender As Object,
ByVal e As System.EventArgs) Handles btnCalc.Click
    ' prompts the user to enter two sales amounts,
    ' then totals both amounts, and then calls a
    ' sub procedure to calculate and display the bonus

    Dim strInputSale1 As String
    Dim strInputSale2 As String
    Dim decSale1 As Decimal
    Dim decSale2 As Decimal
    Dim decSum As Decimal

    strInputSale1 = InputBox("First sale amount",
        "Bonus Solution")
    strInputSale2 = InputBox("Second sale amount",
        "Bonus Solution")

    Decimal.TryParse(strInputSale1, decSale1)
    Decimal.TryParse(strInputSale2, decSale2)
    decSum = decSale1 + decSale2
    Call CalcAndDisplayBonus(decSum)
End Sub
```

TRY THIS 2 (Chapter 16)

```vb
Private Sub CalcBonus(ByVal decS1 As Decimal,
                      ByVal decS2 As Decimal,
                      ByRef decBonusAmt As Decimal)
    ' calculates the bonus

    Dim decSum As Decimal

    decSum = decS1 + decS2
    If decSum > 1200 Then
        decBonusAmt = decSum * 0.1
    Else
        decBonusAmt = decSum * 0.08
    End If
End Sub

Private Sub btnCalc_Click(ByVal sender As Object,
ByVal e As System.EventArgs) Handles btnCalc.Click
    ' prompts the user to enter two sales amounts,
    ' then calls a sub procedure to calculate the
    ' bonus, and then displays the bonus

    Dim strInputSale1 As String
    Dim strInputSale2 As String
    Dim decSale1 As Decimal
    Dim decSale2 As Decimal
    Dim decBonus As Decimal

    strInputSale1 = InputBox("First sale amount",
        "Bonus Solution")
    strInputSale2 = InputBox("Second sale amount",
        "Bonus Solution")

    Decimal.TryParse(strInputSale1, decSale1)
    Decimal.TryParse(strInputSale2, decSale2)
    Call CalcBonus(decSale1, decSale2, decBonus)
    lblBonus.Text = decBonus.ToString("C2")
End Sub
```

Chapter 17

Mini-Quiz 17-1

1. c. `Private Function GetBonus(ByVal(dblSold As Double) As Double`

2. `Return decIncome`

3. `decTax = GetSales(decSale1, decSale2) * .08`

TRY THIS 1 (Chapter 17)

```
Private Function GetBonus(ByVal decTotal As Decimal) As Decimal
    ' calculates the bonus

    Dim decBonus As Decimal

    If decTotal > 1200 Then
        decBonus = decTotal * 0.1
    Else
        decBonus = decTotal * 0.08
    End If

    Return decBonus
End Function

Private Sub btnCalc_Click(ByVal sender As Object,
ByVal e As System.EventArgs) Handles btnCalc.Click
    ' prompts the user to enter two sales amounts,
    ' then calls a function to total both amounts,
    ' then calls a function to calculate the bonus,
    ' and then displays the bonus

    Dim strInputSale1 As String
    Dim strInputSale2 As String
    Dim decSale1 As Decimal
    Dim decSale2 As Decimal
    Dim decSum As Decimal
    Dim decBonus As Decimal

    strInputSale1 = InputBox("First sale amount",
                            "Bonus Solution")
    strInputSale2 = InputBox("Second sale amount",
                            "Bonus Solution")

    Decimal.TryParse(strInputSale1, decSale1)
    Decimal.TryParse(strInputSale2, decSale2)
    decSum = decSale1 + decSale2
    decBonus = GetBonus(decSum)
    lblBonus.Text = decBonus.ToString("C2")
End Sub
```

TRY THIS 2 (Chapter 17)

```vb
Private Function GetSum(ByVal decS1 As Decimal,
                ByVal decS2 As Decimal) As Decimal
    ' totals the sales amounts

    Return decS1 + decS2
End Function

Private Function GetBonus(ByVal decTotal As Decimal) As Decimal
    ' calculates the bonus

    Dim decBonus As Decimal

    If decTotal > 1200 Then
        decBonus = decTotal * 0.1
    Else
        decBonus = decTotal * 0.08
    End If

    Return decBonus
End Function

Private Sub btnCalc_Click(ByVal sender As Object,
ByVal e As System.EventArgs) Handles btnCalc.Click
    ' prompts the user to enter two sales amounts,
    ' then calls a function to total both amounts,
    ' then calls a function to calculate the bonus,
    ' and then displays the bonus

    Dim strInputSale1 As String
    Dim strInputSale2 As String
    Dim decSale1 As Decimal
    Dim decSale2 As Decimal
    Dim decSum As Decimal
    Dim decBonus As Decimal

    strInputSale1 = InputBox("First sale amount",
                    "Bonus Solution")
    strInputSale2 = InputBox("Second sale amount",
                    "Bonus Solution")

    Decimal.TryParse(strInputSale1, decSale1)
    Decimal.TryParse(strInputSale2, decSale2)
    decSum = GetSum(decSale1, decSale2)
    decBonus = GetBonus(decSum)
    lblBonus.Text = decBonus.ToString("C2")
End Sub
```

Chapter 18

Mini-Quiz 18-1

1. `Dim intQuantities(19) As Integer`

2. 19

3. `intQuantities(3) = 7`

Mini-Quiz 18-2

1. `Array.Sort(strStates)`

2. Length

3. a run time error will occur

TRY THIS 1 (Chapter 18)

```
Private Sub btnVerify_Click(ByVal sender As Object,
ByVal e As System.EventArgs) Handles btnVerify.Click
    ' searches the array for a name and then
    ' displays an appropriate message

    Dim strPartyList() As String =
        {"Jacob", "Karen", "Gregory",
        "Jerome", "Susan", "Michele",
        "Heather", "Jennifer", "George"}

    Dim strSearchFor As String
    Dim intSub As Integer
    Dim strFound As String

    strSearchFor = txtGuest.Text.Trim.ToUpper

    intSub = 0
    strFound = "N"
    Do While strFound <>"Y" AndAlso intSub < strPartyList.Length
        If strPartyList(intSub).ToUpper = strSearchFor Then
            strFound = "Y"
        Else
            intSub += 1
        End If
    Loop

    If strFound = "Y" Then
        MessageBox.Show(strSearchFor & " is invited.",
            "Party List", MessageBoxButtons.OK,
            MessageBoxIcon.Information)
    Else
        MessageBox.Show(strSearchFor & " is not invited.",
            "Party List", MessageBoxButtons.OK,
            MessageBoxIcon.Information)
    End If
End Sub
```

TRY THIS 2 (Chapter 18)

```
Private Sub btnCount_Click(ByVal sender As Object,
ByVal e As System.EventArgs) Handles btnCount.Click
    ' displays the number of times a specific
    ' letter appears in the array

    Dim strGrades() As String = {"C", "B", "C",
                                 "A", "B", "A",
                                 "F", "A", "D",
                                 "B", "C"}

    Dim strSearchFor As String
    Dim intCount As Integer    ' counter

    strSearchFor = txtLetterGrade.Text.Trim.ToUpper
    intCount = 0

    For intSub As Integer = 0 To strGrades.Length - 1
        If strGrades(intSub) = strSearchFor Then
            intCount += 1
        End If
    Next intSub

    MessageBox.Show(strSearchFor & ": " &
                    intCount.ToString,
                    "Grades", MessageBoxButtons.OK,
                    MessageBoxIcon.Information)
End Sub
```

Chapter 19

Mini-Quiz 19-1

1. b. False
2. a. `strCapital(1)`
3. a. True

TRY THIS 1 (Chapter 19)

```
Private Sub btnDisplay_Click(ByVal sender As Object,
ByVal e As System.EventArgs) Handles btnDisplay.Click
    ' displays the price associated with the product
    ' ID entered by the user

    Dim strIds() As String =
        {"BX35", "CR20", "FE15", "KW10", "MM67"}
    Dim intPrices() As Integer = {13, 10, 12, 24, 4}
    Dim strSearchFor As String
    Dim strFound As String
    Dim intSub As Integer

    ' assign the product ID to a variable
    strSearchFor = txtId.Text.Trim.ToUpper

    ' search the strIds array for the product ID
    ' continue searching until there are
    ' no more array elements to search or
    ' the product ID is found
    strFound = "N"
    Do Until intSub = strIds.Length OrElse strFound = "Y"
        If strIds(intSub) = strSearchFor Then
            strFound = "Y"
        Else
            intSub += 1
        End If
    Loop

    ' determine whether the product ID
    ' was found in the strIds array
    If strFound = "Y" Then
        lblPrice.Text = intPrices(intSub).ToString("C0")
    Else
        MessageBox.Show("Invalid product ID",
        "Treasures Gift Shop", MessageBoxButtons.OK,
        MessageBoxIcon.Information)
    End If
End Sub
```

TRY THIS 2 (Chapter 19)

```vb
Private intTemps(9) As Integer
Private intHighSub As Integer = intTemps.Length - 1

Private Sub btnGet_Click(ByVal sender As Object,
ByVal e As System.EventArgs) Handles btnGet.Click
    ' gets the temperatures and stores them in the array

    Dim strInputTemp As String

    For intSub As Integer = 0 To intHighSub
        strInputTemp = InputBox("Temperature " &
            intSub + 1, "Temperatures")
        Integer.TryParse(strInputTemp, intTemps(intSub))
    Next intSub

    lblHighest.Text = String.Empty
    lblLowest.Text = String.Empty
End Sub

Private Sub btnDisplay_Click(ByVal sender As Object,
ByVal e As System.EventArgs) Handles btnDisplay.Click
    ' display the highest and lowest temperature

    Dim intHigh As Integer
    Dim intLow As Integer

    intHigh = intTemps(0)
    intLow = intTemps(0)

    For intSub As Integer = 0 To intHighSub
        If intTemps(intSub) > intHigh Then
            intHigh = intTemps(intSub)
        End If
        If intTemps(intSub) < intLow Then
            intLow = intTemps(intSub)
        End If
    Next intSub

    lblHighest.Text = intHigh.ToString
    lblLowest.Text = intLow.ToString
End Sub
```

Chapter 20

Mini-Quiz 20-1

1. `Dim intQuantities(3, 1) As Integer`

2. 3

3. `intQuantities(2, 0) = 7`

Mini-Quiz 20-2

1. d. none of the above

2. a. `decSales(0, 1) += 20`

TRY THIS 1 (Chapter 20)

```vb
Private Sub btnDisplay_Click(ByVal sender As Object,
ByVal e As System.EventArgs) Handles btnDisplay.Click
    ' displays the price associated with the product
    ' ID entered by the user

    Dim strPriceList(,) As String = {{"BX35", "13"},
                                     {"CR20", "10"},
                                     {"FE15", "12"},
                                     {"KW10", "24"},
                                     {"MM67", "4"}}

    Dim strSearchFor As String
    Dim strFound As String
    Dim intRow As Integer
    Dim intNumRows As Integer

    ' assign the product ID to a variable
    strSearchFor = txtId.Text.Trim.ToUpper

    ' search for the product ID in the first column
    ' of the array
    ' continue searching until there are no more
    ' rows to search or the product ID is found
    intRow = 0
    strFound = "N"
    intNumRows = strPriceList.GetUpperBound(0) + 1

    Do Until intRow = intNumRows OrElse strFound = "Y"
        If strPriceList(intRow, 0) = strSearchFor Then
            strFound = "Y"
        Else
            intRow += 1
        End If
    Loop

    ' determine whether the product ID
    ' was found in the array
    If strFound = "Y" Then
        Dim intPrice As Integer
        intPrice = strPriceList(intRow, 1)
        lblPrice.Text = intPrice.ToString("C0")
    Else
        MessageBox.Show("Invalid product ID",
            "Treasures Gift Shop",
            MessageBoxButtons.OK,
            MessageBoxIcon.Information)
    End If
End Sub
```

TRY THIS 2 (Chapter 20)

```
Private Sub btnDisplay_Click(ByVal sender As Object,
ByVal e As System.EventArgs) Handles btnDisplay.Click
    ' displays the sum of the values stored in the array

    Dim intInventory(,) As Integer = {{34, 56},
                                      {75, 67},
                                      {5, 6}}

    Dim intTotal As Integer ' accumulator

    ' total the array values
    For intRow As Integer = 0 To intInventory.GetUpperBound(0)
        For intCol As Integer = 0 To intInventory.GetUpperBound(1)
            intTotal = intTotal + intInventory(intRow, intCol)
        Next intCol
    Next intRow

    ' display the total
    lblTotal.Text = intTotal.ToString
End Sub
```

Chapter 21

Mini-Quiz 21-1

1. Declarations

2. `address.strStreet = "Maple"`

3. `inventory(4).intQuantity = 100`

TRY THIS 1 (Chapter 21)

```
Structure SalesInfo
    Public decSale1 As Decimal
    Public decSale2 As Decimal
    Public decSale3 As Decimal
End Structure

Private Function GetCommission(ByVal company As
SalesInfo) As Decimal
    ' calculates and returns the commission amount

    Dim decTotal As Decimal

    decTotal = company.decSale1 + company.decSale2
    + company.decSale3
    Return decTotal * 0.03
End Function
```

```vb
Private Sub btnCalc_Click(ByVal sender As Object,
ByVal e As System.EventArgs) Handles btnCalc.Click
    ' displays the commission

    Dim companySales As SalesInfo
    Dim decCommission As Decimal

    Decimal.TryParse(txtRegion1.Text, companySales.decSale1)
    Decimal.TryParse(txtRegion2.Text, companySales.decSale2)
    Decimal.TryParse(txtRegion3.Text, companySales.decSale3)

    decCommission = GetCommission(companySales)
    lblComm.Text = decCommission.ToString("C2")
End Sub
```

TRY THIS 2 (Chapter 21)

```vb
Structure Item
    Public strId As String
    Public intPrice As Integer
End Structure

Private Sub btnDisplay_Click(ByVal sender As Object,
ByVal e As System.EventArgs) Handles btnDisplay.Click
    ' displays the price associated with the product
    ' ID entered by the user

    ' declare an array of structure variables
    Dim gifts(4) As Item

    ' declare variables
    Dim strSearchFor As String
    Dim strFound As String
    Dim intSub As Integer

    ' assign IDs and prices to the array
    gifts(0).strId = "BX35"
    gifts(0).intPrice = 13
    gifts(1).strId = "CR20"
    gifts(1).intPrice = 10
    gifts(2).strId = "FE15"
    gifts(2).intPrice = 12
    gifts(3).strId = "KW10"
    gifts(3).intPrice = 24
    gifts(4).strId = "MM67"
    gifts(4).intPrice = 4

    ' assign the product ID to a variable
    strSearchFor = txtId.Text.Trim.ToUpper

    ' search the array for the product ID
    ' continue searching until there are
    ' no more array elements to search or
    ' the product ID is found
    strFound = "N"
```

```
    Do Until intSub = gifts.Length OrElse strFound = "Y"
        If gifts(intSub).strId = strSearchFor Then
            strFound = "Y"
        Else
            intSub += 1
        End If
    Loop

    ' determine whether the product ID
    ' was found in the array
    If strFound = "Y" Then
        lblPrice.Text =
            gifts(intSub).intPrice.ToString("C0")
    Else
        MessageBox.Show("Invalid product ID",
            "Treasures Gift Shop", MessageBoxButtons.OK,
            MessageBoxIcon.Information)
    End If
End Sub
```

Chapter 22

Mini-Quiz 22-1

1. `Dim outFile As IO.StreamWriter`

2. StreamWriter

3. `txtCity.Focus()`

Mini-Quiz 22-2

1. `Dim inFile As IO.StreamReader`

2. StreamReader

3. b. False

TRY THIS 1 (Chapter 22)

```
Private Sub btnSave_Click(ByVal sender As Object,
ByVal e As System.EventArgs) Handles btnSave.Click
    ' writes a gross pay amount to a sequential access file

    ' declare a StreamWriter variable
    Dim outFile As IO.StreamWriter
    ' open the file for append
    outFile = IO.File.AppendText("gross.txt")
    ' write the amount on a separate line in the file
    outFile.WriteLine(txtGrossPay.Text)
    ' close the file
    outFile.Close()
    ' clear the text boxes and then set the focus
    txtGrossPay.Text = String.Empty
    txtContents.Text = String.Empty
    txtGrossPay.Focus()
End Sub
```

```vb
Private Sub btnDisplay_Click(ByVal sender As Object,
ByVal e As System.EventArgs) Handles btnDisplay.Click
    ' displays the gross pay amounts stored in
    ' a sequential access file

    ' declare variables
    Dim inFile As IO.StreamReader
    Dim strGrossPay As String
    Dim decGrossPay As Decimal

    ' clear the contents box
    txtContents.Text = String.Empty

    ' determine whether the file exists
    If IO.File.Exists("gross.txt") = True Then
        ' open the file for input
        inFile = IO.File.OpenText("gross.txt")
        ' process the loop instructions
        ' until the end of the file
        Do Until inFile.Peek = -1
            ' read an amount
            strGrossPay = inFile.ReadLine
            ' display the amount
            Decimal.TryParse(strGrossPay, decGrossPay)
            txtContents.Text = txtContents.Text &
            decGrossPay.ToString("C2") &
                ControlChars.NewLine
        Loop
        ' close the file
        inFile.Close()
    Else
        MessageBox.Show("Can't find the gross.txt file",
            "ABC Company",
            MessageBoxButtons.OK,
            MessageBoxIcon.Information)
    End If
End Sub
```

TRY THIS 2 (Chapter 22)
```vb
Private Sub btnDisplay_Click(ByVal sender As Object,
ByVal e As System.EventArgs) Handles btnDisplay.Click
    ' reads the names from a sequential
    ' access file and stores them in an array
    ' sorts the names and then displays them

    Dim strFriends(4) As String
    Dim inFile As IO.StreamReader
    Dim intSub As Integer

    ' clear the My friends box
    lblFriends.Text = String.Empty
```

```vbnet
        ' determine whether the file exists
        If IO.File.Exists("names.txt") = True Then
            ' open the file for input
            inFile = IO.File.OpenText("names.txt")
            ' start the subscript at 0
            intSub = 0
            ' process the loop instructions until the
            ' end of the file or the array is filled
            Do Until inFile.Peek = -1 OrElse
                intSub = strFriends.Length
                ' read a name and store it in the array
                strFriends(intSub) = inFile.ReadLine
                intSub += 1
            Loop
            ' close the file
            inFile.Close()

            Array.Sort(strFriends)

            For intSub = 0 To strFriends.Length - 1
                lblFriends.Text = lblFriends.Text &
                    strFriends(intSub) & ControlChars.NewLine
            Next intSub
        Else
            MessageBox.Show("Can't find the file",
                "Friends", MessageBoxButtons.OK,
                MessageBoxIcon.Information)
        End If
End Sub
```

Chapter 23

Mini-Quiz 23-1

1. txtAddress.Text = txtAddress.Text.Trim

2. strWord = strWord.Insert(0, "wo")

3. strWord = strWord.Replace("d", "fr")

Mini-Quiz 23-2

1. 3

2. −1

3. strCode = strPartNum.Substring(2, 4)

4. strCode = strPartNum.Remove(2, 2)

TRY THIS 1 (Chapter 23)

```vbnet
strAmount = strAmount.Replace(",", String.Empty)
[or strAmount = strAmount.Replace(",","")]

strAmount = strAmount.Insert(0, "$")
strAmount = strAmount.Insert(2, ",")
strAmount = strAmount.Insert(6, ",")
```

TRY THIS 2 (Chapter 23)

```
Private Sub btnDisplay_Click(ByVal sender As Object,
ByVal e As System.EventArgs) Handles btnDisplay.Click
    ' displays a shipping charge based on a ZIP code

    Dim strZip As String
    Dim intShipping As Integer

    strZip = txtZip.Text.Trim

    ' validate the ZIP code
    If strZip Like "605##" Then
        intShipping = 25
    ElseIf strZip Like "606##" Then
        intShipping = 30
    Else
        intShipping = 0
        MessageBox.Show("Invalid ZIP code.",
                "ZIP Code",
                MessageBoxButtons.OK,
                MessageBoxIcon.Information)
    End If

    ' display shipping charge and set the focus
    lblShipping.Text = intShipping.ToString("C0")
    txtZip.Focus()
End Sub
```

Chapter 24

Mini-Quiz 24-1

1. field

2. c. BindingSource

3. binding

Mini-Quiz 24-2

1. `TblInventoryBindingSource.MoveFirst()`

2. ex

3. b. False

TRY THIS 1 (Chapter 24)

Steps to connect the application to the database:

1. Click Data on the menu bar and then click Show Data Sources to open the Data Sources window.

2. Click Add New Data Source in the Data Sources window to start the Data Source Configuration Wizard. If necessary, click Database on the Choose a Data Source Type screen.

3. Click the Next button to display the Choose a Database Model screen. If necessary, click Dataset.

4. Click the Next button to display the Choose Your Data Connection screen. Click the New Connection button to open the Add Connection dialog box. If Microsoft Access Database File (OLE DB) does not appear in the Data source box, click the Change button to open the Change Data Source dialog box, click Microsoft Access Database File, and then click the OK button to return to the Add Connection dialog box.

5. Click the Browse button in the Add Connection dialog box. Open the ClearlyVB2010\ Chap24\Access Databases folder and then click Employees.accdb in the list of filenames. Click the Open button.

6. Click the Test Connection button. The "Test connection succeeded." message appears in a message box. Close the message box.

7. Click the OK button to close the Add Connection dialog box. Employees.accdb appears in the Choose Your Data Connection screen. Click the Next button.

8. Click the Yes button to add the Employees.accdb file to the application's project folder. The Save the Connection String to the Application Configuration File screen appears next. If necessary, select the Yes, save the connection as check box. Click the Next button to display the Choose Your Database Objects screen.

9. Expand the Tables node and then expand the tblEmploy node. Click the empty box next to tblEmploy and then click the Finish button.

```vbnet
Private Sub TblEmployBindingNavigatorSaveItem_Click(ByVal sender As System.
    Try
        Me.Validate()
        Me.TblEmployBindingSource.EndEdit()
        Me.TableAdapterManager.UpdateAll(Me.EmployeesDataSet)
        MessageBox.Show("Changes saved.", "Morgan Industries",
                        MessageBoxButtons.OK, MessageBoxIcon.Information)
    Catch ex As Exception
        MessageBox.Show(ex.Message, "Morgan Industries",
                MessageBoxButtons.OK, MessageBoxIcon.Information)
    End Try

End Sub

Private Sub frmMain_Load(ByVal sender As System.Object, ByVal e As System.
    'TODO: This line of code loads data into the 'EmployeesDataSet.tblEmpl
    Me.TblEmployTableAdapter.Fill(Me.EmployeesDataSet.tblEmploy)

End Sub
```

Chapter 25

Mini-Quiz 25-1

1. name.LastName Like "A*"

2. Order By name.LastName Descending

3. Language Integrated Query

4. b. Order By

5. d. Where

Mini-Quiz 25-2

1. sales.JanSales

2. Select points.PointsEarned
   Into Average()

3. Min

TRY THIS 1 (Chapter 25)

```vb
Private Sub btnSort_Click(ByVal sender As Object,
ByVal e As System.EventArgs) Handles btnSort.Click
    ' displays records in descending order by the Cost field

    Dim records = From magazine In MagazinesDataSet.tblMagazine
                  Order By magazine.Cost Descending
                  Select magazine
    TblMagazineBindingSource.DataSource = records.AsDataView
End Sub

Private Sub btnDisplayCode_Click(ByVal sender As Object,
ByVal e As System.EventArgs) Handles btnDisplayCode.Click
    ' displays the record whose Code field contains PG24

    Dim records = From magazine In MagazinesDataSet.tblMagazine
                  Where magazine.Code.ToUpper = "PG24"
                  Select magazine
    TblMagazineBindingSource.DataSource = records.AsDataView
End Sub

Private Sub btnDisplayName_Click(ByVal sender As Object,
ByVal e As System.EventArgs) Handles btnDisplayName.Click
    ' displays the record whose MagName field contains Java

    Dim records = From magazine In MagazinesDataSet.tblMagazine
                  Where magazine.MagName.ToUpper = "JAVA"
                  Select magazine
    TblMagazineBindingSource.DataSource = records.AsDataView
End Sub
```

TRY THIS 2 (Chapter 25)

```
Private Sub btnDisplayCost_Click(ByVal sender As Object,
ByVal e As System.EventArgs) Handles btnDisplayCost.Click
    ' displays magazines costing $4 or more

    Dim records = From magazine In MagazinesDataSet.tblMagazine
                  Where magazine.Cost >= 4 Select magazine
    TblMagazineBindingSource.DataSource = records.AsDataView
End Sub

Private Sub btnDisplayName_Click(ByVal sender As Object,
ByVal e As System.EventArgs) Handles btnDisplayName.Click
    ' displays magazines whose name starts with C

    Dim records = From magazine In MagazinesDataSet.tblMagazine
                  Where magazine.MagName.ToUpper Like "C*"
                  Select magazine
    TblMagazineBindingSource.DataSource = records.AsDataView
End Sub

Private Sub btnAverage_Click(ByVal sender As Object,
ByVal e As System.EventArgs) Handles btnAverage.Click
    ' displays the average cost of a magazine

    Dim avgCost =
        Aggregate magazine In MagazinesDataSet.tblMagazine
        Select magazine.Cost Into Average()
    MessageBox.Show("Average cost of a magazine: " &
                avgCost.ToString("C2"), "Magazines",
                MessageBoxButtons.OK,
                MessageBoxIcon.Information)
End Sub
```

Chapter 26

Mini-Quiz 26-1

1. object-oriented programming

2. b. Set

3. c. `Return _strCity`

Mini-Quiz 26-2

1. New

2. `Dim dog As New Animal`

3. a. True

TRY THIS 1 (Chapter 26)

```vb
Public Class Square
    Private _decSide As Decimal

    Public Property Side As Decimal
        Get
            Return _decSide
        End Get
        Set(ByVal value As Decimal)
            If value > 0 Then
                _decSide = value
            Else
                _decSide = 0
            End If
        End Set
    End Property

    Public Sub New()
        _decSide = 0
    End Sub

    Public Function GetArea() As Decimal
        Return _decSide * _decSide
    End Function
End Class

Private Sub btnCalc_Click(ByVal sender As Object,
ByVal e As System.EventArgs) Handles btnCalc.Click
    ' calculates and displays the area of a square

    ' instantiate a Square object
    Dim mySquare As New Square

    ' declare a variable to store the area
    Dim decArea As Decimal

    ' assign input to the Square object's property
    Decimal.TryParse(txtSide.Text, mySquare.Side)

    ' use the Square object's method to calculate the area
    decArea = mySquare.GetArea

    ' display the area
    lblArea.Text = decArea.ToString

    txtSide.Focus()
End Sub
```

Chapter 27

Mini-Quiz 27-1

1. active server page
2. Hypertext Markup Language
3. a. client computer

Mini-Quiz 27-2

1. c. Title
2. b. ImageUrl
3. a. PostBackUrl

Mini-Quiz 27-3

1. d. Right
2. b. Web server
3. a. RequiredFieldValidator

Index

Note: Page numbers in **boldface** indicate key terms.